HISTORY OF THE
DUTCH-SPEAKING PEOPLES
1555–1648

Pieter Geyl, who was born at Dordrecht in 1887 and educated at the University of Leyden, was the greatest Dutch historian of his time, and a scholar of European renown. In 1913 he came to London as the correspondent for a Dutch newspaper, and in 1919 he was appointed Professor of Dutch Studies at London University. He later returned to the Netherlands as Professor of Modern History at the University of Utrecht, where he remained until his retirement in 1958. During the Second World War, he was imprisoned in a German concentration camp, and wrote *Napoleon: For and Against* (1944). He produced many books on Dutch history, including *The Netherlands Divided, 1609–1648* (1936), and several volumes of essays on which *Debates with Historians* (1962) and *Encounters in History* (1963) are the best known. He died in 1966.

Also by Pieter Geyl

Napoleon: For and Against

Debates with Historians

Encounters in History

HISTORY OF THE
DUTCH-SPEAKING PEOPLES
1555–1648

Pieter Geyl

**PHOENIX
PRESS**

5 UPPER SAINT MARTIN'S LANE
LONDON
WC2H 9EA

A PHOENIX PRESS PAPERBACK

Originally published in Great Britain
as *The Revolt of the Netherlands 1555–1609*
and *The Netherlands Divided 1609–1648* by
Williams & Norgate Ltd, 1932 and 1936
This paperback edition published in 2001
by Phoenix Press,
a division of The Orion Publishing Group Ltd,
Orion House, 5 Upper St Martin's Lane,
London WC2H 9EA

A CIP catalogue record for this book
is available from the British Library.

Printed in Great Britain by Clays Ltd, St Ives plc

ISBN 1 84212 225 8

This Phoenix Press edition combines the two volume *The Revolt of the Netherlands 1555–1609* and *The Netherlands in the Seventeenth Century 1609–1648* into one.

The Revolt of the Netherlands 1555–1609 is the first volume in Pieter Geyl's magnificent — but sadly incomplete — *History of the Dutch-Speaking Peoples*. In this superb panorama of politics and war, Geyl tells the epic story of the Netherlanders' heroic struggle against the might of Spain, and of the rise and establishment of the Dutch Republic. As such, it remains the definitive account of one of the central episodes in early modern European history. But it also addresses issues which remain alive and important today: the relation between religious belief and political action, the complex questions of national identity, and the problems besetting a small country struggling to survive in a great-power world. Above all, it is suffused by the author's abiding belief in the vitality of European civilisation.

The Netherlands in the Seventeenth Century, 1609–1648 is the second volume in Pieter Geyl's *History of the Dutch-Speaking Peoples*. In this masterly account of how the Netherlanders finally won their freedom, he describes the uneasy truce with Spain, the arrest and execution of Oldenbarnevelt, the resumption of war in 1621, the uncertain alliance with France, and the eventual establishment of Dutch independence in 1648. At the same time, Geyl also provides an unforgettable portrait of Dutch life during the first half of the seventeenth century — an era of unprecedented domestic prosperity, of extensive colonial expansion in the East Indies and North America, and of outstanding cultural achievement, most brilliantly exemplified in the works of the young Rembrandt.

PHILIP II OF SPAIN
1555–98

CONTENTS

THE REVOLT OF THE NETHERLANDS
1555–1609

THE NETHERLANDS IN THE
SEVENTEENTH CENTURY 1609–1648

LIST OF MAPS

VOL I

VOL II

THE REVOLT OF
THE NETHERLANDS
1555–1609

MAP I

THE NETHERLANDS IN 1555

DUTCH-SPEAKING PROVINCES

1. FLANDERS (Grevelingen, Dunkirk, Nieuwpoort, Ostend, Sluis, Brugge, Yper, Meenen, Kortryk, Oudenaarde, Ghent, Aalst, Dendermonde).

2. BRABANT (Brussels, Antwerp, Bergen-op-Zoom, Breda, Den Bosch, Grave, Eindhoven, Lier, Leuven, Tienen, Diest; in the French-speaking district: Nivelles, Gembloux).

3. MECHLIN.

4. LIMBURG (Maastricht).

5. ZEALAND (Middelburg, Veere, Flushing, Goes, Zierikzee).

6. HOLLAND (The Brill, Delft, The Hague, Rotterdam, Dordt, Geertruidenberg, Gorcum, Schoonhoven, Gouda, Leyden, Haarlem, Amsterdam, Alkmaar, Hoorn, Enkhuizen, Medemblik).

7. UTRECHT (Utrecht, Amersfoort).

8. GELDERLAND—8^1 being the Upper Quarter—(Roermond, Venlo, Gelder, Nymwegen, Arnhem, Grol, Zutfen).

9. OVERYSEL (Deventer, Oldenzaal, Zwolle, Kampen. Steenwyk).

10. DRENTE (Koevorden).

11. FRIESLAND (Leeuwarden, Harlingen).

12. GRONINGEN — Town and Ommelands — (Groningen, Delfzyl).

WALLOON PROVINCES

I. ARTOIS (Arras).

II. WALLOON FLANDERS (Lille, Douai).

III. CAMBRAI.

IV. TOURNAI.

V. HAINAUT (Mons, Valenciennes).

VI. NAMUR.

VII. LUXEMBURG.

TOWNS OUTSIDE HABSBURG TERRITORY: Liège, St. Truiden (BISHOPRIC OF LIÈGE), Köln (ARCHBISHOPRIC ELECTORATE) Cleve, Wesel, Emmerik (DUCHY OF CLEVE), Emden (COUNTY OF EAST FRIESLAND).

PREFACE

The present work is based on my *History of the Netherlandish Race* (*Geschiedenis van de Nederlandsche Stam*), the first volume of which was published by the "Wereldbibliotheek," Amsterdam, early in 1931.

. . . . .

The revolt of the Netherlands is of all periods of Netherlands history the most popular in the English-speaking world. This is no doubt largely due to John Lothrop Motley, whose *Rise of the Dutch Republic* was at one time a favourite with the general reading public. Must not another book on a period to which he devoted seven volumes—four of *The United Netherlands*, 1584–1609, in addition to three of the *Rise of the Dutch Republic*, making in all some 3,400 pages—be considered somewhat superfluous? While disclaiming any ambition to supersede a work that will always remain a classic of historical narrative, I may perhaps be permitted to suggest that the difference in point of view between the nineteenth-century American and the twentieth-century Dutchman is considerable enough to warrant a fresh survey of the same events.

To Motley this upheaval was nothing but an illustration of the eternal struggle between right and wrong. To him Catholicism and Absolutism were Powers of Darkness, while Protestantism was one with Liberty, Democracy, and Light. The contest between the Netherlands and Spain is to him a contest between the principles of good and of evil, in which he feels compelled by the most sacred obligations of morality to join, and of course to join on the right side. The modern historian cannot see matters quite like that. It is not that to him no principles are involved in the great struggles of history, nor that his sympathies cannot be engaged on one of the opposing sides. But he knows that the other side, too, must have had its justification, and he will try to explain its position rather than overwhelm it with ridicule and invective. Speaking for myself, the point where I am conscious of the widest divergence from Motley in what I may perhaps call the philosophy of the subject is in the interpretation of Protestantism, which to me is not the radiant message of liberty and progress which it was to the New England Presbyterian; neither can I see in Catholicism merely the wicked system of mental sloth and persecution that it seemed to him. While, therefore, my sympathies are divided where the religious struggle is concerned, I can the more readily come to the conclusion that other issues were at least equally important with the religious, and that other factors had far more influence in determining the event of the contest. My nationality and the age I live in have caused me to devote particular attention to one great problem of which Motley did not even become aware.

Whoever attempts to trace in Motley's volumes the course of the break-up of Netherlands unity and to establish the causes of the failure of the rebellion in the South and of its success in the North, will emerge from his reading completely befogged. The only explanation that might occur to him would be that in Holland and Zealand Protestants were much more numerous than in the other provinces, and especially than in the South—a conclusion that would be quite wrong in fact. Yet Motley makes this statement in the most extreme form imaginable.[1] It is impossible to indicate in a few brief sentences what is involved for the interpretation of Netherlands history in this tremendous fact—which apparently remained hidden from Motley—that Protestants were only a minority in Holland and Zealand, and not less numerous in Flanders and Brabant. The truth is that Motley, while carrying on his impassioned polemics against Granvelle, Alva, Parma, and above all Philip II, and while enthusiastically putting the case for William the Silent's greatness as a champion of Protestantism, Liberty, and Democracy, was so little interested in the problems of Netherlands history that he never took the trouble to get up the necessary information about them.

It is a most significant fact that Motley ended his first book with the death of William the Silent.[2] The Prince was assassi-

---

[1] E.g. *Rise of the Dutch Republic*, iii. 4.
[2] The observation was made as early as 1862 by the great Dutch historian Fruin: *Verspreide Geschriften*, iii. 126. Motley's faulty composition was

nated at one of the most critical moments of the rebellion,
when the fate of Ghent and Brabant was hanging in the
balance. Yet not a word does Motley say about the situation
in which his hero left the country, or on the issue of the great
decisions that were then pending. Moreover, in his preface
he commits himself to the statement that "the final separation of territory into independent and obedient provinces, into
the Commonwealth of the United States and the Belgian
provinces of Spain, was in reality effected by William the
Silent." One hesitates to say which is the more amazing, the
assertion that William the Silent was responsible for the loss
of Flanders and Brabant, a disaster which he strove to avert
with all his might, or the belief that the separation had already
been consummated at the moment of the Prince's death. When
in his sequel, *The United Netherlands*, Motley attempts a
summing-up of the situation which he had left in the air at
the conclusion of his first great work, he perpetrates a passage[1]
full of the most startling confusions and inaccuracies of
geography and chronology, which, moreover, proves once
again his inability to rid his mind of the contemporary dual
state system of Holland and Belgium. He "assumes, for general
purposes," that Holland and Belgium had already sprung into
existence at a moment when the permanent division along
those exact lines could not possibly have been foreseen. He
looks upon the emergence of the two modern countries as a
foregone conclusion without even noticing how profoundly
the situation he is describing differs from that which resulted
from many more years of war. It is small wonder that this
attitude of mind—which, let me add, has long been common
among Dutch and Belgian historians as well—has prevented
him from offering any explanation of what in reality was a
long and complicated process.

Motley's work will survive the exposition of many more
glaring errors and grievous shortcomings. Nor have I the
slightest wish to attempt killing it. All I have wanted to make

---

nevertheless copied by the Rev. G. Edmundson in the *Cambridge Modern
History*; his chapter on the first stage of the revolt is actually entitled
"William the Silent."   [1] I. 9.

clear by these observations is the reason for my belief that there ought to be room in English historical literature for a modern version of what must still be regarded as one of the most important events in modern European history.

. . . . .

Some explanation is required of my use of certain geographical names. The appellations current to describe the Low Countries, or parts of them, and their inhabitants, have fallen into a chaotic confusion which is a reflection of their chequered history, but which compels the historian to introduce some system of his own if he wants to convey clear impressions to the minds of his readers.

Netherlands: the entire seventeen provinces owing allegiance to Philip II on his accession (see Map I). Nowadays *Netherlands* is the official name of the North Netherlandish State; in this work the word is not used in that restricted sense.

Netherlandish: (*a*) appertaining to the whole of the Netherlands; (*b*) appertaining to the Germanic population of the Netherlands, and especially to their language. The linguistic boundary, north of which *Netherlandish* or *Dutch* and south of which French is spoken, is indicated by a line on each of the maps included in this volume. The use of the word *Netherlandish* in this restricted sense is common in the language itself, which the Northerner generally calls *Hollandsch* and the Southerner *Vlaamsch* (Flemish), but for which both have the official name of *Nederlandsch* (a word first used for the language about the middle of the sixteenth century, and in Flanders). When, however, a distinction is made between Netherlanders of Germanic and of Romance speech, there are obvious disadvantages attached to the use of the word *Netherlandish* to denote the Germanic part, and although I have not been able to do without it altogether, I have more commonly used *Dutch*, a word which presents problems of its own.

Dutch: appertaining to the Germanic population of the Netherlands. In modern English parlance *Dutch* means: appertaining to the population of the Northern Netherlands (commonly called Holland). In this work that use of the word is strictly avoided. There is complete historic justification for the application of the word to the wider area. Etymologically *Dutch* is the same word as *Duitsch* (*Deutsch*), which down to the seventeenth century was used by the Germanic Netherlanders themselves to indicate their own language; to-day in their parlance the word means German. (In the sixteenth century a distinction was beginning to be made between *Nederduitsch*—Dutch—and *Hoogduitsch*—German.) In any case *Duitsch* was never restricted to northern Netherlandish; neither was the dialectical variant *Dietsch* (see p. 28), which on the contrary is used to-day to denote more particularly the unity of race and language embracing Germanic Netherlanders of the North and of the South (Hollanders and Flemings, as modern usage has it). The word *Dutch* has been used in this work as an equivalent of *Dietsch*; and also commonly to indicate the language spoken by Hollanders and Flemings, which in that language itself would nowadays be called *Nederlandsch*.

Holland: the county on the shore of the North Sea, bounded by Zealand on the South, Gelderland, Utrecht, and the Zuider Zee on the East (see Map I). The modern usage by which the name is made to apply to the whole of the Northern Netherlands is strictly avoided in this work.

Hollander: inhabitant of the county of Holland.

Flanders: the county on the shore of the North Sea bounded by Zealand on the North, Brabant on the East, Walloon Flanders and Artois on the South (see Map I). The modern use of the name to indicate the whole of the Dutch-speaking part of Belgium is strictly avoided in this work.

Flemish: appertaining to the county of Flanders. *Flemish* (*Vlaamsch*) was commonly used by the inhabitants of the county to indicate their language, just as the Hollanders called their language *Hollandsch*. Foreigners, Italians, Frenchmen, Englishmen, often used the word in the sense of *Nederlandsch*, or *Dutch*, making, for instance, a Brabander or a Hollander speak *Flemish*. In modern times *Vlaamsch* is commonly used to describe the language, officially *Nederlandsch*, spoken in the whole of the Germanic part of Belgium. These uses are strictly avoided in this work.

Fleming: inhabitant of the county of Flanders.

.   .   .   .   .

I have found it impossible to conform to the English custom of calling all western continental towns by French names; it is utterly senseless to speak of *Bruges, Courtrai, Bois-le-Duc, Treves,* or *Aix-la-Chapelle.* Except, therefore, when there are true English names in current use, like Mechlin (instead of Mechelen), Antwerp (instead of Antwerpen), The Hague (instead of Den Haag), I have used the native names (Brugge, Kortryk, 's-Hertogenbosch, Trier, Aachen).

A list of these names for the Dutch-speaking area with the French translations in the second column is here inserted.

Aalst	*Alost*
Belle	*Bailleul*
Brugge	*Bruges*
Den Bosch or 's-Hertogenbosch	*Bois-le-Duc*
Dendermonde	*Termonde*
Grevelingen	*Gravelines*
Kortryk	*Courtrai*
(River) Leie	*Lys*
Leuven	*Louvain*
(River) Maas	*Meuse*
Meenen	*Menin*
St. Truiden.	*St. Trond*
St. Winoksbergen	*Berghes St. Winox*
Sluis	*l'Ecluse*
Tienen, Thienen	*Tirlemont*
Veurne	*Furnes*

References to the sources of the quotations from contemporary texts will be found at the back, as also a general note on sources and historical literature.

My thanks are due to Mr. S. T. Bindoff, B.A.(Lond.), and Mr. W. D. Robson-Scott, M.A.(Oxon.), for their kindness in reading through my manuscript and suggesting corrections of my English; also to my son, W. F. Geyl, for designing the maps.

P. G.

INTRODUCTION

I

EARLY NETHERLANDS HISTORY

THE NATION AND THE DYNASTY

When Charles V transferred the government of the Netherlands to his son Philip in 1555, delegates of seventeen provinces of varying size and importance composed the assembly of the States-General at Brussels, before which both the old ruler and the new appeared. In the course of Philip's reign practically the whole of this country rose in revolt, but only the seven northern provinces, situated beyond the great rivers that run out into the North Sea, succeeded in establishing their independence. An eighty years' war had to be waged before this independence was unreservedly recognized by Philip's second successor. In the later stages of this war the seven United Netherlands had taken by force of arms certain portions of the adjoining provinces, where in the meantime Spanish rule had been restored. During the lifetime of the Netherlands Republic these districts were administered as subject territory under the name of Generality Lands. To-day the seven provinces and the one-time Generality Lands south of the rivers constitute the Kingdom of the Netherlands, to which certain additional districts in the East, on the Maas, were joined in 1839. The provinces in which Philip II, with the resources at his disposal as King of Spain, succeeded in putting down the revolt, shorn of the acquisitions of the Dutch Republic and of the Dutch Kingdom in the North, of the conquests of Louis XIV in the South-West, of the larger part of Luxemburg in the South-East, but with the addition of the Bishopric of Liège, after centuries of subjection to successive foreign masters and after a short-lived reunion with the Northern Netherlands, form the Kingdom of Belgium as we know it to-day.

When the Twelve Years' Truce was concluded between the Dutch Republic and Spain in 1609, the issue had in its

main lines been decided. It was certain that the North was to
be free and Protestant, and that it was to be separated from
the South, which returned to Catholicism and to submission
under foreign rule. We shall therefore, in our account of the
war from the beginning of Philip II's reign to the Twelve
Years' interval, be reviewing the complete course of events
in which some of the most fundamental problems of Netherlands history have their setting. What is the explanation of the
partial success, as well as of the partial failure, of the revolt?
In how far was the revolt a national one? In how far was
its inspiration religious? Was the emergence of a Protestant
North and a Catholic South in accordance with the aspirations
of the populations concerned, or was it due to factors of a
different nature? Was there, at the beginning of Philip's
reign, a national consciousness embracing all the Netherlands,
or was the specifically Northern consciousness, which acquired
so undeniable a reality after the separation, really in being
before it occurred? These are some of the questions that will
have to be faced as our account of the events between 1555
and 1609 is developed.

But before ringing up the curtain on that great drama it
will be necessary to examine the stage on which it was soon
to be performed. We must know something of the peoples
living in the Netherlands, their races and languages, their
economic conditions, their religious outlook, their political
and cultural traditions rooted in their medieval history. We
must know something of the ruling dynasty, which had created
a political unit of the seventeen provinces—in so far as they
can be called a political unit. For the clash between the tendencies represented by the dynasty and the forces living in the
people was more than the usual conflict between sixteenth-
century monarchy—authoritarian, levelling, centralizing,
modernizing—and the love of particular rights, the tenacity
of vested interests, the conservative libertarianism characteristic
of feudal society. What gives it a distinctive colour is that this
dynasty was of alien origin and had lately become even more
estranged from the Netherlands. The monarchy is to be regarded
as an independent entity, superimposed upon the rich and

varied life of the Netherlands community; and its age-old traditions need to be studied by themselves.

At the outset one great fact claims our attention. It is that in the seventeen Netherlands two races and two civilizations met. By far the larger part of the country was inhabited by a population of Low-Germanic origin and speech. In the southern fringe of provinces, however, in the so-called Walloon area— that is in Artois, Walloon Flanders (Lille, Orchies, and Douai), Tournai, Hainaut, Namur, as also in the southernmost district of Brabant (Nivelles) and in the western half of Luxemburg— French was spoken. Trace a line, starting from the North Sea shore in the neighbourhood of Grevelingen,[1] following the rivers Aa and Leie,[2] then, from a point several miles south of Kortryk,[3] continuing in an easterly direction and crossing the Maas[4] several miles south of Maastricht. That line is the linguistic boundary, north of which French was in the position of a foreign language. This, indeed, is still in the main the position to-day. For many centuries that boundary has hardly moved, so that it still cuts off the northern corner of France and divides Belgium in two almost equal halves. North of it only the towns in the Flemish district annexed by Louis XIV (as for instance, Dunkirk and Belle[5]) and Brussels have in varying degrees become gallicized.

The origin of this line of demarcation can be exactly indicated. It sprang into being at the time of the great Germanic migrations, in the sixth century, when the people of the Franks, coming from the East, out of the obscure depths of Germania, broke through the Rhine frontier of the crumbling Roman Empire. The country north of the rivers had already for a long time been inhabited by Germanic tribes, some of whom had entertained close relations with the Romans and had undergone their influence very deeply. South of the rivers, too, there were numerous Germanic settlements, although the substratum of the population was probably still Celtic. Incessant raids from

---

[1] Grevelingen: in French—*Gravelines*.
[2] Leie: in French—*Lys*.   [3] Kortryk: in French—*Courtrai*.
[4] Maas: in French—*Meuse*.   [5] Belle: in French—*Bailleul*.

the East had in any case so far devastated this region that large stretches were practically empty when the Franks, crossing the rivers Ysel, Rhine, Waal, and Maas, poured down into the valleys of the Scheldt and the Leie. In the course of not very many years they seem to have settled pretty densely most of the land down to the line which still divides the languages. Meantime their most renowned chiefs went on and subjected the Romanized country of Gaul south of that line, which, being more densely populated and more highly organized, succeeded in absorbing their numerous scattered settlements.

Two more Germanic tribes helped to compose the population of the Netherlands north of the linguistic boundary—the Frisians and the Saxons; but it was the Franks who, under the Merovingian Kings and their successors, the Carolingians, created the first political organization in which the whole region found a place, and it was their language that became the expression of its unity. The original area of Frankish settlement stretched over Flanders and Brabant (to use the names of a slightly later date which are still current) right across the rivers into Utrecht and the Veluwe up to the River Ysel. East of that river was Saxon country as far as Friesland and the Ommelands of Groningen, where on the shores of the North Sea the Frisians had their home. At the time of the great Frankish irruption, Holland and Zealand were already settled, but probably very thinly, by Frisians and Saxons. At a very early date, at any rate, that coastal region—with the exception of the small northern part of Holland which long retained the name of West-Friesland—became completely franconized, so that it was differentiated by its language from the northern Frisian as well as from the eastern Saxon areas, while being assimilated to the Frankish territory of Flanders, Brabant, western Gelderland, and Utrecht.

On the basis of linguistic unity there soon arose a common civilization, but political unity proved harder to achieve. In fact, the development of a Netherlands nation and a Netherlands state was from the start seriously impeded by the brilliant career which the leaders of the Frankish race made for themselves in Gaul. Their rise to greatness in that land of superior

civilization divorced their interests from those of the bulk of
their people, who had stayed behind to settle outlying regions—
as they seemed to the dwellers on the Seine and the Loire—
on the other side of the Ardennes and by the North Sea. In
the large empire of the Merovingians and of the Carolingians
after them, of which the centre of power lay among the inheritors
of the Roman tradition, the backward and leaderless Netherlands
could not attain to any individual status. Not even their unity
was respected in the divisions which the successors of Charle-
magne arranged amongst themselves. When the Middle Kingdom of Lotharius had come to the end of its brief career and
the French Kingdom and the Holy Roman Empire of the
German nation were left facing each other, their frontier in
the North followed the Scheldt right across the Frankish area.
Flanders, as the country between the Scheldt and the North
Sea was now called, owed allegiance to the King of France;
all the rest of the Germanic Netherlands, with a large slice
of Walloon land, belonged to the German Empire. These
distant parts proved fertile soil for feudal principalities, which
became practically independent when the power of the French
Kings, and afterwards that of the Emperors, declined. Soon the
Netherlands were a chaos of petty states, each pursuing a
territorial policy of its own and eternally at war amongst themselves. Flanders, while taking a strenuous part in the general
mêlée of feudal anarchy, was from the middle of the twelfth
century subjected to formidable attempts on the part of the
French Kings to restore their authority over it. The French
Kings were then building up a powerful state, and it was only
the unexpected popular strength of the great Flemish towns,
Brugge[1] and Ghent, that defeated their attempts on Flanders,
and, in saving the Germanic character of the most exposed
region, at the same time prevented the French Kings from replacing the imperial authority in the other Netherlands by
their own. What the French monarchy failed to achieve, however, was later effected by a branch of their royal house, which
derived its power from purely French possessions.

Long before the rise of Burgundian power united most of

[1] Brugge: in French—*Bruges*.

the feudal principalities of the originally Frankish area in a political structure, that area was the scene of a distinctive Netherlandish civilization. The great thirteenth-century poet Maerlant, for instance, covered practically the whole of it with his attention and his influence. Himself a Fleming, he composed a wider literary language, which he called *Dietsch*. He enjoyed the protection of the Count of Holland. He addressed some of his finest lyrical poems to ecclesiastics of Utrecht. His truest and ablest follower was a Brabander. At the same time, from this originally Frankish nucleus, political forces of various description stretched eastward, tending to withdraw the adjoining regions from participating in the political and cultural life of Germany. The East-Frankish country on the Maas was drawn into the orbit of Netherlands life by the union of the Duchy of Limburg with the Duchy of Brabant. The Saxon and Frisian country immediately to the north and east of the Frankish land had had special relations with it ever since the diocese of Utrecht had been formed under the immediate pressure of the Merovingian Kings. The town of Utrecht and the surrounding district and even Overysel and the town of Groningen long recognized the Bishop not merely as their spiritual but as their secular overlord, while at an early stage the episcopal see itself had fallen under the political influence of the Counts of Holland. Holland, too, tenaciously attempted to subdue Friesland, and long before—in the sixteenth century—actual political victory was achieved, Frisian language and civilization had begun to give way to Frankish influence, of which Holland was the agent. That some generations after Maerlant's death there existed a wider area of cultural affinity appears from nothing so strikingly as from the great religious movement of the Modern Devotion which, started towards the end of the fourteenth century by Geert Groote of Deventer, who was himself deeply influenced by Ruusbroec, the Brabant mystic, spread over all the Netherlands; the Brethren of the Common Life and their schools were a powerful factor in moulding the spiritual and intellectual outlook of the urban middle class, ever the most fertile of Netherlandish civilization. The Modern Devotion, in fact, also penetrated eastward into the Saxon regions of Westphalia, which never became incorporated with the Netherlands state such as the Burgundian and Habsburg rulers fashioned it. The truth is that there was not on that side any natural racial or linguistic boundary, and that the exact line which in the end came to separate the Netherlands from Germany was the result of political accident.

In the fourteenth century it was becoming clear that the days of extreme feudal confusion were counted. The only question was by whose agency would some sort of larger unity be achieved. Owing to the desertion of the Merovingian Kings, who had gone to seek world power in Gaul, there was not in the Netherlands any such old historic principle of union as was provided by the kingship in France or by the imperial idea in Germany. The four most powerful Netherlands princes, the Count of Flanders, the Duke of Brabant and Limburg, the Duke of Gelderland, the Count of Holland and Zealand (who was also Count of the Walloon country of Hainaut), balanced each other so nicely that it was quite impossible for any of them to raise himself to a position of supremacy. The great European rulers, however, all kept their eyes on that unstable region, whose wealthy towns, trade, and geographical position would inevitably bestow eminent power on its possessor. In spite of the efforts of German Emperors and Kings of England, it was the French family of the Dukes of Burgundy that won. They were descended from a King's younger son, and at first fully supported by the monarchy. In 1378 they acquired Flanders, and soon afterwards got a hold on Brabant. Holland, Zealand, and Hainaut fell to them before 1430, while with Luxemburg and other Walloon provinces they rounded off their Netherlands possessions.

If at first they had been able to use the French monarchy for their own purposes, soon, under Philip the Good, they came into open conflict with the country of their origin, and their design to found an independent state on the flank of France stood revealed. Charles the Bold pursued the policy of his father with a reckless ambition all his own. In the state as as it grew under him the Dutch-speaking Netherlands (though

still without the Saxon and Frisian provinces) were all united.
Not only, however, was French the language of the dynasty
and of the leading class of nobles and officials formed by it,
but the Netherlandish country was linked up with a jumble
of French and German lands with which no union on a sound
national basis was conceivable. The inspiration of the Duke's
feverish scheming was purely dynastic, and his ambitions were
carrying him ever farther away from the Netherlands when
he was overtaken by the disaster for which his great enemy,
Louis XI, the King of France, had been waiting. The crisis
into which Charles the Bold's death in 1477 threw the Burgundian state permanently altered its composition. More than half
of the French possessions were detached from it, the Duchy of
Burgundy among them; the County of Burgundy, Franche
Comté, a French-speaking fief of the Empire, remained under
Charles's daughter and heiress, but the possibility of bridging
the wide gap separating it from the *pays de par deça*—as the
Northern possessions were called—grew very remote. The
Burgundian state became essentially a Netherlands state.
With the Dutch-speaking provinces a number of Walloon
provinces remained united, but Flanders and Brabant, owing
to their wealth and the economic importance of their great
industrial and trading towns, were now the true centre of
gravity once more.

This is not to say that the dynasty became nationalized in
the Dutch-speaking part of the country. Charles's daughter,
in the hour of her distress, had married the Emperor's son
Maximilian of Habsburg; but German though he was, he
readily adopted the Burgundian dynastic tradition, and spent
the energy and resources of his wife's, and after her early death
of his son's, subjects in senseless wars to recover the lost
French possessions. It was to be no less true for the Habsburg
period which he opened than for the Burgundian period which
had come to a close that a principal factor of Netherlands
history was the lack of national solidarity between rulers and
ruled. Founded by foreigners, the Netherlands state continued
to be ruled by foreigners. All along the princes, whose work
for the building up of a Netherlands nationality looms so large

in the eyes of history, pursued other aims which had no connection with Netherlands interests whatever and which could
not but render the whole of their policy suspect in the eyes of
the people. In the revolts with which the great Dukes had had
to deal, especially from the unruly and formidable towns of
Flanders, the contrast between modern equalitarian administration and medieval urban exclusivism and particularism had
always been embittered by the difference of nationality. When
they wanted to ingratiate themselves with the men of Ghent
or of Brugge, the Dukes knew perfectly how to speak Dutch.
When they wreaked their vengeance, when they chastised and
humiliated, the language that made the Flemings tremble
was always French.

No doubt the Burgundians, like the Habsburgs after them,
did much to make the Netherlands people become politically
conscious of their nationality. An indispensable preliminary to
this development was that the resistance of provincial and
municipal particularism should be broken down, and that at
any rate was what their rule began if it did not complete it.
The bureaucracy which they created, instead of being swayed
by purely local interests, envisaged the country as a whole.
They raised up a high nobility which was similarly free from
provincial prejudices. Philip the Good's institution of the Order
of the Golden Fleece was a stroke of genius; it was remarkably
successful in giving a national outlook to the magnates who
were employed as Stadtholders of provinces or in the Prince's
Council. Philip, too, and Charles the Bold after him, had
accustomed the privileged classes—clergy, nobility, and urban
magistrates—of the various provinces to meeting each other
for the purpose of granting subsidies on a quota system: the
assembly of delegates from the various provincial States
(States being the name of the assembly of Estates in each
province) was called the States-General, and it was a most
potent means for developing a common political consciousness,
the effects of which were somewhat disconcerting to the
Dukes.

For they had done all this, not in order to develop the
Netherlands nation in accordance with its inherent qualities

and dumbly groping aspirations, but in order to make it more
amenable to their own dynastic ambitions. The bureaucracy,
the high nobility, the court, which the Dutch-speaking Netherlands owed to them, were very largely French. And though they
educated the Dutch-speaking Netherlands to the political union
for which an unkind history had done nothing to prepare them,
at the same time they connected them with a number of Walloon
provinces, which, by strengthening the class and official position
of the French language in the whole of the country, helped
to corrupt their civilization. Moreover, if on the death of
Charles the Bold most of the more distant provinces were
lopped off, by the marriage of his daughter with the Habsburg
Archduke a link was forged with even more remote interests,
to which the rulers too frequently subordinated those of the
Netherlands.

Small wonder, then, that the Netherlands union which they
had helped to bring about turned against them on the first
opportunity, and that they soon found the States-General,
which they had instituted for the convenience of their financial
administration, facing them in a hostile mood as the personifi-
cation of the Netherlands people. Under Charles the Bold
the political classes of the whole country had already realized
their community of interests as against the grasping dynasticism
of the ruler. But under him dissatisfaction was still countered
by fear. On the accession of the helpless Maria, however, and
again some years later, when after her early death Maximilian
held the regency for their son Philip the Fair, there were violent
attempts to subject monarchical rule to some sort of national
control. It is true that these outbreaks of anti-dynastic opposition were most effective in so far as they appeared in provincial
forms, and in any case they were responsible for a recrudes-
cence of the old particularist spirit. Nevertheless the idea of
Netherlands unity had already obtained so much hold over
men's minds that in no province, either in 1477 or from 1482
to 1490, was the continuance of the association with the others
called into question, except—significant exception!—that the
Flemings not only resented Maximilian's attempts to win back
the French-speaking regions lost in 1477, but even, according

to Commines, would fain have seen their ruler lose what still remained to him of Walloon subjects.

One thing, nevertheless, is made very clear in the critical times through which the Burgundian monarchy passed after Charles the Bold's death—namely, that to build up a firm political structure in opposition to the dynastic policy of the alien ruler was an undertaking that surpassed the forces of the Netherlands people. A groping towards national consciousness there was, and this was beginning to acquire a political significance. But the guidance of a dynasty which could appeal to the medieval feeling of loyalty was as indispensable in the case of the Netherlands as it was in that of any other European nation at that time, when most of the national states were being finally established. The tragedy of Netherlands history was that the dynasty called to this great task never lost its alien character and always pursued objects not only foreign but inimical to the cause of Netherlands nationality. Yet when the nation rose against its rulers, at once centrifugal tendencies appeared which, even though no conscious intention in that direction existed, jeopardized the newly established union of the provinces. In the struggle with Maximilian especially, Flanders, for all its ancient distrust of France, was inevitably driven to look for support in that quarter—a much more dangerous diversion in its case than in that of Gelderland, which also fraternized with the enemy of Habsburg, but which was situated at a safe distance from his territories. In suppressing the rebellion of Flanders, therefore, Maximilian, like the Burgundian dukes before him, unwittingly worked for the future of Netherlandish nationality, to which the reabsorption of Flanders by France would have been the gravest of blows.

For a time the dynasty and the nation seemed to have become really reconciled. When after a devastating war, in which the remnant of a Holland noblemen's party had made common cause with the urban opposition of Flanders, peace had been restored by Maximilian's German commander, Albert of Saxony, when Ghent had been made to feel the ruler's heavy hand as roughly as at any time in its stormy history, the whole collection of provinces, Dutch and Walloon, was in 1492

B

handed over undiminished to Philip the Fair, just growing into manhood. A sharp reaction manifested itself in favour of the monarchy, the restorer of order, the guardian of unity. Philip the Fair, free from the unpopularity that hung around his father as the foreign inspirer of Albert of Saxony's brutality, was hailed as a true native-born prince, the inaugurator of a happy period of peace.

Philip the Fair, it is true, was born and bred in the Dutch-speaking Netherlands, at Ghent and Mechlin. Yet not only was he surrounded by the Walloon nobility with which Philip the Good had filled the Order of the Golden Fleece and which had ever since grown in wealth and prestige, but he was the ruler who by his marriage to a daughter of Ferdinand of Arragon and Isabella of Castile prepared that unnatural connection of the Netherlands with Spain which was to lead to such disastrous results. He died young, before the destinies of his house had come to their full blossoming, but although his son Charles V, grown up at Ghent, was likewise regarded by the Netherlanders with affection as one belonging to themselves, he was nevertheless heir to that immense, multi-national empire, in which the Netherlands were no doubt one of the most valuable assets, but in which interests hostile to theirs too frequently directed policy.

II

UNDER CHARLES V

a. CONTINUED STATE-BUILDING

In two respects especially does it strike the observer how little relation there was between the policy of the ruler and either the mind or the interests of the nation. Charles V was faced by the great religious upheaval that shook the ancient Catholic unity of Europe and by which the Netherlands, as we shall see, were profoundly affected. The severe repression with which he met this crisis was far from being in accordance with the temper of the Netherlands people. It was dictated by what he thought was due to his position as the Holy Roman Emperor, by the fanaticism of his Spanish advisers, by all sorts of extra-Netherlandish considerations which made it inevitable that he should throw in his fate with the South-European Papal Church.

In the second place it is obvious that the wars he waged with France throughout his reign were no more inspired by Netherlands interests than had been the case with those of his grandfather Maximilian, and as a matter of fact they were no more popular. More than once the States became a little restive under the repeated demands for more money that were pressed upon them, and the war policy of the Government always helped to keep alive in them that suspiciousness which made them cling to their local privileges as the safeguards against arbitrary power.

Yet here it must be admitted that this policy, even though its inspiration was partly Spanish and partly German and all the time dynastic, both directly and indirectly advanced the formation of a potential Netherlandish state begun by Charles's forebears. First of all Francis I was forced to renounce the ancient suzerainty of his crown over Flanders. This, while it prevented the Flemings from sheltering any longer behind the Parliament of Paris against the encroachments of their formidable ruler's power, meant the elimination of a very old danger to Netherlands unity, which as recently as Maximilian's days had shown its actuality. At the same time it was really in pursuance of his feud with France that Charles extended Habsburg rule over those regions in the North-East whose continuously threatened independence had been temporarily reprieved when Charles the Bold's death threw the affairs of the monarchy into confusion. It is curious to observe that the States of those provinces which were most concerned owing to their contiguity, Brabant and Holland, never manifested much eagerness for the wars undertaken to subdue those regions. Yet Gelderland, Groningen, and Friesland, although largely non-Frankish, had always been in the closest contact with the Frankish Netherlands, and, once subdued, were destined to form an integral part of the Netherlandish nation. The state-building impulse was feeble in the Netherlanders, who had never been able to recognize themselves in their rulers. As for Charles, he was especially determined to have those provinces because, having been galvanized into action by the redoubtable Duke of Gelderland, Charles of Egmont, they now constituted a dangerous threat in his rear, the more dangerous through their alliance with his lifelong enemy Francis I. One by one they were conquered in a series of little wars, which were nevertheless exhausting and devastating, and which extended over a period of some twenty years, until in 1543 Gelderland itself was added as the seventeenth province under Habsburg rule. It was more than a century and a half since Flanders, more than a century since Brabant, Holland, and Zealand had fallen to the Burgundian Dukes.

The conquest of Gelderland was followed by an interval of quiet. Not that there was any inherent finality about it. East-Friesland and Cleve were both as deeply mixed up in the affairs of the provinces now conquered as these had been in the affairs of Holland and Brabant; they were indistinguishable from them in language and civilization; Cleve, moreover, was now enclosed on three sides by Habsburg territory. It might have been supposed that these regions would be the next to be swallowed, as soon as the latest acquisitions had been digested by the Habsburg system and appetite rose afresh. It was the revolt and the split which checked the eastward advance and caused the Burgundian Circle, such as Charles V created it in 1548, to wear in our eyes the appearance of a thing completed, of a thing expanded to its natural limits. Yet if the eastern frontier which Charles V traced has become the line of demarcation between the Netherlandish and German peoples, this is due to no inner necessity, but to the apparently arbitrary course of political events.

A breathing-space was badly needed, and that not only on account of the devastations which the war had caused in the new provinces and in Holland and Brabant. Force had been the decisive factor in the acquisition of all these new lands. In most cases, no doubt a few leading personages, or a few towns, had previously come to an understanding with the powerful Emperor, and always the contest had been concluded by treaties in which the provinces obtained recognition of their ancient constitutions in exchange for their acceptance of the new prince. Nevertheless time was required, after so protracted a resistance, before the leading classes of these several provinces could accustom themselves to Habsburg rule. No less troublesome were the inter-provincial feuds which the period of unrest had intensified—between Gelderland and Holland and Brabant—between Holland and Utrecht, between Groningen and Friesland.

It may seem surprising that in spite of all these weaknesses the achievement of the Habsburger has nevertheless proved to be so enduring. Yet there is nothing miraculous in this. Long ago the Burgundian Dukes had been greatly assisted in extending their authority over the southern and western Netherlands by the weakening of the particularist principle of the feudal age. The violence with which it had asserted itself once more in the North-East had at the same time exhausted it. Even the turbulent noblemen who had revelled in the guerilla warfare had enough of it for the time being. Submission to the powerful ruler seemed to be the only safeguard against a renewal of the intolerable anarchy which had ruined the country. Thus it was without much difficulty that

Charles in 1549 carried a most important measure which was calculated to consolidate Habsburg rule in the Netherlands even more than the formation of the Burgundian Circle. In all provinces the States assemblies and towns swore fealty to their future prince, his son Philip, who had come over from Spain, while at the same time they ratified a uniform regulation of the succession, a Pragmatic Sanction as it was called, notwithstanding such ancient privileges and customs as might conflict therewith. This was intended to obviate the danger lest differences of opinion should arise at any time as to the succession, or that any provinces, owing to divergent law in this matter, should become separated from the others. The Governess, Maria of Hungary, had previously sought the opinion of the Great Council of Mechlin upon the question whether the Emperor were competent to regulate the succession for his descendants in this way. The Council returned a characteristic reply:

We do not entertain any doubt but that His Majesty may arrange this affair. The measure not only is in accordance with law and reason, but it is founded on the important and inestimable advantage which by preventing dissensions and wars (by which otherwise they might be visited) it will bring to these provinces and subjects.

This utterance deserves to be called characteristic because in it are indicated the principles which inspired the entire policy of the Burgundian-Habsburg rulers in the Netherlands. Against the ancient privileges of provinces and towns, classes and groups—against tradition, in fact—they appealed to law and reason, to the common weal. Under Charles V and Philip II the monarchy was no less eager to reform than it had been under Philip the Good and Charles the Bold, and it still found its principal assistants in lawyers and officials who assailed the usages handed down from former generations with rulings derived from Roman Law and common sense.

In each new province organs of the prince's authority were established, after the usual pattern: Court of Justice, Chamber of Accounts, Stadtholder. Moreover, the central administration was organized anew. In 1531 a famous "Ordinance," expressing the tendency towards specialization which had long manifested itself in the Prince's Council, created three Councils in order to assist the Governess. The Secret Council, which dealt with matters of justice, and the Council of Finance were composed mainly of "long-robed men," while the magnates sat on the Council of State, which was consulted on matters of general policy.

These magnates were at the same time employed as Stadt-holders in the several provinces. Moreover, the Order of the Golden Fleece, to which most of them belonged, still possessed the right of counselling the prince on matters of state. The high nobility thus occupied an important position in the Burgundian-Habsburg polity, and this position was one of general, not merely of provincial or local, significance. Even in the capacity of Stadtholders, for all the independence with which they were allowed to act, they still represented central authority, and as a rule a nobleman did not fill the Stadtholder's office in his native province or in the province where the bulk of his estates was to be found. The policy initiated by Philip the Good with so firm a hand had been continued, and the high nobility had acquired a Burgundian outlook. There was, however, this difference, that Burgundian without Burgundy, lost in 1477, had developed into Netherlandish (albeit with a preponderance of the Walloon element), while at the same time Burgundian interpreted in this guise was no longer synonymous with the dynasty, which had become Habsburg, Imperial, Spanish. Under Charles V this difference still remained hidden, and the nobility served him with entire conviction. Under his successor the contrast was soon to come to light. In any case, apart from the relations with the ruler, the high nobility was a unifying factor in the Netherlands community, although it was at the same time a centre of gallicization.

This whole centralizing effort met with little but opposition from the old political organs of towns and provinces, but indeed the Government, at least under Charles V, walked warily on the whole. A violent incident such as that of the Ghent rebellion of 1539, for which the incorrigible town was mercilessly punished, remained exceptional. Most of the town governments, in all of which the prince had caused the oligarchic system to prevail, entertained good relations with the central authority and its representatives. The privileges of towns and provinces were respected. From the side of the Government, it is true, there was no end of pushing and pressing, to which the subjects often gave way, but when they did hold firm, the Government yielded: it never resorted to downright coercion. This holds good even for the cruel persecution for religion's sake, although as we shall see it led to many clashes. But the fact is that in consequence of the opposition it encountered it was far from being carried out as systematically as the Government would have wished.

His wars with France were doubtless responsible for much in this wise moderation of Charles V. His representatives were everlastingly pestering the States with requests for money. As his reign grew older finance became ever more his predominant care, and there was already so much grumbling about heavy charges that it was necessary to humour the States on other points. In addition to this the Emperor was always fearful lest quarrels with his Netherlands provinces would open the door to French interference. (The people of Ghent had been so unwise as to select for their revolt a moment when Charles V and Francis I were fraternizing.) Whatever the motives, as a matter of fact the Habsburg state in the Netherlands was very far removed from the "French slavery" which before their annexation in 1527 had been a bogey to the magistrates of Utrecht.

We must now face the question as to what was the attitude of the people, or of the various sections of the people, towards the monarchy, how firmly knit was that state of the seventeen provinces, and what were the feelings of nationality which inspired the inhabitants. But first it will be necessary to glance at the cultural movement of the period, and especially to consider the most striking event, the disruption of the age-old Catholic unity which brutal oppression could not heal but only cover up.

b. CIVILIZATION

In spite of civil wars, floods, and plagues, in spite of the painful embarrassment into which large social groups were brought by the devaluation of money—a consequence of the discovery of America—the first half of the sixteenth century was a period of amazing economic development for the Netherlands. Not all the provinces, certainly, had an equal share in this. The North-East resumed a modest and gradual progress only after the conquest, which secured peace. In Flanders the old centres of prosperity had sadly decayed. The silting-up of the Zwin could be checked no longer, and Brugge was a mere shadow of what it had been. The industry of Ghent and Yper had now definitely fallen behind in their competition with the English. The three great towns still possessed much ancient wealth, but their guilds had lost all hold on economic life and struggled in vain against unemployment. But in the country and in the small towns which were now protected by the prince's authority against the tyranny which the three used to exercise in medieval times, a new industry had sprung up which, free from the limitations and restraints of the medieval guild system, and using the cheaper Spanish wool, found markets where the English manufacturers could not follow. The area of this "new drapery" extended from the coast near Dunkirk and Veurne[1] down into Walloon Flanders: St. Winok's Bergen,[2] Hondschoote, Armentières were centres. Moreover, a linen industry began to flourish along the Leie, using Flemish flax for its raw material, and especially in the neighbourhood of Oudenaarde thousands were employed in tapestry weaving, first raised into an art in the Walloon town of Arras and now also practised in Brabant towns, especially Leuven[3] and Brussels. Flanders therefore remained an important industrial region, even though an economic revolution was taking place there which caused a great deal of misery. The new rural proletariat, moreover, scattered as it was, and outside the organization of the guilds, had much less chance

[1] Veurne: in French—*Furnes*.   [2] St. Winok's Bergen: in French—*Bergues*.
[3] Leuven: in French—*Louvain*.

of protecting itself against the increasingly powerful
capitalists.

About the middle of the sixteenth century Flanders still
raised more than any other province under the system of
quotas as introduced by Philip the Good; its share was about
one-third of the total amount raised by what was called "the
patrimonial provinces"—that is, the seventeen without the
recently conquered north-eastern ones. Brabant—without
Mechlin—paid a little less than Flanders; Holland half of what
was paid by Brabant, Zealand one-fourth of what was paid
by Holland. It will be noticed that the Dutch-speaking provinces in the aggregate raised by far the larger half of the total:
the share of the Walloon provinces was not more than about
one-fifth, or, if the north-eastern provinces are counted in,
considerably less. Within the Dutch-speaking provinces,
although Flanders still occupied the first place, the principal
centres of economic development were to be looked for elsewhere—at Antwerp, and in Holland and Zealand.

Antwerp had become the heir to Brugge, the pivot of the
great European movement of exchange of northern for southern
produce, at the same time the port for the Flemish and Brabant
textiles and for the Liège and Hainaut metals. One consequence
of the Portuguese discovery of the sea route to India and of
the Spanish discovery of America was to increase the importance
of this European trade of exchange between North and South:
Lisbon became the staple port of the Indian spices; Sevilla
of the gold and the other products of America. Both Portuguese
and Spaniards made Antwerp their headquarters for the distribution towards the North. The German and Italian bankers
established offices there. The town grew rapidly, although even
by the middle of the sixteenth century it was not a large town
if measured with modern standards: the number of its inhabitants is estimated at 100,000. But in the Europe of its own
time it made an imposing appearance; in European commerce
the place it occupied was unique.

A weakness, however, in the position of Antwerp was the
fact that this great trading movement, which gave employment
of many kinds to the industrious natives and fostered their

prosperity, yet went mainly through the medium of colonies of foreigners. Apart from the French who, without being properly organized as a colony, were to be found there in large numbers, there were at Antwerp colonies of Scandinavians and Germans, Italians, Spaniards, English, and Portuguese (and of them all the Spaniards were most numerous). Add the Walloons, of whom many settled in the town, and it will become clear how important was the non-Dutch element in the Antwerp trading world. Guicciardini, the Florentine, who lived at Antwerp, and in 1567 published his famous *Descrittione di tutti i Paesi Bassi*, notes that French is taught at several schools, and gives it as his opinion that before long that language would be generally spoken at Antwerp. This is the superficial judgment of a foreigner. Even in the business world French was still far from occupying a dominating position. In the administration and in the law courts, in public and intellectual life the town remained as Dutch as it had ever been. The weakness which I indicated was a purely economic one. Although bound as time went on with ever more numerous ties to the labour, the skill, and the capital of the native citizens, trade yet remained as it were a visitor to Antwerp. Especially as there was still another peculiarity about the position.

Just as Brugge had been in her time, so was Antwerp a port without a merchant fleet of her own. The vessels with which she maintained the intercourse with northern and southern Europe either belonged to those distant countries or had their owners in the ports of Holland and Zealand. Those ports were therefore not merely Antwerp's competitors. They were this in so far as they gave the most immediate access to the northern Netherlands and disputed the German hinterland to Antwerp. For certain goods some became the staple ports for wide areas, such as Amsterdam for wheat from the Baltic, Dordt for Rhine wine. But at the same time their merchant fleets served the Antwerp trade of exchange and themselves benefited by Antwerp's prosperity.

The steady growth of the trade of Holland and Zealand is one of the most noticeable phenomena in the economic history of the first half of the sixteenth century. Amsterdam was still far from equalling Antwerp, but it was already an important trading town, and in the Baltic trade its position was a dominating one. Capital flowed into the Holland towns, rousing them to unprecedented activity. The country-side, too, benefited, and cattle breeding and dairy farming still formed the basis of the Holland economic system. Guicciardini grew enthusiastic over Holland. While still possessing a reputation for boorish backwardness, in reality the province, according to him, was a model of ordered civilization. The organization of the dykes and the waterways filled the Italian observer with admiration, and even more so did the appointment of dwelling houses.

To enter their houses and to examine the abundance of furniture and all kinds of utensils, all equally neat and well kept, causes great pleasure and even greater astonishment, for, indeed, there is not perhaps in the whole world anything to equal it. This is what I have heard said by the quartermasters of the Emperor Charles V, who had been over most of Europe with His Majesty; and as everyone knows, they, who in all towns enter the houses, are better able to judge of this than anyone else.

In fact, in spite of local differences it may be said of the whole of the Netherlands in the days of Charles V and Philip II that here was a prosperous and highly cultured people. In 1473 the first printing-presses were founded at Aalst[1] and Leuven. In the next twenty years the number had steadily grown in Flanders and Brabant, but even more in the northern provinces. The country-side was still dominated by nobility and clergy, who were more exclusively the proprietors of the soil, and enjoyed a higher prestige and exercised a greater political influence in some provinces than in others. This was so (leaving out the Walloon area) in all the inland provinces, both north and south. Yet even there the urban middle class, enterprising, well educated, keen on their privileges and liberties, played an important part in economic, intellectual, and political life. Looking at the Netherlands as a whole they appear

---

[1] Aalst: in French—*Alost.*

a veritable land of towns; both in their economics and in their civilization the third estate dominated.

However admirable were some of the features of that civilization, a harmonious development had for some time been beyond its reach. The middle-class basis and conditions were not in themselves the greatest difficulty. But this middle-class society was contained in a monarchical state, and, what was worse, that monarchy was foreign, and, without intending to do so, inevitably alienated from the people the nobility whom it honoured and the officials whom it employed. From the court at Brussels, from the Great Council of Justice at Mechlin, there radiated much stronger forces of gallicization than from the foreign merchants at Antwerp. This is not merely a question of linguistic purity. Whole spheres of intellectual life were closed to Dutch civilization, and, bound to the towns which were themselves kept in tutelage, it could not but begin to wear a certain appearance of localism and particularism. Literature, whose medieval inspiration was running dry, could not in those circumstances easily find the fresh sources that it needed. The Chambers of Rhetoric were almost the sole guardians of Dutch poetry.

These were originally religious institutions which under the Burgundian Dukes had spread from the North of France over the whole of the Dutch-speaking Netherlands owing allegiance to them (that is to say, they were to be found in large numbers in Holland and Zealand as in Flanders and Brabant, but not in the eastern provinces north of the rivers). The part they played in the public and intellectual life of a town was now a large one. On festive occasions they produced a play; when princely visitors were to be welcomed they contributed greetings in verse for which biblical and classical antiquity were plundered. Their "Land Jubilees" became ever more splendid; these were competitions where Chambers from widely distant towns met together and prizes were assigned to the best poems or plays; they were especially frequent in the Flemish and Brabant towns, though Holland and Zealand later on had their share of these festivities. The honour of a town was involved in the appearance of its Chamber on these occasions and the expenses were borne by the municipal exchequer. No more brilliant "Land Jubilee" was ever seen than that held at Antwerp in 1561. An English spectator, obviously impressed, describes the gorgeous entry of the fourteen visiting Chambers from Flemish and Brabant towns, the festive mood which interrupted business for a few days, and the rich banquets. But although the Chambers of Rhetoric bore witness to the ostentatious prosperity of the burgher class, and even to their intellectual and artistic interest, true poetry was not produced by them. A really high standard could not possibly be maintained in the circle of those excellent and merry citizens. Only some verses of Anna Bijns, an Antwerp school teacher, who wrote after the manner of the Rhetoricians, probably without belonging to a Chamber herself, are still alive with the passion with which she defended the Catholic church against the schismatics of her day.

The poetry of the Rhetoricians was an offshoot of the medieval spirit whose inspiration, as I said, was exhausted. We are soon bored by ingenious tricks such as double rhymes and chain rhymes, which had to do service for poetic beauty, by the hollow emphasis, by the cheap pretentiousness of words taken from the French with which the Rhetoricians' language was flooded in Holland no less than in the South. Yet it is possible to see in all this a reflection, albeit a pale one, of the vehement striving after renovation which inspired the cultural life of all Europe at that time. Everywhere there was a searching after new truths and new forms, everywhere the individual detached himself from the community and demanded freedom and space. Dreams were dreamt of a world order in which man would master his fate by means of reason. The Middle Ages had cherished an innocent admiration for Antiquity without being conscious of the profound differences which distinguished its civilizations from their own. Now the restless thinkers and scholars and artists recognized in it their own ideals. Humanism flourished exceedingly in the Netherlands. It is true that it expressed itself only by means of Latin, but its influence made itself felt on the whole of intellectual life. Nevertheless this European movement contained in itself a grave danger. It would not do to impute the disharmony characteristic of sixteenth-century Netherlands civilization solely to the peculiar political circumstances in which the life of the Netherlands race was set. In all countries Renaissance and Humanism, in the exuberance of their joy at new dis-coveries, were brushing aside hopeful cultural traditions, too frequently replacing them by no more than a slavish love of imitation. This was certainly not the essence of the new European spirit. In the noblest minds the contemplation of the wise and beautiful world of Greece and Rome encouraged a loving cultivation of native possibilities. Now and again some Dutch writer, too, possessed enough independence to read the lesson of antiquity aright, and to understand that pride in borrowed feathers was no true wisdom. In 1553, for instance, Jan van de Werve, a well-born citizen of Antwerp, published a *Tresoor der Duitsche tale*, in which he made a spirited attack on the abuse of Romance words:

Help me, I ask you, to raise up our mother language, which now lies concealed in the earth like gold, so that we may prove how need-less it is for us to beg for assistance of other languages.

It should not be overlooked that the man who wrote these words belonged to a higher social class than that which set the tone in the Chambers of Rhetoric. Such utterances in any case long remain somewhat scarce and timid, in comparison with France, where Du Bellay had written his *Défense et illustration de la langue française* in 1548. It is only in a later period, as we shall see, that the true Renaissance spirit together with the desire for intellectual independence assert themselves in Dutch literature.

Architecture and painting were no more able to keep them-selves free from the overwhelming southern influence. The architectural forms of the Italian Renaissance had long been known, as may be seen from the pictures of Van Eyck and Memlinc. But the practice of architecture depended too much on the skill of the artisans as it was handed down from one genera-tion to another to follow suit at once. Now, however, sculptors and decorators began to play with the new Italian-antique

motives. The burgher class wanted to see their prosperity osten-
tatiously expressed in civic buildings, as did the nobility in their
palaces, and the artists revelled as whole-heartedly in the rich
ornamentation of the Renaissance as did the Rhetoricians in
their foreign words and mythological allusions. But if the
enjoyment was of the same character, far greater was the
mastery with which architects and sculptors fashioned pilasters
and architraves, gryphons and medallions, plants shooting
upward from vases. A number of most attractive works came
into existence, as the oaken roodscreen at Enkhuizen, the
porch of the Mint and the choirstalls in the great church at
Dordt, the House of the Salmon at Mechlin. Looking at these
products of the Netherlands Renaissance one is often tempted
to think oneself transported into an earlier period of the great
movement in Italy. And yet this is not always the impression
received. In the famous mantelpiece of the Free District Court
room at Brugge, even more than in that of the Town Court
room at Kampen, these forms adopted from abroad express
a peculiarly Netherlandish quality of feeling, heavier and more
exuberant than that of the more subtle Southerners with their
unfaltering sense of measure. In the general planning of
buildings, moreover, the native traditions offered tenacious
resistance. Not only did the pointed arch long remain pre-
valent, but even at a time when the names of Vitruvius and
his Italian prophets, Alberti and Serlio, were mentioned with
respect—about 1540 Pieter Coecke, of Aalst, published Dutch
translations of their writings—buildings which in details conformed to their precepts yet preserved, with their high roofs,
gables and towers, an entirely unclassical and un-Italian
character. A peculiarly Netherlandish Renaissance style was
thus developed, especially in the South; the Chancery at
Brugge (about 1530) is an early example of this.

Meanwhile, the painter's art was suffering from the evil of
imitation much more severely. By the middle of the sixteenth
century the national tradition was being most woefully over-
grown by the Italian fashion. Yet the native genius for this
art was far from being exhausted. Until 1530 Antwerp possessed in the cultured Quinten Matsys, the friend of humanists,

a noble representative of that generous love of beauty so characteristic of the age. Gossart of Mabuse (Maubeuge), a Walloon who worked at Antwerp for some time—the town attracted artists from all parts—the first who went to Italy in person and preached the undiluted doctrine of Italianism, was himself a figure of undeniable talent. At the same time there were in Holland Lucas van Leyden and Jan van Scorel, the latter working mostly at Utrecht, both men who underwent the Italian influence and yet preserved an individuality of their own. After them, however, a stiff academic spirit grew dominant. An Italian journey became indispensable if a painter wanted to be taken seriously, and an insufferably artificial style compelled universal admiration. The artistic world bowed down before men like Michiel Coxie and Frans Floris, who worked at Mechlin and at Antwerp respectively, and whose art breathes the same spirit as the increasingly conventional and stilted poetry of the Rhetoricians; they were also, as Karel van Mander was soon to relate, equally fond of a pot of beer in their leisure hours. In the North the situation was no better. Instead of having conquered freedom for a more courageous individualism, this generation allowed itself to be swept off its feet by another mighty wave of southern civilization.

And yet this same period witnessed the miracle of Pieter Breughel. Born in a North-Brabant village he worked at Antwerp and Brussels after having been to Italy like everybody else, but in the choice of his subjects as well as in spirit and technique hardly any painter before him was more thoroughly Netherlandish than he; it is true that he owed something in this respect to the Amsterdam master Pieter Aertssen, who had worked at Antwerp for some time. Breughel paints the Brabant peasant and the Brabant landscape with unsurpassed directness. At the same time his work is impregnated with a sense of the tragic which raises it high above mere realism.

Was it the tension caused by Reformation and religious persecution—a tension of which neither the academic painters nor the Rhetoricians seemed to be aware—that was respon-

sible for the tremor one detects in Breughel's art? Here was
another factor, and the most potent of all, to disturb the
harmony of sixteenth-century Netherlandish civilization.

c. THE DISRUPTION OF CATHOLIC UNITY

In the spirit of the time there lurked a danger. In their eager
search for truth and reason men were brought to smash irre-
parably the forms in which State and Church had settled
down, and, when they were checked midway, there resulted
the great disruption which the Reformation betokened for the
whole of Europe north of the Alps and the Pyrenees. The
Church was undeniably in a condition of decadence which the
best minds observed with pain. The Papacy offered a sorry
spectacle. In the Netherlands as elsewhere, too many priests
were worldly and indifferent, thinking only of money and
benefices. The country vicars were hardly less rude than the
villagers, and almost without exception were living openly in
concubinage. The monasteries had lost sight of their spiritual
task. As a result of the economic power which it owed to its
ever increasing landed property, the Church was in continual
conflict with the urban communities and with the Government
itself. Scholastic theology hampered the intellectual movement
which at one time it had supported. The faith that was
preached to the multitude had a mechanical quality and
practices were permitted—especially the trade of indulgences
—which revolted really religious souls. Reformation was sorely
needed. But reformation had been sorely needed many times
and had been effected without a break with the past. Was it
inevitable that now, because men's minds were full of new
longings and expectations, reformation must spell demolition?

In the first decades of the sixteenth century that was certainly not the opinion of those who in the Netherlands were
most keenly interested in those problems. A new generation
of humanists had grown up, trained in the schools of the
Brethren of the Common Life, clerics, rectors of Latin Schools,
men for whom learning and piety had to go hand in hand,
and who held that reformation of abuses would follow from

enlightenment as a matter of course. The mystical spirit of Ruusbroec and Geert Groote worked in them less strongly than the spirit of research and investigation of Wessel Gansfort. Not only therefore did they bitterly criticize the clergy, but they often arrived at unorthodox conclusions. Especially the symbolical interpretation of the communion was frequently foreshadowed by Netherlands thinkers. But the medieval Church left considerable latitude to individual opinions on doctrine, and the Biblical Humanists, as the Netherlands school is often called to distinguish it from the paganistic humanists of Italy, did not dream of secession. On the contrary, their mood was one of hopefulness. Their influence on the educated middle class was indeed great, and it is quite justifiable to speak of a national movement, which nevertheless, since it used Latin almost exclusively, flowed out imperceptibly in every direction into great European currents. This use of Latin at the same time determined the somewhat aristocratic character of the movement. We may quote it as an instance of the fact, which the history of medieval civilization demonstrates again and again, that it was in the sphere of religion that the Netherlands under foreign rule were capable of the most original and valuable intellectual manifestations. It should be noted that in scholarship and through Latin the barriers between the nation and the governing classes were eliminated. Erasmus, the most representative figure amongst the Biblical Humanists, a man whose mind had its roots deep in Netherlands traditions of civilization, and who at the same time enjoyed a European fame such as had not yet fallen to the lot of any Netherlander—Erasmus had his friends amongst princes and noblemen, prelates and high officials, and it was on such that he counted for the carrying-out of his schemes of reform.

Superficially Erasmus of Rotterdam gives one the impression of a complete cosmopolitan. He was overjoyed when he was able to go to Paris in 1495 (just before he completed his thirtieth year). The quickened interest in true Latinity, behind which Greek was beckoning with an even fairer promise, created out of enthusiasts of all countries a republic of scholars in which Erasmus felt completely at home, the more so as he was so generally honoured as its first citizen. Nearly the whole remainder of his life was spent abroad. A couple of years as a dependant in a nobleman's castle near Veere; twice a period of a few years at the University of Leuven; for the rest, after France it was England, then Italy, again England, Germany, and Switzerland. After 1522 Erasmus, who died in 1536, did not see his country again. (By *patria* at first he understood only the County of Holland, but later Flanders and Brabant were also comprised in the term). His most famous works were written and printed abroad. His most intimate friends in the prime of his life were the great English humanists. His letters, in which he discussed problems of scholarship and theology and the affairs of the world with irresistible wit and zest—they were really a high form of journalism, and, going from hand to hand, and soon printed, contributed powerfully to the propagation of his ideas—these letters were addressed to correspondents of all nations.

Yet nothing is plainer than that the opinions of the religious leader—and Erasmus was that no less than he was a scholar, especially during the later period of his life—sprang from a Netherlands tradition, that of Geert Groote, largely as it had been developed by Wessel Gansfort. Subtle disputations about dogma, cold-hearted denunciations on the grounds of theological opinions, were to Erasmus intensely hateful, no less than the excesses of popular religion, which he branded as superstitions. For him Christianity consisted in christian love and christian life. That temper—it can hardly be called a theological system—of which reasonableness, humanity, tolerance were the characteristic features, nowhere penetrated so profoundly as in the Netherlands, where it found the soil prepared, and where, moreover, Erasmus's personal influence counted for more than anywhere else. Here, too, Erasmus came to face the great practical task of his life—a task which he was unable to fulfil, but the enterprise alone ennobles his career. In 1517 he came to Leuven in order to bring about the triumph in his own country of "good letters" and pure piety.

Leuven was a stronghold of traditional theology. Erasmus,

whose fame was at its zenith, was received with distinction, but not without suspicion. He felt himself borne along on the current of the time. A Leuven citizen, Hieronymus van Busleyden, a member of the Great Council of Mechlin, had bequeathed to the University a fund for the establishment of a *Collegium Trilingue*: for the study of Hebrew, Greek, and Latin, the three languages of the Bible and the Fathers. Nothing could have been more congenial to Erasmus, and he exerted himself as much as possible to make a success of the college, whose chairs were occupied by his disciples. Erasmus believed whole-heartedly in academic truth. Restore in its purity the knowledge of the Bible and the Fathers, dispel the dark cloud of scholasticism, and the reign of heartfelt and simple Christianity, such as he understood it, would begin. To him mankind seemed to possess in its reason a key to its own perfection, and to earthly and heavenly happiness. It was a noble dream, but it was rudely shattered by the flood-tide of religious passion set in movement about that very time by Luther in Germany.

Luther was incapable of waiting for the gradual penetration of the influence of "good letters." When after his first indignant protest Emperor and Pope wanted to force him to submission, they drove him to the discovery that the immediate contact with God in which he found his strength had no need of the Church and its means of grace. Taking his stand on that ground he hurled his defiance into the world, and the century in ferment responded with jubilation to the promise of deliverance. Erasmus, although agreeing with Luther on many points, dreaded the consequences of his vehement one-sidedness too much to join in the chorus, but he disapproved none the less of the violence with which the zealots on the other side attacked the daring monk, even before his final condemnation, as if on purpose to drive him on. This was not enough to preserve for Erasmus the sympathies of the many who denounced as half-heartedness all hanging back where Luther rushed forward. At the same time the division which had now come about in Germany caused all conservative forces in the Netherlands as well to adopt a harsher attitude, so that in their eyes, too, the exponent of a reasonable reformation, and the entire cause of "good letters," became suspect. This was a heavy blow, for it was on the persuasion of the powerful that Erasmus had built his hopes, and indeed they had begun to give him their attention. But now they pressed him from all sides to take part in the struggle against Luther. Leuven, leaning on a Government whose determination to maintain orthodoxy was decided by quite other than Netherlandish considerations, came forward as a champion against the heretic. But Erasmus held fast to his conviction that only ruin could result from strife. Rather than abandon his independence, he left Leuven in the autumn of 1521 and retired to Switzerland. His attitude in those years compels the deepest respect. Against Luther as well as against the obscurantists who blamed "good letters" for all the trouble, against fanatics on both sides, he continued to proclaim undaunted the rights of reason and criticism, but also of respect for tradition. The age listened to him no more. In the grip of a furious gale of hatred and misunderstanding it hurried past him, into disasters and disruptions without end.

In Germany Lutheranism was spreading, and in a number of states organizing itself under the protection of the princes; finally, in 1555, even obtaining imperial recognition. The King of England broke away from the Papacy and the English people was by degrees protestantized. At the same time in the Netherlands the ruler, without regarding the opinion of his subjects, obstinately attempted to root out all heretical sentiments by means of force. It was impossible to eradicate Biblical Humanism from men's minds, but the opportunity for its adherents to lead a conservative reformation had gone for ever. As late as 1529 Laevinus Ammonius (Lieven van der Maude), a Carthusian monk of Ghent, addressed to Erasmus at Basel a pressing invitation to come and settle down at Ghent.

All the members of the Council of Flanders (he wrote) are heartily devoted to you; a large number of the monks have abandoned their superstitious practices and have returned to true piety.

But in the following year the writer was expelled by a new prior. Others who could be charged with more decidedly heretical opinions had already made their submission, as for instance Grapheus, the secretary of Antwerp. Some, on the other hand, went over to Protestantism, and had to seek a refuge in Germany; such were Gnapheus, a Hollander, author of a little book of edification in the vernacular that was soon placed on the index (*The Consolation and Mirror of the Sick*), and two Flemings, Berthulfus and Rex, who both had served Erasmus as secretary. The Inquisition, meanwhile, found quite a different kind of people to deal with.

An Episcopal Inquisition had long existed in all countries; but in the Netherlands, where the organization of the dioceses was thoroughly antiquated, this was considered to be entirely insufficient. In 1522, therefore, Charles V, who wanted to make of his hereditary lands an example of what such things should be, organized an Inquisition of his own, and although this had soon to make room for a papal establishment, the monarch arrogated to himself complete control over the clerical heresy-hunters. No doubt he defended orthodoxy for the sake of God's honour, but no less for the strengthening of his own power, which unorthodox opinions seemed to threaten. Side by side with the Inquisition properly so called, which in the face of resistance based on privileges it proved impossible to introduce into certain provinces—Groningen, Gelderland, Brabant—courts of law and sheriffs carried on religious persecution on the strength of the edicts issued by Charles in the plenitude of his sovereign power, and which were binding on all the secular authorities in his Netherlands provinces. From the very first these edicts pronounced draconic punishments on all who were even remotely connected with heresy; every new one was more severe than the last, until in 1550 the limit of frightfulness was reached with the "edict of blood," in which all loopholes were stopped and death was enacted for all trespasses.

It was a monstrous policy, and, if it had been carried out to the letter, it would have placed all Netherlands towns under the continual smoke of the faggots. But the execution could not but meet with endless difficulties in a country where both officials and magistrates were impregnated with the spirit of Erasmus, while, moreover, the latter wanted to protect their citizens against so arbitrary a procedure for the sake of the privileges and of free commercial intercourse. In vain the Government tried to undermine society itself by promising to informers a share in the spoils of forfeitures. In the opinion of those who designed the system, religious persecution in the Netherlands never worked anything but defectively.

Nevertheless, after the first deaths by fire—the victims were two Antwerp Augustinian monks, burnt at Brussels in 1523—the number of the martyrs kept steadily growing, and soon the terror of the persecutions began to cause emigration. Particularly the edict of 1550 made a profound impression. The magistracy of Antwerp, fearing that it would frighten away trade, offered tenacious opposition, but in vain. And yet this horror, imposed by the wish of a practically foreign ruler, achieved no more than that the opinions which it was intended to kill were driven underground. Men who could have given a lead kept quiet or left the country, but the spectacle of the martyrs' sufferings and courage made many thousands of simple souls take the new heresy into their hearts. In the parlour and the market place, in the workshop and in the meetings of the Rhetoricians, passionate discussions went on about the problems of faith. Souls that were inaccessible to the learning of the humanists now thirsted after the new doctrine.

Meanwhile the lead given by Netherlands thinkers did not lose all effect, and while during those early years all heresy in the Netherlands was described as Lutheranism, and, indeed, had been roused by Luther, it nevertheless had a character of its own. On the whole—and this was far from being Lutheran —it had a Sacramentarian tendency, that is to say, the communion used to be interpreted symbolically. In any case men's minds were profoundly affected. Antwerp, with its German colony and trading relations, was an active centre for the distribution of the heresy.

What disputations there are amongst people!
The world is full of error, where shall we flee!
It has come to this, by Luther's poison,
That all that may stir to sin is praised,
While all that may purge the soul is blamed.
Where have we come to! May God take pity on us.

Thus lamented Anna Bijns: "for this sort"—the heretics—
"is fast growing among Dutch and Walloons." Indeed, at the
"Land Jubilee" held at Ghent in 1539, where nineteen Chambers, mostly from Flanders and Brabant, met, a question had
been proposed for the playwrights: "Which is the greatest
comfort to a dying man?", and practically all the moralities
breathed an unorthodox spirit, so that the book in which they
were collected and published at once fell under the Imperial
ban.

But at that time another form of heresy had already sprung
up which even outsiders were able to distinguish from Lutheranism. Anabaptism was persecuted with uncommon bitterness, in which social hatred reinforced religious intolerance.
It, too, came from Germany, where religious excitement had
given rise to all kinds of social movements. It was a creed for
extremists, for simple-minded people with no share of the
world's goods. The Anabaptists renounced society as light-
heartedly as they did the Church, they admitted no other code
of law but the bible, no other tie but faith and love. The
economic difficulties of the period favoured the spread of this
new gospel. In their ecstatic bliss the converts expected the
approaching end of the world. Soon it was the purest religious
mania. The strength of the movement lay in Holland, but it
was at Munster that in 1534 Jan Mathijsen of Haarlem founded
the new Jerusalem, whither the faithful were summoned if
they would avoid eternal damnation. Thousands set out from
Holland, but were intercepted and caught by the troops of
the Government. As long as the fantastic Reign of God lasted
at Munster—Jan Mathijsen had been killed and an even
wilder fanatic, Jan Beukelszoon of Leyden, had proclaimed
himself king—unrest continued in the whole of the northern
Netherlands. With the fall of Munster in the summer of

1535 their high expectations everywhere collapsed. The community, however, survived, but only by reacting sharply against the excesses which had made it notorious. A new leader arose in the Frisian preacher, Menno Simons, an ex-priest, who mostly kept himself in safety in East Friesland (an independent County), but not without risking many expeditions in order to teach and organize "the allies" groaning under Habsburg rule. His influence caused the Baptists or Mennonists to develop into a quiet unworldly sect, with little inclination towards dogma, but greatly concerned about morality, averse from matters of state, all wrapt up in their personal search for the narrow path of God and in the endless quarrels and schisms which resulted from their markedly individualistic belief. In the forties and fifties Protestantism, which did not cease to expand underneath the Catholic surface, was mainly Baptist, and the southern provinces, especially Antwerp and Flanders, now came under the influence of that doctrine as much as the North. In the whole of that period the Baptists supplied the bulk of the martyrs burnt or drowned for the sake of religion. However harmless they had become, the terror of Munster still attached to their name. Soon—for the first time in 1562—the confessions and last letters of the martyrs were collected and printed by the care of their leaders. *The Lord's Sacrifice* (as the book was called) contains moving confessions of those pious and simple souls, small citizens and artisans all of them, men and women from Amsterdam and Rotterdam, from Leeuwarden, Antwerp, and Ghent. In the firm conviction that it is for the honour of God, they steel their hearts to suffer a bitter death; they comfort and admonish their relatives, and refrain from judging their judges and executioners. Theirs was a faith which taught how to bear persecution with dignity, and I should almost say with grace, but which on account of its gentleness as well as of its individualism was unfit for the task of rousing a people to resistance.

That task fell to Calvinism, which began to penetrate in the fifties and sixties from Geneva into the whole of the Netherlands, and also from France into the Walloon region, and thence into the Dutch-speaking provinces. If the Baptists' faith has been little more than an episode in Netherlands history, making room for Calvinism almost without a struggle as soon as the critical times of Philip II began, it was no doubt mainly due to the political sense of Calvinism being more strongly developed. When matters came to a crisis between the nation and the monarchy, Mennonism with its lower middle class appeal could not possibly stand up against this fighting creed, which understood organization and discipline, and which had armed itself with a philosophy for state and society.

The thing that most forcibly strikes the unprejudiced observer to-day in this development of the religious conditions in the Low Countries is the lack of liberty in their spiritual life. For a generation and more the fire is kept smouldering in the depths before it can break out in flames. There is an appearance of constraint about the whole of that period. A harmonious development on national lines was out of the question. Such a development might have been possible, even after the cataclysm in Germany, under the leadership of the humanists and their supporters amongst the officials and the magistrates. When, however, under the influence of German events, the Government, that is to say Charles V and his Imperial and Spanish councillors, wedded the cause of reaction and repression, the schism in the nation's life inevitably extended into this sphere as well. The exchange of thought on the burning questions of the day between the people and its natural leaders was hampered; promising lines of development were cut off. Only the emigrants, living together in large numbers in London, Emden, Frankfort, were able to organize themselves freely. On the whole, unless acquiescing in the orthodoxy that was prescribed and severely maintained, people could look for salvation only in foreign ideas of reform. In the upshot it seems as if the ironic fates of history willed Charles V to prevent the Netherlands people from finding its own way in religious matters for no other purpose than that after his death it should be the less able to offer resistance to French Calvinism.

d. NATIONAL SENTIMENT

To consider at last the question which we left unanswered before—what was the attitude of the people, or of its various component parts, towards the monarchy and towards the state, what was the nature of the sentiments of national consciousness entertained by the inhabitants?

In spite of diverse discontents—over the heavy expenditure necessitated by the endless wars, over the religious persecutions, etc.—Charles V's person was still able to rouse the feelings of attachment to the dynasty which had become traditional in the "patrimonial provinces." It was only in the Netherlands, where forty years ago he had shouldered his heavy task, that he abdicated with public solemnity. The scene is well known. At Brussels, in October 1555, the old Emperor, old before his time as a result of his incessant cares and labours, crippled by gout, appeared before the assembled States of his seventeen Netherlands provinces. Leaning on the shoulder of young William of Orange and surrounded by all the knights of the Golden Fleece, he protested before God that it was not ambition, but a sense of duty by which he had been guided in the exercise of his more than human power. He was aware of his insufficiency. It was not out of fear for responsibility, but because his health was broken and his son had attained the vigour of his manhood, that he now laid down his authority over these countries in the latter's hands.

And here he brake into a weeping (so we are told by an English witness of the scene), whereunto, besides the dolefulness of the matter, I think he was moche provoked by seeing the whole company to doo the lyke before; there being in myne opynion not one man in the whole assemblie, stranger or other, that dewring the tyme of a good piece of his oracion poured not oute abondantly teares, some more, some less.

Yet, notwithstanding these tears at his farewell, the States of the Netherlands provinces under Charles V as well as under his predecessors had always eyed the ruler's authority with that suspiciousness which is natural towards a foreign power. Their constant fear was lest they should be dragged into a dynastic foreign policy. This suspiciousness was a real obstacle to the development of a national state. Always, behind the Government's tireless admonitions to get closer together in order to be the better able to render mutual assistance in case of foreign danger, the subjects suspected that the intention was to extort more money and to encroach on provincial autonomy. In 1534 and 1535, for instance, a project for a closer confederation of the provinces was submitted to the States-General on behalf of the Governess. In case of war all were to contribute to expenditure according to a fixed scale. But great opposition arose. Holland was willing to co-operate with Brabant and the new north-eastern provinces against Gelderland (then still independent under Charles of Egmont), but it refused to let itself be mobilized against France; while Flanders, which since the acquisition of Tournai and Lille was fairly protected against its ancient enemy France, would have nothing to do with the scheme at all. The idea of a standing army to be supported on the fixed contributions of all provinces roused general aversion. In the later years of the reign, when the finances got more and more into confusion, the endless wars meant only one thing to the public, and that was expenditure.

It was the misfortune of Netherlands history that the national forces living in the people found it so difficult to co-operate with the state-building forces directed by the monarchy. But what about these national forces themselves, as we see them at work in the sixteenth century? Now, as before, a lack of harmony seems characteristic of Netherlands civilization. The main cleavage was along social lines, although there also were geographical diversities in the area of Dutch speech, the importance of which in this period, however, tended to grow less.

The chief of these geographical lines of demarcation ran from north to south, and separated the eastern from the western part of the area which is to-day considered to be homogeneously Dutch. Holland and Zealand, which were in any case by their Frankish local dialect related much more closely to Flanders and Brabant than to Gelderland and the

North-East, had moreover been connected with these southern provinces in one and the same political structure a century before the others. They now formed with Flanders and Brabant a real cultural unit, which received most of its more significant influences from the Romance South. The eastern region, on the other hand, during the period of strenuous resistance to the advancing Burgundian-Habsburg power, seemed to have directed its attention eastward more consciously than before. The gentry of Gelderland intermarried with those of Cleve[1] and Gulich[2]; the burghers of Groningen mixed themselves up in the affairs of East Friesland; in the houses and schools of the Brethren of the Common Life no discrimination was made between natives and Westphalians. An eastern literary language was in the process of formation during those years, in competition with that of Flanders–Brabant–Holland. It was used in the Gelderland chancery and in the town hall of Groningen, by the writers of chronicles and of works of edification. It accentuated the unity with the region adjoining on the east, for until vanquished by Luther's southern High German it was current over a wide area of Germany. These conditions were still largely fluid. The religious movements, for instance, as we saw above, crossed these boundaries without difficulty. Even before the conquest Dutch cultural influences radiated from Antwerp eastward together with the town's trade. In the churches of Calcar and Xanten, which never came under Habsburg and are German to-day, one can still admire the beautiful sixteenth-century wood-carvings from Antwerp. The University at Leuven attracted into the circle of Dutch civilisation "Overlanders" (as the Easterners were called), before they had accepted the same ruler. As for Friesland, the Frisian language had now definitely failed to rise to the position of a language of civilization, and not only the administration, but even provincial historiography and religious movements used a language that was in all essentials Dutch. Holland as well as Groningen influence had helped to bring this about. Menno Simons, for instance, wrote a form of Dutch which has no doubt an eastern colouring, but which nevertheless is nearer

[1] Cleve: in French—*Cleves*.   [2] Gulich: in French—*Juliers*.

the Holland–Brabant–Flemish language than is the language
of the Groningen chronicler Sicke Benninghe or of Charles
of Gelderland's chancery.

After the annexation at all events there was no question any
longer of the eastern provinces attempting to maintain their
cultural independence as against the western and southern
region. It is conceivable that they might have done so, although
less deliberately than these things are done in our days, had
they continued to resist Habsburg authority. But, as we saw,
they submitted readily to it, and since then the State, by
promoting economic and intellectual intercourse, and by
bringing Overlanders and Netherlanders together on the same
political stage (where so intensely gripping a drama was soon
to be performed), effected almost automatically the cultural
amalgamation of the new provinces with the old. There remained differences, but there was no longer any danger that
they would become the basis for divergent national development.

As to the West and South, one may notice certain changes
in the parts played by the various provinces in the cultural
movement. Even more than in the fifteenth century Flanders
has fallen behind Brabant. Brabant, with Brussels, Leuven
and Antwerp—the capital, the university town, and the commercial metropolis of the Netherlands—has become the central
region of intellectual life. Antwerp is a place of exchange of
ideas for the whole of the Dutch-speaking country, just as it
is a place of exchange of goods for Europe. The increasing
importance of Holland is making itself felt especially in its
contributions to humanism and to painting; in Dutch literature
the North is still following the lead of the South. But in all
those spheres, how striking is the close intellectual relationship! The Chambers of Rhetoric in Holland and Zealand—
—the only northern provinces in which they flourished—
imitated the example of the South in their organization and
activities, and their archives were stocked with the products
of the rhyming zeal animating the Flemish and Brabant
brethren. There were intimate relations between the printers,
and that is to say the publishers, of North and South. The

Holland painters learnt from those of Brabant, and inversely, as mentioned above, Breughel owed a great deal to the Amsterdammer Pieter Aertsen. These are no more than a few instances taken at random. The development of Erasmus, for whom Leuven came to have such importance, who found as much admiration and support among Flemings and Brabanders as among Hollanders, and who in the end felt himself, as we saw, to be no longer a Hollander but a Netherlander—that development is typical.

A fact deserving especial attention is that the religious development, sketched above, did not anywhere intensify provincial differences. Undoubtedly, a closer examination reveals many-featured variety rather than flat uniformity. But it is a shifting variety. In the reactions of particular regions to the religious problem, the observer finds no constant differences which would suggest the existence of deep-seated internal causes, certainly none which would seem to announce in any way the sharp separation into a northern Protestant and a southern Catholic block which was to result from the fast approaching crisis. In Flanders and Brabant the cultured and politically privileged burgher class was no less Erasmian than it was in Holland. The Baptists, having worked off their ecstatic and revolutionary period in Holland, afterwards spread their influence in the South as well. Calvinism, as we shall see, nowhere found so ready access as it did in Flanders and Brabant, and if in the long run it was driven from the South and subjected the North, it was the result of foreign interference.

Once more, therefore, the facts of the history of civilization reveal the Netherlands as a unit, with as much variety as every cultural area needs for a healthy and vigorous life, but with the north-eastern region attached somewhat more loosely to the closely knit and dominating combination of Flanders, Brabant and Holland. A unit in fact, but whose consciousness was still feeble and obscure. Intellectuals, poets, royal officials, high nobles, these no doubt thought more and more beyond their particular provinces. It is in this period that the language and the country acquire a name of their own. Instead of *Duitsch*, which embraced, of course, German as well—although, as we saw, Maerlant used the dialectical variant *Dietsch* in the more restricted sense—*Nederlandsch* was coming into use. At the same time *Nederlanden*, or even *Nederland* in the singular, was still largely a literary, not an official nor a popular word. A little later *Nederlanders* (*Belgae* in Latin) abroad began to organize apart from the wider Germanic nation—thus, for instance, students at Italian universities. But in this there was still a great deal of uncertainty. When under the influence of the classics the sixteenth century began to idealize the "father-land"—the word was translated out of the Latin about this time—it automatically based the conception on the State, merging it with that loyalty towards the dynastic which had been dear to the Middle Ages, and which still had power over men's minds. That is to say that in the Netherlands the Walloon provinces were included.

It goes without saying that this was less easily done in intellectual intercourse. Walloon painters (like Gossart, whom we mentioned above, or the landscape painter Patinir) worked at Antwerp. Walloons took an active share in the propagation of Calvinism all over the Dutch land. But other religious movements, as we have seen, did not so easily cross the linguistic boundary, and at any rate it was naturally a different matter where literature was concerned. It is significant of the importance of the Dutch-speaking provinces that they could claim the name of the country for their language. Men were nevertheless entirely familiar with the notion of the country being inhabited by two groups, the Dutch-speaking and the Walloons. The Protestant refugees abroad as a matter of course organized their churches in two divisions—thus at Emden, London, Frankfort, Köln. But these arrangements were simply demanded by practical considerations. National sentiment did not rule out the Walloons. In Flanders especially, as the chroniclers bear witness, there existed an old popular hatred against the Walloons, but at this moment it seemed to slumber. The worst linguistic abuses which had characterized the régime of Charles the Bold were avoided by the Habsburg rulers. The quiet infiltration of French was causing no uneasiness.

c

But the test of all this was only to come when the conflict with the monarchy broke out, and national feeling suddenly had to stand on its own feet. For the makers of the Beggars' songs "Netherland" was the country of the Seventeen Provinces: the new North-East as well as the Walloon area were comprehended in the patriotic enthusiasm of the first stage. How this conception fared in the reality of the terrible struggle is a question that will be closely examined in the course of this work.

THE STRUGGLE FOR INDEPENDENCE
AND THE SPLIT

THE PRELUDE, 1555–1572

a. THE HIGH NOBILITY IN OPPOSITION

Just as in the case of Philip the Good and Charles the Bold, so it is usual to make a contrast between Charles V, wise, moderate, and popular, and Philip II, short-sighted, unbending, and detested, and to extend this contrast, with as little right in the one case as in the other, to the principles of their systems of government. Undoubtedly the son lacked those particular qualities which had rendered his father's rule acceptable, and there was moreover that one insurmountable obstacle—he was a foreigner. Brought up in Spain, he could not even speak French, let alone Dutch, and this had been made painfully apparent to his subjects assembled at the solemn gathering at Brussels where the transference of the government had taken place: on that occasion the Bishop of Arras, Granvelle, had had to speak for their new ruler. As soon as the war with France (which Philip inherited along with the sovereignty) was finished, he took the road back to Spain, and the Netherlands saw him no more.

And yet, in the main, Philip simply pursued the policy of Charles, and the forces which so speedily broke out in opposition to him had been gathering under his predecessor. It was, indeed, a heavily mortgaged estate that Charles V bequeathed to him. Discontent was everywhere rife. At the same time the finances were in such confusion that the monarch was wholly dependent on the co-operation of the States, at least while the war with France lasted. At first, therefore, Philip attempted to win over the nobility. A number of the most important were nominated to the Order of the Golden Fleece (now no longer an exclusively Netherlandish institution), and were granted stadtholderships and seats on the Council of State. It was a bitter disappointment to him when these nobles, on whose help his father, though he gave them less power, had always been able to reckon, remained none the less intractable. It was like a return to the days of Maximilian when the nobility in 1556 censured the war with France, alleging that it was waged not in the interests of the Netherlands, but to give Spain a firm foothold in Italy. And soon they were stiffening the States in demands which seemed to the King to attack his power and his honour.

First, in 1558, there was the affair of the nine years' subsidy, which the States would only grant if they were allowed to raise it through their own commissioners. Then, just before Philip's departure, there was the stipulation made by the States-General at Ghent that, now that there was peace, the three thousand Spanish troops, who had got themselves detested wherever they were stationed, should leave the country. This dispute, which mortally offended Philip, stirred up popular feeling to an astonishing degree, and after lengthy attempts at evasion the King had to give way. It was the first mutter of the approaching storm. But this was not how Philip read the signs of the times. By the peace with Henry II of France the two rulers had agreed that they should wage a more vigorous campaign against heresy in their respective dominions, and, apart from this, Philip believed that more amicable relations between Habsburg and Valois would put him in a better position to carry out the complete absolutist programme. But in his absence the high nobility entered almost immediately into systematic opposition.

The King had left behind him as Regent or Governess his half-sister Margaret of Parma, but his real confidant was Granvelle, whom he had made President of the Council of State and who corresponded directly with him. Together with the Presidents of the other two Councils, Viglius, a Frisian jurist, and Berlaymont, a Walloon noble with many children and a short purse, Granvelle formed an inner council of officials, who knew no law but the King's will, and who awaited directions from Madrid for the policy of the country. And a long wait it sometimes was! Philip was slow in coming to a decision and could leave nothing to others. The loss of all initiative, which this dependence on a distant and dilatory master involved, seriously weakened the Brussels Government in the crisis which was now near at hand, and the absurdity of the situation was sometimes vividly illustrated by their helpless hankering after orders from Madrid. And over against this group of servants, by means of whom the monarch gave expression to his will, there now stood the high nobility of the country, glittering with honours, but with sadly restricted power.

Philip, wise by experience, intended the Council of State to be no more than an ornament of the Crown, while the popularity and splendour of the Knights of the Fleece must be used to cover whatever was done by the absolute monarch and the servants he had raised from nothing. But at a time when political questions began to kindle such passions and the trend of the monarchical policy to excite such opposition, it is little wonder that the great nobles failed to be attracted by the rôle assigned them. They wanted to make the Council of State a powerful body and take part in the government, but always they found their president, Granvelle, opposing this ambition and admonishing them in the King's name to be tractable.

In these first years after Philip's departure one thing in particular provoked a formidable commotion, much worse than that over the Spanish troops, uniting all the different elements of opposition present in the Netherlands into an impassioned chorus of complaint and protest. This was the establishment of new bishoprics, which obtained the papal sanction in 1559; in 1561 a second bull worked out the details. It was a striking instance of what the monarchy could do in the way of state building, and exhibits Philip as a diligent worker in the tradition of his house.

The ecclesiastical divisions in the Netherlands, which had come into being with the earliest expansion of Christendom, corresponded little indeed to the later political organization or even to the linguistic conditions. What Philip aimed at in the first place (and here he was reviving an old scheme of Charles V) was the elimination of foreign ecclesiastical authority. Secondly, he wanted to see an increase in the number of bishops so that they might the more effectively combat the growth of heresy. At the same time the right of nomination was taken from the chapters and given to the crown, in order that the bishops might be the faithful servants of the secular power. A provision which gave great offence to the nobility stipulated that bishops should be skilled theologians, so that the episcopal chair should no longer be a resting-place for the sons of great lords. The plan also struck at the independence of the wealthy abbots, who, particularly in the States of Brabant, joined lustily in all opposition to the Government: the new bishops were to be endowed out of the revenues of historic abbeys like those of Afflighem, of Tongerloo, of Marienweerd, while they were to usurp even the abbatial title and sit in the States, where the Government would be able to rely upon them.

It is not to be wondered at that there arose a storm of opposition to a plan which involved such a strengthening of the King's authority at a moment when his designs were viewed with distrust on all sides. Indeed, quite apart from the special circumstances, this concordat, for so the arrangement deserves to be called, implied such a complete subjection of the Church to the State, that liberty, which in the Middle Ages had bene-fited by the antagonism between these two powers, was seriously threatened. The same tendency had already appeared in the organization of the Inquisition. In both cases for that matter, the Habsburger was only following in the footsteps of the French monarchy, which half a century before had already secured papal recognition of its authority over the Church. Elsewhere, in the German states and in England, it was the Reformation which helped to put the seal on absolutism by investing the ruler with supremacy over the Church. Putting aside for the moment such considerations (though it is easy to understand that they were all-important to contemporaries), we can see how greatly this much-maligned measure would have contributed to the consolidation and rounding off of the Netherlands state, had not its future been ruined by the rupture between King and people. Even so this measure did at least free the churches of Brabant and Flanders from their long dependence on Walloon sees.

+++ Boundaries between the Archbishoprics.

---- Boundaries between the Bishoprics.

+++ Linguistic Boundary.

The territory included in the new organization, and therefore subject to the Primacy of Mechlin, has been left white.

Leeuwarden Grozingen

Haarlem UTRECHT Derenter

'sHertogenbosch

Middelburg

Brugge Antwerp

Ghent MECHLIN

Yper

St. Omer Namur Liége

Tournai

Arras

CAMBRAI

MAP II.—THE NEW DIOCESES, 1561

Nearly the whole of Habsburg territory in the Netherlands
—the Bishopric of Liège remained outside the reform—was
taken out of the ecclesiastical provinces of Rheims and Cologne,
and erected into three independent provinces. Cambrai,
Mechlin, and Utrecht became Archbishoprics; the Archbishop
of Mechlin was to be Primate over the whole Netherlands
Church. Of the three provinces under the authority of these
archbishops that of Cambrai comprised the Walloon area, with
four other sees: Arras, Tournai, St. Omer, and Namur; that
of Mechlin, the area as far northward as the great rivers, with
Yper, Brugge, Ghent, Antwerp, 's Hertogenbosch[1] and Roermond; finally, that of Utrecht, the whole of the remaining
territory, with Middelburg, Haarlem, Deventer, Groningen,
and Leeuwarden. The demarcation of the two southernmost
groups of Bishoprics did not conform exactly to the linguistic
boundary, but the sees of the central strip were now all located
in Dutch-speaking towns, and there was the expressed intention of organizing "the churches which use the French tongue"
separately. All together it was a very great measure; its bold
logic and symmetry and its vigorous attack on historic development and ancient rights were thoroughly characteristic of the
spirit of the monarchy and its rationalistic lawyer servants.

Resistance was violent. All classes—the nobility, the clergy,
and the towns—made a great outcry about the violation of their
rights. Abbots and Knights of the Fleece fraternized. The
pensionaries, the legal officers of the towns, industriously ferreted
into old documents and drew up lengthy remonstrances. The
bishops had to be inducted into most of the sees almost by
force. Those in the new eastern provinces—Leeuwarden,
Groningen, Deventer, and Roermond—could, indeed, only be
occupied at the time of Alva, when everything lay crushed
under the heel of the oppressor. Antwerp, where business
interests were greatly disturbed at the prospect of a bishop
residing within the city walls, even sent a couple of envoys
to the King in Spain and obtained a suspension. The reception of the measure showed how inflammable was the state
of public opinion in the whole of the Netherlands. What

[1] 's Hertogenbosch or Den Bosch: in French—*Bois-le-Duc*.

excited the multitude was the fear of keener religious persecution, but the real danger which the Government so blindly
prepared for itself lay in the injury it did to the private interests
of the privileged classes, thereby stimulating their already
awakened spirit of opposition.

Although Granvelle had had nothing to do with the preparation of the reform, he profited more than anyone by it;
he became the first Archbishop of Mechlin and Primate of
the Netherlands Church, at the same time receiving the Cardinal's hat. Moreover, upon him fell the task both of defending
and executing the measure. Thus the affair helped not a little
towards making his name hated, and it was a natural tactical
instinct which caused the malcontent lords to raise the cry
"Away with Granvelle," whereby they could, without openly
attacking the King, give expression to their demand for a
complete change in the system of government. Under the
leadership of the Prince of Orange and the Count of Egmont
they formed a league against the Cardinal; the lower nobility
also began to participate noisily in the movement. The members of the Council of State sent one of their number, Montigny, to the King; Orange, Egmont, and Hoorn addressed a
written request to him, and, when this remained unanswered,
created a popular sensation by withdrawing from the Council
of State until their wish should be fulfilled. Finally, after much
wavering, Philip gave in, albeit with a bad grace. In the beginning of 1564 Granvelle was ordered to leave the country.
Margaret of Parma, to the profound alarm of Viglius and
Berlaymont, undertook to govern with the Council of State.

These great lords, to whom the Netherlands cause now
seemed to be entrusted, were princes both by rank and position, the equals not only of the powerful feudal nobles by
whom the monarchy in France was still surrounded, but of
the greatest of the German princes; and with both of these
they were linked by numerous marriages. For Orange, the
eldest son of a Count of Nassau, the position in the Netherlands to which he succeeded as a child had appeared to be
so great a good fortune that his parents had handed him over
to be educated as a Catholic and set apart the countship for

his younger brother John; in 1561 Orange married a daughter
of Maurice, the Elector of Saxony, the man who had proved
so fatal to Charles V, and this marriage was an event of international importance. Egmont's wife was a Duchess of Bavaria.
For Aremberg first a Princess of Cleve, then a Vaudemont
of Lorraine was thought of for a bride.

The magnates owed their rise and position to the Burgundian-Habsburg monarchy, so that each one's broad lands lay
spread over several provinces. Orange's Netherlands possessions had their centre in Brabant at Breda, but he also owned
land in Holland and Zealand, of which provinces he was
Stadtholder. Egmont's house sprang originally from Holland;
one branch had occupied the ducal chair of Gelderland. But
Egmont's father, a faithful follower of Charles V, had married
a Walloon heiress who brought him estates in Luxemburg and
Flanders, and Egmont, Stadtholder of Flanders, could no longer
be considered a Hollander. Orange was not the only one of
German origin; there was Mansfeldt also. For the rest, the
great nobles mostly belonged to Walloon families, even if they
owned lands in Brabant, Limburg, or Gelderland, and were
known by the Dutch names of these estates. Aerschot was a
Croy, son of Philip the Good's favourite Chièvres; Aremberg,
Stadtholder of Groningen, Friesland, and Overysel, a Ligne;
Meghen, Stadtholder of Gelderland, a Brimeu; Hoorn a Mont-
morency; Hoogstraten a Lalaing; Bergen a Glimes. These men
kept a truly princely state. Aerschot's son, Chimay, when a
student at Leuven, lived in a palace with a governor and a
tutor, besides twelve pages. At his marriage there were present
representatives of the Pope, the Emperor, the King of France,
a number of German and Italian princes, and the States of
Brabant, Flanders, and Hainaut. From their youth onwards
these men were employed in the service of the monarch for
the most important military, diplomatic, and political missions.
The question that confronts us is whether the national cause
was safe with them.

Their zeal in guarding against the subordination of Netherlands foreign policy to Philip's Spanish ideas cannot be
doubted. Themselves Catholics without much fervent con-

viction, they detested the policy which would make of the Netherlands an outpost of a system of Catholic aggression in northern Europe. Philip and Granvelle watched with profound distrust the evidences of Orange's friendliness with his relatives in Germany; but for that matter the nobles as a whole looked at events abroad with very different feelings from the King. They rejoiced, for instance, at every success of the Huguenot nobility in France, where, to Philip's consternation, serious religious strife had broken out after the death of Henry II. In other words, anything which might hinder the establishment of Philip's despotism in the Netherlands was welcome to the nobility; but how weak nevertheless was the leadership they could offer! From the beginning they were divided by jealousies and dissensions. Aerschot held aloof and exercised some influence over Aremberg and Meghen. It was quickly apparent, too, that the victory of the Council of State was not solely the victory of the national principle, but that it was as much the victory of privilege. The monarchy had endeavoured to make great and small alike subject to the law; happy in the consciousness of power regained the nobility now trampled the law underfoot. Particularism, too, raised its head. Gelderland, for instance, immediately attempted to get the "foreigners"—that is, the natives of other provinces—removed from the Court which since 1543 had represented royal authority at Arnhem.

But the worst part of it was that while it lay in the power of the nobility after Granvelle's departure to prevent many things and to create much mischief and confusion, for constructive purposes their victory was only apparent. Far away the silent Philip still remained the arbiter of Netherlands destiny. Armed with the power derived from his other dominions, he could still forbid, and, if need be, command. So, if the nobles were not prepared to carry their opposition to extremes, the development of affairs in the Netherlands was bound to escape from their control. The people still looked confidently to them. But while the exuberance and light-hearted insolence which marked the proceedings of the nobles at times give the impression that they were only playing at politics, the people were in deadly earnest. The new creed of Calvinism was gaining more and more ground, and hatred of the Inquisition became a consuming passion.

To their credit be it said that the nobles were not blind to the feelings which agitated the people. They had too large a share in the Erasmian culture of the country to be able to give the religious persecutions whole-hearted support. The decisions of the Council of Trent, which was just then devoting itself to the task of formulating a stricter Catholic creed and of tightening up the organization of the Church to fit it for the struggle, were repugnant to them, and Philip's command to promulgate these decisions unconditionally appeared impolitic even to the most loyal Catholics among them. But Orange in particular realized that the religious question could no longer be shirked. In full assembly of the Council of State on New Year's Eve, 1564, on the occasion of the drawing up of instructions for Egmont, who had once again to go and discuss the situation with Philip, he made a speech of which Viglius, who was mortally alarmed by it, has left us a short report:

The King errs if he thinks that the Netherlands, surrounded as they are by countries where religious freedom is permitted, can indefinitely support these sanguinary Edicts. However strongly I am attached to the Catholic religion, I cannot approve of princes attempting to rule the consciences of their subjects and wanting to rob them of the liberty of faith.

It needed Egmont's vanity to be deceived by the vague promises which he brought back from Spain. In November 1565 the Governess received the King's final answer in the famous letters from Segovia. Now no one could delude himself any longer. Against the growing unrest Philip recognized only one weapon—sterner repression. Peremptory orders were addressed to all authorities to carry out the Edicts and to assist their execution. Great was the resulting excitement of the people, who had expected much from the intervention of the magnates. A profound impression was created by their refusal to share the responsibility for the government any longer. Orange, Egmont, and Hoorn withdrew once again from the Council of

State, while Bergen and Meghen requested to be relieved of their Stadtholderships. The Governess, the monarch's reluctant agent, was thus brought face to face with the popular movement.

b. THE FIRST OUTBURST

We have already noticed that what Protestantism in the Netherlands lacked was organization and political sense. Lutheranism, which had risen in Germany only by reason of its alliance with the princes, was helpless wherever the Government remained loyal to the old religion. Anabaptism was a creed for long-suffering lower middle-class people. The National Reformers, as the Sacramentalists have been called, remained too individualistic to construct anything. From Geneva there now began to spread over Europe the influence of Calvin.

In the *Institutes*, the first edition of which appeared in 1536, when he was still only twenty-seven, Calvin had elaborated a complete system of Protestant theology. By its logical strength it made a deep impression on an age which in every sphere was bringing reason to bear against long-established traditions. To the Church, appealing to her ancient rights, Calvin opposed the authority of Holy Scripture, which to his mind contained complete and absolute truth for all circumstances and for all ages. Mighty indeed was the driving-power which he gave thereby to a new and individualistic religious life, but at the same time he set narrow limits to its functioning, and entrusted their maintenance to the ministers, who were empowered to fix binding articles of faith. At Geneva, from 1540 onwards, Calvin was able to test his ideas on a living social organism, and to erect a state which should fulfil what was in his conception the highest purpose of the State, namely, the glorification of God. The Church must include the whole body of citizens, and be under the constant supervision of the consistory, ministers, elders, and deacons, the guardians of orthodoxy and of the moral life of the community. Society and State were alike subject to its rule, and freedom of thought was as little tolerated there as in the strictest Catholic countries.

The first Netherlanders to follow the example of Calvin did so outside the Habsburg Netherlands, outside the reach of oppression. At Emden in East Friesland there grew up in the 'forties what may be called the Mother Church, after whose example the Reformed communities "under the cross"—that is to say, hiding from the persecution—were generally modelled. It was a Polish nobleman, Johannes à Lasco, who under the protection of the Countess reformed the national Church of East Friesland after his own fashion, but on the whole in accordance with the Calvinistic ideal, and a number of Netherlands refugees sought shelter there, and were made familiar with the Calvinistic ideas of discipline and co-operation. À Lasco introduced the consistory, the council of elders and deacons under the minister, and the *coetus*, or assembly of ministers, and drew up a catechism. When, as a result of Charles V's victory over the Schmalkaldic League, Germany was re-Catholicized, à Lasco emigrated to London, where a Netherlands Church was established on the same lines for exiles from Flanders, Brabant, and Holland. Here, in the church of the Austin Friars, which still belongs to the same community, now become exclusively North Netherlandish, were sung the first Dutch psalms as rhymed by Utenhove of Ghent. Here also à Lasco drew up in Latin the first comprehensive declaration of faith, which Utenhove likewise translated into Dutch. In his capacity of elder, Utenhove was one of the leaders of the community. He was a man of good family, his father having been president of the Court of Flanders. The ministers were Micronius, also of Ghent, and Delenus, who probably came from Alkmaar.

I do not think [wrote Utenhove] that hitherto our Netherlands nation ever had a community in which the word of God was preached in such purity, the sacraments performed with such sincerity, and Christian punishments so zealously and faithfully administered as in this our community.

According to Reformed ideas he was right. This first bloom, however, was of short duration. In 1553 there began under Mary a Catholic reaction in England, and à Lasco, along with a number of followers, among whom were Utenhove and Micronius, returned to Emden, "the shelter of God's Church," which now, after the final defeat of Charles V, became more than ever a beacon for the whole of Netherland Protestantism.

Many were the preachers who, in the years that followed, went forth from Emden to minister to the Protestant communities in towns throughout the area of Dutch speech, and who introduced the needful uniformity and organization. The advice of Emden was sought on difficult points of Church discipline or doctrine, as, for instance, the consistory of Antwerp did in 1558 when it had a dispute with its minister Haemstede. A remarkable man this Haemstede. A Zealander. of good family, he acquired great influence with the well-to-do citizens at Antwerp. He was the author of the famous *Book of Martyrs* which was published at Antwerp in 1559, and of which many later editions were brought out elsewhere. On one occasion, on the day of the procession of the Holy Sacrament in 1558, he was bold enough to speak before the multitude in the streets, in the sight of the priests passing by. Shortly afterwards he emigrated to London, where he was expelled from the community as a heretic, because he persisted in calling the Baptists his brethren. It is hardly an inspiring spectacle to see the victims of persecution themselves casting out that spirit of tolerance and anti-confessionalism which was a heritage of the Netherlands people, and which could substantiate the justice of their cause in the struggle against Spanish oppression. But do men for their struggles trust to justice alone? Against the might of the enemy the confusion attendant on well-meaning individualism would have been powerless, and, just as Catholicism had done at Trent, so Protestantism had to arm itself with order and unity of belief. No more efficient weapons can be imagined than those of stern Calvinism.

In so far as it came by way of Emden and London, the influence of Calvin operated in the Dutch-speaking Netherlands mainly by means of Dutch speech. But about 1560 a rising wave swept over from France. The peace of 1559 not only freed the Government, as Philip had hoped it would, from the burden of guarding the southern frontier. It re-opened the traffic of Antwerp and Wallonia with France, where Calvinism was just beginning to organize itself on a firm basis. A synod had secretly been held at Paris and a confession of faith drawn up for the French Church. Many were the communities, each with its minister and consistory, scattered throughout the country. Naturally this example made a deep impression on the Walloons. In 1561 Guy de Bray, one of their most zealous ministers, who laboured at Tournai and from there as far as Mons and Lille, drew up a confession of faith for the Netherlands Church modelled on the French confession. The Walloon underwent French influence, but for the realization of his ideas he could not but look northward: the State must furnish the foundation for it, the State which with its persecution set the rising faith its greatest problem. Just as Calvin himself, in his preface to the *Institutes*, had addressed Francis I directly, so de Bray wrote a letter to Philip II, which he caused to be thrown by night, along with the confession of faith, inside the ramparts of the Castle of Tournai. It was childish to think that the monarch, deceived by the enemies of the Reformers, would be led to conclude from the statement of their beliefs that they were peace-loving citizens whose lives he could spare without danger. But what is most striking in this document is the self-assurance with which this man stands before the King and says that "his people" can no longer endure the religious persecution.

De Bray's *Confession*, which was speedily translated into Dutch, acquired much authority among the Reformed communities. In numerous towns there now existed secret organizations on the usual model, and the bonds between them were tightened by means of frequent synods. It would seem that before 1566 the Calvinistic organization proper, with consistories and synodal assemblies, did not extend to the North. Spreading outwards from the Walloon country through the industrial region of Flanders, it had established itself in most of the towns of any importance in Flanders and Brabant, and finally made its headquarters at Antwerp. That Antwerp acquired such importance for the movement was in a measure

due to the existence there of a Walloon community alongside
the native one. The Walloon ministers of Antwerp (since 1565
there was a Frenchman, Franciscus Junius, amongst them),
together with the lawyer Gilles le Clerq of Tournai, the
trusted agent of the Antwerp Walloon consistory, did much
to promote the co-operation between the Walloon and Dutch-
speaking consistories, and, when the time was ripe, the alliance
of both with the malcontent nobility. The organized communities comprised for the most part artisans and small
citizens; the circles of the Rhetoricians probably furnished a
goodly number. No doubt many wealthy merchants were also
touched by Calvinism—I have mentioned the influence of
Haemstede—but they had more to fear from the Edicts, and
had to keep in the background. And, as in France, there were
converts from among the ranks of the nobility who sometimes
introduced Reformed preachers on their estates.

All told, however, the convinced Calvinists still formed but
a tiny fraction of the Netherlands people, and by their side
existed yet other sects: the Baptists, who, however, were to
some extent absorbed by the new Church; and the Lutherans,
especially strong at Antwerp, who were more successful in
maintaining their individual existence. But meanwhile public
opinion assumed an ever more critical attitude towards priests
and monks, religious persecution more and more became an
object of hatred. The terrible scenes witnessed at the stake
aroused a loathing no longer to be controlled. Sometimes there
was resistance, and executioners and sheriffs went in danger
of their lives: as, for example, in 1564 at the execution of
Fabritius (De Smet), a former Carmelite of Brugge, who had
ministered to the Reformed community at Antwerp. At his
examination before the magistrates Fabritius had roundly
admitted his offences.

"So it is not we put you to death," said the Sheriff, "but the King's
decree." Whereupon Fabritius made answer: "Look well to it, then,
that this decree answer for you and protect you at the great and
awful day of the last Judgment." After these words they condemned
him to death in accordance with the edict and decree of His Royal
Majesty, but with such pallid countenances that one might easily
trace therein the misery, oppression, and terror of their consciences.

The judges themselves did not believe in the harsh law which they had to administer. What more natural than that the whole people had watched with anxious expectation the efforts of the nobility to obtain the relaxation of the Edicts, and that the disappointment at the close of 1565 caused a violent commotion? On all sides the Brussels Government was overwhelmed with protests from the authorities in towns and provinces. Flanders, under the leadership of Brugge, was up in arms against the hated inquisitor Titelman. In the northeastern provinces, where it had as yet proved impossible to establish the new bishoprics, although Protestantism had made much less progress there than in the South, the several provincial States made an agreement amongst themselves to offer united resistance. In Brabant wild rumours went abroad of designs to introduce the Inquisition (as distinct from the persecution arising out of the Edicts) there also, and the chief towns, however meticulously loyal the behaviour of their magistrates had so far been, bestirred themselves in anticipation. But out of the masses there rose sounds of fury and revolt. Notes were thrown in the palace of Egmont at Brussels urging him to join the ranks of Calvinism, and holding out the dominion over the Netherlands as his reward. Lampoons were circulated, branding Philip as a perjurer who violated the privileges, and to whom, following the old law of the "Joyous Entry," no further allegiance was due. In Antwerp people were reminded of the ancient ties with the Empire, where the Religious Peace had put a check on persecution.

The driving-force behind all this agitation was hatred of the Inquisition, but whatever discontent there was at the unnational appearance and tendencies of the Government and at its reforming zeal, together with all the social unrest and economic distress, combined with this feeling to swell the excitement to the proportions of a mighty national movement. Mighty it was, but uncertain of its goal. It cried out for leadership. The Calvinists, who alone knew what they wanted, could not openly furnish this. The people looked up to the magnates to be "chieftains unto them."

What did these magnates mean to do? They had taken care

that the King's refusal to give ear to their demands should
be noised abroad, and by applying for their relief from office
they had at the same time made clear their intention that he
alone should bear the responsibility. The violent agitation of
public opinion was not unpleasing to them. But what next?
Egmont was certainly far from any idea of securing for himself
the dominion over the Netherlands. Sulk as he might, he knew
less than anyone what he wanted. Orange looked at events
with a cooler and a clearer mind, but he, too, for the present,
kept himself in the background. The front of the stage was
now occupied by nobles of the second rank, confidants and
servants of the malcontent magnates, partly encouraged by
them, partly bent upon pushing them on.

Already in the summer of 1565 parleys had taken place at
Spa between a few noblemen of decidedly Protestant. persuasion: Louis of Nassau, a brother of Orange, who as a Prince
of the Empire could be a Lutheran with impunity; Nicholas
de Hames, Herald-at-Arms of the Order of the Golden Fleece;
and Marnix, lord of Tholouse, a Brabant noble, who with his
brother Marnix of St. Aldegonde had imbibed Calvinism from
the fountain-head at Geneva; Gilles le Clerq was also there
representing the contact with the consistories.

The possibilities of a league of the lower nobility were discussed. After the arrival of the letters from Segovia, at a
moment when Brussels was the scene of magnificent festivities
in celebration of the marriage of Alexander of Parma, son of
the Governess, to which the nobles flocked from all sides,
there met in the palace of the Count of Culemborch the con-
stituent assembly of the famous Compromise or League of
the Nobility. Besides Culemborch, who was a native of Gelderland, and Louis of Nassau, the most notable personalities
among the assembly were the Count van den Bergh, a brother-
in-law of Orange and also a "Geldersman," and the Hollander
Hendrik van Brederode, all intimately related to the magnates
and of the same social standing, but, not being Stadtholders,
or members of the Order of the Fleece or the Council of
State, less closely connected with the Government. In addition
there were present several of the smaller nobility, such as the

Marnixes and de Hames, Leefdael, Blois van Neerijen, and Bakkerseele, the last three all belonging to the household of Egmont.

All were Protestants or favourably disposed to the new creed, but they resolved to enlist as many supporters as possible throughout the various provinces, and so it was essential not to deter Catholic noblemen. From the beginning the goal they set before themselves was to bring pressure to bear on the Government to obtain the relaxation, if possible the withdrawal, of the Edicts. From the first moment, however, the leading spirits among them were prepared to use force, and all the time they kept their eyes fixed on Germany, where Louis of Nassau could act as their mediator. There was even some hope of Orange himself. Had he not some time before already examined the possibility of prevailing on the Calvinists to accept the Confession of Augsburg, so that it would be easier to co-operate with the Lutheran princes of Germany, some of whom were bitterly opposed to Calvinism? As far as character went, there were marked differences between the various leaders of this new movement. Firm conviction and idealism characterized the Marnixes and de Hames; Bakkerseele was an ambitious intriguer. Brederode, who at Vianen recognized no master above him (as little as Culemborch did in his town), was the perfect example of the blustering, bellicose, mutinous noble, scion of a long line of fighters who had played their parts in the Hookish wars of the previous century. A survival of the Middle Ages, but yet at the same time how modern! Every revolutionary epoch is familiar with his kind.

Meanwhile, in all secrecy, members were recruited. It should not be thought for a moment that the four or five hundred who joined meant harm to the Catholic religion. The Edicts were hated by Catholics and Protestants alike. Moreover, in the tense atmosphere of that year, the appearance of conspiracy appealed strongly to all turbulent elements, to all who execrated the bureaucratic State and the Brussels centralization. This explains why the Compromise made recruits particularly in the North, and nowhere so many as in Friesland.

The Walloon provinces were but scantily represented. Meanwhile, the leaders, in consultation with Orange, determined their line of action. Marnix of Tholouse and Louis of Nassau drew up a petition which was to be presented to the Governess at Brussels in April 1566. With a reference to the ferment among the people, which threatened to break out into rebellion, the request was put forward that the King abolish the Inquisition and the Edicts, and in concert with the States-General take new measures to deal with the religious question; the nobles demanded a suspension of the persecution until the King's answer should be received. The members of the League were urged to attend in as large numbers as possible the presentation of this petition at Brussels.

But before venturing upon this public step, the leaders sought to reach an understanding with the group of magnates who had pursued a common line of action since the struggle with Granvelle. A conference at Hoogstraten served to show, however, that fatal differences of opinion predominated in this group, while Aerschot, as we know, stood apart, and Mansfeldt, too, had virtually withdrawn. Orange advocated an open avowal of the League and support of the petition, but to Egmont and Meghen this seemed to be taking up too antagonistic an attitude towards the Government. In the upshot the great lords decided that the League must bear its own responsibility, but agreed to represent its demands to the Governess in as favourable a light as possible. In other words, when it came to the point, Egmont and Meghen dared not use their position as Stadtholder and Councillor of State against the Government; on the contrary, they felt that this position bound them indissolubly to the monarchy.

Nevertheless, the sudden disclosure of the existence of the League and the announcement that a petition would be presented at first threw the Governess into a panic. The appearance at Brussels in the first days of April 1566 of some four hundred nobles from almost every province of the Netherlands, their solemn procession to the palace of the Governess, the presentation of the petition by Brederode, Berlaymont's derisive remark about the impudence of these "beggars" (*gueux*), cheerfully transformed by the Leaguers into a title of honour, the banquet where they sat with the chains and wooden cups on their breast—all this constitutes a great event in Netherlands history. Never before had the political unity of the Netherlands nation manifested itself in such dramatic manner. What strikes us most in the description of that vivid and colourful scene, as it was played out in the characteristic setting of old Brussels, studded with the palaces of the nobility, is the use of the French tongue. French was the language of Margaret and her courtiers, as well as of the petition which was being presented to her; and although the overwhelming majority of the nobles themselves were of Dutch speech, for them too French was, so to say, the official language, in which the leaders corresponded amongst themselves, and in which were couched all the watchwords and the entire terminology of the movement. And yet a great noble like Brederode, whose library at Vianen is known to have contained little but French books, was still so far from expressing himself easily in this tongue that in the verbal discussions with Margaret a Walloon noble had to come to the help of his leader. But for the moment nobody took exception to these linguistic conditions. *Gueux* was roughly "Dutched" into *geus*, and "*Vive le Geus!*" shouted the mob at Brussels and Antwerp, at Breda, at Delft, and at Amsterdam, to express their gratitude to the nobles. In these nobles they saw themselves and all the provinces, "the whole of these Netherlands," united against the Spanish king. That was in this movement something new, and something of the greatest importance.

All former rebellions or movements of revolt, even when they were so widespread as that which followed the death of Charles the Bold (when, moreover, the north-eastern provinces still lay outside the State), had borne a distinctly local or provincial character. The States-General, it is true, had more than once, by the very nature of the problems with which the policy of the monarch had confronted them, been inspired with a national consciousness and been driven into a national attitude, but never on former occasions had the people participated so generally and with such enthusiasm as they did at this time, when the folk of Holland and Friesland, Gelderland, Brabant and Flanders followed with tense interest the complications between the Governess and the magnates and the nobility, when Orange and Egmont, Brederode and Culemborch had become figures of truly national dimensions.

This is not to say that the movement expressed itself everywhere with the same dramatic intensity. On the contrary, although it certainly drew from all parts the forces that sustained it, Brabant was the heart of the Netherlands, and political life pulsated there at its strongest. Brussels was a focal point because Court and Government resided there; Antwerp because of its own national importance. It is noteworthy, too, that the voice of the people, which spoke with more power and greater political sense there than anywhere else, always made mention of the Netherlands, and, carrying the conflict outside the limits of the old Duchy of Brabant, proclaimed Antwerp as the champion of the seventeen provinces. Netherlands and Netherlandish are now no longer mere literary terms; they have acquired political meaning. The innumerable pamphlets and manifestoes, soon to be followed by the ballads, even though they start from the "Joyous Entry" of Brabant and speak of Antwerp's special privileges, nevertheless extend their view over the whole Netherlands. Nothing is more natural. The State had become too unmistakably the framework of the great political events. No single province could claim the magnates as its own. The religious movement ignored provincial boundaries, and the League of Nobles covered the whole land. National consciousness, prepared for many a year, but now pushed on by the energy of the rising revolutionary movement, broke through with elemental force.

On the first tidings of what was in store for her, the Governess implored the great lords to return to her council, and even before the petition was presented she had deliberated with them and with the high officials, and decided to yield on the most pressing point. All the agents and organs of the Government in the seventeen provinces were instructed to proceed with caution in the execution of the Edicts. This amounted to a suspension, and in the meantime the matter was to be submitted to the King. The nobles celebrated their triumph in boisterous fashion. Orange and even Egmont, who was now veering round once more, appeared at the banquet in the palace of Culemborch, and it was a moment of wild enthusiasm.

But again everything hung on Philip's decision. Two of the great nobles, Bergen and Montigny, were sent to Spain, with the consent of the Governess, to expedite the King's answer— an unfortunate step which was destined seriously to weaken the old union of the magnates in the crisis at hand. Bergen's energy, in particular, could ill be dispensed with at this juncture. Meanwhile the officials and the Knights of the Fleece prepared for the Governess a scheme to mitigate the Edicts, a "Moderation," which might form the basis of a positive religious policy. No one in the Central Government supposed that liberty of conscience, let alone freedom of worship and organization for the heretical sects, was a possible solution, and even Orange dared only very cautiously to hint at this. The scheme of Moderation was known already before the end of April, and it was of such a nature that the people called it the "Murderation." The League was now put to a test in which the sharp cleavage existing between the aims of the Protestant-minded majority among the leaders and the still loyally Catholic majority among the rank and file was soon revealed.

For the Moderation went right against the development of public opinion, which had naturally drawn not a little encouragement from the sensational activities of the nobility at Brussels. All who inclined towards Protestantism considered the Edicts abolished; the refugees, among them many ministers, flocked back from all the neighbouring countries. In May the roads and fields of the textile-manufacturing district of West Flanders began to be the scene of public preaching, a scandal which could never be justified by the promises of the Governess. But it spread like a contagion. While the Governess issued a fresh Edict against the preachers, the consistory of Antwerp resolved to have public worship there also. It was as though a signal had been given. In every province preachers and thirsters after the new gospel emerged from their hiding-places, and that summer saw "hedge-sermons" delivered in the environs of countless Netherlands towns.

Already (this was in mid-July) the Calvinists observed a certain order in their services. The women sat in the middle inside a circle marked out with stakes and cords; their servants and soldiers, who kept guard, formed fighting-order after the sermon, and then they fired stray shots and now and then would shout, *"vive le geus!"* At Ghent the assemblies outside the town were commonly twenty thousand strong, and were attended by people from other places where there was no preaching. And if there should happen to be two successive holy-days, then they stayed the night there, so that they should not have to come back, and cooked their food in the fields. So it was throughout almost all Flanders, Holland, and Zealand.

In this energetic and passionate movement the Calvinists, with their uncompromising theology and with their genius for organization, inevitably became the leaders. Up till now the majority of the Reformers, especially in the North, had not yet joined their ranks. At Antwerp, too, besides the Lutherans, we meet with a figure such as the pastor of the suburb Kiel, who preached after the new fashion without wanting to break away from the Church. Such a middle-position, however, became more and more untenable as popular excitement waxed higher and higher. People wanted to sing the psalms; a new version, based on the French of Marot, had just been published by a West Flemish minister, Dathenus of Kassel. People wanted to listen to the most fiery preachers, such as Moded of Zwolle, who in July had drawn great crowds at Ghent and Brussels, and who came to Antwerp in August.

The Governess looked on in desperation at this breaking down of all barriers. It is true that she had quickly discovered the discord among the great nobility, and there were men about her already advising strong measures. In the States of the Walloon provinces, where nobility and clergy held a ruling position, great annoyance had been expressed at the audacity of the League. Meghen brought some troops into the neighbourhood of Antwerp, and appeared to be contemplating an attack on the town. Thereupon Brederode, with a hundred and fifty followers, all clad in "Beggars' grey," made his way into it; the inhabitants received him with tumultuous enthusiasm as a liberator. It looked as if Antwerp were becoming the starting-point of civil war. However deep her mistrust of him, Margaret was compelled to send Orange (who among his many honorary offices numbered that of Burgrave of Antwerp) to guard the town for the Government. For him Brederode was willing to vacate the place, in him the burghers felt confidence. With the strong support of the burgomaster Van Straelen and the pensionary Wesembeke, he now established order there.

But he was as impotent as anyone to check the march of events. The leaders of the League of Nobles, disquieted by the delay in the King's decision, summoned a new assembly for the middle of July at St. Truiden.[1] Although a goodly number of Catholic confederates held aloof, while others, infuriated at the insolence of the Calvinists, vehemently reproached Louis of Nassau and Brederode; although Orange urgently warned his brother that by encouraging the Calvinists he would ruin everything—nevertheless the nobles and the representatives of the consistories resolved upon close co-operation. The leaders foresaw that it would come to fighting. The Lutheran princes must be won over and troops raised in Germany. The consistories must provide the money, the nobles, claiming the right of resistance as belonging to their rank and competent to wield the sword, must lead the revolt. But the Calvinist community did not let itself be restricted to the passive rôle prescribed for it in these plans. The holding of meetings outside churches did not give sufficient vent to their long-suppressed feelings. They longed for action, and in the breaking of the images they found it.

The movement started on the linguistic frontier, in the area where the new cloth manufacture had created an industrial proletariat, particularly amenable to the propagation of a new creed, and whose religious ecstasy was nearly allied to social unrest. A transport of rage suddenly possessed the multitude. Crowds surged into the churches to destroy all the most

[1] St. Truiden: in French—*St. Trond.*

treasured symbols and ornaments of the old religion. This wave of frenzy swept from village to village, Dutch-speaking or Walloon, throughout that industrialized country, and then turned and engulfed town after town. The first outburst, at Poperinghe, took place on August 14th. On the 18th the storm struck Oudenarde, whence it reached Antwerp on the 20th, Ghent on the 22nd; that same day it swept to Amsterdam (where the mob was roused by the sight of fragments of statuary which two merchants brought from Antwerp); thence to Leyden and Delft; on the 25th to Utrecht, and in the following weeks into Friesland and Groningen. In the Walloon country the movement was less widespread, but at Valenciennes it displayed peculiar energy and raised the extreme Calvinist party, led by two ministers, Guy de Bray and Pérégrin de la Grange, into virtual power. Elsewhere, too, the ministers or the consistories had sometimes directed the operations of the iconoclasts. For the most part, however, these excesses caused surprise and discomfiture to the leaders whose fanatical phraseology had roused the temper of the mob to the right pitch. In any case it was a truly Calvinistic work, fierce and honest, restrained by no respect for art or beauty, striving to purge the land for God's elect from the devilish ornaments of idolatry, and to pull down at one blow a past of a thousand years. Nor did the deed once done lack dour approbation from the side of the intellectual leaders of Calvinism.

It is a small matter, or revenge, thus to have destroyed the images, which are only a species of idolatry, since the ecclesiastics have done us a thousand times more hurt and hindrance through their persecutions which broke those statues which God Himself had made and for which He once shed His precious blood, namely, our dearest friends, fathers and mothers, sisters and brothers.

Thus wrote a man of Ghent, and Marnix of St. Aldegonde in a French pamphlet argued to the same effect.

Meanwhile, almost everywhere the authorities had looked on at this savage scene as though paralysed with fright. The clergy hid themselves. In several places, such as Ghent, Yper, and Antwerp, the churches were in the hands of the Calvinists, and Catholic worship was interrupted. On August 23rd the Governess, who felt as if her world came crumbling to pieces before her very eyes, gave her assent to an "Accord" with the leaders of the Compromise, whereby preaching was permitted in all parts where it was already practised, provided that the people laid down their arms and did not interfere with the old religion. Actually it was the Government that had the best of this arrangement, as it gained time to reassert itself, and would alone have armed forces at its disposal—for even the Compromise was dissolved by this agreement—if differences should arise over the execution of the Accord. But in reality the sudden predominance of Calvinism did not rest on sound foundations. In the Walloon provinces, outside Valenciennes and Tournai, a vehement Catholic temper asserted itself under the protection of powerful Stadtholders. But in the Dutch-speaking provinces, too, the town-magistrates were everywhere as much offended as they were terrified by the outburst.

The exercise of the new or Reformed religion (wrote the pensionary of Leyden, Paulus Buys) has led many people to resort to idleness, to forget the duty of submission to authority, and to bring justice into disrepute.

The Stadtholders, charged with the carrying out of the Accord, did their best to stir the intimidated majority out of their frightened passivity; thus did Egmont in Flanders, and even Orange at Antwerp, though the latter was now distrusted by the Catholics. In his hands the Accord became at Antwerp a formal religious peace between the three persuasions, Catholic, Calvinist, and Lutheran; and, with his eye on Germany, he was particularly careful to encourage this last.

Meanwhile, the Governess had recovered from her fright. She had found in Mansfeldt an intrepid counsellor, while some time ago Philip had sent her money, so that she was in a position to raise troops. And now it was quickly apparent to what an extent the fierce emergence of the Calvinistic element had robbed the movement against the Government of that attraction which it had hitherto exercised over the national

instincts of the Netherlandish community. As soon as the
Governess bravely came forward as the protectress of Church
and Society, she was again accepted as the natural leader of
the nation, and many who had taken part in or sympathized
with the movement of opposition now, frightened, disillusioned,
or indignant, rallied round her.

So when it came to a trial of strength, it was in the most
unfavourable circumstances. And a trial had to come, for the
situation created by the Accord of August 23rd could not last.
Margaret roundly condemned the interpretation Orange had
given the Accord at Antwerp, and she had not a good word
to say even for the agreements concluded by Egmont for
carrying it into execution in the Flemish towns. And then
there was still the King; indeed, in the long run, there was only
the King. No one but a past-master in self-deception, like
Egmont, could believe that the King would ever put up with
even the most conservative interpretation of the Accord. Very
soon there came rumours of the King's anger, of his plans
to punish the Netherlanders—and in particular the great
nobles, whom he regarded as the authors of the disturbances—
and of military preparations. Orange wanted to attempt armed
resistance, and held that a national revolution was still possible
if Egmont and Hoorn would stand by him. Egmont even now
retained the confidence of many Catholics, and might be able
to heal the rupture in the national movement caused by the
image-breaking. But Egmont obstinately refused co-operation.
He persisted in his delusion that the Government would be
moved to call the States-General together, although it should
have been obvious that Philip would know better than to
provide the opposition with such a rallying-point, which had
already proved so dangerous in the time of Maximilian, and
of which he himself had had most disagreeable experience.
Egmont's vacillations had a demoralizing effect. Although it
was plain that the policy of the Governess aimed at the annul-
ment of the Accord, it proved absolutely impossible to recon-
stitute the Compromise that had been so rashly dissolved. On
the contrary, every day erstwhile members came to Brussels
to avow their repentance. On the other hand the Catholic

nobility of the Walloon provinces began to manifest an ever more bellicose attitude in support of the Government.

There remained, of course, a party which could not submit. These were the Calvinists, for whom it was a question of life or death. But they stood alone in opposition to a Government now growing daily stronger. At a synod held at Antwerp and attended by representatives not only of Flanders, Brabant, and the Walloon region, but of Friesland as well, it was determined on December 1st that in the Netherlands a group of vassals had the right, in conjunction with a part of the population, to offer armed resistance to the monarch if he laid hands on the privileges—old Netherlandish doctrine which could now be fortified with Calvin, since he invested the "lower authorities" with the right of resistance. A "group of vassals" could indeed be reckoned on. Brederode, who had removed the statues and introduced the Reformation in his own town of Vianen, was found ready to assume the command of the troops which were to be raised in Germany with the money supplied by the Calvinist congregations.

Orange had been asked first. He certainly had no longer any illusions about the intentions of the Government. At Antwerp and in his Stadtholderships, whither he betook himself in the autumn, he did what he could, ostensibly on the basis of the Accord, to strengthen the position of the Calvinists. He sent reassuring (and false) reports to Brussels on the subject of Brederode's activities at Vianen. With the arrangement he made at Utrecht for Calvinistic worship the States and Court of this province would have nothing to do, so anti-Catholic did it appear to them, while at Amsterdam Orange had to push through the arrangement against the will of the staunchly Catholic town government. But openly identify himself with the Calvinists he would not. He felt too strongly that the national tide was running against them; moreover, he feared that to do so would be to prejudice his connections in Germany, and that was after all where the troops must come from.

The results of the collection of money among the Calvinists were bitterly disappointing. Moreover, the leaders could not control the movement. When in December the Governess went right against the Accord, at the same time pronouncing Valenciennes to be in a state of rebellion and despatching a force under the Lord of Noircarmes to lay siege to it, bands of men sprang to arms as if of their own accord throughout Artois and Walloon Flanders, and in the traditionally unruly coast-land of Flanders. The "wondrous year" 1566 was not yet come to an end, when they were annihilated by Rassenghien, Stadtholder of Tournai, at Watrelos, and by Noircarmes at Lannoy. The remnant fled to Antwerp and took service with the troops which Brederode, from his headquarters at Vianen, was now having recruited.

While the Court party rejoiced over the success of the first encounter, while Egmont slid still farther away from his onetime friends and in Flanders began forcibly to destroy the arrangement, which he had himself carried into effect on the basis of the Accord, Brederode's party girded itself for a desperate effort. In February 1567 the Lord of Bombergen marched from Antwerp and threw himself into Den Bosch. But the chief attack was launched on Zealand. Orange was now looking on from Antwerp once more, still further alienated from the Government at Brussels, to which he had refused to take a special new oath of allegiance demanded of all Stadtholders, high officials, nobles, and officers (Egmont had taken it). It was thought that Orange's covert assistance would be valuable to an enterprise in a province of which he was Stadtholder; once they had conquered this territory, so well defensible from a strategic point of view, the rebels would be able to defy the Government. The leadership of the expedition was entrusted to Marnix of Tholouse. The attempt on Flushing in the beginning of March 1567 miscarried, however, and the troops, disembarked at Terneuzen, wandered about in the neighbourhood of Antwerp. Without a doubt Tholouse had hopes of mastering Antwerp, which after having been the spiritual centre of the movement for so long would then have become the strategic centre as well. But Orange was not to be hustled out of his middle course. With the help of the Catholics and Lutherans, who together formed the great majority of the citizens, and who declined at any price to be

D

drawn into the incalculable hazards of a rebellion, he kept the gates of the city shut. Tholouse and his men were thus still in the open country—at Oosterweel—when the troops of the Governess appeared on the scene; they included some companies of Egmont's and were led by the Lord of Beauvoir. At danger to his life Orange held the excited Calvinists of Antwerp in check, while their brethren were cut to pieces at Oosterweel. Tholouse was killed. The next day Valenciennes surrendered to Noircarmes; De Bray and De la Grange, bitterly denouncing Orange as a traitor, were hanged.

The ill-tidings reached Brederode at Amsterdam, where he had forced his way in and was living on terms of armed peace with the Catholic-minded magistrates. There was no longer any hope for the cause of the rebellion. In the East the Stadtholders—Aremberg in Friesland, Groningen and Overysel, Meghen in Gelderland—had suppressed the preachings and occupied towns which thought of resistance. Orange's position had become untenable. In April he left Antwerp and the country; for the present he went to Dillenburg. For Brederode, too, nothing remained but flight; he went to Cleve. A number of his noblemen fell into the hands of the Stadtholder of Friesland on their retreat across the Zuider Zee. Thousands of others, nobles and citizens, who were Calvinists or in some way compromised in the commotions, followed their leaders into exile.

It was not only from Margaret and the men who carried out her policy that they fled. The Governess was indeed mistress of the country, and Mansfeldt and Aerschot, Meghen, Aremberg, and Noircarmes were triumphant, while the wretched Egmont added a wavering voice to the chorus of rejoicing. But in Italy, meanwhile, there had been gathered together from Naples and Sicily, Milan and Sardinia, four regiments of chosen Spanish infantry, together with 1,200 cavalry, who in the beginning of June 1567 set out, over the Alps, through the Franche-Comté and Lorraine, towards the Netherlands, where they arrived in August. Their commander was one of Philip's most noted military captains and statesmen, the Duke of Alva, the man who in the Spanish Council had always advocated the policy of rigour against the unruly Netherlands and whom Philip, immediately on receipt of the crushing news of the image-breaking, had appointed to carry out his vengeance.

c. THE TYRANNY OF ALVA

The resistance to the non-national tendencies of Philip's rule, to the Spanish troops, to the excessive centralization and to the religious persecution, had proceeded from the politically privileged classes. The national movement had found expression in the activities of the Knights of the Fleece, the lower nobility, the town governments, and of the States assemblies, in which all these could co-operate. Calvinism had at first added a warlike element to the movement, but before long it brought about a split in the nation, and through the image-breaking it scared in particular the politically privileged, the politically active. Thus the Brussels Government had been able to subdue the country with the help of the native nobility (among the most considerable and energetic of whom the Walloons, it is true, were much over-represented), and with the sympathies of a great part of the citizens, particularly of the town governments.

The prospects in the summer of 1567 were therefore as favourable as possible to the distant monarch. Never had there been so much readiness to accept the government of his representative as a national Government. The old watchwords of opposition seemed for the moment forgotten. In the reaction from the violent events of the past year the people of standing and the local authorities vied with each other in their show of loyalty. All the most intractable elements of the opposition had emigrated and filled the German border-towns—Emden, Wesel, and Köln—with their misery and their bickerings. It is easy to understand that many were in a bitter mood.

> We are by all deserted, and forlorn;
> In truth a just reward, which doth requite
> Our talk of Orange's power and Breero's might.
> Right worthy are we now of all men's scorn.

Thus one of the "Beggars' songs" which expressed the varying moods of the party of resistance in those years. Brederode, meanwhile, was diligent enough and travelled round in northern Germany to raise men and money. But the money would not come, and he had soon to disband the troops he succeeded in collecting. Orange sat tight in the ancestral castle at Dillenburg, greatly distrusted by the many who could not forgive him his anti-Calvinistic activities at Antwerp. All told, Margaret of Parma could be very well satisfied, and she was not a little proud of her achievement.

But nothing was farther from Philip's mind than the idea of accepting it as the basis for his policy. Margaret had always governed with the nobility and come under the influence first of one group then of another. Finally, although no doubt circumstances were not a little in her favour, she had taken excellent advantage of the dissensions among the nobles; but Philip detested in his soul the very idea of allowing any part of the nation a say on its affairs. To him it seemed that now was the moment to make the royal authority in the Netherlands completely independent. Alva came not only to visit the evil-doers with merciless retribution and wipe out the last vestiges of sedition and heresy, but to destroy the ancient privileges of the country, the root of all the evil, and to raise up on the site thus cleared and levelled the straight, symmetrical edifice of absolutism, the ideal of the new age. In course of time this attempt was to rouse all the forces of national resistance once more out of their seeming death-slumber, and at the same time to give the exiles, and the radical party in general, a fresh chance to seize the leadership they had lost.

On August 22, 1567, Alva rode into Brussels. Margaret, greatly concerned about her position and deeply offended, had for a moment thought of resisting, although in the country where eight years earlier the withdrawal of the Spanish troops had been so vehemently demanded no voice was lifted against their return. Alva assured the Governess that he only came to assist her, a piece of dissimulation which was necessary in order that the Count of Hoorne, who was away in Germany, should not be deterred from coming back. Hoorne came back

on September 7th. On the 9th he and Egmont, together
with Bakkerseele and Van Straelen, were unexpectedly made
prisoners by the arbitrary command of the Duke. As soon as
the news of the successful *coup* reached Spain (but what a
pity that neither Orange nor Hoogstraten had let themselves
be enticed from their hiding-places!), Hoorne's brother, Montigny, whom the King had thus far held fast by means of the
most flattering pretences, was taken into safe custody; Bergen
had died some time before.

To understand the tremendous impression caused by the
arrest of Egmont and Hoorne, it is necessary to recall what
a position the great nobles possessed in the Habsburg-Bur-
gundian State, how much the people looked up to them, and
how solemnly the personal safety of the Knights of the Fleece
was guaranteed by the privileges of the order. But according
to the political theory preached by Alva nothing could hold
out against the crime of lese-majesty, and on the same theory
all the opposition offered to the King during the last few
years could be brought under that head. Who then could consider himself safe? There was still a small group of Knights
of the Fleece at Brussels; Aerschot, Berlaymont, Aremberg,
Meghen, and Mansfeldt. Of these the three last had once participated in the campaign against the Cardinal. They trembled
and bowed their heads. The protests and admonitions of the
German princes who belonged to the Order were unsupported
by action. Margaret, deeply mortified, could only mingle her
tears with those of the Countess of Egmont, and at the end
of the year took her departure, accompanied by Mansfeldt,
leaving Alva both in name and in practice the ruler of the
country. The other great officers of the Netherlands, however
greatly dismayed at heart, continued to function. It was not
so much that their co-operation served to conceal the brutal
fact of foreign domination as that their knowledge of the
country and people was of value to Alva, and this was true
particularly of Viglius, who, reserving recrimination and
lamentation for his confidential correspondence, continued to
serve.

The Duke's first and chief act of government after the

arrests of the 9th of September was the institution of a special
court to punish those guilty of the commotions of the year
before. Viglius assisted in composing that body, the very
purpose of which was to hack its way through all opposing
privileges. These arbitrary proceedings became even more
insulting when foreigners—Spaniards—were appointed to
membership, and, confident of the Governor's favour, soon
assumed a tone of authority. The Chancellor of Gelderland
and the Presidents of the Courts of Flanders and Artois thus
met at the council board Del Rio and De Vargas, the latter
of whom had incurred a dishonouring sentence in Spain. He
was nevertheless a man after Alva's heart, who in his letters
to the King keeps on praising his zeal, which forms so brilliant
a contrast to the hesitations and the juridical scrupulousness
displayed by the natives. Among the members of the Blood
Council this De Vargas, who knew no French and used to
bully his colleagues as well as his victims in bad Latin, acquired
a notoriety of his own. The phrase which he threw at the
frightened delegates of the University of Leuven come to
protest against the abduction of Orange's eldest son—*non
curamus privilegios vestros*—is still remembered.

At first, since Alva's governing consisted entirely of the
organization and execution of a reign of terror, the Blood
Council was in effect the highest organ of government. The
Duke was not only its president, but his signature was required
to make decisions valid, and the opinion of a minority sufficed.
Neither by law nor equity was Alva guided in planning his
policy, but solely by the interest of the State which, as he
and Philip saw it, demanded that men should be intimidated.
This is what he himself wrote to the King in January 1568,
when the public, downcast as was their mood, were beginning
already to whisper of "a general pardon":

A great deal remains to be done first. The towns must be punished
for their rebelliousness with the loss of their privileges; a goodly
sum must be squeezed out of private persons; a permanent tax
obtained from the States of the country. It would therefore be un-
suitable to proclaim a pardon at this juncture. Everyone must be
made to live in constant fear of the roof breaking down over his

head. Thus will the towns comply with what will be ordained for them, private persons will offer high ransoms, and the States will not dare to refuse what is proposed to them in the King's name.

Morning and night, therefore, he laboured, with Berlaymont, Noircarmes, and Viglius in the Council, drafting the sentences of the emigrant lords, whose estates were seized as well as those of the late Marquess of Bergen; drawing up rules to create new categories of culprits; studying the reports of the commissaries sent out into the provinces. In the meantime Egmont and Hoorne were examined. As to the prisoners of a lesser rank, if it was thought that they were able to implicate the magnates, they were lifted on to and off the rack for months. On one day in March 1568 five hundred new arrests were made all over the Netherlands. It was not long before the executions began, and in the meantime it was Alva's chief concern to stop the emigrations, which started afresh after every act of terror, and obtain the forfeiture of the victims' possessions, notwithstanding the privileges, and at the expense even of their creditors. Most of the signatories of the Compromise, in so far as they had not fled, were left unmolested after submission.

Against the towns, on the other hand, Alva proceeded with extreme rigour. As early as October 1567 he had gone to Antwerp in person, compelling the magistrates, frightened by Van Straelen's fate, to raise a tribute, out of which a castle was built. Indictments were now drawn up against practically all the principal towns, charging them with the crimes of commission or of omission of which their magistrates had been guilty during the troubles. A number of pensionaries—salaried legal advisers of town governments—were successively arrested: Joost Borluut, pensionary of Ghent; Vorroux, pensionary of the States of Namur; Van den Eynde, pensionary of the States of Holland; Jan van der Cammen and Pieter Wasteel, pensionaries of Mechlin; Roeland de Rijcke, pensionary of Leuven. In the end only Vorroux was found guilty, but Van der Cammen and Van den Eynde did not survive their captivity. Dirk Volkertszoon Coornhert, too, secretary to the magistrates of Haarlem, was carried off to The Hague, "pinioned, manacled, and handcuffed like the meanest criminal," and was imprisoned for some time at the Gevangenpoort.

Never was nation subjected to a reign of terror with more calculated deliberation or more systematic persistence. The "Iron Duke's" imperturbable severity had a paralysing effect. The Netherlands people had offered no resistance to the entry of the ten thousand Spanish troops. They now let themselves be maltreated by the man who commanded their halberds and muskets. Only in West Flanders stirred rebellion, strengthened in January 1568 by the return from England of some fifteen hundred refugees. Bands led by rude chieftains roamed over the country, plundering the vicarages and murdering or torturing the priests. It needed only a few regular troops to put down that movement, although for a long time to come Wild Beggars (as they were called) continued to hide here and there in the woods and marshes of that distant region. No good could come of such ferocious outbursts of popular despair. If the country was to be saved, it must be by a great leader and by means of external assistance.

That great leader could be no man but Orange, even though Alva's tyranny had not yet pushed the religious question into the background to such an extent that it was possible for any-one man to possess the confidence of the whole nation. The Calvinists found much to object to in Orange, but they could not do without him, especially when Brederode, the only man they might have tried to raise up in his stead, died unexpectedly in February 1568. As for the Prince, the circumstances in which he now found himself inevitably drove him on towards the Protestant camp. In January 1568 he had been summoned before the Blood Council—together with Count Louis, Hoogstraten, Brederode, Culemborch, and Van den Bergh—a summons which was the sure forerunner of condemnation and forfeiture of goods. He now lived as a Lutheran with his Lutheran relatives in Germany. Were he to raise the banner of revolt, the Calvinist exiles would naturally flock to it from all sides. He could not but appear to the Catholic people of the Netherlands as the champion of Protestantism. But the way things had gone, it was inevitable that Protestants

should man the front ranks in the struggle with foreign domination. Orange at least never lost sight of the great fact that
the nation was still largely Catholic, nor did he ever conceive
the aim of the great movement to be the overthrow of this
Catholicism. What he constantly strove for was the union of
all against the Spanish oppressor, and in the free Netherlands
of which he dreamt there was to be freedom for Catholics
no less than for Protestants. Amongst all the leaders in exile
Orange was the one who held to this view most firmly. Nor
was any of them a European figure in the way he was. None
could make such an impression as he did when he protested
in the face of all Europe against the summons of the Blood
Council and Alva's usurpation—as he termed it—of authority.
None was so true a statesman, able to survey Europe in order
to make use of any political opportunity that might offer itself.

Truth to tell, the readiness to help of the Lutheran princes,
to humour whom he had always kept the Calvinists at arm's
length, fell very far short of his expectations, and as no great
sums were obtained from Antwerp and the exiles either, he
was left to scrape together what money he could with the
assistance of his brothers. The County of Nassau was involved
in heavy debts. The friendship of some leading princes was
nevertheless valuable in that it enabled Orange to make full
use of the anarchy prevailing in much-divided western Germany, where nobody disturbed him when he levied troops and
prepared attacks on the neighbouring Habsburg state. Soldiers
were plentiful and to be had cheap that summer as a result
of the peace ending the French civil war, in which numbers
of German mercenaries had served.

Numerous attempts were planned by Orange and his asso-
ciates in 1568. All were based on the expectation of some
co-operation on the part of the Netherlands people. Several
proved instant failures, but at the end of April the impetuous
Louis, at the head of a small band, invaded the Ommelands
of Groningen from East-Friesland. Only in the town of
Groningen was there a garrison, and that a weak one, so the
Stadtholder, Aremberg, had to wait for Spanish reinforcements
from the South. When at last he was able to advance against

D*

the Beggars, their numbers had been swollen considerably by
local sympathizers, and at Heiligerlee he and his Spaniards
were defeated. Aremberg himself was killed. Alva showed
himself equal to the emergency. He marched north in person
in order to wipe out the impression of the event. But before
leaving he staged a number of executions so as to strike terror
into the hearts of the provinces from which he had for a brief
period to withdraw so many troops. On the 1st of June
eighteen noblemen were beheaded on the Zavel square at
Brussels; some of them belonged to the party which had fallen
into Aremberg's hands on the Zuider Zee more than a year
before; amongst the others was Van Straelen; all had been
sentenced by the Blood Council months ago. The next day
a few more heads fell. Then, on the 5th of June, the execution
of Egmont and Hoorne took place on the Great Market Square
in Brussels. It was not without justification that the Beggars'
song imputed Egmont's fate to his "inconstancy." However
that may be, Alva's severity achieved its object. He was able
to take his army to Groningen-land with an easy mind.

And yet, suppose that Orange had been ready to attempt
his invasion of the heart of the Netherlands and had marched
into Brabant at this moment! But Orange was not ready, lack
of money was holding him back, and Alva was given time to
restore affairs in the North. He pursued Louis' retreating
army into the Count of East-Friesland's territory and annihilated it at Jemmingen. After having made the town of
Groningen feel his fist—he compelled it at last to receive its
first bishop and had a fortress built there as at Antwerp—he
was prepared to march South again and meet the Prince of
Orange.

For Orange would not abandon the enterprise, even though
his German relatives, thoroughly frightened, were now trying
to hold him back. In the neighbourhood of Trier a numerous
army was assembling under his command. It was indeed far
too numerous. Even after pledging all that he and his brothers
possessed and obtaining the meagre contributions of the consistories, he had been hard put to it to raise money enough
for the first month's pay. A crowd of exiles marched along

with the army hoping to return into their country under his leadership. There were Count Louis, escaped from Jemmingen, Hoogstraten, Culemborch, De Hames, and other noblemen members of the Compromise. Eloquent manifestoes announced to the people their liberation, and tried to rouse them to rebellion against their oppressors, against Alva in particular, who was alleged to be acting against the King's wishes. But the mercenaries were driven to join Orange by nothing but the hope of booty, and never did a more unruly and rapacious host set forth to liberate a country. Alva, who had his own smaller army in infinitely better control, decided not to risk a battle and merely kept the Prince under observation. It was certainly against his wish that Orange succeeded in crossing the Maas, but the striking feat (which was not accomplished until the 6th of October) led to no results. In the towns everywhere sympathizers were following the movements of Orange's army with tense expectations. The Spanish party felt that nothing but fear of the garrisons kept the people in check, and every precaution had been taken. In all the most exposed towns—Thienen,[1] Leuven, Brussels, Mechlin—Alva had placed reliable governors, Walloon noblemen every one of them— Hierges (Gilles de Berlaymont, the eldest son of the President of the Council of Finance), Beauvoir and Robles, Bournonville, Aerschot, Du Roeulx, and de Crecques (the last three belonging to the house of Croy)—all with Walloon troops. No doubt, moreover, the excesses committed by the liberators created a bad impression. In any case, not a town stirred. In North Holland a movement in the country-side, not dissimilar to that of the Wild Beggars in West Flanders, but which used the name of Orange, was suppressed by the citizen guards of Hoorn and Enkhuizen. Thus the Prince soon had to retreat without having achieved anything, his army degenerated into an undisciplined mob, starving in the inclement winter, burning, ravishing, and murdering. After having escaped on to French territory he wandered about for months, pressed for payment by the soldiery, until he fled from them by stealth. No more pitiable failure could

[1] Thienen: in French—*Tirlemont*.

be imagined. Profound was Orange's disappointment at the inaction of the Netherlands people. He himself had become the laughing-stock of his enemies. Yet, "my heart hath remained constant in adversity": so the Beggar poet made him speak in these very days. There exists no more noble expression of acquiescence in misfortune, coupled with unshakable faith in the future, than the *Wilhelmus* song, which is still a national anthem in Holland, while the Flemish Nationalists, too, love it as a true expression of their aspirations. A cause which was able to find such a voice at such a moment disposed of greater reserves of power than was guessed at by Alva and the men who humbly did his bidding.

For the time being, however, Alva's authority was firmly established. The reign of terror continued. The Blood Council was still hard at work. The forfeitures constituted a source of revenue that the Government could not do without. But it was one which from its very nature could not flow indefinitely, and so the Duke proceeded to tackle the chief purpose of his mission—the completion of the absolutist system—by making the Government financially independent of the States for good and all. At bottom Alva's extraordinary powers were intended only to make the true Burgundian-Habsburg principles triumph over opposition which in normal times had to be respected. He carried farther the organization of the new bishoprics from the point at which it had been left by his predecessor. He also attempted to create order out of the chaos of the law, which was still purely medieval and differed from province to province. In 1570 the Ordinance of the Penal Law was issued; drafted by the jurists of the central councils, it was to have legal force for the whole of the Netherlands. In many respects it was an excellent piece of work, but its introduction met with powerful obstacles. The financial independence of the Government, however, was conceived as the basis of everything.

Alva had in mind the introduction of a tax which was to be granted by the States once for all. In March 1569 he summoned a meeting of the States-General and demanded their consent to a tax called the Tenth Penny, which had been devised after a Spanish pattern, and by which 10 per cent. was claimed of the value of every article whenever sold. Recalcitrant towns were brought to reason by having the hated Spanish soldiers quartered on them. The States of Utrecht refused obstinately, on the ground that they formed no part of the Patrimonial Provinces, to which with this exception the tax was confined. Alva knew how to deal with such disobedience. The entire States of the province were summoned before the Council of Blood on the charge of having neglected their duty in the troubles of 1566, and after long legal argument were found guilty and declared to have forfeited all their rights. Small wonder if the other provinces, however reluctantly, gave their consent. As usual the real struggle was fought over the execution of what had been formally decided upon. What roused the Netherlanders to opposition against the Tenth Penny was not only the principle of a permanent tax but the nature of that tax, which, suitable as it might be to Spanish conditions, menaced ruin to an industrial and trading country. Even so economic life was seriously incommoded by the troubles, the forfeitures, and the emigration. Now the air was thick with complaints and protests, and the Government officials at Brussels added their own grave warnings. For the time being, therefore, the Governor contented himself with an extraordinary grant raised by the provinces after the old fashion in lieu of the tax; meanwhile the matter was to be further investigated. The period of grace came to an end in 1571; and now Alva, regardless of the difficulties raised by his councillors and of the objections moved by staunch loyalists like Noircarmes and Berlaymont, and even by the Bishops, announced the introduction of the Tenth Penny—in a considerably toned-down version, it is true. In the spring of 1572 a beginning was to be made with the collection.

But the situation was no longer what it had been two years ago. In 1570 a Pardon had at length been issued. It is true that the exceptions enumerated in it embraced practically all the real malefactors, so that it was still out of question for the exiles to return except under the leadership of Orange.

But even so Alva had divested himself of that extraordinary authority which we saw him using against Utrecht, for instance, and men plucked up courage more readily to resist him and his schemes. The spectacle of the divisions of the Central Government, which could scarcely remain concealed, revived the courage of urban and provincial authorities and of all who, whatever their reason, hated the forcigner's system of government. The temper of the Netherlands people was in a ferment.

Scathing remarks have frequently been made to the effect that the Netherlanders suffered the torments to which they were put on account of religion, and only rose in revolt when they felt their purse to be endangered. At the time a Beggar song represented Alva as scoffing:

> They did not care about the ruin of their country
> As long as I let them stay with their fleshpots,
> But now that I lay violent hands on their Mammon
> They want to drive me out of these lands.

And indeed one can understand the exiles feeling thus bitterly. They always talked as if Protestantism was, or ought to be, the cause dearest to the heart of all Netherlanders. But in reality the religious question, far from being a unifying factor, could not but make for disruption amongst the Netherlands people; at least from the moment when, however briefly, the menace of a Calvinist domination had shown its face. Nothing is more natural, on the other hand, than that the Tenth Penny should have proved an efficient means to heal the cleavage. And yet even now the situation remained such that it must inevitably be the Calvinists who would avail themselves of every fresh opportunity, and thereby the others were sure to be deterred once more. The Calvinists were the bitterest enemies of Spanish rule, and in the exiles, who had nothing more to lose and who were all the time looking longingly across the frontier, they possessed a peerless band of picked shock troops.

It is true that Orange was still the one and only leader, or rather, that had once more become his position since he had been able to free himself from the most embarrassing con-

sequences of the disastrous campaign of 1568. He had now
come to an arrangement with his creditors which at least
permitted him to go and live at Dillenburg again. But Orange
had himself drawn closer to the Calvinists. No other allies
equally zealous and reliable offered themselves to him. Even
before setting out on his campaign of 1568 he had concluded
an intimate alliance with the leaders of the French Huguenots,
Condé and Coligny. In view of their Kings' design to root
up "the true religion" and "to establish an unlimited tyranny
on the ruin of the nobility and of the propertied classes," the
two sides had promised each other assistance, and whoever
witnessed the triumph of liberty of conscience in his country
first was to exert himself on behalf of the other as if he were
still in danger himself. Thus, after the failure of his invasion
into Brabant, the Prince had for a while fought in the ranks
of the Huguenots. Since then peace had been restored in
France, and now that Coligny's influence at Court was plainly
rising—Condé had been killed—Orange kept his eyes fixed
on him full of hope for the fulfilment of the agreement of
1568. In the meantime he also entertained close relations with
the Netherlandish Calvinist communities in the German frontier towns. His most useful personal assistants, too, were
Calvinists, namely, the exiled pensionary of Antwerp, Wesembeke, who entered his council early in 1570, and from the end
of that year Marnix of St. Aldegonde, who had just issued
that bitterly antipopish pamphlet *The Beehive*, which has a
place of its own in the history of Dutch prose. As the representative of Orange, Marnix went in 1571 to a synod of exiled
Calvinists held at Bedtbur in the County of Gulich, where he
urged the need of unity, if possible even with the Lutherans.

Yet Orange continued to work for the nation as a whole,
and, indeed, out of its midst non-Calvinist elements did enter
into relations with him. In January 1570 he received an unexpected visit from Paulus Buys, the pensionary of Leyden,
whose unfavourable verdict on the effects of the Reformation
will be remembered. The pensionary faced the dangers of that
journey in order to inform the deposed Stadtholder of Holland
of the temper created among the urban magistrates of that

province by Alva's reign of terror and the threat of the Tenth Penny. A scheme was worked out for the organization of a revolt in the northern provinces; in Utrecht, whose States had suffered more than any from the tyrant's rough handling, even the clergy was involved in the conspiracy. Attempts were planned on a number of towns, money was collected in order to enable the Prince to come to the assistance with an army. It all ended in disappointment. Grievous mistakes were committed, money proved hard to come by, and Orange wrote bitterly that even the German princes asked themselves what had become of the famed love of liberty of the Netherlanders, a people who were reputed to be ready for any sacrifices in the preservation of their privileges.

Why was it that the Prince and his Brabant councillor—for Wesembeke displayed tremendous activity on behalf of these schemes—directed their attention to the northern provinces so specifically? The visit of Paulus Buys, Orange's particular relations with provinces of which he had been Stadtholder, these were contributory causes. But the main considerations were of a different nature, and in order to grasp this fact it should be realized quite clearly that the problem as it presented itself to Orange and his advisers was above all a strategic problem. Protestantism and disaffection were distributed fairly evenly over the whole of the Dutch-speaking Netherlands. The liberator could count everywhere on the sympathy of the population, and no doubt its character was everywhere composed in similar proportions of courage and cowardice, public spirit and egoism. In those respects there was nothing to choose between Hollanders and Brabanders, Flemings and Groningers. The question was, Where could an attacker cause the greatest embarrassment to the occupying Power?

In 1568 Louis of Nassau's raid in the province of Groningen had proved how easily an initial success could be gained in that outlying and inadequately garrisoned region. On the other hand the Prince's own expedition had shown only too clearly that the South, held immediately in the grip of the conqueror and his troops, was unable to do so much as to stir. In 1571 another Brabander, Geldorp, then rector of the Latin school at Duisburg, drew up a statement for the Prince, in which he characterized the invasion of Brabant as a strategic mistake:

country and circumstances were nowhere so favourable for the enemy as there, while, on the contrary, once you have got a foothold in the maritime provinces, it will be easy to resist all attempts at expulsion. Next time, therefore, Holland should be the objective. There is to be found the converging-point of trade routes which he who obtains a firm footing there will be able to command. It will be unnecessary to occupy more than a few towns, by preference in the neighbourhood of the Zuider Zee. That will at once give to our privateers a safe retreat and a market. The enemy, hampered by the rivers and lakes, will not easily surprise us there. Town after town will choose our side and a free trading commonwealth will arise, which will be an example to Brabant and Flanders, tempting them similarly to throw off the yoke, or which, if they prove incapable of doing that, will be able to keep them cut off from all trade and traffic.

Evidently these were the ideas which the year before had guided the enterprises of Wesembeke. They had been aimed mainly at Enkhuizen, which was to have been connected with Germany by means of Zutfen, Deventer, and Kampen; the Maas towns, Rotterdam, Dordt, had also been thought of. It is easy now to see that this was a purely strategic conception, in which the desire to supply the Sea Beggars with dependable harbours had played a considerable part.

Among the forces at the disposal of Orange the Sea Beggars were indeed of the utmost importance. Even when Louis of Nassau advanced into Groningen land in 1568 he had been joined by supporters who had come by sea in their own ships. After the defeat these had turned Emden into their centre of operations, and, sailing along the coasts of Groningen and Friesland, had been plundering monasteries and churches, somewhat after the manner of the Wild Beggars in Flanders. When Orange was forced to disband his army, a number of noblemen joined them. Soon Orange himself, in his capacity of sovereign Prince of Orange, regularized their position by providing them with letters of marque. At the same time he tried to cure them of their fierce pirates' habits and accustom them to order and discipline. A Flemish nobleman,

Dolhain, was commissioned by him to organize them, using England, which was at that time on bad terms with Alva, as his base. That attempt proved a failure. In 1570 Louis of Nassau established a new centre at La Rochelle, the strong port of which the Huguenots had then just made themselves masters.

At a time when the obligations of neutrality could be stretched so far, while moreover the Spanish Government in the Netherlands disposed of no naval power of any importance, it was possible for the privateering of the Sea Beggars to develop considerable activity. Their prize-money was to help the Prince in raising another army. They caused, moreover, great damage to Netherlands shipping, creating a general sense of insecurity and increasing the unrest in the country kept down by Alva. As long, however, as they depended on the favour of foreign rulers who were exposed to the pressure of Spain, their position remained precarious. The advantage which the Huguenot cause gained by the possession of La Rochelle was not lost on the Netherlands rebels.

And yet Geldorp's scheme was no longer consonant with the Prince's intentions in 1571. It is true that he did not disguise from himself the strategic importance of the coastal towns of Holland, but the failure of the attempts of the previous year had caused him to doubt the capacity of the Netherlands people to start a rebellion of their own accord. He therefore based all his calculations on the European situation. Assistance from France—it was this which seemed to hold the only promise of salvation, and it was with a view to this that the warning memory of 1568 was to be disregarded and another direct attack launched on the main position of Spanish power in Brabant.

In France Coligny, the leader of the Huguenots, had since the peace of 1570 gained considerable influence over the mind of the young King, Charles IX, an influence which he used to direct his ambition to the resumption of the old struggle with Habsburg. In 1571 Louis of Nassau came over to Fontainebleau from La Rochelle in order to discuss with the King schemes for the expulsion of the Spaniards from the Netherlands. The

secret of these interviews could not be prevented from leaking
out, and the indignation and uneasiness of Alva may be
imagined. But France as champion of the cause of Netherlands
independence? No doubt in the forthcoming contest the
Netherlands rebels managed more than once to play off successfully against their oppressor the rivalry of Habsburg and
Valois. But these tactics were never without peril, and if the
projects of 1571 had come to be carried out, Netherlands
nationality, still only striving towards consciousness, would
at once have fallen into worse jeopardy than that with which
Habsburg domination threatened it.

According to the English Ambassador at the French Court
—who was informed because the participation of his Queen
was hoped for—it was intended to divide the liberated Netherlands. Flanders and Artois were to fall to the share of France
(it was at least hoped that Charles IX would content himself
with those provinces which had still owed allegiance to his
grandfather), Holland and Zealand were to go to England,
while the government of the remainder was

to be committed to some prince of Germany, which in reason cannot
be but to the Prince of Orange.

In judging this project it should be borne in mind that Louis
of Nassau, in spite of his having devoted his life to the cause
of Netherlands Protestantism, was a foreigner, while it is
improbable that Orange had any knowledge of it. It is certainly a fact that the movement in the grip of which the
Netherlands now found themselves was by no means exclusively
governed by national sentiment, and few were able to distinguish behind the catchwords of "the privileges," "religious
liberty," or "Protestantism" the positive aim of an independent
Netherlands state. Yet it may well be considered significant
of the latent strength of the nationalist factor that in the stormy
times which were beginning no Netherlandish leader ever
meddled with schemes like the one mentioned, and that in
the end the idea of Netherlands unity was only given up under
the stress of superior military power. Nevertheless at the
opening of the War of Independence this incident rises up as

a reminder of the dangers to which French, English, and German interference had exposed the development of a Netherlandish nationality in former centuries, and as a warning that in the travail through which it was now to pass these dangers might well be revived.

Be this as it may, in the year 1572 events chose their own course without minding the deliberations of statesmen.

First of all, against the intention of Orange and Louis of Nassau, the game was set going in Holland, and that far too early, by a force of Sea Beggars who on April 1 captured The Brill, which in those days commanded the entry into the lower Rhine. Queen Elizabeth, who in the end felt not enough confidence in the French to risk the rupture with Spain, had ordered the Beggar fleet away from her ports, and the sensational feat had been the action of hunted and despairing pirates. Their commander was Lumey de la Marck, head of a great Liège family, who through his Holland mother also possessed estates in Holland. It was not he but his second-in-command, Blois van Treslong, a Holland nobleman, who first realized the possibilities of the capture, and at whose instance it was decided to hold the little town in the name of the Prince of Orange.

The true significance of what had happened became apparent only when Flushing called in the Beggars a few days afterwards, and especially when still a little later Enkhuizen broke out into rebellion. Then exiles, provided with commissions of the Prince, came streaming back, and in June and July the Beggars, starting from Enkhuizen, The Brill, and Flushing, brought most of the towns of Holland and Zealand under the authority of Orange.

Meanwhile the Count of Bergh had invaded Gelderland from Cleve. In the course of the summer he subjected town after town in that province and in Overysel, while in August the Frisian towns, too, were beginning to fall into the hands of the Beggars. The entire country north of the rivers was weakly garrisoned, and Alva felt himself compelled, in spite of the growing defection, to denude it still more when on May 24 Louis of Nassau surprised Mons in Hainaut with a band of Huguenots, thereby opening a suitable gate of entry to the threatening French invasion.

Yet this French invasion, on which centred the hopes of Orange as well as the fears of Alva, continued to be postponed. Orange himself, who was raising a large army in Germany, was delayed by lack of money no less than in 1568. On July 23 he took Roermond on the Maas, but had to wait for contributions from the revolting Holland towns before his soldiers, who were clamouring for their pay, consented to be led farther west. During all that time Louis was invested at Mons. A little Huguenot army, which attempted to come to his assistance, had been cut to pieces. After weeks of inactivity at Roermond, Orange at last crossed the Maas on August 27. Unknown to him, the French King, for a sign from whom he had been waiting hardly less than for money, had then given awful proof of his emancipation from the Huguenots and their counsels. On August 24, in the night of St. Bartholomew's, Coligny and his supporters had been murdered. There could be no question any longer of a French war against Spain. Even before his campaign had really started the ground had been cut from under Orange's feet. When he attempted to relieve Mons, the Spaniards on September 9 and 11 dealt severe blows to his army. Nothing remained but to return.

More successful than in 1568, Orange had made himself master of a few towns in Brabant and Flanders. Diest, Zout-leeuw[1] and Thienen had at once opened their gates for his army. Oudenaarde and Dendermonde,[2] had been brought to his side by sympathizers within co-operating with friends without. But to whatever pitch of excitement the temper of the people rose in many other towns, at Brussels, Brugge, Ghent, Breda, prospects were now too cheerless for any further defections to occur. Soon the army of "Duc d'Alve, the tyrant," was released from Mons—Louis of Nassau capitulated on September 19—south of the rivers that army was in complete control of the situation, and popular feeling counted for nothing. Orange, with his scratch lot of mercenaries, was powerless

[1] Zoutleeuw: in French—*Léau*.
[2] Dendermonde: in French—*Termonde*.

against it. At the beginning of October he led his army outside the Netherlands, dissolving it near Orsoy. He himself travelled over Kampen and Enkhuizen to Holland. There and in Zealand —so he wrote to his brother John at Dillenburg—he meant to make a stand and to see what was God's will. There—so he expressed himself a few days later in a more gloomy strain— he meant to find his grave.

II

HOLLAND AND ZEALAND IN REVOLT

The Prince was right in thinking that Holland and Zealand would alone be able to offer resistance. As soon as Mons had surrendered, Alva turned northward against Mechlin, which although abandoned as indefensible by Orange's governor Merode, was nevertheless, as an example for others, given up to the brutality of the soldiers. Unspeakable horrors were committed upon the defenceless citizens. The submission of other disaffected towns in Flanders and Brabant was graciously accepted by Alva. He had meanwhile advanced as far as Nymwegen, and from there sent on his son Don Frederick with the main body of the army.

To a greater extent even than elsewhere, external force had in Gelderland and Overysel been the determining factor in the rising of the towns. As we saw, it was the Count van den Bergh, Orange's brother-in-law, who had invaded those provinces with a little army from Germany. For a start he had, in concert with some citizens within, got hold of Zutfen, but all the other towns were simply captured. Deventer and Arnhem he found garrisoned too strongly to undertake anything against them, and from Zwolle and Kampen, even after the conquest, he experienced more hindrance than support. When, pushing forward, he reached the small northernmost towns of Overysel, some Frisian towns, long prepared by agitators returned from exile and at the same time exposed to Beggar attacks from Enkhuizen, began to join the revolt. At the approach of the Spaniards, however, it did not take the Frisian Stadtholder long to restore order in his province, while farther south there was hardly a thought of resistance against Don Frederick. Only in Zutfen did the Prince's garrison, at whose hands the citizens had suffered a great deal, remain just long enough to provide the Spaniards with the pretext for another spectacular act of severity. The sack of the town was attended with rape, murder, and arson; tremblingly the inhabitants of neighbouring places told each other of "cries of woe" heard over unfortunate Zutfen. The Count van den Bergh fled back to Germany in unseemly haste. Town after town threw itself at the feet of the despot. The magistrates of Kampen even wrote to those of Enkhuizen to counsel them to submit.

But Holland, whither Don Frederick now marched, massacring the inhabitants of Naarden on his way—Holland was another matter entirely. Not because the Hollanders were more anti-Spanish or anti-Catholic, nor because they were more courageous or tenacious than the people of Gelderland or Overysel or Brabant or Flanders. But here stood the great leader of the revolt, with his Beggars and mercenaries, the concentrated power of resistance not of this province only but of the whole Netherlands people, and they were determined to put up a desperate fight. Nor was Holland an indefensible post, but on the contrary a country with unequalled natural advantages for defence and in open communication with the sea. Moreover the Prince and his men were in possession not of a few scattered towns but of the whole province, with the exception—a very important exception no doubt—of Amsterdam, which continued to keep on the Spanish side; and they had had time to place their party in power, sufficiently at all events to enable them to continue the ejection of pro-Spanish elements as soon as it might prove necessary. The Prince and his armed followers it was in any case who made resistance possible; and their party, the party of resistance, was a small party which would not have been able to do anything without them.

Too often when Dutch historians consider those heroic four years during which Holland and Zealand defied the armies of the King of Spain while the rest of the Netherlands looked on, patriotic and romantic rhetoric prevents them from clearly recognizing that this was so. Yet the fact that the actual course of events was in accordance with what history and human nature would teach us to expect does in no way detract from the grandeur of the spectacle. Let us look a little more closely at the happenings of the summer of 1572, when the Holland and Zealand towns came over to the side of the Prince.

It all began with the capture of The Brill, and in this the

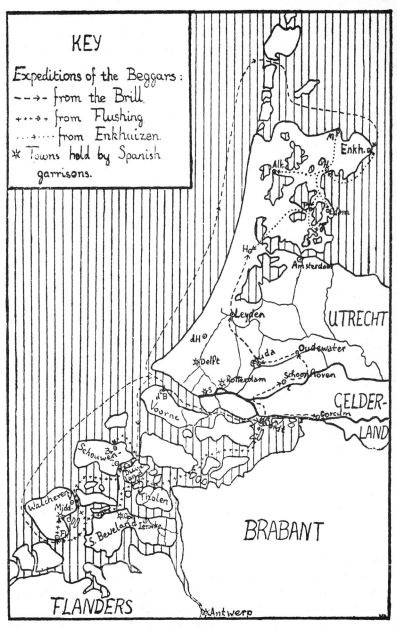

KEY

Expeditions of the Beggars:
--→- from the Brill.
+··+·→ from Flushing.
···→·· from Enkhuizen.
✳ Towns held by Spanish garrisons.

MAP III.—HOLLAND AND ZEALAND IN 1572

citizens had no share whatever. The Sea Beggars, far from being received with open arms as liberators, caused a general panic by their sudden appearance, and the magistrates and all the wealthy citizens, together with the clergy, secular and regular, fled with what possessions they could carry. Less than a week afterwards the defection of Flushing from obedience to the King began, and here we have indeed a different case, although here, too, the scale was tipped by influences from outside. Here, when Alva, mindful of the strategic importance of the place, but just too late, wanted to introduce a Spanish garrison, a real popular commotion was the response to the incitements of Jan van Cuyck, Lord of Erpt, an emissary of Orange's. The construction of a citadel, which was still unfinished, had already caused great resentment in the town. But it was on the fishermen, who were restive on account of the interruption of their trade, that Van Cuyck made the most impression. In vain did the town magistrates strive to keep the movement within bounds; they themselves were pushed onward by the captains of the citizen guards. Van Cuyck went to The Brill for help, soon Treslong brought troops in three vessels, and foreign auxiliaries, too, came pouring in. Tseraerts, a Brabant nobleman, sent to act as Orange's governor, came over sea from France with Walloon and French troops. English troops sailed with the secret approval of their Government and helped to garrison the town:

So that the people of Flushing grew very courageous and had no more thought of opposing the war.

Small wonder if the citizens had at times experienced a sinking of the heart when they reflected on the consequences of their impulsive rebellion; but the influx of soldiers, which they owed to their free connection with the sea, not only raised their courage, it also dragged them irresistibly along into further adventures. From Flushing as a starting-point in the first place the whole of Walcheren must be brought under the Prince. The magistrates of Veere refused to let the Beggar troops in, but here too Van Cuyck succeeded in rousing the fishermen, so that the gate was opened for a company from

Flushing. Middelburg, the seat of the provincial government, was held by a Spanish garrison and had to be laid siege to. In spite of the Beggars' command of the waters it could get supplies from South Beveland via Arnemuiden. Tseraerts therefore attempted to get hold of Goes in order to cut Middelburg's communications with the Continent, the basis of Spanish power. It was then, in October 1572, when the recapture of Mons and the withdrawal of Orange's army had freed Alva's hands a little, that the Spanish commander Mondragon, with three thousand men, made that famous march from Tholen (which can easily be reached from the Brabant mainland) to Ierseke, right across the water of the East Scheldt at low tide. Goes was relieved and the pressure on Middelburg lightened for the time being. Truly a brilliant feat of arms! It had taken five hours to cross the chilly autumn water, which sometimes rose as high as the men's lips. How the affair makes one realize the inestimable advantage which their superiority on the water in that island province gave to the insurgents!

Without the Spaniards being able to do anything to prevent them, the Beggars' fleet had meanwhile raided now this now that part of Schouwen-Duiveland from their bases at The Brill and Flushing, finally laying siege to Zierikzee, where the magistrates and the garrison with one accord offered resistance. For the citizens of that considerable port the situation soon grew unbearable:

We are caught like mice in the trap [so the town government wrote to Brussels]. Many citizens have gone away with their ships, wives, and children, some towards the enemy, some elsewhere. The citizens of good will who have remained in the town are becoming unmanageable.

A summons from the Beggars of Veere that they might free themselves from "the eternal slavery in which you wallow" and might not wait until they, the Beggars, forced their way in, made an impression, although when the end came in August 1572 it was still force to a certain extent which decided the issue. Even though they had been able to relieve Goes, Walcheren remained as inaccessible to the Spaniards as

Schouwen-Duiveland; when the Beggars began to besiege Middelburg next year in real earnest, the town could not be held. Before acquiescing in its loss the Spaniards made a desperate effort to assert themselves on the water. But while warfare on land could be carried on with foreigners, for the fleet they fitted out on the Scheldt they needed Zealanders. It was difficult to procure any while Flushing, Veere, Zierikzee, and Brouwershaven were in the hands of the rebels, quite apart from the fact that the sailors preferred service under the Prince to service under the Spaniard. The fleet which had been assembled at Antwerp with so much difficulty for the purpose of breaking up the. blockade of Walcheren suffered a crushing defeat in December 1573 against the Beggars' fleet under its new admiral, Boisot (a Brussels nobleman, with estates in Flanders). This sealed the fate of Middelburg. The citizens of that town had suffered little less for the Spanish cause than those of Leyden were soon to do for the cause of the country.

In Holland events had meanwhile followed a similar course. The capture of The Brill had been far from leading immediately to further defection. On the contrary, Bossu, Alva's Stadtholder for Holland, Zealand, and Utrecht, on the first report of what had happened had crossed over to Voorne with ten companies of Spaniards in order to expel the invaders, but he had been forced to evacuate the island again somewhat hurriedly when the Beggars began inundating it. Yet he had been able to summon the States of Holland to The Hague and to obtain a subsidy from them for the war against "the pirates." This in spite of the fact that what was called "the Rotterdam massacre" had already occurred on his retreat from Voorne: instead of marching through Rotterdam as had been agreed upon, he had, at the cost of the lives of several citizens, taken possession of the town, a deed which had everywhere intensified the hatred against the Spaniards as well as the fear of garrisons.

The first town where anything happened was Enkhuizen. Just as at Flushing, the fishers and skippers were in a disturbed mood through lack of employment. The burgomasters, scenting danger, wished to take in a garrison from the Count of Bossu, a precaution which seemed to be all the more necessary as Enkhuizen was the principal naval port on the Zuider Zee, and the Stadtholder was at that very moment having men-of-war fitted out there. But on the first suspicion of their magistrates' intention the citizens flew to arms. For weeks Enkhuizen vacillated between Bossu and Orange. At one time the citizens seized the Spanish warships, or even laid hands on the admiral, then again on the admonition of their burgomasters they let them go. A company of townsmen taken into pay by the burgomasters proved insufficient to keep order. The citizens' guard was indispensable, but it was so divided as to be in constant confusion. The first report of the disorders had caused a number of exiles to hurry to Enkhuizen. The Lord of Sonoy, whom Orange in anticipation of possible developments had appointed to be his lieutenant in North Holland, was levying troops in East Friesland. Beggars' ships made an appearance off Enkhuizen. At last, on the 27th of May, matters came to a crisis, in which former exiles played a leading part. The magistrates were placed under arrest in the Prince's name, appeals for help were sent to the Beggars in the Vlie and The Brill. On the 2nd of June Sonoy arrived in the town and took command.

It was his first task to provide the revolt with a broader foundation. By June 8 Medemblik had been taken; nearly the whole body of the citizens fled into the castle, but by pushing their wives and children in front the Beggars compelled them to surrender. Next came Hoorn, where the citizens were facing each other in arms, and after this one little town of the Northern Quarter after another was brought over to the side of the rebellion.

If Bossu, already hard pressed by The Brill and Walcheren, had any intention of venturing between the lakes and meres of North Holland against this second set of intruders, it certainly did not survive the emergence of yet another threat, for soon a thrust was aimed against the very heart of his provinces—against South Holland. On the 18th of June the Lord of Swieten, a nobleman who as a landed proprietor

had possessed considerable influence in the neighbourhood
of Leyden, but who had been attainted by Alva, threw himself
into Oudewater with a little band of Beggars, all come from
The Brill. A few days afterwards he came and occupied Gouda
by agreement with the citizens; the town had long been in
a disturbed condition. Now disaffection suddenly began to stir
on all sides. At Leyden returned exiles appeared in arms before
the town hall in order to prevent the magistrates from taking
in a Spanish garrison. For a few days longer the town government opposed the admission of a Beggar garrison either, then
they twice let in a few hundreds. At the same time (June 23)
Dordt, where "the commonalty" had long been agitated by
letters from Flushing, concluded an agreement with Jonkheer
Barthold Entes, a lieutenant of Lumey's. Bossu, all the time
entrenched at Rotterdam, did not dispose of the naval power
needed to cut those communications. Without loss of time a
Beggar expedition set out from Dordt against Gorcum, which
by reason of its situation on the confluence of Maas and Waal
was of great strategic importance. Here the castle, where the
clergy and Catholic citizens had sought shelter, had to be
taken by dint of hard fighting. Simultaneously from Enkhuizen
and from Leyden pressure had meanwhile been put on Haarlem.
On July 3 burgomasters and corporation, impressed by what
they had been told of the growing power and the plans of
Orange and urged on by part of the citizens, concluded with
the Prince's plenipotentiaries (former exiles of their town) an
agreement similar to that of Dordt. A few weeks afterwards
Dordt took it upon itself to call together the first assembly
of the insurgent States of Holland. On July 19 Marnix appeared
before it as the representative of the Prince of Orange, who
was recognized in his former capacity of Stadtholder. About
that very time Alva, in order to concentrate the whole of his
forces against the menace on the French frontier, summoned
all troops from Holland. Rotterdam, Delft, and Schiedam were
evacuated; and with the troops, the Court of Justice and other
official bodies from The Hague, together with many priests
and faithful Catholics, four thousand people in all, retired to
Utrecht in seven hundred carts. The three evacuated towns

at once joined the revolt, which now embraced the whole of Holland, with the notable exception of Amsterdam.

One thing appears at once from this outline—namely, that in the extension of the revolt the Beggars fulfilled a function of the greatest importance. Everywhere the magistrates had to be compelled to recognize the Prince, and it was not often that the party of the revolution, which most easily found support amongst the lower classes, was able to apply sufficient pressure from within the walls. It was the Beggars, under their aristocratic chiefs, who spread the revolt from town to town; and if occasionally a town did come over to the Prince spontaneously, their assistance was immediately required to confirm it in its choice. Nor should it be thought that all these Beggar bands did was to reveal the towns to themselves. The two were by no means animated by the same spirit. The Beggars were the men of '66, the Iconoclasts; men who had suffered on account of their faith and who bore a grudge not merely against the Spaniards but against the Church; men whose Calvinist faith found vent most readily in hatred against priests and papists. But the bulk of those who called in the Beggars most certainly had no thought of breaking with the country's Catholic tradition. To the town populations on whom Orange called in the summer of 1572 his cause meant detestation of the Spanish garrisons and the Tenth Penny. We have seen how the fear of garrisons helped to set Flushing and Enkhuizen on the road to revolt. When the burgomasters of Gouda, in their anxiety at the approach of the Lord of Swieten, cautiously sounded part of the citizen guards as to whether they were ready to defend the town, all the reply was:

No; for the Tenth Penny we won't lift a finger.

The Beggars on their part soon made it clear that five years of a piratical life had not softened their manners. The Brill, under Lumey, became a veritable den of robbers, whence the Beggar vessels sailed to plunder churches and catch priests and monks. Treslong's troops entered Flushing dressed up in desecrated vestments. The whole of Europe was horrified by the massacre of twenty monks captured at the conquest of the Castle of Gorcum and thence dragged to The Brill. Here Lumey showed great personal interest in their fate. He himself interrogated the unfortunate captives, placing before them the choice of apostasy or death—for no crime but that of their faith and calling was brought up against them—harassed them, put them to the torture, and in the end had them hanged:

to the great dissatisfaction and annoyance of the good citizens, who had a great aversion from such cruelty.

The good citizens had only too much occasion for annoyance in those early days. The clergy and faithful Catholics suffered most in those towns where the Beggars had made a forceful entry with the help of sympathizers from within. But in many cases, as we saw above, at Dordt, Leyden, Haarlem, for instance, the town government concluded an agreement with the Beggar chief who came to liberate them from Alva before opening the gates for him, and in these agreements there was always an express guarantee for the safety of the lives and goods of ecclesiastics and for the exercise of the Catholic religion. But no sooner was the Beggar chief inside than the agreement, which was nevertheless in such complete harmony with the wishes of the Prince, was violated, churches and monasteries were plundered, and priests murdered. Next there came, sooner or later, the expulsion of magistrates who were considered too favourable to Catholicism. Generally some men who had just returned from exile were waiting to take their places. In any case these were filled with reliable Calvinists.

Lumey, who looked upon himself as the begetter and leader of the revolt, appeared before the States assembly at Dordt, not a fortnight after having cooled his courage upon the "Gorcum martyrs," armed with a commission by which the Prince of Orange appointed him to be his lieutenant in the Stadtholderate of Holland. It had not been forgotten in that document to enjoin him to protect Catholics as well as Reformed and compel the two to live in peace. That was indeed putting the wolf in charge of the sheep! When Lumey soon afterwards went north to besiege Amsterdam, it was not long before the lamentations of the country people round Haarlem

reached the States, who dispatched their secretary to inves-
tigate. This was no less a person than Coornhert, who after
his imprisonment in 1566 had secretly served the Prince. Now
he soon fled from Holland to escape the rage of Lumey.

Orange, when he appointed Lumey, could not yet have had
any knowledge of the Beggar chief's goings-on at The Brill.
As soon as he arrived in Holland, towards the end of October,
the Prince at once became the protector of all the oppressed,
the support of all who wanted to found the new order on
respect for private rights. Sonoy, whose conduct in North
Holland had been little less reprehensible than Lumey's in
South Holland, mended his ways, for a while at any rate. With
Lumey, after more shocking misdeeds—the murder of Father
Muis on his flight being the most wicked—matters came to
a crisis. At the risk of goading the Sea Beggars to a rising
on behalf of the chief with whom they felt their interests to
be bound up, and of irritating the fanatics and the plunderers
who saw in him a man after their own hearts, the Prince, in
January 1573, after consultation with the States, had Lumey
and a few of his lieutenants arrested. It was thought inex-
pedient to deal with Lumey, Prince of the Holy Roman
Empire, after his deserts. In May 1574 he was allowed to
retire to Germany, where he returned to the Roman Catholic
Church.

It was easier for Orange to suppress excesses which
threatened to bring the revolt, no less than the regime against
which it was directed, into conflict with human and social
order, than to realize the purpose of which he had formed
so admirably clear a conception. No doubt this conception,
so truly noble, which he expounded with such splendid
eloquence in his manifestoes, speeches, and letters, had an
elevating influence on the whole movement. It is due to this
great leader more than to anyone else that the national significance of the revolution asserted itself in spite of everything.
That the reality fell short of the ideal cannot, however, be
denied. A free Netherlands community, safeguarded exter-
nally against the King and his Spaniards, by the ancient
privileges under the watchful supervision of the States-General,

κ

and internally against divisions and civil war, by religious peace—such was the programme that William of Orange advocated. It was neither the introduction of Calvinism, still less the suppression of Catholicism, that he called upon the Hollanders to achieve, but

to restore the entire fatherland in its old liberty and prosperity out of the clutches of the Spanish vultures and wolves.

"The entire fatherland." In the assembly of the insurgent States at Dordt the Hollanders had not merely recognized the absent Prince as their provincial Stadtholder and leader against "the Albanian tyranny"; in pursuance of his instructions the Prince's commissary, Marnix, himself a Brabander, made them, as it were, abjure their provincial particularism and promise that they would also support Orange in his task,

as a principal member of the General-States of this Netherland, to protect the said Netherland against all invasions and oppressions on the part of foreigners, they being ready, as far as lies with them, to consult and agree thereupon with the other regions and provinces.

That same day (July 20, 1572) the States resolved, in accordance with what Marnix had "stated to them to be the intention of his Princely Grace":

that freedom of religions shall be observed, as well of the Reformed as of the Roman religion, and that everyone in his house or in public, in churches or chapels (such as shall be ordained to be most convenient by the local authority) shall enjoy free exercise of his faith, and that the ecclesiastics shall be left in their state and unmolested. Unless they proved to be hostile.

The *unless* sounds an ominous note. As a matter of fact the fair promise of this resolution was not long honoured. Even now that the Beggars' rule of terror had been ended, the mob showed an inclination to break out against all manifestations of Catholicism. Conscience remained free, this was a precious gain of the revolt which was never again to be lost, but in the spring of 1573 the exercise of the Catholic religion was prohibited on the pretext of the interests of public order.

Meanwhile the replacement of Catholic by Reformed magistrates proceeded apace, and the complexion of the States of Holland, which were nothing but a reflection of the town governments, grew ever more Reformed in consequence. In April 1573 Orange himself joined the Reformed Church; yet he was never completely identified with the stricter sort. Among the town "regents"—as the magisterial class was called —there were many who left the Catholic Church without ever joining the new community, while others conformed but outwardly.

At first sight the Protestantization of Holland is an amazing spectacle. There can be no doubt that the Reformed constituted a minority, and even a small minority, and this continued to be so for a long time to come, for generations in fact. As late as 1587 they were estimated at one-tenth of the population of the province. How did they manage to retain the ascendancy which in 1572 they had obtained by surprise, because they happened to be the only armed force in the country? How was it that in the long run they even succeeded in winning the majority over to their side? This phenomenon becomes intelligible only through the state of war, a condition under which detestation of the enemy can cause a society to submit to harsh but purposeful leadership against its real inclinations.

At the beginning of December 1572 the enemy had set foot on Holland soil. They came by way of Amsterdam. It was not by any garrison that Amsterdam was kept on the Spanish side; on the contrary, it had obstinately refused to take in a garrison. The magistrates maintained order with companies levied in the town itself. A number of the wealthiest merchants, who had some years before complained to the Governess about corruption in the municipal administration, had in 1567 been forced to flee and had since served the Prince of Orange ashore or afloat. If Amsterdam went over to the Beggars they would inevitably come back into power. It was only in accord with Spain, therefore, that the magistrates could maintain themselves, and none realized this more clearly than they. That their citizens continued to follow their lead in spite of the disastrous effects on the city's trade resulting from the

Beggars' control of the Zuider Zee, is a most remarkable fact. It proves, just as does the case of Middelburg, that there existed in Holland and Zealand, no less than in the other provinces, a strong anti-Beggar undercurrent, which could easily have come to the top had the war taken a different course. Lumey's attempt to gain possession of the town had failed, without giving rise to disturbances within. And now Amsterdam opened to the Spaniards a road straight into the heart of Holland.

Here Orange, in the six weeks since his arrival, had done what was possible to bring order out of the chaos caused by Lumey's misrule. His first task had been to inspire even his supporters with the will to resistance, for under the impression of the defeats in the South the most prominent and active among them were thinking of flight.

But with the coming of the Prince the faint-hearted were now so much encouraged that they no longer flinched from peril. To the States (whom he met at Delft) he afforded such hope and satisfaction in everything that they declared themselves content to venture with him all that they possessed in the world.

Yet the very first town against which Don Frederick led his troops from Amsterdam—Haarlem—nearly opened its gates for him. On the approach of the army stained with the blood of Mechlin, Zutfen, and Naarden, the frightened corporation had decided by a majority to send delegates to Amsterdam to arrange a surrender. Behind their backs, however, the Beggar commander of the town, the Groningen nobleman Wigbold van Ripperda, engineered a local revolution. It was possible to argue from the past massacres the uselessness of surrender as well as that of defence. Ripperda's advocacy of resistance made an impression on the citizen guards. The garrison, too, was quickly strengthened, and Orange informed of what was happening. The Prince sent Marnix, who changed the magistrates in his name. The delegates were arrested on their return, and, notwithstanding their plea of having acted on the instruction of the corporation, they were beheaded at Delft.

For seven months Don Frederick lay before Haarlem,

though he had not expected that seven days would be needed. Assaults were beaten off. To exhaust and starve the town proved difficult on account of its communication with the Lake, across which fresh troops and provisions could be freely carried to it from Sassenheim. With all its lakes still awaiting reclamation Holland was hardly less an island province than Zealand, and operations on water covering a wide area played a decisive part in the siege of Haarlem, as in those of Zierikzee and Middelburg. In the end the Spaniards, at great labour, transported the whole of their Zuider Zee fleet under Bossu to the Haarlem Lake. Sonoy at once tried to utilize the command of the Zuider Zee, which was thus left to him, by making a move from Enkhuizen and occupying the Diemen Dyke, in order to cut the communications between the Spanish army and its base in Utrecht. But Amsterdam citizen companies drove the Beggars from that post, and at the end of May the Beggar fleet on the Lake suffered a crushing defeat at the hands of Bossu. It was only then that the investment of Haarlem could be made watertight, and when an army which attempted relief overland was scattered in an engagement on the Manpad (end of June 1573), the town was doomed irretrievably.

Since earlier severity seemed to have inspired Haarlem with the courage of despair, Don Frederick decided to try moderation this time, and the citizens' lives were spared. Five executioners were nevertheless set to work on the soldiers, and finally, when arms had grown too tired to wield the sword, those that remained were thrown, bound back to back, into the River Spaarne. Ripperda was beheaded.

The long duration of the siege was almost as serious for the Spaniards as failure would have been. Consumed by impatience, Alva had been waiting in the South, knowing full well that only by a show of power were the obedient provinces kept quiet, and at his wits' end how to obtain the money required to satisfy his soldiers. Yet it seemed reasonable to hope that the fall of Haarlem, which with Amsterdam cut Holland in two, would dishearten the other towns. And indeed when a few days later a small contingent of Spaniards appeared before Alkmaar, which could be reached from Haarlem by a march along the border of the sea downs, that little town fell into the greatest confusion and panic. It had for some time refused to admit within its walls Jonkheer Jacob Cabeliau with his troops, whom Orange had designated to be its governor. (No more than Marnix, Lumey, Boisot, Sonoy, or Ripperda, by the way, was he a Hollander: he hailed from Ghent.) And now neither the magistrates nor the citizens knew what to do.

If the Prince has been unable to relieve the brave town of Haarlem, what will he do for us?

This plaintive question was asked of the Beggar chief himself, when with Ruychaver and a few more officers he appeared before the corporation, assembled in the town hall, in order to press them to take in his troops who were waiting before the Friesland gate, rather than the Spaniards who were knocking at the Kennemer gate. The chronicler, Bor, tells a vivid story of the irregular way in which the decision was at last forced through by one of the burgomasters supported by a group of citizens.

They were so frightened that they could not resolve anything. A great crowd of citizens had assembled in front of the town hall, waiting for the resolution of the magistrates. When this had gone on for a long time, Ruychaver said with anger in his heart: "This is not the time to deliberate any longer, tell us briefly what you will do or not do." Upon which Floris van Teylingen, one of the burgo-masters, said: "With Prince and citizens I live and die," and imme-diately he went with Captain Ruychaver out of the town hall. Many citizens crowded in front and behind, Meerten Pietersen van de Mey, the town carpenter, among them, with axes and sledge-hammers, and they hacked the Friesland gate open and let in the men of the Prince of Orange, and the next moment the Kennemer gate was opened so that these soldiers could make a sally against the Spaniards.

The Spaniards slunk back, but after a few months (wasted in a mutiny) they returned for a regular siege. Now, however, Cabeliau had the situation well in hand, and there was no more question of hesitation. After three assaults had been beaten off, Sonoy, careless of the opposition of the peasants, had sluices opened and dykes cut for the purpose of flooding the land. The Spaniards, who had never felt at ease between the canals and meres of North Holland, retreated before the rising tide, just as a year and a half earlier Bossu's troops had fled from Voorne. Thus, as people said, "at Alkmaar began victory." Almost at the same time the Amsterdamers were disappointed in their hope that the Zuider Zee fleet, which had returned from the Haarlem Lake, would succeed in opening up a passage to their trade again. Although a huge effort had been made to reinforce that fleet, it was defeated and Bossu carried to Hoorn as a captive. Before the year came to an end, Boisot, as has been mentioned above, won the battle on the Slaak, and early in the next year Middelburg had to surrender to the Beggars.

Not two months had elapsed before tragic proof was forthcoming of the strength which Spanish military power could still display when circumstances were less unfavourable than those provided by the soil of Holland and Zealand. Orange, who never cherished the illusion that the two provinces would be able to continue the struggle indefinitely on their own resources, not only made tireless attempts to move France and England to come to their aid, but also managed once more to raise a mercenary army in Germany. Louis of Nassau was to lead it into the Netherlands. Hurriedly the Spaniards withdrew their mobile troops from Holland and elsewhere, and close to the frontiers of the Netherlands, near Mook, on April 15, 1574, a battle was fought, in which the German auxiliary army was annihilated, and in which Louis of Nassau and another brother of Orange's were killed. But at the same time it became apparent that Spain, through lack of money, was beginning to lose control of that admirable weapon which was the Spanish Army. After the victory, instead of taking immediate advantage of the dejection it caused in Holland, the Spanish soldiers demanded the pay still owing to them and began to mutiny. It was a repetition, only much worse, of what had already occurred after Haarlem. Under an *electo* the mutineers marched through the subjected provinces, robbing as they went, and finally entered Antwerp, which they proceeded to terrorize, until the Central Government succeeded by a great effort in finding some money to satisfy them. Then they were once more sent into Holland, and before long the main body was again immobilized for months by another siege —that of Leyden.

Alva had departed in November 1573. The fact could scarcely be glossed over that his rule had ended in dismal failure. He was replaced by Don Louis de Requesens, also a Spaniard, but at least not so detested that his name alone was enough to frustrate every attempt at reconciliation; for a change of policy was now announced with much blowing of trumpets. In reality this signified nothing. Requesens might have been found ready to .grant real concessions. The new Governor was alarmed by what he discovered concerning the temper of the subjected provinces, which must provide him with his foothold for the struggle with the two rebellious ones. Moreover, he experienced the public penury directly, so much so that there were moments when he was unable to pay the tradesmen of his own household. But it was the King, shut off from all contact with reality in his convent-like palace, from no reality so distant as from that of his Netherlands, who nevertheless indicated the lines along which Netherlands affairs had to move; and on the point of religion, at any rate, he was immovable. Requesens himself, it is true, believed that the Tenth Penny was the real cause of the revolt. However much truth there might be in that view, the abolition of the Tenth Penny and a General Pardon were no longer sufficient to pacify public feeling even in the subjected provinces, and at any rate to the Calvinists who had got control of Holland and Zealand the religious question was of no less importance than it was to the King. There was nothing for it but to continue the trial of strength.

The siege of Leyden put the revolt to another hard test. The town could be approached by the Spaniards via Amsterdam and Haarlem, and in order to close it in towards the south a wide circle of the country-side was occupied. Part of the population of The Hague, which was unfortified, fled to Delft; the rest welcomed the Spaniards with manifestations of joy. Leyden had no garrison, but the citizen guard had been reformed in 1572, and consisted of zealous adherents of the new state of affairs. The town government, too, which in that year had given so hesitating a consent to the introduction of the Beggar regime, had undergone some change. Van der Werff, a new man, returned from exile, during which he had served the Prince on missions full of danger, had been included among the burgomasters. Yet, on the whole, the government was still lukewarm and lent a ready ear to refugee citizens— "glippers" as they were called—who transmitted from the Spanish camp promises of mercy in case of submission. In September, after more than three months of the siege, distress was already gripping the population while there were no signs yet of the relief announced by Prince and States. If in those circumstances surrender was not decided upon, it was due to a few men of determination, who could count on the civic guard. These were, besides Van der Werff, the secretary of the town, Jan van Hout, and his literary friend, the nobleman Jan van der Does (both of whom we shall meet again, Van der Does under his scholar's name of Douza, when considering the intellectual activities of the period); and the latter's cousin Jacob. The Prince's governor, Bronkhorst, who had caused a gallows to be erected in the Breestraat as soon as any murmuring began, died in these same critical days. Jan van der Does, writing to the Prince, spoke bitterly of

the great unfaithfulness of some from among the magistrates, who presume daily more and more to incite the needy and hungry commonalty to disobedience by means of idle and false promises taken from the enemy's letters, contrary to the oath they have sworn to your Excellency and to the States.

But he and his friends stubbornly resisted all such attempts, and the town held out until Prince and States saw the fruits of their efforts. Towards the end of September the autumn winds swept the waters of the Maas, through the gaps cut in the dykes, over the land of Schieland and Delfland, and at last of Rijnland also, so that the Zealand Beggars, under Boisot, in their flat-bottomed vessels, were able to approach the town.

E*

The soil of Holland's polder-country becomes living history in the story of that expedition. The advanced posts of the Spaniards at Zoetermeer and Zoeterwoude suddenly saw the water rising all around them, the Beggars in boats and armed galleys threatening to cut off their retreat across what yesterday was land. As at Voorne, as at Alkmaar, the Spanish Army fled terror-stricken. For a while they continued to hold The Hague; but they soon broke out into mutiny again, and marched through Haarlem and round Amsterdam to Utrecht, subsisting on the peasants there and in Gelderland, at times engaging in bloody fights with the troops of the royal Stadtholders, until Requesens had once more scraped enough money together to come to some arrangement with them.

The relief of Leyden was a great event. The courage and self-confidence of the rebels were immensely stimulated. Very gradually their position acquired a certain stability. The country-side had naturally suffered terribly from the inundations and from the expeditions of the Spaniards right across the province. The trade of the towns, too, was impeded. And yet they were better off than the trading towns still on the Spanish side, Amsterdam and Antwerp, for the Beggars held the sea, preventing any ships from passing in or out, so that if the inland provinces wanted overseas goods, they had to connive at importation from the rebel towns. It is a curious spectacle to see a new social order in course of formation in the midst of the convulsion of war. Nothing is more striking in this connection than the foundation of a university—at Leyden, as a reward for the perseverance shown during the siege—which was to be for the new Reformed Church what Leuven was for the Catholic Church. But this was no more than a detail in the great work of building up a Reformed Church organization. Calvinism had been weak in Holland before 1567. At a general Netherlands synod held at Emden in the period of exile shortly after that of Bedtbur, the Holland ministers had joined in signing the confession of De Bray as an instrument of unity. Now that Holland and Zealand were an open field for their activities, nothing could stand against the rigid organization and determination of the Calvinists.

They had laid hands on the positions of power in the two provinces; for their part the authorities recognized the Reformed organization as the State Church which could unite the people in the struggle against Spain, and on whose behalf the goods of the old Church were seized. In 1574 a general synod took place at Dordt. In close co-operation with the local authorities Reformed congregations were organized in all the towns. At first the Reformed Church was almost exclusively an urban affair, and, indeed, in this new order of society the towns were of even greater importance than they had been in the old.

This was emphasized by the political developments as well. In the peculiar position of a Stadtholder representing the sovereign against whom the country was waging war without having repudiated him (for the fiction was that arms had been taken up against "the Duke of Alva and his adherents"), the Prince of Orange was, practically speaking, the depository of sovereignty, and in 1575 the States actually invested him formally with it, using the expression "High Authority"; this was after the breakdown of the negotiations, about which more hereafter. But he never strained their confidence unduly, and did nothing without consulting them. The result was that the States came to exert not only a political influence but immediate administrative powers such as they had never possessed before. Now in these States the urban oligarchies ruled supreme. The popular uprising had not found expression in any greater and more regular popular influence on the Government. The oligarchies in power had bowed so low before the storm that they had not been broken. In so far as changes had taken place, they had been changes of individuals. Many "regents" of too pronounced Catholic sentiments had been removed, and their places had been taken by exiles and other new men whom the Reformed party trusted, and to whom, once placed into power, they left the management of affairs. The nobility had been greatly reduced in numbers by proscription and emigration, and their influence in the provincial administration was to a certain extent supplanted by that of the burgher oligarchy. Side by side with the six large towns which of old

"had session" in the States of Holland, twelve small ones took
part henceforward, so that the "College of Noblemen," purged
of Catholic emigrants, was now only one—though it retained
the dignity of being the first—of nineteen members of the
States. The political power which had been set free mainly
by the efforts of the nobly born Beggar chiefs and the lower
class of the people thus fell to the share of the town "regents."
The Reformed community found itself face to face with the
States as a self-contained power, which later on would prove
to be animated by quite other than Reformed ideals. Indeed,
amongst the most daring and sturdy leaders of the revolt in
its early days there were those—I need only recall Jan van
Hout and Jan van der Does—who traced their spiritual descent
from Erasmus rather than from Calvin, and for whom the aim
of the struggle was not Reformed theocracy but liberty. After
the wild confusion of the beginning, conditions in Holland
thus developed under the banner of Calvinism in a remarkably
quiet way.

The state of public feeling in the subjected provinces, on
the other hand, was growing more and more alarming to the
Spaniards. Negotiations, carried on for a year through various
intermediaries, had really made it clear above all else that the
programme of the revolt as formulated by Orange and the
States of Holland and Zealand was the national Netherlands
programme. While ready to acknowledge the King's authority,
the Hollanders demanded the restoration of the privileges, the
departure of the Spanish soldiers and officials, and liberty of
conscience. As to the first and second points, these were the
very concessions for which the States-General, summoned to
Brussels by Requesens to assist him in his financial need, were
clamouring without showing much gratitude for the dropping
of the Tenth Penny. And while they certainly continued to
speak fair words about the maintenance of the Catholic religion,
the Governor noticed sorrowfully that there was no sincere
dislike of liberty of conscience. All he could think of in that
disastrous winter of 1574–75 was to make another attempt at
negotiating, in a more formal manner this time. So desperate
did the situation appear to him that he undertook to do this

without the express consent of Philip, who, as so often at critical moments, took refuge in a profound silence. At Breda, in the spring of 1575, delegates of the two sides met in the presence of an Imperial Ambassador, a circumstance which added even more prestige to the rebels. The instructions of the States of Holland and Zealand to their delegates laid down that they must treat only in writing and use the Dutch language; three of these delegates were Brabanders: Marnix, Charles de Boisot, brother of the admiral, and Dr. Johan Junius de Jonghe. The object of their diplomacy—here we can detect the master-hand of Orange—was to bring out still more clearly the essential unity of interests and feeling between the rebellious and the other provinces. The religious question was not pressed to the front; nay, the Holland and Zealand delegates were empowered to declare their readiness to submit it to a free States-General, on condition that the Netherlands were first evacuated by the Spanish troops. When the other side had to admit that the King could not withdraw these until order and the supremacy of the Roman Catholic Church had been restored, the negotiations could safely be broken off. Orange had achieved his object.

However, despite the disapproval with which even official circles in the obedient provinces and towns regarded the policy of the Government, all exhortations to cast off the yoke addressed to them by the States of Holland—especially to Flanders and Brabant, and to Amsterdam—remained without effect. In that same year, 1575, indeed, the Netherlanders saw a striking demonstration of the formidable strength that the Spanish military forces could still display. Although many foreign bankers had been driven away from Antwerp by the disturbances and uncertainty of the last few years, so that the money market was woefully weakened, Requesens had once more managed to raise enough funds at a high rate of interest for a desperate attempt to break down the revolt by main force. Attacks were launched at three points. An invasion of North Holland led to nothing—except to the infliction, on Sonoy's responsibility—of horrible tortures on a few Catholic peasants who were wrongly suspected of an understanding with the enemy.

Hierges, who had been appointed to replace Bossu, after the latter's capture, as royal Stadtholder of the provinces of Holland, Zealand, and Utrecht, next proceeded from the town of Utrecht and captured Buren, Oudewater, Schoonhoven, and the fortifications near Krimpen on the Lek, only to be held up by Woerden. In the autumn the Governor-General himself undertook the conquest of the island of Schouwen-Duiveland, marching through the water from Tholen, as Mondragon had done a little more towards the south three years before. Bommenede and Zierikzee, both strongly garrisoned, offered heroic resistance, and after a winter spent in hard fighting—both the Boisots were killed in attempts at relief—the troops were still lying before Zierikzee when Requesens died, on the 5th of March, 1576. Thus the government of the Netherlands devolved upon the Council of State, which soon gave proof of being unequal to it.

Yet as late as the end of June the Spanish troops, now under Mondragon, managed to get inside Zierikzee, but immediately afterwards they broke out into mutiny and abandoned the conquest which it had taken them nine months to achieve. That mutiny caused the practical collapse of the Spanish dominion over the Netherlands. The Beggars of Holland and Zealand had not brought about this great event directly by force of arms, but it resulted from the financial exhaustion into which their obstinate perseverance had plunged the entire Spanish Empire. For it was not the Netherlands provinces alone which were suffering from the penury owing to which the soldiers' pay was twenty-two months in arrear. On the contrary, Requesens bitterly reproached the States-General for the close-fistedness which compelled the King to send millions, far above his means, from Spain. As a matter of fact, by declaring in the autumn of 1575 a bankruptcy of his exchequer, Philip had dealt the final blow to the credit of his Governor as well; his precaution of soliciting beforehand the approval of the Pope, who gave it in consideration of the extortionate rates of interest paid so far, did not sufficiently impress even the most faithful Catholics among the bankers.

The changed state of affairs in the rest of the Netherlands suddenly freed Holland and Zealand from all immediate danger. Seventy years were to pass before Spain gave up all claims to sovereignty over those provinces, but never again was a Spanish force to tread their soil. There was to be plenty of time for the stabilization of the condition which we have seen growing up with and as a result of the armed resistance against foreign domination; the Reformed ruling class was given the opportunity of consolidating its position.

The phrase "ruling class" does not do justice to the actual state of affairs. There was a community of active citizens, the only ones who, according to their own opinion, had a right to activity, and who as emphatically identified themselves with the nation as do the Fascists in present-day Italy. For while the Reformed accepted William of Orange's nationalist ideology, they permeated it with their particular notions, and then went on to lay exclusive claim to it. In that way the Catholics were pressed down relentlessly to the position of second-class citizens. A most unnatural state of affairs—yet it is difficult to see how the revolt could have stood this four years' test of fire had it not been for the iron courage and energy which the Reformed owed to their faith in the country's being elected to become a temple for God's word. Later the divergence within the ascendancy party, which has been hinted at above, was to become apparent and to cause great strife and trouble in Holland. For the time being nothing was shown outwardly but Calvinism and an inclination to spy in every Catholic a suspect, a potential friend of Spain.

The problem presented in 1576 with pressing insistence by the sudden but temporary breakdown of Spanish power was the problem of "the entire fatherland." The independent position, however, which Holland and Zealand now occupied in the Netherlands, and the peculiar politico-religious character they had been developing, complicated this problem not a little. William of Orange was already familiar with the difficulty of uniting the two religious parties against the Spaniard. Would it prove an easier task now that one of them had acquired a firm foothold in a particular region? The Prince was the man called by fate to undertake the attempt in the new circumstances created by the death of Requesens, but at no time would he be able to forget that Holland and Zealand, such as the last four years had fashioned them, provided him and the revolt with the most reliable support.

III

"THE ENTIRE FATHERLAND" IN REVOLT

a. UNDER THE PACIFICATION OF GHENT

After having taken Zierikzee the Spanish troops, as mentioned in the previous chapter, began to mutiny, and in spite of Mondragon's objurgations marched off to the Continent. At Roosendaal their comrades from Goes joined them, and together they went farther into Brabant, threatening Mechlin, then Brussels, and when both towns made brave preparations for resistance they turned westward and suddenly entered Aalst, where they entrenched themselves strongly. This was not the first time that the bloodhounds of Philip II had broken loose and wildly attacked his obedient subjects. Indeed, these Spanish mercenaries were men of convictions, and, without making much distinction between the rebels and the other Netherlanders, they looked upon that whole nation as sullied with heresy and turbulence, heinous vices which inspired them with a sincere aversion. Not all the horrors they perpetrated had weakened their faith in the cause for which they fought. The less fiery Catholics of the Netherlands looked on astonished at their scourging processions. Even during their mutinies their piety asserted itself. Their *electo* and his advisers were solemnly sworn in at the altar. They prepared for their worst massacres with prayer and carried them out under a banner from one side of which Christ, from the other the Holy Virgin, looked down on them. This time, the more readily because the Central Government, under the care of the many-headed Council of State, was clearly seen to be tottering, their excesses called forth a violent reaction.

Brussels took the lead. The furious and excited citizens brought so much pressure to bear on the Council of State that this body, notwithstanding the protests of the Spanish member De Roda, towards the end of July, declared the mutineers to be public enemies. At the same time the States

of Brabant had already begun levying troops on their own
account. Orange came to Middelburg, so as to be nearer the
fire, which he fanned with all his might. The Lord of Heze,
who commanded the Brabant troops, carried on a frequent
correspondence with him. The Abbot of St. Gertrude among
the clergy, Heze and Glymes among the nobility, the pensionary of ˙Leuven, Roels, among the town delegates—these
were the leaders of a powerful party in the States of Brabant
who looked to the Prince for salvation. Meanwhile a popular
agitator, De Bloyere, was working for him among the Brussels
citizens. The Council of State was powerless. Out of Spain
there came no better comfort than the announcement, five
months after the death of Requesens, of a new Governor:
no less a personage than Don John, the King's bastard brother,
was to come—only patience!—and he would, so Philip assured,
bring with him "the true remedies" for a disease which nevertheless under the King's doctoring had for twenty years been
going from bad to worse. Meanwhile the Spaniards at Brussels
went in danger of their lives. A secretary of De Roda's was
murdered in the streets. De Roda himself sought safety elsewhere, and now Heze, without a doubt at the instigation of
Orange, placed the remaining members of the Council of
State under arrest.

At this moment the States of Brabant made a move which
recalls that of Dordt in July 1572: they addressed a summons
to the other provinces—excepting the two with which a state
of war still existed—to send deputies to an assembly of
the States-General. Soon, however, a few of the imprisoned
councillors were released—not Viglius or Berlaymont, who
were still kept in confinement—and the Council of State,
thus doubtfully restored, in which the Duke of Aerschot was
the leading personage, lent its authority to give that summons
a semblance of legality. This had already proved to be indispensable. Only Flanders and Hainaut had appeared on the
invitation of Brabant. The States of Gelderland, for example,
who with the other north-eastern provinces did not join until
a few months afterwards, took good care to underline the fact
that the summons which they accepted had been sent to them

by the Council of State, "charged with the general government of the Netherlands by His Royal Majesty our most gracious Lord."

Meanwhile the States-General, still representing only Brabant, Flanders, and Hainaut, had resolved at their first sitting (September 25, 1576), and as their very first act, that in the country's distressful condition a chief was required, and had appointed Aerschot to act in that capacity. Aerschot was a man of little perspicacity or character, whose importance lay wholly in his rank and fortune. It will be remembered that he had taken little part in the national movement of the magnates before the coming of Alva. The rivalry of his own house of Croy with Nassau-Orange obscured his understanding of the greatest national problems. In accepting the commission of the States-General he caused the Greffier of Brabant to take good note of his declaration

that he does by no means understand to take upon himself this charge for any object but the maintenance of God's service and of the old Catholic Roman religion and of the service and obedience of our Lord the King and to the greater profit and prosperity of the country.

Yet at that moment the movement had already gone beyond taking measures against the Spanish mutineers. De Roda, who was now lodged in the citadel at Antwerp under the protection of its Spanish garrison, declared the full power of the Council of State to be residing in himself as its only member not exposed to violence or undue pressure, and he protested his utmost against the action of Aerschot and his colleagues. The Spanish commanders, not only in the citadel of Antwerp but also at Haarlem, and in the citadels of Ghent, Valenciennes, Maastricht, and Utrecht, obeyed De Roda, and so did, though more hesitatingly, a number of German and Walloon garrisons scattered over the whole country from south to north-east. The consequence was that the mutineers were no longer isolated, and the States-General therefore began its career with the prospect of a serious war. Troops had to be hired. For that matter, among the noblemen siding with the States-

General there were, since Aerschot covered the movement with his name, several in official positions, and these sometimes carried their soldiers, especially the Walloons, with them. Hierges, the Stadtholder of Utrecht and Gelderland, for instance, joined in the hope of obtaining the release of his father Berlaymont.

Nothing more natural than that others, whose dislike of Spanish rule was more sincere, at this critical juncture looked towards Orange, the master of tried troops, with which during four long years he had kept the Spanish armies in check. Soon there came to Middelburg the Lord of Haussy, a brother of Bossu (himself still a prisoner at Hoorn), to ask, in the name of Du Roeulx, the Stadtholder of Flanders, for help against the Spaniards in the Castle of Ghent. Orange was eager to comply with the request. And, indeed, the States-General themselves had placed the restoration of peace with Holland and Zealand in the forefront of their programme; and in October, in that very town of Ghent where Orange's troops had already entered to help besiege the Spanish garrison, negotiations for that purpose were begun. Don John, the new Governor, was now on his way. It was essential that the negotiators should reach a conclusion before his arrival.

The veneer of legality which the authority of Aerschot and his Council of State was intended to spread over these activities cannot really hide the fact that with the unauthorized meeting of the States-General the Netherlands had taken the first step on the road towards rebellion against the King's rule. It is nevertheless well worth our while to observe how profound was the difference between the beginnings of this revolution and of that which four years ago had overtaken Holland and Zealand. That difference did not proceed from any inherent difference between the two maritime provinces and the rest of the Netherlands, but from the circumstances in which the two events took place.

In Holland and Zealand we have seen that the revolution was brought about by the Beggars, who came in from outside and directed developments. The revolution of 1576, on the other hand, was made by the established authorities under the pressure of their own people. An attempt could therefore more readily be made to consolidate it on the basis which before the coming of the Beggars had existed in Holland and Zealand too—namely, on a Catholic and conservative basis. The slogan announced by Aerschot gave complete satisfaction to most members of the States-General. All they wanted was the restoration of prosperity, and no one objected to the service of the King and the maintenance of the Catholic religion. In Holland the Beggars had constituted the only armed force. In the other provinces, on the contrary, it all began with the raising of an army by the States themselves, and the noblemen who were placed in command over it bore little resemblance to those country gentlemen returned from their exile for religion's sake who had played a leading part in the revolt of Holland and Zealand; they belonged to that nobility of courtiers and officials which possessed such power in Flanders and Brabant, although, as we know, generally not of native but of Walloon origin; even more exclusive, indeed, was its ascendancy in the Walloon provinces. This does not mean that the Netherlands outside Holland and Zealand knew no Beggar movement. On the contrary, feeble though it was, for example, in Gelderland, Overysel, and Groningen, and hardly noticeable any longer in that Walloon region which ten or fifteen years ago had been active in introducing Calvinism into the Netherlands, it was vigorous in Flanders and Brabant. But in order to come into power it had to wage a severe struggle with a social order whose powers of resistance had not been taken by surprise.

In these circumstances there could be no question of any recognition of Protestantism in the provinces now seeking a *rapprochement* with Holland and Zealand, nor could Orange even ask for such recognition. The negotiations at Ghent were regarded as a resumption of those of Breda, which only the King's obstinacy had caused to fail. The principals at Brussels were still hesitating whether to ratify what had been arranged by their delegates, when all scruples were removed by a terrible event at Antwerp. A few weeks earlier Maastricht had had to suffer a massacre for risking an attempt to rid itself of the Spanish garrison in the castle. Now it was Antwerp's turn. Simultaneously the troops of De Roda from the castle and the mutineers from Aalst fell upon the town, expelled the troops of the States, and plundered and murdered for days on end. The so-called Spanish Fury struck a heavy blow at Antwerp's long-threatened prosperity. Less than a week later the Pacification was signed.

It was a treaty of peace between the provinces of the States-General on the one side and Holland and Zealand on the other, and at the same time an alliance for the repulsion of the Spanish soldiery and other foreign oppressors. The Prince of Orange was recognized in his Stadtholderships dating from before Alva's time; the towns belonging to them which had not yet accepted his authority (Amsterdam being the principal) were to do so after having received "satisfaction" from him on points in dispute. An extraordinary assembly of the States-General was to be called together in order to settle everything, the religious question included, and this in Holland and Zealand no less than elsewhere. Until then the Edicts against heresy were everywhere to be suspended. The States of Holland and Zealand promised not to undertake anything against the Catholic religion outside their provinces. The exclusive rule of Calvinism in the two provinces was, for the time being at any rate, recognized implicitly; in a clause about secularized Church lands almost explicitly.

Here was a victory indeed for the rebels of 1572! But at this very moment the new Governor had arrived in Luxemburg, and the question arose what was to be done. The States-General did not dream of admitting him without imposing their terms. The fame of Don John's martial glory and of his attractive and romantic personality were far from making that impression on which he himself had counted. There were other facts which had more weight, as, for instance, that he came without troops and without money, and that he could not hope to achieve much, even if they were of a mind to obey his orders, with the scattered Spanish garrisons—that of Ghent capitulated in these very days. The noblemen who had the lead in the States-General, the Croys, the Lalaings, the Hennins, Catholic and Royalist as they were, intended to make the most of this splendid opportunity to carry out the traditional pro-gramme of the nobility and to shackle the representative of absolutism. Don John would have to treat. For that matter, he had been authorized to treat by his brother the King. To the ambitious dreamer, who had coveted the Netherlands government especially because he wanted to cross over from the Scheldt to England, and to set free and perhaps marry Mary Queen of Scots, the humiliating delay in Luxemburg was a grievous disappointment. The most galling demand made to him was that he should ratify the Pacification and send away the Spanish troops, which alone could help him to secure real power. Meanwhile, province after province joined the States-General, and in January 1577 a Union was concluded at Brussels by which nobles, abbots, and town deputies signed their names to a pledge to stand by the Paci-fication. Don John realized that there was no other way for him. In February he accepted the Pacification, by the so-called Eternal Edict, and the Spanish troops were ordered to leave the country. Only when they had actually departed was Don John permitted to make his festive entry into Brussels. It was then May, and the Governor's patience had worn very thin. The capital in which the States received him was still guarded by their own troops.

But if the situation was far from agreeable for the Governor, Orange, too, had plenty of reasons to feel uneasy. He had been against all negotiations. In his frequent correspondence with adherents and prominent men outside Holland and Zealand he had been tireless in sowing the seeds of distrust against Don John. He had caused intercepted letters to be published so that all might see that treason was brewing. Nor had his attempts been fruitless. A burgomaster of Zutfen, Van Thil, travelling to Brussels to attend the States-General, went by way of Middelburg to meet the Prince. Afterwards, writing to his principals from Brussels, this man expressed the greatest concern at the decision, which had then just been taken, that the assembly should move to Namur in order to speed up the negotiations. The citizens of Brussels insisted that only part of the deputies should go,

for they fear that if we came there all in a body, it might end in a Paris affair [St. Bartholomew's Massacre].

Van Thil himself was no less fearful of it, but he comforted himself with the reflection:

Dulce est pro patria mori. If I do not return, your worships may have a mass read for my soul.

If this was how a staunch Catholic felt, with how much more anxiety must the Reformers watch Don John make his entry, even though the Spaniards marched away; especially because it could not be denied that the States-General, in their eagerness to come to an arrangement, had made light of the clause in the Pacification concerning religion. The Eternal Edict spoke of the restoration of the Catholic religion in the whole of the Netherlands without mentioning any previous extraordinary assembly of the States-General. That was the basis on which already in January the Union of Brussels had been founded. Now the agreement with Don John was concluded without the Brussels leaders awaiting the consent of Holland and Zealand.

There was not, in fact, much chance that this would ever have been given. About this very time a person sufficiently simple to expect that this clause in the Pacification might result in the expulsion of heresy was met by a Brabant Calvinist with the scornful reply:

Will the Hollanders suffer themselves to be robbed by means of a vote of what they have not suffered to be taken from them by force of arms?

Indeed, it was not likely. The Hollanders and Zealanders were still sitting behind their water defences, their army and navy ready to act, governing themselves under their States and Stadtholder, and not at all inclined to let themselves be dissolved in the community of the States-General except on their own terms. Haarlem (taken by the Spaniards in 1573), Schoonhoven (in 1575), and Goes (which had never as yet sided with the Beggars) had received treaties of "Satisfaction," in accordance with the Pacification, and had submitted to the States of Holland and of Zealand; in all these "Satisfactions" protection of Catholicism was asked for and promised; in Haarlem the Bishop still resided. Amsterdam alone, blocked in now on all sides, stubbornly refused to join the rest of Holland; it still hoped for relief from Don John. Meanwhile the Prince was trying to strengthen the outer defences of the position. His troops still lay at Ghent, where he had supporters who were ready for anything. Negotiations were being carried on with Utrecht, which had been freed from the Spanish garrison in the Vredenburg Castle only in January 1577, and which, so the Prince maintained, by virtue of the Pacification ought to revert under his Stadtholderate. The States of that province, however, in which nobility and clergy possessed much power, and which were traditionally afraid of being overshadowed by Holland, preferred to keep Hierges. Holland envoys travelled to Gelderland in order to put the States on their guard against Don John's intentions and to propose a closer alliance with Holland. At Brussels, at Antwerp, everywhere the Prince's agents were agitating and intriguing.

Don John, who had started negotiations with "the arch-rebel," soon discovered that he would never of his own free will make any concessions on the point of religion. What was worse, like Requesens, the new Spanish Governor found that the Netherlands nobles who surrounded him were not averse from liberty of conscience, and were little enamoured of the prospect of a renewed struggle with the two maritime provinces. They irritated him terribly, these nobles, who were holding him in strings. How different was this Governorship from what he had pictured to himself:

fit for a woman, like Margaret of Parma. Only a renewal of the war could make the situation bearable, only by possessing Holland and Zealand and thereby commanding the trade of the Netherlands, can one be Governor of the Netherlands in reality.

In fact, he was so far from enjoying any real power that already after a few weeks, aggrieved by the hostile and suspicious attitude of the citizens, he had left Brussels. For a time he resided at Mechlin, but his position became unbearable, and on 24th July, 1577, he unexpectedly captured with his body-guard the citadel of Namur. An attempt on that of Antwerp failed. From Namur he now demanded fuller power, the removal of suspect personages like Marnix from the States-General, and assistance against Orange. An outburst of popular rage was the response, and while Don John could only wait in impotence for the troops which he begged Philip to send back, but which were slow in coming, the citizens at Antwerp, Utrecht, and elsewhere pulled down the hated citadels, and the country threw itself into the Prince of Orange's arms.

The policy of co-operating with Don John, or rather of using him, had been the policy of the high nobility. The peace of the Duke of Aerschot, that was the name given to the Eternal Edict. As in the days of Margaret of Parma after Granvelle's departure, the nobles had under Don John carried everything with a high hand. Now that he himself tore up the Pacification and called back war and Spaniards, the party of the Catholic nobility was plunged into the greatest confusion. Some who had kept aloof from the States-General movement, or had no heart in the business, Mansfeldt, Berlaymont and his son Hierges, Meghen, and the others, rallied round Don John. The majority, Aerschot himself among them, could not so readily renounce the programme of the Pacification of Ghent and the Union of Brussels, but they now found themselves, half un-willing and somewhat disconcerted, more patently in opposi-tion to the King's authority than ever before. At the same time their prestige with the public had seriously suffered. The Prince of Orange was now the wise man who had foreseen it all. His adherents triumphed. Not only had his warnings been justified by the events, but, moreover, now that it was to be war once more, the two provinces of Holland and Zealand, strongly situated, vigorously led and formidably armed, offered an unshakable support in the rear that could not but appear of the utmost value.

For the time being there still prevailed in the States-General at Brussels a good deal of confusion and vacillation. In fact, it was from outside the circles of the politically privileged that the great moves towards drastic change were now to proceed. All over the Netherlands, in the towns at any rate, the people began to stir. First of all at Utrecht, where the burgher cap-tains (captains of the civic guard) presented a threatening address to the endlessly deliberating provincial States, urging them to hasten the negotiation about a "Satisfaction," and even to invite the Prince to visit the town. The popular party at Utrecht had ever been turbulent. Yet there was not lacking, even in this address, the assurance that everything must be done

without injury to the Catholic Apostolic Roman Religion or to the due subjection to His Majesty.

Orange came to Utrecht even before an agreement had been reached over the Satisfaction, and was received rapturously. He also tried once more to establish relations with Gelderland. The States of that province, hard pressed by the garrisons of Kampen, Deventer, and Roermond, which remained loyal to Don John, were fain to concert common measures of defence with their Catholic neighbours of Utrecht, Overysel, and Groningen; but even so they were still a little shy of Orange.

Now, however, the citizens of Brussels suddenly broke the deadlock. The government of that town consisted of three "members," the third of which was that of the nine "nations" or guilds. These nations had appointed a committee of "Eigh-teen Men," and these, under the leadership of the lawyer Van der Straeten, who was in close touch with Marnix and through him with Orange, lorded it over the town and bombarded the States-General with petitions and opinions. It was under their immediate pressure that this assembly invited the Prince to come to Brussels in order to assist it with his counsel. The States of Holland were loath to see him go. Their independent position had become dear to them since 1572, and was it not to be feared that Brabant and Flanders, now that they rallied to the Prince, would resume their ancient leadership in the Netherlands community? All Orange's activities in the South in the ensuing years were to be watched with jealous eye by Holland and Zealand.

This was nevertheless a proud moment in the life of William of Orange, when he, the exile of ten years ago, after first having been received with tempestuous joy at Antwerp, made his stately entry into Brussels. At Vilvoorde already the Brussels rhetoricians welcomed him with their symbolic representations on barges—the journey from Antwerp to Brussels was made by water—the famous "Rhetorician" Jan Baptista Houwaert greeted the Prince in flowery Dutch rhyme, just the kind of poetry to which he had been treated at Utrecht; for the rest of the journey to Brussels· a citizen guard of honour marched on either side of the canal; at the gate of the town were waiting representatives of the States-General, the States of Brabant and the municipal government; Aerschot himself rode beside Orange through the densely crowded and gaily bedecked streets, amid cheers and blessings, to the palace of Nassau, which, plundered and gutted by Alva, was yet home to its returning master. It was Aerschot again who welcomed him on the morrow in the States-General, although in effect the Prince had come to transplant the "chief" elected by that assembly a year ago.

He came just in time to frustrate negotiations with Don John into which the States had entered out of fear for the master they were giving themselves. Orange's strength lay in the people. He knew how to make himself liked. The Eighteen Men he invited to his table; in the street, on the walls, he talked to the civic guards familiarly and in a human way, using at times the great words of Liberty and Fatherland which went straight to their hearts. And when shortly afterwards another scheme came to light with which Aerschot hoped to deprive him of the power to harm; when it appeared that the young archduke Matthew, a brother of the Emperor's, nephew of Philip's, was on his way to the Netherlands, having been invited by a number of the high nobility to come and assume the governorship in order to save the country at least for the Habsburg dynasty and for the Catholic Church, then the people of Brussels were immediately ready to maintain the Prince against those intrigues as the trusted man of the nation. Reinforced with delegations from Antwerp, Leuven, and Den Bosch, the three other chief towns of the province, the men of Brussels pushed their way into the meeting-chamber of the States of Brabant and forced through the appointment of Orange to be "Ruwart" of Brabant—an office corresponding to that of the Stadtholder in the other provinces; as the residence of the Governor-General was in Brabant, that province had no Stadtholder in ordinary circumstances. The appointment was confirmed by the States-General acting under similar pressure. Aerschot and the entire conservative party were profoundly irritated.

Aerschot had just been made Stadtholder of Flanders by the States-General. He thought that post gave him a *point d'appui* for a counter-attack. In fact, he caused the provincial States assembly at Ghent to protest against Orange's appointment. But here his rival had the same kind of allies at his disposal. The popular party, fired by the recollection of the heroic traditions of their town's past, burned to imitate the example set by Brussels. Two members of the Ghent municipal aristocracy, Hembyze and Ryhove, aspired to the rôle of tribunes of the people, like in days gone by Artevelde, with whom Hembyze claimed family connection. He had long been in touch with Orange. It was with the Prince's help that he had just succeeded in obtaining from the States-General the restoration of the privileges which Charles V had torn up in 1540. This had caused great rejoicings at Ghent. The people expected next to see guild rule re-established in a legal manner. Aerschot, the new Stadtholder, looked askance on that claim, but Hembyze and Ryhove, having made sure of Orange's secret approval, now ventured upon their great attempt. On the 28th of October they arrested Aerschot and the principal members of the States of Flanders, among them the Bishops of Brugge and Yper. The old democratic town government was resurrected, but at the same time a revolutionary committee of Eighteen Men was instituted.

These developments caused not a little consternation in the States-General at Brussels, and everywhere they hastened that estrangement from the cause of the revolt which had already begun among nobles, clergy, magistrates. While Orange had Aerschot (and Aerschot alone) released from prison, during a visit to Ghent he showed himself openly the friend and ally of Hembyze, Ryhove, and the guilds. Indeed, he had for a second time marched troops into the town from Zealand, and it was on these that the revolutionary regime now rested. Meanwhile the States-General were still entirely under the thumb of the Eighteen Men of Brussels, who declared masterfully that the national cause was the cause of the people, and therefore their concern. The Commune of Paris, two centuries and more afterwards, during the French Revolution, would not be able to put it any better.

It was in this confusion that the organization of the new government under Matthew, which was to be independent of Spain, had to be elaborated. The two most vital decisions were forced through by new tumults. It was in spite of themselves that the States-General included in the new Council of State avowed adherents of Orange like the lawyer Liesvelt and Marnix. And it was in spite of themselves that they appointed Orange to be Matthew's lieutenant, an arrangement by which in effect the Governor, intended by Aerschot to control him, was delivered into his hands.

A Netherlandish government was now in being. After Don John, after Orange himself, Matthew could make his festive entry into Brussels, and under him Orange was the real ruler. It was a government in which old national tendencies were realized. As we saw, the States-General had taken it upon themselves to appoint a Council of State. In spite of all loyal declarations with which even now they were not chary, they laid hands on a considerable part of the royal prerogative. The Governor took an oath to Philip, but also to the States-General. He promised that even when fortified by the advice of the Council of State he would consult them before committing any important act of government, and he acknowledged their right, as also that of the provincial States, to assemble of their own accord. In case these conditions were violated, the States would be at liberty to take up arms—who does not recognize here the inspiration of the Brabant Joyous Entry? It was a veritable constitution. But was this constitution of a nature to secure sufficient strength to the Central Government?

The Burgundian Dukes, as we have seen, had imposed the Central Government upon the Netherlands people as a foreign organism which—certainly not without great gain to national development—went right against historic subdivisions which may appear arbitrary now, but to which political life had accustomed itself. Now this superimposed Central Government was to a large extent pulled down and a new one formed, but as the vitality of these historic subdivisions was far from being exhausted, the new Central Government was conceived as the resultant of the old groups coming together in freedom. No doubt a true feeling of community manifested itself in opposition to the provincial particularism which had always caused so much trouble to the rulers, but the difficulty was that the States-General, without whom the Governor was nothing, were so much the immediate creature of the provinces that in cases of conflict they could do little but admonish and implore. As for the Prince of Orange, it was impossible that he, in spite of his eloquent declarations, should be generally accepted as a national leader; in the eyes of many he was bound to remain the chief of a party. The worst weakness of "the Generality," however, was its lack of money. The States-General reproached the provinces situated a little away from the Brabant centre with not contributing anything to the federal exchequer. These provinces retorted that the States left them to battle alone against their particular perils. Gelderland, for instance, still had serious trouble with the garrisons, mentioned above, of Kampen, Deventer, and Roermond, and the Gelderland deputy, Van Lier, wrote home from Brussels in his German-flavoured East Netherlandish:

According to my humble opinion there is but little help and comfort to be expected for us from their lordships the States here. I give your worships to consider, therefore, whether it might not be better that we provide ourselves with the help and assistance of the neighbouring provinces.

And the new regime, thus beset by the problems of these

strong centrifugal tendencies, had hardly begun to function when the military power of Spain administered a blow to it which set it tottering. The Netherlands were not to be left to work out their own destiny.

Don John had had to use a great deal of patience, but at length in January 1578 three thousand of the Spanish troops which he had sent away after the Eternal Edict came back, and without losing a moment he marched from Luxemburg in a north-westerly direction. At Gembloux, just across the Brabant boundary, he fell in with the much more numerous army of the States. Many of its noble officers were at Brussels attending a wedding. The Walloons threw away their arms almost at once. The defeat became a rout. Nivelles, Diest, Thienen, Leuven capitulated; Maastricht was held, like Brussels, where the people insulted the nobles, calling them traitors; Don John did not yet dispose of a sufficient number of troops to attack the capital. Yet the States-General, with Matthew and the Prince of Orange, withdrew to Antwerp. What might not have happened had Don John been able to follow up his success! But while the course of events in his Netherlands was once again crying out for speedy decisions, Philip was sitting lost in the disentanglement of his half-brother's vague projects against England; he suspected him of treason, had his agent Escovedo murdered in Madrid, and instead of reinforcements sent him congratulations. The States-General and the Prince of Orange obtained a respite to put the country in a state of defence.

An almost desperate undertaking; not only on account of the feebleness of central authority, which has been indicated, but at this very moment, partly as a result of the shock of the defeat, the country slid into an indescribable confusion. The savage forces set free by the political and religious passions of the time no longer let themselves be controlled by the ingenious devices of the States-General and of Orange. Their sudden irruption, which threatened society itself with collapse, dealt shocks to the young community of the Netherlands which weakened its powers of resistance not a little, just when it needed them against the renewed attack from outside.

b. RELIGIOUS STRIFE AND SEPARATE UNIONS

The Pacification of Ghent, as we know, had attempted to settle the religious question on regional lines. A really satisfactory solution could hardly be obtained in that way, for even though the events of 1572 had brought the Reformed party into power in Holland and Zealand, there were Catholics there just as much as there were Protestants in the fifteen provinces that were officially considered as Catholic. Both sides now had the consolation that conscience was free, but 'for the rest all they were allowed to do in those provinces where they were not in control was "to keep quiet." Their respective attitudes showed how much the tendency of the time was with the Protestants. In spite of the fact that the suppressed Catholics in Holland and Zealand constituted a majority of the population, the Protestants stirred much more vigorously and created a far more urgent problem in the provinces where they were kept under, small minority though they were there too. The example of Holland and Zealand acted as an inspiration to them. Numerous Flemish and Brabant exiles, who had done their share in the building up there of the new Reformed State, now brought to their own towns the tales of the victory they had witnessed. It was inevitable that the democracy, which Orange had helped to put on its feet in Brussels and Ghent, and which he had let loose against the conservative and Catholic States assemblies, should move towards Calvinism. Both the Catholicism of its adversaries and the Calvinism of its Holland allies and of the returning exiles drove it in that direction. In the eyes of the democrats, too, the national cause, which they already identified with the cause of democracy, became one with the cause of the Reformation. At Ghent the report of the defeat near Gembloux had the immediate effect of causing the Eighteen to have the monasteries occupied by their soldiers, and this was only the first of a long series of acts of violence against the Catholics.

At Ghent, under the leadership of Hembyze and Ryhove, and after the fashion in which the same work had been done in 1572 and 1573 in Holland and Zealand, Calvinism was in

the course of the spring and summer of 1578 raised to exclusive
dominion. Monasteries were closed and their properties con-
fiscated, monks sent into exile, all offices filled with Calvinists,
churches emptied of decoration and whitewashed for the
Reformed service, finally the exercise of the Catholic religion
prohibited. Ghent's traditional claims, which had been vigorously revived by the revolution of the year before, combined
with religious enthusiasm to drive the movement outside the
town. Oudenaarde, Kortryk, Brugge, finally Yper as well,
were surprised, generally with the help of sympathizers within
the walls, and gradually the whole of Flanders was forcibly
subjected to Calvinism, the democratic form of government,
and at the same time to the hegemony of Ghent. Needless
to say the process was attended with a good deal of violence.
The Ghent preacher Regius—De Koninck, a native of Kortryk—on contemplating the finished work, found comfort in
the thought that the worst things

were done by those who know of no religion. In fine (so he must
nevertheless admit) Babylon (meaning Rome, Catholicism) could not
be annihilated without a Babylonish confusion.

In July, when public preaching had only just begun, this man
had felt very unhappy over an interview at Antwerp with
Villers and Taffin, court preacher and councillor to the Prince,
who had warned him that what was happening at Ghent
"greatly displeased" Orange.

With many arguments and high words they begged of us that we
should at once abstain, if we would not cause His Excellency the
greatest trouble and to the Fatherland the most notable peril.

Nothing more natural than that the Prince should be alarmed
to observe the breaking forth of Calvinism in Flanders. The
entire Catholic and aristocratic party in the Netherlands were
aghast and at the same time indignant, and protested with all
their might against the tearing up of the Pacification. Orange
had not scrupled, when there seemed to be a fair opportunity,
to administer shrewd blows to these men, but now he judged,

and rightly, that caution was necessary, especially because they were in almost exclusive control of the Walloon provinces, which consequently—and this was an exceedingly dangerous development—began to form a block in the States-General. But however readily one may understand the Prince's urging patience and moderation, no less obvious is it that the Calvinists could not at his bidding check themselves in midway. God's work must not be hindered by human considerations. Everywhere the Protestants began to stir, and after a synod at Dordt, presided over by Dathenus, a formal request for freedom of religious exercise was presented to Matthew and the Council of State.

The Prince now flattered himself with the hope that concessions would get the better of the extreme claims of the Reformed party. In July the States-General resolved to lay before all the provinces a project of Religious Peace. Even though this was merely a project, over which each province was to retain the final decision, the resolution met with the opposition of Hainaut and Tournai, and needed Orange's urgent insistence to go through. According to it, public exercise of the second religion would have to be conceded, of Catholicism where the Reformed were in control, of Calvinism where the Catholics ruled, in all places where a hundred families so desired.

At Antwerp, under the eye of the Prince, the project was introduced, and for the time being only there. One cannot wonder that the Catholics in those provinces where they still had the upper hand, especially the Walloon area and Groningen, Gelderland, and Utrecht, saw in it merely a sly contrivance for the introduction of heresy and in the long run for the dethronement of Catholicism. That was the way they saw things going all over the country! The example of Flanders and Holland and Zealand was instructive: there was no thought there of granting to the Catholics that liberty which in the Catholic provinces the Religious Peace was to bring to the Protestants. Thus the Walloon provinces grew more and more embittered, and events rolled on irresistibly in their fatal course. The Walloon troops which had acquitted themselves

so badly at Gembloux had been removed to the boundaries
of Flanders and Hainaut, and there, long unpaid, and declaring
that they were intentionally neglected by the States-General,
in August they began to mutiny. They had since been living
at the expense of the peasants in southern Flanders. On
September 28, under the command of the Baron of Montigny,
a brother of the Count of Lalaing, who was Stadtholder of
Hainaut, they captured the little Flemish town of Meenen.[1]
Montigny gave them a watchword: they called themselves
"Malcontents," and fought for the Catholic religion and for
the Pacification. Soon the situation developed into a real civil
war with the troops of Ghent under Ryhove, while the Walloon
provinces acclaimed Montigny as their champion.

What complicated matters still more was the activity of
John Casimir, the Elector Palatine, with his auxiliary troops.
After the defeat of Gembloux the States-General had redoubled
their efforts to obtain assistance from foreign princes. Lalaing
had invited the brother of the French King, the Duke of
Anjou, to Hainaut, but although the States-General had
decorated him with the title of "Defender of Netherlands
Liberty," he achieved nothing for the good cause. It was his
interference nevertheless which, by rousing England's ever
wakeful jealousy of France, made Queen Elizabeth forget both
caution and economy so far as to subsidize the warlike and
zealously Calvinistic Casimir towards leading his army to the
Netherlands. The English money did not, however, go very
far, and Casimir, having reached Brabant by way of Zutfen
with his undisciplined troops, had nothing more urgent to do
than to demand payment of the States, and when this was
not forthcoming, achieved no more against the enemy than
Anjou. With all the more fervour, however, did he throw
himself into domestic party strife. In October, at the instance
of Dathenus, who had been employed in the Palatinate during
his exile after 1567, and who was now the minister of the St.
Bavo church at Ghent, Casimir came to that town and backed
Hembyze notwithstanding the admonitions of the States-
General and of Orange. In the eyes of the Flemish Cavinist

[1] Meenen: in French—*Menin*.

he was the man of God. Orange, on the other hand, who wanted to tolerate Catholicism, who in spite of the St. Bartholomew's massacre was still hankering after an alliance with France, was for these zealots a worldling, an atheist. Dathenus rated him from the pulpit for making the State into his God, for changing his religion as other men would change a suit of clothes.

In these circumstances, and "having understood that the heretical provinces of Flanders, Holland, Zealand, Gelderland, and others are planning a separate union," the States of Hainaut in October took the initiative for negotiations with the other Walloon provinces in order to work out a similar alliance on a Catholic basis.

At that moment events escaped the control of Orange completely. The Spanish army had during the summer been driven back some way out of Brabant by Bossu, whom the States-General had entrusted with the command-in-chief over their troops. But while Don John, again in the neighbourhood of Namur, was eating his heart out over the way in which his brother the King was crossing his plans, the States Government lacked the cohesion it would have needed to collect its scattered forces for a decisive blow. Orange had to give all his attention to the war the Walloons were carrying on with the Flemings and to their threatening defection. It is true that he succeeded for a moment, by playing off Ryhove against Hembyze, in making Ghent submit to his policy. In December he came to the town in person and had the Religious Peace proclaimed. But in the meanwhile he had to leave the affairs of the North to his brother John of Nassau, who, no less zealous a Calvinist than Casimir of the Palatinate, was as little inclined to think of national unity, and in accordance with the Prince's policy to respect Catholic feeling.

John of Nassau, the eldest, and now the only surviving, brother of Orange's, had always assisted him in his perilous undertakings up to the extreme capacity of his lands of Nassau and beyond. When the Prince in 1577 went to Brabant, he had wanted to leave John as his lieutenant in the Stadtholderships of Holland, Zealand, and Utrecht, but the States of those provinces had not been agreeable. In June 1578, however, John

had become Stadtholder of Gelderland, which had been without a Stadtholder since Hierges had gone over to Don John.

How is it possible that the States of that eminently Catholic
province had let themselves be saddled with so vigorous a
Protestant? When they had begged Matthew to indicate a
suitable person for the post, they had been careful to stress
their desire to see the Pacification respected; that is to say,
they professed themselves to be averse from religious innovations. The fact is that Gelderland was in desperate straits.
Lords, knights, and towns, divided into four "Quarters," for
the most part disliked the idea of submission to Don John;
but even apart from a secretly pro-Spanish party, they were
torn by faction and could not unite on any decision, particularly not on a selection for the Stadtholderate. Yet at the same
time they were painfully aware of being unequal to the military situation created by the garrisons of Kampen, Deventer,
and Roermond. Only Orange, only Holland seemed to be in
a position to render assistance against those dangers. Orange's
brother appeared as the messenger of that assistance, and for
the moment his religion was overlooked. In Overysel, of which
province Hierges had also been Stadtholder, the States were
really making the same calculation when they asked to be
allowed to take as his successor the Lord of Rennenberg, who
was already, since the end of 1576, on behalf of the States-
General, Stadtholder of Friesland and Groningen. This was
indeed a more natural choice than that of John of Nassau, for
Rennenberg, a scion of the great Hainaut family of the Lalaings,
for all that he was closely connected with Orange, who loved
him as the younger brother of his late friend and fellow-exile
Hoogstraten, was at the same time a staunch Catholic. Between
them the two Stadtholders now obtained troops from Holland
—which were commanded by no less a person than Sonoy—
and in the second half of 1578 first Kampen and then Deventer
were besieged and captured under Rennenberg's direction.

This eliminated a serious danger, but there still existed the
chief menace, that from the South, where Roermond in Upper
Gelderland was still in Spanish hands. John of Nassau therefore applied himself vigorously to the task, entrusted to him

by his brother, of securing Gelderland by binding it more closely to Holland.

Mention has been made more than once in the preceding pages of this idea of a separate union between Holland and Gelderland and other northern provinces. It was promoted by Orange and Holland—there is no doubt that Van Lier's suggestion quoted above was inspired by the Prince—not because they felt more closely related in spirit to Gelderland than to the provinces south of the rivers, nor indeed because they had any intention of seceding together from those southern provinces. On the contrary, their insistence, repeated more than once, and each time suspiciously repulsed by the Catholic States of Gelderland, sprang from their realization of the strategic importance to Holland of the maintenance of Gelderland, coupled with their fear lest the province should prove too weak and too much divided to work out its own salvation. Against an attack from the south, Holland and Zealand were safeguarded by nature, but as soon as the enemy was able to take the offensive he was sure, just as in 1572, after a circling movement through Gelderland, to attempt an attack from the east. Gelderland was therefore described as "a propugnaculum," a bulwark for Holland, Zealand, and Utrecht, and attention was drawn to the fact that

the enemy directs most of his effort against Gelderland, thinking thereby to acquire the four rivers, to wit, the Rhine, the Maas, the Ysel, and the Waal, and in course of time to get at Holland.

It was John of Nassau himself who instructed an envoy of his to represent these facts to the States of Holland, it was he who, a little while after his elevation to the Stadtholderate, renewed the negotiations. In doing so he was by no means acting as the executor of the wishes of the Gelderland States. On the contrary, how to overcome their persistent opposition to the idea was his great problem. John of Nassau stood in Gelderland as an independent power, by many hated and feared in equal measure, but, strong through his relations with Holland, whose auxiliary troops now formed a potent factor in the struggle of forces in Gelderland, he carried through his policy with high-handed determination. This was the moment when the relations between Catholics and Protestants were becoming infinitely more strained than they had been since the Pacification; the events at Ghent by no means had that effect in the South only. If as a consequence many Catholics, affected by the temper of the Malcontents, began to look to the King's Governor, this again produced increasing suspicion on the part of the patriots against all Catholics indiscriminately. Nobody did more to strengthen this vicious circle than Count John. He exerted himself greatly to persuade the States of Gelderland to accept the Religious Peace, and when they obstinately refused, he yet helped the Reformed wherever possible to possess themselves of churches, overlooking antipapist violence on the part of the troops. A number of towns from the Quarters of Roermond and Zutfen addressed to the States-General a complaint about "the exorbitant innovations" with which, since the new Stadtholder had taken the oath, they were "overrun" by the action of the soldiers. The Stadtholder had on his own authority dissolved the Court of Justice of the province. No doubt this court was a hotbed of Spanish intrigues, yet in the eyes of many who had no use for Spain the deed was an unheard-of violation of the ancient constitution. In a similar fashion Count John, regardless of their kicks and struggles, forced upon the States that bitter medicine, the Union.

In September a meeting of the States was held at Arnhem, where, at the invitation of the Count, envoys of Holland and Zealand were present. Here the obstinacy of the men of his own province, who persisted in appealing to the Pacification of Ghent to justify their refusal, so angered him that he burst out:

Smear yourselves all over with the Pacification of Ghent, I see too well what is going on.

The Count of Culemborch, the Beggar of '66, who assisted him, gave even more explicit utterance to the suspicions of the Protestant party, fulminating:

"It is all due to the fact that a handful of idols have been thrown down [the military had been guilty of iconoclasm at Arnhem], that is why we see this distant manner. You had better take the Duke of Anjou, he will protect you, he is a Catholic, he drives the shaven band"—and more such words.

All these passionate sallies did not move the States of Gelderland to give in; but neither did their blank refusals make an end of the negotiations, which were continued by their Stadtholder. The project which served as a basis had been drafted by the Advocate of the States of Utrecht, Floris Thin, and had the approval of Orange. The Hollanders and Count John, however, altered it flatly against the Prince's intentions. Instead of, in accordance with his wishes, protecting and reassuring the Catholics as much as possible, the exclusive dominion of Calvinism in Holland and Zealand was first of all expressly recognized, while in the second place the Religious Peace was made the normal condition for the other provinces. The Religious Peace might not be in accordance with the Pacification, it had at least been sanctioned by the States-General. In the new project for the Union, however, a further step was taken: the provinces were allowed to do what seemed to them to be required by the interests of public order; at the same time, by clauses concerning the secularization of ecclesiastical goods, clerical apostasy was positively encouraged. So all that the opposition of the Catholic States of Gelderland effected was that the Union was prepared in Protestant conclaves, for in the end they were unable to prevent the alliance from being concluded.

Don John had died in October 1578. Alexander of Parma, the son of Margaret, had taken over the government, an arrangement which the King confirmed. In the last days of the year he marched against the Upper Quarter of Gelderland. The Knighthood of the Upper Quarter (constituting one of the "members" of its States) declared at once

that this principality is entirely powerless to resist the enemy, and has fallen into such utter confusion that they cannot do without neighbourly assistance.

At the Gelderland Diet only Zutfen and the knights still opposed the despatch of delegates to Utrecht, where the final

negotiations about "the Holland Union" were to take place.
Fear of the Protestants, fear of Holland supremacy, everything
had to give way before the need of Holland troops and Holland ships. On 23 January, 1579, the Union was signed at
Utrecht. But even though the States of Gelderland had sent
a delegation, they had not empowered it to sign, and it was
Count John who with his solitary name on the document
boldly represented the whole province. At Utrecht, shortly
before, the municipal authorities had prepared for the conclusion of the Union by placing under arrest several of the
clerical members of their States. Rennenberg and his provinces,
who had taken part in the first discussions at Arnhem, ab-
stained now that matters had taken this turn. Only the Ommelands, always at variance with the ultra-Catholic town of
Groningen, at once participated. So also did Ghent, which had
eagerly sent delegates to attend the final discussions and which
formally adhered a few days afterwards. Holland and Zealand
were the fixed point round which this so-called Closer Union
crystallized.

As a matter of fact the alliance formed at Utrecht did constitute within the Pacification a far tighter organization. The
participators bound themselves to be "for ever as one province."
They organized a committee of their own to deal with military
matters, and took into their service troops paid out of their
own contributions and commanded by their own general, the
German Count of Hohenlohe. The provinces allied at Utrecht
continued to sit on the States-General, yet the latter were
practically relieved from all responsibility in the territory of
the Union, and it is only when one remembers how feeble
was their rule and how incapable of acting with any speed
that the founders of the Union can be understood to have
been moved by other motives than a desire to secede.

The territory united on 23 January, 1579, while it was
seeking to expand its boundaries, at the same time needed
itself a good deal of confirmation and purification. In accordance with the opinion that had now come into sway, this meant
the suppression of all influence of the Catholics, potential
friends of Spain. It was practically by force that Count John

got the Quarters of Gelderland to consent to the Union he had already concluded in their name. Into several town administrations he introduced Calvinists. At Zutfen, which remained recalcitrant longer than any other town, Sonoy's soldiers seized the churches for the Reformed. Sonoy admitted that

no doubt some idols were taken down somewhat roughly,

but nevertheless gloried in that work. Within the Union territory the public exercise of the Catholic religion was thus restricted more and more. So far in Holland and Zealand the towns which had come under the Prince's authority by Satisfactions had for some little while occupied an exceptional position. Amsterdam, whose citizens in 1577 had beaten off with considerable loss of life an attempted surprise by the troops of the States of Holland, had not come over to their side until February 1578, and then only on terms which included the continued suppression of all religious services except the Catholic. But these Satisfactions were torn up one after the other. At Amsterdam, as early as May 1578, the old government, together with the priests and monks, had been driven out of the town, where the exiles of 1567 now formed a new government and introduced Calvinism. They since supplied to the new regime in Holland, and even to the Union, some of the most prominent among many vigorous personalities; for example, Reinier Cant, who became a member of the Committee of the Closer Union. At Haarlem, on Corpus Christi 1579, the garrison assaulted the procession, invaded the cathedral, killed a priest, smashed the statues; the Bishop fled for his life. One of the offending soldiers was subsequently hanged, but in spite of the murmurings of the Haarlem Catholics, who appealed to the Satisfaction, public exercise of their religion was now prohibited and the churches were given to the Reformed. In the province of Utrecht, Amersfoort would not submit to the Union nor introduce the Religious Peace. Commissioned by the new regime, John of Nassau came to lay siege to the little town. On 10 March, 1579, it surrendered. New magistrates were appointed and the Religious Peace proclaimed. On the 11th of June following the statues were removed out of all the churches, and once again the Religious Peace had led to the exclusive domination of Calvinism. At Ghent, too, in March 1579, the Religious Peace which Orange had caused to be accepted there was brought to an end, and Hembyze and Dathenus were once more in control.

> They who at first asked for no more than to live in freedom,
> Now have their liberty, but will not give it to others.

Thus bitterly wrote Spieghel, the Amsterdam poet, who himself constantly refused to serve in any capacity under a regime based on the violation of the Satisfactions.

Orange—nothing else could be expected—looked on these developments with profound concern, and refused to join a Union which had been so utterly alienated from his intentions. Seen from where he resided, from Antwerp, the situation appeared gloomy indeed. In southern Flanders the Walloon Malcontents were advancing, while Parma's troops from the Upper Quarter of Gelderland marauded over the entire country-side of Brabant. Although the Prince, therefore, still considered "a good Union" to be imperatively necessary, at the same time he roundly declared to the envoy who came (at the end of February 1579) to ask for his signature to the Utrecht agreement and for his help in obtaining those of the magistrates of Antwerp:

this one is no good.

In spite of which, a little over two months later, he joined all the same, and not only Antwerp but Lier and Breda and the whole of Flanders followed suit. Circumstances were too strong for him. Once more his efforts to make Protestants and Catholics co-operate had failed; once more, now that there appeared to be no remedy for that, he had no choice but to go on with the Protestants alone. It was in any case too late to hold back the Walloons. No less by what had been done at Utrecht than by the proceedings at Ghent, they were irretrievably alienated.

We saw how the first rumours of a "heretical" Union had served as an excuse to the States of Hainaut in proposing a

Catholic one. This argument continued to be used, while in its turn the Union of the Walloons served the same purpose in the North. Here, too, was that vicious circle which Orange could not break through. In the end the Walloon provinces had come to an agreement at Arras before the others at Utrecht. At the basis of their Union was the wish to have the Pacification respected in a strictly Catholic sense. Since this was the very purpose of the Eternal Edict, which had been expressly confirmed by the King, the conclusion was obvious that between the Union of Arras and the legitimate Sovereign it ought to be possible to restore peace. The fact that Don John, who by his attempt on Namur had broken the Eternal Edict, was no longer among the living made an agreement even easier of achievement, and Parma showed himself to be an accomplished diplomatist. First, Montigny with his troops was reconciled—with him went that de Hèze who in the first stage of the revolt, not three years ago, had been Orange's man at Brussels—then the Walloon provinces of Artois, Hainaut, and Walloon Flanders concluded at Arras in due form a peace with the King. The great lords of those provinces made excellent terms for themselves. This was not a small temptation for their equals who still, at the cost of daily irritations and humiliations, held the side of the States-General. What a scene, for instance, when on Corpus Christi 1579 at Antwerp (where the Religious Peace was supposed to be in force), Aerschot and the Archduke Matthew himself, with all who took part in the procession, were, to the anguish of Orange, molested by the Beggar mob! For the rest, the peace of Arras, like the Eternal Edict, solemnly confirmed all the old privileges and promised the removal of the foreign troops. Was it not the true national policy which triumphed there? No, for the most precious thing was lacking, namely independence. But independence was not what the Netherlanders had set out to win with any clear consciousness of purpose, and in any case the triumph, under the Catholic banner, of the interests of the nobility and the States, of the old privileges, was bound to make a profound impression all over the country.

The secession of the Walloon provinces is an event in the

history of his people which rouses mixed feelings in the heart
of the Netherlands historian. He is tempted to discern the
possible beginnings of a sounder political organization. In the
convulsions of the war of independence the French-speaking
and the Dutch-speaking regions seemed each to be waking up
to their own individuality. Not all was religion in these
developments. That becomes evident at once from the exactitude
with which the separation coincided with the racial boundary.
After the Union of Arras the only Walloon deputies remaining
in the States-General for a little while longer were those of
Tournai. But, in fact, the Walloons were beginning to remember
their ancient feuds with the Dutch-speaking Flemings, and
became more conscious of their racial community as against
that of the central and northern Netherlands. These for their
part were heartily sick of the gallicization of the Central Government which had been the consequence of the conjunction
with Walloon countries; this is true especially for the north-
eastern provinces, whose nobility and magistrates were less
familiar with French than those in the others. The States-
General—was it on account of the deputies from Tournai?—
continued to use French for some time longer, but as soon
as the Dutch-speaking provinces—from Flanders to Friesland
—were left among themselves, Dutch was introduced as the
official language. (In the provincial States, even of Brabant and
Flanders, it had of course never lost that position, in spite of
the influence of the nobility transplanted from Wallonia.) I
am not suggesting that this linguistic and racial factor played
any considerable part in the shaping of events, only that
developments revealed its existence and sometimes fell in with
it. The primary importance of the religious motive will clearly
appear as soon as we come to consider affairs in the North-
East. But even so we may, from the point of view of our later
experience, point out what a blessing it would have been for
the future of Netherlandish civilization in Flanders and Brabant—of the native civilization of those regions, in other words
—if their leading classes had had to collaborate in politics with
those of the North, and had been detached from the corrupting
association with the Walloons. But while we cannot overlook

these possibilities contained in the peace of Arras, even though they have not materialized, another reflection offers itself even more insistently. It is that if the Walloons had to cut loose from the Dutch-speaking Netherlands, they could not have chosen a more unfortunate moment. Their action hastened the development of a conflict between the cause of independence and the cause of Catholicism, a process as harmful to the one as it was to the other. And it provided the foreign ruler, whose commander so far had had to stay in the poor and distant region on the Maas, with far more important resources and a base of operations from which not only the towns of Brabant but those of Flanders as well came within his immediate reach. One circumstance, finally, deserves some notice, namely, that these Walloon provinces which by their defection were going to exercise so fatal an influence on the course of the war in the South and on the future of Flanders and Brabant, to-day for the most part do not even belong to Belgium. Of the four that made peace at Arras, two (Artois and Walloon Flanders) were wholly, while a third (Hainaut) was for about one-half, annexed to France, and for good, by Louis XIV.

The revolt thus found itself in a sad plight in 1579. Serious inroads were already being made on the Dutch-speaking Netherlands. Parma did not at once continue his attack on Gelderland, but turning round he first besieged Maastricht. After an obstinate resistance the town was taken, and suffered for the second time in a period of three years a horrible sack and slaughter. Meanwhile the Catholic party gained the upper hand at Den Bosch and Mechlin, so that these towns left the side of the States-General. A negotiation which was conducted at Köln that summer, once more under the Emperor's mediation, again stuck on the unsurmountable difficulty of the religious question. But this time a number of highly placed personalities, particularly the Duke of Aerschot and the Abbot of St. Gertrude, took the occasion of its failure to disengage themselves from an unbearably false position, and instead of returning to the States-General made their personal peace with Parma.

One most dangerous loss the revolt still had to suffer, as

a direct consequence of the unhappy contrast between Catholic and Reformed.

Friesland, Drente, and Overysel had joined the Union of Utrecht, district by district, and amid loud quarrelling. Rennenberg, who had at first resolutely refused to do so, invoking the example of Orange, had given in when the Prince himself changed his mind. He had then even forced the town of Groningen to submit and introduce the Religious Peace. Yet he did not feel comfortable when matters took this turn. It was not to be expected that he should! The Walloon nobleman could hardly remain insensible to the example set by his cousins the Baron of Montigny and the Stadtholder of Hainaut (Lalaings like himself), and by how many others! The faithful Catholic was greatly offended by the proceedings of Sonoy and of John of Nassau. Nor for that matter was he the only one. At Groningen, at Leeuwarden, Kampen, Zwolle, everywhere, the Catholics were afraid that the Calvinist minority, leaning on the Holland auxiliary troops, would proceed from Religious Peace to suppression of the Catholic services, and everywhere they felt their courage rise with the Malcontents movement, which had now found a protector in Parma. Members of the dissolved Law Courts of Friesland and Groningen, noble *émigrés* from the whole region east of the Zuider Zee and the Ysel, surrounded Parma and entertained relations with their friends who had remained behind, to whom they promised the King's and his Governor's pardon. The whole of that area, where many looked upon the Union of Utrecht as a yoke imposed by the Hollanders, was in a dangerous ferment. Rennenberg certainly must not be represented as the disinterested champion of an idea. Before taking the leap he made careful arrangements with Parma, as had done all his friends, about his rank and his possessions and his honorary titles. Nevertheless his "treason," as it is called in the North Netherlandish history books, was no mere personal act. It was an act of policy for which he could count on widespread acclamation in the provinces of which he was Stadtholder.

In March 1580, at Groningen, ever a stronghold of royalism in the North, he announced his defection from the States-

General. All his helpers and councillors were natives of Groningen, Friesland, and Overysel. His action caused a tremendous sensation. Everywhere the dislike of the patriots for Catholicism was doubled. At Leeuwarden, at Zwolle and Kampen, at Utrecht, priests were insulted and statues in the churches broken to pieces. The States of Friesland and those of Utrecht now prohibited the exercise of the Catholic religion in the whole of their provinces. The Catholics, on the other hand, longed only the more fervently for the coming of the liberator. But Rennenberg's intention had been guessed a good while before, and measures had been taken accordingly. The Prince of Orange, deeply shocked by the faithlessness of a beloved younger friend, had already come north as far as Kampen, accompanied by the Committee of the Closer Union. Holland was ready with an advance of money for the soldiers' pay, and the troops were withheld by Barthold Entes, the former Sea Beggar, from following Rennenberg. Erelong he was being besieged within Groningen by Sonoy and William Louis, John of Nassau's son; and even though without troops to overawe them, not a single town in Friesland, and especially in Overysel, could be relied upon, for the moment the defection had been checked. Only the Overysel country-folk, harassed by the States' troops little less than by the Spanish, rose to arms in their thousands, and had to be struck down in bloody fights by the Count of Hohenlohe's cavalry: seven hundred peasants were killed in the first engagement.

Immediately afterwards, however, Hohenlohe was faced by a harder task, when Parma sent a small army from the Upper Quarter of Gelderland round the east to relieve Groningen; it was led by Schenck van Nydechem, with a staff of Frisian and Groningen *émigrés*. Hohenlohe, trying to stop this force, was defeated, the siege of Groningen had to be raised, and now more than ever the entire North-East was in jeopardy. The majority of the citizens of Zwolle nearly succeeded in bringing the town over to the Malcontent side—for that name was now used here too. Oldenzaal threw its garrison out and called in Rennenberg. Koevorden and Delfzyl opened their gates for him. Steenwyk was held thanks to a vigorous commander, and the States troops could also safeguard Friesland and the Ysel towns. But everywhere citizen stood over against citizen, exiles returned while other groups went into exile (as did almost the whole of the Ommeland nobility, which had ever been zealous in the cause of the revolt), and a wide area was exposed to raids from either side.

A man like Coornhert, the poet and philosopher, the friend of liberty, was alarmed to see how the Reformed, by their consciousness of constituting "by far the smallest band," were driven to ever sterner repression of the "wronged" Catholic majority. In the end, he feared

the town populations which have let in the Beggars, hoping for better from them and experiencing worse, will again help to drive them out and will open lands and towns to the enemy. So that they will, together with the oppressors of their consciences, see this delightful country once more subject to Spanish slavery.

How is it that events have not taken this course? How is it that in part of the Netherlands, at any rate, that "small band" has managed to maintain itself, and in the long run even to fashion the majority after its wish? At the moment when this chapter is closed no equilibrium has been established between the contending parties. But in the forces which will make themselves felt from now on the military factor is much more prominent than it was in those to which the enormous losses of the States in 1579 and 1580 were due. No doubt the religious divisions still remained a source of weakness to them; in the loss of Zutfen, Doesburg, and Nymwegen, for instance, and also in that of some of the Flemish and Brabant towns which Parma won in the coming years, the dissatisfaction of the Catholics was to play an important part. But the great moral issue had been decided. Netherlands liberty was to be anti-Romish. That was the doing, despite Orange, of the Calvinistic regime of Holland and Zealand through the Union of Utrecht, and of the Calvinistic regime of Ghent through the subjection of Flanders and the co-operation with Brussels.

It is undeniable that sentence of death had thereby been pronounced over Netherlands unity, but it should neverthe-less be observed that the line which we have now seen drawn by the Malcontents movement between Flanders and Wallonia, and between the extreme North-East and the neighbouring region, was not to be the final line of separation. The defection of the North-East represented little less clearly than did the defection of the Walloon provinces the spontaneous refusal of the Netherlands people to sacrifice its old religion to liberty. Nevertheless Groningen and Oldenzaal, like Zutfen, Doesburg, and Nymwegen, were in course of time to become free and Protestant; Flanders, and Ghent itself, not less Protestant than Holland and Zealand, were on the contrary destined to slide back under Spain as well as under Rome. How was it? Because, as has been said, the military factor now became paramount; and in the trial of strength between Spain, based on the wide perimeter of the Netherlands—from Grevelingen over Nivelles, Leuven, Maastricht, and Roermond to Groningen—and the revolt, based on the maritime provinces of Holland and Zealand, the geographical configuration of the country, in particular the inestimable strategic importance of the great rivers, was to be the determining factor.

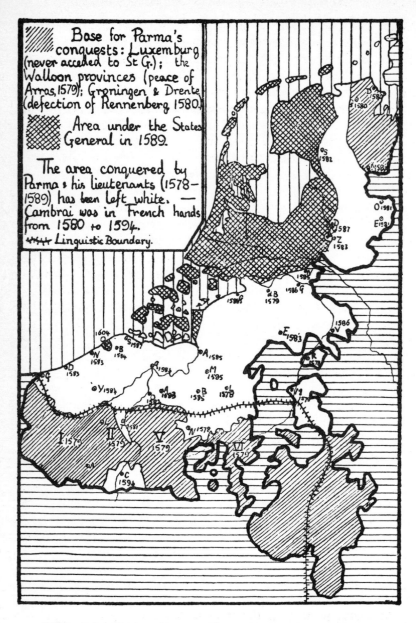

Base for Parma's conquests: Luxemburg (never acceded to St G.); the Walloon provinces (peace of Arras, 1579); Groningen & Drente (defection of Rennenberg 1580.)

Area under the States General in 1589.

The area conquered by Parma & his lieutenants (1578–1589) has been left white. — Cambrai was in French hands from 1580 to 1594.

✠✠✠ Linguistic Boundary.

MAP IV.—THE CONQUESTS OF PARMA, 1578–89

IV

THE SPLIT

a. PARMA'S CONQUESTS, 1580–1589

Thanks to the energy displayed by Orange and the delegates of the Closer Union, together with their military commanders, the revolt had for the moment withstood the shock of Rennenberg's defection. Rennenberg died in 1581, in the bitter consciousness of failure, after having been forced to raise the siege of Steenwyk. Nevertheless the outlook for the States was indeed gloomy. On the land side their territory was now encircled by the revived power of Spain, although Venlo and Upper Gelderland, firmly secured by John of Nassau, still hampered the communications between Parma in the South and Verdugo, the successor of Rennenberg, in the North-East. In the South the enemy took Kortryk by surprise, but as against this Mechlin was recovered by a movement from Brussels and soon resumed its place in the States-General. Flanders and Brabant were threatened with continual attacks and raids from Kortryk and Leuven, while in the North-East not only was the greater part of Groningen, Drente, and Overysel either actually lost or in imminent danger of falling into enemy hands, but Friesland, Gelderland, and even Utrecht had to endure the intolerable vexation of troops, their own being scarcely less troublesome than those of the enemy.

Despite the scant good done in 1578 by Casimir or Anjou (both had departed somewhat ignominiously in the following year), more than ever the feeling asserted itself that without foreign help the revolt must collapse. Already early in 1580 Orange had prevailed on the States-General to draw up a new constitution which must serve as a basis of negotiations for conferring the sovereignty on the Duke of Anjou, and which, no less than the constitution of 1578 had done with respect to Matthew, met all the fears of the privileged class and of the provinces now grown accustomed to their independence,

lest in the new monarch they should give themselves a new
master.

Yet it still required endless patience to get the harassed
Netherlands to welcome their French deliverer. The great
objection was not to the revolutionary nature of the action
demanded of the States in disposing of the sovereignty which
had hitherto been considered as Philip's inalienable possession;
for, whatever the opinion of the nation, in the States there
now sat only men who had abandoned all thought of reconciliation with the King. It was about this time that Philip
issued against Orange the ban by which he armed all mur-
derers against him, promising huge rewards in case of success.
But to choose for sovereign a Catholic and a Valois, and one
with the personal reputation of Anjou! It was hard. No more
than anyone else did Orange cherish illusions about the ability
or reliability of this tainted scion of a despised house, but a
dispassionate contemplation of the state of Europe persuaded
him that there was no alternative, and he accepted the inevitable conclusion. From the German princes there was nothing
more to expect. It might seem even more surprising that
England was not more ready to help, for who could doubt
that the safety of her Protestant Queen was bound up with
the maintenance of Netherlands freedom? But evidence of
the understanding between her Catholic subjects and Philip II
frightened Elizabeth as much as it angered her, and she had
shaken all Orange's confidence in her by her jealous and
capricious policy. A royalist writer railed at the Prince thus:

> Of the English Jezebel you get no audience,
> She leaves you in need without any defence,
> She has turned her coat . .

Anjou, on the other hand, was personally full of zeal. And not
only should his position in France make it possible for him
to raise a host of adherents and adventurers for a private
campaign, but Orange could even hope (it was the old dream
of 1572) that his influence at the court of his royal brother
would enable him to provoke a war between France and Spain,
and that would have decided the issue. Thus the Prince defied

all the suspicion and opposition which he incurred as a result of his support of Anjou's candidature, and yet the affair progressed but slowly. The treaty was not concluded until the autumn of 1580, and in the spring of 1581 the Duke ratified the agreement; not even the most serious limitations on his power had sufficed to discourage him. Under that treaty Holland and Zealand retained their special status and their particular relationship to Orange.

A whole year had been wasted, and it was fortunate that Parma was hindered by the very conditions of his first great success, the Peace of Arras; for by that treaty, as we know, he had agreed to send the Spanish troops away again. But the Walloon provinces were now too deeply interested in the recovery of the King's territory not to let themselves speedily be persuaded to assent to their being recalled once more. Besides, after the occupation of Portugal, which had engaged much of his attention during 1580, Philip again had means at his disposal to carry out those designs in the Netherlands to which he clung so tenaciously. It was thus an excellent thing for the States that Parma was compelled in 1581, as Alva had been in 1572, first to turn southwards for fear of a French invasion. But Anjou's performance was disappointing from the start. With an army for which he demanded subsidies from the beggared States, while his brother would not be hustled out of his neutrality, the whole campaign was spent in the siege of Cambrai, in which France had a more direct interest than the Netherlands. Then, while Parma took Tournai, the last Walloon province remaining in the States-General, the Duke went off to England to court the elderly Elizabeth. There again he achieved nothing, and so in February 1582 he appeared with a brilliant retinue at Flushing and made a festive entry, first in Middelburg and afterwards in Antwerp.

The majority of the provinces now did homage to Anjou as ruler. To make this possible Matthew had departed, and the preceding summer the States-General, assembled at The Hague as it chanced on this occasion (though naturally there were delegates from Flanders and Brabant present), passed the famous resolution, whereby Philip, on account of his tyrannical

rule and his trampling underfoot of the privileges of the
country, was deposed from dominion over his Netherland
provinces. Following this resolution all authorities, officials,
military commanders, and the like, were required to take a new
oath, in the absence of Anjou, to the United Provinces. This
was obtained without much difficulty throughout the Dutch-
speaking Netherlands, while in the North as well as in the
South the Catholic population looked sullenly on. There were
those who argued that unconditional obedience to the King
was the duty of every Catholic, but it would be hard indeed
to square this view with the facts of medieval history. In
reality the "Placard of Dismissal," drawn up by the Brabander
Van Asseliers, was a brilliant, though late, expression of the
sturdy medieval tradition of freedom, which was everywhere
losing ground before the encroachments of modern absolutism,
rather than a manifestation of the specifically Calvinistic spirit.
No doubt Calvinism, with its strong consciousness of individual
rights, which in the Netherlands fell in quite naturally with
the old tradition of privilege, was responsible for much of the
energy which the carrying through of the principle demanded.
Moreover, the revolt was now so closely identified with the
Calvinist movement that the abjuration could not but be
obnoxious to the Catholics.

The Catholic Duke of Anjou entered indeed into a strange
position as lord of a land where the Catholics were suspected
and excluded from all influence. There were, it is true, among
the leading spirits in the States-General, besides Orange, still
some men, like the Fleming Van Meetkerke and the Geldersman Leoninus, who either from indifference or from a well-
understood patriotism put policy before religion, and were able
to co-operate wholeheartedly with Catholics. But this attitude
of mind was a rare one, at any rate outside the circle of
prominent magistrates and jurists. Wellnigh everywhere the
Religious Peace had now come to an end, and the Calvinist
ministers were working tirelessly at the organization of the
new religious community. It was a difficult matter always to
satisfy the demand for efficient ministers of the Word. Nevertheless, as early as 1581, there were ministers in the classis

of Brugge alone, besides in the town itself, at Sluis, Damme, Aardenburg, Oostburg, St. Kruis, Westkapelle, Oostkerke, Knokke, Heist, Wenduine, Groede, Meetkerke, Zoenkerke, Moerkerke, Dudzeele, Lissewege, St. Pieters op den Dyke. The support of the secular authority, which had appropriated ecclesiastical property, was indispensable. It was also expected to lend a strong hand for the expulsion of the old religion from its last hiding-places in the country-side. Thus we read in the minutes of a meeting of the classis of Ghent as early as November 3, 1578:

On those of Ghent asking how the Roman religion may best be impeded everywhere in the surrounding villages, answer was made that the notables of this town shall be requested in the name of the classis to prohibit by open letters all priests of the Mass from exercising their Roman religion.

This work, which was carried on no less zealously in Holland and Zealand and all the other provinces than in Flanders itself, was still far from finished a few years later, and under Anjou went merrily on, certainly not to his edification. It was with great difficulty that the Duke prevailed upon the magistrates to re-establish a church for his co-religionists even at Antwerp, which was, since 1578, virtually the capital, and Anjou's usual place of residence. How heartily the Netherlanders and their new ruler distrusted each other became apparent when an attempt was made at Antwerp on the life of Orange—the first-fruits of the ban—and the general impulse was to regard the French as the instigators of the crime, so that Anjou and his compatriots had to be protected against the popular fury.

It would have been impossible, even had there not been the treaty limitations on his power, for this man ever to establish that strong central authority of which the Netherlands people in their distress had so great a need. The tragedy of their history repeated itself. Once more a foreigner was sovereign. For his sake the Council, which the States-General placed beside him, had again to use French—Orange, too, no doubt preferred it—though in the now purely Dutch-speaking

States-General the vernacular ruled supreme. But this difference in language was merely symbolical of a divergence of interests and a complete lack of mutual confidence.

Despite the unfavourable circumstances—and this is a fact well worthy of note—the Netherlands provinces continued to manifest a feeling of solidarity. At the same time it can hardly be called surprising when this sentiment, forced into the old channels of provincialism by the very origin of the rebellion, exposed to the storms of war and under distrusted leadership, failed to give itself enduring forms. The Council of State just mentioned was at any rate an attempt to tighten the bonds of General Union, which had undoubtedly been loosened by the Union of Utrecht.

It is true that the Union of Utrecht now embraced almost the whole of the territory of the rebellion, and had furthered the Protestantization of the South as well as of the North. But so far as its original object, that of defence, was concerned, it remained mainly a North Netherlands grouping. Holland and Zealand supplied the driving-force behind it, and they took an interest first and foremost in the defence of the helpless eastern provinces, which were of such great importance for their own safety. The Committee of the Closer Union, which in its own territory virtually replaced the central authority, had, especially since the defection of Rennenberg, almost limited its activities to the theatre of war north of the great rivers, although Flemings and Brabanders continued to serve on it. In any case the administrative changes rendered necessary by the coming of Anjou were seized upon to put an end to this state of affairs. Now that the States-General no longer formed a battle-ground, as when the Union was concluded, between the Reformed and Catholic factions, but presented a homogeneous appearance as a result as well of the secession of the Walloon provinces and Groningen as of the triumph of Calvinism in the remainder, there was a desire to dissolve the Union of Utrecht in the General Union. Thus, simultaneously with the institution of this new Council of State, the Committee of the Closer Union was abolished; but the necessity for dealing separately with the problems of the war in the North was so keenly felt that there was established, under the Council of State, a new Council "East of the Maas" (north of the rivers). In practice nothing came of the subordination of this new Council to the Council of State, and actually it simply took the place of the Committee of the Closer Union, while the activities of the Council of State (and this remained so after the arrival of Anjou and his assumption of the government of the country) were limited to the southern provinces and the southern theatre of war.

The dual organization thus emerged again the moment after it had been suppressed. What does this signify? No more than that the duality of the strategic problem with which the provinces were faced dominated the situation. It was inevitable that the fighting on the southern and eastern fronts should be conducted as two distinct wars. In the first place, they were separately financed. The Union of Utrecht had prescribed uniform taxes—"general means"—for the Union treasury, but these could never be put into operation. The provinces continued to raise their own taxes, and they had to be spurred on severally for their contributions. In proportion as their exhaustion increased, it became more necessary in every single case to specify a definite object which touched each particularly. The central authorities—Anjou and the Council of State —who resided for the most part at Antwerp or even at Ghent, were almost overwhelmed by the cares of the war on their own side. Not only did they lack the power to assert themselves against Holland, the unassailable province which had pursued its own course since 1572, and entrenched itself more firmly in its own exceptional position with every change of government, but, indeed, they were not sorry when Holland took eastern affairs off their hands.

How inevitable such a development was can be understood only if this exhaustion and the consequent impotence—one may say the paralysis—of authority are clearly visualized. Holland and Zealand were the only provinces not directly exposed to the raids of the enemy, but they could no longer cope with the importunate appeals of their neighbours for assistance. The cosmopolitan soldiery, not very numerous, but too numerous to be paid regularly, became useless by reason of mutiny and disorder:

All mutineers, who cried out for money when they were ordered to fight.

Hohenlohe, the commander in the North, a fighter but no organizer, and a lover of women and wine, was not the man to maintain discipline. Following his example, throughout the army

virtue of life was derided and explained as lack of courage. [At the same time] the States everywhere lost their authority, no less over the soldiery whom they did not pay than over the townsman and farmer whom they did not protect.

It was inevitable that in these circumstances centrifugal forces should get free play, but this fact does not teach us anything about the desires or inclinations of the people. It was simply that in the difficult days of its birth the young Netherlands state had as little control over its limbs as a newborn babe. This naturally meant a considerable weakening of its ability to resist Parma, whose own leadership, for that matter, met in the subjected provinces with a resistance scarcely less unwieldy. But this is not to say that the split which in the ensuing years was to rend asunder the Dutch-speaking Netherlands proceeded from any internal urge or from any inherent failing of the people. The line which this split was ultimately to follow was determined by the interplay of force and counter-force, and these conformed, not to the disposition of the people, but to that of the soil. The Union of Utrecht had nothing, the great rivers everything, to do with it.

Anjou was unable to hold Parma in check. His brother Henry III persisted in his neutrality, while the few French troops, partly Huguenots, partly adventurers of all sorts and conditions, which Anjou had been able to lead into Flanders, played havoc with the people. In April 1582 Parma took Oudenaarde, in August treachery made him master of Lier, while in the East Verdugo took Steenwyk and other places.

But however ineffectual Anjou's help, the case was rendered

still worse when the helper suddenly turned against those he should have protected. Anjou's position was false and disagreeable. The oppression of his co-religionists, the ever recurring suspicions of the men of Antwerp and Ghent against himself and his entourage as Frenchmen and Catholics, the rigorous enforcement by the States of that clause in their agreement with him which debarred foreigners—that is, Frenchmen—from holding office in the Netherlands, all these things irritated him beyond measure. The French nobles at his court, whom the Netherlanders had wanted to exclude even from there, filled his ears with complaints and promptings. In January 1583 he made an effort at one blow to break the bonds of his agreement with the States, and to make himself indeed master of the land, just as in July 1577 Don John had tried to free himself from the Eternal Edict by a *coup d'état*.

The French troops made simultaneous attempts on several places. The Duke, who up to the last had shown a friendly countenance to Orange, himself took charge of the principal enterprise, namely, against Antwerp, but this miscarried badly. While the French nobles and soldiers were rushing through the streets with cries of "Vive la messe! Ville gagnée," the citizens organized a stout resistance and in the end drove them with heavy loss out of the town. Anjou had to retire with great difficulty to Vilvoorde, which his followers had succeeded in taking, and thence via Dendermonde to Dunkirk. Meanwhile a great fury possessed the people, not only at Antwerp but all over the Netherlands, especially in the South, against their treacherous protector and all his countrymen. He was suspected, not without reason, of an intention to come to an agreement with Parma, with the towns he occupied as the price of the bargain. Suspicion of the Catholics was stirred to new life. Meanwhile Anjou was no longer considered as sovereign, and the States urged Orange to put himself at their head. But the Prince, however deeply moved with indignation, held fast to the idea that only with the help of France could the revolt be saved and persuaded the States to open negotiations, which actually led to a provisional agreement. He had made play with the prospect that a French force would be

available for the relief of Eindhoven, which was of importance
as a strong place wedged between the power of Spain in the
South and in the East. The French force, however, came too
late and Eindhoven fell. Shortly afterwards Dunkirk was also
lost; Anjou, discouraged and embittered, had recently left it
and returned to France. And now the cry of treachery went
up more fiercely than ever against the French. Orange, who
continued stubbornly to advocate the necessity of continuing
the negotiations with Anjou, did so at the cost of a good deal
of his popularity. Thus writes an Antwerp rhetorician in a
ballad—the customary opening of the final couplet "O Prince"
here obviously levelled against Orange:

> O Prince, mark well God's Law. Beware
> Thou lead'st us not into the snare
> Of this French fellow.

Such was the prevailing temper that Orange left Antwerp for
Middelburg, from where he soon moved on to Delft. The
Hollanders disliked Anjou no less than did the Flemings or
Brabanders, but the Prince's remonstrances and appeals to
reason made more impression on their oligarchic town governments than on the democracies of the great towns in the
South. In Flanders, where excitement reached the highest
pitch—Nieuwpoort had been taken by a movement from
Dunkirk, and thus Yper was almost cut off and Brugge directly
threatened—the ministers admonished the people from the
pulpit:

That they had to expect no help or blessings from the said Duke,
seeing that he was of contrary religion, and that God promises His
help to Kings and Lords who walk in fear of Him.

Thus there arose really fundamental dissensions to aggravate
the confusion and to weaken powers of resistance. In their
distress, and as if to give expression to their mistrust of
Orange's collusion with Anjou, the Flemings chose as Stadtholder a man who had ingratiated himself with them by
energetic professions of zeal for Calvinism and hatred for the
French; this was the Prince of Chimay, Aerschot's only son,
who in 1582 had ranged himself on the side of the States.

Whether he aimed at treachery from the beginning is not clear. What is certain is that he was soon involved in relations with Parma, and paved the way for the surrender of Brugge by the removal of men loyal to the States and the introduction of partisans of Spain. In Gelderland the Count Van den Bergh had got himself appointed Stadtholder in 1581 in succession to his brother-in-law, John of Nassau, and in his case there is no doubt that this had been arranged with Parma. The first-fruits of his treachery was Zutfen, which was tricked into the hands of the enemy in September 1583, but before he could do more mischief he was apprehended and sent to Holland by Leoninus, the Chancellor of the province.

The treachery of Chimay was scarcely less obvious, but while the Bailiff of the Free Land, and Casembroot, a burgomaster of Brugge, were urging Orange to render him harmless, Chimay got ahead of them and threw the leaders of the party of resistance into prison. At that moment, March 1584, Parma had already for a considerable time been besieging Yper, and shortly afterwards, threatened with starvation, that town surrendered. Now Chimay was free to proceed, and on May 22nd the agreement was concluded at Tournai whereby Brugge and the Free Land once more resigned themselves to the King of Spain. Three of the four "members" of Flanders were lost.

Parma took care that their example should make the desired impression on the rest of the province and of the Netherlands. With Alva's departure the system of barbarous severity had been discarded. Parma, it is true, could not tolerate Protestantism, and the exclusive reign of Catholicism was re-established by the terms of each capitulation. But the Inquisition did not return, and the Reformers were given the choice, either to realize on their possessions and depart or else to submit. An exodus of ministers and of the faithful followed each conquest, but the greater part of the citizens conformed to the new change without difficulty. They had after all merely undergone the Calvinistic Reformation, nor was this more the case at Brugge or Zutfen, which were now once again Spanish and Catholic, than at Dordt or Utrecht, which were still

"States" and Reformed. And, indeed, did not this new change bear the appearance of inescapable finality? The revolt seemed like a passing nightmare, and its watchword, the retrieval of the ancient welfare of the Netherlands, sounded a mockery in the midst of the miserable confusion which prevailed. With a sigh of relief the people could submit themselves again to the old authority, which seemed to have unlearned its excesses and to be ready to respect the privileges. Were not rest and peace to be found there, and there alone?

But however grave the doubts which assailed the spirits in the most exposed towns, the party of resistance was everywhere too firmly seated in the saddle to be lightly thrown out. It is true that Ghent, whose supplies Parma now obstructed on all sides and whose population, swelled by thousands of fugitive peasants, began in consequence to suffer privation, was seriously threatened by treachery; and it was none other than the old zealot Hembyze who, after having been carried to power on the tidal wave of anti-French Calvinism and with the aid of insinuations against Anjou's friend Orange, was now intriguing there with Parma. But he was seized just in time by his indignant fellow-citizens, and a few months later ended his life on the scaffold. Ghent prepared itself for defence. But the attack which followed was a formidable one, and did not aim at this town only.

Meanwhile the Reformed who would have none of Anjou met with another grievous disappointment. In Germany, where they had placed great hopes upon the Archbishop of Cologne, who had gone over to Protestantism, everything miscarried, and a staunch Catholic was installed in the archiepiscopal see. Orange saw in the event a vindication of his French policy. But the envoys who went for the third time to urge Anjou to make haste with his assistance no longer found him among the living. He had died on June 10, 1584. It was still an open question what would now be done with the sovereignty, which had thus reverted once again to the States-General, when just a month later, on July 10, the Prince of Orange was assassinated at Delft. Only a little while before, in a long exposition of the distressful situation, the defection of selfish noblemen,

the disproportion between the power of Spain and that of the
States, he had written that as for himself he

would take his stand unperturbed against those dangers. For no
dangers can for me and mine be compared with a base desertion
of such a noble cause—the honour of God, the peace of the provinces,
the freedom of the Fatherland—and the abandonment of the sacred
and honourable side which I have up till now followed.

"Faithful until death"—the *Wilhelmus* had prophesied it. But
at what a moment was William of Orange called away from
the people he had served, and how must the danger of Flanders
and Brabant have oppressed him in his last moments!

The enemy rejoiced. To them the revolt seemed personified
in the Prince, his ambition its mainspring, his guidance indispensable. That was the idea which had inspired the ban, and
so now it was hoped that the revolt would soon collapse. An
utter miscalculation! The rebellion had its own life. Invaluable
had been Orange's services in animating and giving direction
to the national feeling, even though the passions of the time
had, alas, only too frequently paid little heed to his admonitions.
Certainly his position had been in no sense that of a dictator.
His death interrupted plans for investing him with the Countship of Holland, but the conditions on which this was to be
done placed the sovereign authority no less effectually under
the surveillance of the States than had the treaty with Anjou;
reference was indeed expressly made to that treaty and to
the "Joyous Entry" of Brabant. In a crisis occasioned by the
abuse of monarchical authority, Orange's greatness as a leader
of the Netherlands people lay precisely in his unsurpassed
talent for co-operating with the States assemblies which, by
the former misgovernment, had been impelled to go beyond
their appointed places in that people's ancient constitutions.
Persuasion was what he excelled in. Many were the long
memoranda which he wrote to refute objections to his views;
in the council-chamber he was clear and firm, but also resource-
ful and patient. Thus it was that under his auspices the new
oligarchy had been able to form itself into a real ruling class,
in which, owing to the defection of so many nobles, the town

G

element had become predominant. Several who were too firmly
fixed in the government of their provinces not to see everything
primarily from a provincial standpoint had yet, by the circumstances which demanded the weightiest decisions from
both provincial States and town governments, been taught to
grapple with problems of general policy. Moreover, in close
intercourse with Orange, there had arisen from out their midst,
in the States-General and in the Councils, a group of truly
national statesmen of a different character from the official,
noble, mostly non-Dutch class which the monarchy had reared.

When their leader fell, these were the men who at once did
what they could to prevent the courage of the provinces from
failing. On the same day letters were sent out in every direction
by the States-General giving, together with the dreadful tidings,
the assurance that determination remained unshaken, and that
the enemy would reap no advantage from the crime; the
Fleming Van Meetkerke presided over the assembly, where
among others Aerssens represented Brabant; Mechlin, too,
was present. Shortly afterwards, in consultation with the provinces, a new attempt was made to put the government in the
united provinces on "a uniform basis," as it was expressed,
and a solemn resolution was taken to remain united "according
to the Union of Utrecht," notwithstanding the death of His
Excellency the Prince. This resolution, in which Brabant and
Mechlin participated, was, so far as Brussels and Mechlin were
concerned, like an accession *in articulo mortis* to the Union
of Utrecht, and the dual character of the Government was still
further reduced by the abolition of the Council East of the
Maas and the institution of yet another Council of State,
which, under the presidency of the young Maurice of Nassau,
Orange's son, was to exercise the government until a new ruler
should be found abroad.

For now Parma was straining his energies to the utmost
to possess himself at one blow of the South: the siege of
Antwerp began in August 1584, at the same time Brussels and
Mechlin were invested and communication between them
hindered by the capture of Dendermonde: Ghent was completely cut off, and while the whole of Flanders and Brabant

was thus beset by the most imminent danger, the States-
General had once more to attempt to interest a foreign Power
in their cause. They addressed themselves first to the brother
of Anjou, Henry III, King of France. Especially the threatened
towns of the South pressed for the removal of all hindrances
to these negotiations, which, after the fashion of the time,
dragged on through many months. Necessity alone drove them
to it, for how vigorously had they themselves censured Orange
for his partiality to the French! Out of Holland there now
came another voice, harbinger of many miseries for the
Netherlands people.

Even if they of Brabant and Flanders, through impatience of their
sufferings (whereby all good counsels are hindered) would desperately
adventure a lost cause, are we bound to plunge ourselves and so many
thousands of brave men into sure ruin and decay along with them?
. . . Was it for this that the noble defences of Antwerp were raised
up, and is not the finest town in Europe worthy of some suffering?
Let them come and take courage from Holland, where the little town
of Alkmaar engaged the whole might of Spain, and where nearly half
the brave citizens of Leyden perished of hunger for the sake of their
freedom. Did we rely on any princely power then? or have we suffered all this in order to be delivered up in the end to the French?
Then we may well bewail to God that the noble Prince of Orange
and so many brave men have died for us and for a cause which we
are not resolved to maintain to the end. . . . And however great the
evil which afflicts them of Flanders and Brabant (especially do we
pity the great city of Brussels), nevertheless the enemy does not
rejoice so greatly over what he has conquered there, that he would
not willingly yield it all provided he could have for it the one island
of Walcheren.

The remonstrance of the town of Gouda, drawn up by her
pensionary François Vrancken, from which the above passage
is taken, is without doubt a spirited document, and there is
only too much truth in its argument that no reliance was to
be placed on French help, and that the menace to religion
and freedom from France was scarcely less dangerous than
that from Spain. And this quite apart from the fact that a
separate national existence, based on a specifically Netherlandish culture, would have been under no ruler so difficult
to achieve as under the King of France. Nevertheless, how

strongly does one feel here that their exceptional strategic position not only gave the Hollanders confidence, but, aided by the legend which had already grown up around the events of 1572 to 1576, created a self-righteous feeling that could be dangerous to the cause of unity! It is true that this attitude produced its most harmful consequences only after the split had become a fact, since for the time being the arguments of Holland particularism found no acceptance, and the States of Holland and Zealand both did what lay in their power to prevent the cleavage. To begin with they let themselves be prevailed upon to relinquish, in conformity with the demand of the French King, the special position they had maintained as against Anjou—no mean sacrifice—and thus the offer of the sovereignty could be made in due form by an embassy of all the provinces. By that time the starving population of Ghent had already compelled the town government to make peace with Parma on the usual favourable terms—a serious loss, also on account of the war-material which fell into the captor's hands. And when finally the embassy executed its commission, Henry III, who was now himself hard pressed by the ultra-Catholics and their League in his own kingdom, declined the offer which at first he had striven so hard to obtain.

The entire winter was thus wasted, and now the whole thing had to be done all over again with England, for Elizabeth, disturbed at the prospect of seeing the full might of Spain restored on the other side of the water, had for some time given to understand that she might now be found ready to do something. Not before June 18 could an embassy sail for England, whereupon it quickly appeared that the Queen still shrank from a complete break with Spain, such as would be the inevitable consequence of an acceptance of the sovereignty. Then negotiations for simple assistance began, and it was August 20th before the treaty was signed whereby the States were promised 4,000 infantry and 400 cavalry, against the cession to England of The Brill and Flushing as cautionary towns for the repayment of the expenses incurred. The commander of this force (the Earl of Leicester obtained the appointment), arrayed with the ambiguous title of "Governor-

General," was to have access, along with two other Englishmen, to the Council of State. A most onerous agreement! The
English commander who entered Flushing in 1572 had been
instructed from home to make himself master of that town,
and to prevent the French auxiliaries from doing so, rather
than to fight the Spaniards. Now the English were laying hands
on the mouths of the Maas and the Scheldt in exchange for
very niggardly promises, and without Elizabeth's being willing
to make herself answerable for the country's future. What
would she do in course of time with the strategic position
afforded her by these cautionary towns?

Sadly, indeed, had the States' affairs deteriorated during
these procrastinations. In March Brussels, suffering no less
from hunger than had Ghent, and after making one last
pitiful appeal to Holland for relief, surrendered to Parma.
Mechlin followed in July. It was easy for François Vrancken
to talk: the fact was that the sieges in Holland and Zealand
which he recalled with such pride had been rendered difficult
for the Spaniards by nothing so much as by the inundations,
and by the lakes, canals, and rivers which gave free play to
the naval power of the Beggars. To strike a blow which would
have forced Parma to let go his prey in Brabant, Hohenlohe
would have had to move outside the river-area, and that he
was incapable of doing. All the more serious, therefore, was
the loss of a town inside that river-area. Nymwegen was not
pressed overmuch by the enemy, but in April 1585 the Catholic
citizens broke with the Count of Nieuwenaer, the new Stadtholder of Gelderland, a Calvinist just as intolerant as John
of Nassau, and, after making themselves masters of the town
government, thrust the States' garrison out of the gates. The
same thing happened at Doesburg, while Arnhem had to be
secured for the States by surprise. The worst blow was nevertheless inflicted by the arms of Parma: just before the envoys
in England signed the treaty with Elizabeth, Antwerp had
surrendered.

The siege of Antwerp was a long drawn out tragedy. At
the end of 1583 Orange had sent Marnix there as "External
Burgomaster" in preparation for the expected siege; subse-

quently he had urged the necessity for cutting the Kouwenstein cross-dyke and the Blauwgaren Scheldt-dyke. Antwerp
lay on the edge of the Netherlands water-area, and had to be
victualled and relieved from Zealand. To that end, however,
it would be useful to submerge the broad border-land north
of the Scheldt which these dykes protected; otherwise everything would have to come along the river itself. Private interests,
which found unrestrained expression in the democratic town
government (for Marnix wielded only a very limited authority),
had prevented the cutting of these dykes. So Parma, who
sought to invest the town (since an assault was out of the
question), promptly seized them, and when, to the astonishment of the Antwerpers, he subsequently succeeded in driving
a strong bridge over the river just below Calloo, the unwisdom
of neglecting Orange's advice was made clear. All attempts to
reach the town must now involve the forcing either of this
bridge or of the Kouwenstein dyke, and on them they all spent
themselves in vain.

The Hollanders and Zealanders did their best. Everyone
recognized what a disaster the fall of Antwerp would be. But
reverse followed reverse. Early in 1585 the power of the
Zealand fleet was crippled by a vehement dispute between
Treslong, now admiral of the province, and the regents deputed
to deal with naval matters. After that an enterprise against the
bridge, broken through by Gianibelli's famous fire-ship drift-
ing down from Antwerp, failed owing to a misunderstanding
of signals. Finally, in May a new attempt was carefully prepared. The States of Holland sent some of their own number
to supervise everything—among them was the pensionary of
Rotterdam, Oldenbarnevelt, a rising man. The Kouwenstein
dyke was taken by hard fighting; Hohenlohe from Zealand met
Marnix from Antwerp, and together the two were rowed over
the flooded land to the town to announce the glad tidings.
Their rejoicings were cut short by the news that the Spaniards
had recaptured the dyke and made it fast again. Never was
victory more recklessly thrown away. Elizabeth, too, bore a
heavy responsibility. Had she, in anticipation of a treaty, sent
over a couple of thousand men, Parma, who had barely suffi-

cient troops, would certainly not have been able to make good the losses he suffered.

Now Marnix threw up the game as lost. The poorer classes in the town had long been suffering privation, and the fresh disappointment at the failure of relief led to rioting. The Broad Council resolved to negotiate, but for weeks they maintained a demand for the freedom of the Reformed religion. Parma received the envoys, and particularly Marnix, with every mark of honour, but on that point he was inflexible. In spite of this the impressionable and vacillating Marnix let himself be so captivated by the Duke that to the fury of the Reformed, who already disliked his French leanings, he became at Antwerp the great advocate of surrender.

There was not one assistant in the said assembly of Great Council but gave attentive ear unto the relation Monsieur de St. Aldegonde made, and not a little marvelled to see and hear him in that sort vehemently exalt the virtues of that Prince, naming him to be full of benignity, clemency, and void of all dissimulation, adding for his opinion, that he did believe all that the said Prince had told him. . . . As these persuasions to a reconciliation with the King of Spain, through the good opinion he hath conceived of the Prince of Parma, did not greatly please the ear of those in the Great Council, much less it did unto these Colonels and Captains [of the citizens], the most part thinking it was a dream unto them to see and hear Monsieur de St. Aldegonde speak in that sort. . . .

For a year Marnix had succeeded in checking all sedition and in making all the well-disposed co-operate. What was it that now caused him to despair? Like Orange he had placed his hopes on France, and thus the success of the Catholic League in that country was a grievous blow to him. From England he expected nothing. Moreover, throughout that disastrous year, as town after town fell, the Flemings and Brabanders had been complaining bitterly that Holland and Zealand were leaving them to their fate. Van den Tympel, the governor of Brussels, for instance, after the capitulation of that town, had spoken vehemently in this strain to the deputies of Brabant assembled at Antwerp. Doubtless Marnix was affected by this bitter feeling. The tragedy was that the Hollanders and Zealanders were doing what they could. Certainly, had the

Prince of Orange still been there to compose disputes as to
competence and quarrels between individuals, they might have
done more. The Council of State, under the young Maurice,
was powerless; everything devolved upon the provincial States.
Nevertheless, the complaints of the Southerners were only
an expression of that universal human disposition to cast on
to friends and supporters the blame for an overwhelming
flood of misfortunes. Here, too, Orange's death proved a
disaster: he might have preserved Marnix from this weakness.
A man of determination in' the position of the "External
Burgomaster" could have postponed the surrender for weeks.
And the Hollanders were only waiting for a favourable wind
in order to make a new attempt at relief, nor would the tardy
English troops have tarried for ever. But the Broad Council,
thrown into confusion by the attitude of its appointed head,
let itself be intimidated by the cry of "Peace" from the starving
multitude gathered in the square before the town-hall, and on
August 17, 1585, was signed the treaty by which the town
resumed obedience to Philip. Catholicism was re-established,
but the Reformed were granted four years before they had
to depart. All privileges were restored, no Spanish garrison
was to be placed in the town, and the citadel, which was
rebuilt, would be pulled down as soon as Holland and Zealand
were likewise subdued. Marnix betook himself back to Zealand;
it is, indeed, not to be wondered at that he was overwhelmed
with reproaches and accusations from Holland and Zealand.

Antwerp, still, in spite of the many shocks it had suffered
since 1566, by far the largest and wealthiest town of the Netherlands, from 1578 to 1583 the capital of the rebellion—Antwerp
had fallen! It was everywhere expected that the subjugation
of Holland and Zealand would soon follow. But, behind the
rivers, these provinces lay sheltered from a direct attack. They
were themselves masters of these waters, and Parma was at
once made to feel the importance of naval power. The Beggars
of Zealand had not been able to force his bridge, but now that
Antwerp was once again in Spanish hands they could cut her
off inexorably from the sea. The town which Parma, thanks
to his indomitable spirit, his military genius, and his knowledge

of human nature, had succeeded in conquering, now withered, as it were, beneath his hand. Thousands left Antwerp, not only for the sake of their religion, but because the stoppage of all trade struck at their means of livelihood (just as thousands had left Brugge, Ghent, Brussels, Mechlin, and all the other towns which had fallen into Spanish hands), and the majority of them came to Holland and Zealand, where they strengthened the Reformed element and at the same time brought a wealth of capital, knowledge, and enterprise. The peace and order which Parma gave to Flanders and Brabant very much resembled the stiffening of death. On the other hand all the best vital forces of the Netherlands people drew together in the small area north of the rivers.

Holland, Zealand, and Utrecht, Gelderland within the 'Waal and Ysel, the Ysel-towns of Overysel and Friesland, a couple of coastal towns in Flanders and Brabant, a single isolated place, Venlo, that was all the territory which now remained to the States. In the beginning of October 1585 the English troops arrived, and the Earl of Leicester followed in December. During the two years of his governor-generalship there was never any question of his being able to recover the lost territory. He could not even keep intact the little that remained. In 1586 Grave and Venlo were lost. During his absence in England in 1587 two of his lieutenants (Yorke and Stanley) betrayed Deventer and the entrenchments by means of which the States had controlled Zutfen since it had become Spanish. When he returned he failed to relieve Sluis, which gave the Spaniards a foothold on the Scheldt estuary; after his second departure mutinous English troops sold Geertruidenberg to the enemy. Nevertheless there can be no doubt that the slackening of Parma's advance during Leicester's unquiet governorship—we shall presently consider its importance for the establishment of a North Netherlands state—was partly due to the strengthening afforded by the English auxiliaries. The first explanation must, however, be sought in the fact that Parma's conquest had reached the rebellion's last natural line of defence. On all sides he was confronted by water, as far as Friesland, where lakes and morasses took the place of rivers. It is true that the States held several places on the other side of this natural line, Ostend and Bergen-op-Zoom, for example, but, thanks to the water, these too were within immediate reach of their forces, whose wide arc now more than ever reposed on the unassailable and sea-faring province of Holland.

But the position was not one of equilibrium. The North-East had not been conquered by force of arms; situated on the farther side of Maas and Rhine, it was too far from Parma's base for that; it had fallen to him by Rennenberg's defection and the disposition of its inhabitants. Nymwegen had since afforded him a better line of communication with that distant region, yet his hold on it remained uncertain. Nevertheless contemporaries can hardly have expected its reconquest from the North-West that was soon to take place. To them it must have seemed much more probable that the country east of the Ysel would serve Parma as a base for an attack on the last refuge of the revolt. Sluis and Geertruidenberg also seemed the prelude to a thrust at the heart, for the two places respectively threatened Zealand and Holland. But there the friendly element was of greater help to the rebels than anywhere else, and a break-through from the East seemed the more imminent danger. With Zutfen and Deventer the enemy impinged on the line of the Ysel, and the Spanish cavalry raided over all the Veluwe as far as Utrecht. Friesland, too, was threatened from Steenwyk and Groningen.

The position which Parma had won by 1589 was a position for further attack. How came it that he was unable to use it, and that on the contrary the Northerners, leaning on their Holland base, could wrench it from him, soon even pressing across the inmost and uncertain line of defence, and not content with the outermost strategic boundary, that of the great rivers, managed to secure it by the capture of the fortresses to the south of it? The amazing economic development, which along with political consolidation took place in that north-western sea-territory, was an important factor. But without the opportunity which Philip's unwisdom offered, when he first exhausted his resources in a mad enterprise against England, and then instructed Parma to divide his forces in order to intervene in the French civil war, the success of the northern provinces would be inexplicable.

b. THE ESTABLISHMENT OF A NORTH NETHERLANDS STATE

When the Earl of Leicester came to the Netherlands he had not only a military task to perform. The treaty gave him a vague political position, and Elizabeth had urged him to effect certain modifications in the constitution of the nascent state, as, for instance, a strengthening of the position of the States-General as against the provinces. Indeed, an excellent instruction, but one difficult to carry out if, as she also wished, he was at the same time to abstain from assuming greater political power. Hardly had he landed in Holland, however, when Leicester saw this power thrust upon him by the hard-pressed States. His governor-generalship was made a reality; early in February 1586 he was invested with a truly sovereign position, with less restrictions than those which had irked Don John or Anjou. He, too, was a foreigner (knowing neither Dutch nor French), but he was at least a Protestant. Moreover, he stood high in Elizabeth's favour, and the States, notwithstanding all their experience of this woman, as self-opinionated as she was incalculable, made the mistake of thinking that by exalting Leicester they could involve his Queen in the war more deeply than she intended. Above all, confusion had become worse confounded, and everyone was ready to believe that only a strong personal government could save the country.

But that is not to say that everyone was prepared to submit to whatever the new Governor might dictate. There existed at that moment markedly divergent and well-defined ideas as to the policy to be pursued, different parties, each of which expected support from Leicester. The revolution had done much more than remove the royal government or even over-set the Catholic Church. It had thrown the whole of Society, as well as the State, into confusion. All the bonds which the monarchy had forged between province and province were broken. The leading classes in the towns, in each province, in the whole of the Netherlands, had been partially swept aside, and the remainder had to strengthen itself with "new men." That, following these shocks, all kinds of new problems arose and were approached in an impassioned and contentious spirit is less wonder than that the main lines of the social and political structure resisted the convulsion, and that what was new for the most part masqueraded in old dress. Although the States arrogated to themselves an authority which by no means appertained to them historically, they were—especially those of Holland—in the main a conservative force, and they proved well able to hold out against the attack that was directed against them.

This attack did not come from the mass of the Catholics who had been robbed of their rights. In fact the States of Holland stood in the breach to defend what position still remained to them; but they themselves remained passive in the midst of all this agitation. The attack came from the zealous Reformers, who were especially strong among the urban lower middle class, led by the ministers. These people looked upon themselves as the true exponents of the rebellion, even of the national idea; the State was their State, dissenters must be kept down as much as possible. Their own religious zeal seemed to them the only effective patriotism; in no other way could the enemy be held at bay. We have seen how deeply this idea had influenced the course of events, but it is now time to notice that it was nevertheless continually and strenuously resisted from within the circle of those who accepted and led the revolt, and that it was only very imperfectly realized.

Orange, as we know, had never submitted to it. But the town oligarchies of Holland, which remained oligarchies, in spite of the sudden change of personnel brought about by the revolution, looked on it with no more favour. They had, it is true, accepted the Reformation and suppressed Catholic worship, but they viewed things very differently from the true zealots of the new creed. Some had themselves been swept into office on the flood-tide of the Reformation; the majority had done no more than adapt themselves to the new circumstances, or had hardly even done that. On the whole they felt themselves much more, as of old, the representatives and protectors of the whole body of the citizens, the guardians of the privileges and welfare of town and country, than the champions of a particular new religious faith. In other words, they regarded matters from a secular standpoint, and, while the new Church had in their scheme of things its indispensable place, they felt it incumbent on them carefully to circumscribe this place. From one point of view—especially in Germany and England can this be clearly seen—the great European movement of the Reformation was a revolt of the lay community under the leadership of their rulers—a revolt, that is to say, of the State against priestly influence. When they required theories to justify secular supervision over the new Church, of which for a long time to come not even all of them were members, the Netherlands "regents" did not therefore have far to seek.

But indeed, in Holland, though the political tendency of the revolt had in 1572 been temporarily overlaid by the religious tendency, it had preserved its identity and maintained its ideology. William of Orange had greatly assisted it in doing so, but the town governments and the States also gladly appealed to liberty as well as to religion as the issue in the great struggle. *Haec libertatis ergo* inscribed on the emergency money which was issued at Leyden during the siege epitomized a political programme. Two kinds of patriots were distinguished:

those who are attached to our cause through love either of freedom or religion.

And these "Libertinists," as the former were called, were not merely "Politiques" (the name of the party in France which wanted to keep peace between the two warring religious parties); they could meet the zealous Reformers on their own ground and clothe their ideas in religious garb. An anti-confessional theology came naturally to the land of Erasmus, and in the North, amidst stress and conflict, it was now formulated and developed.

The outstanding figure among the "Libertinists" of these

years was Coornhert, who had returned to Holland in 1576, and whose utterances on religion attracted attention if only on account of his political relations. Coornhert refused to join any religious community. He frankly declared, both in his numerous pamphlets and in public disputations held under the eye of authority, at Leyden in 1578 and at The Hague some years later, that knowledge of the truth was withheld from man. He inveighed vehemently against the ministers who demanded precise assent to the dogmas laid down in the professions of faith. Such words certainly echoed the sentiments of many, and the regents listened the more readily to Coornhert since, despite his aversion from all forms of coercion, his fear of the tyranny of the ministers made him willing to call on the secular power for assistance. At the request of the government of Leyden he wrote a couple of vigorous remonstrances to prove the justice of their case in a dispute with one of their ministers over the appointment of the consistory, and in them he hurled bold defiance at the Synod, which had presented to town and States a vindication of the Church's right to govern itself.

The Synod attempts to make itself the head of the Government.

That was the conclusion he drew from its demand that magistrates should be of the Reformed religion; for the Synod claimed the right to determine what was meant by "Reformed." At the same time the supervision of the ministers over education would result in their becoming "the hereditary masters" of all the people. The secretary of Leyden, Jan van Hout, was himself a good "Libertinist," and under his influence and that of Coolhaes, a minister whom the Synod excommunicated on account of his unorthodoxy, the Leyden government pursued the quarrel with astonishing acerbity and high-handedness.

It was apparent that no agreement existed on the elementary principles which should govern the relations of Church and State. The Church wanted to keep her doctrine undefiled; she wanted to be able to censure, and, if necessary, expel those who were lax, careless, or unorthodox, even when they sat in the seats of the mighty. She regarded it as the godly duty of the secular authorities, under her direction, to give effect to the precepts of Calvinism in the life of society and to suppress dissenting groups. Naturally the State was no longer wholly free with regard to a Church with which it had struck an alliance against Spanish domination. At Leyden, for example, Van Hout was unable to carry through a project to put the care of the poor wholly in secular hands; town governments and consistories jointly administered this potent means of gaining over the mass of the poor to the new religion. But, as far as they were able, the oligarchy wanted to protect their own freedom and that of the people, whether or no they belonged to the Church, and so while they never applied very stringently the repressive measures against dissenters, they hindered the Church as much as possible in the use of corrective measures against its own members. This, together with the whole supervisory power exercised for the purpose by the State, seemed to the Church party an intolerable infraction of its independence. Is it to be wondered at, however, that the secular power, whose help had been as indispensable to the formation of the Church as it was to her continued welfare, and which had, moreover, laid hands on the ecclesiastical property from which the new organization was maintained, did not suffer itself to be used as an inanimate tool?

This conflict, whose last echoes, despite the profound change of circumstances, have not yet died away in North Netherland, has had an inestimable importance for the spiritual life of that country. Each of the parties concerned stood for something of value, and the conflict between them, which sometimes assumed heroic forms, strained mind and soul of the contending sides to the utmost of their power. There lay a mighty strength in the stiff-necked conviction of the Precisians, but, had they been able to enforce their programme, North Netherlandish civilization, which was soon to exhibit so fresh and vigorous a diversity, would have been narrowed down to something very rigid and monotonous. As against that, the protection afforded by the "Libertinist" oligarchy to the multiplicity of forces still springing out of the old cultural traditions was an invaluable asset. But in its turn the power of that oligarchy itself threatened at times to become a stifling bond, and then the stubbornness of the strong Calvinist, who had no conception of conscience in general, but to whom his own conscience was an inviolable sanctuary, was an unqualified gain for the independence of spiritual life.

The States of Holland, indeed, were not inspired by a pure zeal for the freedom and rights of dissenters; they feared the Church as a potential organization of the people, whose last remaining political organizations they had themselves reduced to impotence; since 1581 they had forbidden town governments (it was certainly no longer necessary for most of them) to consult on provincial matters with guilds or corps of civic guards. One of their objects in keeping the Church under their supervision and control was to bolster up their own new political authority; the struggle between Church and State coincided with a struggle between democracy and oligarchy. Other factors added their weight to these. The States of Holland were not only at variance with their own "commonalty"; in most of the smaller provinces too there prevailed a feeling of intense irritation against them.

Holland was rich, strong, inviolate. It pursued trade in the midst of the war. Its harbours gave access to all seas. Indeed, so dependent were the inland provinces on the imports which came through these harbours that Parma had to connive at them in the areas which he recovered; even in Spain itself Philip could not do without the ships of his rebellious subjects. Now that Antwerp was shut off from the sea, the towns of Holland and Zealand—and in the long run particularly Amsterdam—assumed the rôle which the great city of the Scheldt had hitherto played in the economic life of Europe. After the loss of Brabant and Flanders the expenses of the war fell largely on Holland and Zealand. With Groningen, Overysel, and Gelderland wholly or in part occupied by the enemy, and Friesland exposed to predatory incursions, Holland alone contributed nearly two-thirds towards them. No wonder that at times it acted somewhat independently. In 1585, for instance, it had invested the young Maurice with the Stadtholderate, the appointment to which hitherto the States-General, as having stepped into the King's place, had always

kept in their own hands. The States of Holland now made
this office, which carried with it traditions of supreme power,
subordinate to themselves. In the circumstances it was a quite
natural development. In other matters, too, Holland felt that
it had no need to let its needy allies in the States-General
dictate to it. But the provinces which, without the assistance
of Holland, would not have been able to continue the struggle
for another month, complained bitterly that Holland was not
doing enough.

The Flemish and Brabant refugees swelled this chorus. They
belonged to the most zealous section of the Reformed; moreover, they were full of bitterness, and apt to detect cowardice
and treachery everywhere—the true exile mentality:

before they had quite settled down,

as a shrewd Zealander, who had had much to do with them
at Middelburg, remarked, as it were in extenuation. In the
Generality Colleges (from which, as their provinces fell, the
Brabanders and most of the Flemings had nevertheless been
compelled to resign, though Van Meetkerke still sat on the
Council of State) every reverse was attributed, with all too
much readiness, not merely to the lack of a powerful central
authority, but definitely to the indolence and selfishness of
Holland.

The orthodox, the democrats, the inland provinces, the
exiles, the politicians and officials of the Generality—all were
agreed that salvation would only come with a ruler who could
ride the States of Holland on the curb, and such a man they
thought had been vouchsafed to them in Leicester. His religious
inclinations as well as his dislike of a burgher-administration
indeed disposed him towards this ambitious plan. Yet the
haters of Holland mistook their man, while he for his part
was similarly at fault in his estimation of the forces which
contended for the mastery in the foreign land he came to
govern.

Received at first without suspicion by the States of Holland,
Leicester quickly plunged into the party-struggle, and fell into
the hands of a faction who wished to overthrow the provincial

oligarchies and set up in his person a National Reformed dictatorship. In the Council of State the Governor placed faith only in the Fleming Van Meetkerke and the English members, besides the Secretary De Borchgrave, who was also Flemish. Further, he relied on the ministers of religion and the democratic party.

The latter succeeded in making themselves masters of Utrecht, which became Leicester's centre of action. The burgher captains of this town, now no longer concerned for "the Catholic Apostolic Roman religion,"[1] but zealously Reformed, and spurred on by a crowd of Brabant refugees, of whom Prouninck, of 's Hertogenbosch, was the leader, stood strongly in opposition to the magistrate and the provincial States, who were no less "Libertinist" than in Holland. For years the "regents" had maintained a minister, one Duifhuis, who remained outside the establishment of the Reformed Church. But in 1584 the democrats had managed to raise by force the Stadtholder of Gelderland, the Count of Nieuwenaer, to the Stadtholderate of Utrecht, and with his assistance, now reinforced by that of Leicester and his English troops, they held in check the aristocratic and Libertinist party, with which the Prince of Orange used to work, and subjected Utrecht to an intensive Calvinizing process. How bitter were the feelings of these men against the Hollanders was made clear, before the coming of Leicester, by a remonstrance which they had presented to the States-General against what they described as the "shameless" violation by Amsterdam of an edict prohibiting trade with the enemy, which could only proceed (so they asserted) from the subordination of the common interest to that of individuals, from self-righteous contempt for the authority of the States-General, perhaps even from secret leanings towards Spain.

This question was the first in which Leicester openly showed his hand. In April 1586 a stern edict against this trade was promulgated, and confiscations and penalties followed. The Holland merchants protested, and the Holland oligarchy put its back to the wall in defence of this protest. Did it do so

[1] See p. 155.

merely because it was so intimately linked with the mercantile class, because its own particular interests were at stake? Were its motives purely selfish? The Utrechters, and the Flemings and Brabanders who had thrown in their lot with them, seeing how bad was the condition into which the provinces subdued by Parma had fallen—in Flanders and Brabant in 1586 the farmers could not be got to sow the land—thought that it needed only a few more turns of the screw of starvation to compel the Spaniards to negotiate. The Hollanders maintained that the only people to benefit would be their foreign competitors, that Flanders and Brabant could easily be victualled from elsewhere, but that in that case *their* trading towns would lose the revenues without which the war could not be carried on. Out of the licence-money raised from this trade, moreover, were defrayed the expenses of the naval force which commanded the rivers and coastal waters. Although the war-contractors were undoubtedly far from scrupulous in their methods, and private interests sometimes exerted far too great an influence in the States, the Holland case was not lacking in strength. Yet the zealots who had Leicester's ear only replied with wild accusations of treachery, popery, even atheism. Leicester arbitrarily instituted a General Audit Office, whose chief function would be to inflict fines on smugglers; a Brabant adventurer with a very suspicious past, one Reingout, had held out to him the prospect of treasure from the activities of such a body, and this man was the leading spirit in it. A strengthening of the Central Government was precisely what the Union needed, but by associating this College with a policy which appeared ruinous to the welfare of the most powerful province, Leicester dealt a blow at the idea of unity, and drove Holland into defending itself with the help of its provincial rights and its actual superiority of power.

Thus there originated an antagonism so sharp that it threatened to lead to a split, if one party did not get the better of the other. But that was exactly what Leicester and his supporters wanted to put to the test. In June they gained complete mastery of the government of Utrecht: Prouninck became burgomaster, another Brabander sheriff, while Floris Thin and

sixty other members of the States party were exiled; Paul
Buys, the foremost representative of Holland's point of view
in the Council of State, was imprisoned—although he had
worked harder than most men for the treaty with England,
he was now generally referred to by some such word as traitor,
papist, and atheist in Leicester's correspondence. The moment
had come when the people in Holland were to be called upon
to rise against the oligarchy, and when the English troops were
to take a hand in the business.

Had Leicester's supporters been able to look into his confidential correspondence with the Queen, they would have seen
what a dangerous game it was for Netherlands independence.
The favourite, who when he accepted the title of Governor-
General had presumed too much on his favour, now made
it up by slavish submission to the will of his mistress. He
advocated the possession of a couple of towns in North
Holland,

which [together with The Brill] will be such a strength to you that
you may rule these men, make war or peace as you list . . . peace
with the King of Spain so as to restore his authority here again.

Leicester does not indeed commend such a peace, but leaves
everything to the wise disposition of Elizabeth.

Few or none but yourself may be privy to your full mind, especially
if you shall not mean to go through with these people.

The position of power into which he was to be placed by the
most zealous Calvinists must only serve to make the unreliable
Elizabeth the judge of their cause! But when the moment
came to act, he shrank back. He was not, after all, the true
Gideon to redeem Israel. Did he already perceive that the
States of Holland were more firmly seated in the saddle than
he had thought? In any case it was his own mistakes of judgment which had enabled them to take their stand not only
as the champions of the oligarchic system but as the guardians
of the commercial prosperity of the whole nation. A strong
hand had grasped the control of their affairs; Oldenbarnevelt,
the first great statesman to spring from the North Netherlands

people, had become Advocate of the province of Holland. What further strengthened the position of the States not a little was the fact that Maurice and Hohenlohe, together with William Louis of Nassau, now Stadtholder of Friesland, took their part; that gave them the control over the greater part of the army. Leicester in any case did not dare to push matters farther; and when in November 1586 he sailed for England, delegating his authority to the Council of State, he left behind him an unsolved crisis and complete confusion.

He had not been gone long when the English governors of Deventer and of the trenches at Zutfen betrayed their posts to the Spaniards; the most alarming reports came in about the attitude of the badly paid English garrisons in several other places. The States of Holland now felt themselves borne along on the strong tide of anxious and indignant public opinion. Oldenbarnevelt acted. Setting aside the authority of the absent Governor and of his distressed Council of State, Holland entrusted its Stadtholder, Maurice, with special powers and demanded a new oath of the soldiery. In vain did the English member of the Council, Wilkes, protest, denying to the States of Holland the right to act as they were doing:

The sovereignty, or supreme authority, in default of legitimate prince, does not belong to you, gentlemen, but to the commonalty.

It was easy to match theory with theory, and Vrancken's ready pen now formulated for the first time the thesis of the absolute and independent sovereign right of the States of Holland. His historical arguments only reveal the complete ignorance of the Middle Ages characteristic of his time, but however wrong he was about the past, the States of Holland, led by Oldenbarnevelt, were undeniably the only purposeful force in the Union at the present, the only one able to save the country from complete anarchy in the face of the enemy. The States-General were persuaded by the States of Holland to give, out of the fullness of their sovereign power, a new composition to the Council of State, by which Van Meetkerke and De Borchgrave were barred. This was a serious encroachment upon Leicester's supreme authority, and yet the need of foreign assistance was still felt so keenly that negotiations were opened at once to obtain his return. The popular party of Utrecht, too, which had not yet given up the game for lost, implored him to come and restore his authority.

He came in the summer of 1587 with some fresh troops; Sluis, as mentioned before, he could not save. And now he was forced into the execution of the *coup d'état* he had shirked the year before. Utrecht was still devoted to him, and so were the ministers, who never hesitated to impute to the States all blame for the loss of the important fortress on the mouth of the Scheldt. Yet Leicester was approaching his great enterprise in most unfavourable circumstances. His Queen, for ever hesitating, was busy negotiating with Parma, and Leicester, after having stoutly denied the fact when taxed with it by the States, had now not only to admit it, but was also compelled to invite them to take part in those negotiations on an entirely unsatisfactory basis. This exhibition cost the hero of the exiles and of the ministers most of his prestige. The commonalty, whose rights his henchman Wilkes had advocated so eloquently and whom he wanted to lead against the States, were bewildered when he spoke of compromise with Spain. The attempt against the States had nevertheless to be made, and in September Leicester came from Utrecht to Holland, where he tried to possess himself of a number of towns. Sonoy, at Medemblik, was his faithful supporter, and refused to obey the orders given by Maurice in his capacity of Stadtholder, but nowhere did the people stir. At Leyden some South Netherlanders, Van Meetkerke and the professor of theology Saravia, with part of the garrison, undertook in consultation with Leicester an attempt, which was, however, discovered in time. Van Meetkerke and Saravia escaped, but a few others from amongst the principal plotters were punished with death by the Libertinist town government acting in concert with the States of Holland and with Maurice. Leicester, humiliated and embittered, soon left the country for ever.

Confusion was even worse confounded now than after his first departure. With Utrecht and Medemblik and the places garrisoned by English troops recalcitrant to the States' authority, the situation hardly differed from civil war. Only when Leicester's letter of resignation arrived early in 1588 were the States able, with the help of Maurice, William Louis, and Hohenlohe, to break that opposition. Sonoy submitted. For Van Meetkerke and De Borchgrave there was no political future left. At Utrecht the popular party was brought down, Prouninck had to leave the town, and the aristocratic States regime was restored there too. The ministers of religion were defeated along with the Flemings and Brabanders and the popular party. In 1586 a Synod had drafted an ecclesiastical constitution after their own hearts, but although Leicester had confirmed it, on the strength of his authority, it was now shelved. When a number of ministers presumed to offer to the States an admonition calling for unity, Oldenbarnevelt, with insulting hauteur, begged them not to meddle with affairs of state. In Utrecht the restored States rudely interfered in the administration of the Church, which had threatened them in their authority, and held it under vigorous control. Leicester had hopelessly compromised all the causes which he had advocated.

Thus there emerged out of all this strife the oligarchic, erastian, decentralized Republic of the Seven United Provinces. The treaty with England was preserved, English troops still remained in the country, and their commander with two more Englishmen had still access to the Council of State. But the idea of delegating supreme authority to some foreign ruler went under with the popular party. The States were now sovereign in reality. They had learnt the lesson that if the old liberties of Netherlands society were to be saved, the country would have to stand upon its own feet. Following the States of Holland, themselves led by Oldenbarnevelt, the States-General set out on their independent course.

For by the course of events we have described yet another matter had been decided, namely, that Holland was to occupy a preponderant position in the Union, and that therein was to reside the strongest unifying force. Oldenbarnevelt, who owed to his courageous lead against Leicester an uncommon prestige in his province, inspired the States of Holland and through them the States-General. But in the inland provinces the Stadtholder's authority still counted for much beside that of the oligarchy represented in their various States, and here the death of Nieuwenaer in 1589 gave Oldenbarnevelt the opportunity for a great stroke of policy. He persuaded the States of Utrecht, Gelderland, and Overysel, to offer Maurice the Stadtholderate over their provinces. Thus, he pointed out to them, military affairs would be better co-ordinated, and Holland assistance more easily obtainable for the conquests required for the restoration or safeguarding of their territory. Just as he had used Maurice against Leicester, so he used him now for the purpose of guarding under Holland leadership against the worst weaknesses of federation. It was a fortunate circumstance that the only other Stadtholder now remaining in the Union, William Louis in Friesland, was bound to his cousin and brother-in-law Maurice by a firm tie of friendship, and was animated by too high a sense of duty to let jealousy of the younger man's greater position inspire his actions.

Constitutionally speaking, the influence exercised by Holland through its great Advocate and through the authority of Maurice as Stadtholder of a number of provinces was no more than a palliative for a disease the effects of which would none the less one day make themselves felt. An organ of government like the Council of State, through which unity might have found a more regular expression, was thrust into the background. The States-General, in which the provinces sat side by side as free equals, became not only the bearer of the collective sovereignty, but the actual and daily government of the Union. Later, when the national vigour which now kept the cumbrous machinery going began to relax, it was to appear only too clearly how woefully unfit they were for that task. It is, moreover, difficult not to feel some sympathy with the cheated democrats and the disillusioned exiles. But they had had in Leicester an impossible champion for their ideals, while on the other hand the Holland regime was in the imme-diate future to prove equal to the demands of the war. Can one expect of a statesman, confronted with so urgent a crisis as Oldenbarnevelt was in these years, that he should build his system for a distant future? Flanders and Brabant were not regained. But would Prouninck and Van Meetkerke have had better success in that respect than Oldenbarnevelt?

c. THE CONQUESTS OF MAURICE

We have indicated the lines along which the independent North Netherlandish state was to develop in the future. On Leicester's departure, however, the first question still was whether that state had a future at all.

It was not only the internal divisions which made this appear uncertain, but danger threatened also from the English auxiliary troops which by their possession of the cautionary towns of Flushing and The Brill, added to their positions on the land-side frontiers, commanded the entries to the country. If Elizabeth came to an agreement with Spain, the Netherlands revolt was lost. And even if the English continued to assist, so far their help had proved insufficient to check Parma's advance, and now, with the Ysel-line broken into, and Sluis in Spanish hands, the main stronghold of Netherlands independence, Holland-Zealand itself, seemed threatened.

It was great events outside the Netherlands which caused the Spanish attack to waver at this very moment, and Parma's progress not only to be checked midway, but to be converted into a retreat. When in 1589 Geertruidenberg was given up to him by English mutineers—a gate of attack straight against Holland—the worst danger that had threatened from the English side had nevertheless subsided: Elizabeth no longer hesitated, but was engaged in open war with Spain In 1588 Philip had thrown off the mask, and while the Pope deposed the heretical Queen, the King undertook the long-prepared expedition of conquest by sending the Armada against England. Much against his inclination Parma had had to waste the campaigning season by concentrating his army at Dunkirk and Nieuwpoort; the Holland and English fleets prevented its crossing, while the cumbersome Armada could not come near the shore. The disaster which finally overtook the Spanish fleet was a formidable blow to Spanish prestige. The scheme, for the sake of which Philip had withdrawn his attention from the Netherlands, had proved a chimera, and as for Elizabeth, she was cured for good of the illusion that peace with him was possible. For the Netherlands, this was an important consequence of the affair, even though it did not mean that she now became free with her money or even carried out the treaty of 1585 to the letter.

Events in France exercised an even more profound influence on affairs in the Low Countries. We saw how in 1585 Henry III had been compelled to refuse the sovereignty offered him by the States-General out of fear of the growing power of the Catholic movement in his kingdom. Since then the League, under the Duke of Guise, had become master of Paris. In 1588 the King had Guise murdered, a deed by which the Catholic party was even more intensely embittered. In 1589 the King himself was murdered, and a situation developed which was serious indeed, for Henry III's successor was Henry of Bourbon, King of Navarre, a Huguenot, nay more, the leader of the Huguenots. The League, which controlled a large part of France, refused to recognize the heretic as King, and it was inevitable that they should seek the support of Spain.

It is clear that Philip's interests were vitally concerned in that crisis. A victory for Henry IV would create the situation which William of Orange had always hoped for: it would mobilize the power of France against Spain's position in the Netherlands. No matter, therefore, how keenly Parma felt that the whole issue in the Netherlands remained uncertain so long as Holland and Zealand held out; no matter how fervently he wished to complete his task there, he had to obey Philip's positive orders and turn southward. For some time already he had been supporting the League with money and troops which he could ill spare. Now in 1590 he marched into France himself with his main army in order to protect Paris against Henry IV. Finally, in the winter of 1591 to 1592, he had to go south once more in order to secure the election to the French throne of Isabella, Philip's daughter by his first wife, who had been a French princess. No less a stake was now gambled for, and at last there seemed to be a prospect of fulfilment for the scheme that Philip, as long ago as 1558, had arranged with Henry II, of France side by side with Spain beginning to work for the suppression of heresy in Europe. Only, time and again the hopes of a decisive defeat of Henry IV were dashed to the ground. Thus the Spanish interference in France offered a splendid opportunity to the North Netherlandish provinces, and the vigour with which they availed themselves of it, compelling Parma in spite of the policy imposed upon him to turn his attention northward again, in its turn benefited Henry IV. In the course of a few years the Spanish cause was sadly impaired in the Netherlands as well as in France, and Parma, triumphant for so long, at the end of 1592 died in disgrace and despair, like Don John before him.

International circumstances thus became in 1588, and especially in 1590, favourable for the revolt as they had not been since the deceptive spring of 1572. Yet the young Republic might not have been able to make use of them but for the internal developments which had just carried the vigorous personality of Oldenbarnevelt, supported by the whole weight of Holland, into a position of real power; and no less important was his happy co-operation with the high-born Stadtholders, Maurice and William Louis. The moving force behind everything that was done in those years was the powerful mind of the Advocate of Holland, but the two Stadtholders were far more than convenient tools through which he could impart unity of policy to the entire body of the Northern Netherlands. Their great merit lay in what they did together for the improvement of the army, while, moreover, Maurice handled with masterly skill the weapon they created for themselves. After the Hohenlohe regime the mere fact that the young commanders had a sense of order and discipline was a boon. The greater regularity in public finance and the wise self-restriction of the States, who reduced the size of the army so as to be better able to pay what remained, created a favourable atmosphere for their work of reorganization. But they also introduced all sorts of novelties which at first gave rise to mockery, but soon were imitated all over Europe. In the classical authors they read of military movements in which they strenuously trained their troops. They improved the armament, and with a just sense of the nature of the land where their services were required, they accustomed the soldiers to do the digging which until then the military had considered beneath them, and which used to be carried out by peasants hired for the purpose. Maurice had followed at Leyden the lectures on mathematics of Simon Stevin of Brugge, and he was profoundly aware of the importance of a scientific study of engineering. The commissariat, the means of transport on land but especially on water—everything had their attention, so that when the moment came to strike they could strike home.

In 1590 everyone felt that the moment had come. The Council of State, whose activities were now practically limited to military matters, pointed out to the States-General

the good occasion and opportunity which present themselves for doing the enemy an injury, and for carrying out successfully some attempts, caused by the present diversion of the enemy's armed forces.

The States-General decided to levy additional troops. After so long a period of defensive warfare, after years of giving ground, men longed for an offensive. A successful attempt on Breda had a stimulating effect. Maurice was less fortunate with respect to Nymwegen, but in September 1590, while Parma was in France, he took in addition to Steenbergen a number of small places and fortresses on the Maas near Den Bosch. The next year witnessed the real beginning, although Parma remained in the Netherlands, with half his attention riveted on France it is true. Zutfen and Deventer were unexpectedly surrounded by the Dutch forces and quickly surrendered, and although an attempt on Groningen failed, Delfzyl and other strong places in the North were taken. The army then hurried southward to prevent Parma from taking the entrenchment of Knodsenburg opposite Nymwegen. With this the campaign seemed at an end, and the troops went into winter quarters. To the enemy's complete surprise, however, Maurice sud-

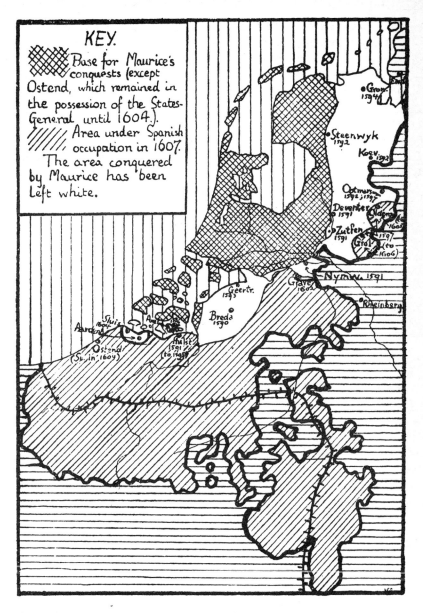

KEY.
Base for Maurice's conquests (except Ostend, which remained in the possession of the States-General until 1604.).
/// Area under Spanish occupation in 1607.
The area conquered by Maurice has been left white.

Grow. 1594
Steenwyk 1592
Koev. 1592
Ostmar. 1592;1597
Deventer 1591
Oldenz. 1605
Zutfen 1591
Grol 1591 (to 1606)
Nymw. 1591
Grave 1602
Rheinberg
Geertr. 1593
Breda 1590
Sluis 1604
Aarden.
Am...
Ostend (Sp. in 1604)
Hulst 1591 to 1596

MAP V.—THE CONQUESTS OF MAURICE, 1590–1606

denly collected a little army and appeared before Hulst in
Flanders, which capitulated. Nor was even this the end. As
unexpectedly he laid siege to Nymwegen and took that town
as well. It was only an effective use of the waterways that had
made possible those disconcertingly quick movements.

In 1592 Parma had again to go to France, and the Spanish
commander in the North-East was, in spite of his warnings,
left to his own devices. Steenwyk and Koevorden, however
strongly fortified, proved impossible to hold. Here Maurice's
scientific methods of siege warfare first showed themselves in
their full glory. The possession of those two places not only
safeguarded southern Friesland from marauding raids, but cut
Groningen off completely from its base in the South.

In 1593 Maurice, to the great resentment of the Frisians,
who wanted all forces concentrated against Groningen first,
besieged Geertruidenberg, by which the Hollanders felt themselves to be threatened, and which he took in spite of all
attempts at relief. The irritation of the Frisians assumed such
violent forms, and without heeding William Louis' efforts to
calm them down they protested so passionately against "Holland tyranny" that one can plainly see there were as sharp
particularist contrasts left in the area which still belonged to
the revolt as there had formerly been in the greater area of
all the Netherlands. Only, within the northern state success
was to compose them. In the winter of 1593 attempts were
undertaken against Brugge, Den Bosch, and Maastricht, all of
which failed, but Groningen, whose turn came in 1594, had
to capitulate after a siege of two months; Friesland could be
easy in its mind. Joyful homage was paid to Maurice on his
return; in the Holland towns through which he passed the
Rhetoricians performed symbolic shows in his honour. It was
in vain that the citizens of Groningen, on whom the defence
of their town had mainly fallen, had sent urgent petitions to
Brussels for an expedition of relief. Renewed mutinies of
unpaid troops, which again exposed large tracts of country in
the South to the excesses of the soldiers, had kept the Government paralysed.

After Parma's death in December 1592 the government

had been temporarily in the hands of Mansfeldt. A Netherlands magnate, no doubt, but under the cover of his name
the real ruler was Fuentes, a Spaniard, brother-in-law of Alva,
and a man of his school. He had been sent by Philip to replace
Parma (who had died just in time to be spared that indignity);
and yet another Spaniard, Ibarra, was, to the intense displeasure
of the native nobility, and indeed against the provisions of the
Treaty of Arras, placed on the Council of State. It was Parma's
reluctance to use the forces at his disposal for interference in
the French civil war, a reluctance shared to the full by the
unhappy people of the Southern Netherlands, which explains
Philip's decision to restore Spanish control. At the same time,
however, the country had to be used as a means for the
tightening of his relations with the German Habsburgs, required by the interests of the King's world policy. His cousin,
the Archduke Ernest therefore, a brother of the new Emperor
Rudolph (as also of Matthew, who nearly twenty years ago
had come to Brussels in rather different circumstances), was
made Governor, while the prospect was opened to him of one
day obtaining the hand of Philip's daughter Isabella, and with
it the sovereignty over the Netherlands. The new ruler's
attention, however, was at the same time directed to France
more insistently than ever, for although Henry IV had now
embraced Catholicism, Isabella's claims were by no means
given up. The subjected Netherlands none the less heartily
acclaimed Ernest when he arrived in 1594: in their helpless
state they expected every new master to save them. At his
entry into Antwerp there were staged on "scaffoldings" dumb
shows which brought the people's hopes in visible form before
his eyes:

Seventeen maidens representing the seventeen provinces, of which
the United ones were made fast apart at one string, and the others
which are still under the King at another string, both groups being
introduced to him, Ernest, by the *Nimpha Belgica* (the Netherlands
Virgin), so that they might once more be joined together.

And indeed Ernest soon wrote to the States-General at The
Hague a smooth letter inviting them to enter into negotiations.

The States, however, or rather Oldenbarnevelt—for he was the author of the striking document—replying with a plain refusal, pushed aside the well-meaning Archduke to discover behind him the old enemy of the entire Netherlands people—Spain.

Unhappily the southern half of the Netherlands people, kept down by the Spanish armies, robbed of all its most vigorous elements, and by the difference in religion separated from the ruling class in the North, was no longer able to raise its head against that old enemy. No doubt the unending misery of the war and the prospect of an open rupture with France were again causing bitter dissatisfaction. Ernest did not dare to call together a complete assembly of the States-General, but a meeting which he summoned of none but nobility and clergy voiced the grievances with sufficient vehemence, exclaiming against the foreigners in the administration, against the mutinies, against the unnational foreign policy. Aerschot, the hero of 1576, the deserter of three years later, was again the leader. The people of the South had got him back with the conquest. But his aristocratic love of opposition indeed benefited them but little. When Ernest died early in 1595, in the midst of confusion and discouragement, Fuentes himself emerged from his obscurity to take the government into his own hands until a new Archduke should come to play to the finish the part of the deceased. There was no thought of resistance to the hated Spaniard, and soon it became strikingly apparent that the Spanish military forces, if only led by a firm hand, still disposed of great reserves of strength.

The States had hopes of turning the dissatisfaction in the South to their advantage by undertaking military operations in the region of the Maas, in the direction of Liège. The plan was to establish communications with Bouillon in France, whither they had just sent an auxiliary corps for Henry IV, but also to open a breach in Brabant and Limburg. In enterprises of this kind, far from his base, Maurice, cautious and methodical, did not excel, and Fuentes easily frustrated the scheme. But more than that, exhausted as the subjected Netherlands were, pushed back on all sides from their natural fron-

tiers, and secured against the unrest of their own people and
the attacks of the Northerners solely by their numerous fortresses, the Spanish Governor, quite in accordance with his
master's wishes, still managed to use them as the starting-point
for an offensive against France. Henry IV, at last sufficiently
in control of his kingdom, in this year 1595 had declared
open war. In the next year an alliance was concluded between
France, England, and the States-General. Those same States-
General, who only a few years ago had come as supplicants
first to the Crown of France, then to that of England, to offer
the sovereignty over themselves, were now admitted on a
footing of equality. It is true that Elizabeth had at first objected on the ground of the special position which the treaty
of 1585 secured to her in the Netherlands. With so much the
greater earnestness had the King of France favoured the
Netherlands statesmen's ambitions towards recognition. Once
more the mutual jealousies of France and England where the
Low Countries were concerned proved a benefit.

Much direct advantage certainly this alliance did not yield.
The States made such an effort to assist Henry IV on his war
front that their power of attack on their own side was paralysed.
And yet Fuentes succeeded in taking Cambrai, and in 1596
the new Archduke, Albert, just come to assume the government, even captured the still more important town of Calais,
which, with Nieuwpoort, Dunkirk, and Sluis (Ostend being
still in the hands of the States), formed a serious menace to
the shipping of England as well as of the Northern provinces.
After this success Albert turned north and retook Hulst, but
the losses suffered there exhausted him for the time being.
A new bankruptcy of Philip II's exchequer made his situation
still more difficult.

So in 1597 it was Maurice's turn again, and while the Spanish
army was fighting in France he, after a famous cavalry skirmish
near Turnhout, completed the conquest of the Eastern provinces. He first took possession of Rheinberg, which commanded
the crossing of the Rhine for an attack on the Eastern frontiers.
It belonged to the archbishop of Köln, who had now to
acquiesce in an occupation by the States substituted for one

H

by the Spaniards. Marching north from thence, Maurice captured without much difficulty Grol, Enschedé, Oldenzaal, and all the other places from which the enemy could still lay Gelderland and Overysel under contribution. There was great rejoicing in the North. "The fence of the Netherlands is closed," so ran the phrase in which the situation was summed up. It meant that the entire territory north of the natural line of defence of the seven provinces still represented on the States-General was now cleared of the enemy. The Upper Quarter of Gelderland, which was situated south of that line, remained in his hands.

The success came none too soon. In 1598 Henry IV concluded peace with Philip. Elizabeth's close-fisted policy had discouraged him, and in any case, after a generation of wars of religion, France stood in need of rest. Philip, on his part, realized at last that it was beyond his power to dispute the succession of the former heretic, and he even restored Calais in his eagerness to get his hands free against the seven provinces once more. For the first time since 1590, therefore, the Spanish commanders in the Netherlands were able to turn their undivided attention to affairs in the North, but the strategic position which Parma in his happier years had prepared as a jumping-off ground for an attack on the main stronghold of the rebellion now lay in ruins. Even so the eastern frontier was still the weak point in the Republic's armour, and the first vigorous onrush, which the Spanish forces made in that same year 1598, was again directed to break through there. The attempt almost resulted in serious trouble with the neighbouring German princes, whose territory the attackers had to cross. It was nevertheless, as we shall see, repeated in 1605 and again in 1606, and each time, in spite of the enemy's remoteness from his base, which inevitably weakened the force of his thrust, people in Holland itself were alarmed as though the very existence of the young state had been at stake. The Reformed "regents" in Gelderland, Overysel, Groningen, felt their authority over their still so largely Catholic populations tottering.

The plans originally formed for Ernest had after his death

been carried out for the benefit of Albert. He had married Isabella, and Philip, who died in 1598, left to them the Netherlands in sovereign possession. In reality they were by no means cut free from Spain, but the nominal independence of "the Archdukes" nevertheless removed, in the eyes of Catholics in the North as well as in the South, some of the hateful character which with the Spanish name had so far clung to the champions of Catholicism in the Netherlands. The Archdukes soon became popular in the South in spite of all the misfortunes of the war, and in the North the Catholic clergy at least felt no aversion from regarding them as the legitimate rulers of the country. This is not to say that they always actively worked for them, or that even in their feelings they were always consistent.

The Catholic clergy in the North were again exercising some influence. A revival had followed the bewilderment and disorganization caused at first by the overthrow of the domination of the Catholic Church. In 1583 Sasbout Vosmeer was appointed Vicar of Utrecht, the first Archbishop under the reorganization of 1561 having died in 1580. Vosmeer, who became Apostolic Vicar in 1592, and in 1602 Archbishop *in partibus infidelium*, worked indefatigably at the re-establishment of the ecclesiastical organization. The spirit of Netherlands society was so much averse from persecution for the sake of religion that Catholic priests, even though they were suspect as enemies of the State, could move about fairly freely so long as they took some elementary precautions. The scope of their labours was nevertheless confined within narrow limits. All that Vosmeer and his helpers could do was to inspire with new courage a little band of faithful souls and keep them together as a nucleus. They could not prevent the indifferent majority from gradually slipping away to where the active Reformed organization, supported by the State, could catch them up. Especially in the country-side, where their movements could more easily be watched, the Catholic priests were unable to achieve much. A further great difficulty was created by the bad relations, soon leading to open quarrel, between the secular and the regular clergy. Of these latter especially the fiery Jesuits were detested by the States as the instigators of political assassination, and were persecuted more bitterly than the others. Vosmeer's activities were seriously hampered when in 1602 the States got hold of evidence showing that he had been received by the Archdukes, and had appealed to them for support in order to have the Archbishopric of Utrecht restored. This was, not unnaturally, considered an act of high treason. Vosmeer had to fly, and thenceforward he led Catholic mission work in the United Netherlands from Köln. His principal helper, Elbertus Eggius, was kept imprisoned in the Gevangenpoort at The Hague for a couple of years.

While the Catholics were thus able to save a few small remnants, the Reformed Church, with the support of public authority, went through a period of rapid expansion. In all conquered towns and districts the Reformed Church organization was introduced without delay. The Protestantization of the people was considered as an indispensable guarantee of their loyalty to the States regime. Small wonder when one remembers the way in which Nymwegen had gone over to the other side in 1585, or when one has observed the zeal with which during the siege of Groningen the Catholic population of that town supported their magistrates in the resistance against the States' army; they had been greatly influenced by the exhortations of some Jesuits who had come to Groningen a few years before. Groningen remained for years a weak member of the body politic. Reunited with its old partner and enemy the Ommelands, it had been admitted to the Union under William Louis as Stadtholder. But the town remained so unmanageable that the States-General had a citadel built to control it, to the consternation of the citizens, who had gone through the same experience under Alva. The Reformed organization was similarly a means for the safeguarding of the State.

In all towns that fell into the power of the States the exercise of the Catholic religion was at once suppressed, and the churches were seized for the Reformed and "purged" in accordance with their ideas. In the country-side, even in

Utrecht and in those parts of Gelderland which had long been freed from the Spaniards, the Reformed Church was in the nineties hardly yet in being. As late as 1599, for instance, the Court at Arnhem had to order that "in the districts of Veluwe and Veluwezoom the altars, images, holy water basins, etc., shall be removed from the churches, as also the crucifixes and chapels, standing in forests or along roads, shall be pulled down." In the town itself, indeed, even in the following year the magistrates had to prohibit the use of pictures or crosses on palls at funerals. The slow progress in the country districts was partly caused by fear for enemy raids, partly by a more general difficulty, namely, the shortage of suitable ministers. In wide tracts of the country the peasant population had to manage for the time being without any spiritual guides at all.

A shift was generally made with the old priests, who were placed before the choice of either "holding their peace" on a small pittance, or submitting to an examination before being admitted as Reformed minister. In Groningen Province this plan worked very well; less so in Drente.[1] Here, in 1598, the Stadtholder, William Louis, having been authorized thereto by the States-General, summoned all parish priests and other secular clergy before a committee of ministers and representatives of the Stadtholder's authority. "They were solemnly asked whether they had embraced the Reformed religion in their hearts, and if so, whether they were willing to give proof of their knowledge of the pure evangelical doctrine. Many gave insufficient answers, others submitted to a theological examination, a few were even ready to be tested on the spot." Only three, however, were admitted, and not without important reservations being made. Two years afterwards a few more were passed.

In 1593 a committee instituted by the States of Utrecht made a tour of that province in order to examine the ministers and former priests. It consisted of a nobleman with two ministers and an elder of the town of Utrecht. Its report gives

---

[1] Drente, which was really the eighth province, had its own States assembly, but no session in the States-General, being too poor and sparsely inhabited. It contributed one above every hundred paid by the seven provinces.

a vivid picture of the varied and frequently very peculiar
conditions prevailing. In the large majority of villages the old
rectors were still living. Many of these expressed their willing-
ness to conform, but some were obviously still hankering after
the old practices, others had come over half-way and failed,
either through ignorance or obstinacy, on some particular
point. Of one priest, whom the committee consider to be

an honourable man, having small children, whose mother has died,

the report says:

In baptizing and marrying this rector does not follow one way, but
still accommodates himself according to people's inclinations.

Several boldly refused to submit and still used to administer
"the popish sacrament" at Easter, or at least manifested 'a
suspicious reluctance to marry their "housewives." One declared
that

he did not wish to have violence done to his conscience either by
the States or by anybody else.

The report continues:

He has not yet married his housewife, notwithstanding our Noble
Lordships the States have ordered him to do so. He even said
expressly that he will not publicly marry her, adding that he was
willing to give her up, as he could easily live without her, nay, he
offered derisively to make a present of her to anybody who had a
use for her.

To remedy all these and suchlike deplorable conditions the
committee looked to the intervention of public authority, just
as fifteen years earlier we saw the Ghent Synod ask the magistrates of the town to take measures against "the priests of
the Mass," just as in all the seven provinces Reformed Synods
were now exhorting States and town governments to proceed
more vigorously against "superstitions, idolatries, abuses, and
profanations."

It would be especially serviceable to this purpose [thus concluded
the Utrecht commission] if all church masters were ordered by edict
or in any other way to have their churches purged immediately and

within a certain fixed time of the remaining altars and other relics
and filth of popery. Also, the superstitious bell-ringing at noon and
in the evening should equally be abolished. Etc., etc.

It is evident that, after the first spontaneous period under the
oppression, the progress of the Reformation had become an
essentially different movement. It is evident that the majority
of the North Netherlandish people have only abandoned
Catholicism under the pressure of public authority. This is
not to say that there was no longer any moral force at work
in the Reformed Church. The ministers' zeal for education
is noticeable. No doubt they saw in education, first of all, a
means for driving the old religion out of people's minds.
Papist schools must be rooted out as much as possible. In the
village the beadle of the new Reformed Church appeared to
be the man indicated to keep school. At any rate classis-
meetings and synods never tired of urging the authorities to
make better provision for public instruction, and their efforts
helped to form a generation which was able to follow the
sermon and to read the Bible. Without a doubt they represented a higher intellectual and moral standard than that of
the priests they ousted.

But that was so only because in the Northern provinces the
Counter-Reformation had had no time to make its influence
felt. Shaken by the attack that was directed against it, the
Catholic Church had pulled itself together. The foundation
of the Society of Jesus, the decrees of the Council of Trent,
the organization of the new bishoprics in the Netherlands—all
these were so many attempts to strengthen by a friendly
reformation the powers of resistance against the hostile one.
The opposition to the new bishoprics, which had so greatly
retarded their actual institution; next Alva's regime of terror,
which had created an atmosphere in which no religious revival
could flourish; finally, the revolt—these interruptions had long
hampered the effect of the Counter-Reformation on the Netherlands people. It was only in the train of Parma's conquests
that this great movement made its entry in full strength.
Consequently, while the North was being Protestantized under
the protection of Maurice's sword, the reverse process was

carried on in the South. It was by no means completed with
the expulsion, immediately after the conquest, of the most
convinced Protestants. Great energy was spent, under Parma,
under the Archdukes, on the rebuilding of the Catholic
Church. Materially and spiritually, everything lay in ruins.
No matter how much impoverished the country was, keen
rivalry was shown in the restoration of buildings and works
of art; architects, painters, sculptors were flooded with commissions. The great abbeys had suffered heavily under the
revolt, in which at first they had taken part so whole-heartedly,
and had to be reorganized from the bottom. Capable and
devoted men were placed in the episcopal sees. Strict supervision was given to the fitness and conduct of priests. The
Jesuits, protected by the Court, established themselves in all
the principal towns and obtained great influence over the
well-to-do middle class as confessors and teachers. Besides
the thousands who emigrated, there naturally remained behind
other thousands who submitted out of mere worldly considerations. The majority, however, settled down to the restoration
of the old conditions quite comfortably. Fatigued by the years
of distress and weakened by the departure of so many vigorous
characters as had gone to strengthen the new civilization and
society in the North, they were eager to seek rest and comfort
in an order of things in which Roman Church and absolute
monarchy supported each other.

Under those auspices a much more complete unity could
be attained than was possible in the independent provinces.
Here as well as there, it should not be forgotten, the substratum of the people's life was still in the main Catholic.
But, moreover, compulsion on the part of public authority
could make itself felt much more severely (even though the
Inquisition and the stake belonged to the past) in a monarchical and Catholic country than in a Republic which, however closely bound to Calvinism, yet recognized liberty of
conscience expressly as a basic principle of its constitutional
law. The difference nevertheless was one of degree only. In
the last resort the position of the Reformed ascendancy in the
seven provinces was based on power, just as power was the

foundation of Catholicism in the South. Power not only preserved the state of the free Netherlands north of the rivers; power not only kept the southern provinces under Spain. It was power no less that brought about along the rivers, by which the course of the war had been determined, this profound moral cleavage within the Netherlands people, for which native traditions had in no sense prepared the way.

For now a stalemate had come into being. Maurice had fenced round the territory of the new Republic with a tenable strategic frontier. To push forward much beyond the rivers was as hard for him as it was for the enemy to force them. But it was to take a few years more before both sides were ready to acquiesce in the accomplished fact of the split.

d. STALEMATE

It was not only to Maurice's conquests that the North Nether-landish Republic owed its power of resistance. If the States regime had been able to check the decline to which it seemed to be succumbing at the time of Leicester's arrival, it was due, in addition to them and to Oldenbarnevelt's vigorous leadership, to the wonderful economic development that took place.

It is known to all the world [so the Amsterdam burgomaster C. P. Hooft wrote a little later] that whereas it is generally the nature of war to ruin land and people, these countries on the contrary have been noticeably improved thereby.

Behind the "fence" Holland and Zealand had been enjoying an absolute immunity ever since 1576, and while the mercenaries were garrisoned in the frontier towns or lay in camps and manœuvred on the other side of the rivers; while the sailors kept watch off Flemish ports from which privateers used to sail—Dunkirk, Nieuwpoort, Sluis—the whole of Holland and Zealand was humming with activity, and the merchant fleets, finding access to Antwerp barred, were sailing to and fro in steadily growing numbers. Communications with Germany were restored by the conquests of the Ysel towns and of Nymwegen. But trade still mainly hinged on the exchange between the Baltic countries on the one side, and France, Spain, and Portugal on the other. In 1590 for the first time Holland merchantmen ventured to pass through the Straits of Gibraltar and to enter the Mediterranean. This was the beginning of an enormous expansion. Stimulated by the overseas trade and by the money it brought into the country, activity and prosperity increased by leaps and bounds on all sides. The towns were enlarged, new harbours were dug, in North Holland there began the reclamations which in a few decades, by the removal of the lakes, were to change the face of the land. In the Zaan region thousands found work in the shipbuilding yards. Haarlem and Leyden became centres for the linen and woollen industries which had to leave Flanders when life grew insecure there and access to the sea was barred.

The sea was a great factor in this amazing development. It was in their traffic with the sea that the Hollanders could make the most of the possibilities of their new condition. It was the sea that opened them the way to wealth and to power, to adventure and to greatness. They were conscious of it.

In the command of the sea and in the conduct of the war on the water resides the entire prosperity of the country.

Thus averred the States of Holland in 1596. It does not follow that naval matters were in a satisfactory condition. There were no fewer than five Admiralty Colleges, a striking instance of the harm done to sound administration by the jealousies between provinces and towns, each of which must have its particular interests satisfied. Three of these Colleges were in Holland (North Holland, Amsterdam, and Maas), one in Zealand, and one in Friesland. They had powers delegated to them by the States-General, and only too frequently hindered each other's work in the fitting-out of men-of-war. They obtained their incomes out of the duties levied on trade, and particularly on trade with the obedient provinces, the so-called "convoy and licence" duties, in the management of which a great deal of corruption took place. The great and

permanent problem before them was created by Dunkirk.
Never did more courageous sailors go out to sea than the
Flemish privateers belonging to that port. Fate disposed that
their courage should not, like the zest for the sea of the
Hollanders and Zealanders, contribute towards the building
up of a national system for their compatriots. It was Parma
who, after the capture in 1583, had transformed Dunkirk from
a peaceful little fishers' town into a veritable robbers' den.
The war between the Dunkirk privateers and their fellow-
Dutchmen of the North was waged with fierce inhumanity.
The permanent blockade of the port laid a heavy burden on
the navy of the Republic, nor was it very effective. The States-
General themselves made liberal issue of letters of marque,
and the North Netherlands privateers, who mostly belonged
to Zealand ports, were often indistinguishable from pirates.
In a few cases they even joined the Barbary pirates who were
infesting the Mediterranean.

More edifying than these savage doings, which demoralized
the skipper class, were the expeditions sent out by the States
against Spain herself, and which had more success than fell
to the share of Philip's Armada in 1588. The first of these
was undertaken in concert with the English in 1596. The most
famous is that of 1607, when the States' fleet, under the command of Jacob van Heemskerck, attacked and destroyed the
Spanish fleet on the roadstead of Gibraltar and under the
batteries of the castle. While the warfare on land, with the
foreign auxiliaries, the innumerable foreigners even in the
States' pay, the foreign noblemen surrounding the princely
commander, could never create a really national tradition—
not during the whole period of the Republic's existence—these
activities at sea were the beginnings of a great story in which
the people would see their own kindred glorified. Wealthy
Holland was beginning to attract mercenaries and adventurers
from all sides, and many Germans and Scandinavians served
in the navy too, but the leading positions—in striking contrast
to conditions prevailing in the army—were always occupied
by Netherlanders, generally promoted from before the mast.

The same is true of the colonial enterprises which began

about this time, and which were of course intimately connected with the merchant service as well as with the navy. A man like Heemskerck, for instance, had graduated in that school. These expeditions were the beginnings of a splendid adventure, which was to demand of the Netherlands people, in so far as they had escaped from the stifling embrace of the foreign monarchy with its bureaucratic and aristocratic regime, the highest tests of enterprise and organizing ability, of war and of statecraft. Quite apart from the material advantages, the heavy task, of which even to-day has not seen the completion, was to call forth a wealth of personalities out of all classes of the Netherlands people; it added treasures to the store of national legend; it broadened the national horizon.

The navigation to America and the Indies sprang in the most natural fashion from the trade in Europe. While Castile maintained a monopoly for the intercourse with America, Portugal, which since 1580 also owed allegiance to Philip, barred the Indian Ocean to all would-be intruders. The Hollanders, however, were indispensable to both, so much so that although the Spanish Government once or twice yielded to the temptation to strike at the rebels by seizing their ships in the Spanish and Portuguese ports, it could not long maintain the embargo. These measures nevertheless whetted the desire of the Holland and Zealand merchants to establish direct communications. The Atlantic Ocean was soon crossed for the profitable smuggling trade in Brazil. The route to the Indies, however, ran right through the Portuguese sphere of influence, and seemed so beset with perils that between 1590 and 1595 the States of Zealand, the States-General, the town of Amsterdam financed several expeditions for the purpose of discovering a navigable way round the north of Asia. Maurice took a keen personal interest in these ventures. But in 1595 a consortium of Amsterdam merchants sent four vessels south under the command of Cornelis Houtman. Jan Huigen van Linschoten and Petrus Plancius assisted in preparing for the voyage; the former had been at Goa in Portuguese employment, and had just written his famous description of the Portuguese Empire; the latter, a Reformed Minister, driven out of Flanders by Parma's conquests, had made profound studies of geography and navigation. In 1597 three of Hout-man's four ships returned with a cargo of pepper and other spices obtained in the Malay Archipelago. Proof had been furnished that the thing could be done. Forces of energy and capital, long contained, immediately burst forth. Several "Companies of Afar" sprang up overnight. In 1598 no fewer than twenty-two ships sailed to the Indies from the Texel, the Maas, and the Scheldt. A new world opened for sailors, traders, adventurers—a wonderful world with new beauties, new peoples, new dangers. Journals and accounts of the voyages were eagerly read. Merchants scented profits, states-men saw the enemy's power hit in a·sensitive spot.

For the one purpose as well as for the other concentration and co-operation soon proved indispensable. In lands where the Portuguese held most of the strategic points strongly occupied and where native society was constantly kept con-vulsed by wars and general insecurity, unbridled competition could not but lead to disaster. It was desired, moreover, to establish monopolies. The natives, especially in the Spice Islands, the Moluccas, were to be forced to trade with the Dutch to the exclusion of every other nation. Power was needed. In the young Republic, born out of opposition against an oppressive central authority, all private interests fought their own battles without caring much for unity or govern-ment, and circumstances were so favourable that this was on the whole the best way for the nation's vital forces to develop. The idea of a privileged Company was uncongenial therefore, and in spite of the energetic intervention of the States-General much persuasion was required before the various Companies could agree to combine. The United Dutch East India Com-pany, which was formed in 1602, is one of Oldenbarnevelt's greatest creations. The capital subscribed was very consider-able; the Company was given a monopoly of trade between the Cape of Good Hope and Cape Magelhaes; complete sovereign rights within the same area were delegated to her. Possessing vessels of war, and soon fortresses and troops, the Company, which disposed of a great freedom of movement while in the last resort remaining dependent on the States-General, was a formidable weapon in the struggle with Spain as well as a capable gatherer of wealth. Many small purses had contributed to the capital, but the shareholders had no real control over the directors. The constitution of the Company gave to the magistrates of the trading towns in which the various "Chambers" were situated a large say in the appointment of the latter. The Company thus became intimately connected with the "regent" oligarchy of the two maritime provinces, which in course of time owed to it an increase in both political power and wealth.

In the whole of this brilliant economic movement the share of the South Netherlandish exiles was most considerable. Without the capital of the Antwerpers who had come north after the fall of the town, without their commercial knowledge and relations, Holland, small and in some respects still backward area, could not possibly have risen to the opportunities that were offered her so suddenly. Under Leicester's government, as we saw, the Flemings and Brabanders had not yet quite "settled down," so that they formed an element of political unrest. Soon, however, most of them were infected with the fever of money-making which was getting a grip on Holland and Zealand, and they prospered too well to spend all their time looking back longingly to their own provinces. In all bold enterprises, requiring initiative and breadth of vision, the exiles did their bit. No man worked in closer contact with the States and Maurice for the expeditions round the north than Balthazar de Moucheron, an Antwerper of French origin, who after the siege (during which he had been one of the colonels of the citizenship) had settled at Middelburg; he also undertook expeditions to Guinea planned in a strikingly big fashion. Another enterprising Antwerp merchant was Isaac Lemaire, whose name survives, however, mainly on account of the conflict into which he got later on with the Company's monopoly. But countless are the smaller men of Flemish and Brabant origin who rose to fortune by trade at home or made their way in the Company's service abroad.

What a contrast is presented by the bright and colourful

life of the North, in which the emigrants played their parts
with so much zest, and the dreary dullness of the land where
the foreigner had succeeded in restoring his rule! If Holland
and Zealand flourished, it was partly because they fed on the
best vital forces of Flanders and Brabant. The war, which
"noticeably improved" them, had truly "spoilt" the Southern
provinces. Trade was at a standstill, the towns impoverished
with countless houses empty, wide regions lay open to the
States' cavalry, which now (like the Spanish had been wont
to do some years previously in Gelderland and Friesland)
from their bases at Breda, Ostend, and other places, laid
Flanders and Brabant under contribution. Meanwhile the
Spanish soldiery had not changed. They still were formidable
to the enemy when they had a mind to fight, but too often
they broke out into mutiny and made themselves formidable
only to the obedient populations. In 1598 the Antwerpers
were rudely reminded of the events of 1576. The garrison of
the citadel mutinied and demanded payment of the citizens
by firing cannon-shots.

Which made many people flee with their money and most valued
possessions, being in great anxiety and at all hours of the day uncertain of their lives and goods. The Spaniards grew so bold that
they considered it to be a great courtesy on their part when, instead
of summoning the magistrates by means of canon-shots to come to
them as they would call their lackeys, they wrote letters to these
gentlemen: "A los de la casa de la Villa," that is to say, "to those
of the town-hall," without giving them any title.

Small wonder that the Southerners longed fervently for the
end of the war, and that, much more than did their more
fortunate brethren in the North, they treasured in their hearts
the memory of the lost unity of the Netherlands.

In 1598 the States-General were called together to Brussels
in order to learn from the Archduke Albert that he was to
marry Philip II's daughter Isabella, and that the King intended
to cede to them, with the approval of his son and heir, the
sovereignty over the Netherlands. Albert set out to fetch his
bride, too late to find Philip alive. The old King, who had
for forty years pursued the visions of Spanish world power

and of a Catholic Europe—indissolubly connected in his mind
—had died at the moment when his policy had definitely come
to grief. Just as in his father's life so in his, while a single
great aim is tenaciously kept in view, one scheme is generally
coming up before the other has been done with, until all
together threaten to go under in financial catastrophe. Yet he
left the tradition in its full strength to his heirs, and the transference of the Netherlands by no means meant that they would
no longer be expected to act as an advanced post in northern
Europe in the service of his double ideal.

It was only in outward appearance that Philip met the
Netherlands' desire for independence. He hoped, and so did
the South Netherlanders, that this would be enough to win over
the rebels. Richardot, the new President of the Privy Council,
a Burgundian like Granvelle, and the marquess of Havré, a
brother of Aerschot (who had died shortly before), used the
good offices of an emigrant Antwerper, Daniel van der Meulen,
in an attempt to make the North Netherlandish statesmen see
that it must now be possible to conclude peace. They too—
so they gave to understand—were heartily sick of the Spaniards;
a bare recognition of the Archdukes' right would be sufficient;
everything could remain as it was, the Nassaus and the States
in power, free exercise of religion. But as soon as Van der
Meulen, who visited Brussels with a passport, wanted to
know whether the Reformed would be allowed to return to
the South, he was met with evasive replies. What could be
the use of a reunion when in the two parts opposite principles
of government were to remain in force? Such an arrangement
could the less appeal to the States since they still felt far from
certain of their population, which would in the event of a
peace on those lines be exposed to influences from the re-
Catholicized South. But the principal objection was that the
independence of the Archdukes was a mere sham, and that,
no matter what Richardot and Havré said about the Spaniards,
the States understood perfectly well that the Southern Netherlands remained on the leash of Spain. Indeed, all precautions
had been taken that they should never fall to another dynasty.
In case Albert and Isabella came to die without issue, the

country would revert to Spain; the Spanish troops remained in the principal fortresses; for the carrying-on of war the new state was, as much as the former dependency had been, dependent on the subsidies, and therefore on the behests, of Spain.

How was it possible to think that the free States-General would let themselves be deceived by that appearance? It was merely inviting an utterly useless humiliation when, at the solemn assembly of the States-General at Brussels to welcome the new sovereign, benches were placed for deputies from the seven Northern as well as for those from the other provinces. And when they remained empty, the Archduke still could not leave it at that. He addressed to his unwilling subjects a letter not less mild than the one to which his brother Ernest had received so crushing a reply. At the same time the Brussels States-General, too, wrote to those at The Hague. The reply, given almost a year later, in March 1599, pitilessly exposed the weak spot in the position of the Southerners. The insufferable excesses committed, since the receipt of their letter, by the Spanish soldiery at Antwerp, thus wrote the Northern States-General, had caused them to hope that "their Reverences, Excellencies, and Worships," the States-General of the South, recognizing the single aim of the Northerners,

to wit, that we might one day see the Netherlands as a whole truly liberated from the Spaniards and their adherents, your and our sworn enemies, would have declared yourselves against the aforesaid horrible practices. But since we observe ever more clearly that the Spaniards and their adherents possess among your Reverences, Excellencies, and Worships so much power that they can prevent this happening, we, after thanking you for your good favour and affection and commending ourselves to you in right friendly fashion, do not know what to reply except that we firmly believe your Reverences, Excellencies, and Worships to be as well aware of the means and ways needed for your and our common liberation as we are ourselves. Meanwhile we beg your Reverences, Excellencies, and Worships to hold it for an incontrovertible truth that the Spaniards and their adherents cannot be got out of the Netherlands by means of any negotiation or treaty, but only by force of arms.

The letter ended with an assurance that in case of the Southern

States "taking up arms with us against the common enemy,"
they would be left free to settle religion and administration
in accordance with their own views. The exhortation to revolt
found no echo in the disheartened and enfeebled South. So
desperate was the situation, however, that the Archdukes—in
1599 Albert had brought Isabella home to Brussels—were
compelled to swallow the insult contained in the Hague
States' reply, and in 1600 once more invoked the help of an
assembly of the States-General in order to lure the Northerners
into negotiations. In the ensuing discussion between the new
sovereigns and the deputies of their faithful provinces it
became clear at once how well the position had been understood at The Hague. The Brussels States attempted to arm
themselves with a little independence in view of the forthcoming negotiations: they desired to be authorized to conclude
with the Northern States a peace or a truce. It deserves attention that the Walloon provinces opposed this pacifist policy,
which was promoted by Flanders, Brabant, and Upper Gelderland; the Walloons suffered less directly from the war, but
at the same time the idea of Netherlands unity appealed to
them less strongly. In any case there was not the slightest
possibility of the Brussels States being left to act thus un-
tutored. When the Archdukes refused to let the decision pass
out of their hands, the States had to be content with the more
modest task—but which in view of the temper in the North
was bound to fail—of opening a conversation in order to
consult with their sovereigns about the reply. So they drew
up a letter (and asked obediently for the Archdukes' approval
of it), in which they said no more than that they hoped it
would be possible to find a way out of the labyrinth of war,
if only they could come together "in talk and negotiation."
As it was known by previous experience that the Northern
States refused to accept from the Southern letters composed
in French, the letter, which had been drafted in that language
for the benefit of the Walloons and the Archducal Court, was
translated into Dutch.

The reply, no less than that of 1599, went straight to the
heart of the difficulty, which the helpless deputies of the South

had on the contrary done their utmost to cover up. The Hague States showed not the least eagerness to meet any delegates of the other side, and observed:

To the great regret of all patriots we learn from a reliable source that the coming of your delegates would be directed under the authority of the Archdukes, and that a promise has been given to do nothing that might be prejudicial to their authority. From which it is concluded that this commission of yours (as tending towards the promotion of such illegitimate and harmful authority) utterly conflicts with the prosperity of the Netherlands.

Before a reply could be sent from Brussels to enable the appointed negotiators to undertake the useless journey—the Archdukes overlooking the fresh insult—an attempt of a quite different nature to restore peace and unity was undertaken by the North.

Oldenbarnevelt and the Northern States had, it will be easily understood, concluded from their correspondence with those of the South that the Archdukes' authority must be tottering. That consideration was a factor towards the decision they took to send Maurice with his army on a bold enterprise into Flanders. As the Spanish army was once again paralysed by a serious mutiny, they could wish for no better opportunity. The principal aim of the expedition was to be the capture of the privateering ports, Nieuwpoort and Dunkirk, but it was hoped at the same time that the appearance of the States' army would rouse the people of Flanders and that the position of Yper, Ghent, and Brugge would become untenable, if not at once, then after the occupation of the coast-line. Unfortunately Maurice held a different view. The plan seemed to him unsound, and he prepared for it reluctantly.

Relations between Maurice and the States, which unswervingly followed the lead of Oldenbarnevelt, were in many respects difficult. They were the sovereign, theirs was the responsibility for the conduct of the war, for which, moreover, they had to find the money—a heavy task in spite of the prosperity of the country. Yet Maurice was more—and he knew it—than simply a soldier in their service. He was the son of the great William of Orange, who was to have been the sovereign.

His campaigns had brought to him an enormous personal popularity. He lived in princely style, his income from war contributions and privateering being very large. In the army camp he was surrounded by hundreds of French and German noblemen who, attracted by his fame, came to learn the art of war under him. In that circle the supreme authority of the burgher States was looked upon as a freak. Undoubtedly he himself often chafed at his position, but actually it was in consultation with the States that he drew up all his plans of campaign, and he recognized their right to give orders to him, which, in fact, they did not hesitate to do when necessary. On a later occasion, for instance, being engaged in a deliberation with the States-General and Council of State about a certain projected enterprise, he described it as "not feasible and too hazardous," but he adds:

Unless the worshipful States were pleased to order them [meaning himself and William Louis] to act otherwise, in which case they, as being the servants of the worshipful States, will be found willing to conduct themselves accordingly with all possible zeal, industry, and duty.

Differences of opinion nearly always turned on this, that Maurice was thought too cautious by the States, or that he blamed them for recklessly staking their army and his reputation. The expedition into Flanders of 1600 fortified each side in its judgment of the other. To me, however, it seems undeniable—and there lies the importance of the event in this history—that Maurice failed to give its due to the last chance of breaking through the fatal equilibrium in which the split of the Netherlands was beginning to be stabilized.

It is certain that the States had underestimated the dangers. In spite of the flying leaflets announcing the coming of Maurice's army to deliver them from the Spanish yoke, the population of Flanders did not stir when the Northerners marched southward, almost touching Brugge. The full assembly of the States-General had gone to Ostend in order to be able to confer with Maurice. Already he had passed that town, when most unexpectedly the Archduke appeared with a con-

siderable army. Isabella herself had succeeded in persuading
the Spanish mutineers at Diest to return to their duty. Near
Nieuwpoort Maurice found himself cut off from his base at
Ostend, and had to give battle in order to avoid a disaster.
He gave battle on the beach and won a complete victory.
Instead of making use of it, however, he soon broke up the
siege of Nieuwpoort, undertaken after the battle at the insistence of the States, and embarked with his troops at Ostend
to be carried back to the Scheldt.

The States had departed before him. Oldenbarnevelt and
a number of deputies (three emigrant Brabanders among them)
had gone to Bergen-op-Zoom, where they met the envoys of
the Brussels States: the Count of Bassigny (Brabant), Colonel
Bentinck Lord of Bicht (Upper Quarter of Gelderland), and
Codt (pensionary of Yper). The chasm separating the position
and ideas of the Northerners from those of the Southerners
was revealed without delay. Oldenbarnevelt, as if continuing
the correspondence in which the parties had been engaged,
remarked that the Southern negotiators apparently lacked
powers to conclude anything without the Archdukes, so that
negotiating with the former really amounted to negotiating
with the latter, and ultimately with Spain, since the Archdukes
were inseparable from Spain. Codt, who had been among
Hembyze's prisoners at Ghent in October 1577, replied un-
compromisingly:

that the aforesaid States [at Brussels], being subject to their natural
princes, could not withdraw their allegiance and dutiful obedience
from them.

There was the rub. At Bergen-op-Zoom sovereigns faced
subjects. No matter how urgently Oldenbarnevelt exhorted
the Southerners to turn Maurice's victory to their advantage
and to rise, the reply was that the removal of the Spaniards

could be effected in a better and more Christian way by a good peace
than by violence, by which we should plunge this unfortunate country
into a new war.

This left, indeed, no more to be said on either side, and
although the majority of the Brussels States-General on re-

ceiving the report of their deputies wished to write to The Hague once more, the Archduke now intervened and made an end of the negotiations—if negotiations can be called what from the side of the Northerners had been no more than exhortations to rise.

The Netherlands historian may hesitate whether to criticize the Brabant and Flemish deputies for their submissiveness or to blame the Hollanders for having been too inflexible. However much he may deplore the confirmation which the split of the Netherlands received from an impact like that of Bergen-op-Zoom, he will have to admit that neither side could have acted differently. Consciousness of common nationhood was certainly not lacking in that tragic meeting. Oldenbarnevelt was continuing the tradition of William the Silent when, leaving aside the religious differences, he called upon all Netherlanders to join in the fight against Spain. But the fact was that he and the Northerners stood there as free republicans, accustomed to administer their own affairs and to give orders to their princely army-chiefs. And although silence was kept about religion, none the less did they stand there as Reformed, whose position in their own country still seemed to require active enmity against Spain.

The Southerners, on the other hand, were no more than the representatives of a defeated people, impoverished and exhausted. Twice had the South risked a revolt, both times it had been struck down. It had lost its economic prosperity, and its bravest and most enterprising men, who were now steeling the strength of the North. It is not to be wondered at that the idea of a new revolt could not inspire the Brussels States. The spring had been broken. Besides, their impotence was not merely moral, it was physical.

The States of Brabant, Flanders, etc., mastered by castles and garrisons, had no other means for promoting the peace than their humble remonstrances, setting out how needful peace was to them, wretchedly lamenting about the war and the unpaid soldiery.

Thus writes the chronicler Van Meteren, with respect to the situation of a few years later, and Buzanval, the French

Ambassador in The Hague, in this same year 1600 deprecates
the possibilities of a revolt in the South, recalling

the gripping bit by which they are held.

There was one thing more. It was all very well for the
Northerners to make solemn promises that in case of a successful rising in the South they would leave religion and
government as they were. But experience had shown that
revolt inevitably threw up a new leading class to be the bearer
of Protestantism. The members of the States of Brabant,
Flanders, Upper Quarter of Gelderland, clergy, nobility,
magistrates, felt that their personal positions were at stake.
Just as nearly thirty years earlier the magistrates of Amsterdam, just as less than ten years before the magistrates of
Groningen, they felt that they would be unable to maintain
themselves without Catholicism. That being so, they had to
take the Archdukes, and even the Spaniards, into the bargain.

And yet they imagined that they could still carry on the
old policy of opposition. Being good Netherlanders they were
offended by the servile ceremonial at court, in accordance with
which Richardot addressed the Archdukes kneeling. They
desired to supervise the Spanish troops and to have a share
in the administration of the subsidies, which they were indeed
still obstinately refusing. Then to their consternation Richardot
came to dismiss them in the name of his masters, telling them
at the same time that the subsidies asked for would be looked
upon by the Government as having obtained their consent.
In their conflicts with the true wielders of power in their own
country as well as with the true States-General in the North,
the Brussels States appeared to be no more than a shadow-
show. They vanished uttering idle protests, and thirty years
were to elapse before, in even more depressing circumstances,
they were again called together—so that they might go through
the same hollow performance once more.

The Southern Netherlands were no longer the masters of
their souls. No share was left to the people in the direction
of the country's higher interests, nor could it be otherwise
since this direction was still determined by Spain. The privi-

leged classes had to console themselves with the miserable
local self-government saved from the wreck, but a class of
national statesmen, reared in an atmosphere of active and
enlightened interest in national policy, such as existed in the
North, was beyond the reach of the enslaved Netherlands.

Battle was joined once more between the Northern States-
General and the Archdukes, who indeed stood for Spain. It
has been briefly noticed above that the respective forces kept
each other balanced on land. Philip III's zeal for the war
equalled that of his father, but Spain was too severely exhausted
to be able to profit by the isolation into which the Republic
was falling. It was considered necessary, first of all, to get hold
of Ostend. Maurice's invasion of Flanders had shown up the
dangers inherent in the continued occupation of that place by
the Northerners. The States of Flanders raised special subsidies in order to be rid of that post from whence a wide circle
of their country could be laid under contribution. But as the
defending troops could be continually supplied, strengthened,
and replaced, owing to the free communication by sea with
the North, the siege, to the astonishment of Europe, was
dragged out for three years and swallowed treasures of blood
and money. While the enemy was being kept riveted to that
place, Maurice took Grave and Rheinberg (the latter town had
changed hands once more since he ejected the Spanish garrison in 1597), and just before the end Aardenburg and Sluis.
By the capture of these two places south of the Scheldt the
menace to Zealand was eliminated, the approaches to Antwerp
were more strongly guarded, and new *points d'appui* were
gained, not less useful than Ostend itself, for laying the Flemish
country-side under contribution.

The man to whom in 1604 the blackened ruins that had
been Ostend were surrendered was Ambrosio Spinola, of
Genoa, who had come, with his brother Federigo, to place
his fortune and his talents at the service of Spain and of the
Catholic Church. Federigo, who some years earlier had conducted his own Mediterranean galleys to Sluis, had already
been killed when Ambrosio was entrusted with the direction
of the siege and showed himself to be a born general. In 1605

Philip III compelled the Archduke to leave the command-in-chief to Spinola. At the same time the Genoese upstart, created Marquess and Knight of the Fleece, was designated to be the King's Governor in the Netherlands in case the sickly Albert came to die. The childless Archdukes were overshadowed by the brilliant stranger who enjoyed the confidence of Spain. Hardly the semblance of independence was left.

In the two years following upon the conquest of Ostend, when, moreover, the international situation had grown even more unfavourable for the North owing to the peace concluded between Spain and England after Elizabeth's death, Spinola led his army against the eastern frontier of the Republic. He proved to be a formidable adversary. Maurice followed his movements carefully all the time, secured the Ysel against an attack with masterly tactics, but avoided any direct engagement. In 1606 Spinola, after having recaptured Grol, marched away to take Rheinberg once more. In his absence Maurice lost no time in laying siege to Grol, but when Spinola, even though his army was weakened by yet another mutiny and his troops thoroughly fatigued, returned to drive him away, he broke up at once without giving battle. This made a painful impression in the Republic. The year ended with Oldenzaal and Grol in Spanish hands.

On both sides meanwhile the feeling was growing in intensity that no decision could be come to in this way. The net result of nine summer campaigns (1598–1606) was a few towns gained and a few towns lost. Nothing was altered in the large lines of the situation. The statesmen of the Republic felt concern about the state of the finances. Much more depressing, however, was the condition of the subjected Netherlands, and the Archdukes were longing for the end of a war which seemed to hold out no prospects. Spain, too, was panting for breath. The penury of the public exchequer became unbearable. The young navy of the States—it was in 1607 that Heemskerk's fleet carried out its famous coup off Gibraltar—gave rise to fears for the safety of the Spanish Plate Fleets from America. Spinola himself was discouraged and wished for peace in order to get back the large sums of money he had advanced to Spain.

e. CONCLUSION OF THE TWELVE YEARS' TRUCE

The first moves were made as early as 1606. The States replied that no negotiations were possible so long as the other side continued to maintain any claims conflicting with the resolution of abjuration of 1581 and with the established right of the Netherlands, which had been recognized as a free state by the greatest kingdoms. So the Archdukes signed a statement in which they expressed their readiness to negotiate with the United Netherlands

in the capacity of, and as taking them for, free lands, provinces, and towns, against which they claim nothing.

On that basis an armistice was at once concluded in April 1607 on conditions wholly favourable to the North. It still cost some trouble to obtain the assent of Spain, and so it was not until February 1608 that peace negotiations could begin at The Hague. There was now no longer even a pretence that it was the representatives of the South Netherlands people who came to meet the Hague States-General. The preliminary exploration of the ground had been made for the Brussels Government by Dutch-speaking Netherlanders, of whom the Brabander Father Neyen became the best known, and he continued to play a very secondary part in the latter stages. But throughout, everything was done in the name of the Archdukes and of Spain. During the negotiations proper Spinola and Richardot were at the head of a delegation representing Philip III as well as Albert and Isabella. It was agreed fairly easily, although the Archdukes had hoped to get back the fragments of Flanders and Brabant occupied by the States by exchanging them for Oldenzaal and Grol, that the territorial separation would be effected on the principle of *uti possidetis*. The demand which resulted in a deadlock was one in which only Spanish interests were concerned, although Richardot had to stand by it. It was the demand that the North Netherlanders should abandon the navigation to the Indies. There also was a serious dispute over the position of Catholics in the Republic. Philip III (and in this no doubt the Archdukes were whole-heartedly with him) felt that it was due to his honour to obtain freedom of worship for his co-religionists; the States, however, declined all interference with their domestic arrangements. Yet the really unsurmountable obstacle was the question of the Indian trade, and in September the negotiators left The Hague. France and England, however, who had played the part of mediators throughout, now intervened somewhat more emphatically. Now that peace appeared to be unattainable, they put pressure on the States to consent to a truce for a number of years.

Public opinion in the Republic was violently agitated. There was a war party, which had from the first followed the negotiations with vociferous suspiciousness, launching bitter attacks and insinuations against Oldenbarnevelt, whom everyone knew to be the moving spirit. A stream of pamphlets burst forth. From the pulpit there resounded denunciations of the bad patriots. To many zealots any treaty with Spain appeared to be a betrayal of the cause of the revolt. It cannot indeed be denied that a truce or a peace, concluded while the Spaniards still kept their grip on the Southern Netherlands, signified an acquiescence in the partial failure of the national programme. But was it possible for the Republic, especially now that France and England were threatening their displeasure, to bear the financial burden of a continuation of the war, let alone to drive the Spaniards out of the Southern Netherlands? Maurice's last campaigns were hardly of a nature to inspire any such hopes.

Yet Maurice, after having privately worked against Oldenbarnevelt's policy for some time, in September 1608 openly came forward as leader of the war party. The letter which he sent out to the States of those provinces of which he was Stadtholder deserves our attention. Uttering a warning against the deceitfulness of the Spaniards, he merely pleaded for the necessity of an absolute recognition on their part of the independence of the United Provinces—that is to say, he declared against the compromise of a truce. It would, in his opinion, result in an ambiguous situation, in a "reunion" full of dangers. That is all he had to say on the question of Netherlands unity. The hope that Flanders and Brabant could still be liberated, and especially that they could still be united on the only terms acceptable to the war party, namely, through Protestantization—that hope had become faint indeed after the disappointment of the Flanders expedition and the negotiations of Bergen-op-Zoom.

The objections to the truce came mainly from those who in the spirit were living in an earlier period, when the party of resistance, strongly impregnated with Calvinist zeal, still had to found the state. Those men had difficulty in adapting themselves to the new situation in which the state existed and in which the need was for normal conditions. Maurice still felt that his own position and the entire constitution of the state were the products of the war, and were dependent upon it for their consolidation. In the letter mentioned above he gave as a principal reason why it was impossible to do without Spain's absolute recognition of Northern Netherlands independence, the following:

in order to make it plain to our own citizens that they must not expect another sun to rise, which, failing that recognition, they will be told will happen.

Van Meteren is even more explicit when he writes that fears were entertained especially on account of

those of Gelderland, Overysel, and Groningen, who had come to arms under compulsion; in which provinces the nobility has the most votes, and these, having their possessions in the country-side, would keep out of the danger [of a renewal of the war] and seek the support of the most powerful.

Maurice's attitude in this affair brought him the acclamations of the very groups against which in the days of Leicester he had let himself be used, and which were now overjoyed to see him make a stand against their old enemy Oldenbarnevelt. Only it should not be thought that what this party wanted was a restoration of the Netherlands community which the war had torn asunder. No doubt the Flemings and Brabanders, in so far as they belonged to the Reformed Church, still constituted a chief support of the ministers who were now again fulminating against the States. In their new surroundings they still hung together as a distinct group, with which orthodoxy and an irreconcilable hatred of Spain had become traditional. At the same time, however, most of them were now too well off in Holland and Zealand to worry seriously about returning to the South, even though their acquiescence was mingled with that wistfulness which is suppressed but not concealed in some beautiful lines of Van Mander. After having recalled the church spire of his native village in Flanders, the poet says:

> But this is done. I now will deceive myself
> And consider all that country covered with salt sea.
> To have exchanged it for this is now no sorrow to me.

Van Mander, it should be added, was not a Calvinist, but a Baptist. All that the bitter-enders were able to do, at any rate, was to make even more irretrievable the moral separation which had already entered upon the heels of the political events. If need be they would admit the accomplished fact of the re-Catholicization of the South, but in their eagerness to complete the Protestantization of the North they looked upon the resumption of normal relations as so much the more objectionable.

Inevitably material interests were mixed up with these considerations of a higher nature. Powerful groups saw their advantage in a continuation of the war. In the first place the military; next the privateers, in whose activities the Zealand trading world was deeply concerned; also the war contractors of all descriptions. Finally, there were those who had for a considerable time already been preparing for the foundation of a West Indies Company, a project directed against Spain's own colonial territory in America, and which Oldenbarnevelt therefore, as soon as the negotiations were opened, strove to suppress. The Antwerper Usselinx was the fervent propagandist of that scheme. In his imagination he saw prosperous settlements, which would transplant to America Netherlands nationality and Reformed religion, thus providing the mother country with vigorous assistance as well as with valuable markets. Unfortunately the theory of colonization, such as Usselinx developed it in masterly pamphlets, never appealed to the rulers of the North Netherlands state, and the Amsterdamers who made use of his services certainly were more interested in privateering raids at the expense of the Spanish colonies than in the founding of settlements of their own race. In any case the project was inconsistent with either peace or truce, and it had therefore to give way before the need of rest which actuated Oldenbarnevelt's policy, and which, indeed, was so generally felt that the opposition to the negotiations proved to be a good deal less firm that it was violent. Even before the end of the year 1608 Maurice, Zealand, and Amsterdam accepted the inevitable, and in March 1609, after further conversations at Antwerp, a truce was concluded for a period of twelve years.

It was for the Seven Provinces an astonishing victory. On practically every point that had been under discussion the Archdukes and Spain gave way. The recognition of independence with which the negotiations had opened (and which, even though on account of the word *as* it could not be called absolute, actually left little to be desired) was repeated. Trade with the Indies was not explicitly prohibited. The Catholics in the North obtained no protection, except, by a separate agreement, those in the districts torn from Brabant, which the States-General kept. The Scheldt was not explicitly thrown open for navigation to and from Antwerp. To the Southern Netherlands the treaty gave nothing but twelve years of rest. How much more did it give to the Northern provinces!

There the Netherlands race had acquired a territory—unfortunately no more than half of that on which it had a claim in nature—where, under its own political direction, it could form its own civilization. The Republic had succeeded in maintaining its independence, in the course of a generation of war, against the most powerful monarchy of the world. More, that empire had almost bled to death from the wound it had received in the Netherlands. The self-confidence of the North Netherlands people was heightened, and indeed the other European Powers, too, were impressed, when they saw proud Spain in so much need of a breathing-space as to submit to the humiliations of the Treaty of Truce. The territory of the States—the entire history of the last thirty-seven years went to prove it and is itself explained by the fact—was strongly situated. The eastern frontier was now lightly encroached upon once more, and in any case was not yet based very firmly upon the great rivers—the Rhine being in States' possession only up to Schenkenschans, the Maas only up to Grave. But apart from that, the natural strategic lines of defence had not only been attained but had been confirmed by the occupation of posts beyond. The States had even continued the movement of expansion of the Burgundian-Habsburg rulers, and had pushed on outside the seventeen provinces. Rheinberg had not ultimately remained in their possession, but, making use of the dissensions between the town of Emden and the pro-Spanish Count, they had in 1595 occupied several places in East Friesland. This looked like the beginning of an annexation, and in any case directed the political life of that country towards The Hague for a long time to come. Everywhere the Netherlands remaining under Spain had been pushed back from the water, except for the seacoast, which from Heist to Grevelingen had now been freed from States' occupation. But this flat and straight Flemish coast had never been the true entrance to the country. That was the Scheldt, which on both sides was held by the States—albeit with the English for the time being at Flushing—and in spite of a general guarantee of free intercourse between North and South in the Treaty of Truce, the States, and especially the States of Zealand, took advantage of their position to force any ships on their way from or to Antwerp to break cargo. Antwerp remained a big dead town. It was now mainly the motive of commercial competition that inspired the Scheldt policy of the Hollanders and Zealanders, but the original motive had been a different one and it still counted: Antwerp could not be left free to become a busy port again, where a native merchant fleet might be developed, as long as it was not what nature had meant it to be, a Netherlands town, but on the contrary was a weapon in Spanish hands.

Next to the geographical configuration of their country, it was to their superiority at sea and on the rivers that the Northerners owed their independence. Under the provisions the Truce, which left to the States the most part of the river-courses in the Netherlands as well as all the estuaries and sea arms, and which, moreover, did not prevent their navigation to the Indies, that superiority could be fully developed—and always with the help of the trading resources in men and capital that had been wilfully expelled from the South. In the next generation or two the Republic was thus to rise to undreamt-of heights of prosperity and power, but it must be added that the international constellation created, during most of that time, exceptionally favourable circumstances.

Yet these could not but be temporary. As soon as they began to fail the Republic, it became apparent that she, with all her advantages of situation and of trade, was a small-sized state, very small indeed in the midst of the Great Powers of Europe. North Netherlands historians have often praised the fate by which the forces of the whole of the Netherlands people were drawn together on that small territory north of the rivers, since as a consequence this narrow strip of land became the scene of an incomparable splendour of political, economic, and intellectual life. This view betrays a sad lack of imagination. Those whom it satisfies must turn a blind eye on the political, economic, and intellectual misery which that concentration was to bring to the southern half of the Netherlands people. We shall in our last chapter see something of the contrast that was provided during the last decades of our period by the buoyant intellectual activity in the North and the desolation in the South. It would be difficult indeed to look upon that unnatural spectacle and rejoice.

It is true that at the time the North seemed so much the darling of fortune that not even the emigrant Flemings and Brabanders could fully realize that the split was a disaster to the Netherlands people as a whole. As a matter of fact the consequences to the South were without comparison heavier. Brabant and Flanders, only a generation earlier the heart of the Netherlands people, the rich source out of which had been drawn so many of the best forces now helping to build up the young state in the North, were lying overpowered and disheartened, under the cloak of a national Government subjected more helplessly than ever to a foreign ruler and destined only to serve his policy. No doubt the Catholic spirit, which owed to the conqueror its triumphant return, again possessed spiritual creativeness now that it had been rejuvenated by the Counter-Reformation. As soon as the worst war misery had subsided, during the Truce, a cultural life of marked character grew up in the South, Antwerp and Leuven being the centres. But circumstances were really too unpropitious. The deadness of economic life, the lack of independence paralysing political life, the renewed conjunction with the Walloon provinces under a foreign court, the gallicized nobility possessing greater influence than ever, and this at a time when the war and the difference of religion were raising obstacles in the intellectual intercourse with the suddenly emancipated North—all these factors could not but weigh heavily, to the detriment of the entire Dutch-speaking community, on the civilization of Dutch-speaking Flanders and Brabant.

In addition to this the unnatural restriction of its territory involved dangers for the North and its state and society. Exhaustion soon followed upon the overstrain of "the golden age"; that splendour was short-lived. Speaking politically, the weakness of the Southern Netherlands was very far from being an unmixed benefit to the Dutch Republic. That unhappy country was but a fragment of the Burgundian state which fate had overtaken in its rise, a fragment with indefensible frontiers, which, as it were, offered a standing invitation to invaders. Had the Archdukes been able to pursue a truly South Netherlandish policy, they would have sought the friendship of the North in order to be covered on one side at least. Since they were but the agents of Spain, the war with the Republic was resumed after the Truce, and the menace of France, reinvigorated under Richelieu, held therefore the greater danger. Long before the peace of Munster, the northward expansion of France at the expense of the Southern Netherlands began to rouse uneasiness at The Hague.

I

No more proof can be required that the split of the Nether-lands had not merely weakened the powers of resistance of the Southern provinces, but that it had compromised the safety of the whole of the Netherlands race, which in the Middle Ages already had found in Flanders a bulwark against the French advance.

After the account given in the last three chapters it is un-necessary to subject to a set criticism the view, which has long been current, and according to which the split was determined by some inherent divergence within the Netherlands people. A Protestant North (not without numerous Catholics however) and a Catholic South were not predetermined by the natures of the populations. Those two great cultural currents of Catholicism and Protestantism originally mingled their courses in both North and South. It was only the outcome of strife, of war with the foreign ruler, which brought about that fatal redistribution of forces which was to estrange the two regions for so long. That outcome was not determined by any greater courage possessed by the North, or even by Holland and Zealand alone (for the conventional view conveniently over-looks the fact that the Eastern provinces had to be reconquered for the Republic by force). That outcome was determined by the great rivers. Brabant and Flanders lay open for the enemy, and soon therefore their Protestants went to strengthen those in the impregnable river area. Gelderland, Overysel, and Groningen, much less affected by Protestantism than Flanders and Brabant, could not be held for the Catholic Church because the swords of Parma and of Spinola lost their striking-force when stretched precariously beyond the rivers.

North Netherlands historians have been slow to see these matters in their true colours, because the dazzling brilliance of the Dutch seventeenth century prevented them, as it had prevented contemporaries, from discerning failure in the course of events. National and Protestant self-consciousness, more-over, seemed to require the carrying through of a contrast as against "Belgians" and Catholics. Certain Belgian historians, on their side, wanting to give a respectable historical back-ground to present-day Belgium, which they look upon as the natural state organism for both Walloons and Flemings, cannot but welcome the emergence of the Southern Netherlands, which I pictured as an indefensible and subjected fragment, but in which present-day Belgium can for the first time be unmistakably recognized. To them this must be an inevitable development—nay, a fulfilment.

We need not occupy ourselves with views which are so clearly artificial and inspired by later political prejudice. The split was a disaster brought upon the Netherlands race by foreign domination. Time was to show what misfortunes lay hidden in the situation that resulted from it.

REVOLUTIONS IN NETHERLANDS CIVILIZATION

About the middle of the sixteenth century one revolution was, as has been described above, well under way. The Renaissance had made its entry from more southerly regions. Painters and architects were eager to carry out the precepts of Italy. In literature the new spirit as yet manifested itself mainly in feeble imitations, although we saw the first signs of a better understanding of the true meaning of the Renaissance in the opposition to the bourgeois and moralizing prosiness of the Rhetoricians and in the attempts of some daring spirits to stand on their own feet. But this great change was not to be left to run its course undisturbed and in accordance with its own laws. From the start two other revolutions interfered with it: firstly, the Reformation; and secondly, the political troubles, which about the middle of the period under review led to a forcible shifting of the cultural centre within the Dutch-speaking Netherlands.

As far as the Reformation is concerned, it is true that the first thing to be noticed is the length of time during which it continued side by side with the Renaissancist intellectual movement without making much impression on it. The two great movements were in many respects intrinsically antagonistic. The Renaissance was fundamentally worldly. Full of admiration for the old pagan civilization, it accepted life and nature, and its joyful cult was devoted to beauty. Often beauty was conceived in an exuberantly sensuous manner, and the worshippers revelled in a fullness and richness of expression which seem to us excessive. The life of that generation was in all its manifestations permeated by this spirit, and the surprising thing to us is the absence of any clear consciousness of the contrast between it and the moral tendency of Protestantism. The gorgeous displays of the Rhetoricians, for which on great social occasions poets and painters lent their services, bore the same character whether they were intended to celebrate the entries, into Brussels or Antwerp or The Hague, of Orange, Anjou, Leicester, or of Matthew, Ernest, Albert, and Isabella. These were the externals of Renaissance civilization which could most readily be brought to the attention of the masses. Behind them there was a keen and courageous intellectual activity; individuality, arising eagerly, asserted itself. These intellectual tendencies were doubtless closely allied with the forces that were breaking up Catholic unity, but no sooner had the new Church been organized than it attempted to ban within narrow limits the searching spirit to which in part it owed its existence. And even more definitely did that Church range itself against the sensual inclinations of the Renaissance. In Calvinism was reborn the ideal of primitive Christianity, according to which truth, having been revealed, could do without the free development of human reason, and nature and the world were of the devil.

But as' has been suggested, that conflict did not come to light at once. In the minds of many men of that period the principles of the Renaissance and of the Reformation lived peacefully together. As long as the Reformation appeared to be primarily a movement of opposition against the tyranny of Spain and Rome, we are struck by the vigour with which the forces of the mind continued to strive after freedom and beauty; and this in spite of the rival claims made on spiritual and intellectual energy by rebellion and war, and by vehement theological disputes. But as soon as the Reformation had apparently triumphed, those who most truly embodied the new ecclesiastical conception, the ministers of the Word, entered upon a systematic struggle with the forces of the time and attempted to fetter society and civilization afresh. Then it became clear at once that the intellectual movement, however completely it had seemed to be under the influence of the Reformation, followed the impulse of its own principles. The roots of the Netherlandish civilization which was now beginning to blossom north of the rivers extended not only outside the region to which Parma's armies restricted its growth, but also outside the religion which was aspiring after dominion in the young Republic. Liberty was dearer to the hearts of poets and thinkers than orthodoxy, and neither they nor the artists could regard the world, man, and nature as mere corruption outside God.

Considered by themselves, the ministers of religion present an important and highly characteristic appearance in the Netherlandish cultural movement of the second half of the sixteenth century. In the cult of Catholicism the sermon had never held a very conspicuous place, even though, for instance, the Dominicans had always made much of it, and the Modern Devotion had frequently made direct appeals in the popular language to the hearts and minds of the faithful. In the Reformed cult the sermon, along with psalm-singing, counted for everything. It was Dathenus, the Flemish minister, whose translation opened up the world of the psalms to the Netherlands people. Meanwhile the preachers up and down the country expounded to the congregations that Biblical view of life which taught the Reformed to look upon themselves as the chosen people, as the New Israel. This concept became a source of confidence and courage to them, and on it they built up their strong and narrow national sentiment. The influence which was thus exercised by the Reformed ministry cannot easily be overestimated, but as soon as we direct our attention more particularly to literature, art, and scholarship, we are struck by the paucity of strict Calvinists among the leaders in those spheres.

This latter development can be traced to its natural conclusion only in the Northern Netherlands, although the origins, as we know, are to be found in the South no less. Parma's conquest for a while concentrated all living cultural forces on the northern section of the Dutch linguistic area, preparing at the same time for the civilization of the South a future on the basis of the Counter-Reformation. There is no organic connection at all between his interference and Netherlands intellectual life; it was extraneous and by its nature physical and accidental. Yet it created insurmountable barriers in what ought to have been a continuous development, and we cannot but accept in our survey of the civilization of the period the division which is marked by them.

a. BEFORE THE SPLIT

During the first decades of Philip II's reign, Netherlands unity manifested itself in the sphere of intellectual life no less freely than in the political agitation which swept all the provinces along with it. As of old, it was in Flanders and Brabant that the heart-beat was strongest; yet its rhythm made itself felt ever more insistently in the North, especially in Holland.

In painting, little that was new appeared in the years before the great parting, except that Breughel, whom I mentioned above, came to his full development only then. But Breughel was a figure apart from the fashion of the time, which was to be a slave to Italianism and classicism for many years to come. Coxie and Frans Floris were still regarded as the great men. Good work was done in portraiture by Frans Pourbus and Adriaan Key, who both lived at Antwerp. But far superior to them was a master who, in a way very different from that of Breughel, remained somewhat outside the general movement of Netherlandish art—namely, the Utrechter Antonie Mor, one of the greatest portrait-painters that the country has ever produced. There is in his work a subtlety and a distinction which are entirely foreign to the bourgeois society of the Netherlands and which obviously owe much to Italian schooling, and yet Mor cannot be described as Italianate. He came to be the painter of the aristocracy, and the Dutch-speaking area soon grew too small for him. Even Antwerp could not retain him for long. He worked a great deal at the King's Court in Spain; even to-day his name is generally given in a Spanish form (Antonio Moro). Philip himself, Alva and Granvelle sat to him.

In architecture attempts were still being made to reconcile the rules taken over from Italy with the native traditions. A purely classicist current maintained itself, of which the little town hall at The Hague, built in 1565, is an example. But side by side with this a more playful and whimsical style was developed, which left greater room to the display of native character. The most famous building of the period was the town hall of Antwerp, built in 1564 by Cornelis de Vriendt, a brother of the painter Frans Floris; and although the ordering was rather severe, so that the whole building makes a somewhat chilly impression, it yet contains decorative detail which, though really incongruous, was to have a great future in the Netherlands. The influence which spread from the Antwerp town hall was considerable; yet if the bold decorative effects which broke through the severe classicist style were soon to be adopted all over the country, this was largely due to the inexhaustible inventiveness of the designer, Hans Vredeman de Vries. Born in the North—de Vries means the Frisian, and, in fact, Vredeman's father was a German mercenary soldier who came to Friesland with Albert of Saxony and settled there—Vredeman de Vries worked mostly in the South, in Antwerp and Brussels, until Parma's conquest drove him to Germany. There, too, his influence made itself felt, and from there we shall see it, saturated with the traditions of those parts, penetrate during our second period into the Northern Netherlands. Vredeman's work consisted mainly of collections of designs, displaying an inexhaustible fertility in variations of those cartouches and grotesques which went right against the purely classicist taste of the early Renaissance in the Netherlands and replaced its cheerful and delicate chasteness with a certain heavy luxurious exuberance. Yet at the same time he carried on the line of Coecke and proclaimed the rules of Vitruvius. The Hospital of St. John at Hoorn (1563), in which classicist window pediments are placed in a brick façade with a pointed and stepped gable, and statuary and cartouche work on the steps, is a good example of the hybrid building which sometimes resulted. Vredeman himself never attained to a profound harmonizing of the various elements, but he nevertheless did great service in preparing the way for the really brilliant, if brief, period of Netherlandish architecture the beginnings of which we shall notice in our last paragraph.

In literature, too, the noteworthy events during the sixties and seventies took place in the South. It was not a time of great achievement in this sphere. But from the point of view of later developments it was undeniably most important that attempts were made to give Dutch verse mastery over the new

Renaissance forms—real mastery, moreover, which would not
rest content with the superficial imitation in which the Rhetoricians took pleasure. These attempts were made by some
South Netherlandish poets, especially De Heere, of Ghent,
and Van der Noot, of Antwerp. They scarcely produced
beautiful poetry, and moreover the results of their pioneer
labour were largely lost in the convulsion caused by rebellion
and reconquest. Before we glance at their work, which was
solely intended to serve literature, and which will always
appeal to those who come to the past with minds set on literary
discovery, some attention must be given to the numerous
writings to which the troubles themselves gave rise. Sometimes
the writers, with no conscious literary intention, yet by true
passion and profound humanity, achieved literature.

I am inclined to mention in this connection Marnix van
St. Aldegonde and even Dirk Volkertszoon Coornhert. Both the
Brabant nobleman and the Haarlem engraver and notary
public were certainly writers of exceptional gifts, both attended
most carefully to problems of style—both, for instance, purged
their language of the foreign words in which the Rhetoricians
indulged and which sound so hateful to modern Dutch ears;
but to both public affairs and the questions which agitated
the people were the principal incitement to writing. Marnix
was inspired by his hatred of popery and zeal for the Reformation; Coornhert by his aversion from all coercion of conscience,
including that applied by the Reformed, and by his yearning
after rational philosophical convictions in the midst of the
theological disputes that raged all round him. Coornhert, born
in 1522, and so older than any of the other writers here mentioned, did not reach his full development until the second
period discussed in this chapter. Marnix, too, who was born
in 1538, completed his translation of the psalms only during
the retirement following upon the cutting short of his political
career after the surrender of Antwerp; but his *Beehive of the
Holy Roman Church* appeared as early as 1570. In this virulent
pamphlet Dutch prose was for the first time employed for the
purpose of bitter satire, and this by a man who was at home in
French and classic literature. It goes without saying that not

even the truest passion or the profoundest humanity will always enable writers to express themselves in literature. If an example were needed, Dathenus' translation of the psalms —made in 1566, not after the original, but after Marot—would suffice. No more deplorable hack work can be imagined, and it says little for the literary discrimination in Reformed circles that this translation was not only adopted by the new Church, but actually retained for two centuries despite the claims of several better versions.

Many Beggar songs are little better, yet taken as a whole these productions of mostly anonymous poets constitute a collection for which Dutch literature has reason to be grateful. Now hopeful, then despondent, stately or vehement, expressing scorn or hatred, sorrow or confidence, these songs preserve the memory of an arresting period of Netherlands history with a freshness unequalled by chronicles or documents. The North, which alone won independence during that period, has as it were appropriated that treasure, of which the *Wilhelmus* song is the most precious jewel. Yet Flemings and Brabanders had their share in making the songs no less than in doing the deeds which gave rise to them, and the *Wilhelmus* itself is almost certainly the work of a Brabander, possibly of Marnix.

Many of these songs were made by Rhetoricians who were swept beyond the narrowness of rhetorical convention by the compelling reality of their theme. But at the same time that convention was still diligently pursued in the Chambers, numbers of which continued to flourish in spite of the suspicion with which they were regarded by the Government. They took themselves with profound seriousness, these Rhetoricians, and if they were to be believed, the collection of moralities published after the Antwerp Land Jubilee of 1561 proved that, compared with former times,

wits in these Netherlands are brighter, all arts plied with greater skill; many are the poets, and the lovers of literature without number; so that one might truly say that Mount Parnassus now rises up in our midst and *Castalides Nimphae* have chosen this country as their dwelling-place.

The brightest of all these bright wits was in the judgment of the "lovers of literature," or rather of Rhetoric, Jan Baptista Houwaert. Homer, Virgil, Ovid, Petrarch—no venerated name sounded too great to be applied to Houwaert. In sober truth he was a rhymer of the usual pattern, who tried in vain to invigorate his spineless verse and to add lustre and an appearance of modernity to his conventional thought by a liberal use of classicist allusions and foreign words. By his very addiction to foreign words he proved himself to be a poet of the old stamp. A Brusseler of good family, the owner of a country house in the Sonien Forest, Houwaert, like so many others, was in 1568 imprisoned in the Treurenborch by the Blood Council and cruelly maltreated. In those days he inclined to the heresy then current. In 1577 we saw him act as organizer of the festivities on the occasion of the Prince of Orange's entry into Brussels. But later on, in 1594, he acted in the same capacity when the Archduke Ernest made his entry. At that time he was a councillor in the Brabant Chamber of Accounts and obedient to both Roman Church and Spanish Government.

North Netherlandish historians have sometimes applied scornful conclusions drawn from Houwaert's career to the character of the South Netherlandish people as a whole. They forget that, had political disasters overtaken the North, his type, which is of all nations, would inevitably have made its appearance there too. How many exiles could be quoted, on the other hand, to prove that Flanders and Brabant were not the homes of time-servers only, but of characters of a more stubborn type! This much may be said, however, that the political vicissitudes of Flanders and Brabant had a depressing effect on the tone of the intellectual life in those provinces. It was not Catholicism, or the Counter-Reformation either, it was the defeat and the restored authority of the foreigner: men had to bow down or be broken.

The lives of the two poets to whom I alluded when mentioning the development of Dutch prosody contain further striking illustrations of this fact. For although the inspiration of those men was essentially literary, this does not mean that they could keep aloof from the great religious and political revolution of their time, or that the conditions of their whole being were not, partly at least, shaped thereby.

Lucas de Heere was a painter of Ghent (1534–84), who, in a volume published in 1565, *The Garden and Orchard of Poetry*, had been the first to try the strict iambic metre, and who wrote odes, epigrams, and even sonnets. Soon afterwards he had to flee to England on account of his religious convictions. Having returned after the Pacification he accepted an official position in his native town, to die soon after the recapture by Parma during a second exile. Different, but hardly more enviable, was the fate of Jonkheer Jan van der Noot, "patricius of Antwerp" (1538–95). In 1566 and 1567 Van der Noot had been conspicuous among the most zealous Calvinists; during his exile—also in England—he manifested as bitter a hatred of Catholicism as did Marnix himself. But exile and poverty broke his conviction though not his pride, or at least his pretensions: on his return after the Pacification he conducted himself as a Catholic once more; and after Parma's reconquest of Antwerp, which he applauded, his Catholicism became positively fervent. Meanwhile he begged the administrations under successive regimes for support in his need, and occasionally received a small sum, both on account of his rank and because of

his great industry in imitating the French poets.

Van der Noot was a more important poet than De Heere. He too experimented and played with the new forms, and he did so with less visible effort, with greater mastery. The replacement of the old free verse by the iambic metre which, as it was put, involved "counting the feet," had a deeper significance than might be thought at first sight. It was one more sign of the desire of that generation for order and discipline in the conduct of their mental affairs, it was a means of expressing their joyful sense of having gained a firmer control over themselves and over life than was possessed by their predecessors. In this way it was a European phenomenon.

But in these Dutch poets the dependence on the French is marked indeed. Van der Noot not only repeatedly imitated

Ronsard, his ambition was to do for Dutch literature what the *Pléiade*—for he had mov d on beyond Marot—had done for French literature. It was through them that he came to Petrarch. It was with their eyes that he read the classics. Their sense of the high value of the poet's office, their proud consciousness of speaking for the ages—in a man who had not really anything to say, all this became a hollow pose. A delicate sense of verse, that undoubtedly Van der Noot possessed, but what he lacked (possibly the time, too stern for poetry, destroyed it in him) was character. In his volumes *Theatre* and *The Thicket* of about 1568, in his great work of 1579, the *Olympias*, Van der Noot won new beauties for the Dutch language such as were not dreamt of by his friend Houwaert. Unlike the Brussels councillor, he never, for all his imitation of the French poets, indulged in the abuse of Romance word forms. But the fame of this other Homer, Virgil, and Petrarch (the comparisons in this case are his own) penetrated but little beyond a small group of adulators, so that with the catastrophe which soon came to upset the intellectual life of Antwerp his work sank into deep oblivion.

In science and scholarship, too, the South maintained down to that catastrophe its supremacy among the provinces of Dutch speech. In those spheres the middle of the sixteenth century was a rich and vital time. The scientific sense of the men of the Renaissance, their appreciation of facts and their courage in facing logical consequences undeterred by respect for tradition or fear of authority, were no longer manifested only in the literary criticism of the classical authors, in which the humanists had exercised those qualities. In art a similar attitude of mind had long won triumphs. Now men came in the same way to the study of nature and of the world around them. Netherlanders took a brisk part in that activity. For many years there lived at Mechlin, his native town, the physician, Rembert Dodoens (born in 1517), who, in 1554, published at Antwerp a work on botany in the popular language (*Het Cruyd Boeck*), which helped to lay the foundation for the scientific treatment of that subject. He lived to see several later editions through the press, mostly in Latin; his own name he latinized into Dodonaeus. At an advanced age he went to Vienna to take up the post of Court physician to the Emperor, and towards the end of his life he answered a call from the University of Leyden. A man of even greater significance was Mercator (Gerard de Cremer), who was born at Rupelmonde in 1512, learned the geography of Aprianus of Ingolstadt from the Frisian Gemma at Leuven, and at a very early age founded in the last-named town an institute for cartography and geometrical instruments. Having been troubled by the Inquisition in 1544, Mercator spent the remainder of his life at Duisberg under the protection of the Duke of Cleve. His maps and atlases excelled in the careful incorporation of all the knowedge about distant and nearby countries then available, but, moreover, he introduced new methods which helped the science of geography to make further progress. At Antwerp lived his colleague Abraham Ortels, a little younger than he (Ortelius, 1527–98), and a less original mind, but whose *Theatrum Orbis Terrarum*, a large world atlas, achieved an enormous success (1570; Dutch edition, 1571). It was published in all languages and a popularized version in Dutch by Pieter Heyns of Antwerp became almost equally famous. Ortelius was a man of means with many scientific interests, who was in correspondence with a large number of scholars in the Netherlands and abroad. His cabinet of "medals" became one of the curiosities which visitors to Antwerp must see. The antiquarian and engraver, Hubert Goltzius (born at Venlo in 1526, generally living at Brugge), had assisted him in forming the collection.

A man who did more even to make a centre of learning of the great town was Christophe Plantin, a Frenchman (born in 1524) who founded a printing business at Antwerp about the middle of the century which was destined to become world-famous. He established his reputation by the publication, with papal sanction and royal support, of a Bible in the original languages together with the Latin translation. It was a work in many volumes, on which huge sums were spent, and a number of scholars were engaged on it for years. The financial success of the firm rested on the monopoly which Plantin obtained, in all the Spanish lands, of liturgical books printed in accordance with the precepts of Trent. But this royal and Catholic publisher belonged in secret, as did Ortelius also, to a heretical sect, "the Family of Love." He had no difficulty in adapting himself to the changes occurring at Antwerp in his lifetime. After 1576 he became printer to the States-General and to the town, in 1583 even to the University of Leyden; and yet after 1585 he returned to Antwerp to spend his last days in the strictly Catholic atmosphere of the subjected town. His son-in-law Moretus (Moerentorff), who was to continue it after his death, had by that time acquired a large share in the direction of the firm. But Plantin had rendered his greatest services to learning before 1585. It was he who published the later editions of Dodoens, as of Ortelius, Guicciardini's description of the Netherlands, and the works of Hubert Goltzius. Furthermore his fund contained Hebrew dictionaries, collections of laws and ordinances, and the works of the great Latinist, Justus Lipsius (1547–1606). Lipsius was a Brabander, who left Leuven when it was threatened in 1577 by the Spanish troops, to go and add lustre to the young University of Leyden. Disturbed by the disputations with which theologizing Holland resounded, he was to return later on, in 1591, to Leuven, which had then found security under Parma. Since 1558 Plantin employed as corrector Cornelis van Kiel (Kilianus, 1528–1607), who issued in 1574 his famous Dutch dictionary, to the third impression of which he gave in 1599 the title of *Etymologicon Theutonicae Linguae*.

In these two men, Lipsius and Kilianus, the renowned professor and the simple amateur, may be seen the representatives of two currents in the Netherlands Renaissance which, sprung from the same source and frequently mingling their courses, are yet clearly to be distinguished, and of which one was in the long run to have a much more fertilizing effect on Netherlands civilization than the other.

Justus Lipsius was a high priest of that cult of the ancient civilization out of which the renovation of intellectual life had largely arisen. At this juncture, it found equally zealous worshippers, but—more than had been the case some generations earlier—they worshipped for devotion's own sake. It is true we saw Maurice and William Louis studying Caesar for lessons in military tactics, and Vitruvius proclaimed as a guide for architects. Yet the great humanists themselves rarely made so immediate a connection with practical life, they did not grapple so powerfully with the ideas of their contemporaries as their predecessors, such as Wessel Gansfort or Erasmus, had done. A man like Lipsius certainly got involved in the theological strife of his time—more so than was agreeable to him—but it was simply as a Latinist, as a master of conjectural criticism, as the editor of Tacitus and Seneca, that he was venerated. We find it hard to understand the almost superstitious respect with which a great classicist was surrounded; the figure which a Lipsius cut in the world leaves us puzzled. We must remember that the hopeful, vigorous, and vital Renaissance was stiffening —without the contemporaries being conscious of any change— into a mere subjection to pure Latinity. A crowd of scholars shut themselves up in an ideal world, the world of the classics; the education of the rising generation amounted to an introduction into that magic circle. The joy of discovery, which had found vent in heightened intellectual energy and love of adventure, was beginning to settle down, and a hard and fast convention was being forged, which would soon prove as cumbersome to the national movement of civilization as the first contact with the classics had been invigorating and inspiring.

There were also, however, those who applied the lessons of the ancients with a little more independence and tried to use the new methods of research and the new spirit of interpretation for the building up of the national tradition. That was done partly by means of Latin, for most humanists were unconscious of the conflict here indicated. They did not see that the exclusive use of Latin must harm the popular language and the national civilization. An example is the Hollander Adrianus Junius (1511–75), a man of an older generation than Lipsius, who praised him on account of his learning as a second Erasmus. Junius—a Haarlem physician, whose real name was De Jonghe—began a great work, entitled *Batavia*, in which he proposed to treat the oldest history of his province, of Holland.

This was, of course, an enterprise in the true spirit of the Renaissance: historical interest was stimulated, if only by the example of the classic historians, to imitate whom people turned to their own past. At first there were few signs of a really new attitude of mind. Little more criticism was applied than had been done by the medieval chroniclers, whose work was used as almost the only source. It also proved beyond the powers of vision of these writers to look across the boundaries of their own province and view the Netherlands as a whole. The name of Johannes Goropius Becanus, of Antwerp (Jan van Gorp van Hilvarenbeek; as it chanced, another physician), is still remembered for the solemn argument set out in his *Origines Antverpianae* (published by Plantin in 1569) to prove that the oldest language, from which all others are derived, is Dutch.

Interest in the popular language manifested itself in more fruitful fashion than this. It has been shown how, since the protest raised by Jan van der Werve of Ghent (which was mentioned in the introductory chapter), the best poets banned foreign words—a reform of the literary language which demanded thought as well as enthusiasm. Van de Werve's work had been continued by several others. Coornhert, for instance, sounded the alarm against the foreign intruders in 1561. Moreover, spelling rules as well as etymologies were proposed. As early as 1550 a *Nederlandsche Spellynghe* had been published at Ghent, by Joas Lambrecht; in 1576 Anton Tsestich published an *Orthographia Linguae Belgicae* (that is, of the Dutch language) at Leuven; in 1581 Pontus de Heuiter, of Delft, issued a *Nederduitsche Orthographie* with Plantin at Leyden. The mother tongue was beginning to be regarded as a worthy object of study. The importance of Kilianus lies in the fact that he more than anybody was the founder of the true scientific study of the Dutch language. He dabbled in rules and precepts less than most of his contemporaries, and apart from etymologies, which were no better than was usual at the time, his work consisted of collecting, classifying, and interpreting, all done with great care and acumen.

The scientific and scholarly movement described above was

mainly carried on in the South. Even though Lipsius returned to Leuven, and Kilianus never stirred from Antwerp, we shall see in the next paragraph that it was mainly continued in the North, partly by refugees from the South. Already in the seventies the insecurity prevailing in Brabant and Flanders interfered with the careers of scholars as well as artists and men of letters—we have come across several instances in the preceding pages. At the same time the foundation of the University of Leyden—a sign of the enhanced importance and self-confidence which resulted from Holland's separate rebellion —meant the creation of a new centre for the movement of learning in the Netherlands. With the definitive subjection of the South and the exile of so many of the most vigorous-minded Brabanders and Flemings, there ensued a veritable revolution in the respective positions of North and South, as far as their contributions to the common stock of Netherlands civilization were concerned. Nay more, the unity of that civilization itself was endangered, and a duality was introduced which was, however, too directly in conflict with Netherlands history as it had been shaping before these catastrophic events ever to be carried through to its logical conclusion.

b. AFTER THE SPLIT

In Flanders and Brabant during the eighties, as a result first of the war, then of the conquest and the emigration, all cultural activity was paralysed. Holland, on the other hand, the stronghold of the truncated Netherlands community which was still maintaining its independence under Protestant leadership, was already offering a sufficient measure of that order and security without which civilization cannot flourish. There was more than order and security; there was a brisk economic movement which, as sketched above, created prosperity in the midst of war. It was especially Amsterdam that inherited the position of Antwerp as a trading centre, but at the same time great new enterprises, partly planned by South Netherlanders, brought the rising town, and indeed the whole of Holland, into direct contact with the colonial world, increasing the intensity of intellectual, together with that of economic, life. The textile manufacturers, employers and workmen, who had left the South, settled mostly at Haarlem and Leyden, where they greatly increased the population and the trade. And while Brussels had been the capital under the alien regime of Burgundians and Habsburgs, The Hague had now become the centre of a domestic political system, essentially Netherlandish, even though the Court added a foreign note to it—not so much through the Stadtholder, who never married, and who in the summer was generally away in the field, as through his stepmother, William the Silent's widow, Louise de Coligny. In any case Holland had suddenly become fertile soil for all the activities of civilization.

By no means all the abundant growth that was soon now to be observed there presented a character distinct from what had gone before, either by specifically North Netherlandish or Protestant features. In many ways it was the continuation —certainly in rather different circumstances, in a still more preponderantly urban and middle-class society, which for that reason alone was more exclusively Dutch—of the common Netherlandish cultural tradition, strongly influenced by the Romance South, which until then had found a more favourable soil in Flanders and Brabant. Catholic inspirations and associations could not have been suddenly cut out of that tradition without killing it, and although Protestant conceptions and Protestant conditions of life at once made their influence felt, Protestantism, let alone strict Calvinism, was far from dominating cultural life in the North during these decades. And not only did building proceed on the old, "general Netherlandish" foundations, but among the builders we shall come across innumerable Flemish and Brabant immigrants. As a class these men, as we know, were generally the strictest Calvinists, and they had a profound influence on the development of the Dutch Reformed Church in that sense. But when one tries to estimate their influence outside ecclesiastical history, how varied do their contributions and stimuli appear to have been! Sixteenth-century Holland was, compared with Flanders and Brabant, a small town community; there were certainly few aristocrats among the immigrants; yet they introduced a larger, and a more ostentatious, mode of life. Hollanders of the old stamp frequently grumbled against, or mocked at, these characteristics of the refugees. Yet undoubtedly the latter helped to brighten up "the dull Hollanders"—the old Brabant nickname for their northern neighbours. In any case the Brabant invasion helped to bring about that quickening of the rhythm of life, that bursting of old bounds, and that colourful variety, which were to count for so much in the rich charm of the civilization of Holland in the seventeenth century.

More than any other intellectual or spiritual activities, painting and architecture demand settled social conditions. In Flanders and Brabant, for twenty years exposed to the excesses of Beggars and Malcontents, of Spanish, German, and Walloon mercenaries, the old centres were rudely uprooted, and in the order, such as after a while it was, restored by Parma, the former prosperity was still too much lacking for these centres to spring into being again very readily. Nevertheless Antwerp, which had indeed been gradually monopolizing all such activities during the preceding period, remained, in spite of the paralysis of its trade due to the closure of the Scheldt, a large town with a great deal of old-established wealth; and here Parma's conquest, which meant the triumph of the Catholic Church, opened another period of brilliant prosperity for painting. The Calvinist interregnum had robbed the painters of Church patronage. Now, on the contrary, religious pieces of all descriptions were in great demand for the restoration of the sacked and emptied churches: the studios were soon active as they had not been for long. In the work then done, the spirit of Frans Floris still set the fashion. Italianate and academic as it is, it has not much to attract us to-day. Mindful of the great time which was soon to begin for the Antwerp school of painting under the leadership of Rubens, the modern art lover will watch especially for signs of the baroque breaking through the stiff forms of the ageing Renaissance. We know that soon the fervent, though externalized, religious life of the Counter-Reformation will produce its own style. About this time, young Rubens was already at work in his native

town, before his departure to Italy in 1600; his masters were
Tobias Verhaecht, Adam van Noort, and Vaenius. Is it possible
to find in the paintings of those older men any rays of light
announcing the rising sun? The work of Otto Vaenius, despite
his deficient sense of colour, yields most to this questioning.
Interesting from this point of view are also two other contemporary painters, the brothers Francken: especially Hieronymus
Francken, who in 1589 painted the martyrdom of St. Crispin
and St. Crispinian for the cathedral of Our Lady at Antwerp;
this is a picture with the true baroque vehemence of expression.
(The centre piece is now in the Antwerp Museum.)

Otto Vaenius, or Van Veen (1556–1629), Parma's court painter,
deserves a moment of our attention. He came of a good Leyden
family. His father had been burgomaster before 1572, but had
gone into exile when the Beggars arrived. (This is by no means
the only instance of a migration in the opposite direction from
that of the Protestant Flemings and Brabanders who settled
down in the North.) No painting was—under the double
influence of the Counter-Reformation and of Italy—more
completely divorced from realism, more conventionally idealistic
and grouped in a more theatrical way, in short none was more
what would later be regarded as typically "Flemish" and "un-
Hollandish" than the work of this exile from Leyden, who had
received his first lessons in his native town.

During this period there was little inclination to build in
the South, but in the North architects found plenty of work
before the end of the sixteenth century. Towns were expanded,
well-to-do merchants wanted houses in accordance with their
wealth, new municipal buildings were required, weigh-houses,
shooting galleries for bowmen's companies (doelens), town
halls. Two style currents continued side by side. In so far as
a separate Flemish element had existed in each, this was now
completely absorbed into the Northern tradition; first by
means of imitation, as in the Flushing town hall (since demolished), for which that of Antwerp had served as a model;
or in the house called "De Steenrots" at Middelburg (1590),
which is reminiscent of the classicist style fashionable at
Antwerp or Brugge for buildings of that kind: and secondly,

by means of the original work of masters born or schooled in the South, who were driven North by the troubles. For example, the son of Hans Vredeman de Vries, Paul, born at Antwerp, was now working at Amsterdam in his father's style. A really great figure among these refugees was Lieven de Key, of Ghent (1560–1627), who became town architect of Haarlem. He used both manners of building between which the time hesitated. If the weigh-house at Haarlem was classicist, the meat hall, in which the interplay of brick and stone creates an incomparable effect, is a triumphant instance of that peculiarly Netherlandish Renaissance style, which had come into being before the great political change, but which could attain its full development only in the circumstances of the liberated North. For us, at any rate, it is hard not to regard that style as the true expression of the time. How eminently suited are its brave and cheerful forms to the mood of the prosperous burghers who were emerging from the struggle as the real victors. Nevertheless, as has been hinted above, there were, at the same time, strong German influences at work on this style. It is uncertain how large a share De Key had in the planning of the famous Leyden town hall (built in 1598, recently destroyed by fire), but probably the principal man engaged in the actual building of it was an "Easterner"—that is to say, a North German—Luder van Bentheim, who had done most of his work at Bremen. To this, no doubt, Van Mander alluded in his *Schilderboeck* (about which more will be said later on) when he wrote:

It is a pity that a new, foul, modern manner of building after the German fashion has once more come into use; we shall be hard put to it to get rid of it, but in Italy it will never be adopted.

For he, like many others who wanted to be considered connoisseurs, continued to regard the classicist style, such as Pieter Coecke had expounded it after Serlio, as simply "the right manner of building." In spite of this condemnation by the orthodox, colourful and gaily decorated buildings continued to spring up in every town, and another great master of the Dutch Renaissance style rose to fame, namely Hendrik de Keyser, of Utrecht (1565–1621), who became town architect of Amsterdam. Before the Twelve Years' Truce he built—or at least began—the South Church, the East India House, the Exchange (demolished in 1838), all at Amsterdam. His work has a gracefulness of its own. He made freer use of Italian architectural forms than did De Key, so that in the next period, when public taste turned more in that direction, he was better able to maintain his prestige.

It is a surprising thing that painting in the North survived not only the passing unrest of the seventies, but the permanent loss of Church patronage. It shows how firm a tradition had already grown up in Holland and Utrecht no less than in Flanders and Brabant. Not only were there well-established studios and schools, but the public, the middle-class as well as the aristocracy, had learned to love pictures and wanted them to decorate their interiors. A good deal of work was done even for export, for instance, to the Frankfort Fair. In Haarlem, Leyden, Utrecht, Amsterdam, the old groups of painters managed to maintain themselves and work could even be found for the numerous newcomers from the Southern provinces; soon other towns, Dordt, Delft, The Hague, became important centres. In all this activity the old Holland traditions were inextricably intermingled with those of the South Netherlandish schools; in any case, of course, all had sprung from the same source and had always greatly influenced each other. Lines in which the Flemings used to excel now found their best continuation in the Holland school; as, for instance, lands capepainting. Here Gillis van Coninxloo (1544–1607), who moved from Antwerp to Amsterdam, constituted a link; later, his Kortryk pupil, Roeland Savery, who settled down at Utrecht, continued the chain; but Breughel's work, which became known through engravings, also exercised influence. A genre which had early found a favourable soil in Holland was further developed as if in preparation for triumphs still to come, namely the group portrait, in which members of municipal committees or of civic guard companies sat together. Good work was done in this line by Cornelis Ketel of Gouda, Aert Pieterszoon, the son of Pieter Aertszoon, and Cornelis van Haarlem. The last-named, as a rule, revelled in large theatrical compositions and Michelangelesque nudes, but it is pleasant to see him once in a while forgetting this romantic showiness when painting the portraits of soberly attired Haarlem burghers. Another national trait was the penchant for the illustration of scenes from domestic life; before Aertszoon had made it into an accepted genre which Breughel soon carried to undreamt-of heights, the primitives had shown an inclination for it even in their religious art; and now we have, for instance, David Vinckeboons, a native of Mechlin (1576–1629), who worked at Amsterdam. In the Antwerp school those tendencies were certainly by no means lost, yet neither the spirit of society, through Spanish rule and Counter-Reformation in open communication with the Romance world, nor the patronage of Church and aristocracy, was favourable to their development. Conditions in the North, on the contrary, as it were, invited the painters to cultivate a loving pride in everyday environment. In the South everything pressed towards narrowing down art to one attitude of mind. The North inherited the Netherlands traditions in the full wealth of their variety.

For that Italian-classicist style which triumphed at Antwerp was by no means abandoned in Holland and Utrecht. It still ruled in several studios, and the power of literary fashion caused the most cultured art lovers to regard it as the true and only style. I mentioned Cornelis Corneliszoon van Haarlem (1562–1638) as a representative figure. Another one was Hendrik Goltzius (1558–1616), a member of the same Venlo family to which the antiquarian Hubert Goltzius belonged. He too worked at Haarlem, where he had learned engraving from Coornhert.

Goltzius, home from Italy, had so firmly impressed on his memory the beautiful Italian paintings that he still saw them as in a mirror whenever he wished to and wherever he found himself. Now he enjoyed the angel grace of Raphael, then the natural fleshes of Correggio, or again the surging heights and receding depths of Titian, the fine silks or other well-painted materials of Veronese; beside all this the native painters seemed disappointing and less perfect to him.

So does Karel van Mander sketch the true "Romanist." He,

the Fleming (1548–1606), also settled at Haarlem, felt no less veneration for the Italians and the classics than did his friend Goltzius, but in his *Schilderboeck* (Book of Painters; 1604) he nevertheless described, proudly and lovingly, the lives and works of "the native painters"—naturally he did not discriminate between Northern and Southern Netherlandish. The very fact of his undertaking this task (conceived after Vasari) proves the emergence of an entirely new conception, namely, of art as a highly important matter, which adds to the honour of a people. The book itself brims over with pleasant anecdotes and with particulars about the painters' work and methods. It is most enlightening about the ambitions and opinions of the artists of the time. They and their patrons, the *liefhebbers* (art lovers) with their "cabinets," live on in Van Mander's pages.

A book like this extended the boundaries of Dutch literature, which had been perilously narrowed down during the alien rule of the Burgundian-Habsburg dynasty, when history and politics had been more and more reserved for treatment in French. The Renaissance, as we know, in spite of the overwhelming admiration for the classics and the Italians which it enjoined, had quickened the interest in national intellectual possessions. But it is obvious that the political and economic circumstances in which the North now found itself must no less powerfully promote the spirit of independence and of enterprise in intellectual matters. How immediately these circumstances influenced literature can be seen from the accounts of voyages to which expeditions to the Indies and America gave rise, and from the chronicles, which were not slow in appearing, of the great events through which the country was passing.

It is true that the literary value of most of the voyages is nil, although Gerrit de Veer's account of Heemskerck's and Barentsz's expedition round the North, to give only one instance of the more successful few, will always charm by its straightforward and sincerely human tone. But it was a thing of importance in itself that this wonderful new world and the epic of its exploration and conquest were described in Dutch, however unskilled the writers were in the use of the pen. As a matter of fact the work with which this new kind of literature opens, Jan Huygen van Linschoten's description of the Portuguese empire in the Indies, is a masterpiece of observation and insight, which still has considerable historical value.

As to the chronicles, under the pressure of the stirring times they were at one blow cut free both from the petty local and from the un-Dutch and dynastic tradition. Pieter Bor, of Utrecht (1559–1635), Emanuel van Meteren, of Antwerp (he lived in London; 1535–1612), and Everhard van Reyd, of Deventer (1550–1602), constitute a remarkable trio. The first part of Bor's work appeared in 1595, of Van Meteren's in 1599; both spent the remainder of their lives in writing sequels of it. Van Reyd's book was not printed until years after his death. Bor is the matter-of-fact registrar and collector; although not infrequently (the reader has met with some instances above) by a simple remark or some description very much to the point he throws light which the modern researcher has looked for in vain among the documents. Van Meteren, who was a cousin of Ortelius, and in touch with the whole of that cultured circle, strove to write something like a connected story and was more alive than Bor to problems of causation; he was particularly interested in economic conditions. Van Reyd was councillor to Stadtholder William Louis and relates vividly all that comes within his particular circle of vision. Of the three, he is the most individual writer.

Many scribblers [as he puts it himself] seek the glory of being called impartial. Yet the pen can ill be so governed that inclination do not sometimes appear. Therefore do I boldly declare that with my counsel and actions I have always supported the party of religion and liberty, but with my pen only that of truth, hiding neither the virtues of enemies nor the shortcomings of friends.

How confidently this writer speaks his mind in the mother tongue on a problem which the preceding generation would hardly have presumed to tackle but in Latin! And, indeed, there was now a public consisting not of international scholars, or of French-cultured noblemen and royal officials, nor exclusively

of the writer's own townsfolk: an historian of the formidable
events of the immediate past could count on the attention
of citizens and citizen magistrates in all the provinces of the
Union.

But not in this direct way only did circumstances affect
Dutch civilization. Far more important in its consequences
was the awakening of national confidence. Deeply stirred by
the great trials they had gone through, men felt that the nation
was called to a brilliant future. In all spheres of the mind
this mood had a stimulating effect. The determination grew
that all should be opened to a people which had gloriously
defied the mightiest monarchy of the earth. Many of the best
minds realised that the national language must be the key.

The exhortations of Van de Werve, the complaints of
Coornhert, had certainly found some response. But when
Hendrik Laurenszoon Spieghel of Amsterdam in 1584 published his *Dialogue of Dutch Literature*—Coornhert had been
delighted to write a preface—a whole generation was ready
to receive the message and to act upon it. The influence of
that essay was immediate and profound. The language was
stripped of the abuse of foreign words as of a parasitic growth
and after the operation appeared in pristine purity. It is true
that the watchword was not accepted so readily for non-literary
purposes; in town halls, States assemblies, merchants' offices,
a much less pure language remained in use. A standard had
nevertheless been set up which was never again to be lost.
Nor was this reform limited to the Northern Netherlands.
There was very little literary activity in the South during
this unhappy period, but as soon as circumstances permitted
a revival of literary interest it appeared that writers in re-
catholicized Flanders and Brabant had adopted the same
conventions as their brothers in the North. In fact, the movement had been begun before the split, and by Southern writers;
and, moreover, the prestige of the poets of Holland soon came
to stand high in the subjected provinces.

For, as a matter of fact, much more was done in the North
than to cultivate respect for the language and to purify it
from "bastard words." This was but one condition for literary

achievement. The important thing was that the achievement itself followed. It had been centuries since the Netherlands produced such a group of striking personalities who used Dutch as their medium of expression. Take only Marnix, Coornhert, Van Mander, and Spieghel.

Marnix, the temperamental Calvinist nobleman, had retired to his country seat at West Souburg in Zealand after the disastrous end to his active career; there he spent his time translating the Bible, writing political and theological essays, and, above all, a masterly version of the Psalms, in which he sought a durable form for that confidence befitting a chosen people, however severely tried, which had proved too hard for him in reality. Van Mander, the artist, lover of life, not content with painting and with describing the painters, chased beauty in poetry as well; his *Scriptural Songs* long remained popular with his co-religionists (the Baptists), but he himself could not rest satisfied with them, because, as he put it, "he could not take pleasure any longer in our common old lame manner of writing verse"; he was nearly fifty before he reached a "true understanding of the French metre" and was able to write real Renaissance poetry. Coornhert, the wisdom-loving engraver, notary public, and politician, of Haarlem, indefatigable defender of liberty, undaunted fighter against Catholic and Protestant intolerance, found time in the midst of so much strife and polemical activity for other work even than the building up of a pure Dutch language, freed from the conventions of the Rhetoricians; his great achievement was a book published in 1586, *The Art of Well-living*, an untheological, Christian-stoical system of morality, in which, in the teeth of the Protestant doctrine of man's corruption, he maintained the attainability of virtue; this earnest and biglyplanned book, utterly different from the religious writings of preachers and mystics, was another *novum*, by which the area of Dutch prose was expanded. Spieghel, the Amsterdam merchant who, far from allowing himself to be worried out of the Catholic Church, declined public office as a protest against the breach of faith involved in the tearing up of the Satisfactions, yet recognized in his country's independence

the condition for the independence of his intellectual development; averse from incongruous decoration, be it French or
classical, a stern servant of truth, he made a sober appearance;
in his principal work, *Hertspieghel* (The Mirror of the Heart),
he confessed in verse of most individual tone and imagination
to a conception of life closely akin to that which his elder
friend Coornhert had expounded in prose.

A quartette, these two South Netherlanders and these two
Hollanders, of which any literature might be proud. Of the
four, Marnix was the most isolated; his relations were mainly
with the scholars, the theologians, and the statesmen. Van
Mander was surrounded by a group who made their bow in
a volume, *De Nederduytsche Helicon*, which was published in
1610, a few years after their leader's death. They were mostly
refugees. In Haarlem, Leyden, and Amsterdam, the Flemings
and Brabanders had founded their own Chambers of Rhetoric,
while entertaining close relations with the native poets; in
De Nederduytsche Helicon, for instance, are published poems
of Scriverius and Douza (both of whom we shall meet later on).
It must be admitted that most of the refugees were rhymers
of the old stamp. Spieghel's group were men of a different
calibre. He, too, was a member of a Chamber of Rhetoric, for
which, in fact, his *Dialogue* of 1584 had been written. The
"Chamber of the Eglantine," with the motto, "Flowering in
Love," was generally called the "Old Chamber," in contra-
distinction to the "Chamber of the White Lavender," which
was the chamber of the refugee Brabanders at Amsterdam.
A number of men from the "regent" circles of Amsterdam
belonged to the Old Chamber, which moreover disposed of
more talent than did its Brabant sister institution. Fellow
member with Spieghel was his friend Roemer Visscher, also
a merchant and a Catholic, whose epigrams achieved great
popularity. But Spieghel was the master mind, strong in his
clear conception of the unity of life, the whole of which he
wanted literature to master. It was this that gave him his
influence over the younger men, and it was to the younger men
that the Chamber "Flowering in Love" was to owe its fame
in Dutch literature. Even before the end of our period, the

poetry of Pieter Corneliszoon Hooft (1581–1647), the son of burgomaster Cornelis Pieterszoon Hooft, himself a member, roused the delight of lovers of literature. Never before had Dutch verse attained to that full Italian beauty. Gerbrand Adriaenszoon Breero (1585–1619) and Samuel Coster (1579–1655) were soon to raise the Amsterdam stage to an unparalleled position in the literary and intellectual life of the Netherlands. Meanwhile the greatest of all those figures who were going to illustrate the next period belonged to the Brabant Chamber, namely Joost van den Vondel, of Antwerp (1587–1676); but his poetical development, too, was to owe a very great deal to the circle of "the Eglantine."

With what keen understanding Spieghel and his friends tried to promote the construction of a sound and many-sided Dutch civilization appears from the request which in 1585, the year after the *Dialogue*, they addressed to the University of Leyden, begging that the courses might be given in the mother tongue,

so that we Hollanders might at last enjoy learning in our own speech, which we must now with great labour cull from unknown tongues.

But there was, unfortunately, no chance of that request being acceded to. The Latin tradition was too powerful and it had made of Leyden a stronghold for itself. Yet even here something was achieved. No man was ever a more enthusiastic advocate of the use of Dutch for scientific purposes than Simon Stevin (1548–1620), a refugee (although a Catholic) from Brugge, who in the eighties worked and taught at the University of Leyden. His works, written in Dutch, on mathematics and mechanics, prepared the way for important developments, especially of the latter science. Their immediate practical value too was considerable, and Maurice caused Stevin to be appointed (in spite of his religion) to the post of Engineer and Quartermaster with the States army. When in 1600 the Prince founded a school for engineers at the University of Leyden, it was Stevin who drafted the statutes, in which it was laid down that the medium of instruction should be the mother tongue.

But as a whole the University and the scholars who formed

part of it remained unalterably addicted to Latin, and that is one of the principal reasons why that little world so often makes the impression of a colony leading its own life fenced off from the rest of Dutch society. The use of Latin erected a partition between scholarship and the nation. On the other hand it enabled the Leyden professoriate to attract foreigners into their lecture rooms and to admit them within their own circle, while they could freely carry on intellectual intercourse with their equals over the whole of Europe.

But the intellectuals of those days gave hardly a thought to that language problem. It was possible to share the new feeling of nationality and at the same time to be a confirmed writer of Latin. For men of that way of thinking the glory of a great scholar—and nothing could impart such glory to a scholar as service to the mystery of Latinity—was reflected quite automatically on to the entire nation. Douza, who was a curator of the University, and himself a humanist who combined an intense national sentiment with his enthusiasm for antiquity, declared that his work in keeping out the Spaniard during the siege did not constitute so great a service to the country as his success in bringing Lipsius to Leyden. And when Lipsius absconded after a stay of thirteen years, it was thought a complete compensation for the disaster when the great Frenchman, Scaliger, was prevailed upon to leave his disturbed country (this was in 1593, before Henry IV restored order), and to come to Leyden. The negotiations that took place over that appointment, in which Prince Maurice and King Henry intervened, the conditions that were offered, and according to which the famous scholar would not even be obliged to lecture, the splendid reception at Leyden when at last he appeared with a suite of noblemen—all that makes one realize the respect that was felt for the study of the classics. The succession of Lipsius and Scaliger was continued after the latter's death in 1609 by his favourite pupil, Daniel Heinsius, of Ghent (1580–1655), and gave to the young university uncommon prestige in the international world of scholars. There were, indeed, several men who did excellent work in other subjects. It has been mentioned above that Dodoens—

Dodonaeus—came to Leyden when quite an old man, and after his death in 1589 botany was taught by Clusius. Snellius was a famous mathematician, although later on to be excelled by his son; Bonaventura Vulcanius, a good Greek scholar. In 1586 Raphelengius was appointed professor of Hebrew; he was a son-in-law of Plantin, who had left to him, who belonged to the Reformed Church, his Leyden printing firm when he returned to Antwerp; Raphelengius studied the Koran in Arabic.

If I stressed the fact that Latin was the language used at Leyden and that the outlook there was in many ways cosmopolitan rather than national, I do not for a moment mean to suggest that the existence of so brilliant a centre of learning was of no account for Dutch intellectual life generally. It would be difficult to trace the effect in all its ramifications, but without the shadow of a doubt the treasures of knowledge and of ideas gathered at Leyden enriched the national civilization. Moreover, after having noticed that the scholars in a sense kept themselves apart, one must not overlook the numerous relations which nevertheless existed between them and Dutch society in general and the exponents of the new cultural aspirations in particular.

The thing that involved them in the life of the nation more than anything else was their position in the great European struggle between Protestantism and Catholicism. Leyden was an advanced post of Protestantism not in Holland alone but in the world. It is true that in the early years the theological faculty had to contend with greater difficulties than any of the others. The need for ministers was urgently felt, but the office was of little account socially, and not until a system of scholarships had been instituted could the training of Reformed preachers be taken seriously in hand. A college was founded for theological students, but its history was marked at first by stormy incidents, which throw a lurid light on the rowdyism of youth, and even Calvinist youth, in those days. But when these gales had been weathered the faculty encountered even heavier seas. One might say, however, that it was the dissensions among the Reformed which brought the University and the nation into the closest contact.

The disputes within the Church, of which we have heard
something above, never quite died down, and when in 1602,
beside the strictly Calvinistic professor Gomarus, of Brugge,
the Hollander Arminius was appointed to the second chair
of theology, strife flared up almost at once, and the training
for the ministry came to be the very object of contention.
Years before, certain sermons which Arminius had delivered
at Amsterdam on the subject of grace and election had caused
a considerable stir. His appointment to a chair at Leyden
carried into the very heart of the Reformed system in Holland
opposition to the extreme doctrine of the corruption of man
and the setting apart as the elect of the small group who regarded
the State as having been made for their sake alone. Gomarus
and his supporters soon raised the cry of popery, and in fact it
was the essentially Catholic tradition of Erasmus that Arminius
continued, even though there was no thought of a reconciliation
with Rome. The Truce had not long been concluded before
this theological quarrel developed into a great political conflict
which shook the very foundations of the Republic.

Until that crisis at any rate, which was to give to the orthodox party a firmer control over the University, more latitude
was allowed in the matter of religion at Leyden than in most
other Universities in Europe. The town Government and the
States of Holland, on whose authority the curators acted, lived
up to their libertinist principles. After the very first years no
religious test was demanded of either professors or students;
as far as the latter were concerned, that remained the position
even after the synod of Dordt in 1619. This liberty unmistakably benefited the University. Lipsius, for instance, in all the
thirteen years that he spent at Leyden, never once partook of
the Reformed Communion, and was able afterwards to maintain
that he had never receded from his Catholic convictions. Yet
the case of Lipsius shows that there were inevitably limits to
this liberty.

Lipsius was not by nature a fighter. In a disturbed and
cruel age, tranquillity was what he wanted. At first he believed
he had found it at Leyden and was full of praise for the tolerance
prevailing there. But he soon began to fear the ministers and

K

their tyrannical proclivities. To his Libertinist friends, Van Hout and Douza, a strict upholding of the rights of the secular power seemed to be the only safeguard against this danger, and now Lipsius himself expounded this point of view in such a way that his book (*Politica*) caused another Libertinist, the passionate Coornhert, to take up arms against him, protesting that Lipsius wanted to reintroduce the killing of heretics. The great Latinist was profoundly disturbed by that attack, the more so as it was couched in the popular language, which seemed to him derogatory to his dignity as well as fraught with danger. It made him reflect that the tranquillity he coveted so heartily was, after all, to be found only in a Catholic country, under the double authority of Pope and King, and soon he was back at Leuven, which was now again enjoying security behind the shield of Parma. To a man who felt no spiritual affinity with the Reformation, Leyden, in spite of liberty, could scarcely be a home. Nor can such a man have been readily accessible to the influence of that new feeling of nationality based on the Northern Netherlands which might have prevented Lipsius from calling the Hollanders rebels and from paying such unrestrained homage to the Habsburgs as he did after his transition.

Non-Catholic scholars, whether Libertinist or orthodox, were for all their Latinist cosmopolitanism unable to escape that influence altogether. They showed the effects of it in many ways, both by their connections and their own works. The strongest link between the academic world and those poets in Dutch who were most deliberately building up a national civilization was formed by Douza and Jan van Hout, those doughty comrades in literature and arms. Curator and secretary to the curatorium of the University, they were at the same time in constant intercourse with the poets of their own town and of Haarlem and Amsterdam. Both also wrote Dutch verse, but perhaps the most fruitful work that they did for Dutch civilization was their scientific study of the older national history; Scriverius, of Haarlem (Pieter Schryver, 1576–1660), who later on moved to Leyden, shares this honour with them. Inasmuch as they limited their attention to their own province, they continued the Batavian tradition of Junius. But the method of research was carried by them far beyond Junius's limits. With a detachment without precedent they assailed the tradition of the chronicles at whose meaningless lies they scoffed mercilessly. They went to the original charters. In 1591 even, Douza, in conjunction with Spieghel, whose interest extended to these matters too, published the medieval chronicle in Dutch verse by Melis Stoke, which had been so completely forgotten that on the appearance of the book the clever ones suspected a hoax; the author's name was unearthed only much later by Scriverius. The publication of this chronicle was an event also for the study of the medieval Dutch language. Douza wrote a preface for it in Dutch verse. (He generally wrote in Latin; Scriverius, however, very frequently in Dutch.)

Scriverius was a convinced advocate of the use of the mother language for the higher functions of intellectual life. In the universal estimation he never did greater service to that cause than when he persuaded Daniel Heinsius, a few years after our period (in 1615), to publish his Dutch poems. Heinsius, of course, primarily served the Latin muse. Ever since the beginning of the sixteenth century the Netherlandish humanists had been active in that service. The results, however, in general amounted to no more than an utterly lifeless stylistic exercise. Latin was no longer handled so freely as in the Middle Ages (the same is true for prose); Latin poetry therefore was all imitation and erudition. Many who had read his poems in manuscript knew that the famous Heinsius sometimes deigned to rhyme in Dutch. What a triumph that he should not think it beneath him to let these poems be publicly printed! There is little real poetry to be found in the *Nederduytsche Poemata*. Interesting, apart from the fact of its publication under so illustrious a Latinist name, is the tone of vigorous patriotic pride sounded, for instance, in a poem celebrating Heemskerck's heroic death off Gibraltar in 1607. Heinsius—born as has been said at Ghent—was so much aware of his origin in the lost provinces as to write:

Wherever you (Spain) are not, there is our fatherland

Yet he confidently claimed his share in the glory of the Republic, and when he boldly asserts that "we were born to be free," he identifies himself with the successful Netherlanders of the North. Heinsius' mood was typical of the generation that had grown up with the war of independence. Another young man who served Latin and patriotism with equal conviction was Hugo de Groot (Grotius, 1583–1646), of Delft; he had been as great a success at Leyden as Heinsius himself, but was soon called away to enter upon a "regent's" career. This Hollander already identified without a qualm the *Respublica Batava* with the fatherland. In a poem addressed to Douza (and written before the latter's death in 1604) he abjured classical history (which he had served by editing some texts) and vowed himself to the study of the *fasti* of his native country. But he did so in Latin, and indeed it was but seldom that Grotius was to use Dutch in the whole course of his life.

It is hardly surprising that the Catholic Brabander, Lipsius, could not accept the patriotic ideal of the Reformed Fleming and the Libertinist Hollander. It would not be fanciful to represent him as having remained faithful, in the face of the triumphant dualism that was going to divide the Netherlands for so long, to the older sixteenth-century national sentiment, which embraced all the provinces. When he made his choice in 1591, the prospect in front of the rebellion was still far from hopeful, and he might reasonably expect the power of Spain to heal the fissures in the Netherlands. Even when shortly afterwards Parma's chances of conquest came to nothing, he still prophesied that a truce would cause grave religious quarrels to break out in the Republic—had he not seen at Leyden how the heretics hated each other!—that the new state would collapse and the Archdukes be enabled to extend their authority over the whole country. But those expectations were confounded. For the time being duality was confirmed in the Netherlands. And in the South, whither his fears had driven (and certainly his heart drawn) him, Lipsius found a society weighed down, not only by adversity in war and economic distress, but also by alien rule and a religious coercion infinitely worse than that which he had seen threatening in the North. A society which might afford tranquillity to the scholar, but in which for the builder of a healthy national civilization— a part, it is true, for which Lipsius never felt any ambition —circumstances were sadly unpropitious.

THE NETHERLANDS
IN THE SEVENTEENTH CENTURY
1609–1648

Preface to Second Edition (1961)

The Netherlands Divided has been long out of print. I had often had evidence of continued interest in the book and I am glad that the publishers have decided to reprint it.

The book is presented to the public under a new title. The original title was perhaps too closely connected with the problems arising out of the separation of the Netherlands to make an immediate appeal to the English reader. No doubt these problems occupy a central position in the story as I have told it. But for all that I have attempted to picture the period in the fulness of its many aspects and interests. That instead of calling the book *The Netherlands in the First Half of the Seventeenth Century* I can call it *The Netherlands in the Seventeenth Century, Part I*, is explained by the fact that the publication in English of the next part of my *Geschiedenis van de Nederlandse Stam*, covering the period from 1648 to 1702, is planned for the next year.

The present edition is not identical with that of 1936. The text has been gone over carefully and numerous slight corrections as regards both style and contents were the result. With real gratitude I acknowledge the discriminating and patient assistance given me in this laborious job by Mr L. Russell Muirhead. Moreover, some insertions have been made, mainly after the revised Dutch edition of 1948.

One point should be mentioned particularly. In the version of 1936 the French names by which so many towns or rivers in the Dutch-speaking area are referred to in English were replaced by the Dutch forms. I still think that it is unfortunate that the English should be addicted to the use of French geographical names for non-French-speaking countries on the Continent. The habit extends even to German places: e.g. Aix-la-Chapelle for Aachen. But I have come to realise that it is presumptuous, and in any case a hopeless undertaking, for a foreigner to try to improve the English language. I have therefore used the current French names throughout and here append a list of them, each followed by the form by which the towns are known to their inhabitants and compatriots.

Alost	Aalst
Bailleul	Belle
Berghes St Winox	St Winoks Bergen
Bruges	Brugge
Cassel	Kassel
Courtrai	Kortrijk
Furnes	Veurne
Grammont	Geraardsbergen
Gravelines	Grevelingen
Hal	Halle
Lierre	Lier
Louvain	Leuven
(River) Lys	Leie
(River) Meuse	Maas
Menin	Menen
St Trond	St Truien or St Truiden
Termonde	Dendermonde
Tirlemont	Tienen
Ypres	Ieper

I have retained the name *'s Hertogenbosch* (*Den Bosch* is the more current form) which is frequently used by English writers, although one will often meet the French version *Bois-le-Duc*.

P. G.

Utrecht, 1961

Preface to First Edition (1936)

LIKE *The Revolt of the Netherlands* (Williams & Norgate, 1932) the present work is based on my "History of the Netherlandish People" (*Geschiedenis van de Nederlandse Stam*), and more particularly on the first half of the second volume, which was published by the Wereldbibliotheek, Amsterdam, in July 1934. It continues the story where *The Revolt of the Netherlands* left off, but it deals with a well-defined period and can be read independently. References to the sources of the quotations from contemporary texts will be found at the end of the volume, as also a general note on sources and historical literature.

My thanks are again due to my son, W. F. Geyl, for designing the maps; and to Mr. S. T. Bindoff, the translator, for the patience and devotion displayed in our collaboration.

Introduction

IN 1609 Spain, thoroughly exhausted, had been compelled to conclude with the States-General of the Seven United Provinces a truce for a period of twelve years. The proud Spanish government had not given up all hope of recovering these provinces as, in the days of Parma, between 1579 and 1585, it had recovered those situated south of the rivers, but the weary years following upon Parma's spectacular successes had so far subdued its spirit that it had consented to treat with its rebels (for so it continued to regard them) 'as if ' considering them a free and independent power.

In the young Republic, which had in so unique a way found it possible, not only to survive against mighty Spain, but to thrive upon war, there had not been lacking those who scouted the subterfuge and opposed the Truce as a trick by which the Spaniards sought to recover their strength in order to resume the attack at a more opportune moment. Foremost among them was Maurice, the son of William the Silent, Stadholder of Holland, Zealand, Utrecht, Gelderland and Overysel, and Captain-General of the Union. His immense prestige was based on the brilliant exploits by which, in the 'nineties of the previous century, jointly with his cousin, the Stadholder of Friesland and Groningen, William Louis of Nassau, he had turned to account the embarrassments of Parma and Parma's successors and driven the Spaniards from their position north of the rivers, thus firmly securing the defensible northern group of provinces by a strong frontier. Maurice's opposition was that of the military man. There were, besides, the zealous Calvinists, stronger among the lower middle class than among the ruling set of 'regents' who composed the town governments and, through those, the States assemblies of the leading provinces, especially of Holland. To the Calvinists all truck with the Spaniard seemed to be damnable weakness. Finally, the opposition had been strengthened by certain commercial interests, strong especially at Amsterdam and in Zealand, where it was regretted that the Truce would interfere with plans for the foundation of a West India Company, a company which in fact was to have been a privateering enterprise at the expense of the Spanish colonies.

The man who had braved these powerful opponents and seen the negotiations for the Truce to a successful conclusion was Oldenbarnevelt, the Advocate of Holland, that is to say, principal officer of the States of that province and permanent leader of their delegation on the States-General. In the time (1585–87) of the ill-fated governorship of the Earl of Leicester, who had tried to fuse the provinces into a firmer union, and for that purpose had leant on the popular and orthodox party, Oldenbarnevelt had come to the fore as the leader of the Holland oligarchy, and the consolidation of the Republic as a loose confederation in which the preponderance of the province of Holland, ruled by its burgher aristocracy, was the principal unifying factor has been largely his work. Maurice, a youth at that time, and always more interested in military than in political affairs, had allowed himself to be used by the Advocate. Their disagreement over the conclusion of the Truce was to prove the beginning of a tragically serious divergence.

There had never been any love lost between Oldenbarnevelt and the Reformed ministers. The Advocate was the embodiment of the secular feeling so strong among the regents, who regarded the ambitions of the new Church with suspicion and were determined to keep it under control. The ministers, on the other hand, protested against the freedom left to dissenters and papists and were inclined to explain the moderation and toleration of the regents' regime as the outcome of secret leanings towards Catholicism or even atheism.

The South, meanwhile, was subjected to the full force of the Counter-Reformation, promoted and directed by the Spanish government re-established at Brussels.

'The South' now means a conglomeration of provinces in which the modern eye observes before everything the lack of linguistic unity. Side by side with the Walloon provinces, Artois, Cambrai, Hainaut, Walloon Flanders (Lille, Orchies and Douai), Namur, Luxemburg (in part of which the popular speech was German), there were the Dutch-speaking provinces, Flanders, Brabant and Upper Gelderland. Down to the actual split Flanders and Brabant had not only been the wealthiest and economically most developed part of the whole Seventeen Netherland Provinces, but they had held the lead in the cultural movement of the Dutch-speaking area.

It is a point worthy of note that within the orbit of the partly Dutch-speaking, partly French-speaking Burgundian-Netherlands State there had been an active and creative cultural unity covering the whole of the Dutch-speaking area, that is, the area embracing Flanders, Brabant, Zealand, Holland and Utrecht. The Eastern group, Gelderland, Overysel, Groningen, where the Saxon dialect is spoken as it is in the adjoining German lands, stood somewhat apart, but within the Frankish area (covering, therefore, the Western parts of the present Kingdom of the Netherlands and the Northern half of the present Kingdom of Belgium) a cultural unity was unmistakable. The Dutch literary language had been formed largely on the basis of Flemish-Brabant dialects.

How was it that the cleavage, confirmed by the Truce of 1609, and enduring down to the present day, came to run right across the Dutch-speaking area, severing Flanders and Brabant from Holland and Zealand, and leaving them associated with the Walloon provinces? It has long been usual to explain this development by vague references to a supposed difference in national character between 'Flemings' and 'Hollanders', more particularly apparent in the faithfulness with which, in the critical period of the sixteenth century, the former clung to Catholicism while the latter spontaneously embraces the new doctrines of Calvinism. It was one of the objects of my previous volume, *The Revolt of the Netherlands*, to show how very far from the truth is this traditional view.

In actual fact, as long as the provinces were together under Spanish rule, Calvinism was no less strong in Flanders and Brabant than it was in the Northern provinces. If it was first established as the ruling religion in Holland and Zealand, as it was after the rebellion of 1572, this was due to the fact that the Sea Beggars, the shock-troops of Calvinism, recruited from all over the Netherlands, selected those provinces as the stronghold where they had the best chance of resisting Alva's offensive return after the disaster of the massacre of St. Bartholomew had led to the collapse of William the Silent's larger plans. Their choice was determined not so much by the temper of the population, which did not differ from that of Flanders and Brabant, as by the geographical situation of Holland and Zealand, further away from the centre of Spanish military power, possessing in the rivers, lakes and marshes splendid natural advantages for defence and offering above all the inestimable advantage of open communication with the sea, that is to say, with the rest of Protestant Europe. The presence of this armed force of extremists enabled a vigorous minority to seize power in the name of the Prince of Orange and in course of time to fashion the majority after its ideals.

But while the fiction of a spontaneous desertion from Catholicism on the part of the Holland people is thus disposed of, the idea that the Flemings and Brabanters were by nature proof against Calvinism is no less erroneous. After the general rising of 1576 it was not long before determined Calvinist minorities came to control all the towns of Flanders and Brabant in exactly the same way as they had done after 1572 in Holland and Zealand; only in Gelderland, Overysel and Groningen (in regions which are to-day among the most solidly Protestant of the Kingdom of the Netherlands) did Catholicism show greater powers of resistance. The final distribution of the two religions, Catholicism prevailing to the exclusion of everything else south of the rivers, Protestantism in a dominant position north of them, resulted from the course of the war between the rebellious States-General and their tenacious King. Parma succeeded in re-establishing Spanish power in Flanders and Brabant, not because they were more inclined to Catholicism than the Northern provinces, but because they were more exposed to his attack.

In fact, he also reconquered the outlying North-Eastern provinces which were farther removed from the unassailable centre of the rebellion, Holland. Similarly, when Philip II's unwise policy of diverting Parma's forces towards France, combined with the disaster of the Armada, gave Maurice his chance to resume the offensive, he succeeded in recovering these North-Eastern provinces, which were difficult to hold from Brussels, but failed to penetrate far south of the great rivers, where Spanish power was most strongly entrenched. In neither case did the inclinations of the inhabitants greatly influence the result. The Groningers resisted Maurice's army with all their might; in the Flemish and Brabant towns there were not lacking well-wishers to his cause.

It was the rivers that brought about a strategic stalemate; it was this stalemate, in the end confirmed by the Truce, which enabled the secular power on either side to strengthen the position, here of Catholicism, there of Protestantism. The Spanish government was much the more determined about this task. Every conquest of a Southern town in the 'eighties was followed by the conversion or expulsion of the Protestants. Thousands upon thousands left Ghent and Bruges, Brussels and Antwerp, mostly to settle in the North, where they strengthened the most zealous wing of Calvinism. Without resorting to the same methods of compulsion, the victorious side in the North put very severe pressure on the Catholic majority of the population. Their church organisation was dissolved, public exercise of their religion prohibited. Adherents belonging to the governing class were excluded from public office (not too systematically at first, but later on, as we shall see, more so), while the appropriation of the possessions of the old church gave the dispensers of charity opportunities to influence the lower strata. Schoolmasters and university professors, of course, were subjected to tests, and education played an important part in the long process of protestantisation.

The splitting of the Netherlands, then, was brought about by the interference of a foreign power—Spain. The divergence in religion, which deeply influenced political and cultural feeling and relations between the severed parts, was not the cause but the result of that split. The consequences of the violent disruption of a natural whole and its replacement by a different mentality and national outlook in each of the severed halves, in the North the triumph of Protestantism and the development of a particularist, North-Netherlandish patriotism, in Brabant and Flanders the re-establishment of the Catholic Church in all her Counter-Reformation militancy, these constitute a slow process which I shall attempt to trace in the succeeding pages.

I

The Gulf in Religious and Intellectual Life widens

POLITICALLY, when the Twelve Years' Truce had been signed, in March 1609, the Netherlands were split in two by a dividing line cutting right through the Dutch-speaking area. This cleavage, resulting in the triumph of Protestantism in the North and of Catholicism in the South, was indeed already being reflected in social and cultural life, although there still remained lines of religious and intellectual cleavage running through both halves and cutting across the political frontier. No sooner were hostilities suspended than thousands from the North flocked with their children to Antwerp or 's Hertogenbosch (then still within the Spanish Archdukes' territory) to have them confirmed, while many Reformers came northwards from Antwerp to worship at the States' fort of Lillo on the Scheldt. On both sides the danger of defection from the established faith and of traffic with the other half of the country awakened fears. Take, for instance, the title of a pamphlet by the Middelburg minister Willem Teellinck:

> Timotheus, or a devout admonition against the vexatious gaping at the idols and the idolatrous worship of the Papists; which most rashly is committed by many of the Reformed faith in Brabant and Flanders on the occasion of this armistice.

It was indeed precisely the period of the Truce, which was to witness in both North and South a stricter enforcement of the systems that had truimphed in each, and consequently an increasing divergence between the two. In the South the government addressed itself immediately and with unfaltering determination to this task. In the North this was the programme of one party alone, which was hard put to it to get that programme carried through, and which, even after the victory that appeared to give it a free hand, exercised very much less power than did the Archducal government in the South.

A. THE SOUTH UNDER ALBERT
AND ISABELLA

THE seeker after the governing principle in the 'loyalist provinces' is brought first to the silent, sober palace of the Archdukes. Transplanted from Spain, and Spanish to the end, these rulers not only received their orders from Spain in matters of foreign policy; they used the power which the old Burgundian Habsburg governmental machine gave them in the domestic field to direct the development of social and cultural life in a Spanish sense.

The two forces which from the sixteenth century onwards had worked side by side, though never very harmoniously, on Netherlands soil, finally to clash irreconcilably, the force from below in its many local and provincial forms, and the force directed from above by the centralising and regularising monarchy, had as a result of the cleavage obtained control each in one half of the Netherlands. In the North we shall see the one blossom forth to its full extent in a wealth of intellectual and social life, yet at the same time so anarchical as to threaten dissolution to the State. In the South the other continues its work, producing not only order but a monotonous conformity, and weighing so heavily upon initiative and individualism that in the long run it seems likely to stifle everything.

Not that the government of the Archdukes had no other goal than administrative efficiency. On the contrary, it was imbued with a living idea, the idea of the Counter-Reformation. The Archdukes not only aimed at strengthening the monarchical-bureaucratic principle in the government of the country; they were determined at the same time to impregnate the population with the Catholic faith, newly reborn throughout South Europe. But in the practice of the seventeenth century, which did not scruple to employ political authority for spiritual coercion, such an endeavour could not but lead to inertia and atrophy. The fact that the government of the Southern Netherlands stood ranged under the banner of Catholicism is not the real point there. The system by which the Archdukes sought to realise their religious ideal was fundamentally the same as that which the Synod of Dort had in view. The real difference is, that whereas in the

North the Synod was only able to carry its programme through to a very limited extent, in the South we can observe the system working smoothly and at full pressure under the impulse of a strong central authority.

The Archducal government was not, of course, a despotism. The old Netherland traditions were weakened, the princely authority brought in from abroad had become the real motive power in political life. But these old traditions were not completely uprooted. Even some time later, when the King of Spain had resumed the direct government of the country, Puteanus, Lipsius' successor at Louvain, could thus address his sovereign:

In some countries thou art master, here thou art father; elsewhere thou mayest rule by the rod, here thou rulest by good will; for the condition of the Netherlands is wholly different from that of other nations (*he must have been thinking especially of Naples, Sicily and Portugal*). With the Netherlanders, where there is less of subservience, there is more of service; freedom makes others (*here he seems to be alluding to the North Netherland provinces*) intractable.

South Netherland society, no less than that of the North, was still permeated by the medieval idea of privilege, that is to say, by a conception of law which caused all groups and all individuals within those groups to stand firm against sheer arbitrary power. In municipal and provincial life, beyond whose borders few indeed ever looked, this priceless and typically Netherland heritage was saved out of the disaster of the war of independence, and in its mutual enjoyment the parts now wrenched asunder could still remember each other.

For we are all Netherlanders (*so a Holland pamphleteer could write even much later*) and apart from being neighbours, bound one to the other both by ancient kinship and common ties, of the same speech, way of life, temper and condition, and enjoying practically the same privileges. . . .

And yet to speak as Puteanus did meant shutting one's eyes to much that was humiliating in higher political life.[1] In the

[1] Even to-day Belgian historians willingly do the same. Thus Pirenne writes in the historical survey prefaced to his *La Belgique et la guerre mondiale* (1928), p. 18: 'Rien n'est plus faux que de considérer la Belgique, avant le xixᵉ siècle, comme soumise à la domination étrangère. Le régime qu'elle a connu a été un régime d'union personelle et non point du tout un régime de conquête.' How untenable this thesis is will appear at every turn in the present narrative, where we shall see the great problems of foreign policy treated not from a South Netherlandish but from a Spanish point of view, more often than not by Spaniards without South Netherlanders having any say in them. One cannot call such a regime one of 'personal union' without doing violence to the words.

theories of the native legists, who served the State in the central
and provincial courts or reared up new generations of lawyers
at Louvain, the ancient customs and privileges still found their
wonted place; nevertheless the Roman law concept of the
omnipotence of the sovereign, regarded as the embodiment of
the State, became more and more their veritable inspiration.
For their own part the Archdukes were on the whole shrewd
enough to keep up appearances. The Spanish character of their
Court was indeed hard to conceal. Only with difficulty could
they express themselves in French, while of Dutch they knew
absolutely nothing. For military affairs there stood beside them
a Spaniard responsible to the King. The father-confessor of the
Archduke Albert was another Spaniard, the Dominican monk
Fray Iñigo de Brizuela, and since the Archduke believed the
salvation of his soul to depend no less on his political steward-
ship than on his private life, this father-confessor was consulted
on all matters. The Papal Legate, Cardinal Bentivoglio, bore
witness to this in 1612:

> Seeing that the Archduke imitates the government of Philip II as closely as
> possible and conforms in everything to the usages of the Spanish Court,
> where the father-confessors of royal personages commonly possess very great
> authority, he has readily allowed the influence of Fray Iñigo to increase: it
> can be said that this person holds a supreme tribunal before which all matters
> are brought.

Such was the reality, and it was quite unaffected by the
employment of natives for other ministerial offices and for
diplomatic missions. The attachment shown by Peckius,
chancellor of Brabant, to the idea of national liberties was sadly
lacking in practical significance, even though it was made a
grievance against him in Spain. Maes, since 1614 president of
the Secret Council, was as devoted a servant of the monarchical
regime as Viglius had been in the previous century. The Secret
Council had gained in authority what the Council of State had
lost since the troubles, and this supplanting of the organ of the
great nobility by that of the jurists symbolises the evolution of
the regime.

How little indeed the aspirations and material interests of the
subjects counted with the Spanish counsellors and the Spanish
overlord of the Archducal government, the following case may
serve to illustrate.

Since the end of the sixteenth century the English Company

of Merchant Adventurers, who held a monopoly in the wool trade of that country, had maintained their Continental headquarters at Middelburg. This was a valuable asset to Holland as well as to the Zealanders, for English woollen cloths came over unfinished and were dressed at Haarlem, Leiden and elsewhere. This arrangement was a thorn in the flesh of the English government, whose efforts to keep the finishing process in English hands had repeatedly led to reprisals on the part of the States-General. Now in 1615 the luckless city of Antwerp, casting round for ways and means of lifting her trade out of its profound depression, perceived an opportunity of turning to her own advantage the disputes between James I and the United Provinces. Forty English woollen merchants wanted to come over with their families from Middelburg. They were heretics, but they were prepared to forgo the public exercise of their religion. Antwerp sought the consent of the Archduke to the scheme, laying no little emphasis on the distress of her population. The Archduke took plenty of advice. The Netherlanders—De Robiano, Treasurer-General, formerly burgomaster of Antwerp, and Peckius, even Netherland theologians like the Louvain professor Jansenius and the Jesuits Lessius and Scribani (this last, like Robiano, a Brabanter, in spite of his name)—saw no harm in the plan. But the Spaniards opposed it tooth and nail. The Spanish ambassador wrote to his sovereign that these people were heretics, which was enough for him. The Spanish commander of the citadel of Antwerp also wrote to the King to remind him of the expulsion only a few years before of the 150,000 Moors from Valencia, a measure in which he, Philip III, had surely taken no count of material gain or loss. Antwerp went on appealing and the Archduke deliberating and seeking advice, but the permission was never given, and when a few years later the English government itself took up the proposal it was turned down.

You may permit the transference of the English wool comapny from Middelburg to Antwerp (*the King had written to the Archduke*), but above all you must avoid anything which would prejudice the Catholic faith; this claims the first consideration.

How different this from the situation in the Northern Netherlands! In the Republic synods and congregations might remonstrate and admonish, but even after the Calvinist victory of 1618 no responsible government authority would have thought of consulting them or any eminent theologians on matters political. Only compare the position of Antwerp with that of Amsterdam: Antwerp, compelled willy-nilly to hand over the control of her interests to a foreign prince surrounded by foreign diplomats, military commanders and ecclesiastics; and Amsterdam, powerful enough, as we shall see later, to thrust her interests, time and again, upon the government as the motive power of policy.

Of resistance to the Archducal government there was hardly any question. The leading class, purged of rebellious elements a generation before, felt itself dependent on the Archduke. One crisis there was, in Brussels itself, which caused Albert to look up the precedents of the last rebellion at Ghent in the time of Charles V. This time the nine 'nations', that is, the gilds—now as in the days of the Pacification the unruliest group—refused their assent to a new tax and asserted that the consent of the other 'members' of the city (the magistracy and the Great Council) and of the duchy (the remaining three towns, Louvain, 's Hertogenbosch and Antwerp, the nobility and clergy) could not bind them. Committees of 'Eighteen Men' (as in 1576[1]) negotiated with the government. The agitation lasted for weeks, but the movement collapsed when at last Spinola's troops marched in. Throughout the proceedings not only the officials, Maes, Peckius, De Robiano, with the nobles and the ecclesiastics, represented in the persons of the Duke of Aerschot and the Abbot of Park, but also the city burgomasters, aldermen and councillors, all stood shoulder to shoulder with the government, and it was on the motion of the last-mentioned that the ringleaders were banished without trial. The municipal patriciate made common cause with the government when it was a question of crushing out the last vestiges of the old Brabant democracy. Indeed, the 'nations' themselves can no longer be simply identified with the cause of democracy. The economic development had long since passed the gilds by and they now comprised only a privileged class of artisans in small trades who had succeeded in escaping capitalisation and proletarisation.

The term 'leading class' which I have used also requires some explanation. I was thinking of town governments and high

[1] See *The Revolt of the Netherlands*, p. 145.

officials, who hung very closely together, and of the nobility, which was continually being reinforced by fresh elements from those two groups. But although a certain resemblance to conditions in the new Republic is not to be denied, we must nevertheless note the differences, and it then strikes us that those, whether commoners or noblemen, who still played their part in the old municipal and provincial colleges—town councils and States assemblies—only 'led' in a limited social sphere. Political and social decisions of real importance came within the sole purview of the central councils serving the royal government, to which the older provincial colleges were subordinated, an arrangement in every respect the opposite of what obtained in the North.

There the class which led socially also governed in a political sense through the sovereign authority of the States assemblies; and there the old provincial councils and courts, once instruments of the royal authority in the separate provinces, stood independent of one another and without any central organ, except perhaps the States-General, to instruct or dictate to them, but each so much the less able to stand up against its own provincial States. There, moreover, both the intrinsic position of the nobility and its relation to the town regencies were totally different. In the North the nobility took part in the independent States' government on an equal footing with the town oligarchies, but in the political organs of the weightiest provinces they formed an insignificant minority. True, the social position of the nobility was recognised in political life and noblemen had a claim to high diplomatic and military office; but on the other hand they were in a sense debarred from wielding real political power, which was reserved, by reason of the preponderance of the States of Holland and Zealand, to the municipal governments of those provinces. At the same time an unbridgeable gulf separated nobles and town regents. The regents might indeed begin to give themselves lordly airs and call themselves after their estates—a habit which was to grow upon them later—but there was no authority in the Republic which could ennoble them, so they often made shift with foreign titles. Nevertheless the native nobility in the North was to become more and more an exclusive caste.

In the South, on the other hand, the appetite for noble rank among the socially successful—officials, town regents and capitalists—was satisfied by their own government. This of itself tended to undermine the independence of the municipal oligarchy as a class. Moreover, it was the towns that had suffered most from the calamities of the previous generation, while the recovery which accompanied the advent of more settled conditions, and especially the breathing-space of the Truce, in large measure passed them by. As a result the economic importance of the towns as against the countryside suffered a sharp decline. The prosperity of agriculture, which astonished foreigners, and the success of new industries, notably the production of luxury articles such as lace and tapestries, testifies to the indomitable spirit of enterprise among the population, which, throughout all its disasters and humiliations, maintained the traditions of a highly civilised community. But the point I want to make here is that even this development strengthened, directly and indirectly, the position of the nobility. In the long run the whole upper stratum of society throughout the South acquired an aristocratic complexion. The common people resigned themselves to the new order with a meekness hitherto unknown. The attempt of the Brussels 'nations' did not for the time being excite emulation, and for many years the ancient medieval organisations were to make themselves little felt in the political sphere, existing, so it seemed, principally for good-fellowship and display. At the same time the revivified Catholic faith not only permeated the people with the spirit of submission, but quite naturally adapted itself to the colourful features of social life and gave them religious sanction.

What a different picture from the North! Yet all these differences sprang from the fact that the population of the South was no longer in a position to utilise any of its indigenous social and economic formations for purposes of independent political activity, but must needs leave that to an alien monarchy, whose instruments (and at the same time to some extent whose inspiration) were the priesthood and the lawyer bureaucracy. In the long run this regime was destined to press with leaden weight on the intellectual and spiritual life of Flanders and Brabant, but for efficient administration it offered undoubted advantages. That is as true for this period as for the early years of Philip II.

In the previous volume I mentioned the reform of the criminal law, already promulgated in the time of Alva.[1] Owing to the speedy outbreak of the troubles, little had been done towards applying, let alone extending, this measure, but now the Secret Council took seriously in hand the codification, and as far as possible the unification, of civil law. Legal study, as the preparation alike for an official and for a political career, became more than ever the fashion, and at the university of Louvain, drastically purged of abuses and standing on the threshold of a new era of prosperity, no faculty was so important as that of law. Economic recovery, too, save where religion or foreign policy intervened, was intelligently promoted, as, for instance, in the construction of canals between Ostend, Bruges and Ghent, although it is true these were designed primarily to serve the strategic schemes of Spinola and the Spanish government.

But what has for us an especial interest is the way in which under the direction of the Archducal government the triumph of the Counter-Reformation was completed and made secure; for the results of that process were to dominate the social and cultural life of Flanders and Brabant for many generations, and, coupled with the more gradual and less thorough penetration of Calvinism north of the Moerdyk, were to clinch the real estrangement of North and South.

The State and the Church—the Archdukes, the Bishops (following Philip II's concordat nominated by the former) and the Papal Nuncio—worked together to eradicate what might remain of previous heretical fallacies and to stimulate a vigorous religious life. Generally their collaboration was cordial enough, despite conflicts of competence in which the officials of the great councils usually adopted a stiff-necked attitude. The edicts of Charles V and Philip II had never been withdrawn, but their bloodthirstiness was no longer in agreement with the times. Yet that generation threw itself into a new folly of cruelty— witch persecution. It is a remarkable testimony to the critical spirit which conditions in the North had fostered that these ludicrously solemn trials of miserable old women never went to such lengths there as they did almost everywhere else in Europe about this time, in Calvinist Scotland as much as in the Catholic

[1] See *The Revolt of the Netherlands*, p. 108.

Netherlands. Heresy, nevertheless, was now persecuted some-what less severely. Religious convictions as such were no longer inquired into; but all the same the new edicts issued by religious and political authorities maintained intact the principle of insistence on strict outward conformity to Catholicism.

At the beginning of the Truce, which threatened to facilitate traffic with heretics, strict regulations were prescribed even for foreigners, and we have already seen that no exception was allowed even in the interest of Antwerp's trade. But in the case of the natives themselves the system went much further. Priests were enjoined to report such of their parishioners as failed in their Easter duties, and imprisonment or exile might follow. Midwives were bound by oath to see that the new-born babe should be baptized according to the rites of Holy Church. Sunday observance was decreed by episcopal order. Education was taken vigorously in hand: at least one school to every parish; no one allowed to teach except after religious examination and profession; care that the children should go to confession; compulsory Sunday schools. The synod of the diocese of Mechlin prohibited all discussion of religious subjects by lay-men, and the Archbishop confirmed the prohibition for the whole country. It was enforced by a censorship on printers and booksellers such as was quite unthinkable in the Republic. The regulations for printers in Antwerp, based on a general precept of the synod of the whole ecclesiastical province of Mechlin, were typical. No one might set up as printer or bookseller without a licence from the Archbishop, approval of the Bishop and magistracy, and proof of orthodoxy; nothing was to be printed except what had been approved by the Archbishop's or Bishop's censorship; and at any moment the episcopal super-intendent might conduct a search of printers' and booksellers' premises.

Such was the regime which, as I have said, and as we shall later see, the Synod of Dort could not succeed in establishing amid the political conditions of the North, and which indeed represented another disfiguring blot on Puteanus' idealised picture of a free Southern Netherlands. The Spanish reconquest had restored the Catholic Church to its supremacy there, and systematic governmental pressure now drove the victory home.

But that is not to say that every feature of this process came either from outside or from above; far from it. The priests, of sound education and irreproachable private lives, inspired with that new zeal which Trent had given to the Church, laid hold of the mind and spirit of the people. Of great importance in this connection were the Jesuits. Let us observe one outstanding figure.

Born at Mechlin in 1532, Father Costerus taught for years at Cologne, which in his youth was the principal centre of Jesuit activities in Northern Europe. He came back to the Netherlands during the revulsion of feeling following upon the Breaking of the Images, and in February 1567 his preaching in St. Bavo's cathedral at Ghent drew large crowds. But Alva distrusted the Jesuits, and it was only under Parma that Costerus' career in the Netherlands began in real earnest. Immediately after the fall of Antwerp in 1585 he had settled in that city as Chief of the Netherlands "province" of his order. His influence on the religious life of the provinces reduced to obedience was considerable. But it was especially in the last period of his life, when he lived in retirement at Brussels, that he developed an enormous activity as preacher and as publicist. Apologetics and polemical exchanges with Protestants, especially of the North, went hand in hand, and the series of folio volumes in which between 1597 and 1616 he collected his sermons was aimed not least at those who lived in the disobedient or rebel countries among the heretics and must do without God's word.

Written in forceful, vivid Dutch, this work is evidence of the heartfelt conviction with which the restoration was promoted. Here is not only the derision of the heretics—among whom "Harry Everyman treats of the scriptures", and who are like "ladies who change the fashions of their dresses every year"— but also the example set of fervent devotion to the Catholic faith. Here too speaks a deep concern at the disasters suffered by the Church, and at times the lukewarmness of his compatriots oppresses Costerus:

Praying, preaching, disputing and expounding, crying out and weeping, we search for you with penitence, and you make no response.

It was first and foremost through education, however, that the Jesuits tried to mould public opinion. The education of the upper classes in the towns passed almost entirely into their hands, and everywhere they founded their colleges. Even the catechism prescribed for general use by the diocesan synod of Mechlin in 1607 was the work of a Jesuit, Father Makeblyde of Poperinghe; in the North, too, this catechism came into vogue, Father Makeblyde labouring there himself from 1611. There was much jealousy of the Jesuits on the part of the secular clergy. There was also, especially at Louvain, fundamental opposition to their particular creed, aiming as it did more at social organisation than at the intensification of individual faith; even in the mysticism which was encouraged by Loyola's example all the stress was laid on the 'spiritual exercises'. But the Jesuits were protected by the Court and their influence spread powerfully throughout the Catholicism of the Southern Netherlands. A remarkable feature of the new religious zeal were the brotherhoods or sodalities in which groups of laymen, bound by social or professional ties, assembled under the direction of a priest and in the name of Mary for the purpose of venerating the sacraments. Besides the old social groupings, the gilds and companies of archers were likewise absorbed into religious life, more readily than was possible under the Reformed regime. Characteristic, for instance, was the way in which the Archduchess, who at the Zavel shooting festival at Brussels in 1615 herself brought down the bird, commemorated that popular success by instituting an annual procession, in which the six chaste maidens whom she undertook to present each year with a dowry had to take part in two successive years. In such ways civic life was sanctified and an ardent piety manifested itself in which the Archdukes, foreigners though they were, could be one with their subjects. It was with feelings of respect and emotion that people saw them take part in the processions which were celebrated with unheard-of magnificence, and the public shared their devotion for such pilgrim-shrines as those of Hal and the Scherpenheuvel at Sichem. The vogue of this last was due to their patronage; at their instance Lipsius and, after his death, Puteanus described the miracles wrought there at a statue of the Virgin, and it was they who built the circular basilica which attracts pilgrims to this day.

Writers and artists, indeed representatives of all branches of culture, enrolled themselves in the service of the new ideal. As a result the observer receives a much greater impression of unity than in the North. Here is nothing of that turbulence and those cross-currents, nothing of that individual seeking and thinking. Whereas in the North the ruling opinion still has to struggle against the opposition of a refractory society, in the South everything is absorbed into the broad stream of the Counter-Reformation.

Thus it comes about that, strong as was the humanistic tendency in the culture of the North, in the South humanism exercised an incomparably more exclusive sway. The spirit of Catholicism, triumphantly restored to power, was able to adapt to itself the search for beauty of form, the rhetoric and the stateliness of the old civilisation. Moreover, it was in Southern Europe, in Italy, that both movements had arisen and merged in the most striking harmony, and it was on the South, therefore, that their particular religious development caused Flanders and Brabant to focus their whole intellectual and artistic attention. But if we search their literature for any individual utterances, anything which promises an independent growth for the future, distinct from what is common form in Counter-Reformation Europe, then the harvest is indeed meagre.

No doubt it is worthy of note that the 'rhetoricians'[1] of North and South sought contact with each other during the Truce, exchanging questions for prize competitions and the rhymes submitted in answer to them, and even attending each other's festivals. But neither in Holland nor in Brabant and Flanders is the really fruitful culture to be looked for any longer among the rhetoricians. Whether there was anything apart from them, or perchance anything developing out of them —that is the question. In the North we shall see that the outstanding figures already mentioned at the close of the previous volume—partly of Southern extraction!—were only the precursors of a still more brilliant generation. In the South there are only a few feeble efforts, leading in the end to nothing of consequence.

One poet, long forgotten, but recently brought to light again, wrote some really beautiful things: Justus de Harduyn of Ghent, whose *Weerlijcke Liefden tot Roose-mond*, a collection of youthful verses, appeared under the auspices of the Chamber of Alost in 1613, six years after his consecration as priest. This

[1] See *The Revolt of the Netherlands*, pp. 45–6, 266, 285.

work has an immediately arresting sound, but to the mastery of form there is added no correspondingly significant content, several of the sonnets being simply translations from Du Bellay and other French Renaissance poets. De Harduyn did not forsake poetry when he ceased to be a layman, but his *Goddelijcke Lofsanghen* (1620) consist mainly of adaptations of his love-poems and fresh translations. A pure talent, but a feeble personality. From his pastory at Oudegem, near Termonde, he had some contact with like-minded rhetoricians and humanists. There *were* some such, and the work of piecing together the scraps of information to be found in prefaces, dedications and the like, about their mutual relations and their vision of a Netherland poetry has been well worth the doing, just as was the publication of De Harduyn's smooth-flowing verses; but to talk about 'a general Renaissance of literature' and 'a general efflorescence' is to lose all sense of proportion. Nothing is more noteworthy perhaps than the encouragement which De Harduyn received as early as 1608 from Puteanus, the great classical scholar of Louvain and successor of Lipsius. Just before, on his appointment as professor, he had pronounced an oration in honour of the Dutch language which testifies to an unusual insight into the relationship between the vernacular and culture, but at the same time goes to show that the vernacular was already in a bad way in Flanders and Brabant.

What may be called preliminary questions, which in the North had practically been answered by Spieghel, Van Hout, Van Mander and Heinsius[1]—such questions as the seemliness of an educated man's writing in the vernacular, the repudiation of Latinisms and the use of the regular iambic metre—still busied men's minds in the South. Van Liefvelt, lord of Opdorp, a Brusseler, who later took military service with the North, demonstrated with great zeal that it was possible to write in Dutch without using bastard words, but the work he published in 1609 was merely a translation from the French. Jacques (so he called himself) Ymmelost, lord of Steenbrugge, from Ypres, made his début in 1614 as an iambic theorist; for a professed pioneer his appearance was belated, and he found it necessary to write in French on the reform of French and Flemish poetry. An Antwerp painter, Guilliam van Nieuwland, saw his drama

[1] See *The Revolt of the Netherlands*, pp. 283–7.

Saul produced by the 'Olive Branch' Chamber of Rhetoric in 1615. The attempt to follow the example of Seneca was new, but in truth Van Nieuwland had picked up his classicism in Amsterdam.

> Do we not see the Antwerp stage hung round about with fresh green laurel once again? Is it not as if it were wrought of gold, while heretofore it was merely wood for the playing of foolish farces?

Thus De Harduyn. The priest could whole-heartedly welcome religious dramas, which in the North the minister regarded at best with suspicion. And yet *Saul* heralded no dramatic revival, while we shall see later how vigorous and how varied was the drama at Amsterdam. Painful as is the contrast, it must be pointed out, and we have to recognise that now for the first time in the history of Netherland culture all the stimuli to new enterprise and all the models came from Holland. The altered circumstances were beginning to leave their mark: here life and wealth, there poverty and stagnation.

From the point of view that we are taking, this means in the North health and in the South decay. Not only has this specifically Netherland culture a particular charm for us; in our estimation it actually surpasses in importance the general humanistic movement, for we know that this had no future and can discern in it already the symptoms of withering and decay, of degeneration into an intellectual pastime, into a barren academicism. But the circles which at that time set the intellectual tone of Europe still disdained national cultures and paid little heed to their manifestations. In so far as it employed Latin, the culture of Flanders and Brabant was not far behind that of Holland. It could boast no such outstanding figure as Grotius, but in Puteanus it had a worthy rival to Heinsius, and the high level of humanistic interest and attainment among the governing class, officials, priests and municipal magistrates, was remarkable. When in 1621 Grotius came to Antwerp following his escape from Loevestein, he found there a circle such as neither The Hague nor Amsterdam could have offered him. He was welcomed by the 'external burgomaster', Nicolaas Rockox, the patron of Rubens, who himself soon arrived to pay his respects. The Latinists did their utmost to honour one in whom they saw not only a great colleague but an opponent of the Calvinist regime of the North. Among them was the old Jesuit Schottus;

Hemelarius, canon of the cathedral; the jurist and councillor Woverius; the philologist-poet Gevartius, who was to be pensionary of Antwerp before the year was out; and the historian Miraeus, nephew of the Bishop of Antwerp and now Court Chaplain to the Archdukes at Brussels, who had not lost touch with the Antwerp group. Brant, too, the municipal secretary and father-in-law of Rubens, was a Latin author. Rockox himself collected old coins and statuary and corresponded with a large circle of intellectuals.

None of these people held the Dutch language in much esteem. Latin was their normal medium for correspondence. When Rubens must needs have recourse to Dutch, he opens with an apology:

> My reply in the Dutch tongue will sufficiently show that I do not merit the honour which Your Excellency does me with your letters in Latin. (*Thus he wrote to Gevartius in 1627, at the same time tacking on just enough Latin to show that he was no ignoramus:*) My exercises and *studia bonarum artium* are so far distant that I must needs *veniam praefari soloecismum liceat fecisse.*

Rockox wrote in French for preference, Rubens in Italian; Rubens even signed himself 'Pietro Paolo' at the end of letters in Dutch. Italian could indeed still dispute with French the first place among the languages of culture. Antwerp had a brotherhood of 'Romanists' established in 1572 at the church of St. George with SS. Peter and Paul as patron saints, to which only those who had visited Rome could belong. Rubens was introduced into it by 'Velvet' Breughel on his return to Antwerp in 1609.

The whole cultural life of Antwerp and the loyal provinces, where the ruling class and the intellectuals vied with one another in their zeal for Catholicism, their worship of antiquity and their admiration for Italy—this whole cultural movement found its most radiant expression in art.

The Counter-Reformation needed art and was sympathetic towards it. The lavish rebuilding and decoration of its ravaged churches and monasteries was an integral part of the revivification of Catholicism. It was only with the Truce, when funds became more plentiful, that activity in this sphere began in earnest; and the new spirit manifested its self-confidence in a new style, vehement and emphatic, a style which although utilising those classic forms in which artists had been working now for generations, yet in its strongly marked rhythm and feeling for the dramatic presented a sharp contrast to the Renaissance proper—the Baroque. In painting we saw it heralded already during the preceding period. In Italy it had for some time been in the ascendant, and under Italian influence it was now to dominate South Netherland architecture. It was from Italy that the Archdukes, who, like the clergy themselves, were alive to the great significance of art for religion, summoned home their Court architect, Coeberger of Antwerp; and soon he was called on to build the Scherpenheuvel church mentioned above. His (much younger) brother-in-law, Frankaert, like him many years resident in Rome, was also attached by the Archdukes to their Court and was responsible among other works for the Augustinian church at Brussels. He also wrote in favour of the new architecture, which, by introducing a circular ground-plan behind an ornate façade, and a cupola in place of towers, at last broke radically with the Gothic tradition. The Jesuits had a considerable share in the introduction of this new style, which is not surprising when we remember how much they did in general towards inculcating the new spirit, and at the same time how profoundly conscious they were of their dependence on Rome. At Amsterdam De Keyser was still building Protestant churches which were nothing else than Gothic churches in Renaissance garb (first the South, then the North and West churches, all delightful pieces of work). Meanwhile, during the Truce, Coeberger and Frankaert found themselves outstripped by the Jesuit Huyssens of Bruges, whose church of St. Charles Borromeo at Antwerp made a great impression on his contemporaries.

In a country where the towns languished there was little need of new churches, although the century was to witness the rise of a fair number. Most of the activity was directed towards the embellishment of existing Gothic churches. There began a transformation, which was to continue for a century or more, and which to this day has the effect of mentally transplanting those who visit South Netherland churches into the period of the Counter-Reformation and of the Baroque much more than into the Gothic Middle Ages. The image-breaking had made room for this change, but nothing was safe, either, from the assurance and self-confidence of the new generation of sculptors and decorators. Altars, choir and chapel screens, pulpits, stalls and monuments were built, totally out of keeping with the style of the original church-building; with heavy horizontal lines, circular arches and curving scrolls, the very black-and-white of their marble in contrast with the surrounding grey, and with vivid figures striking pathetic attitudes, the sweep of their gestures conceived in an utterly different rhythm from the ethereal soaring of the Gothic. De Keyser's mausoleum of William the Silent in the church at Delft, erected at this time, shows that the North had found no other solution of this problem of church ornament; but then the Reformers needed none, neither altar nor chapel having found a place in their worship. It was solely as a result of this difference in the requirements of the cult that the interiors of old Gothic churches in Calvinist hands were in course of time to present such a contrast to those of the Flemish and Brabant churches.

The Archducal regime, I repeat, witnessed only the beginnings of all this activity, and out of many names I select only those of the sculptors Urban Taillebert of Ypres and Koenraad of Noremberg. The first-named was responsible, among other pieces of work, for the lovely choir stalls (1598) and the monument of Bishop de Hennin (1624) in the church of St. Martin in his native town; the second built the great screen for St. John's at 's Hertogenbosch (1610–12), which was removed during the restoration of 1866 because it seriously obstructed the view of the altar, and which is now a show-piece in the Victoria and Albert Museum in London. Designed after the model of a screen built before the close of the sixteenth century by one of the Van den Broeks for the cathedral church of Our Lady at Antwerp and later likewise removed, it consists of a gallery supported on three arches springing from four pairs of columns; it is in red, white and black marble, the statues and reliefs being of alabaster. Cumbersome as it must have been in a Gothic church, there is no denying its impressiveness, the statuary in particular being of unusual beauty. The fate of a statue of St. John by De Keyser, originally intended for the church of St. John at Amsterdam, but there rejected as papistical (the church itself had in the end to be called the North Church), shows how thankless was the lot of the sculptor in the Republic.

Head and shoulders above this multitude of artists towers

the figure of Rubens. By nature and disposition in complete harmony with the spirit of the age, Rubens was no seeker nor struggler, no dealer in new ideas, but a man who, readily and unhesitatingly accepting the conventions of his time, glorified them in his art with an awe-inspiring energy, with a never-failing mastery of composition, and, above all, with a joyous and unflagging faith. His is not the quiet, introspective devotion of a former age, of Memlinc or Van der Goes, of Geertgen tot St. Jans or Gerard David; it has all that sense of the dramatic, all that joyous vehemence and assertiveness which characterised the Church victorious after the shock of contradiction and conflict. Yet within the bounds now set, the Church had triumphed so convincingly that fierceness and bitterness were utterly lacking. Rubens loves life and finds it beautiful, and everything he touches glows with life and colour. Even in such a work as the famous Descent from the Cross in the cathedral at Antwerp, which he painted for the gild of crossbowmen, and in which he renders the poignant tragedy of the scene in masterly fashion, one can feel his delight in the composition and the contrasts, in the portrayal of a sinewy body, in the hang of a dress, in the dignity of a bearded head. Besides his altar-pieces, Rubens also treated secular subjects, preferably classical and mythological, in which his feeling for sensuous beauty found outlet even more readily.

In his realism, his colour and his portrait-types a Nether-lander; in his mastery of design and composition as well as in his acceptance of a norm of beauty a pupil of the Italians; and in his vigorous movement and delight in contrast a child of his age, Rubens holds a unique place in Netherland art. So great was his influence and so numerous his following that people are sometimes tempted to identify the Flemish school with him and to regard him as above all 'pure Flemish'; the more so since Holland art, which had hitherto formed an indissoluble unit with the art of the Southern Netherlands, now, under the influence of social and religious conditions in the North, and in spite of the admiration which the Hollanders entertained for Rubens, broke away from the common precedents and went its own way; part of it did, at any rate, but this is precisely the part which to-day we most admire. Rubens was certainly 'pure Flemish', an Antwerper to the core, but taking for granted his mighty creative power, his art was the outcome of a wide European movement, conditioned much more by time and circumstance than by regional tendencies.

In any case Antwerp and the Southern Netherlands fell for him enthusiastically. Commissions flowed in on him in such a spate—from abroad, too, one of his clients being Sir Dudley Carleton, English ambassador at The Hague, whom we shall shortly meet again—that, with assistants and pupils to help, he had his hands full and commanded high prices. More youngsters aspired to a place in his studio than he could take; one of his pupils, Van Dyck, quite early displayed a talent which rivalled the master's. But what is significant is the social position which the painter enjoyed in his native city. Married at thirty-two, in the year of his return (1609), to the daughter of the municipal secretary Brant, who was himself a nephew of Peckius, the chancellor of Brabant and a humanist of repute, Rubens moved in that circle of intellectuals, ecclesiastics and notables of which I have spoken above not only as an equal but as one of whose fame—a world-wide fame—all were proud. Appointed Court painter by the Archdukes, honoured by his own city government, Rubens cut a striking figure at Antwerp. The house he built for himself just off the Meir ranked with that of Balthazar Moretus, Plantin's grandson and heir, as one of the sights of the city. It was a real Italian palace, with lovely courtyard and garden, the façade on that side and a triple gate richly embellished with figures of classical heroes, gods and goddesses, and the rooms themselves a regular museum of Italian and classical art.

Foreign with a vengeance! But then who can blame Rubens for it? The circumstances which rendered the South defenceless before those influences were not of his making. We ought rather to rejoice that Rubens himself was able to absorb Italy and classical antiquity without violating his own nature, and that his art, however heterogeneous it appears under analysis, was inspired by a pulsating life which could in its turn generate life. At the same time his position at Antwerp proves the aristocratic tone of society there: cultural contact between the intellectuals and the ruling class, no matter whether it was Spanish or native, sufficed to create the unity out of which alone such a position as Rubens' could arise; the people did not count. In the North a phenomenon like Rubens was in any case unthinkable, as well by reason of the fundamental disunity of Northern society—for all the ambitious claims of Calvinism—as because of that society's middle-class character; for the military Court of the Oranges was connected with it by but the loosest of ties.

B. THE RELIGIOUS DISPUTES IN THE NORTH

WHAT a change it is from this tranquil and somewhat hothouse-like atmosphere, charged with sultry and exotic perfumes, to turn to the North! There fresh winds and even tempests blow, ideas buffet one another heavily and noisily, developments are born out of conflict; but all that grows there is redolent of the soil.

The religious disputes which dominate the history of the Republic during the Truce are foreign to the present-day reader. His first reaction is one of dismay at this squandering of so much passion on such incomprehensible issues. When he has browsed a little in the musty library of polemics bequeathed by legions of theologians and divines, he is at a loss to choose between astonishment and disgust at the virulence with which these Christians fell upon each other, and at the dry-as-dust argumentations, cram-full of quibblings and hair-splittings, with which they sought to approach the eternal verities. This, of course, simply means that we of the present, to whom that bygone generation can still speak so directly through its poetry or its art, find its theological terminology hopelessly antiquated. If we only take the trouble to decipher these weird symbols we find them full of a profound human significance. The struggle becomes one between enduring principles, and in the combatants we discern an infinitely enthralling diversity of personalities, whose minds and characters take shape and colour before our eyes. The religious disputes are no longer an extraordinary lapse in an otherwise rich and fruitful age. They are themselves an expression of this wealth and fruitfulness; the age lives in them, and even in its apparently most accessible manifestations is not to be understood without them.

The clash of arms was hushed as if to focus attention upon

the warrings of the divines. The international situation was, indeed, still in the highest degree uncertain, and the hovering threat of a renewed Habsburg onslaught, combined with the uneasiness inspired by the existence of a large Catholic population at home, kept alive the passions aroused by the conclusion of the Truce. And now there arose a new danger in the East.

For more than a generation the German Reformed princes had felt confident of their safety in the system of equilibrium established by the Religious Peace of Augsburg, and in that security had done little to support the revolt of the Netherlands. Now, however, it appeared that this equilibrium was tilting against them. Catholic princes felt equal to planning the reconquest of districts long ago lost to Protestantism. True, the position of the Imperial authority in its own hereditary dominions, hopelessly weakened as it was in the course of the long reign of the feeble-minded Rudolph, constituted a serious defect in the Catholic cause. When in 1610 the succession to the counties of Cleve, Gulich and Berg, directly on the eastern frontier of the Republic, fell vacant, and the Protestant claimants had to maintain themselves against an Imperial decision, France and the States-General could see in this an opportunity to turn the scale of German politics against the encroachment of the Counter-Reformationist forces. Henry IV was not so good a Catholic but that the feud with Habsburg was with him, as it had been with Henry II, the first consideration. How closely in the Dutch Republic internal discords were connected with this state of tension on the European stage, appears from disturbances occurring at this juncture at Utrecht.

The man who was there raised to the burgomaster's office by popular acclamation, Dirk Canter, and his associate Van Brakel, a nobleman who was trying to be re-admitted to the States, were no doubt largely animated by personal ambitions. Canter had made his way into the town government shortly after the Leicester episode as a champion of the provincial States against the Reformed ministers and the burgher captains. Having fallen out with the ruling group, he now looked for support to the citizens who blamed the oligarchy for their corrupt dealing with the secularised possessions of the old Church and who regarded the new ministers of the Arminian persuasion as no better than the regents' lackeys. But simultaneously Canter needed the help of the papists still so numerous at Utrecht. In *their* minds the thought was stirring that now that it was peace they could not in fairness be denied the freedom to practise their religion, and Canter, the friend of the rigidly Calvinistic citizen guards, encouraged them in this. The monstrous alliance between Calvinistic democracy and papism seemed to Oldenbarnevelt to threaten the foundations of his political system, and when Maurice, called to the town as the province's Stadholder, was visibly wavering, the demonic energy of the old Advocate got the States-General to interfere forcibly. Henry IV's and James I's ambassadors were involved in the negotiations with the rebellious town, as if to show the world that the maintenance of the oligarchy was regarded as a matter concerning the whole of anti-Habsburg Europe. The Utrechters, however, were not to be cowed in this way, and so the States-General dispatched troops which, Maurice being unwilling, were commanded by his brother Frederick Henry. Fighting was avoided. A capitulation was arranged, and once the town had admitted troops inside its walls, the old magistracy was soon reinstalled. The heterogeneous composition of the malcontent party had paralysed its strength, but the incident and its immediate epilogue—a new conspiracy, prosecutions and confiscations, also the organisation of a carefully purged civic guard—reveal in a flash the narrowness of the basis on which the new State rested.

Vigorous action, not only at home, but also beyond the frontiers, in order to check the swelling tide of the Counter-Reformation, was therefore felt to be all the more necessary. Very shortly after Utrecht had given in to Frederick Henry's little army, conditions in Europe were brought to a much more menacing pass by the assassination of Henry IV (1610). France was plunged into confusion, and the ultra-Catholic party, which leant on Spain, was brought to power at the French Court. Thus it was a States' army under Maurice which was called upon almost unaided to put both claimants in possession of the duchies, and when in 1614 these two princes fell out, and one chose the Catholic side, it was again the States who supported the other, the Elector of Brandenburg. Nor was it the Emperor himself, but the Archdukes Albert and Isabella (and that meant Spain) acting in his name, who aided Brandenburg's rival, and a States' army under Maurice and a Spanish army under Spinola each occupied a line of fortresses in the disputed territory without coming to grips with one another. As advanced defensive works against the menace rising ominously from the German chaos, the States kept Gulich, Emmerich, Rees and other strong places occupied; indeed, the Spaniards now sat entrenched in Aachen and Wesel. Their position in the last-named town especially was regarded in the Republic with serious misgivings, and Olden-barnevelt's acquiescence in that outcome—for it was he who in effect handled the whole of this affair—was resented by many. After what had happened at Utrecht it is somewhat surprising to hear suspicions of Spanish proclivities voiced against the old Advocate. It seems obvious that the situation did not permit a more active policy, since no reliance was to be placed either on France under the regency of Marie de Medici or on England under the weak and conceited James I, whom Spain was keeping in leading-strings with the famous marriage plan.

Relations with England were in fact beginning to present their own difficulties. The community of interests against Spain came in course of time to be overshadowed by the rivalry of the mercantile classes. Many Englishmen were growing uneasy at the swift progress of their former protégé, and what was especially hard to bear was the knowledge that the prosperity of Dutch shipping was based on the herring fishery ('the great fishery') off the Scottish coast in the North Sea, which from early times had been regarded as under the English Crown. This old medieval theory of England's dominion over the narrow seas was revived as a weapon against the Dutch fishers, and although James never got as far as using it, time and again the question led to the most ticklish negotiations. Then there were the Indies, where the expansion of the young Republic was not only pushed forward, despite the Truce, at the expense of Spain and Portugal, but led to bloody conflict with the English, whose rivalry although coming late seemed the more dangerous for the future. But these events are of such importance—for only now were the foundations of a Dutch East Indian empire truly laid—that I shall deal with them separately later.

The outbreak of a Church quarrel in the province of Holland, which now claims our attention, had been long preparing. We noticed in the previous volume[1] that Arminius, one of the theological professors at Leiden, taught views on predestination which deviated from strict Calvinism, thereby causing his colleague Gomarus to show signs of uneasiness. This uneasiness spread to the ministry, and as early as 1605 the South Holland synod approached the curators of the university with a request to put certain questions to the professors for elucidation. The curators, however, members of the Leiden magistracy and of the Holland States, fobbed off the petitioners: only a National Synod, they replied, was competent to handle such matters.

No National Synod had met since the time of Leicester, but now the ministers asked the States-General to authorise one to meet. It did not accord at all with the view of authority, however, to countenance an ecclesiastical arraignment of Arminius and his supporters scattered among the ministry. Under the influence of Oldenbarnevelt, the States therefore, while giving permission for the assembly of a synod, prescribed as its object the revision of the Heidelberg Catechism and of the Netherland Confession.[2] This was wholly unacceptable to the majority of the ministry; it was by those very documents that they wanted to test the orthodoxy of Arminius and his followers. The Arminians, like the 'libertinists' before them, denied that the written creeds had any binding force or could be used as formularies to compel uniformity. When, therefore, the States-General in 1607 called together for advice a preliminary assembly of seventeen theologians representing several provinces, four Arminians amongst them pronounced in favour of revision on the lines of the States' original resolution, thus preventing unanimity. That was enough for the States to abide by their decision, while the majority of the ministers rejected a synod on those conditions. This majority—the Church, as it called itself—had many other ways, failing a synod, of thwarting its opponents. The examination before the 'classis' committee, which young theologians just down from Leiden had to pass before being admitted to the office of minister in any particular district, was an especially useful weapon. Arminius' students often had a rough passage. For their part the Arminians stoutly

---

[1] See The Revolt of the Netherlands, p. 289.
[2] The Confession originally drawn up by De Bray. See The Revolt of the Netherlands, p. 68.

maintained, both now and later on, that they deviated only on points of secondary importance, and while they maintained fraternal communion with the majority, untroubled by conscientious scruples, they challenged the others' right to cut them off on account of the points in dispute.

Was the difference really so small? In 1609—the Truce had just been concluded and Arminius, still only in middle age, but a consumptive, had less than two months to live—there was arranged, in the hope of reconciling them, a conference between the two Leiden professors, each seconded by four ministers, in the presence of Oldenbarnevelt and a committee of the States of Holland. It served only to widen the breach. One of Arminius' seconders, the Hague court preacher Utenbogaert, the man of the world, who was listened to by Oldenbarnevelt and the States, and at this time by Maurice also, later complained that

it was there declared that Arminius' doctrine of justification is worse than that of the Jesuits, that it is contrary to Christ's honour, that *they* would not dare to appear with it before the Judgment Seat of Christ.

The opponents of predestination, although somewhat less aggressively inclined, themselves gave vent at times to feelings of real abhorrence.

You turn God into a tyrant and an executioner,

a 'libertinist' or 'moderate' theologian at Leiden had thrown at a Calvinist colleague a generation before, and the gentle Arminius himself flared up against what he called the 'blasphemy' of a student who had declared, under the influence of other teachers, that man could offer no resistance to God's resolve that he should transgress the law.

Indeed, pursued to their logical extremes, the two principles led to two completely different worlds of ideas. On the one side there were those who sacrificed all humanity to the dizzy edifice erected by Calvin to the honour of God. With these nothing counted save the eternal decree whereby God had lifted them, unworthy as they were, from out the universal perdition of the human race. In the face of haters and seducers they clung to the conviction that, no matter what they did, they could not fall lastingly from grace, nor anything deprive them of salvation. For them and for the Reformed Church alone Christ had died and the Republic of the Seven Netherlands been delivered out of Spanish chains, for so it had pleased God to decree for all eternity. As against that, the others were unwilling to ascribe that certain power for good, which they too felt within themselves, so exclusively to an arbitrary working of God's will; and the smallest encroachment which they ('contrary to Christ's honour') allowed themselves in that direction was like a door wide open to the whole world of mankind outside the narrow community of their little Church, to love joy and beauty. Each side accused the other of pride. The Arminians uttered the warning

that the dreadful doctrine of predestination renders useless all remonstrance and punishment and destroys all zeal for godliness.

It was a favourite taunt of theirs that the spirit of the papist inquisition seemed reborn in their opponents; but the Gomarists wanted to know who was to draw the line between important and unimportant differences, and asserted that the slightest relaxation must inevitably lead to 'doctrinal liberty'. As a matter of fact, Libertinists and 'free-thinkers' outside the Church everywhere stood ready to support the campaign against 'exactitude' and to carry it on to much more sweeping conclusions.

> You call the Pope the Antichrist,
> But are there not other such to find?
> Methinks that all who deem it good
> Our spirits with their dreams to bind,
> Are chickens of the self-same brood.

Utterances of that nature could not fail to rouse the Contra-Remonstrants, and they warned their countrymen that the principle of Arminianism led directly to pelagianism, papism, socinianism and atheism, and of these the most dangerous in the eyes of the congregations was papism, for did not papism imply pro-Spanish feeling? Oldenbarnevelt might be broad enough to see

that among papists, too, there are numbered many loyal upholders of the fatherland.

But he said it only to the French ambassador; the view did not move him to any positive action. And indeed in a community which saw the Catholic supremacy being restored in the surrounding countries, the fear of a like fate made the pursuit of a policy of confidence impossible. At the same time the disabilities imposed upon Catholics rendered it difficult for them to identify themselves with the existing order. How little they did so appears from the instructions which their exiled leader Vosmeer[1] concerted with the Jesuit provincial at Brussels in 1610, and which served as the rule of conduct for both priests and Jesuit missionaries in the North. Among the things which they were to represent as unfitting for believers were: studying at the heretical universities of Leiden and Franeker, taking shares in the Dutch East India Company, and furnishing supplies to armies which fought against Catholic monarchs. The knowledge that new generations of priests were being reared up outside the States' territory, at Cologne and especially at Louvain, was quite sufficient to arouse the suspicions of Northern patriots, and in this atmosphere no assertion went home so dangerously as that the Arminian was himself a disguised papist, a concealed Jesuit.

In the serious theological discussions, it is true, the potent conflict of principle seems to get lost in the fine-spun webs of argument. Arminius especially was inclined to minimise it. In the disputes during his Amsterdam period[2] he had stopped the mouth of Plancius, his foremost opponent there, with the admission that even innocent children are liable to damnation for original sin. It was one of his opponent's charges that he would not come straight out into the open in defence of his opinions, but spread his heresies secretly, in an underhand way, among his students. His was no fighting nature, and exposed as he was to a formidable heresy hunt by the grim and explosive Gomarus and the great majority of the ministry, it is not surprising that he twisted those views, which he yet could not bring himself to renounce, into words approaching as nearly as possible to accepted opinion. On their side the strict Calvinists were extremely sensitive to the reproach that they made God the creator of sin, and in their defence they sometimes appear to soften the rigidity of their system. But all the same the difference was there, and following the death of Arminius it developed irresistibly.

It was impossible for authority to keep out of the conflict. Peace and unity in the State Church were universally considered

[1] See *The Revolt of the Netherlands*, pp. 226-7.
[2] See *The Revolt of the Netherlands*, p. 289.

a major political interest. Just now I mentioned the meeting of theologians in 1609 before a committee of the States of Holland. This was not the first attempt of its kind made in that province, where the dispute raged most fiercely. As early as 1607, shortly after the abortive conference arranged by the States-General, Gomarus and Arminius had appeared before the High Council of Justice (a Holland body), and the following year each professor had developed his views in a long address before the full assembly of the States of Holland. The death of Arminius in October 1609 did not bring about reconciliation; on the contrary, the funeral oration pronounced by Bertius, Regent of the States Seminary (for intending ministers) at the University had incensed Gomarus, and the majority began making matters even harder for the Arminians. So in 1610 the Arminian ministers took a step of the highest importance. There can be no doubt that it was concerted with Oldenbarnevelt through the medium of Utenbogaert. Under Utenbogaert's direction forty-four ministers meeting very privately gave their approval to a 'Remonstrance', setting forth their views on the vexed question of justification by faith, to be forwarded to the States of Holland along with a request for protection. Following this profession of faith they were henceforward called Remonstrants. What really mattered was the request for protection.

The States' first and instinctive reaction could not fail to be in favour of granting that protection. Here was a dispute among theologians, difficult for laymen to comprehend even in an age infatuated with theology, but the least theologically-inclined regent could predict the result of leaving the Church to deal with it on her own. The Remonstrants would be expelled, doctrine defined in exact terms, and an even more arrogant supervision exercised over the orthodoxy of the authorities and of their proceedings. Memories were carried back not only to the days of Leicester, but to what had happened in Flanders before then.

If the secular authority can be thus countermined, things will go as in Flanders in your time,

wrote Oldenbarnevelt somewhat later to Caron, the States' envoy in England, who was a Flemish refugee.[1] The freedom claimed by the Church meant not merely freedom within her

[1] cf. *The Revolt of the Netherlands*, pp. 162-5. See also below, p. 62.

own sphere, but the right to set the tone in the State at large. This was how regents had looked at it from the first days of independence, and, in common with Protestant governments everywhere, they had been on their guard against this danger.[1] Leicester had in 1586 pushed through a "Church settlement" more or less in accordance with the orthodox ministers' desires, but it had not survived his brief governorship. The ministers had continued to regard the regents' attitude as an insufferable ambition for power, and the opposing views were so little to be reconciled that, despite an earnest attempt in 1591, it had not been found possible to effect an adjustment of the relations of Church and State in the form of a Church settlement accepted by both sides.

The theological dispute now brought this old question again to the fore, and in a more dangerous shape than ever, for, although the States of Holland did not yet grasp this, it was becoming more than a ministers' quarrel: it was beginning to arouse the passions of the religious community. For that reason all efforts at reconciliation and peace-making were doomed to failure, were regarded, indeed, by the more numerous group, which was prevented from availing itself of its strength, as intolerable interference. Worse still, in the long run the States themselves, exasperated by the obstinacy of the orthodox party, gave rein to anger, so that their measures assumed an unmistakably dictatorial and coercive character. With a heated stubbornness developing on both sides, the tension increased from one year to another, until nothing but an explosion could clear the air.

In 1610 the States of Holland actually granted the protection which the Remonstrants had demanded. The States admonished ministers to leave in peace those candidates at classis examinations who would not go beyond the five points of the Remonstrance, and at the same time to cease raking up in their sermons

those lofty and mysterious questions which are at present, God help it, all too much in dispute.

It will be remembered that the Archdukes were able to enforce a much more comprehensive prohibition of theological discussion. In Holland the States' resolution was like a word

[1] See *The Revolt of the Netherlands*, pp. 204-5.

spoken into the storm. The majority of the ministry now followed the minority's example and began to organise itself in order to influence the authorities. In 1611 the States of Holland summoned a fresh conference between six ministers from each side, and here it was that the orthodox party—their leader was Festus Hommius of Leiden, the fiercest among them Plancius of Amsterdam—presented the Counter-Remonstrance in which their views on election were set forth. No agreement was possible. The Contra-Remonstrants were all the time urging that the Church should settle the matter herself, but this the States of Holland could not permit. The Contra-Remonstrants in Holland now reinforced themselves with the assistance of those in the other provinces, and joint petitions were addressed to the States-General for permission to convoke a National Synod. But although most of the other provinces, where Arminianism had made little or no headway, were ready simply to act on the advice of their ministers, the influence of Holland and of Holland's Advocate was sufficient to rule out an assent to this demand.

With one 'reconciliation conference' after another leaving the ministers more acutely divided against each other than ever, the States of Holland were irresistibly drawn further along the path of intervention. The Remonstrants, to whom the States' protection was all-important, practically invited them to arrogate to themselves legislative powers over the Church. Almost simultaneously with the Remonstrance Utenbogaert had published his *Treatise of the office and authority of a High Christian Government in affairs of religion*, in which he insistently urged the States of Holland not to let fall in abeyance, but vigorously to maintain, that authority over the Church which they had received from God:

God has made you into gods over your people. . . . See to it, and take care, how your subjects are being instructed, and what is offered to Christ's poor sheep to eat; and look to it earnestly.

This admonition did not fall on deaf ears. In 1612 the States resolved to empower municipal and other authorities to conduct themselves conformably with that Church settlement which the regents, flushed with their victory over Leicester and his allies the ministers, had drafted in 1591, but which they had not after all, in the face of the protests of the synods, dared to put into operation. What this meant in practice was soon clear from one sensational case after another. Thus, at the village of Warmenhuizen a Remonstrant minister was forcibly inducted by the lord of the manor with the help of the sheriff of Alkmaar. At Rotterdam the minister Geselius, who refused to live amicably with his Remonstrant colleague Grevinckhoven, or to hold his peace about the 'lofty and mysterious questions', was first cautioned and then suspended by the magistracy, and when after that, egged on by the fiery Ds. Smout, he still continued to edify his stalwarts in private devotions, he was banished from the town without form of trial. Henceforward the Rotterdam Contra-Remonstrants went outside the town gates to worship, and were ridiculed as 'Mud Beggars'.[1]

Meanwhile, Oldenbarnevelt judged it necessary to proclaim his system yet more explicitly and impressively. In January 1614 there was promulgated a resolution of the States of Holland setting precise limits to what might be taught in the Reformed Church. Extremes on either side were condemned, namely,

that God the Lord created any man unto damnation, (*or on the contrary:*) that man of his own natural powers or deeds can achieve salvation; both tending to God's dishonour, and to great slandering of our Christian Reformation, and conflicting with our considered intention.

Liberty of disputation was left to the universities, but

we do not intend that those lofty disputations which may give rise, contrary to our aforesaid order and considered intention, to the above-mentioned preposterous deductions and extremities, should be brought into the open, or into the pulpit, or otherwise before the commonalty generally.

Whoever in the course of such disputations refused to go 'higher' than the doctrine of the Remonstrance, might not on that account be molested,

the said doctrine being also sufficient unto salvation and meet for Christian edification.

Well might Trigland say (the Amsterdam minister who was to chronicle these events from the strict orthodox standpoint)

that the authors of this resolution take upon themselves to declare what doctrine is sufficient unto salvation, which is about as much as constituting oneself master of the word of God and of the rule of life there laid down for us.

---

[1] Beggars, of course, to be understood as an allusion to the fighting men of the sixteenth-century Revolt.

In the seventeenth century, when the Church claimed that the State should uphold her doctrine as the one and only verity, such presumption on the part of the State could certainly be explained as a measure of self-defence. Oldenbarnevelt, calling to mind the rise of Protestantism, considered it simply preposterous that anyone should contest the authorities' right of decision.

Now to regard as ignorants the magistrates, who were once so seriously summoned on their conscience and their office to adopt the Reformation and to take the matter of religion to heart; to deny them any understanding, and to want them to see through other eyes; is by many considered not to be right or reasonable.

And in truth Oldenbarnevelt did not stand alone in that opinion, and took good care that it should be known. He sought to cover himself with no less a name than that of the King of England. It had come to him as a most unpleasant shock when in 1611 James I had declaimed with surprising vehemence against the appointment of the German theologian Vorstius to Arminius' chair. Vorstius was Utenbogaert's nominee, and the Contra-Remonstrants, who thus had an objection to him in any case, were not a little rejoiced at this unexpected intervention on the King's part. James, who prided himself on his theological learning, detected Socinianism in Vorstius' writings and reprimanded the States with more than paternal severity for their unconsidered decision. Winwood, the English ambassador at The Hague, declared that the religious tie uniting the two countries had been severed. However offended he might be at the King's tone, Oldenbarnevelt was forced to give in, and the unlucky Vorstius, who had already resigned his German post, passed years at Gouda composing defences of his orthodoxy. True, the Contra-Remonstrants were no better off with Episcopius, the young and able Hollander who was now appointed. Gomarus had quitted Leiden in high dudgeon, and although he was succeeded by a Contra-Remonstrant, the majority of the Church still felt it a crying scandal that youths preparing for the ministry were liable to be led away from the straight and narrow path by his colleague.

But Oldenbarnevelt, the wiser for the Vorstius case, now prefaced the resolution which was to set the coping-stone to his work with a full-dress diplomatic action. Whatever the relations between the Contra-Remonstrant theologians and the Archbishop of Canterbury might have achieved in the Vorstius case, it remained a fact that the authority wielded by the King of England over his own Church was not less extensive than that which the Contra-Remonstrants begrudged to the States, and so in 1613 the Advocate managed to elicit a letter from the King recommending to them, as the only way to peace, a prohibition of any discussion of the disputed points in the pulpit and the enforcement of mutual forbearance respecting those points. To this James had added, after a study of the five points submitted to him by Caron in Utenbogaert's French translation, that the doctrine of both parties was compatible with truth and with salvation.

It was under distinguished patronage, therefore, that the resolution was released upon the bewildered Contra-Remonstrants, and many of them accepted the ruling. Fortunately for the country's spiritual life many others resisted it strenuously. So instead of peace the resolution produced a new crop of untoward incidents: municipal governments mulcting refractory citizens for holding unlawful assemblies—how very distressing was it for members of the State Church to find themselves more rigorously dealt with than Lutherans, Baptists or even Papists! but then, what those sects did was no concern of the State—and turbulent ministers being warned, threatened, suspended, dismissed, exiled. One of the worst cases took place under the very nose of the States, indeed, as a result of their interference: the case of Rosaeus, Utenbogaert's colleague at The Hague, who refused to partake of the Lord's Supper with him. Twelve hundred members of the congregation petitioned the States in 1616 for 'restitution' of the dismissed minister, but Utenbogaert threatened to resign if they surrendered to

so temerarious a slighting of their Noble Mightinesses' authority.

Henceforward the malcontents could only 'walk out' to Ryswyk (a village near The Hague) on Sundays. Such methods gradually aroused an ugly spirit among the Protestant multitude, however permeated it might be with a profound respect for authority. The forbidden doctrine of predestination, declared by authority to be unessential to salvation, was clung to with growing fervour as almost the sole essential, and those who

belittled it were held to be atheists and papists. It was said that
Utenbogaert and Arminius had been promised the cardinal's
hat by the Pope if they succeeded in bringing the Dutch Church
back under Rome. It is obvious that the doctrine of Arminius,
which ascribed to man a capacity to contribute something to his
own salvation, might in a way bridge the chasm separating
Protestantism and Catholicism. And as a matter of fact there
were adherents who opposed the view current among the
Reformed according to which the Church of Rome was totally
estranged from Christianity and the Pope identical with Anti-
christ. This is something still very different from being ready to
be reconciled to the old Church, and even though some few
isolated individuals went that way later—Bertius for instance,
and perhaps also Grotius—the large majority of Arminians
stood fast by the Reformation. Nevertheless insinuations to this
effect were fraught with danger to their position in the prevailing
atmosphere. Of Oldenbarnevelt it was whispered that he stood
in the pay of Spain; had he not forced through the Truce? Even
apart from such slanders, the policy of Holland appeared to
many in the light of a danger to the country. How was the
Republic to survive, if the Church in one or two provinces was
forced along a divergent course and the States-General shrank
from summoning a National Synod to restore unity? Oldenbarnevelt himself was too much of a *politique* of the school of
William the Silent to regard strict religious conformity as an
indispensable basis for the State, and among the regent class
that was certainly not an unusual view.

The most serious weakness in Oldenbarnevelt's position,
nevertheless—more serious than either the fury of the Calvinist
community or the censure of the other provinces—was the fact
that the ruling class in the province of Holland was not of a
single mind. The resolution of January 1614 had not been adopted
unanimously; Amsterdam, Enkhuizen, Edam and Purmerend
had not accepted it. It was therefore not a proper resolution,
argued the more implacable of the Contra-Remonstrants,
and in any case the ministers in the opposing towns need not
bother about it, for the magistrates of a voting town did not
allow a majority resolution of the provincial States to lay down
the law to them. Amsterdam, with its nine ministers, all Contra-
Remonstrants, among them Plancius and Trigland, was a

stronghold of the whole party. In 1616 an attempt was made to bring the Amsterdam government to other views: Hugo Grotius appeared before the town council as spokesman of a solemn deputation from the States of Holland, and delivered a long address urging his audience to fall into line with the majority in favour of the resolution of 1614.

Hugo Grotius, then still in his early thirties, enjoyed international repute as classical scholar, theologian, historian, and lawyer. A year or two before, at the request of Oldenbarnevelt, he had become pensionary of Rotterdam in order to assist the old Advocate in the States of Holland. A whole-hearted supporter of Oldenbarnevelt's religious policy, he had helped to draft the resolution of 1614 and now defended it in an erudite but crystal-clear argumentation before the rulers of Amsterdam. The town council resolved, nevertheless, 'by a majority of a few votes', to adhere to its former standpoint.

We may well ask why it was that these Amsterdam regents of all people should reject the thesis of the supremacy of the secular authority so attractively presented by Grotius. So typical a libertinist as ex-Burgomaster C. P. Hooft (who was now kept outside the burgomastership every year) had been an authoritative figure among them. Why did they now encourage their ministers in their zeal for strict doctrine and in their exaltation of the free synod above the States? That they feared the rage of the Amsterdam populace, which broke up Remonstrant meetings, is improbable; it was precisely the liberty of action they allowed the ministers which caused that violence. The ministers' disposal of Church funds, so said the opponents, came in useful for that purpose. There were, moreover, other sections of the population whose support the burgomasters, had they so wished, could have relied upon. It is true that the Reformed community alone was sufficiently strong in organisation and possessed enough self-confidence to become a real political danger. But, apart from the Remonstrants, there were the Catholics and the Baptists, there was the old tradition of libertinism. As in the days of Spieghel and Roemer Visscher,[1] the Amsterdam intelligentsia were averse from rigid Calvinism; we shall consider this point in detail later. Here we need only observe that Samuel Coster and his Academy, who took up so

[1] See *The Revolt of the Netherlands*, pp. 172, 283–6.

determined a stand against the ministers, evidently had not only intellectual but popular force at their disposal; and that the consistory, deprived of the support of the burgomasters, would have availed little against free expression of opinion and free teaching. Once again, then, why did the town government side with those who repudiated a conception so favourable to its authority?

The burgomasters, who at Amsterdam more than in other Holland towns were the all-powerful directors of municipal policy, represented only a majority, and a small majority, of the Amsterdam town council; the minority, led by the upright but all too gentle ex-burgomaster Hooft, was systematically excluded from 'the burgomasters' room'. This majority did include a certain number of whole-hearted supporters of the Contra-Remonstrant cause, whose leader was the ambitious and passionate Reinier Pauw. But were not others actuated by wholly different considerations? As we saw in the previous volume, Amsterdam had tried to prevent the conclusion of the Truce, a policy in which Calvinist hatred of Spain had coincided with economic interests.[1] The town had had to bow to the authority of Oldenbarnevelt, but many of its leading men were still feeling sore. Clinging obstinately to the scheme for a West India Company, which the peace policy had ruled out, these now—so we may suppose—made use of the opposition to the Advocate's religious policy to bring about his downfall. Many other considerations of municipal policy, in which 'self-seeking' was the deciding factor, produced a situation in which Pauw could bring the weight of Amsterdam to bear on national policy after his own good pleasure and could act on his conviction

that it was high time to let a good breeze blow over the country.

And, indeed, a crisis was coming to be the only way of relieving the unbearable tension. There was another factor besides the attitude of Amsterdam which was not conditioned solely, nor even primarily, by religious considerations, but which, nevertheless, when the crisis did arise, determined the issue against Oldenbarnevelt and his party. This factor was the attitude of the Stadholder.

Early in 1617 Prince Maurice, who had hitherto kept aloof

[1] See *The Revolt of the Netherlands*, pp. 253–4.

from the dispute, unconditionally chose the side of the Contra-Remonstrant extremists. To doubt that he was brought to this decision by deep religious conviction does not necessarily involve labelling him a hypocrite. Nothing that we know of Maurice, neither his manner of life nor any utterance of his, would lead us to suppose that religious problems had any profound conscientious significance for him. It was otherwise with William Louis, Stadholder of Friesland and Groningen; it is indeed only natural that John of Nassau's son had much earlier taken a strict Calvinist line. William Louis exercised a certain influence over his cousin at The Hague. But that was by no means all.

We saw in the previous volume[1] how the negotiation of the Truce had brought Maurice into sharp conflict with the Advocate, whose lead he had so far followed in the political sphere, and how he had on that occasion fallen into line with the Calvinists, against whom he had let himself be used by Oldenbarnevelt early in his career. The West India Company group at Amsterdam at that time already belonged to the opposition alliance. It was almost inevitable that when, with the dispute becoming more and more acute, Maurice found himself forced to make a decision, he should have entered the camp where he had found himself before in 1608.

And the more so since in the meantime he had differed from the Advocate, and again in company with the strict Calvinists, on yet another question of foreign policy. What attitude was the country to adopt towards the civil commotions in France following the death of Henry IV which refused to subside? The Dutch Calvinists saw in the Huguenot nobility, rising time and again against the Catholic government, the natural allies of the Republic. Oldenbarnevelt, on the contrary, was convinced that trouble-making was all that was to be expected from them; as he saw it, a strong French government, even though Catholic, would not be so pro-Spanish—and that was all that mattered—as one embarrassed by Huguenot turbulence. So far from wanting the Republic to support the Huguenot nobility, he judged that its interest, in the threatening situation then preparing through the concert between the Spanish and the German Habsburgs, demanded the maintenance of a good understanding

_____
[1] See *The Revolt of the Netherlands*, p. 251.

with the French government. During the first years of the Truce the States' ambassador, Aerssens, had deeply offended the French Court by his intrigues with the rebel notables. By replacing him in 1614 Oldenbarnevelt had gained the French Government's goodwill, but from that moment he had in Aerssens an implacable enemy. Maurice fell very much under the influence of this unscrupulous man, who served as a link between him and one of the leading Huguenot malcontents, his own brother-in-law the Duke of Bouillon. It was these French complications which, combined with the settlement of the Gulich-Cleves succession quarrel by which Wesel was left in Spanish hands, lent credence to the charge that the old Advocate was the accomplice of Spain in seeking to reintroduce Catholicism. We heard the cry of 'Popery!' being raised as an outcome of the theological dispute; now the conduct of foreign policy seemed to confirm these fears.

And yet another foreign country was mixed up in the domestic crisis. To play off against the French ambassador at The Hague, the coalition against the Advocate could rely on the ambassador from James I. From 1616 Sir Dudley Carleton filled this post. His sovereign was deeply offended over a transaction into which Oldenbarnevelt had wheedled him that year, namely, the evacuation at a relatively low compensation of the 'cautionary towns' (Brill and Veere) which had been in English hands since 1585. No less obnoxious to James was the protection which the Dutch East India Company enjoyed from Oldenbarnevelt and his party in its struggle with the English Company (of which we shall later treat in detail). They, again, bore in his eyes the odium of the States' defence of the Dutch fishermen's traditional right to fish in those waters which he was pleased to call his own. Grotius' *Mare Liberum* had been in fact aimed at the arrogance of the Spanish and Portuguese, who wanted to appropriate the oceans, but the cap fitted James and he put it on; he never forgave Grotius his 'extravagance'. The recurrent conflict over the English wool trade—which Antwerp would so dearly have loved to turn to its advantage[1]— heightened his feelings still further. All the more readily, therefore, the King, enlightened by the Contra-Remonstrants, now considered himself to have been duped over the letter which

[1] See below, p. 22.

Oldenbarnevelt and Utenbogaert had got him to write so as to place the resolution of 1614 under his patronage. That letter was now repudiated, and Dudley Carleton made one representation after another to the States in favour of a synod as the only way out of the difficulty, while at the same time seeking contact with the Stadholder.

Maurice was thus getting accustomed to looking upon the Calvinists as his allies in purely political affairs. And now the happenings in the congregation of The Hague confronted him with the choice of declaring either for the supporters of Rosaeus or for the States of Holland.

The Hague 'sufferers', in the view of the States schismatics, in their own eyes the true Church, had grown tired of trooping out to Ryswyk for their Sunday services. Firmly determined all the same to hold no communion with Utenbogaert and the Remonstrants, they had a house in the town fitted up for their services, in spite of the regulations to the contrary, and even threatened to take possession of a church. In January 1617 the Commissioned Councillors (the standing committee of the States of Holland), who were responsible for law and order in The Hague, asked the Stadholder to assist in maintaining the civil authority and enforcing the resolutions. Maurice told the greffier to read out of the register the article of the instruction which he had sworn in 1585, laying upon him the duty of protecting 'the true Reformed religion', and then said:

So long as I live, I shall keep my oath and defend that religion.

A weighty pronouncement this, whereby the Stadholder, the commander of the army, implied that he did not recognise as orthodox those Remonstrant ministers whom the States regarded as representing 'the true Reformed religion' just as much as the others.

This matter is not to be settled by many orations and flowery arguments (*Maurice declared somewhat later in the full assembly of the States of Holland, after Oldenbarnevelt, Grotius and others had put their point of view*); but with this (*slapping his sword hilt on this word*), with this will I defend the religion which my father implanted in these lands, and I will see who shall hinder me!

This was, to be sure, an arbitrary use of the memory of William the Silent, who in his time had been the patron of all 'latitudinarians' or 'libertinists' and the advocate of the political, the national, conception of the Revolt. But it had now become an article of faith with the Contra-Remonstrants that they were the veritable 'Old Beggars' and that the War of Independence had been waged for their sake, a claim which not only the great Orange himself, but many of his boldest supporters, men like Coornhert, Van Hout or Van der Does, would have flatly rejected and which deeply offended men still living, such as old Hooft, once an exile, or Oldenbarnevelt, who had fought before Haarlem. But as Maurice had rightly said, the course of events could no longer be moulded by arguing this way or that; it was might, it was the sword, which would decide. From the moment that he threw in his lot with them, there was no checking the progress of the Contra-Remonstrants.

At Amsterdam, meanwhile, where the Remonstrants could not expect any but Contra-Remonstrant sermons in the churches, they arranged, after the example set by the Calvinist secessionist congregations in towns under Remonstrant magistracies, for religious services to be held in a warehouse. The town government did not prevent these meetings, but neither did it lift a finger to restrain the mob that had been egged on, one day in February, to invade and ransack the house of a prominent Remonstrant citizen, Rem Bisschop, brother of the Leiden professor Episcopius. The incident created quite a sensation all over Holland.

In the Hague dispute the 'sufferers' impetuously kept pressing on still further forward. No warehouse for them: on 9 July 1617 they took forcible possession of the Abbey church, already set apart for them, and the second Sunday after that the Stadholder himself, with a large retinue of nobles and womenfolk, attended service there. In many other Holland towns Contra-Remonstrants struggling with Arminian governments felt encouraged by his support, and turbulence increased. At the same time a majority of the provinces in the States-General adopted a resolution to summon a National Synod, despite Holland's appeal to the Union of Utrecht, which did indeed guarantee provincial autonomy in religious affairs.

Against the oncoming tide of religious passion the Advocate set his face. Already in March 1617 the States of Holland had passed a resolution by which the two High Courts of Justice— the Court of Holland and the High Council of Holland and

Zealand—were forbidden to take cognisance of any application of a citizen against his municipal government. It was especially the measure of expulsion—a purely political measure, which town governments claimed they could resort to without any judicial procedure whatever—against which the victims frequently had recourse to these high bodies. There were precedents for this resolution, but it is obvious that it had very questionable aspects. In order to preserve "peace within the Church" not only the consistories' right of appointment and the ministers' freedom of action were limited, the Church's freedom in other words compromised, but the irresponsible power of the town oligarchies over their citizens was buttressed. The most serious threat to the States system that had to be supported in this way came, nevertheless, from the disagreement existing in their own midst. This resolution had again to be forced through against the protests of a minority. Dordrecht, Amsterdam, Enkhuizen, Edam and Purmerend had gradually come to constitute a group, which in all ways obstructed the policy of the majority and called its legitimacy into question.

More was considered necessary by the redoubtable Advocate and his friends. On 5 August 1617 the resolution was driven through (again against the opposition of the five towns) which became famous as "the Sharp Resolution". In the face of the manifest unwillingness of the Stadholder, this resolution was designed to provide other means of enforcing the States of Holland's system. It expressly confirmed the right of towns to take into service troops of their own—*waardgelders*—for the preservation of order and furthermore ordered the commanders of the regular army to co-operate to that end with the States of the province, or the magistracy of the town, where they were stationed, *notwithstanding any orders to the contrary*.

If we fail to realise that the Advocate sincerely believed himself to be fighting for lofty principles, then his offer of battle with such scanty forces against so powerful an array will give the impression of blind obstinacy. But he was defending the system to which his entire political life had been devoted, and under which he had watched the Republic grow in power and prosperity. He believed not only in the justice of their lordships the States of Holland's cause, but in the absolute necessity of their authority to save the country from the tyranny of the unreasoning mob and of the divines lusting for power. In the same way, not only did he believe that the cause of his province was founded in right, but he held that the attempt of the weaker provinces to force through their policy by weight of majority was bound to overthrow the Union, which owed its all to Holland.

None the less, he now provided Maurice with a cause into which the Prince could throw his whole personality with much better founded conviction than into the religious issue. Maurice saw in the Sharp Resolution an attack on the army itself and on the unity of the Republic. "Notwithstanding any orders to the contrary", even if its application was restricted to the task of maintaining order, placed the States of a province—of the province that acted as "paymaster" for more than half of the army,[1] above not only the Captain-General but also the States-General. Maurice was cut to the quick. From now on he acted no longer merely as a protector of the Contra-Remonstrants; he became a principal and threw himself into the conflict intent on breaking the power of the Advocate and his party.

Another year elapsed, however, before he forced an issue. Throughout that time the civil authorities were at such cross-purposes—the majority of the States-General ranged against the minority, with the minority of the States of Holland ever active on the side of the majority in the States-General; townsfolk banded against town governments and garrisons in opposition to militia; and everybody wrangling all the time over non-payment of taxes or denial of justice—that the State seemed to be visibly crumbling, to the concern of its friends and the delight of its enemies abroad. Meanwhile, there was let loose against the Holland regent party in general and against Oldenbarnevelt in particular a flood of vilification which does little honour to the great principles at stake. Only if we remember the state of semi-warfare in which the country was placed, as well as the multitude of Catholics by whom the predominant set knew themselves to be surrounded and about whose thoughts they were in the dark, do these crazy suspicions become explicable as the product of

[1] The provinces did not pay their several quotas in so far as army expenditure was concerned into the Union exchequer. Particular regiments were assigned to them, and the sums spent in providing the soldiers' pay were accounted to them as fulfilment of their quota obligation. Holland's quota was of some 56 per cent.

nervous strain. Even Maurice did not scruple to heighten them by talking about a choice between Orange and Spain. Sermons and pamphlets echoed, in elaborate variations in every key, the theme of the pro-Spanish tendencies and treasonable activities of the Advocate and his friends.

At length Maurice, in close concert with his cousin William Louis and with Burgomaster Pauw, working in accordance with a well-thought-out plan of campaign, as prudently and methodically as he did in the field, proceeded to decisive action. In January 1618, availing himself of those vague traditions of sovereignty, which still clung to the Stadholder—a legacy of the monarchical period—as well as of his command of the armed forces, he confirmed the position of the Contra-Remonstrant party in Gelderland by dismissing the Remonstrant magistracy of Nymegen. This done, he repeated the process in Overysel. Holland being thus more and more isolated, the majority of the States-General, actively supported by the minority in the States of Holland, took seriously in hand the preparations for a National Synod. A visit to Amsterdam, where he was enthusiastically received, was a sign that the powerful province was not escaping the Stadholder's attention. To break Holland's unflinching opposition, the States-General in July resolved, on the advice of the Stadholders and the Council of State, to disband the *waardgelders*. A beginning was made in the execution of this measure with the weaker province still following the lead of Holland, namely, Utrecht. Grotius, despatched there post-haste by the States of Holland to urge the friendly States to stand firm, could not succeed in preventing Maurice, armed with his authority as commander-in-chief and supported by the English garrison, from winning an easy victory. The Utrecht town government was changed. Now at last it was Holland's turn.

The States of that province were now prepared to give up the *waardgelders* and to co-operate—but still only on conditions—in the calling of a National Synod. But this no longer satisfied the other side. On 28 August Maurice, holding a warrant from the States-General, had Oldenbarnevelt, Grotius and a few others put under arrest. After this, accompanied by a large suite and at the head of troops, he moved about Holland from town to town, ejecting supporters of Oldenbarnevelt's policy from the councils and replacing them by men of the other persuasion, as he had previously done at Nymegen and Utrecht. In this manner the States of Holland, to whom, as their only sovereign, the arrested men were appealing against what they considered the States-General's monstrous overstepping of their authority, were converted against them. However much the new members, too, might be set upon their provincial rights, the States thus transformed gave their assent to the trial of their eminent subjects before an extraordinary Generality court, on condition that half its members should be Hollanders.

There is much that is attractive about the elevation of the Generality idea above provincial particularism. The only drawback was that, as the Union of 1579 had not provided for a regular Generality court, this extraordinary court had now to be improvised. Composed as it was for the most part of politicians, almost all of them hostile to the Advocate, the Hollanders not less than the others (Pauw presided!), justice was not to be expected from it, only vengeance. The whole official life of the aged statesman who, after William the Silent, must be called the founder of the Republic, was subjected to malevolent scrutiny. The authorisation from his masters, the States of Holland, which he had never lacked, was not taken into account. In his examination, which was protracted for months, he was seriously asked to explain himself about the most contemptible slanders; the most blameless political transactions were twisted against him. Finally, seeing that

he the prisoner has dared to jeopardise the position of the faith and greatly to oppress and distress God's Church; . . . making hateful the true brethren in the faith as well within as without the country with the names of foreigners and Puritans,[1] who want to imitate the Flemings and stir up the subjects against their rulers; and that he the prisoner, thinking all these things not sufficient to compass his aforesaid evil designs, has dared at the same time, with his accomplices, to jeopardise the position of the State, attempting to cast the governance of these lands into disorder and confusion,

Oldenbarnevelt was on 12 May 1619 sentenced to death. The charge of connivance with the enemy, which the court had not dared to mention in the sentence, was nevertheless insinuated in a letter from the States-General to the provinces. Grotius was sentenced to life imprisonment.

[1] By comparing the Contra-Remonstrants with the English Puritans the Holland States party had sought to enlist the support of James I against them.

> Is this the wages of the three-and-thirty years' service that I have given to the country?

demanded Oldenbarnevelt of his judges. And the following day, on the scaffold on the Binnenhof, he declared:

> Men, believe not that I am a traitor. I have borne myself uprightly and honourably, as a good patriot, and the same shall I die.

c. UNCALVINISTIC TENDENCIES IN RELIGIOUS AND INTELLECTUAL LIFE

THE EXECUTION of Oldenbarnevelt followed a few days after the close of the Synod, which in accordance with the States-General's resolution had assembled at Dort in November 1618, and which, as was to be expected, had thrust the Remonstrants out of the Church. Before we consider the proceedings of the Synod and their results, it will be useful to review briefly the religious and intellectual forces present among the North-Netherlands people in so far as they manifested themselves outside the Church. A feature that strikes the observer at once is that these forces worked to a large extent independently of, and were often indeed hostile to, that religious regime which, nevertheless, in 1618–19 obtained control even in Holland.

By its nature Calvinism stood in a very different relation to culture from that of the Counter-Reformation. This is especially apparent in the case of the plastic arts, which Calvinism could not turn to its own ends and which it could at best exclude from the sphere of the Church. We have already seen that De Keyser was forced to sell his statue of St. John to the cathedral of 's Hertogenbosch. In the rifled and white-washed churches of the provinces north of the rivers there could be no place for 'feeble puppetry and lifeless paintings' (to quote the poet-minister Revius of Deventer). Not all pictorial art was so flatly rejected by the ministers, but a close spiritual tie such as existed between ecclesiastics and artists in the Catholic Netherlands was impossible. During the years of the Truce the old traditions of Renaissance and Humanism flourished unchecked in the North. If no mighty genius such as Rubens rejuvenated and invigorated them, yet the most celebrated studios at

Utrecht (Moreelse, Bloemaert), Amsterdam (Pieter Lastman), Haarlem (Cornelius Corneliszoon) were pure Italian-academic in outlook, secular, sensuous, ceremonious. The new national art which was to become the glory of the century was still only in the first bloom of its youth as practised by Frans Hals and Willem Buytewech, by Hercules Seghers and Jan van Goyen. But it, too, in its humanity and its naturalness, was governed by principles wholly different from those of predestination.

With literature and philology—to leave the natural sciences out of consideration for the time being—the case was indeed otherwise; there a closer connection was at least possible. Nevertheless, the most eminent of the great humanists belonged to the Arminian camp: besides the most famous of all, Grotius, there were the Leiden professor Gerard Vossius and the theologian with whom Latinity was soon to oust theology, Caspar Barlaeus. Daniel Heinsius at this time was still a zealous Contra-Remonstrant. And among the Dutch-writing literary men there was Jacob Cats, the prosperous Zealand advocate and politician, who in 1618, when already forty, brought out the first of his great moralising poems; Constantyn Huygens of The Hague, nearly twenty years Cats's junior, was only on the threshold of his career. But the real spirit of Calvinism, in its unimpeachable austerity, in its ferocity as well as in its self-abnegation, was personified in Revius, whose verdict on painting I quoted above, and who dedicated his poetry solely to the glory of God and the service of Church and Country. These personalities, however, represent only one tendency. A Calvinist surveying society and culture during the years of the Truce could be little satisfied even with literature. The Jesuit doing the same in the loyal provinces would observe with satisfaction Rubens and Puteanus, the entire intellectual movement, sodalities, gilds and crossbow companies, all devoting themselves to the glorification of the Mother Church. The Calvinist in the North saw a vigorous and colourful society, a surging of desires and opinions, an irresistible effervescing of forces which cared neither for election nor for predestination.

Nowhere was this more the case than in thriving Holland, open to influences from every side, and in Holland nowhere more than in Amsterdam, for all its being the bulwark of the Contra-Remonstrant party throughout the province.

A great period of Dutch literature was opening, and Amsterdam furnished a vital centre where views were exchanged and tastes formed, such as neither Ghent nor Bruges, nor even Antwerp itself, had ever been. Three of the greatest poets our people has ever produced were working there, Pieter Corneliszoon Hooft, Gerbrand Adriaanszoon Breero, and Joost van den Vondel. The last, indeed, born only two years after Breero, who died in 1618 at the age of thirty-three, had hardly yet carried his slow development beyond the stage of absorbing impressions and attempting earliest exercises in expression. The spirit in which these Amsterdam writers regarded literature was still the spirit of Spieghel and Roemer Visscher. Visscher was still alive, and his daughters Anna and Maria Tesselschade were beginning to lend his home a new charm 'for painters and artists, for singers and poets'.

Among a host of lovers of literature, who helped to create the atmosphere in which the great ones breathed, there stood out two figures less gifted poetically but important for their personality and influence, those of Dirk Rodenburg (he called himself 'Theodore') and Dr. Samuel Coster. Of all these Amsterdammers, Rodenburg alone sided with the Contra-Remonstrants, and even he, so far as one can judge from his work, less because of a real affinity than as a result of his feud with Coster. All things considered, what strikes one about this outburst of cultural activity is how little store its leaders set by the rigid system which the Reformed ministers wanted to press upon the nation. Everywhere the fresh green came pushing up through it and over it.

A great, at times almost an exuberant, love for natural life (held by the Heidelberg Catechism to be of the devil) was what inspired these poets, and how brimful of it does that early seventeenth-century society still appear in their works, untroubled by the new rigidity.

It was a music-loving age. If the synods had had their way, the organs would have been removed from the churches; in 1578, and again in 1581, they had issued orders to that effect. But fortunately the possessions of the old Church had passed, not into their hands, but into those of the secular authority, and burgomasters as a rule protected organ and organist. So, at Amsterdam, in the Old Church, Jan Pieterszoon Sweelinck was

able to exercise his art and to win a European fame. Still, the
limits set by the new church service were so narrow that there
was no future for organ music and church song in the Northern
Netherlands, and it was mainly through his German pupils that
Sweelinck could make a school. Outside the church walls, too,
triumphant orthodoxy was to silence music, but at this time
the old love of song was still very much alive and seemingly
free of care. The ministers were not always consistent, and a
strictly Contra-Remonstrant *domine* from Kampen, Baudartius,
was still able to have his joy at the zest with which Sweelinck,
in his house at Amsterdam, kept playing on the harpsichord all
through an evening, repeating the song of *The Merry May is
now in its Season* in as many as twenty-five variations.

There is something infinitely attractive about the feeling for
songs of that kind. Song-books with such titles as *The Court
of Love* and *The Lover's Song-book* were in every hand at the
gay young people's parties. Since the sixteenth century the
Renaissance had been at work on the songs themselves as well
as on the music to which they were set, but the traditional folk-
songs were still universally known and many of the new songs
were written to their tunes and wholly in their style. At the same
time the literary fashion which the Renaissance had brought in
throughout Western Europe made its influence felt, a style of
heavy frills and forced wit, of surprising twists and turns, of
violent contrasts and inflated metaphors. The love-song in
particular had much to suffer from it. Not, however, with a man
like Hooft. He, thoroughly grounded in the classics and from
his own experience conversant with Italy, consciously, unlike too many thus favoured, devoted all his study and all his
talents to the service of developing a nobler Netherlands
culture; he succeeded in creating a lyric poetry endowed with a
distinction of style and a purity of tone such as had never before
been wedded in our tongue. On others, however, this discipline
lay rather heavy; Breero, for instance, wrote a great deal of
sonorous and jingling bombast. But if the new harmony of the
true Dutch Renaissance poet personified in Hooft was beyond
his reach, when he gave rein to his natural style of direct self-
expression and of passionately interested realism—and happily
he did so in much of his work—then Breero too showed himself
a consummate master. However humbly he might all too often

bow the knee to fashion, on that true ground of his own he moved with confidence. Brought up in the Spieghel sphere, he could proudly defend the use of ancient words against the deadening precepts of

certain Latinists, who learned foreign tongues earlier and better than they learned Dutch.

His daring in making direct personal experience and workaday life into the stuff of poetry springs from the same source. It was not only against the 'Latinists' that this attitude of mind required to be defended. The English-born Starter, Breero's echo, who had established a Chamber of Rhetoric at Leeuwarden on the model of the Amsterdam Eglantier, was driven out of Friesland at the instance of Dr. Bogerman, whom we shall soon meet as the president of the Synod of Dort. And indeed the tone of this love-poetry, wherein natural love reigned unchallenged, often has a frankly pagan sound.

Yet Breero did not go deliberately against the religious-moral ideal of the Reformers. Just as between what was his own and what was foreign, so also between his worldly inclinations and his religious ideas there was conflict within him, and he never won through to harmony. In the year of his untimely death he gave us the play *The Spanish Brabanter*, which after his earlier plays on the Franco-Spanish-Italian conventional-aristocratic model, was a triumph for the national, for the homely and genuine in his art; no doubt the failure of the true dramatic element makes one conscious of the loss of that brilliant tradition of the medieval stage, which had been primarily South Netherlandish. Now in this play, a masterpiece in its depiction of life, Breero gives full reign—all sorts of loosely-inserted moralisings apart—to his artistic craving for natural life even in its crudest manifestations. And how crude life still was! How sensuous and licentious that swiftly-developing society as he, and his friend Samuel Coster likewise, saw it! The petty bourgeoisie in the prosperous province of Holland had the virtues and vices of simplicity and virility. Restless under the moulds which were being forced down on him from elsewhere, your real Amsterdammer felt an aversion to the airs and graces of the South Netherland refugees, of which at times he quite rightly gauged the hollowness. Breero's conception of

Jerolimo, the Spanish Brabanter in the play, is the revolt of the
Hollander in him; and exactly similar was the reaction of Coster,
who, in a crushing reply to his Southern kinsmen's favourite
nickname of 'heavy Hollander', pointed to the success of the
young Republic:

> Let them try to heave out the Spaniards. I will give them three tries.

Yet we have already seen that the Hollanders, too, became the
apprentices of the foreigner in order to pose as men and poets of
the world. The North may have struggled free of Spain; nevertheless, there was still that discord in its culture which we
noticed throughout in the Burgundian Netherlands and which
in the reconquered South our previous chapter revealed under
the cover of a patently foreign veneer. A figure like Rodenburg
is interesting because he provides a caricature of this peculiarity
alike in his poetical and in his social appearance. His violently
romantic dramas, botched together after the Spanish model,
are no less a masquerade than is his clumsily elegant portrait
with stiff pointed ruff and Burgundian knightly chain. Hooft
presents the exact reverse of this; in him, in the poet as well as
in the man of the world, what was once foreign has become his
own. He, the Sheriff of Muiden, host and letter-writer, was the
pattern of genuine Netherlands distinction, his classical and
foreign schooling notwithstanding. National consciousness
gives a beautiful unity to the life of this cool-headed, purposeful
man, who was already making preparations for writing the
history of the great epic of the generation before him.

But the point I particularly want to make here is that this
whole poetical movement so obviously ran counter to the
ideas of the religious party whose cause the Amsterdam
government was defending in the States of Holland. Not only
on account of the erotic glow, whether grossly sensuous or
refined by the Italian feeling for beauty, and the delight in the
realities of human life, but also because of the philosophic
system which Spieghel and Coornhert had built up for themselves under the influence of the classical Stoic writers and of
Erasmus, and which attached so much importance to man's
free will. This still exerted great influence over many minds;
Hooft himself was its most conscious exponent. And at last all
that meant most in the Amsterdam literary world came under

Coster's leadership into open conflict with the consistory, the assembly of Reformed ministers and elders.

During these years poets still belonged to one or other of the two Chambers of Rhetoric, the Old (the Eglantier, 'Flourishing in Love'), or the Brabant (the White Lavender), although the latter, save for Vondel's membership, was no longer of much significance. But now the Eglantier too was torn by disputes; their why and wherefore is not always clear, but they certainly sprang mainly from the more individual spirits' impatience with the routine of the old rhetorical tradition. However that may be, Hooft and Breero accompanied Coster when in 1617 he launched a new institution, the Dutch Academy, intended to be a 'Netherlands training school'. While Rodenburg of the spectacular drama remained the leading light of the Eglantier, the Academy saw the production of Hooft's *Warenar*, Breero's *Spanish Brabanter*, and Coster's *Iphigenia*. But the enterprising doctor wanted to go further. He hoped

that here the sciences too would bring their industry to bear, to edify the citizenry for love's sake and to enlighten it with the torch of the Dutch language.

Higher education in the Dutch tongue, for which Spieghel and the Eglantier of his days had vainly looked to Leiden, that was what this Amsterdam institution would supply. Hebrew was taught there, and mathematics to 'an incredible multitude of people', while there were plans for many other branches; it was to be a regular national university. But the consistory espied the enemy—not a little aided by the fact that the first two professors at the Academy were Mennonites—and the burgomasters let themselves be persuaded into prohibiting this teaching, which might otherwise have meant so much for the growth of a healthy Netherlands culture. The Academy's theatre lived on, in spite of continual opposition from the ministers, and in the meantime Coster's *Iphigenia*, in a Greek garb worn so carelessly that a chorus is even made to mention 'pulpit and town-hall', had been a stinging challenge to his adversaries.

O high-born people, that never was constrained beneath the world's tyranny! And are you now forced to bow under the heavy yoke of foolish popery? (*A generation ago already a Libertinist had mocked at Calvinism as being no better than "inverted popery"*.) . . . O heroes! 'twere better far never to have begun the war, for more has been lost than gained by fighting.

And by means of a parable—the world is a vicious horse ridden by authority and curbed by the whip of the law and the bridle of religion; put the bridle into the hands of a second rider, the Church, and the horse will bolt—Coster develops the pure Remonstrant theory of the relations of Church and State. It was a theory which appealed to the cultivated all over Europe. Their fear of the unreasoning multitude and its excesses of religious excitement everywhere redounded to the benefit of the claims to absolute authority put forward by the secular magistrates; by the monarchs elsewhere, here by the States.

Where there existed a vigorous intellectual life, and where Catholics and Protestant dissenters were still bold enough to allow themselves an opinion on matters political, there, if it came to a choice between two tyrannies, the tyranny of ministers of religion aroused the greatest repugnance. Thus it was Holland, the province of large towns and of an active intellectual and economic life, and with a population plentifully admixed with extraneous elements, it was Holland that, notwithstanding the attitude of the Amsterdam government, formed the centre of the resistance to the further Calvinisation of the country. As we have already seen, the Synod of Dort had to be imposed on Holland with the help of the outer provinces. The carrying out of its decrees during the next generation met with less resistance in those provinces, in spite of the fact that the Catholics were so strong in some of them.

D. THE SYNOD OF DORT AND THE CONSOLIDATION OF CALVINIST SUPREMACY

THE SYNOD was composed exclusively of orthodox Calvinists. Besides the Netherland ministers there were present representatives of Churches abroad, so that all business had to be transacted in Latin, to the no small embarrassment of the delegates present on behalf of the States-General. The Frisian Bogerman was chosen president. The Remonstrants were not admitted to the deliberations; thirteen of them were summoned before the assembly and treated as accused before their judges. Utenbogaert having fled at the threat of prosecution for political misdemeanours, Episcopius appeared as their chief spokesman. Not that there was ever any discussion of the points at issue. For six weeks Episcopius and his friends put up a dogged resistance to the efforts of Bogerman and the 'politicians' (the delegates from the States-General) to threaten or cajole them into acquiescence in a form of procedure which would have drastically limited their freedom of speech. At last, on 14 January 1619, they were driven with contumely out of the assembly, so that the Synod might examine and condemn their errors in their absence.

> Ite, ite, dimittimini! (*thundered the fierce Bogerman with a sweep of the arm; but as they went out Episcopius said:*) I shall hold my peace on all this with Jesus Christ my Saviour, and God shall judge between us and the Synod.

While the accused were forbidden to leave Dort, the Synod, deliberating for the most part in secret, reached agreement on doctrine, though not without difficulties. From now onwards the Netherlands Church had her own *canones*, which were accepted by the States assemblies of each of the seven provinces as the rule of public worship. The Church was defined, in accordance with Calvinist theory, as the community of the elect. She also obtained an authorised translation of the Bible; the Synod appointed a committee which after years of labour produced the famous States' version. But the question of a 'Church settlement', that is to say, a settlement of the relations of Church and State, appeared difficult of solution even with 'politicians' who had allowed a doctrine to be defined. The States would not hear of the short-lived settlement of 1586,[1] belonging to the Leicester period, which the Synod favoured. In her own estimation the Church did not succeed in 'freeing' herself even under the enemies of Oldenbarnevelt; neither the traditionally Contra-Remonstrant regents of the landward provinces, nor the newly-appointed ones in Holland, would suffer her to abrogate the rights of patronage. It remained a source of bitter complaint that lords of the manor and town governments continued to have a voice in the nomination of ministers of religion.

For the time being, however, this was hardly noticed when the authorities brought to bear such zeal on another major issue, the suppression of the proscribed doctrines. On their refusal to

---

[1] See above, p. 47.

promise to abstain from preaching, the ministers summoned before the Synod and awaiting the verdict in Dort were banished from the country. Next a host of other unorthodox ministers were ejected, often despite protests from their congregations. Leiden university was 'purged'. Bertius, the Regent of the States Seminary, was forced to resign. Academic teaching was subjected to much stricter supervision than before.[1] An edict was issued forbidding Remonstrant conventicles and putting a price on the head of ministers who defied the prohibition. For the proscribed sect was not so easily disposed of. At Antwerp they established a Remonstrant Brotherhood under the leadership of Utenbogaert, and several ministers braved every danger to keep in touch with their persecuted congregations. Informers, sheriffs and constables had their hands full, and the military were required to keep Remonstrant towns in order (there were towns where a majority favoured the Remonstrant side) and to disperse open-air meetings. The other sects and the Catholics also had a much worse time of it now. Not that the great principle of freedom of conscience was even now rejected; not even the enforcement of conformity to the State Church was contemplated, such as we have seen operating in the South (and such as was applied in England, too, for example). The unbroken existence, through it all, of *béguinages* in towns like Amsterdam and Delft gives an idea of the tolerance of public life. Prohibition of worship and exclusion from office for the well-to-do and from all sorts of benefits for the poor was as far as matters went. Enough, indeed, to activate the policy of protestantisation, which was in this period, under the incessant urging of synods and consistories, carried on more vigorously than ever, and with increasing effect.

As far as the Remonstrants were concerned, however, the policy adopted in 1619 led to actual persecution, a deplorable spectacle in a country which prided itself on its record of resistance to the Spanish Inquisition. In practice, the outlook of regents, officials and jurists was not so deeply affected by party passion as to preclude considerable hesitation in the prosecution of this campaign, and here and there even determined opposition. At Amsterdam in particular, as we have seen, many regents

[1] For the relative freedom enjoyed by Leiden professors until then, see *The Revolt of the Netherlands*, p. 289.

had taken part in the onslaught against Oldenbarnevelt from motives that had nothing to do with religion. Now that their goal was reached, they did not gladly bear the yoke of church rule which their alliance with the Calvinists proper had imposed upon them. Nor was the orthodox position strengthened by the sore embarrassment into which the State's new leader, Maurice, was brought by those problems of foreign policy with which hitherto Oldenbarnevelt had had to wrestle.

Maurice, as leader of the victorious party, with such men as Aerssens, whom he pushed into the Holland nobility, Reinier Pauw and Count William Louis to advise him, wielded an authority such as no man had ever enjoyed in the Republic before. It fell to his lot to cope with the renewed onslaught of the allied Austrian and Spanish Habsburgs, who, after years of menacing manœuvres, now launched their offensive in Germany. So perilous did the situation become after the expiry of the Truce that Maurice found himself forced to seek the aid of Catholic France, even at the price of assistance against the French Huguenot rebels—the policy for which Oldenbarnevelt had been blamed so heavily. This did Maurice's reputation no good, and what made things worse was the continued ill-success of the war.

When he died in 1625, moreover, he was succeeded by his much younger brother Frederick Henry, who with his mother Louise de Coligny had always leaned towards the side of the Arminians and France. The war soon began to go better now, and this gave the new Stadholder the prestige necessary to enable him to break with the policy thus far pursued. But Frederick Henry was a cautious man and, despite the brilliance of his position after the capture of 's Hertogenbosch in 1629, he eschewed anything that savoured of a counter-revolution. Hugo Grotius, for instance, who had escaped from Loevsetein soon after his sentence and had since lived in exile, was disappointed in his hope of now being allowed to return. And indeed this would have looked as too much of a humiliation for the party of 1618. Shortly after his escape from Loevestein, in 1622, he had published, in Paris, an apologia that they found hard to swallow. *Justification of the Lawful Government of Holland* was the title, and in it he not only reiterated the argument that he had put forward so often when his party was still in power, defending the course followed on grounds of public law and precedent as well as of reason, but he also reinforced it with deadly criticism of the irregularities (and worse) committed in his own and the other gentlemen's trials and with a scathing analysis of the sentence. The impassioned, though outwardly cool, and crystal-clear pamphlet had not been forgotten in a year or two; indeed, a later generation of States supporters venerated the book as their political bible. To its author, however, even when conditions began to wear a different aspect, it blocked the return home. Religious persecution, nevertheless, came to an end in most towns with the accession of Frederick Henry. Men of less rigid principles were gradually and systematically reintroduced into the town councils; worship at Arminian conventicles was winked at, nor did the Captain-General any longer allow the military to be used to put it down. In 1631 even Amsterdam, in the area of its own jurisdiction, expressly suspended the operation of the States-General's edict.

What had happened at Amsterdam did, indeed, wear the appearance of counter-revolution. We have seen what a variety of motives had coalesced there in the campaign against Oldenbarnevelt. Now that the object was achieved—not only the hated statesmen out of the way, but the West India Company established on the renewal of the war—the unorthodox among the regents, who had made common cause with the Calvinists, no longer suffered Pauw to retain his dictatorial position. The new groupings now lording it at the town-hall were careful at first not to irritate the ministers and the Calvinist populace. With the advent of the new Stadholder, however, the 'free-thinkers' were no longer content to brood in silence over their wrongs, and they had at their service a voice which was to ring across the centuries. Again the fighting spirit of the Academy flared up, and Coster now had a formidable ally in Vondel. In October 1625 Vondel flung his *Palamedes* into the arena, a defiance to all who had taken part in 'murdering the innocence' of Oldenbarnevelt. Victorious power hauled before the poet's judgment seat—this work created a profound impression. The Amsterdam government refused to hand Vondel over to the fiercely Contra-Remonstrant High Court of Holland, which would certainly have meted out merciless punishment. Hooft was living in dignified and active tranquillity at Muiden, but the name of

Hooft was made into a battle-cry: Vondel extolled the memory of the burgomaster, the poet's father, who died on 1 January 1626, as the model of the good regent. He similarly honoured Frederick Henry, the defender of liberty, in alexandrines of exuberant Renaissance pomp.

The antagonism grew apace. In 1626 a Remonstrant meeting was interfered with by the mob; one minister alone complied with the government's request and reprimanded his flock from the pulpit. He was immediately suspended by the consistory. In the town government, however, where the magistracy was every year renewed by the town council, the election of February 1627 brought the anti-Calvinistic party definitely into power. In Andries Bicker it found a dauntless leader. The orthodox, instructed by the consistory and counting on the support of the civic guard, continued for some years to make trouble. Petitions against the freedom left to Remonstrant conventicles created so dangerous a feeling that the burgomasters invited Frederick Henry to the town in the hope that the spectacle of their cordial relations with the Prince of Orange would quieten the people. The sobering effect was of brief duration. Meanwhile, poets and intellectuals had thrown themselves whole-heartedly into the fray on behalf of the town government, in whose cause they saw the cause of liberty. Vondel lashed and stung the ministers with joyous vehemence. The trial of strength came when the burgomasters appointed a regent of undisguised Remonstrant sentiments as captain of the civic guard.

Indignation went beyond grumblings. A number of malcontent guards laid before the Synod[1] the question whether it was permissible for them to take an oath of loyalty to an enemy of the Church. The Synod consulted the theological faculty of Leiden University, which was of opinion that this was not permissible. The danger of the Church dictating to the State had never appeared so clearly. The town government expelled the questioners from the civic guard. A few of these, accompanied by citizens of some standing, now went to The Hague and applied to the States and to the Stadholder. These, however, upheld the town government. Unexpectedly, but in concert

---

[1] That is, of course, the provincial Synod; or rather, the South Holland Synod, for in Holland there were two Synods; the National Synod of 1619 had been an exceptional case, which was not repeated in the life-time of the Republic.

with the burgomasters, Frederick Henry threw troops into Amsterdam, whereupon the burgomasters expelled five of the trouble-makers from the town (early 1629).

Among the ministers Smout, whom we met before at Rotterdam,[1] even now kept agitating. From his pulpit he thundered against the regents seated below him. It had again become necessary to lend Richelieu assistance against Huguenot rebels in order to put him in a position to renew his struggle with the Habsburgs, and a States' fleet was sent to La Rochelle. This betrayal of the principles which had triumphed in 1618–19 angered the ministers beyond measure, and Smout did not hesitate to attribute to it the danger to which the country was exposed in 1629 when during Frederick Henry's siege of 's Hertogenbosch an Imperial army penetrated from the east as far as the Veluwe. His was the language of Dathenus and Moded fifty years before, but practical politicians were no more intimidated now as then.

> We have the word of God, hearken therefore to what we say unto thee. We are thy shepherds, we shall speak unto thee nothing save the truth. Thou shalt not listen to the Poets, Jurists, Orators and Politicians. Thou shalt listen to us, hence it must come.

Thus Smout from the pulpit. But the burgomasters, firmly led by Bicker, did not shrink from another measure of vigour. In 1630 Smout was banished from the town, just as Geselius had earlier been expelled from Rotterdam (and the Rotterdam magistracy too went once again to the same extreme). At the same time the Amsterdam town council sent delegates to attend meetings of the consistory to keep it in order. Protests to the Synod and to the States of Holland were of no avail; the tyranny of ministers at Amsterdam was at an end. In 1631 there followed the suspension of the States-General's edict, as already mentioned; the year before the building of a Remonstrant church had been started. In 1631 an Athenaeum Illustre was established under municipal auspices, a university on a small scale, which gave shelter to those two eminent humanists and Remonstrants, Barlaeus and Vossius, expelled from the now strictly orthodox University of Leiden soon after Dort had spoken. It was Coster's 'training school' revived, only it was not 'Dutch'; that attempt had been nipped in the bud, and in the meantime Latin

[1] See p. 49.

had still further strengthened its hold on all higher culture, and especially on scholarship. But, as far as the spirit of the teaching went, the Athenaeum could hardly have been less Calvinist. Grotius himself was able to move freely at Amsterdam and was even received most courteously by the town government; the majority in the States of Holland, however, again set a price on his head, so that once more he had to seek safety abroad. Observe that the opinion of the States-General was no longer asked.

After this recital my readers might jump to the conclusion that the revolution of 1618–19 must have been no more than a violent interlude without lasting result. As far as the constitutional issues are concerned, this view can indeed be defended. Oldenbarnevelt's system had suffered a shock, but all the same it survived him. Maurice had been satisfied with bringing down the presumptuous one and filling the States of Holland with supporters; he had had no thought of altering the foundations of the government, of revising the constitution. Personally, he was all-powerful; so long as he lived, the Republic was in fact a monarchy. Yet he was only the leader of a victorious party. Nor was the Generality idea worked out in any permanent form. Holland had been brought low, a dramatic demonstration had been given of the superior power of the Generality; but nothing further was done, and the circumstances which had made that demonstration possible—the passions aroused by religious controversy, the disunion of the powerful province, the support of the Stadholder and his army—passed away.

Oldenbarnevelt had complained, at his trial, that he was prosecuted on the strength of principles which had not been valid when he was in office. Grotius, chafe as he did against his exile, could see from France the old principles, as if they had been suspended only to overthrow his party, come into honour again. Everything fell back into the previous equilibrium. Now that the storm had subsided, that state of affairs was fortified by the inclination, natural to each organism (to the States of Holland, in this instance, whether composed of Remonstrants or of Contra-Remonstrants), to preserve its rights or functions once established—an inclination that found support in the conservative spirit of the age.

Concerning the opinion of some that, if all the provinces were submitted to one sovereign authority, the government would be the more stable and effective, this is the answer: that the sovereignty of the provinces should not be judged in the light of imaginings as to what might seem to be the most useful or not; but it should be judged by the laws and usages. . . . Very wise and perspicacious authors teach us that not all laws, and especially not the fundamental ones, should be altered, even though the alterations were an improvement: since the improvement cannot be so advantageous as the alteration will be harmful, the latter being bound to weaken authority, which is rooted in perdurance.

This is what Grotius wrote in his *Justification*, and it was language after the heart of the large majority of his contemporaries, whatever view they might take of the Sharp Resolution. Indeed for the next hundred years and more this was to be current wisdom of politics, and pleas for reform were only rarely and timidly to contend with it.

In any case the new Holland regents, Contra-Remonstrants though they might be—and many were so only in outward appearance, while as time went on family ties helped many more such into office—were not inclined to surrender for ever the provincial position as against the States-General or that of the oligarchy as against the Stadholder. All that Maurice had achieved for the future was that in the contest with the Holland regent class, which was to recur inevitably, albeit in connection with different questions, the House of Orange had found new allies in the Reformed ministers; that alliance was to survive the disappointment which Frederick Henry's attitude meant to the latter.

Even in the relations between Church and State that basic readjustment which the strict Calvinists would have wished was far from having been achieved. It was principally owing to this continued subordination of Church to State that the persecution of Remonstrants and the concurrent stricter treatment of other persuasions did not go to greater lengths and that it came to an end in relatively so short a time, for as for consistories, classes and synods, they did not cease to dun the authorities for the punctual enforcement of the edicts.

Yet, if we strike the balance, we shall see that the revolution of 1618–19 did indeed produce certain permanent results. The character of the Church and the character of the regent class were indeed changed, and from this a profound influence gradually spread over the whole of the society and of the civilisation of the Seven Provinces. The Church was tied much more straitly to her creeds; in her the Calvinists set the tone for several generations to come. The Remonstrants, separately organised in a sect which was in the end merely tolerated by the State, could not make themselves felt as before in public life. The regent class was purged of openly Remonstrant, libertinist and Catholic elements. It did not thereby lose its essential regent spirit; that is to say, it retained a sense of its being called to care for the interests of the whole community, including the non-Reformed sections; moreover, the purge was not really thorough-going, not even outside Amsterdam (where we already noticed this), and its effect was soon in part neutralised. But men were at much greater pains than before to preserve an appearance of orthodoxy, and this increasing homogeneity, even though in large measure only apparent, rendered the civil authorities more accessible to influence from the likewise more homogeneous Church. Thus the Church could now·bring not only greater zeal, but more power, to the task of moulding after her own ideas a society still permeated with so much that was unorthodox.

We can observe that process at work in two main directions. First, Catholicism was forced still deeper below the surface and the Catholic tradition still further weakened; and second, a puritanical outlook on life was imposed upon that Dutch people so inclined (as had been sorrowfully admitted at the Synod of Dort) 'towards liberty and pleasure'.

The Catholic influence was combated first and foremost in the political field. In Holland, in the first impetus of the revolution of 1618–19, Catholics were, equally with Remonstrants, dismissed from posts of authority, in which large numbers were still to be found, especially in the country districts. In Overysel and Gelderland, where the nobility was still largely Catholic, Catholic noblemen were only now systematically excluded from provincial commissions and appointments. In Friesland, where the States were still based upon a system of election by land-owners—noblemen and freeholders—Catholic owners of *horn-legers* (vote-carrying estates) were deprived of their franchise. These are merely examples of a process that was not so soon arrested after the crisis period of 1618–19. In 1621 the renewal of the war gave it a fresh impulse. Straightway there was a sensational case: a conspiracy, detected in time, to deliver Tiel into the hands of the Spaniards, the prime movers in which were three Catholic noblemen holding important provincial offices in Gelderland.

That the priests continued to regard the Archducal, or as it had again become by 1621, the Spanish, government as their lawful sovereign, was apparent from numerous public actions. Rovenius of Deventer, the successor of Sasbout Vosmeer, who had died in 1614, was at first appointed by the Pope only Vicar Apostolic (i.e. papal), since the Archdukes, respecting the Truce, would not use their right under the concordat of 1559 to make an appointment to the archiepiscopal see of Utrecht. But in 1622, at Forest near Brussels, Rovenius was consecrated Archbishop of Philippi by the Nuncio, assisted by the Archbishop of Mechlin (Jacob Boonen) and the Bishop of Antwerp. He afterwards performed his solemn entry at Oldenzaal, in that corner of the archbishopric of Utrecht which Spinola had recovered shortly before the Truce. Rovenius himself had here laboured before his appointment as Vicar, spurring on the Spanish authorities to the suppression of Baptist and Reformed worship. Catholics from the dioceses of Utrecht and Haarlem besought the King of Spain, in a petition carried to Spain by the Louvain professor Jansenius (a native of Aquoy near Leerdam, in Holland), to invest Rovenius with the plenary title of Archbishop of Utrecht; and soon he bore that as well. His retreat from Oldenzaal when Frederick Henry occupied that town in 1626, and from Grol when this was in its turn captured by the Stadholder in 1627, symbolises his relations with the States government. Afterwards he lived in concealment at the Castle of Hazenberg near Utrecht, which belonged to a Catholic lady of the noble house of Wassenaar. In the meantime, Reformed classes and synods never tired of lodging complaints against 'popish effronteries' and of calling the attention of the authorities to the religious devotions that took place here, there and everywhere with the connivance of bailiffs and sheriffs, who filled their pockets over these transactions. The continual revelations of traffic between their own Catholic notables and the Brussels government impressed the States, and, little inclined to persecution as they were, they always concurred in principle with the ministers.

And here a vicious circle was at work. The dismissal of

Catholic regents, although not universally carried out even now, was in any case a logical consequence of a revolution which had re-emphasised the view of the State as being first and foremost a Protestant State, and which saw treachery in the suggestion that Catholics might be reconciled. The majority of the Flemish and Brabant exiles and their descendants supported a movement which could not fail to intensify the estrangement of North and South. That was not, indeed, their intention, any more than it had been the intention of the Beggars of Ghent and of Holland, or of John of Nassau with his Union of Utrecht; but the conception of the revolt as a religious struggle, which now triumphed anew over William the Silent's political and national conception of it, was automatically bound to widen the gulf between the two halves of the Netherlands once a political frontier had been drawn between them.

The Reformed Church in the North attempted to subdue intellectual life by means of the University of Leiden and the no less orthodox younger Universities of Franeker (1583), Groningen (1614), and later especially Utrecht (1636). At the same time she also tried to bring about a reformation in morals, which in the long run was to leave a deep impression on North Netherland society. Church members were subjected to super-vision by the consistory, which did not shrink from interfering in the most intimate matters. War was declared on all ancient folk-customs which seemed to perpetuate a popish love of tradition or which gave expression to an unchristian enjoyment of life, and in this campaign the public authority was constantly called upon for support.

However, the social and intellectual life of the wealthy Netherlands, engaged in busy intercourse with the outside world and governed by a multitude of independent authorities, was not to be fashioned so easily in accordance with the ideas of Dort as was that of smaller or more primitive communities such as Geneva or Scotland, or the New England colonies. When we come to consider the culture of the period more specifically we shall find abundant evidence of this. If here and there the material yielded, in other places it remained refractory. In the country-side and in the smaller towns, and in other provinces more than in Holland, the ministers were on the whole successful. How strong a centre of resistance, on the contrary, there was in

Amsterdam, we have already seen. No more willing was the Stadholderly Court under Frederick Henry to conform to the dictates of those who, while ready to see the providential protector of God's Church even in an Arminianising Orange, were sometimes shocked by the sound of dancing and merry-making. Intellectual and artistic life were both too deeply rooted in their own traditions to yield without resistance to the dictates of the dominant trend, even though Leiden had been too effectively purged to be able to offer the resisters much support.

Yet the ultimate result of this persistent pressure by the Church in the new order of things brought about by the revolution of 1618–19 was that the middle class and peasantry in the Northern Netherlands acquired an unmistakably Reformed and Puritan cast of thought and conduct. That the Church found the seeds of corruption in her very triumph, that the influx of new members and the strict spiritual supervision were to weaken the independence and to taint the freshness of her religious life—this we shall discuss later on. Here I am pointing only to the imprint that this potent ecclesiastical regimentation was setting on the habits of Dutch society. On the relationship with the South this could not but have far-reaching effects. The accelerated de-catholicisation of public life in the North was loosening one spiritual link with the South, and now there was being created a positive difference as well, which in the course of a long evolution was to render the severed groups foreign and unsympathetic towards each other. But the period which we are now considering, the dozen years following the Synod of Dort, witnessed only the very beginnings of this process. It needed the work of generations before the North Netherland people was well set on its divergent road, while the Southerners, under the guidance of their priesthood, were continuing in the old direction.

The slow process of spiritual development is often determined for generations to come by catastrophic political events. The process which we are here considering still reaches back for its origins to the capture of the Brill in 1572, to the conquests of Parma and the reconquests of Maurice. The reinforcement of the strict Reformed element in the government of the North which resulted from the crisis of 1618–19 contributed in its turn to the failure of opportunities, which were to present themselves during the course of the war, even at this later stage, of rescuing Flanders and Brabant from the yoke of Spain and of re-uniting the severed halves of the Netherlands.

II

The War (1621–1648)

A. THE MENACING POWER OF THE HABSBURGS

IN 1621 THE WAR was renewed, as we know, in circumstances highly unfavourable to the Republic. There had, indeed, been some talk of extending the Truce. Among the party in the North which had secured the twelve years' respite and which, though since brought low, still counted for a good deal, there were naturally some on whom the prospect of renewing the endless struggle weighed heavily indeed. In the Southern Netherlands, where war's miseries were all too well remembered, that feeling was even stronger. Negotiations were set on foot through a zealous intermediary, a Madame 't Serclaes, who as a Catholic Hollander, the widow of a Brabanter exiled for the cause of the Revolt, and with married daughters living at Brussels, could not but smart under the splitting of the Netherlands. The Archdukes made a show of encouraging her efforts, but in reality the decision rested, as ever, with Spain, where shortly before his death Philip III laid it down that no extension of the Truce was to be thought of unless the North Netherlands conceded three points: freedom of worship for Catholics, the opening of the Scheldt, and the evacuation of the East and West Indies.

This last demand, dictated by the interest of Spain alone, was sufficient to unite everyone in the North in the determination to continue the war, and although some would have been ready for an agreement on the basis of the first two, which would have opened up the possibility of a renewed combination of the whole Netherlands, we must be careful not to over-estimate their influence. The interests of Protestantism and of trade would brook no sacrifices for the sake of Netherlands reunion. On the other hand, we must also preserve our critical sense in evaluating those expressions of the sentiment of Netherlands solidarity in which the spokesmen of the South frequently indulged. An attempt was made, for instance, to establish contact with Utenbogaert and his comrades in misfortune. The bishop of 's Hertogenbosch (then, of course, still Spanish), and Peckius, the chancellor of Brabant, uttered fair words about the manifest injustice of religious persecution and the possibility of coming to a mutual compromise, but the Remonstrant minister was shrewd enough to see that the intention was only to use him to promote dissension in the North. Spinola himself and the Spanish ambassador at Brussels added honey-sweet words to those of the Brabanters, whose pratings were of no significance so long as they had no hand in directing the foreign policy of their unhappy country and did not dare oppose the Spaniards.

An official mission of Peckius to The Hague, immediately before the fatal zero-hour when the sword would again be called into play, showed that on either side the positions were still what they had been twenty years before at Bergen-op-Zoom.[1] Peckius spoke very touchingly of 'the Netherlands, our common fatherland', when addressing the States-General, but at the same time invited them to come to a settlement 'under acknow- ledgment of the natural sovereigns'. No wonder Their High Mightinesses listened to him with head-shakes and signs of amazement. How could they have recognised the moribund Archdukes, whose sovereign authority the King of Spain was about to take into his own hands again? How could they believe that any treaty which restored the sovereignty to him would protect them against his arbitrary will? Peckius took his departure, guarded not without difficulty against the fury of the populace of Delft and Rotterdam. Shortly afterwards Albert died, and Isabella, who in her widowhood presently devoted herself to the Franciscan rule, henceforward ruled the Southern Netherlands as Governess for her nephew Philip IV, who succeeded to the throne almost at the same time. As though the disasters and disappointments of the previous generation had never been, this young man preserved inviolate in his mind the pretensions of his father and grandfather.

This renewed war with their Northern brothers into which Flanders and Brabant were now dragged was only part of the last great attempt made by the Habsburgs to extend to its

[1] See *The Revolt of the Netherlands*, p. 245.

utmost limits, by dint of armed force, the Catholic counter-
offensive that was everywhere driving Protestantism back. The
most ardent protagonist of that policy was Ferdinand, who
became Emperor in 1619 and worked in close alliance with the
Court of Spain. Despite corruption and economic depression,
despite their chronic straits for money, Austria and Spain, led
by sovereigns who, however incapable, held an unshakable
confidence in their mission, put forth a mighty effort. In the
German Empire, the Protestant Princes, following the defeat of
their leader Frederick of the Palatinate, the 'Winter King' of
Bohemia, collapsed with a completeness which recalls the
situation after Charles V's defeat of the League of Schmalkalden.
In South Germany the Counter-Reformation carried all before
it, while the Imperial armies under Tilly (a South Netherlander)
and Wallenstein laid down the law far into North Germany.
Denmark proved but a rickety support for Protestantism
driven back upon the Baltic, and when King Christian, despite
subsidies from the Dutch Republic, withdrew defeated, the
Habsburg power seemed to reign supreme in the North, and
even the sea to lie open before it. The Edict of Restitution now
proceeded to restore to the Church her lost power throughout
the German Empire (1629).

In face of this surging flood-tide lapping her Eastern frontier,
the Republic of the United Netherlands appears like a rock.
Nothing more natural, however, than that this cataclysmic
spectacle, in which so much they felt to be akin was swept away
before their eyes, should fill the people with anxiety. The
outlying posts held in the Empire, in East Friesland and on the
Middle Rhine, were stoutly defended, only Gulich, which lay
much too far to the south, being lost at once in 1621. Taking it
altogether, the outlook was perilous enough, and the rejoicing
with which the North in 1622 greeted the relief of Bergen-op-
Zoom against the 'Spanish hordes' (as the song has it) gives
the measure of the anxiety which beset men's minds. So
dangerous was the situation that, as we have already seen, the
new Calvinist directors of the country's policy were driven to
lean on the Catholic government of France, so soon as it seemed
at all ready to face the Habsburg menace. In 1624 they were
able to negotiate an alliance with France, where Richelieu had
just come into power. But the danger was not yet past. In 1625

Spinola succeeded in recapturing Breda, which had been the first-fruits of Maurice's military success thirty-five years before; now the Prince vainly tried to relieve the town, and just before it surrendered, he died.

His five provinces elected as Stadholder in his place his much younger brother Frederick Henry, whom the States-General appointed Captain-General. His was a troubled heritage: there were the still smouldering embers of the religious conflict; there was the military situation. In the military sphere, however, the new Stadholder was quickly able to register considerable successes. As early as 1627 he captured Grol, thus closing the breach in the Eastern frontier that Spinola had made before the Truce. The careful preparation and skilful prosecution of the siege showed the world that the States' army had been confided to a master-mind. It was a misfortune, all the same, that on England under her new monarch Charles I—James had died the same year as Maurice—no more reliance was to be placed than before; the colonial issue had just aroused bitter feelings there owing to the massacre of Amboina (about which later). As far as France was concerned, Richelieu was still distracted from his anti-Habsburg plans by the necessity of first strengthening the royal power at home against unruly nobles and Huguenots. When in 1628 the whole resources of France were brought to bear against the Protestant stronghold of La Rochelle, it needed great confidence in the Cardinal's motives not to believe (and we saw already that many of the more fanatical Calvinists did believe) that he too was aiming at the destruction of Protestantism, whose strategic position in Europe was threatened with the simultaneous loss of its bases in the South-East, the South-West and the North-East.

B. FREDERICK HENRY CAPTURES 'S HERTOGENBOSCH (1629)

SUCH were the circumstances in which Frederick Henry and the States-General determined in 1629 to lay siege to 's Hertogenbosch. The previous year had witnessed an event of an entirely different character, which encouraged the Northerners to undertake the costly enterprise of besieging so considerable a town in direct communication with the enemy's main base : I refer to the capture of the Spanish Plate fleet by Piet Hein, acting for the West India Company. Everyone knew how much the world policy of Spain depended upon the half-yearly shipments from the American mines. It could thus be hoped that Hein's marauding enterprise would cripple the resistance of the Southern Netherlands during the following season, while at the same time it filled the treasury of the North, and in particular strengthened the credit of Holland, the mainspring of every military undertaking.

Early in May 1629, after a winter spent in making plans and preparations, Frederick Henry appeared before 's Hertogen-bosch with an army of nearly 30,000 men. Ranking by tradition with Brussels, Antwerp and Louvain as one of the four chief towns of Brabant, 's Hertogenbosch could muster some 4,000 or 5,000 citizens under arms towards its own defence, while the governor, a Brabant nobleman named Grobbendonck, disposed of a garrison of nearly as many again. Moreover, situated as it was between the rivers Dommel and Aa, surrounded by swamps and defended by forts, the town was exceptionally strong. On the north the besiegers could use the river Maas as their base-line, the Crèvecœur fort having been in the States' hands since 1600. To the south-west, however, they had to camp on open moorland, exposed to attack by Spanish forces, and here as a matter of fact there soon appeared the army for which the Brussels government, in default of money from Spain, had managed to extract extraordinary subsidies from the States assemblies of the loyal provinces. Spinola had left the Nether-lands the year before—and died before he could return. He had been succeeded in the command by Count Henry van den Bergh, who as the son of that Van den Bergh, Orange's brother-in-law, who had played a far from heroic part in 1572 and had afterwards turned traitor, was first cousin to Frederick Henry. He was Stadholder of the Upper Quarter of Gelderland, where lay his ancestral castle of 's Heerenberg. More than ever the war assumed the appearance of a civil war.

Van den Bergh did not venture a direct attack on the States' army, and the siege works went forward undisturbed. Never before had the Orange brothers' laborious and scientific siege-methods been displayed upon so impressive a scale. A dyke was built across the swamps to connect two camps; both the rivers were dammed up and a host of water-mills built to drain the marshes. Thousands of peasants were employed upon the work, and the States, in consultation with their deputies attached to the commander, had to supply money unceasingly.

But after three months of this there came a sudden and dramatic change in the situation. Van den Bergh had dashed away eastwards to co-operate with Imperial forces in attempting an invasion from that side, of old the side on which the Northern Netherlands were hardest to defend. For the sake of the siege the river Ysel had been to a great extent denuded of regular troops. On 23 July a Spanish detachment succeeded in crossing the river at Westervoort; after a vain attempt to repulse the invaders, Arnhem gave way to panic. The Court there, the executive authority of Gelderland, distributed the scanty forces available among the threatened towns, thus handing the country-side over to the invaders. The Veluwe was completely overrun by Van den Bergh's army, reinforced by Imperial forces under Montecuculi. The enemy in the heart of the country—that was something unheard of! The Southern Netherlands were accustomed to such raids right up to their town walls, while Hooft wrote of Germany:

The unhappy Eastland is exposed to endless incursion and never free from horses' hoofs!

But the Republic had since the conquests of Maurice been immune from such outrages, and excitement was intense throughout the country. Panic and confusion were everywhere. Like Gelderland, the province of Utrecht failed to take energetic steps to defend itself; the town of Amersfoort capitulated without any attempt at resistance. The fact that so many of their notables were Catholic undoubtedly had a great influence on the attitude of these provinces. Jesuits appeared in the wake of the invaders, prophesying to the people that the end of the rebels' power was at hand. But the spirit of the Hollanders was more than equal to the test. Under their inspiration the States-General held firm. The Assembly approved Frederick Henry's courageous determination not to be drawn away from 's Hertogenbosch, and in his absence organised a vigorous defence of the canalised Rhine and Vecht, of the Zuider Zee and Ysel towns, and of the Betuwe. Fresh troops were enlisted, bands of *waardgelders* formed. The West India Company raised men and money, and Amsterdam contrived to produce a continual stream of both money and supplies.

And then the position was as suddenly reversed. On 19 August a small detachment under Van Gendt van Dieden surprised the town of Wesel, an indispensable link in the chain connecting the invaders with their base. Before the month was out they had evacuated the territory of the Republic, now no longer tenable, and on 14 September 's Hertogenbosch capitulated. The terms of the capitulation included the Meiery, the extensive district comprising Tilburg and Eindhoven over which the town had of old exercised jurisdiction. The Brussels government, however, denied that the town had any right to dispose of it, so that for a time the troops of the two sides disputed with one another the possession of this unhappy region.

In both Northern and Southern Netherlands, and throughout Europe, this conquest made a deep impression. It was the first important gain since Maurice had 'closed the fence' of the Northern Netherlands a generation ago. Throughout this interval the great rivers had roughly formed the frontier and, side by side with the seven provinces, Flanders and Brabant had maintained themselves practically intact. Now Brabant was shorn of an important town, the seat of a bishop, along with a large tract of countryside.

Conscious of its weakness, the Brussels government had acted upon an authorisation it held from Philip IV and opened negotiations even while the siege was still in progress. In the North the prospect of a settlement with Spain immediately aroused the old party passions of Holland mercantile interests and Protestant militancy to renewed opposition. 'Trevists' and 'Anti-Trevists'[1] assailed one another in scores of pamphlets. What in particular inclined the merchant class towards peace was the ravages inflicted by the Dunkirk privateers, against which the North Netherland navy could never furnish complete protection. The war party argued that Spain was only seeking a respite in the Netherlands the better to be able to co-operate with her Austrian ally in the conquest of Germany, after which the two would unite their forces to subjugate the Netherlands.

---

[1] After 'trêve', the French word for truce.

There is no doubt that such a danger was now inherent in any peace that left Spain in possession of the South. Every enemy of the Habsburgs, therefore, and especially France and Sweden, worked against the negotiations, and although they dragged on for years, mostly in secret and through all kinds of only half-acknowledged intermediaries, they were never taken really seriously by the States-General; the less so because another sort of peace appeared to be possible, one which would not leave Spain in possession of the hitherto loyal Netherlands.

For in the South itself the loss of 's Hertogenbosch aroused profound dissatisfaction with the Spanish regime. Since the accession of Philip IV not even the pretence of a national government, as under Albert and Isabella, had been kept up. The Council of State was excluded from everything; all matters of importance went through two *juntas*—the Spanish name is symbolic—one consisting of Spaniards, the other of well-disposed native officials. The most powerful man in the country was the Cardinal de la Cueva. He had formerly been ambassador to the nominally sovereign Archdukes, but now he represented the royal power more directly, standing next to the Governess Isabella, as Granvelle had once stood next to Margaret, and at the same time directing both *juntas*. All this was resented the more now that the burden of the war fell principally on the Netherlands, and Spain proved unable to protect the loyal provinces against the rebels. The great nobles, Aerschot, Egmont, even the commander-in-chief Henry van den Bergh, were as discontented as their grandfathers had been seventy years before. The privileged classes, which composed the provincial States-assemblies, the ecclesiastics, the nobility and the town magistracies, were offended by a hundred-and-one proofs of Spanish mistrust added to Spanish inefficiency. And now there came this mutilation of the old Duchy of Brabant to alarm and inflame men's minds.

Never (*wrote a Spaniard, a member of the Brussels government, to a compatriot*) have these provinces been more bitter in their enmity towards Spain. If the Prince of Orange and the rebels were not kept by their fanatical intolerance from granting liberty of worship and from guaranteeing their possession of churches and Church property to the clergy, then a union of the loyal provinces with those of the North could not be prevented.

Alas! while the Spaniard's indignation of the intolerance of the heretics may well raise a smile, he was none the less correct in his perception that the treatment of 's Hertogenbosch and the Meiery would be an obstacle to the coming together of the sundered Netherlands. The people of 's Hertogenbosch had hoped that they would be admitted to the Union on a footing of equality and granted freedom of worship. What an effect such an example might have had on other towns in the South! But the Calvinist party in the States-General was still sufficiently strong to rule out this policy. While the siege was still in progress the ministers had been on the watch. The South Holland Synod had memorialised the States and sent one of its leaders, Gisbert Voetius, to army headquarters to warn the Prince and the Field Deputies

that the Christian authorities, in the war which they are waging for the sake of religion and of the State, must take thought not so much to conquer lands and towns as to spread the word of the Lord and to propagate His Church.

By the terms of the capitulation, therefore, while the town government was confirmed in its ancient customs and privileges, in the matter of religion the town had to submit to the edicts. That meant liberty of conscience, no doubt, but liberty of religious exercise was ruled out completely. Just as Rovenius had retreated from Oldenzaal and Grol,[1] so now Bishop Ophovius had to quit 's Hertogenbosch. Under the gaze of thousands of sightseers who had assembled from all the seven provinces, he left the town the day after the surrender, with the governor and the garrison, at the head of a large concourse of priests and monks, followed by wagons laden with ornaments and relics —the 'puppetries' as the victors contemptuously called them —removed from churches and monasteries. The cathedral of St. John and all other churches and chapels were taken over by the handful of Reformed, mostly intruders from the North, servants of the new regime. On 19 September Ds. Conradus Markinius preached in the ex-cathedral on the text from Isaiah:

And I will give thee the treasures of darkness, and hidden riches of secret places, that thou mayest know that I, the Lord, which call thee by thy name, am the God of Israel.

It goes without saying that the suppression of Catholicism, in a town where there was hardly a Protestant to be found, rendered the promise of municipal self-government, too, in

---

[1] See above, p. 80

practice inoperative. In order that the new magistracy might consist of Protestants, fortune-hunters of all sorts had to be brought in from outside ('carpet-baggers', to borrow a term belonging to the Reconstruction episode after the Civil War in America), while the gilds, which according to Brabant usage—it was otherwise in oligarchic Holland—still played an active part in municipal government, were now excluded from it, despite the terms of the capitulation, because otherwise the Catholic element simply could not have been shut out. The first act of sovereignty in the Meiery was an edict instructing all priests to make way for Protestant ministers.

It was the same policy that had been carried out thirty and forty years before, following Maurice and William Louis' conquests in the Eastern provinces. What made it now appear so much more unpleasant was its fruitlessness. Not that Brabant was in any sense more firmly rooted in the Catholic tradition than Overysel or Gelderland had been; but the position of Catholicism in the Netherlands generally was now different from what it had been in the 'nineties of the previous century. The resistless slide towards all-conquering Protestantism which at that time had still been possible was now stopped by the barrier that the Counter-Reformation had thrown up under the auspices of the Archducal regime. It proved impossible to assimilate 's Hertogenbosch and the Meiery, just as Grol, which had also been under the Archdukes during the Truce, would remain an island of Romanism in the Protestant East. The policy of Protestantisation could no longer serve the building up of a North Netherlands nationality; it had become a policy of vexation and suppression. Everybody, down to the orphan children of 's Hertogenbosch, who straightway passed into Protestant keeping, resisted this coercion of souls.

There were, indeed, in the North those who realised the unwisdom of this policy, and foremost among them was Frederick Henry. In his general approach to the religious question, Frederick Henry adhered, as we have seen, to the tradition of William the Silent, which Maurice had abandoned. During these years the prospects of large conquests in the South caused him to understand more fully the practical importance of the way the Catholics were treated. After the capitulation of 's Hertogenbosch he was instrumental in smoothing over and softening down all kinds of minor points—temporary residence of priests, their subsistence out of commandeered Church property, and the like. But this could not prevent exiled priests going to Antwerp and elsewhere and spreading terror of the conquering heretic. And on top of that the pugnacious Voetius waged a boisterous pen-and-ink warfare across the frontier with the Louvain professor Jansenius, which, to an accompaniment on both sides of less theological but not less bitter satires and pamphlets, is unlikely to have won over a single citizen of 's Hertogenbosch to the Reformed Church, but which did stir up mutual antagonism and distrust all the more.

c. UNSUCCESSFUL EFFORTS AT REUNION

DURING the next few years, nevertheless, the Spanish regime in the Netherlands was once again in a tottering condition. The idea of reunion moved into the centre of practical politics. But no less auspicious a prelude to this crisis was conceivable than the treatment meted out by the States-General of The Hague to 's Hertogenbosch and the Meiery. Amid all the talk of restoring peace in the Netherlands and all the whispers about casting off the yoke of Spain, this manifestation of Calvinistic assertiveness could not but dampen the zeal of the South Netherland population in the face of those who at the same time posed as its saviours and protectors.

So the Governess was able in 1629 to ward off the danger with some apparent concessions. She dismissed the hated Cueva and brought the Council of State more into affairs again. But the new Spanish representative, the Marquis of Aytona, although personally of opinion that the wishes and the self-respect of the natives should be taken more into account, was in no position to force a radical change of system upon the Madrid government. He himself, moreover, distrusted the only native who held a position of independent authority, the Count van den Bergh, who early in 1631, to his own intense indignation, was relieved of the supreme command, which was given to a Spaniard again, the Marquis of Santa Cruz.

Meanwhile the siege of 's Hertogenbosch had so depleted the Republic's treasury that the following year saw it unable to put an army into the field. In 1631 an invasion of Flanders was ventured upon, only to be abandoned as soon as the Spanish army appeared on the scene; whereupon the Spaniards themselves undertook an attack upon Zealand which was bloodily repulsed on the Slaak. It was clear—Frederick Henry fully realised this—that in order to escape from the stalemate brought about by the establishment of the river-line as a result of Maurice's conquests, the Republic needed the co-operation of the South Netherland population.

In 1631 a 'blue-dyer' of Ghent by name Jaatsem (Joachim) Pyn got into touch with the governor of Sluis and with the Prince himself, offering his aid for a surprise attack on his town. His plot was discovered, however, and the town government showed an exemplary zeal in punishing him for what it described in his death-sentence as

a naked and detestable treason against your natural sovereign and your own fatherland.

But in the spring of 1632 a conspiracy was set on foot by personages of much greater importance than the unlucky Pyn, and this, moreover, at a moment when the military position of the Spanish rulers of the South, as well as that of their ally the Emperor, was seriously weakened. Gustavus Adolphus' invasion of Germany had since 1630 brought about a sweeping change in the situation. The best part of the Spanish army had been sent from the Netherlands to the defence of the Palatinate, where, following the annihilation of the Imperial army under Tilly at Breitenfeldt, a linking up of French and Swedish forces was threatening. Gustavus Adolphus had become the Protestants' hero, and even the South Netherlanders felt fortified against their Spanish masters by his victories. Such were the circumstances in which there came to The Hague, in all secrecy, the Count of Warfusée, the president of the Brussels Council of Finance, who, speaking also in the name of the Count van den Bergh, put before Frederick Henry and Grand Pensionary Pauw, as well as the French ambassador, a plan for the liberation of the Southern provinces from Spain. Warfusée himself admitted that what moved him to this was the injustice done

him by the Spanish government in matters of finance; Van den
Bergh for his part chafed at the loss of the supreme command.
Both of them wanted considerable sums of money and the
promise of great titles and offices from France and the Republic
before they made use of their influence over the people and the
army. The nobles who had let Parma reconcile them to the King
fifty years before had bargained in just the same way, and it was
the usual procedure among the great nobility and princes of the
blood who took part in the French disturbances. This private
self-seeking in no wise alters the fact that the schemes of
Warfusée and Van den Bergh were connected with a strong
current of feeling in the Spanish provinces.

What they proposed was that all the French-speaking
provinces should be joined to France, all the Dutch-speaking—
naturally with safeguards for privileges and religion—to the
Republic.

The Walloon nobility would only feel at home under the
French monarchy; they hated the prospect of coming under the
middle-class government of the North. At that very moment
a group of the greatest Walloon nobles was in contact with the
French government itself through the medium of François
Carondelet, Dean of Cambrai. On the other hand, in the Dutch-
speaking provinces, in Upper Gelderland, but especially in
Brabant and Flanders, the town governments were of more
importance than the nobility, and while they were even more
averse to the French than to the Spanish system of government, they were at the same time powerfully attracted
towards the republican forms which had triumphed in the
revolted territories. What, indeed, is more natural? One sees at
once with what longing the weight and dignity of the Holland
burgomasters and town councils—not to mention the thriving
trade of their towns—must have filled the impoverished and
humiliated town-magistracies of the South. But there is no lack
of direct evidence from various witnesses on this divergence
of aspirations between the Dutch- and the French-speaking
groups in the South.

In the upshot, however, France was restrained from active
co-operation by fresh domestic upheavals, and it was the North
alone which sought to make use of the assistance of Van den
Bergh and Warfusée. The money they demanded was paid, and

towards the end of May 1632 the States-General to the Southern
provinces issued a proclamation admonishing them

to follow the praiseworthy example of their forefathers in liberating themselves from the heavy and intolerable yoke of the Spaniards and their
adherents, and of their own free will to join themselves unto these United
Provinces; to which end we offer them our strong and effectual assistance by
the army which we have put into the field under the wise and courageous,
and withal prudent, leadership of His Excellency the Lord Frederick Henry
Prince of Orange; and we herewith religiously and irrevocably promise unto
the aforesaid provinces that we will conserve and maintain the towns and
members of the same, likewise their inhabitants, as well spiritual as secular,
of whatever state, quality and condition they may be (who shall join themselves unto us as aforesaid), in their privileges, rights and liberties, as well as
in the public exercise of the Roman Catholic Religion, desiring for ourselves
to live, deal and converse with the same as good friends, neighbours and
allies.

For the moment, therefore, the policy of militant Protestantisation was tempered down. The opportunity to rid themselves
completely of Spanish power in their neighbourhood seemed too
good for even a Contra-Remonstrant States-General to reject
it out of hand for the sake of the chimera of a de-Romanised
South.

Frederick Henry led the army into the region of the Maas.
Here Van den Bergh, as Stadholder of Upper Gelderland, could
be of most service, and it was indeed due to him that Venlo and
Roermond surrendered without firing a shot, thus enabling the
Prince to appear before Maastricht as early as 10 June, much
sooner than anyone had expected. But the powerful garrison of
Maastricht remained loyal to the Spanish government, and
Frederick Henry was forced to undertake a regular siege. When
not only Isabella's own troops were recalled from the Palatinate,
but a strong Imperial army under Pappenheim advanced to the
relief of the town, the position of the besiegers, so far from their
base, became critical, and it required all the commander's skill
and experience, and especially all his strength of mind, to bring
the enterprise to a successful conclusion. But it was done, and
on 22 August Maastricht surrendered. Following 's Hertogenbosch here was another conquest to impress all Europe; the
fame of the cautious but persevering Frederick Henry bade fair
to rival that of the dashing Gustavus Adolphus.

So far everything had had to be done without that help from
the South Netherlanders which the conspirators had promised.

From Liège Van den Bergh had been issuing manifestoes to the troops who had been under his command, and to the inhabitants.

There shall be fire and flame (*he wrote in his German-flavoured Eastern dialect to his brother-in-law in North Gelderland, Culemborch*) when they talk about me among the ministers (*meaning the Governess's advisers at Brussels*), but not among the commonalty, who are wholly in favour of a good peace.

But whatever sympathy the commonalty might feel, they did not stir, and but few soldiers ranged themselves under their late commander. The main factor in causing this disappointing result was undoubtedly the abstention of the French government; to the Walloon nobles, who were awaiting a signal from France, that was conclusive. As for the inhabitants of the Dutch-speaking provinces, they had forgotten how to move a single step without the leadership of the great lords.

So long as Frederick Henry was occupied with the siege of Maastricht, therefore, the government easily retained control, although there was a strong feeling of tension. The Hague States-General's promise to respect the people's religion had made a deep impression. One night in June a signboard showing the King of Spain's head was torn down, and the cry of 'Long Live the Prince of Orange' resounded in the streets of Brussels. The government judged it necessary to demand a new oath of loyalty from the citizenry and from the States' deputies at Court, both high nobles and prelates. Throughout all this the common people's devotion to Catholicism did not falter, and the strongest link between them and the government was formed by the piety of the Governess, impressively demonstrated on the occasion of a four days' adoration of Our Blessed Lady of Laeken. But in the government's view the issue depended mainly on the secular and ecclesiastical dignitaries, and it was they who came in for its chief attention. Nobles who had sulkily withdrawn, as in the days of Granvelle, to show their disapproval of the exclusively Spanish character of the regime, were coaxed back into the councils with words of flattery. The Governess staged banquets for them. To the most eminent it was whispered

that they ought to set more store by the titles and appointments which are in the gift of the House of Austria and of the Catholic King (*the King of Spain*), and that they should disdain a simple States' government, where a loutish and ill-mannered burgomaster can often lay down the law.

So hard pressed did the Governess feel, that although knowing full well how obstinately opposed her nephew the King was to the summoning of the States-General—in his eyes this was a surrender to sedition—she nevertheless yielded to the insistence of Aerschot and the Archbishop of Mechlin. The States-General opened their session at Brussels on 9 September 1632. They had not met since 1600. Now, as then,[1] they regarded it as their principal task to enter into direct peace negotiations with the Northern States-General; and now, as then, the Spanish government was constrained to allow this, although making the States promise that in the negotiations, which in appearance they were to carry on independently, they would not transgress the bounds of the loyalty due to the King.

Would they keep this promise? Now that France held aloof, the nobles who had been party to Van den Bergh and Warfusée's partition-scheme were suspicious of the North, and this was naturally not less true of the ecclesiastics, also strongly represented in the Brussels States-General. The freedom of worship promised in the Northern States-General's proclamations was not enough for them. In the Republic the Reformed Church enjoyed more than freedom of worship, it enjoyed an exclusive right to freedom of worship; in the South, 'under the Spanish yoke', the Catholic Church tolerated competition just as little, or even less. The regime that the Northerners were proffering so grandly found ominous illustration for devout Southern Catholics in the handing over of two churches to the Reformed as stipulated in the capitulations of Venlo, Roermond and Maastricht. This added bitterness to the reproach cast at the Spanish government by the Archbishop of Mechlin and his suffragans, that it was no longer able to protect the faith, and there floated before their eyes the vision of the Southern States-General's arresting the march of the conqueror with a declaration of independence.

But even for that, the co-operation of the Northerners whom they distrusted so much was essential. The Southerners would have liked them flatly to refuse to negotiate with Spain: then the declaration of independence could be represented as being forced on the South, and the odium of rebellion against the lawful sovereign, which weighed much more heavily in the

[1] See *The Revolt of the Netherlands*, pp. 242–6.

quiescent and formal seventeenth century than in the aspiring
and turbulent sixteenth, could be avoided. A Catholic Republic
which should ally itself with its neighbours and would have the
support of England in maintaining its independence against
France as well as against the Seven Provinces—this was the
theme of much discussion in States circles at Brussels.

But would the Hollanders meekly adopt the policy thus laid
down for them? On the fall of Maastricht, the position of the
victorious States' army, its freedom of action regained, seemed
a menace to these plans as well as to the Spanish regime. A
westward sweep by Frederick Henry—and would not the towns
of Flanders and Brabant far sooner throw in their lot with the
North on the basis of the proclamation than attempt to form an
independent State with the Walloon lands? They did, indeed,
regard union with the North very differently from the Walloon
nobility and the ecclesiastics.

> . . . the Catholic States were jealous of some of their members of States,
> principally of those of Flanders, and some of Brabant, suspecting that they
> might incline to join themselves with the Hollanders; for proof whereof, his
> Majesty will be pleased to recall to mind, that when the deputies of the
> Catholic States were sent to Maestricht . . . in consideration the third deputy
> was the pensioner (*Edelheer*) of Antwerp, a town much affected to the
> Hollanders by reason of hopes for traffic, the Catholic States imparted
> nothing to them of their secret design to move the Hollanders to cause to the
> said Catholic States, by arms, the necessity for their declaration.

Thus wrote later, in his almost unintelligible English,[1]
Balthazar Gerbier, the Hollander of French descent, who as
English resident at Brussels did his utmost to encourage the
formation of this South Netherland State, for England feared
the accession of power which reunion with Flanders and Brabant
would mean to the young Republic, her rival in trade and
colonisation. Soon after the proclamation by the Hague States
Gerbier warned his principals that people at Brussels were only
waiting for the arrival of Frederick Henry, and a Zealand regent
wrote later:

> Many towns were looking for our arrival, as if with the keys in their hands.

But they looked in vain. Before September was out, the
Brussels States-General had sent emissaries to Maastricht to

---

[1] The meaning of the passage quoted is that the States-General at Brussels,
knowing Antwerp's preference for a union with the Northern Republic,
found it necessary to keep the pensionary of Antwerp in the dark as to their
plan for founding an independent State.

open negotiations with Frederick Henry and the Hague States'
Field Deputies accompanying him. In October there followed
in their wake a more numerous delegation headed by the Duke of
Aerschot and the Archbishop of Mechlin. All this time the
Stadholder was lying idly with his army near the town he had
just captured; he remained there until disease in the army
prompted him to lead it back into winter quarters, while the
States-General transferred the negotiations, which were making
no headway, to The Hague. The same Southern delegation
made its appearance there in the beginning of December. But
how the situation had changed! The States' army, which had
struck such terror into the South, now withdrawn, and Gustavus
Adolphus dead at Lützen. In Germany the power of the
Protestant party crippled and awe of Habsburg everywhere
revived. How came it that the critical moment had been thus
let slip?

The Prince afterwards in his *Mémoires* had hard things to say
about the States-General, who had refused to send full powers
to him and the Field Deputies at Maastricht and had finally
transferred the negotiations to The Hague. In this way, he
complains, they made it impossible to conclude peace under the
pressure of the army at Maastricht. But with whom did the
Prince want to make peace? He and the deputies, who were all
his personal supporters, had set the negotiations with the
Southern envoys on a basis which satisfied neither the Northern
haters of Spain nor the party in the South who wanted independence following a refusal by the North to negotiate with
Spain. Although ostensibly calculated to put the power of Spain
in the Netherlands under the closest restraint (there was a reference to the Pacification of 1576), the nine points which the
Prince drew up at Maastricht seemed to be designed much more
to beguile the Hague States into negotiations, not with the
Brussels States, but with Spain. According to Aitzema (the
chronicler, writing in 1658), even before the arrival of Aerschot
and his colleagues, he had let a Spanish envoy convince him
that the idea of a revolution in the Catholic Netherlands was an
illusion, and his own trusty henchman Heenvliet had confirmed
that view from Brussels. Thus undeceived (again according
to Aitzema), he abandoned 'further invasion' and tried to
bring the Northern States assembly, through the medium

of the emissaries from the Brussels States, into parley with Spain.

Was Frederick Henry right? His idleness at Maastricht certainly astonished his contemporaries. In the Zealand letter from which I have already quoted, this sentence followed:

> It is a source of undying regret to all good men here (*at Middelburg*) that the unexpected occasion of joining the Provinces unto one another was as it were kicked aside.

And as early as October the English ambassadors, Carleton and Boswell, wrote from The Hague that in States-General circles grumblings were current to the effect that

> . . . whereas there was a resolution taken to act somthing of importance with the army and the Count Henry de Berg should have gone along and ioyned in the enterprise, things are now at a stand, neither is it imputed to other cause then an amusement given to the Prince by the coming of these deputies of Bruxells and the expectation he remaines in to heare from hence (*i.e. The Hague*) what to doe with them.

It is difficult to avoid the impression that if political considerations did indeed help to determine Frederick Henry's conduct during these critical weeks following the fall of Maastricht, they were reinforced by those characteristics which marked him as a military commander. Great organiser that he was, methodical and persevering, he had even less feeling than Maurice for the strategy of the open field. Whereas Gustavus Adolphus, careering all over Germany with his little army, demonstrated what enormous shiftings of power could result from daring movements, even though he had to leave fortresses with enemy garrisons in his rear, the Dutch commander went beyond the shelter of his fortresses only reluctantly and, so to speak, step by step. The sweep through the Liège country to Brussels which was expected at The Hague, and even at Brussels itself, was against his nature; his tarrying in the captured town, which he caused to be strongly fortified, is paralleled by numerous hesitations which crippled his other campaigns. If 1632 really offered a chance of reunion, or at least of driving the Spaniards right out of the Netherlands—and certainly everything points to that—then that chance was lost by Frederick Henry's excessive caution.

In December, as already stated, the South Netherland delegation appeared at The Hague. But with the circumstances so radically changed in the meanwhile, the renewed negotiations never offered any real chance of agreement. The Southern deputies now found the nine articles, which at Maastricht had seemed so attractive to them,

of such a nature that, in the event of their being accepted, the King would keep only the bare title, as he is King of Jerusalem; and that they must therefore scruple to accept them.

We need not believe that they really felt repugnance for stipulations which would have put the King's authority under restraint. It was that they lacked the courage and strength to compel their government to accept them. Early in 1633 that government was reinforced by the arrival from Spain of a trusted servant of the King's, the jurist Pieter Roose, himself an Antwerper, but as stout a champion of the royal authority as any Spaniard. The deputies who early in January 1633 went to Brussels to report on behalf of the whole delegation hardly dared to communicate the new North Netherland proposition, according to which in the event of the King's refusal to ratify the forthcoming treaty between North and South the Southern Netherlands should be released from their oath of loyalty, and they crumpled up before the hectoring reception which the new President of the Secret Council accorded even their timorous circumlocutions.

It was becoming more and more difficult to keep up the pretence of negotiations between 'States and States'. It weighed too heavily on the Southerners themselves, who did not want to be regarded as other than plenipotentiaries from their sovereign, and it was on this basis that the negotiation was now carried further. Groningen and Friesland protested against this; Zealand, too, was greatly opposed to it; but Holland, supported by the other three provinces, wanted to explore this way to get out of the war.' Frederick Henry advised in the same sense; everything, in fact, points to his having foreseen and favoured this course from Maastricht onwards.

But even this was now no longer to be achieved. Spain felt relieved from the immediate threat to her hold over the Southern Netherlands, and thus in no mind to forget her interests elsewhere. The Spanish government at Brussels had made another attempt to secure direct contact with the North. No less a person than Rubens, a great favourite at Court, with

whom Frederick Henry had already had conversations at
Maastricht, was to have come to The Hague—the Northern
States-General and the Stadholder were now ready even for
this—, had not the Southern States-General protested violently
against this intervention by the Governess; and for that matter
they played Spain's game well enough themselves. Their
deputies at The Hague, now nothing better than spokesmen for
Spain, had no choice but to claim back Pernambuco, which the
West India Company had captured a few years before, thereby
making a serious inroad on the Portuguese Empire in Brazil.
Spain's desire to recover the territory of her discontented
Portuguese subjects is understandable, but was it likely that the
Dutch Republic in the heyday of its success would forgo this
new opening for expansion in the West Indies?

Never was people more unhappily placed than the South
Netherlanders now. Their sovereign was sacrificing them to
interests which they did not share, for they were excluded from
the Brazilian trade, just as from the East Indian, which a
quarter-century before had nearly cost them the Twelve Years'
Truce.[1] Nor was the policy which now prevailed in the Republic
less selfish. The idea of Netherland unity was not dead. Within
sight of possibilities such as had not been offered for a generation, it once again found emphatic expression. But its advocacy
in the States-General was left to the two Contra-Remonstrant
provinces where Frederick Henry did not exercise the Stadholdership. In their protest against the negotiations with Spain,
Friesland and Groningen declared themselves impelled

to add something here on the advantages and good fortune which such a
pacification and general union of all the Netherlands provinces will present
unto the state of the United Netherlands. (*In the third instance they mention:*)
Lastly, this pacification and general union will create such a Republic as
shall be strong enough to procure and to maintain a general peace throughout
all Christendom and to frustrate and set bounds to the ambitious designs of
all Kings and Potentates who should seek or contrive to perturb that general
peace and welfare.

The compilers of that document were not unmindful that

a good part of the subjected Netherlands were of old our allies in the Union
of Utrecht, (nor that) the war was begun to free all the Netherlands from the
yoke of Spain.

---

[1] See *The Revolt of the Netherlands*, pp. 250-1.

But then they, self-styled champions of 'the old Beggar maxims', went on to speak of the importance of their policy for 'God's Church' and for 'the propagation of His Sacred Word', phrases which must have sounded less attractive to South Netherland ears. It was indeed the ministers in their pulpits who declaimed the most fiercely against peace with Spain; it was the party responsible for the treatment meted out to 's Hertogenbosch which, paradoxically, made the unity of the Netherlands its battle-cry. The document put in by Friesland and Groningen certainly mentions the proclamation addressed to the Southerners in 1632, but one searches in vain for any reiteration of the recognition of their Catholicism contained in that document.

The Southerners experienced even colder comfort, however, from the other party, which now directed the negotiations, led, with the Stadholder's at least temporary approval, by the Grand Pensionary of Holland, Pauw (son of Oldenbarnevelt's enemy, but himself more Amsterdammer than Contra-Remonstrant). One of the reasons which made Holland and Zealand averse to a policy aimed at a reunion with, or even at independence of, the Southern provinces, was the fear that the rise of the South might lead to

a diversion of trade, if the subjected provinces should come to enjoy freedom of government, religion and commerce, especially upon the rivers Hont and Scheldt.

From now on, therefore, we have to reckon with a body of opinion in the Republic, and strongest at Amsterdam, which held that the economic interests of the North demanded that the South, Antwerp to be precise, should remain under Spain, since it would be less easy to lay upon a free sister-republic, let alone upon allied provinces, the servitudes which were judged essential. The Frisians and Groningers, who warned the Hollanders against 'the wrath of God' if they made an idol of trade after this fashion, were none the less themselves of opinion that the permanent closure of the Scheldt could be stipulated as the price of freedom.

Thus neither with the one party nor with the other was there any escape from that condition, and the South Netherland negotiators conceded it along with other provisions involving economic exploitation. The territorial demands, too—

recognition of the States' possession of the Meiery and cession
of the barony of Breda required to link it with Bergen-op-Zoom
—they were ready to accept. But nothing was of avail so long as
they had to insist on the restoration of Pernambuco (ostensibly
in exchange for the districts to be ceded in Brabant). They did
do so loyally; they made a merit to the King of thus subordinat-
ing their own interests to those of his other dominions, and
besought him in return to show some complaisance and to
grant them peace. He listened no more than did the Northern
States, and so the negotiations dragged aimlessly on.

There was, indeed, a stir when in May 1633 Frederick Henry
took the field with the new season, but instead of striking a blow
at the heart at last, he took himself off to Rheinberg, the Cleve
fortress, which had been in Spanish hands since Spinola took it
in 1606 and was, since the loss of Wesel and Orsoy, the last
Spanish stronghold on the Rhine. Not until he had taken it,
did Frederick Henry move towards Brabant, only to idle six
weeks away at Boxtel awaiting Swedish reinforcements. A fresh
proclamation by the States-General to the population of the
South seemed to indicate a return to the policy of 1632, but
when the Prince finally moved—September had already come—
it was only to make a few timid manœuvres. A frontal attack, so
contemporaries believed, would at once have exposed the pitiful
weakness of the Spanish army under d'Aytona and made
Brussels untenable. Frederick Henry let himself be intimidated
by the brave countenance of the Spanish commander—or was it
that he did not want the much talked-of revolution in the
South? Anyhow, he soon brought his army back into winter
quarters. Once again the Spanish regime in the Netherlands
had escaped; once again the Brussels States-General found
themselves alone with their masters.

Less than ever were the latter inclined to give way to the
States'feeble clutchings at the helm of affairs, and they were now
better informed of the treasonable relations which the noble
members in particular of that assembly were keeping up with
foreign powers. In the summer of 1633 Gerbier had betrayed it
all for a large sum of money. The Duke of Aerschot himself was
involved in the disclosures, and the first result was that the
Archduchess rallied to the helpless States-General's plan of
sending Aerschot on a mission to the King. He set out in

November. Isabella herself died shortly after (4 December 1633) and the direction of affairs passed into the hands of a council on which the Archbishop of Mechlin alone represented the Netherland element amidst a crowd of Spaniards. Before the year was out the Northerners broke off the negotiations, which had long since lost all meaning. Aerschot, soon after his arrival at Madrid, where he had actually begun by making serious efforts to secure for the States full powers with respect to the negotiations, was clapped into prison—just as Bergen and Montigny had been nearly seventy years before[1]—and died a prisoner in 1640. The tidings of his arrest reached Brussels along with the King's order to dissolve the States-General. As in 1600, they dispersed in dejection.

A tragic end to this attempt of the South Netherland pro-vinces, the last before the Brabant revolution of a century and a half later, to escape from foreign domination; but an end which in its want of anything spectacular or heroic corresponded only too well with the feebleness of the attempt itself. The hand of Spain now lay more heavily than ever on 'the loyal provinces', at least, as far as their own population was concerned, for although revolution had been averted, it remained a question whether, now that the struggle for overseas trade had made peace with the Seven Provinces impossible, conquest could in the long run be avoided. And despite the singular inactivity which Frederick Henry once more displayed in the campaign of 1634, that question began to assume a more threatening aspect owing to the attitude of France. For the sake of keeping the Republic in the war Richelieu was now prepared to risk an open breach with Spain. On 15 April 1634 a subsidy treaty was concluded whereby the States-General of the Republic promised not to resume for the space of a year the negotiations with Spain recently broken off; and before that period had elapsed the States succeeded in bringing France into the war, but at the same time surrendered their own freedom of action once and for all in the celebrated treaty of 1635.

[1] See *The Revolt of the Netherlands*, p. 101.

D. THE FRENCH ALLIANCE OF 1635

WE HAVE seen what valuable assistance France had more than
once rendered at critical moments, so that Calvinist prejudice
against an alliance with the Catholic monarchy had had to be
brushed aside. But this time the intervention of France meant
something quite different. At the end of 1632 and in 1633 the
Republic presented the appearance of a State so divided against
itself that it could neither wage war nor make peace. The French
alliance served to help the war party back into the saddle. From
the beginning of 1633 there was a French ambassador-extra-
ordinary in the country with instructions to foil the conclusion
of armistice or peace, if necessary by the offer of large subsidies
for the prosecution of the war. The activities of this diplomat,
the Baron de Charnacé, give a far from edifying impression of
political life in the Union. The ambassador established contact
especially with a few of the Stadholder's intimates—Aerssens,
De Knuyt, the Prince's representative as First Noble in Zealand,
Musch, the Greffier of the States-General—and with their
assistance the entire Contra-Remonstrant party and the West
India Company were mobilised on behalf of co-operation with
France. In the process French titles and pensions were distributed with lavish hand. The Prince himself hesitated the whole
summer through; perhaps he was only feigning, in order to
encourage France to greater concessions. In the end, however,
he definitely abandoned the peace policy and came forward
as leader of the Anti-Trevists—which meant of the friends of
France, for continuance of the war was no longer to be thought of
save in terms of close understanding with France. Charnacé was
soon avowing that if the Prince himself had been the King's
ambassador he could not have pleaded the cause of the treaty
more forcefully. In explanation of this change-over, the Frenchman alleged motives of self-interest, and in particular he believed
he had made an impression with the argument that the Stadholder would be able to rely on the goodwill of France and on
the French auxiliary troops to ensure his dynastic interests in
the Republic. We shall soon see that subsequent developments
bear out the likelihood that such reflections had occurred to

Frederick Henry's mind. Meanwhile, it is clear that the impotence of the Brussels States and the stubbornness of Spain had in fact made the Trevists' policy impossible to carry through. When Frederick Henry abandoned it, it was lost. Nevertheless, the Holland trading towns continued throughout 1634 to obstruct the negotiations with Charnacé, which now held the field in the place of those with the Southern deputies. Pauw still acted as the spokesman of these Holland towns—now patently in opposition to the Stadholder.

Their primary motive was certainly war-weariness linked with that narrow commercial approach to which I have already called attention. But combined with these were other considerations which seem less unacceptable to the present-day observer. Many Hollanders were afraid that France might soon grow into a power more dangerous than Spain. In that they were right, and the alliance of 1635, by which the parties mutually contracted not to make a separate peace, ushered in an era of French expansion which to no people was to cause more calamities than to the people of the Netherlands.

But that vague fear of something which still lay in an uncertain future had to yield place to the immediate danger. In Germany, following the death of Gustavus Adolphus, the situation had once more turned in favour of the Habsburgs. Spain might be spent economically, but her spirit remained indomitable, and fresh Spanish troops were coming from the Milanese to the assistance of the Austrians. The commander of the second reinforcement was the Cardinal-Infante Ferdinand, brother to Philip IV, and by him appointed Governor of the Netherlands. He first helped to annihilate the Swedes at Nordlingen in September 1634, and then came north with his victorious army to Brussels. Along with the new governorship great military plans were set on foot. Thus for the time being the French alliance was received with relief almost everywhere in the anxious North; at the last moment even Holland and Pauw co-operated towards it.

The treaty (February 1635) provided that the oppressed Netherlands should be granted a short period in which to liberate themselves with the help of the allies, after which—and here was the real objective—these would proceed to conquer and partition them. The partition-line now adopted deviated considerably from the linguistic frontier, which had been followed in Van den Bergh and Warfusée's plan of three years before. The instruction for the States' ambassadors might indeed lay down

that the provinces in which the French tongue is generally spoken should be assigned to the Crown of France, those remaining should and ought to be left to the United Provinces,

but even in this document, as soon as the States came down to details, they suffered community of language to be over-ridden by strategic and other considerations. In the treaty itself, Brabant and Mechlin were assigned to the Republic, but almost the whole of Flanders went with the Walloon provinces to France, the projected frontier running from Blankenberge northwards of Bruges to Rupelmonde. If the treaty had ever been carried out, a big slice of Dutch-speaking territory, with Dunkirk, Ypres and Grammont in the South and Bruges, Ghent and Termonde in the North, would have been consigned to France and gallicisation.[1]

What a change from the hopes and schemes of 1632! Conquest took the place of reunion. One point in the treaty gave umbrage to the North Netherland war-party: the promise that the Republic would leave undisturbed the position of the Roman Catholic religion in the territories assigned to her. The Cardinal de Richelieu, bitterly attacked as he was in his own country for his co-operation with the Protestant powers in Europe, could not indeed forgo this demand, but so closely had Frederick Henry now attached himself to the Contra-Remonstrants that in practice, as we shall see later, the promise came to nothing. The gesture of Venlo, Roermond and Maastricht was not repeated. Then how hollow rang the admonition still issued from time to time to the South Netherland population! Flanders, assigned to France, could not but look to the Spanish government at Brussels, as to a guardian for the maintenance of its particular character; Brabant, threatened with annexation to the Calvinist Republic, for the maintenance of its religion. Not that there occurred a sudden revulsion in the relations between the two separated parts of the Netherlands. The factors which predominated after 1635 had all been

[1] See map on p. 153.

present before. But to us, who know what course affairs were to take, that year nevertheless appears to mark the beginning of a new period. Before entering upon it, let us for a moment glance backward at what the crisis ended thus inauspiciously has to teach us about the feelings and ideas of North and South regarding one another.

e. NORTH AND SOUTH FACE TO FACE

REUNION had miscarried, but that does not alter the fact that the idea of Netherland unity was still a force in politics. I hinted above[1] that Peckius' appeal in the States-General at The Hague to 'the Netherlands, our common fatherland', could hardly be called other than loose rhetoric in view of the circumstances of his mission. In 1632 there was at least the semblance of action on the part of the South Netherlanders, and when, therefore, on the first appearance of the Southern delegation in the Hague States we find the Archbishop of Mechlin delivering an oration in Dutch in which the same phrase occurs, we are the more disposed to bear in mind that even such commonplaces have their significance in political relationships. There can be no possible doubt of the sincerity with which the South felt the war to be a disaster destructive of the old welfare of the Seventeen Provinces. In the North people were too prosperous—the remark applies to this no less than to the previous generation[2]— to idealise the past after the fashion common in the South, but the remembrance of the lost unity, especially as it had found expression in the Pacification of Ghent, could yet give direction to thought among the politically minded. It finds its clearest expression in the document drawn up by the deputies of Friesland and Groningen from which I have quoted; the utterance of the Zealand regent cited above is also significant. The notion of community between North and South, with only the Spanish hold on the South to disturb it, clearly lives on, too, in some of the pamphlets occasioned by the peace negotiations; thus

[1] See above, p. 85.
[2] See *The Revolt of the Netherlands*, pp. 238–9.

Diogenes, in a *Dialogue between Diogenes, Momus and Menippus*, thinks that the object of opening negotiations is

to restore and to conserve the Seventeen Provinces once again in their old bloom, traffic and prosperity, with maintenance of their liberty, privileges and rights. Thereunto have States (*assemblies*) entered into communications with States (*assemblies*), Netherlanders with Netherlanders, natives with natives.

The 'Seventeen Provinces'—then the Walloons were not excluded from that feeling of unity? Sometimes, indeed, they were. When a few years after the alliance the French struck a heavy blow by capturing Arras (in 1640), the Amsterdam publisher Hondius, son of an exile, wrote to a cousin at Ghent:

I hope that the loss of Arras and other places besides, which stand to follow, will open the eyes of the States on that side (*the States of the loyal provinces*), and that they will unite with us well-buttered Hollanders to form a single body and to be good friends, for we have never been enemies save by accident, which being removed, we shall have peace. The Walloons have always been French before; let them be French still, and let those who speak Dutch join and unite with us who speak Dutch, each part preserving its liberty. We should then set a pale to the Frenchman which he would not jump over. Oh! that it might come to pass!

There the dividing line was drawn sharply enough, to be sure! The pamphlets may more than once mention community of language as an argument for co-operation between North and South, and strong cultural currents (as we shall see later on) might be continually sweeping back and forth from one to the other, yet one seldom hears so clear-toned an utterance as this; generally the expression is much vaguer, and consciousness of linguistic unity as we understand it is scarcely to be found. If the people of Flanders and Brabant on the one hand, and those of Hainault, Artois, and so forth, on the other, confirm their dualism by feeling drawn in the different directions of their respective neighbours of kindred speech, the aversion of the Walloons for the Northern Republic is expressed in social terms, while Antwerp explains her inclination towards union on the grounds of economic interest. And as far as the North is concerned, we have seen how grievously the treaty of 1635 if carried into effect would encroach upon the unity of the Dutch-speaking area, so that Hondius' call to the man of Ghent to join in setting a pale to the Frenchman sounds painfully false. Had not the States themselves agreed that Ghent should lie within the Frenchman's pale?

Through it all the idea of Netherland unity persisted. It

speaks again out of a letter to Hondius from the priest Sanderus
(whose *Flandria Illustrata* Hondius published), when he writes,
apparently in equal ignorance of what the unholy treaty of 1635
stipulated:

> The French will seek to do great damage to us this year, and then the
> raindrops from that quarter will begin to fall on the heads of you gentlemen
> as well, for they will spare nobody and will try to swallow up everything they
> can. *Tunc tua res agitur, paries cum proxima ardet.*

The idea of Netherland unity persisted. Yet when it came to
the test, all kinds of other motives—economic advantage,
colonial expansion, religious intolerance—weighed more heavily
on both sides; and fate had now determined that these other
factors, and especially the last, should operate within the Dutch
linguistic area almost consistently against the idea of unity.
It was not only the Spaniards who perpetuated the division,
although certainly in the last resort the South Netherlanders
were not masters of their destiny. From the beginning of the
revolt the religious factor had stood in the way of the national,
and when force of arms had once brought about the separation
and the two contending principles had firmly rooted themselves
each in one of the two parts, it was that which proved (at least
during the period when European history was dominated by the
Catholic-Protestant struggle) the greatest obstacle to their reunion.

Again and again have we seen how strong was the view in the
North which regarded the war as a religious war. Libertinists,
Baptists, Catholics might be indifferent or even hostile to it,
but the Reformed were in control of the State and they used
their position to build up gradually a political outlook, a conception of North Netherland patriotism, from which the others
could not wholly escape. Take the Catholics, the most difficult
group, one would think, to assimilate in this respect. We have
seen how in religious matters they continued to look to Louvain,
Brussels, Antwerp, and how their priests maintained close
contact with the hierarchy in the South, nay even disputed in
principle the very authority of the Northern States and still
recognised the title of the former sovereigns. Yet a hundred-and-
one ties came to bind their followers to Northern society, which
after all granted them full civic liberty; in practice they could
not keep up their aloof and unbending attitude. And whatever
their feelings or desires, politically speaking they formed a

passive element; the public opinion which counted in political
life was Protestant.

Actually, moreover, the specifically North Netherland
patriotism which thus grew up on the soil of the Republic and
of Protestantism did have a counterpart in the South. The old
tradition of loyalty to 'the natural sovereign' was far from dead;
it survived all grievances and troubles, and, given an appropriate
person and favourable circumstances, it could be infused with a
fresh zeal. It has been suggested above how important in this
respect was the imposing figure of the old Archduchess.
Aerschot displayed her portrait on the wall of his residence in
the monastery of St. Servatius at Maastricht when he entertained the Northerners there. Even Vondel, then leaning
towards Catholicism, commemorated her at her death as a
Netherland princess, who had striven earnestly after peace.
But the young Prince-Cardinal, crowned with the laurels of
Nordlingen, who at the head of his Spanish troops made his
entry in 1634, holding a naked sword, evoked an outburst of
perhaps even more lively emotion and attachment. Neither in
the one nor in the other case was this mere traditional loyalty.
There was genuine Catholic enthusiasm for the cause of Habsburg, which, notwithstanding all the shortcomings of kings and
emperors, and despite adversity and defeat, was a truly great
cause. Already under the Archdukes this showed itself in the
form of a South Netherland nationalism, which drew pride and
vigour from the consideration of the mighty European drama
wherein the country was under Spain playing its part. 'Thou
think'st', so a (still completely 'rhetorical') poet addressed the
Winter King of Bohemia after his overthrow:

Thou think'st to bring the noble house of Austria in ruin to the ground
with thy false practices; but God shall exalt it and humble the rebels.

It was a source of satisfaction to people in that frame of mind
to see South Netherland noblemen, Tilly from the Brabant
family of 't Serclaes, Bucquoy from Artois, fighting in the
German war under the banner of the Emperor.

Such feelings could not but turn against the enemies of the
King, against the heretics and rebels of the North, who (so ran
the party version already at the waning of the Pacification[1]) had

[1] See *The Revolt of the Netherlands*, for instance p. 176.

engineered all the miseries that were desolating the Netherlands. If the events of the long-drawn-out war between North and South called forth from Flemings and Brabanters no such fine or famous Dutch poems as Vondel, Huygens or Revius were writing from the other side, that was because poetry in the vernacular enjoyed no esteem in the latinising Counter-Reformation atmosphere of the South; a number of more or less clumsy popular versifications show that there was no lack of effort. The pamphlet-literature of the South, where the censorship was not to be trifled with and where participation in the broader political happenings was altogether so much more limited than in the North, is too meagre to furnish much material. In 1633 a fierce anti-Holland diatribe made its appearance in answer to Puteanus' *Statera belli ac pacis*, in which the author, though wrapping up his meaning in typically pseudo-classicist allusiveness, had recommended peace with the Hollanders. We know that this bitter retort was inspired by the government; but we need not for that reason, nor yet because the Brussels States, bent on their peace parleys, wanted it suppressed, doubt that it voiced the feelings of many when it called the maltreatment of 's Hertogenbosch a strange manifestation of Holland's much-vaunted love of freedom and tried to disparage Frederick Henry's military prowess with scornful references to his oft-manifested reluctance to meet the Spanish forces in the open field. When, as we saw, even the North Netherland Catholic priests felt obliged to work against the States' military enterprises on the frontiers and in Asia, what is more natural than that in the South religious zeal should intensify veneration of the 'natural ruler' and abhorrence of the Northern enemy?

Yet we have seen in 1632–33 the spirit of rebellion communicating itself even to the clergy, and the Archbishop of Mechlin himself involved in the plans for the establishment, with the aid of the independent provinces, of a South Netherland republic. The apparent contradiction is resolved when we remember how powerless the Spanish regime appeared at that stage. For loyal Catholics those plans were nothing but a policy of despair. Professor Jansenius, on being asked for his opinion, thought them compatible with religious obligations, but when the circumstances had changed, when the Republic and France

were collaborating no longer towards liberation, but towards
partition, while at the same time Spain seemed to have discovered a new power of resistance, then in his *Mars Gallicus* he
sounded an ardent call to battle under the Habsburg banner
against the deceitful French monarch and his Cardinal-Minister,
who were lending aid to the heretical rebels of the North against
their lawful sovereign. The breakdown of the negotiations of
1632–33, the coming of the Prince-Cardinal, the Franco-States
alliance of 1634–35, together these meant a turning-point in the
relations between North and South. They brought about a
reaction in Southern opinion in favour of the Spanish regime,
with which the country's fortune seemed indissolubly linked.
The priest-poet Justus de Harduyn, who, with his friend the
antiquarian Van der Linden, drew up the festival plan for the
Prince-Cardinal's entry into Ghent, declared that His Highness
must bring the protracted war to a close by

overpowering the enemy and bringing the errant provinces back to their
bounden duty of loyalty.

This motif comes out even more clearly in an anonymous
poem prompted by the burning and sack of Tirlemont in 1635,
which accompanied the first joint invasion of Brabant by the
new allies, 'the courtly French and our worthy brethren', as
the title scornfully has it.

The Beggar is always cruel, the Frenchman always treacherous,

declares the poet, carefully pointing to the difference of religion
to the one side (for that is what the word Beggar implies) and
to that of national character on the other. The moral he draws
from the events of the last few years is that for the South
Netherlanders to let themselves be stirred up to revolt against
Spain would be merely to play into the Beggars' hands. It is
thus with complete conviction that he hails the Prince-Cardinal
('his is Spanish and Netherland blood') as the man for Church
and Country.

It was inevitable that the war should thus envenom feelings.
We must, it is true, be on our guard against transposing present-
day conditions into the seventeenth century. The civilian
population was then immeasurably less involved in warfare.
Professional armies invested frontier towns and marched hither
and thither during the summer season to launch a surprise or

undertake a siege. Even for the rural population of the frontier regions the war was regularised by means of a recognised system of contributions; if they duly paid up their quota, villages within reach of the enemy—and thanks to the Republic's strong strategic frontier that meant South Netherland villages within reach of the States' forces—were left in peace. 'Executions', that is to say, burning and plundering raids meant as the penalty for non-observance of the arrangements, such as the one Frederick Henry when a cavalry commander had led far into Brabant in 1622, were very seldom necessary. But this relatively humane system was completely overthrown by the dispute about the Meiery. When the Spanish government proceeded to levy taxes there, the States authorised 'extraordinary contributions' for a yet wider circle of Brabant territory, to the very gates of Antwerp and Louvain, and when Spanish troops harassed the new sheriffs and Reformed ministers in the Meiery, the States' forces made regular expeditions from Bergen-op-Zoom to hunt down sheriffs, priests and monks in the entire contribution area. This reprisals system, which raged especially between 1632 and 1642, naturally created bad blood. However, war excesses are never very lasting in their effects, and in this case they certainly did not leave any deep mark on men's minds. The problem remained fundamentally the same: the political crisis of 1633–35 brought no final solution. We shall see that during the last stage of the war the question of Spain's position in the South was raised anew, and that once again it was the States' refusal to compromise with the Catholics that hindered a *rapprochement* between North and South.

And there is still an entirely different note to be heard. A North Netherland author, as we saw above, had made one of his characters, Diogenes, appeal to the sense of Netherland solidarity,[1] but his opponent in the dialogue derides him for his credulity, exclaiming: "What 'States with States'?"

If one would speak frankly, one must say: sovereign States with dependent ones. States of full age and free of wardship with States still under age, and held in tutelage, in short, freemen with slaves. For who lords it over the others? The King of Spain. Who holds them in tutelage? The King of Spain. Whose slaves are they? *Ad idem*, the King of Spain's. And do you still think it possible to negotiate with these people without first throwing the King of Spain and his Spaniards out of the country? I do not believe it.

---

[1] See above, p. 112.

Such a view reflects a feeling of superiority which the circumstances could scarcely fail to engender. However noble the cause
which the South Netherlands served, not all the panegyrics
and the battle-songs, not all the triumphal gates and arches, nor
yet all those gallant Walloon and Dutch-speaking warriors which
they furnished to the Emperor and the King of Spain, could
alter the fact that they were merely being dragged along in the
war. The Northerners, on the other hand, had an active share
in shaping their own destiny under national leaders. The
impotence of the so-called States-General of Brussels, which
either could not or dared not allow their deputies to move a
single step without the approval of Spain, was bound to fill the
sovereign deputies of The Hague with disdain. This attitude on
the part of those who counted in the political life of the North,
coupled with the resentment which it aroused in the South, was
in the long run to do the cause of Netherland unity grave harm.

f. THE WAR DRAGS ON, 1635-1644

THE DOZEN summer campaigns which Frederick Henry under-
took under the new alliance with France bore meagre fruit.
I have already alluded to the unfortunate events of 1635. A
French army which had pushed its way through Luxembourg
joined hands with the States army in the neighbourhood of
Maastricht, and together they carried out that invasion of
Brabant which, if undertaken immediately after the capture of
Maastricht, might have had such tremendous results. The sack
and burning of Tirlemont made the worst possible impression
in the South. The siege of Louvain which followed had to be
raised almost immediately on the approach of an Imperial army
from the East. During the ignominious retreat to States' territory the French officers complained bitterly of the Prince's lack
of enterprise, but their own troops degenerated into a mob of
ragged vagabonds. Then, suddenly, the Republic was startled
by a breach of her strong river frontier: the Prince-Cardinal
signalised his arrival in the Netherlands by capturing the
Schenkenschans on the Waal, and during the following winter
and spring all efforts had to be concentrated on recovering this

fortress. Apart from that nothing happened in 1636. In 1637 sufficient resources had been mobilised for the siege of Breda; like those of 's Hertogenbosch and Maastricht, it was a great feat of engineering, and like them it was brought to a successful conclusion. An important gain, no doubt, but while Frederick Henry was busy there, the Prince-Cardinal had snatched back Venlo and Roermond. For 1638 another great plan was prepared, this time against Antwerp. The Prince had wanted first to make himself master of Hulst, but the Field-Deputies prevailed upon him to attack Antwerp directly. The detachment under Count William of Nassau-Siegen sent forward to occupy the Flanders bank of the river opposite the town was driven back by a sudden Spanish onslaught and annihilated at Calloo. All that the Prince did for the remainder of the summer was to attempt to capture the town of Gelder at the other end of the theatre of war, but in that too he was unsuccessful. The year 1639 brought further unlucky ventures, first in Flanders, against Hulst, which since the defeat at Calloo appeared more than ever indispensable as a preliminary at Antwerp, afterwards in Upper Gelderland, and then finally against Hulst once more. Yet that year witnessed one achievement of prime importance, this time at sea.

Since the disaster of 1635 the French had directed their assault on the Habsburg power eastward rather than northward, and had secured a position in Alsace and Lorraine which blocked the overland route for bringing Spanish troops to the Netherlands, the route which the Prince-Cardinal himself had followed in 1634. Once again, just as fifty years before, the Spanish government at great effort equipped a powerful fleet in its harbours, designed to set sail for the northerly seas to carry to the Prince-Cardinal the reinforcements he so urgently needed.

The main problem which faced the North Netherland navy was Dunkirk, although for a fleeting moment the menace of English ambitions reared its head. Charles I had visions of using his fleet, paid for out of arbitrary taxation (for since 1629 he had governed without Parliament), to compel acknowledgment of that dominion of the sea which his father before him had never tired of proclaiming. In 1636 these pretensions were announced to the world at large, with the King's full approval, through the

medium of Selden's *Mare Clausum* (the title itself was a challenge to Grotius), while at the same time Charles demanded
tribute from the Dutch fishermen, the Earl of Northumberland
sailing northwards with the fleet to collect it. The States
straightway despatched their own fleet to Scottish waters to
protect the fishermen—even against themselves, for whereas
the fishermen were only too willing to pay up to be left in peace,
the States would have no sort of recognition given to the
English thesis that the sea was not free to their subjects. A
collision was avoided, however, for Charles was too uncertain
of his position with regard to Spain and to his own subjects to
be able to take a firm line, and so the real task of the Netherland
navy remained focussed on Dunkirk.

Soon after the expiry of the Truce the Brussels government,
then still propelled by Spinola, had decided to give all possible
aid to privateering from that port. Of the various harbours on
the Flemish coast—the only ones remaining to the Southern
Netherlands now that the Scheldt estuary was sealed up—
Dunkirk was the easiest to defend. At Mardick, situated some
distance farther west on the principal mouth of the so-called
Scheurken (the Rift), a channel formed by the 'Shoal' extending
before Dunkirk, the Spaniards constructed a fort like a sea-
jetty, called the 'Wooden Doublet', and laid down a squadron
of twelve 'King's ships', as distinct from the privateers proper.
The visit which the Governess herself paid to Dunkirk in 1625
showed the importance attached to the enterprise. There were
also grandiose schemes for encouraging peaceful trade, which
could not end in anything but disappointment: the Northerners
were too completely masters of the sea. But the enormous
expansion of the Holland and Zealand mercantile marine was
precisely what made privateering so extraordinarily remunerative. Besides the private shipowners, among whom the Van de
Walles, father and son, were the wealthiest and most enterprising, the town magistracies of Dunkirk and of the little
inland town of Bergues engaged in it. An Admiralty college,
first established at Bergues, but soon afterwards transferred to
Dunkirk itself, and a Council at Brussels, exercised strict
control over the fitting-out even of privately-owned privateersmen and over all their operations. In time the King's ships
came to number thirty or so, and the private ones totalled

hardly less. The light Dunkirk frigates, crank and fast, won Flemish shipbuilders a good name abroad. Sometimes they served with the Spanish fleet in southern waters, where also they were renowned. Their crews, like those of the North Netherland navy, were a rough collection, including many foreigners, often deserters from the Republic's service. Hope of booty drew men to Dunkirk.

Here some seamen have already waxed so rich that they may henceforth live like lords in lust and luxury. Wherefore the number of brave fellows doth greatly increase day by day.

Thus wrote the Antwerp newspaper *Nieuwe Tijdingen* of Abraham Verhoeven in 1622, in the tone of the recruiting-sergeant. But the captains, especially of King's ships, Flemings like those of the privateers, were sturdy fighters and excellent seamen; the best among them, like Jan Jacobsen, who fell in one of the first great naval battles after the renewal of the war, or Jacob Colaert, the King's admiral until 1637, served the cause of the old religion and of the lawful sovereign with no less conviction than Mooi-Lambert or Houtebeen, Evertsen, De With or Tromp, brought to their heavy task on behalf of the liberated provinces.

A heavy task it was. First, the merchant vessels, forbidden by the States-General to sail otherwise than in fleets, had to be given convoy. More than once the convoying warships were themselves attacked, and they did not always have the better of it. Then in addition a regular blockade was kept up to shut the privateers in their harbour. A few ships cruised off Nieuport, Ostend and Gravelines and a large squadron of eighteen sail or more off Dunkirk, outside the Shoal and in the midst of the sandbanks stretching into the sea beyond it. It was extremely difficult cruising-ground, and by night and in rough weather the swift privateersmen were always slipping in and out. On the renewal of the war the States-General had ordered the barbarous practice of 'foot-washing' to be followed and if captured Dunkirkers were not thrown overboard, they were hanged on shore. The result was that the Brussels government ordered full measures of reprisal. The prison at Dunkirk was always too full of North Netherland seamen, hoping for ransom or exchange, to allow the States to keep up for long the treatment of privateers as pirates: their own crews became worse demoralised than the enemy by the horrible prospect. The most vehement outbursts against the cowardice of the sailormen which their lordships the States indulged in from the safety of their council chairs, the most rigorous disciplinary measures against captains who forgot their duty, could not alter the fact that the defenders of that rich trade-flow had less chance of booty than the attackers; and indeed they could not even be sure of always receiving their regular wages. The Northern navy was a source of endless disappointment; it could not master the Dunkirk pest. In 1632—by no means an exceptional year—two hundred North Netherland ships large and small were taken or sunk by the Dunkirkers, the great majority by individual privateers. The other side lost two King's ships and thirteen privateers, but such losses were easily made good out of the proceeds of the prizes. Nothing exposed the government of the Republic to sharper criticism from 'the commonalty' than the unsafety of the neighbouring waters. Holland, the Generality and the Admiral-General disagreed about remedial measures, and a conflict ensued which will once again illustrate how radically the political life of the Republic differed from that of the loyal provinces.

The excessively decentralised system under which the States-General had entrusted the control of the navy to five Admiralty Colleges scattered over three provinces,[1] was often enough grievously felt to be inefficient, but the weaker's fear of being swallowed up by the stronger—the fear of Friesland and Zealand for Holland, of the colleges of the Northern Quarter (of Holland) and of the Maas for that of Amsterdam—prevented the much-needed fusion. As the separate interests were seldom reconciled into a transcending unity in the States-General, it was natural to look to the supreme command, exercised by the Prince of Orange in his capacity of Admiral-General, to provide a real Generality naval administration. But his influence proved totally insufficient to induce harmonious co-operation between the colleges, each supported by its provincial States or municipal government.

Apart from this the Princes of Orange were decidedly less happy in their naval administration than in their control of the army. Their dilettantism in the former element is illustrated by

[1] See *The Revolt of the Netherlands*, p. 234.

their customary choice of men of birth with no experience of the sea to represent them as admirals in Zealand and Holland. This regime of the 'knights' was highly unpopular in the two seaward provinces. When, during the years which followed the expiry of the Truce, one disaster after another in the war with the Dunkirkers demonstrated the ever more urgent need of reform, the pressure of the States-General and the States of Holland caused Frederick Henry in 1629 to appoint a 'Jack Tar', no less a person than Piet Hein. Hein brought plenty of spirit to the task of suppressing all manner of crying abuses, but that same year he fell in action against the audacious privateers. Thereupon Frederick Henry appointed another knight, Jonkheer Philips van Dorp, who as the Prince's admiral in Zealand had already proved himself an impossible person, had been hooted at by the Zealand mob and finally dismissed by the States of that province acting on their own authority. It was a most injudicious choice. Van Dorp met with the same contempt from the Holland public and the Holland seamen as from the Zealanders, and at last in 1636 the Prince was compelled to drop him and to replace him by a second Jack Tar in the person of Maarten Harpertszoon Tromp.

Notwithstanding the appointment of an efficient, energetic and respected admiral, however, the defects from which the navy suffered still continued for a long time to defy remedy. The main source of the trouble lay outside Tromp's control, outside even the Prince's control: it was the inadequacy of the financial resources at the Admiralties' disposal.

The proceeds of the so-called 'convoys and licences', import and export duties, which the Admiralties themselves were charged with collecting, and on the proceeds of which they were supposed to manage, had in fact to be supplemented by subsidies from the Generality, that is to say from the provinces each in proportion to its quota. Now on their contribution for this purpose the landward provinces were perpetually in default. Year after year Holland had to threaten to withhold its contribution towards the summer campaign in the field in order to extort some money for the navy, and even so the landward provinces fell steadily further into arrears while the Admiralties got deeper in debt. The offending provinces were not wholly to blame; they took refuge, at least, in complaints of the

corruption which reigned in the Admiralty colleges. Not so much
the personal corruption, though in 1626 the members of the
Rotterdam college provided a really shocking case of this, which
made a great stir among 'the commonalty'; an echo can still be
heard in Vondel's bitter poem *Roskam*; on this occasion the
judiciary intervened with heavy punishments. But, besides,
the colleges as such too often connived at wholesale evasion of the
convoys and licences in the interest of their town's trade. That
was the reason why the landward provinces so eagerly embraced
the scheme put forward by a group of Amsterdam merchants in
1628 and again, somewhat toned down, in 1634, for a Company
of Assurance. A company was to be formed which was to undertake the responsibility of convoying merchantmen through the
dangerous waters to the Mediterranean in return for the right
of levying a percentage on trade. In this way the duties levied
on trade would be handled by business men who had an interest
in preventing evasion, while the landward provinces, which
took little part in trade, would go free.

No wonder Holland and Amsterdam itself opposed the
scheme tooth and nail, while Frederick Henry's support can
only be explained by the fact that he despaired of ever seeing
the landward provinces contribute regularly towards the
Admiralties and that he was, moreover, always inclined to take
their part against Holland. The same purpose was meant to be
served by a less objectionable scheme, namely, the leasing out
of convoys and licences, which at least would not have entrusted
the actual convoying to a private organisation; but Holland
would not hear of this either, and even took upon herself to
cancel the lease which had already been introduced with respect
to a quarter of them, an action which gave rise to vehement
disputes with the States-General over their respective rights.
Plans for unifying naval administration under the Prince and a
Central College inevitably got mixed up with this clash of
interests. Early in 1639 the States-General went so far as to
'send a deputation' on these matters to Amsterdam, a real
crisis-measure generally resorted to in the hope of rousing
against some stubborn local authority a minority in its midst
as well as the public opinion of its citizenry. In this case a
further complaint was to hand, well calculated to make an
impression, namely, that shipowners of Amsterdam (belonging

to regent circles, so it was whispered) were hiring out their ships in the Mediterranean to Spain. It was even proposed to vest jurisdiction over such misdemeanours in a Generality organ, the Council of State. But the Amsterdam burgomasters refused the members of the deputation admittance to the town council, declaring

that having come in this manner, they were not competent to be received in the Council, still less so with the object of making propositions to an individual member of the assembly of Holland (*namely, the town of Amsterdam*), without the knowledge of the States of that province, which was a sovereign assembly and was only in alliance with the general States.

The States-General's solemn deputation had to return to The Hague, deeply offended. However, attention was quickly diverted from this quarrel, of which the navy was at once the subject and the victim, by the fresh danger which called so imperatively for its services. In the course of 1639 there came news of the great fleet being equipped in Spain. And now was demonstrated how effectively this loosely-constituted State could function in time of need. A vigorous national spirit swept all before it. The disputes over procedure were suspended. The States-General followed the lead of Holland, and the Prince worked in the same sense. Of good courage, Tromp put out to sea to meet the expected enemy.

On 15 September, while on the look-out in the Channel, he sighted the Spaniards, and, although much their inferior in strength, attacked them. There followed some days of furious cannonading the like of which the sea had never heard, until the Spanish admiral, d'Oquendo, fearful of being driven on to the sandbanks off the Flemish coast, ran with his undiminished, but disabled and dispirited, fleet into the Downs roadstead, between Dover and the North Foreland, under the protection of the English coastal batteries and of an English fleet. The Dutch fleet promptly closed in on the Spaniards; the Dunkirkers alone effected their escape. There now followed that remarkable action, which so dramatically revealed to contemporaries the resources, both moral and material, at the disposal of the Republic, and in which she triumphed simultaneously over Spain and England.

Charles I, embarrassed by a rebellion in Scotland, the precursor of one in England itself, was less than ever in a position to maintain the English pretension to the dominion of the seas. Resolved at least to turn the presence of the helpless Spanish fleet to political or pecuniary advantage, he negotiated with each side for recompense either for protection or betrayal. But the States-General had given Tromp instructions to attack the enemy as soon as he thought the moment ripe, without heeding the intervention of a third party, and while the English monarch was playing his double game and the Spaniards lay inactive, on the rivers Scheldt, Maas and Y thousands were feverishly working at the fitting out of merchantmen for war—a transformation still practicable in those days. Not for nothing had Holland developed into the greatest shipping country in the world and Amsterdam into a centre of trade in guns and munitions of war. In less than a month Tromp's fleet, originally not more than two dozen in number, had grown to some seventy ships. Straightway he went into action, using his fireships to drive a number of the unwieldy Spaniards on to the English coast and dealing fearful destruction among those that chose the open sea. D'Oquendo, his own ship a wreck, brought no more than nine others into Dunkirk. The English, mortified and humiliated, could only splutter impotent protests.

It was a brilliant demonstration of the corporate capability of the North Netherland people—or should I say of the people of Holland and Zealand? In the Prince's absence in the field, the magnificent effort which had tripled Tromp's fleet and amply satisfied his every need, had been directed by States assemblies, Admiralty colleges, town governments, Companies, all working as one.

For Spain the defeat was a heavy blow. Indeed, during these years the whole Habsburg cause went into a decline. The French were now directing their attention southwards as well, and in 1640 it looked as if the Spanish Empire would collapse even in its Iberian base. First there came a revolt in Catalonia, which joined hands with France. Soon afterwards Portugal seceded, together with all her old colonies—or what remained of them after the conquests of the Dutch East and West India Companies; the losses they had suffered at the hands of the Dutch in the Indies, Africa and America had increased the bitterness of the Portuguese against the impotent Spanish government. In the same year, 1640, the French secured an important gain on their northern frontier by the capture of Arras, capital of the province of Artois. We have already seen from the correspondence of Hondius and Sanderus what an anxious time that heralded for the Flemings. Yet, despite these cumulative disasters, Spain persisted in stubborn defiance of her enemies, and indeed her powers of resistance in the Southern Netherlands remained astonishing. Even the early death of the Prince-Cardinal in 1641, serious loss though it was, did not cripple the Brussels government.

Frederick Henry, at any rate, could manage little more against it than before. His campaigns of 1640–43 were no more successful than those of 1638–39, although in 1641 the bells were rung and thanksgivings ordered for the capture of . . . Gennep, the Spaniards' most northerly outpost on the Maas, in the land of Cleve! It is a rather wearisome spectacle, this fruitless warfare endlessly renewed summer after summer. Now it was directed against Gelder, now against Hulst; now Ghent and Bruges were in their turn threatened. But no sooner did the Spanish army make its appearance than Frederick Henry fell back on the defensive. That feeling for the offensive which inspired Tromp and the States-General who gave Tromp his instructions, was utterly lacking in the commander-in-chief on land. True, he was hampered at every turn by lack of money. The burden of war was weighing more and more heavily on the provinces, and the landward provinces in particular needed the constant spur of ever more drastic warnings from the Council of State and from Holland to pay up their 'consents'.[1] The Prince, moreover, now approaching sixty and a victim to gout, was rapidly ageing; strategic boldness, strategic imagination were less than ever to be expected from him.

In these far from encouraging circumstances, with war-weariness growing among the people, there once more appeared the prospect of a great change in the political situation. Early in 1644, following the death of Richelieu and Louis XIII, the alliance with France, now directed by Mazarin, was renewed and the promise not to conclude a separate peace reaffirmed.

---

[1] After the provinces had, in the States-General, 'consented' to the budgetary propositions prepared by the Council of State, they were often very slow in acquitting themselves of the obligations which each had thus, to the limits of its quota, assumed; and this not only with the respect to the requirements of the Navy, where we observed it already.

This was the war party's last important victory, but what assisted them was the fact that peace negotiations were now beginning in earnest. There assembled at Münster a congress in which the Habsburgs met all their enemies, and the politicians at The Hague, to whom the idea of ending the war by a separate peace was nothing new, could not help thinking that France might be before them in that game and that the best way to keep her true to the alliance would be to make a fresh military exertion. But in reality France was still but little inclined towards peace. In 1643 the Duc d'Enghien had won his famous victory at Rocroy, on French soil, over the Spanish force under de Mello, the Prince-Cardinal's successor. Never before had Spanish infantry met with so decisive a defeat. Spain's power in the Netherlands was seriously shaken, and under Mazarin French ambitions strove northwards much more eagerly than they had under Richelieu. In 1644 and the following years the French, supported by Tromp's fleet, pressed forward along the coast of Flanders, and since Frederick Henry had himself captured Sas van Gent in 1644 and Hulst in 1645, the way to Antwerp now at last seemed to lie open before him.

To understand why he nevertheless did not succeed in realising this aim we must consider further the domestic situation within the Republic. The position of the Stadholder in the Republican constitution, the power of the States of Holland, the intentions of the one and of the other, their rival claims to pass for the representative of the country's true interests and their mutual jealousy and suspicion, all these deserve discussion before we proceed to the story of the final breakdown of the French alliance policy and the conclusion of the Peace of Münster.

G. DISCORD BETWEEN HOLLAND AND FREDERICK HENRY

THE LONGER Frederick Henry's Stadholdership lasted, the more the rivalry of the Prince of Orange and the States of Holland became, as it had been during the Truce, the determining factor in the political life of the Republic. Religion had little to do with it this time. It was now much more clearly personal authority, and in particular an individual foreign policy, which was the real issue. But, as under Maurice, the struggle assumed the largely illusory forms of a conflict between Generality and provincial sovereignty.

We have seen that Maurice had not carried out any thorough-going reform of the Republic. His victory threw into relief the principle of the supremacy of the Union, but no more than before were there any organs to support that supremacy. There was no federal law-court competent to proceed against individuals or provinces failing in their federal obligations; indeed, there was hardly any federal government at all. It was the States-General that functioned as such: they instructed the ambassadors and the commander-in-chief. But they were nothing more than a permanent assembly of the deputies of the seven sovereign provinces, tied to the mandate of their 'principals'[1], incapable of taking rapid decisions in emergencies, and exposed to minority obstructionism in carrying out any policy of general scope. The medieval principle of the autonomy of small groups, which was everywhere giving way to monarchical centralisation, and which in the loyal Netherlands now only slumbered on in petty local forms under the shadow of Spanish domination, was enjoying a remarkable heyday in a Republic born out of resistance to this very conception of the modern State. We cannot fail to recognise how intimately both the brimming intellectual life and the bustling economic activity, which make the seventeenth century so great a period in the North, are bound up with this principle, but it is equally clear that the anarchical system of loose federation that was for ever appealing to the Union of Utrecht and its provisions buttressing provincial sovereignty was all along

---

[1] That is, the respective provincial States assemblies.

highly embarrassing to the State in the society of States. We have already had an instance of this in the negotiations of 1632-33, when the rival opinions in the States-General prevented either party from pushing through a consistent policy. Another example is furnished by that paralysing conflict which we have seen being fought out over the organisation of the navy. Wonders might certainly be wrought under the imminent threat of a great crisis, but no one will argue from the battle of the Downs that the constitution did not need a more powerful cohesive force. It became Frederick Henry's ambition to build up an effective Union government round his own person.

What were the foundations of Frederick Henry's authority? Looked at from a strictly constitutional standpoint, his position was full of contradictions. He filled his principal dignity, the Stadholdership, in five only of the seven provinces, and in each of them it was a provincial, not a Generality, office. In Holland he thus owed his chief source of authority to his appointment by the States of that province. True, the tradition of sovereignty which the office retained from the monarchical period tended to render him independent of his masters, and his having a say in the appointment of magistrates who subsequently composed and instructed the States assembly accorded ill with the conception of the Stadholder as the servant of the States. During the years following his first great success, the capture of 's Hertogenbosch, the various provincial States one after another showed their respect for Frederick Henry by settling the succession to his Stadholderly dignity on his son, born in 1626. With many good republicans that went against the grain, and in Holland it was not brought about until 1634, in Zealand later still. In any case, when it came to forcing through a Generality policy against provincial opposition, the Prince would need to be able to rely on powers beyond the States of the recalcitrant province.

He found such powers first and foremost in his position as Captain- and Admiral-General, for in these two capacities Frederick Henry was an officer of the Union. With regard to the Admiralty, we have already seen that provinces and even single towns could use the Admiralty colleges to dispute with him the direction of the navy. In military affairs his position was infinitely stronger. Here, too, the provinces kept the purse-strings firmly in their own hands by means of the 'repartition' system[1] and founded on their financial control over particular regiments a right of say in the appointment of officers and in the movement of troops across their territory. Moreover, every plan of campaign was drawn up in concert with the States-General, that is to say, with the provinces, and carried out under the supervision of their Field Deputies. But these things did not alter the fact that the actual administration of the army was in the hands of the Captain-General, working with the one real Generality college, the Council of State, and that in everyone's eyes he bore the heaviest responsibility in the field, so that the honour and the glory fell to his share. It was above all to his military exploits that Frederick Henry owed, like Maurice before him, the great figure that he cut in the life of the nation.

The princely position, too, which he was able to occupy in this republican society rested chiefly on his Captain-Generalship. His share of the war contributions and booty almost doubled his income, which even so was barely sufficient for the sumptuous Court in which his masterful and worldly-minded wife, Amalia of Solms, took special delight. The building of new palaces such as that of Honselaarsdijk, and later of the House in the Wood at The Hague, and the embellishment of the old palaces of the Binnenhof and the Noord Einde at The Hague, swallowed money. A striking feature of this Court life, which made up during the winter for the hardships of the army camp, was the predominance of the foreign element. Certainly there was plenty of native nobility to draw upon; its sons held most of the officers' commissions in the Netherlands regiments. But half or more of the army consisted of French, English or German regiments. The House of Orange was linked in marriage with a multitude of great French and German noble families. 'Nassaus and Solmses, Hanaus and Dohnas, Châtillons and Trémouilles, La Tour d'Auvergnes and Rohans'—nobles with whom few natives could compete in rank and fortune—crowded with their suites to the festivities with which the Prince and

---

[1] Under which the army was not paid directly by the Generality exchequer but each regiment was assigned to a particular province which then became responsible for that regiment's pay, thus indirectly acquitting itself of its Generality obligations; always within the limits of its quota. Holland thus acted as 'paymaster' for about ten times as many troops as some of the smaller provinces.

Princess of Orange, and (all too often for their impoverished treasury) the Bohemian shadow King and Queen as well, enlivened the Hague season. And these foreigners set the tone. Morals were loose and unrestrained. The language was French. Maurice had occasionally addressed in that language even members of the States-General; Frederick Henry, son of a Frenchwoman, certainly used it by preference. His correspondence is preponderantly French; his *Mémoires*, which have been mentioned above, were written under his supervision by a French officer; his small son's education he entrusted to a French divine, Rivet, Professor of Theology at Leiden. Here again, no greater contrast can be conceived than that between the worldly and cosmopolitan appearance of Frederick Henry amidst his Court and army entourage and the sober Protestant and purely Swedish figure of Gustavus Adolphus.

French is not synonymous with immoral, nor is Dutch of itself better than French. But the gallicisation of Frederick Henry's Court is the cause of its having exercised no influence whatever on the cultural life of the Netherlands. That boisterous company was like a foreign colony camping out in the middle-class society of the Netherlands, which it could merely endow with a French phrase or two, but could not help to civilise or refine, as did the Courts in the England and France of this time. At times no doubt the foreignness and licentiousness of the Court disposed Dutch and strict Reformed spirits against the cause of Orange. But in the main people were dazzled by the splendour of it all, and the native nobility was swept away by it. French became the language of aristocracy again to a much greater extent than at any time since the separation. The French —and soon the English—nobles also imparted to the Court and to the whole army a monarchical tone, which often filled republican regents with misgivings. The French government, on the contrary, encouraged this. Early in 1637 it rewarded the Prince for his work on behalf of the alliance, and at the same time tried to bind him closer to itself, by addressing him with the title of Highness. Hitherto the Oranges had had to be content with Excellency, and at a time when much importance attached to questions of precedence the change was of real significance to the Prince's position. Just as in 1618 Maurice had been able to rely on the English regiments, so from 1635

Frederick Henry could rely especially on the French. We have already seen how Charnacé tried to win him over to the alliance with the promise that additional auxiliary troops would assist him in his dynastic schemes.

Under the cautious Frederick Henry, however, it never came to the violent measures contemplated by the Frenchman; with him it remained a struggle of influence and prestige. Here, too, the silent menace of the army counted, but more important was the popularity which, as already observed, accrued to the Prince through his military career. The strict Reformed might look askance at his Arminian and worldly leanings; everyone without distinction hailed the victor of 's Hertogenbosch and Maastricht. True, no direct political results followed upon the favour of 'the commonalty'. The municipal oligarchies and the nobility, which formed the basis of the sovereign States assemblies, were, as far as the forms of the constitution went, completely independent of public opinion; in actual fact they were, especially the first, far from indifferent to it. If we have seen the burgomasters of Amsterdam coolly dismiss a Generality deputation recommending a policy which had the Prince's support, they found the courage to do so because the trade interests involved assured them of the support of their citizenry. It was, indeed, a weakness in Frederick Henry's position that the Generality idea had after all little more hold on the masses in the various provinces than it had on their regents, and he was not the man to appeal either to their as yet unawakened democratic instincts or to their all too inflammable religious passions. Yet proposals which he as Stadholder might make to a States assembly gained no little weight from his prestige with the citizens outside oligarchic circles.

But his objective, I have said, was to build up a real federal government round his own person, and to that end he worked with patience and tact within the framework formed by the oligarchy. As commander-in-chief, member of the Council of State and Stadholder in five provinces, he had an important position to build upon. The thing was to bring under his own control the sovereign authority which as far as foreign affairs were concerned rested with the States-General. To that end the Prince first set himself to win over the officers of the federal authority. The Council of State fell completely under his influence: Aerssens van Sommelsdijk, now his confidential adviser as he had previously been Maurice's, found a place on it. Van Goch, the Union Treasurer, Musch, the Greffier of the States-General—this last notorious for his venality—waited upon the Prince's nods. Since 1631 an independent man had filled the Grand Pensionaryship of Holland: Adriaan Pauw. We have seen how he led the opposition to the policy of the French alliance, even after the Prince had embraced it. But Pauw's reign did not last long. With the triumph of the policy that he had resisted, he was brought down; it availed him nothing that at the eleventh hour he had himself co-operated in bringing the alliance into being. In 1636 there came in his place the docile Cats, Musch's father-in-law, and whatever striving after independence of policy remained in Holland had to do without the leadership of the Grand Pensionary.

It was over foreign policy especially that the Stadholder succeeded in securing control. The ambassadors abroad corresponded privately with him. From 1634 onwards important issues in the domain of foreign affairs were regularly entrusted by the States-General to a standing committee, the *Secret Besogne*, consisting of one member from each province and several from Holland, to work in conjunction with the Prince. Decisions of this committee were to have equal force with 'resolutions' of the States-General. Frederick Henry managed for the most part to get appointed to it men acceptable to him, supporters, or dependents. Members were sworn to observe secrecy about the transactions of the Committee, even, and indeed especially, with regard to their "principals", or mandatories, that is to say their respective provincial States. In the full assembly of the States-General the deputies were bound to consult the principals before giving a final opinion on proposals of any importance. This oath of secrecy, therefore, was a striking innovation in the constitutional life of the Republic. It was, of course, explained as necessary to ensure quick decisions. But at the same time it enabled the Stadholder to make himself the real master of the Secret Committee and thereby of the foreign policy of the Republic.

Why was it Holland in particular which resisted this evolution of a federal government in monarchical form and after a few years, as we shall see, plucked up courage to put an end to

it? We need not believe that the interests of the other provinces
were in reality always opposed to those of Holland, nor that
Holland was more afflicted than they with provincial egoism.
The history of the Republic is thickly strewn with instances
of grossly particularist behaviour on the part of the smaller
provinces. Occasionally their presumption was allowed to pass,
as when in 1636 Zealand reopened trade with Antwerp, which
had been stopped for military reasons, without waiting for the
consent of the States-General. At other times strong measures
were taken against them, as when about the same time Friesland,
torn by party strife, was guilty of grave negligence in the
discharge of its obligations to the Generality, and the Council of
State, supported by the Prince of Orange and backed by a show
of military force, appeared there to change the magistracies.
But whereas the smaller provinces could make trouble over
minor issues which were of vital interest only to themselves,
Holland alone was capable of setting up a positive political
principle as an alternative to the principle of federal government
under the Prince's control.

Frederick Henry's collaborators certainly included men who
were inspired by genuine faith in the Generality idea, yet the
methods which he employed to collect a following were better
fitted to degrade the officials and deputies at The Hague into
the obedient servants of a rising autocracy than to embody the
idea of 'the general interest' in a really reliable organ. All the
influence he could bring to bear as Stadholder on the appointment of magistrates and officials, all his influence as Captain-
General on the promotion of officers, Frederick Henry used to
reward his dependents. That was not without result even
in Holland, but it was especially effective in the landward
provinces, with their politically powerful but not very well-
to-do nobility. The numerous and wealthy town oligarchies
of Holland could preserve their independence when the States
of the other provinces were falling more and more under the
Prince's control. Even these could still stick obstinately to their
guns where their provincial interests were concerned, but the
Stadholder troubled his head little about that; he was satisfied
if they sent him well-disposed men to The Hague. Thus the
States-General came to be packed with men who added 'amen'
to everything the Prince said, with the exception of the Holland

deputation, which still for the most part eluded his control, and which was, besides, much more directly under the eye of its principals than were those from provinces more distant from The Hague.

Did the Prince, by whatever means he acquired his power, at least use it disinterestedly in the service of the State? On general grounds, it is hard to blame a powerful political class, like the Holland regent class, intimately connected with great trading interests, for not tamely surrounding its independence of judgment to a prince surrounded by landed gentry and foreigners. But to this must be added that Frederick Henry himself was sometimes swayed by wholly other motives than those of pure Generality interests. In particular; his conduct of foreign policy was subordinated to his dynastic ambitions.

The dynastic element in Frederick Henry's policy begins to appear quite clearly when he seeks an alliance with the royal house of Stuart. If in 1641 Charles I gave his eldest daughter Mary in marriage to the youthful William of Orange, it was solely in the hope that Frederick Henry, although no more than the chief dignitary of a Republic, would have the power to put the States-General's resources at his disposal in the ever more closely threatening conflict with his subjects. When the English civil war finally broke out in 1642, the Princess Royal, who, still a child, had been left behind in England by her bridegroom after the marriage ceremony, was brought by her mother to The Hague for safety. A new Court was now established there, radiant with the halo of royalty, in spite of the sorry fortunes which attended the royal cause in England, and even less Dutch in character than the Stadholderly Court itself; for Mary, withdrawn behind her royal pride and surrounded by her fellow-countrymen, never learned the Dutch language.

What was worse, the Stadholder now actually bent every effort to bring his country's resources to the help of the hard-pressed Stuarts. It was a policy diametrically opposed to both the interests and the sympathies of the North Netherland people. The most important part of England, including London, together with the national merchant fleet and navy, sided with the Parliament, while the King had to maintain himself in the thinly-populated and rural Midlands and North, with revolted Scotland all the time threatening him in the rear. A war on the

King's side would have been a great naval war, to which mercantile Holland was naturally opposed. Moreover, the Reformed in Holland and elsewhere were aware of spiritual kinship with the Parliamentary party, then still led by the Presbyterians. Charles's alliance with the Catholic Irish was abhorrent to church-people in the Netherlands; the Anglican bishops with their robes and ritual seemed little better than papists, and the Catholic Queen, who remained in the country till 1643 to spur on Frederick Henry to greater efforts in assistance, was the worst person conceivable to render the Stuart cause acceptable outside Court circles.

The religious question was not the only one. The republican tradition held great sway over men's minds. The Holland regents in general saw in the marriage matter for 'umbrage'; and there were even strong-principled republicans who went further and would not be satisfied unless the general displeasure, which in itself they could only welcome, were firmly based on 'solid grounds of State and Liberty'.

True, the common people, with their first-hand experience of the many unpleasant features of that system of 'Liberty', were not sorry to see the Prince of Orange raised high above an oligarchy which so often excited their jealousy, even though in reality he did nothing to reform abuses. But on the whole the idea of overturning the Republican constitution remained foreign even to Orangist Contra-Remonstrants. Take, for instance, what a strictly religious author, in a book dedicated to Frederick Henry himself (1632), recommended as the true national policy:

First, the zealous maintenance of the true Christian Reformed Religion; secondly, temporal prosperity and welfare, under which is chiefly to be reckoned the Golden Freedom of our Fathers. (*In that freedom the writer includes:*) our aristocratic government, which closely agrees with the form of government instituted by God himself among Israel . . . God was not a little wrathful when Israel would overthrow the form of government by Him established, and would set a King over itself.

How wide a gulf yawned between such ideas and the high-monarchical notions which Prince William's bride and her English courtiers came to represent at The Hague! According to Aerssens van Sommelsdijk, who was on a mission to England, Charles I himself had airily dismissed the government of the Republic as 'a populace, without discretion'. The circles in which the young Prince moved found it intolerable that 'brewers, bakers and felt-makers' should presume to the sovereign authority over a King's son-in-law.

Religious and republican feelings thus combined with commercial interests to form so widespread an opposition to Frederick Henry as has seldom been directed against a Prince of Orange in the history of the Republic. In the States of Holland the resistance now offered to his Stuart policy was far more solid and more vehement than had been the opposition to his French alliance policy in 1634. Throughout wide circles, generally inclined to follow the Stadholder's lead, the States of Holland now appeared as the champions of the country's true interest. All observers, native and foreign, agree that the Prince's position was seriously shaken.

In 1642, to the Queen's profound disappointment and indignation, he had been unable to prevent the States-General from declaring their neutrality in the English civil war. But that resolution of the sovereign body in no wise deterred him from continuing to promote the royal cause with the aid of his supporters among the deputies of the landward provinces and among the Generality officials, by supplying arms, by granting leave to officers to proceed to England, and even by lending warships to keep open communications with Holland. By such means, combined with a general policy of pin-pricks—refusing to receive the Parliamentary envoy in the States-General and favouring the royalists through the mediators, his own faithful followers, sent to England by the States-General—he tried to drag the Republic gradually (*insensiblement*, as he himself put it to an emissary from Charles I) into the war.

No wonder the States of Holland in 1643 drew up instructions for their deputies charging them to see to it carefully that no encroachment was made on the sovereignty of the province, and to bring anything tending towards that or towards the 'prejudice, damage or harm' of Holland subjects to the immediate notice of the provincial States or their Standing Committee. It is significant that the only one of the nineteen 'members'[1] to oppose this was the one representing the nobility. The

---

[1] Each 'member' was composed of several individuals; each of the eighteen 'voting towns' of the province constituted one 'member', the nobility being the nineteenth, or rather the first.

nobility, in fact, as the shrewd and well-informed chronicler Aitzema observes,

were wholly dependent on the Prince, being either army men, or enjoying or expecting advancement from His Highness.

No one will deny that a resolution such as this of Holland's was calculated to shackle still more the power of the central authority. It killed the *Secret Besogne*, from which so much might have been expected: it made it impossible for any deputy of Holland on the States-General to take the oath of secrecy, and without Holland's concurrence (even if only nominal) nothing could be done. At the same time we must recognise that what provoked this resolution was the abuse made of the States-General, which from being an organ embodying the federal principle looked like being degraded into a tool of the Stadholder.

Relations between Holland and Frederick Henry were further embittered by conflicting views on the line to be taken over a war between Denmark and Sweden. Denmark was the power whose possession of Norway and Scania gave her the key of the Baltic, and who vexed the Baltic trade by arbitrarily raising the Sound dues. At this time more than half that trade was carried in Dutch ships, and negotiations on the subject with Denmark had long been carried on in vain. When, therefore, at the end of 1644 Denmark went to war with Sweden, Amsterdam could not fail to see in this a splendid opportunity of making the toll-collector of the Sound listen to reason. There were Amsterdammers whose interests in the matter went deeper still. Louis de Geer, who had become the owner and exploiter of Swedish mines, Lord of Österby, Finspång, etc., in Sweden, but whose world business in armaments was centred in Amsterdam, fitted out there an entire battle-fleet for the Swedish government. To the chagrin of the Danes, nothing was done to prevent this fleet from sailing, and it quickly brought success to the Swedes. But now arose the danger that they would impose a peace whereby Dutch interests would be no better served than before. Two of the envoys sent to the Baltic by the States-General—one of them was Andries Bicker of Amsterdam —returned post-haste, therefore, with a Swedish proposal that the Republic should join her forces with theirs. Holland now sponsored in the States-General a policy of intervention on the side of Sweden. But Denmark was the very power on which the English Royalists had built their greatest hopes, and she had an important place in the schemes which Frederick Henry was still concocting with them.

We can now see that, although the progress of the French along the Flemish coast and his own capture of Sas van Gent offered the Stadholder so good a strategic basis for the 'great design' against Antwerp planned for the summer of 1645, the political situation hampered him at every turn. In protesting against 'this new war' he could not adduce the connection between Denmark and Stuart, but he worked openly, though without much result, on the fear that the 'great design' might suffer harm from a Baltic adventure. Most of the other provinces readily accepted Holland's proposal, and Frederick Henry was reduced to blocking it in the States-General with the help of Zealand, where his influence was stronger than anywhere else. But that was a game in which Holland held much the stronger trumps, and that province straightway made clear that it would contribute to the 'great design' of the military campaign only on condition that its Baltic policy were accepted,

the freedom of commerce to the East (*i.e. to the Baltic*) being of more importance than the capture of a town in Flanders.

The Bickers of Amsterdam and Jacob de Witt of Dort (as envoy in the North) pursued this anti-Danish policy with vigour. There were violent scenes. In one of their conferences with the Prince the Holland deputies threatened

to show that the States were master in the land above His Highness; as a trusty friend (*thus Van der Capellen, a Geldersman, in his 'Memoirs'*) told me at length, who even declared that he had warned His Highness not to stretch this rope too tight lest worse should come of it.

In the end the Prince gave way. A strong fleet under the command of Witte de With sailed for Denmark and conducted the merchantmen entrusted to its protection, to the number of three hundred, through the Sound without payment of dues, while the Court and citizens of Copenhagen watched the unwonted spectacle helplessly from the shore. De With's instructions did not, however, permit actual hostilities on the side of Sweden. A treaty regulating the Sound dues was concluded with Denmark at Christianopel, but the Treaty of Brömsebro at the same time gave Sweden a much stronger position in the Baltic, which she proceeded to use for the discomfiture of Netherland trade. In Holland this only partially satisfactory result was imputed to the shackles in which the Stadholder, even after his surrender, had still held the national policy.

What kept the Stadholder even now so zealous for the Stuarts, and for their ally Denmark, was not only the favour already received in his son's royal marriage, but also the prospect of yet another royal marriage, of his daughter with the Prince of Wales. Even in their deepest distress the Stuarts managed to dazzle him with this suggestion. After Naseby (1645) the royal cause seemed lost, but during late 1645 and early 1646 the Prince continued to lend powerful aid towards the equipment of a fleet at Amsterdam to carry troops across, for which he sought the help of France. It was a purely personal policy which Frederick Henry was thus pursuing, far exceeding his constitutional competence and justified by no national interest.

But now matters hastened towards the crisis. The Danish and English episodes had helped to create the state of mind for it, but what provoked it was the biggest question of all, the question of relations with France and the prosecution of the war.

H. BREAKDOWN OF THE FRENCH ALLIANCE

THE FRENCH ambassadors who at The Hague had succeeded in renewing the alliance betook themselves thence to Münster, but nearly two years were to pass in negotiations between the provinces on the drafting of instructions to their delegation to the peace congress, on which every one of the seven was to be represented. Zealand in particular, under the Prince's influence, proved difficult, and it was not until January 1646 that the Netherland envoys arrived at Münster. Each summer, therefore, saw a fresh campaign set in motion. In 1644 and 1645 the French conquered, in addition to Gravelines and Mardick already mentioned, the whole of South Flanders, Cassel, Ypres, and

Menin. With Spain in such obvious straits, much greater gains might also have been expected for the invader from the North than Sas van Gent in 1644 and Hulst in 1645.

The failure of Frederick Henry's great plans (in effect cramped because they had sacrificed the county of Flanders beforehand) is to be attributed to various causes. There was Holland's suspicion of his aims. There was, too, the fear of the growing might of France. There was Amsterdam's fear of Antwerp. But not less important was the anti-Catholic policy of the States, which emanated principally from the provinces other than Holland and which, while it inspired horror in the South, also had a disturbing effect on relations with France.

The edicts against exercise of the Catholic religion, judged necessary by some zealots, in the spirit of the Old Testament,

in order not to provoke and anger that great and jealous God by the toleration of idolatry,

were defended by most regents only as emergency war measures. In practice they failed utterly to prevent the Catholics (who in 1619 were estimated at one-quarter of the population of Holland, in 1624 at one-third of that of Friesland and Groningen) from performing their religious obligations; their several hundred priests, too, laboured undisturbed, assisted by thousands of *klopjes* (devout women who, now that the nunneries were dissolved, lived together in small groups and applied themselves to education and other religious work). Sheriffs and bailiffs took regular payment for 'keeping their eyes shut'. But the ministers never ceased urging stringent execution of the edicts, warning that the papists were out to destroy the peace of Church and State. Ministers and regents certainly saw things from very different standpoints. When in 1642, for instance, the governor of 's Hertogenbosch, Johan Wolfert van Brederode, and the town magistracy compelled the ancient and wealthy Fraternity there to admit Protestants, and the Catholics afterwards sat down with the intruders to the usual banquet, there soon rang out a vigorous protest from Voetius (now professor at Utrecht), not against the violence done to the Catholics, but against so dangerous an association for purely profit-seeking reasons.

If anyone, knowing you, shall see you sit in the temple of the idolaters, shall not that same person's conscience, being weak, be emboldened to eat of those things which are offered to the false gods?

So rigid a view was not for the States; there were even theologians (especially the Groningen professor Maresius) who defended the 's Hertogenbosch incident.

Nevertheless, the States' relations with their Catholic subjects were more rather than less strained about this time. In 1640 the Vicar Apostolic Rovenius was sentenced at Utrecht for treason (traffic with the Spaniards), though by default, since he had managed to keep in hiding. Following this, and after much pressure and argumentation, the High Court of Holland instituted an inquiry into the working of the edicts which showed how largely they remained a dead letter. The French ambassador d'Avaux, one of the two who renewed the alliance (it was now 1644), let himself be prevailed upon by the anxious Catholics to urge toleration on the States-General.

> The rigour (*so he declared*) which you use against them regarding the exercise of their religion, the strict prohibition of all religious assemblies, the covetousness of your commissioners and the scorn which they often show for those things which we hold most sacred, have caused some minds to become embittered. Would you win them back? Would you again join up this part of your State, which is now cleft from it? Would you make good citizens of them? Then soften the rigour of your edicts and ordinances. The names of Catholic and Hollander can go together. It is possible to be an enemy of the King of Spain without being a Protestant.

A Frenchman brought up in the school of Richelieu and Mazarin could not feel otherwise. But in the Republic d'Avaux's speech aroused the violent opposition of the Church party, which still held Protestantism to be the one and only justification for the State and for the war. This was the party with which the Prince and the French had co-operated most closely since 1634, but all its traditional mistrust of the Catholic ally—mistrust which had caused William the Silent and Oldenbarnevelt so much difficulty—was now revived. The libertinist regents of Holland, who could accept the ambassador's line of argument, were yet not so zealous for religious freedom that their annoyance at his unseemly interference would not override their agreement with his reasoning. The request was therefore flatly rejected and the treatment of Catholics became for some time stricter rather than milder. But the principal outcome of d'Avaux's ill-advised step was the serious disturbance it produced in the relations between the Republic and France at a moment when events were already conspiring to give renewed strength to the opposition of 1634.

The 'great design' of 1645 was, as we have seen, directed primarily against Antwerp. A small Spanish army was enough to make the Prince desist for the time being from a serious effort, but he toyed for a moment with the vision of making himself master of Ghent. Supporters inside the walls were in touch with him. But according to the unfortunate treaty of 1635 Ghent was part of the French share. The States' fleet might help the French to press forward along the Flemish coast, because the prospect of seeing Dunkirk rendered harmless, no matter how, was irresistibly attractive; but to bring the redoubtable ally into Ghent, right on the Republic's frontier, when his advances in the Lys region were already causing uneasiness, this was too alarming a prospect when it came to it. Frederick Henry secured from d'Estrades, the French ambassador who was accompanying him in the field, the assurance that France would leave the States in possession of the town until the final division of the spoils—which meant that the settlement of 1635 was still to be maintained; and to even this doubtful concession was attached the condition that the Catholic religion must be left unmolested there. The States, consulted by Frederick Henry, were far from satisfied with this arrangement. Yet it was not obstruction from the States of Holland that nipped the attempt on Ghent in the bud. Suddenly, a French detachment appeared on the canal between Ghent and Bruges. So great was the mutual jealousy of the allies that the Prince would only carry through his plan against the Flemish town if the French returned to their own theatre of operations, and this they refused to do. Co-operation in an attack on Antwerp dissolved in mutual recrimination, and when the French at last fell back on Menin —it was already October—Frederick Henry was only able to lay siege to Hulst.

The surrender of this town served once more as a warning to all other towns in the South, which in their dire straits (the case of Ghent is an instance in point) were again hovering on the brink of rebellion against the tottering Spanish regime. Try as he would, the Prince could not move the States to promise, as they had done in 1632, free exercise of religion to towns that came over to their side. For the strict Contra-Remonstrants the suppression of Catholicism continued to be a duty in conscience.

It is better not to possess the town of Antwerp than to win and hold the same with admission of the Roman religion.

So said Dr. Rosaeus, once Oldenbarnevelt's opponent at The Hague, to Frederick Henry; it was exactly what Voetius had declared in the name of the Synod of Holland before the surrender of 's Hertogenbosch.[1] The Prince replied 'with a forbidding countenance' that he could not agree with Rosaeus' opinion. But he was powerless. Despite the stipulations of 1635 and the pressure of d'Estrades, supported by the Prince, the States resolved to allow the Catholics in Hulst no freedom of religious exercise. The impression created in the South appears from the fact that in January 1646 it proved possible to arrange among the notables of 'the obedient provinces' a subscription to support the Spanish government in the new campaign. The initiative was taken by men 'zealous for the Catholic faith and the service of His Majesty'.

Although one would hardly think so from his manner of waging war, there can be no doubt that the Prince passionately desired before he died to possess himself of Antwerp. It has long been a tradition with Orangist writers to blame the Hollanders for their half-heartedness, and nowadays writers pre-occupied with the problem of Dutch-Flemish relations are doing the same thing. But apart from the fact that Calvinist intolerance probably constituted a much greater obstacle than Amsterdam trade jealousy, this view depends upon a rather too ready assumption that in the existing circumstances the capture of Antwerp would have served the cause of the Dutch-speaking peoples.

What most alarmed contemporaries was the danger that the war would (as Aitzema put it) tend 'more to the greatness of France than to the good of this State'. How had the power of Spain crumbled away and that of France increased since the signature of the alliance of 1635! Pamphleteers might still make play with the horrors of the Inquisition and of Zutphen and Naarden[2] to fan hatred of Spain, but no practical statesman could any longer base his policy on such memories, although

---

[1] See above, p. 92.
[2] In 1572. See *The Revolt of the Netherlands*, pp. 119–20.

the Council of State dragged into its 'petition' (or war-budget) for 1645 even the cruelties perpetrated by the King of Spain in the West Indies. No wonder such clumsy propaganda was laughed at. There were still, of course, powerful groups whose interests were bound up with the prosecution of the war, just as there had been before the conclusion of the Truce. The Zealand ship-owners, for instance, paid particular attention to privateering in South American waters and found in it a never-failing source of profit. From our present national point of view, one would certainly have liked to see the Northerners setting before themselves as a war objective the liberation of the South. But apart from the fact that the party which talked loudest about that was also the one least inclined to leave the Catholics their freedom, since 1635 the States could no longer in decency echo the pamphleteer who wrote that

honour and oath forbid us to forsake them (*Flanders and Brabant*); we are bound to help them to their former proper freedom, and to reunite them to the body from which they have been forcibly torn asunder.

Of those two great provinces, had they not in 1635 bartered Flanders away to France? France was, in fact, already busily grabbing larger slices of Dutch-speaking territory assigned to her by the treaty than Frederick Henry had conquered since 1635, and the position was now such that any weakening of Spain's position on the northern frontier of her Netherlands and certainly the loss of Antwerp, must necessarily bring greater losses on the southern frontier as well. Nor was that all.

At the Congress of Münster the Netherland plenipotentiaries quickly reached agreement with the Spaniards on many points, but on 26 February 1646, two of them, Pauw and De Knuyt, appeared at The Hague to report upon an affair which threw their hearers into the greatest agitation of mind. It appeared that the French and Spaniards had a plan afoot to put an end to the war by means of a marriage and by the exchange of Catalonia, which had gone over to France in 1640, for the Southern Netherlands. Thus for the first time the Republic would have France as an immediate neighbour. France would acquire not only the county of Flanders, which was due to her under the partition scheme of 1635, but all that still remained of the loyal provinces, and perhaps even the title to those which had liberated themselves! The truth was that Spanish diplomacy had set a trap here for Mazarin. He had greedily snatched at the bait, which the Spaniards had held out with no other intention than of enlightening the Hollanders at the right moment and thus sowing dissension between the allies. An outburst of rage at the faithlessness of France was indeed the result, but the exposure was hardly less damaging to the position of the Prince.

Without knowing the rights of it, people suspected him of being party to the secret and of having let himself be won over to this arrangement, so ruinous from a Netherland standpoint, by the prospect dangled before his eyes of gaining Antwerp. This suspicion was well-founded. D'Estrades had let the Prince into the secret and had secured his promise to support the scheme in the States, who were to be offered as an inducement no more than Antwerp, in exchange for which they would still have to give up Maastricht. The French had always believed that the Prince could be won over, provided he were assured a special position at Antwerp—as Marquis. They knew that he would regard a neighbouring France not as a menace but as an advantage. With Antwerp for base and with France behind him, he could have laid down the law to the States. But what would have become of the very independence of the North Netherlanders confronted by this mighty patron of Orange?

The sudden exposure of the plot by Pauw and De Knuyt compelled the Prince to inform the States of what he had heard from d'Estrades, at the same time rejecting the scheme with a horror which he had been very far from showing to d'Estrades himself. The duped French hastened to give the States equally comforting assurances. After some hesitation Holland therefore agreed to the financing of a new campaign. Frederick Henry marched into the Southern Netherlands—it was for the last time—and, with Hulst as an effective base, threatened Antwerp with a few movements begun only to be immediately abandoned. Yet one may say that the false alarm of the proposed Franco-Spanish exchange had spelt the end of the alliance of 1635 and the end of Frederick Henry's personal policy. Everything collapsed together. The same spring saw the publication by the English Parliament of letters captured at Naseby which exposed the Prince's most secret negotiations with Charles I; and in May the King was forced to surrender in person to the revolted Scots.

But his involvement in the Franco-Spanish exchange plan was alone sufficient to break Frederick Henry. The French were mortified to see the States of Holland, and not the Stadholder, now assume command. Deputies of those States and their principals roundly told the Prince that all his dealings with France had been designed only in order "to oppress them". The fact that the States of Holland now took charge meant that the peace negotiations at Münster were to be pushed forward in earnest without France being allowed to hold them up. The Prince was too scared and dispirited, besides being worn-out and ill, to work any more on behalf of the war. His wife thought only of getting her share of the concessions with which Spain was prepared to purchase peace on the northern frontier of the Netherlands. On the southern frontier things went from bad to worse. Courtrai was lost and the French—with Tromp always at hand—followed this up by taking Dunkirk. At the very moment when Spain was abandoning the struggle with the Republic, that notorious nest of privateers passed—though not yet for good—to the power which in more than one war to come would put it to like service against the Republic.

Before 1646 was out, the North Netherland envoys at Münster had drafted a complete treaty of peace with the Spaniards. All the provinces concurred in it with the exception of Utrecht and Zealand. In the first, the ministers, Voetius and his followers, who saw in the French alliance and the war with Spain a religious duty, wielded great influence; in the second, the interest of the shipowner-regent class in privateering in Spanish colonial waters was at stake. Since the other provinces had only given their approval conditionally, in the expectation that Spain would also come to terms with France, there was plenty of scope for mutual wrangling and for interference from both sides. Frederick Henry died in March 1647, and his youthful successor, William II, at first lacked the influence seriously to hinder the peace-making. The struggle was chiefly one between Pauw as spokesman of the peace party and the French ambassador, Servien, who came over from Münster. Spanish money served to stiffen the one party as much as French did the other.

In the Europe of the seventeenth century it was nowhere unusual to accept money from a foreign power, but there is no period in the history of the Republic in which international alignments were so unashamedly turned to private profit as in the period of Frederick Henry. The breathless money-making that went on in the trading towns of Holland and Zealand had its effect on the tone of public life both there and elsewhere. The growing custom of regarding office as the private concern of the regent class blunted the feeling for integrity in affairs of state. All the same, the oligarchy was soon to prove itself capable of a reaction which suggests that the unwholesome influence of the Prince's own governmental methods was also a factor. The use he made of appointments and promotions was demoralising, the example of his dynastic policy far from edifying. The covetousness of the Princess was well known. No more venal personages were to be found in the Republic than Musch, the 'Court sparrow',[1] as some poet mockingly called him, and De Knuyt, Frederick Henry's representative as First Noble in Zealand. Altogether, the circumstances amid which the peace was brought into being make a far from attractive picture.

It would be foolish, nevertheless, to think that the resolutions of the assemblies of state were really determined by foreign money. That generation was too profoundly and vitally concerned with the matters that were at issue.

The conviction that this was a war waged for the Reformed religion still ruled the minds of the Contra-Remonstrants. But their position was not a little embarrassed by the insistence of the French ally that the Catholics should be left freedom of religious exercise in places conquered; by the treaty of 1635 the States had indeed made a promise to that effect. But how meddlesome was this popish France! Had not—as related above—a French Ambassador ventured to ask for this freedom in the seven provinces themselves, to the indignation of the States-General? And how unreliable! That had appeared only too plainly from their intrigue with Spain in 1646. So even the Contra-Remonstrants—of old the war party!—could not help being impressed by the argument that continuation of the war might bring that dangerous ally into a position from where it would be even better able to make its influence felt in the affairs of the Republic. The Contra-Remonstrants clung obstinately to their demands that Spain should abandon the

---

[1] *Musch* is Dutch for 'sparrow'.

Meiery of 's Hertogenbosch, even though the general principle of the *uti possidetis*[1] on which the two sides had agreed was thereby exceeded: since the conquest of the town in 1629 the claims of Brussels and of The Hague to the district had remained in conflict. They insisted, moreover, that Spain was not to receive any promise regarding the treatment of the Catholic population of the contested territory. It was hard work to get the unfortunate Spaniards to accede to these demands, but when they gave in on both points, how could even the most fervent adherents of the war policy in the North decline the peace? True, the split of the Netherlands was thereby confirmed, but the alternative was no other than that the French would establish themselves in the larger part of the Southern provinces.

To those who saw in the war, not a war of religion but a "war of state", it had long been obvious that prolonging it only meant working for France and for the Prince of Orange, who counted on France for the aggrandisement of his own position.

The vehemence with which France insisted on observance of the engagement of 1635, renewed so recently as 1644, whereby the two allies had undertaken not to conclude peace separately, still caused some hesitation in the States, although Pauw and many others were rather irritated by it. In fact, that French policy was out to make the Republic serve its own wide-ranging ambitions became ever more obvious.

Utrecht and Zealand still opposed the peace. The Union of Utrecht provided that decisions about war and peace could only be taken unanimously. In spite of this, the Assembly ignored the protests of the two provinces. Acting upon instructions passed by the majority of the Assembly, the delegates at Münster signed the treaty on 31 January 1648. Before the ratification on 15 May Utrecht joined the majority, and before the promulgation on 5 June Zealand did the same.

---

[1] *Uti possidetis*: 'as you are in possession'; on the basis of actual military occupation.

MAPS OF THE NETHERLANDS

IN 1609 AND IN 1648

IN Map I the numbers on the Seven United Provinces indicate their order of precedence in the 'High and Mighty' Assembly ('Hun Hoogmogenden', 'Leurs Hautes Puissances') of the States-General. The eighth province, Drente, though self-governing, was not represented in the States-General.

'Fl.' and 'Br.' indicate the parts of Flanders and Brabant occupied by the Northern Republic, and administered as 'Generality Lands' in the name of the States-General.

Map II shows the increase in the 'Generality Lands' as a result of the conquests of Frederick Henry. Note also the disappearance of the lakes in North Holland, which had been reclaimed. Certain southern portions of the Spanish Netherlands were already in French hands, but the new frontier was not fixed until the peace of 1659.

KEY

The territory of the Republic and of the Spanish Netherlands is unshaded.

The territory of France, Liège and other non-Habsburg states of the German Empire is shaded.

▲▲▲▲▲ Frontier between Republic and Spanish Netherlands in 1609.

―――― Other political frontiers.

〜〜〜〜 Linguistic boundary.

THE NETHERLANDS IN 1609.

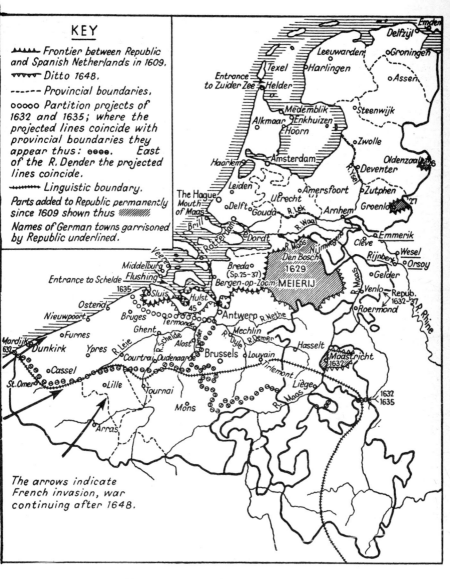

Emden
Delfzijl
Leeuwarden
Groningen
Entrance
to Zuider Zee
Texel
Harlingen
Assen
Helder
Medemblik
Steenwijk
Alkmaar
Enkhuizen
Hoorn
Zwolle
Oldenzaal '26
Amsterdam
Deventer
Haarlem
Leiden
Amersfoort
Zutphen
Utrecht
Groenlo '27
The Hague
Delft
Gouda
Arnhem
Mouth
R.Lek
of Maas
R.Waal
Brill
Emmerik
Rotterdam
Cléve
Dordt
R.Maas
Nijmegen
Wesel
Veere
Den Bosch
Rijnberg
Orsoy
Middelburg
Breda
1629
Flushing
(Sp.25-37)
MEIERIJ
Gelder
Entrance to Schelde
Bergen-op-Zoom
R.Maas
1635
Sluis
Venlo
Repub.
Ostend
Hulst
1632-37
45
Antwerp
Roermond
R.Rhine
Nieuwpoort
Bruges
R.Nethe
Furnes
Ghent
Termonde
Mechlin
R.Dyle
Hasselt
Mardijk
'52
Alost
R.Demer
Moastricht
Dunkirk
Ypres
R.Leie
Brussels
Louvain
1632
Courtrai
R.Schelde
Oudenaarde
Cassel
Tirlemont
St.Omer
Lille
Liège
1632
Tournai
1635
Mons
R.Maas
Arras

The arrows indicate
French invasion, war
continuing after 1648.

THE NETHERLANDS IN 1648.

j. THE PEACE OF MÜNSTER

THE PEACE of Münster confirmed the separation of the two halves of the Netherlands. This is the first and foremost point for us to notice. In the first article the King of Spain declared and recognised

that the Lords States-General of the United Provinces, and the respective Provinces thereof, with all their associated Territories, Towns and dependent Lands, are free and sovereign States, Provinces and Lands, unto which, as unto their aforesaid associated Territories, Towns and dependent Lands, he the Lord King makes no pretension, nor shall his heirs and successors for themselves, either now or hereafter, evermore make any pretension thereunto.

We see a profound distinction made here even within the territory of the Republic. There were the seven free and sovereign provinces north of the rivers, represented in the States-General, and there were the 'associated' territories and towns, the slices carved out of Flanders, Brabant and Limburg. (The Meiery of 's Hertogenbosch was now expressly ceded by Philip IV.) To the bitter disappointment of North Netherland Catholics the treaty included no safeguard for their position in the Republic. One might perhaps think that it would be so much the easier for the States to let drop the anti-Catholic provisions, which were usually defended on purely political grounds, now that their Catholic subjects would owe that concession solely to the States' own initiative. But there was no question of it. Though many regents might appreciate the logic of such a step, the ministers were more than ever determined to preserve the Protestant character of the State; and in proportion as they had further estranged the Church party by the conclusion of the treaty, the States were now the more disposed to ingratiate themselves with it. Their recognition of the validity of the Catholics' claim was, in truth, hardly more than academic, and its application would have raised practical difficulties for them as well. Once Catholics were elevated to the status of equal citizenship, would not many ancient patrician and noble families (such as were everywhere still numbered among the Catholics) demand to be readmitted into the government? Those who were now in possession of political authority were naturally little inclined to enlarge their privileged group. The same attitude prevailed towards the conquered territory, whose population was still largely Catholic even though the local administrations were now composed of Protestants. No attention was paid to the requests from the North Brabanters to be admitted to the States-General as an eighth province. On the contrary, these areas—the Generality Lands, as they were now called; in addition to North Brabant there was also the northern strip of Flanders on the Southern bank of the Scheldt and Maastricht with the surrounding district—did not even receive self-government, but remained directly under the States-General. The States levied the taxes there, which weighed very heavily on agriculture, although at the same time industry and trade were in the interests of the free provinces systematically kept low. The Council of Brabant at The Hague was nominated by the States-General, and appeals from it also came before them. The tax-gatherers from the North made themselves bitterly hated south of the Moerdijk. As early as 1656 the magistracy of 's Hertogenbosch—for in fiscal matters even the Protestant 'carpet-baggers' soon showed themselves good Brabanters—accused the States-General of having exceeded the provisions of the capitulation treaty on as many points as it contained articles. But so long as the Republic lasted, there was no redress for the conquered territories.

While a strip across the middle of the Dutch linguistic area—Zealand-Flanders, North Brabant and the Land Beyond the Maas—had thus fallen into a state of helpless subjection to the provinces north of the rivers, it was, together with its masters, completely cut off politically from the territory to the south, with which it had until recently stood in the most intimate union. All the rest of Flanders and Brabant, besides the Upper Quarter of Gelderland, remained united with the Walloon provinces under Spain. (Venlo and Roermond, captured in 1632, had been lost again, as we saw, in 1637, and a stipulation in the peace treaty that Spain should exchange Upper Gelderland for an 'equivalent' was never carried out.)

This splitting of the seventeen Netherlands into two political units only confirmed what had been settled already in 1609. For the Southern Netherlands, however, the situation legalised by the Treaty of Münster was in every respect more unfavourable than that of the Truce. Frederick Henry's conquests had pushed the frontier much further south: the strategic barrier of the great rivers was lost, while Maastricht opened a gateway for invasion from the East. The Republic had not been strong enough to drive the Spaniards right out of the Netherlands, but she had left them in a position of decided inferiority compared with her own, and in this inferiority of their masters the loyal provinces naturally had to share. The closure of the Scheldt and Zwin was now expressly confirmed in the treaty as though for all eternity; and in order to close all outlets for South Netherland trade the King even had to undertake to levy no smaller duties at the ports on the Flemish coast than those which should apply to the Scheldt.

Thus cramped and crippled, the country still had to face the continued assault of France on the other side. But here the peace of Münster, in other respects so disastrous, meant salvation for the future of the Dutch-speaking people: at least it broke the unholy alliance between the Republic and France, which otherwise would have resulted in France annexing practically the whole of the county of Flanders. The Republic's withdrawal from the war at once increased Spain's power of resistance on the Southern frontier of the Netherlands. In the same year (1648) Courtrai was recovered, although Ypres was lost at the same time, and Condé—for so the d'Enghien of 1643, the victor of Rocroy, was now called—again defeated the Spanish army with great slaughter at Lens. Other events were necessary to save Flanders. I shall in a succeeding volume relate how the attacking power of France was for some years crippled by the disturbances of the Fronde, and how the young Stadholder William II, who persisted in plans to revive his father's policy and to overthrow the settlement of Münster, was removed by an untimely death. So 1648 remained in the history of the Netherland people a date of first importance. If it does not immediately usher in the great period which was to see the North Netherlands under William III leading Europe against France to prevent the annexation of the Southern Netherlands, at least it marks the end of the co-operation so preponderantly to the advantage of France; it introduces a period of transition, in which the statesmanship of the Republic, under the Grand Pensionary De Witt, seriously hampered by the hostility of

England, will attempt, first by amicable agreement, afterwards by diplomatic combinations, to stem the tide of French expansion.

The long struggle with the South from which this North Netherland Republic emerged, had stopped, or at least checked, the eastward expansion that might have been predicted for the Netherland State of Charles V. Yet the garrisons in East Friesland and in the territories of Cologne and Cleve still seemed to hold out promises in that direction. When following the later course of events, one can observe how here again it was the splitting of the Netherlands, and the threat which this brought from the South, that prevented their fulfilment.

III

The North Spreads Out

THE LAST decades of the Eighty Years' War were a time of tremendous economic growth for the North Netherland people. That process which in the previous volume[1] we saw follow immediately upon the closure of the sea-approach to Antwerp was carried on in quickened tempo during, and still more after, the Truce. I purposely mention the closure of the Scheldt here, for it was this measure which caused the overseas trade of the North to be reinforced by that of the South, and from overseas trade the whole economy of the North derived its prime motive power. Trade brought accumulation of capital, and capital in turn set thousands of hands at work in every variety of business, thus promoting further trade. In this way that small tract of country experienced an astonishing outburst of activity, which took Hollanders and Zealanders all over the world and gave them the mastery of trade-routes throughout wide stretches of Europe, Asia and Africa.

A remarkable spectacle, and to us who are attempting to trace the vital destinies of the Netherland people, one of manifold interest. Under the impulse of this economic process the North grew rapidly in wealth and prosperity. This rising standard of living and the busy relations with the outer world combined with other purely political circumstances to shape the conditions in which the Northern Netherlands—above all, Holland, and in Holland among a group of towns especially The Hague and Amsterdam—could become the home of a culture markedly different from what had flourished there before. Here, too, I was able to indicate the beginnings in the previous volume. Already with the shifting of the centre of gravity from South to North towards the end of the sixteenth century, the civilisation of the North had lost much of its provincial character. But Holland the centre of a colonial empire, the home of wealthy and powerful merchants and bankers—this was a

[1] See *The Revolt of the Netherlands*, pp. 233-8.

development that could not but strongly influence intellectual life, enabling the Hollander to think beyond the bounds of his own town and country, without at the same time losing his firm grasp of that which was his own.

One feature of this development, however, cannot be noticed without giving rise to uneasy reflections. The world-wide trade which created the conditions for it (and in which the provinces outside Holland scarcely shared at all) was an uncertain possession, dependent on outside factors. The Republic, under the influence of the trading-interest, ever more powerful at home, would indeed attempt to 'bend these foreign factors to her will, and thus this economic expansion was destined to bring the North Netherlanders into contacts with the leading peoples of Europe and Asia that were not confined to exchange of goods but led to the most serious political repercussions.

Political relationships had so far been dominated by the war of independence against Spain, with which, indeed, the rise of the East and West India Companies was directly connected. In the period now beginning, however, economic relationships tended to determine political ones. Several European powers were better placed to aspire to that trade-monopoly which the Hollanders had, so to speak, taken by surprise, and the leading statesmen of the Republic felt that its maintenance was a matter of life and death to her. The years after 1648 were therefore to see the economic rivalry with England, the dissatisfaction which France, too, felt at the economic preponderance of the North Netherlands, the opposition of aspiring Sweden to the Holland merchants' position in the Baltic, the Companies' struggle with Portugal for Brazil and the Indies, all constituting powerful factors in international politics. Not that the South Netherland question, shelved but not solved by the peace of Münster, ever left the sundered North in peace; indeed, it finally thrust itself to the fore again with irresistible force. In any case, it is now time for us to consider this economic development itself, which set the Republic's feet in so many quarters of the globe and raised up so many jealous rivals for her.

A. TRADE

During the Truce, through our thrifty and shrewd management, we have sailed all nations off the seas, drawn almost all trade from other lands hither, and served the whole of Europe with our ships.

Thus declared a group of Amsterdam merchant ship-owners to the States of Holland in 1629. The process which had begun with the war—did not Burgomaster C. P. Hooft observe that this country belied the general rule that war ruined land and people?[1]—was continued under the Truce and was not checked on the renewal of the war. The Dutch merchant fleet grew. It could sail more cheaply than the 'Easterlings' (the Baltic peoples) or the English, and in time it came to dominate not only the Baltic, where of old the Hollanders had occupied so important a position, but also the French, and to almost as great an extent the English, ports. The war notwithstanding, the South Netherlanders had to send and receive their wares by way of the North (the war merely supplied the Northerners with a pretext for levying extra taxes on them); for Spain herself it was impossible to keep the rebels' ships out. Since 1590 the Hollanders had entered the Mediterranean with entire fleets, supplying Italy with Norwegian timber and Russian grain, and offering their colonial wares, brought round the Cape, even to the Levant, cheaper than the overland caravans could deliver them.

There have come down to us from the seventeenth century a number of estimates of the size of the North Netherland merchant fleet, on which indeed very little reliance can be placed, but which none the less bear witness to the respect which it inspired in contemporaries. We have accurate information only for the Baltic, by the publication of the Sound dues registers for the years 1578 to 1657, from which it appears that already by the beginning of that period more than half, and later usually some 60 to 70 per cent., of all ships passing through the Sound came from the Netherlands, the majority from a multitude of small North Holland towns, but owned undoubtedly for a great part on Amsterdam account.

[1] See *The Revolt of the Netherlands*, p. 233.

The Netherlanders soon engaged in much more than purely freightage operations. In the early years of the seventeenth century Holland was rapidly surpassing all other countries of the world in accumulation of capital. Amsterdam began, first to rival, and then to outstrip, Genoa and Venice as the great international money-market. The town government had done its best to promote this by the establishment in 1609 of the Bank of Exchange, designed to reduce the hindrances to international commerce arising from the uncontrolled state of national currencies; this Bank's paper everywhere took the lead. During the Truce important foreign State loans had been placed in the Netherlands, such as those of Sweden and Brandenburg. The participation in the Thirty Years' War of both Sweden and Denmark was to a great extent financed by Dutch capital. Occasionally the Dutch capitalist was even more deeply involved in the affairs of countries weak in capital. The classic example is that of Louis de Geer, exploiter of Swedish metal-mines and Amsterdam armament-dealer, whose equipment of an entire fleet for Sweden in 1644 has been mentioned earlier.[1] But even wealthy France, land of ancient civilisation, not only saw Holland ships sailing in and out of her harbours, but had to suffer Holland merchant-colonies at Nantes and elsewhere making themselves masters of her own export trade in such commodities as wines and silks; French merchants were driven out even from the traffic between the mother-country and the West African and Canadian settlements.

These developments were assisted by confusion prevailing on all sides abroad. Except in Germany, where the Thirty Years' War brought fearful devastation in its train—and Dutch trade was far from being directed in the first place towards Germany—this confusion did not affect the world's purchasing power, but it did make governments incapable of undertaking or at least of carrying through any vigorous effort at breaking the hegemony of Holland. We have already seen how the Republic was able to play Denmark and Sweden off against each other when their energies were no longer monopolised by their German policies. Richelieu might have his moments of annoyance, but his life-work of bringing Huguenots and nobles to order and of uniting the forces of France against the Habsburgs

[1] See p. 139.

—and this shoulder to shoulder with the Republic—left him
no freedom of action. As far as England was concerned, we have
already heard about the difficulties put in the way of Netherland
fisheries by James I, about tension over the rivalry of the two
East India Companies and the massacre of Amboina, about
Charles I's ambitions to enforce England's dominion over the
Narrow Seas. In spite of these tendencies, which certainly met
with widespread support among the trading and shipping
sections of the country, England did not throughout this period
present much danger, save that, as we shall see later, she outstripped, for the time being in peaceful fashion, the Dutch
colonisation of North America. In the earlier years this may be
explained by the character of James I, peace-loving and fearful
of pushing matters to extremities, and afterwards by Charles I's
ever-increasing discord with his Parliament.

Thus it was that the world became covered with Holland and
Zealand ships and with 'factories' of Holland and Zealand
merchant houses, and that the North Netherland trading towns
grew in wealth and size. In particular, Amsterdam became a
world-town of more diverse economic significance and incomparably greater political power than Antwerp had been in the
previous century.

The activity of the harbour of Amsterdam (that river Y so
difficult of access along the Vlie, Zuiderzee and Pampus), the
stream of goods from all parts of the world into her warehouses,
the confused jumble of races, tongues, religions—all these made
a profound impression upon contemporaries.

> How com'st thou, golden swamp, by the abundance of heaven:
> Warehouse of East and West, all water and all state,
> Two Venices in one, where do thy ramparts end?

Thus the poet Huygens (who was secretary to Frederick
Henry); and quotations expressive of admiration and wonder
might easily be multiplied.

Already by the beginning of the seventeenth century,
Amsterdam, belying the typical small-town aspect which its
main square still presented, had grown to a town of 100,000
inhabitants. (At the same time Antwerp had declined from
100,000 to 50,000.) Thereafter it went on increasing rapidly,
and the boundaries had to be extended again and again. The
religious liberty which the municipal government accorded—

not least with an eye to the welfare of trade—drew foreigners of every description. Among them none presented a more motley appearance than the Jews, who had started coming from Spain and Portugal before the end of the sixteenth century and who greatly assisted in promoting commercial relations with the Mediterranean. The Baltic trade remained the principal source of Amsterdam's prosperity, but the town became in addition the centre of the West and East India Companies' trade. The wealth of Holland was concentrated in Amsterdam nearly as much as that of the Republic was concentrated in Holland; if Holland bore 58 per cent. of Generality expenditure, Amsterdam accounted for about one-half of Holland's revenues. Outside Holland the Zealand trading towns were in decline. They suffered from the decay of the Brabant-Flemish hinterland, which they themselves had helped to bring about; privateering continued to bring them profit for the time being, but this they stood to lose as soon as peace should be restored. Within Holland the small northern ports, Hoorn, Enkhuizen and Medemblik, still flourished, but fell more and more under the control of Amsterdam capital. Rotterdam was progressing at the expense partly of Dort, which had of old dominated the Rhine trade, and partly of Middelburg and Veere, which it was crowding out of the trade with England. Taking all together, Holland continued to benefit by the trading activity.

Navigation stimulated shipbuilding and the allied trades, and the general increase of prosperity and the growth of towns gave all kinds of work to thousands of hands. Yet apart from fish and cheese, which went both to North and South Europe, the only real export-industry was that of wool and linen at Leiden and Haarlem. The Leiden textile industry had its roots in the middle ages, but it owed almost as much as did the Haarlem bleacheries to the influx of capital and labour from the disturbed centres of the unhappy South. The raw material for the woollen industry came mostly from Spain and a great deal of the finished product returned thither.

At Haarlem and Leiden industrialisation brought the usual evils in its train: a swarming proletariat without property or culture, horrible living conditions, child-labour recruited even from the orphanages. Elsewhere the gilds clung stubbornly to the old regulations concerning hours, wages and the number of apprentices. The modern historian, both in Belgium and Holland, often betrays impatience at this opposition to the rise of the independent large-scale capitalist; for the Belgian historian encounters the same situation at Brussels or Louvain as the Dutch historian at Amsterdam or Delft. But no matter how much narrow-mindedness and prejudice and routine-spirit there may have been behind it, and however greatly that opposition certainly retarded the rise of capitalism, it was yet a blessing that the growth of a rightless and propertyless rabble and the bitter class-warfare known to subsequent history were thus to some extent avoided. 'Bourgeois' is the usual description; 'prosperous' may perhaps serve as well; for nowhere was there a broader class of people with a sufficient economic grasp on life to allow themselves and their children some self-development and to build up a tradition of self-respect.

At Amsterdam the great merchants were now soaring above the mass of medium- and small-propertied people, with fortunes undreamt of by former generations of Hollanders, but it is noteworthy that as late as about 1630, The Hague, only one-sixth as large, counted nearly as many big fortunes as were to be found in the commercial capital, and among them some of the biggest of all. Both the war—through prize-monies and army-contracts—and high government office—more through normal perquisites on State revenues and opportunities for speculation than through deliberate corruption—supplied remunerative occupations. In the seventeenth century, moreover, purely capitalistic possibilities were still limited by this very rigidity of industrial organisation mentioned above. So great was the surplus of capital at Amsterdam that it could not all find employment in commercial enterprises or government loans. Thus it came about that merchants who waxed rich made large purchases of land, an investment which also attracted them because of the social distinction and the lordly rights and titles attaching to it. This was one of the channels whereby the trade-boom reached the countryside, which, moreover, found a readier market for its produce in the growing and increasingly wealthy towns, while the wages obtainable there served to pro-cure a higher standard for rural workers. The land-reclamations bear witness to the prosperity of the countryside in the seaward provinces. The hydraulic engineer Leeghwater made his name with drainage-schemes in North Holland; Usselinx[1] lost a fortune in these undertakings, but few were so unlucky; Cats did well in the poldering of Zealand. The shape of the Zealand islands altered apace, and one after another the lakes of North Holland disappeared. In the landward provinces no similar economic development took place. The landed gentry there fell behind the rich Holland burghers in wealth and became the more dependent on an army career and the favour of the Stadholder.

All things considered, the economic history of the North Netherlands in the seventeenth century offers a rich spectacle. It is a bustle and tumult, an interplay of thrusts and forces, which no other period can parallel. In contemplating it one does not know whether or not to lament the circumstance to which I have referred, namely that trade was not fed by home production. Only a large-scale industrial development cutting right across the resistance offered by the gild privileges could have altered that, yet what could have been worse suited to the peculiar character of Netherland society? All the same, there is something unhealthy in this one-sided commercial development; and that vital and strenuous community did indeed lack the power of foresight and self-restraint by which it might have attempted to restore the equilibrium.

The State of the United Netherlands was not cast in a form—we have had ample evidence of this—that would have facilitated the pursuit of any fixed line of economic policy. Here, too, it bore the imprint of the adverse circumstance of its origin in reaction to modern absolutism, that enemy of liberty, which was yet capable of viewing the whole field of political activity and of devising measures, injudicious at times maybe, but intended at least to promote the welfare of the whole. The liberty that reigned in the Republic was the medieval liberty of groups and interests, sheltering behind privilege and ancient custom. The abolition, for instance, of the regulations prohibiting industry outside the all-powerful towns was as unthinkable as the abolition of the gild-regulations which hindered the rise of large-scale industry within those towns. Internal tolls and staple-duties hampered inland traffic.

One powerful interest alone could from time to time, and

[1] See below, p. 189.

increasingly, impose itself upon the political authority, could give it direction and driving power: the interest of overseas trade. In the States of Holland, owing to their composition, that interest found its most powerful expression: the industrial centres of Haarlem and Leiden usually stood shoulder to shoulder with the trading towns, while the small market towns were too insignificant and in truth too much under the influence of commercial capital to be able to formulate any other policy; in fact this was to some extent true even for the nineteenth (or rather, the first) 'member' of the Holland States, the nobility. The Orange party could occasionally assert itself, even in the States of Holland, with a political, but never with an economic, alternative to the policy of Amsterdam. In any case, the States party quietly identified the interests of trade with those of the community and the State. We have already seen an instance of this in the policy of trading with the enemy, which Holland clung to despite the censure of Leicester[1]; the same difference of outlook manifested itself in the clash between Amsterdam and Frederick Henry over the hiring out of ships to the Spaniards in the Mediterranean. The motive of private gain naturally came into play here, and it was sometimes with downright obtuseness that the merchants and their political representatives urged upon the State their narrow group-interests as the only criterion.

It was possible, however, in all sincerity to elevate into a system of statecraft the rule that trade interests must always take precedence. Their overseas trade was indubitably the most impressive feature of the national economy of the Northern Netherlands. Who, seeing what it wrought for them, can remain indifferent to the glorification it received from statesmen, publicists and poets? There was, too, much that seems attractive in the influence which commercial interests exercised over foreign policy. It was by no means confined to the direct effects of private self-seeking. The States-General became the champions before the world of a system of economic intercourse and maritime law which, as a conception, had its greatness. No doubt one can argue that it suited them because the Netherland trader and sailor, with his long start and with his country's capital resources behind him, stood to profit by it. It is a bracing

[1] See *The Revolt of the Netherlands*, pp. 210/11.

spectacle to see Grotius defending the freedom of the seas against the Spaniards and Portuguese, and later against the English—even though his countrymen forgot those theories when they themselves had achieved a position in the Indies. No power did so much to liberate international trade from Sound dues and Mediterranean pirates as the power which itself—again it must not be overlooked—closed the Scheldt. Every usage tending to deliver commerce to the arbitrary power of belligerent States or to those which were simply hard pressed for money found in the Republic a staunch opponent. Right and left she attempted to fix by treaty the principles of a new maritime law which should forbid the disturbance of peaceful commercial navigation by vexatious visitations or reprisals for private damage. In opposition to the rule hitherto followed by both France and England, that a belligerent might confiscate a neutral ship and cargo so soon as enemy goods should be found on board, she upheld the rule that the flag covers the goods. It is easy to show how much every one of these ideas was dictated by the interests of the great international freighting and trading country into which the Republic had developed and again how all of them were transgressed by the Netherlanders themselves where in special cases the interest of the moment demanded a different procedure. This does not alter the fact that the work of diplomats and jurists, among whom Grotius was the first and the most eminent, built up a tradition which acquired a positive significance in international life and which, regarded from the national point of view, may be called a harmonious fusion of economic interest and political idealism.

B. THE EAST INDIA COMPANY

i. Coen: Batavia and the Banda Islands

DURING the Truce the East India Company had experienced a veritable crisis. It had to withstand dangers which threatened to destroy its position in the East, but once having overcome them, it emerged all the more formidable. The man under whose direction this struggle with fortune was undertaken, and the real founder of the Netherland colonial empire in the Indies, was Jan Pieterszoon Coen, of Hoorn.

In the course of a few years the Netherlanders had built up for themselves a mighty position in the wide spaces of the East, round the Indian Ocean and the China Sea. Yet this position remained unstable; at any moment, amid the many conflicting interests and the ever-shifting forces of that tumultuous world, the foundations might give way under it.

Trade was the Dutchman's objective, but from the start all attempts at trade with the East needed the backing of force against the Portuguese, and for the Dutch State, which had helped to bring the Company into existence, the challenging of the Portuguese monopoly had certainly been an important secondary aim now that Portugal had come to form part of the Spanish monarchy (since 1580). Even apart from that, however, trade could not venture out into the East unarmed. Just as the pioneer commercial enterprises of the Portuguese had led to the foundation of a colonial empire, so did the expeditions of the Europeans who came after them, of the Dutch, and in the long run of the English and French, though these at first tried to stop short of empire-building. This was an inevitable development, not so much on account of the Europeans' lust for dominion—their imperialism, as we call it now—as because of the political and social backwardness of the peoples with whom they came into contact.

The numerous kings—rajahs or sultans—in India, Farther India and the Malay Archipelago, held their authority only too insecurely, threatened as they were from without by neighbouring princes and from within by nobles, high officials or claimants to the throne. So long as they did hold it, they exercised that authority in the most arbitrary fashion. To cope with the foreign traders competing with one another in deadliest rivalry was altogether beyond the power of these native States; no law or treaty could withstand the pecuniary temptations with which Portuguese, Dutchmen and Englishmen sought to outbid each other; ministers and harbour-masters were always to be bought, unless the prince had them sufficiently in hand to pocket the profits himself. In short, the meeting of Western commerce with Eastern society meant that modern capitalism, after having grown up amid relatively stable political conditions and become accustomed to them, found itself as it were thrown back into the early feudal, or even the late Carolingian, period. Inevitably, therefore, trade had to look to its own protection. Many Eastern sovereigns accepted this as self-evident; at all events, they negotiated with the Company, whose servants did not fail to invoke the authority of the States-General and the Prince of Orange, as one power with another, and concluded treaties and contracts allowing trade on certain conditions and granting certain privileges, while in some cases they raised no objection to the fortification of the foreigners' 'factory' or 'lodge' so as to make these proof against attack. But conditions were too unstable for the Dutchmen to remain satisfied with positions thus early acquired. They had to contend with so much corruption, lawlessness and breach of contract, both from the natives and from their own European rivals, that they could not but strive after consolidation.

Consolidation led naturally to expansion, the more so because practically from the start it was not security alone, but the lure of monopolies, which drove the Dutch forward. Every means was used to cajole the princes into contracts granting to the Company the exclusive delivery of the native products, pepper, rice, indigo, spices; and when Portuguese or English nevertheless attempted to establish relations, force was generally necessary to prevent evasion of the contract. It was not long before the Dutch were aspiring, just as in Europe, to the control of the freight-trade between the Eastern countries themselves—at the expense of Chinese, Arabs, Indians and Indonesians—and here, too, they naturally availed themselves of their sea-power as the readiest weapon against undesired competition.

By the beginning of the Truce it was clear that what the Company particularly needed in its sphere of operations was concentration of authority and administration. It was also clear that the strong central point—usually spoken of as the *rendezvous* —which would need to be established somewhere for this purpose must come in the neighbourhood of the Strait of Sunda. Hitherto the scattered heads of factories and forts had been subject only to the authority of the commander of the fleet sent out once a year, and soon off home again; among men thus left to themselves, discipline was hard to maintain. It required great strength of mind, indeed, for a man who had been uprooted from his normal surroundings and planted in a foreign civilisation bristling with temptations, and under the strain of an enervating climate, to give loyal service in his duties as trader and chief. Cowardice, corruption and drunkenness were all too common among the badly paid and unsystematically chosen officials. A new regime was introduced in 1610 with the appointment of a Governor-General resident in the East, assisted by a Council of the Indies. The first Governor-General was Pieter Both. His instructions ordered him to select a permanent residence as soon as was practicable, but neither he nor his next two successors, Reynst and Reael, found that possible; instead, they travelled with the fleet to and fro between Bantam and the Moluccas.

Bantam and the Moluccas, these had already become the pillars on which rested the whole Company system in its chartered area. True, there were widespread trading operations developing in other directions, for the Netherlanders were pushing their way in wherever the Portuguese had no strong position to make it dangerous to approach them too closely: in North India, where the Great Mogul had recently established one of the strongest of Asiatic empires, on the Coromandel coast, in China. But attacks on the strongholds of the Portuguese position, such as were regularly undertaken during the first years following the Company's foundation, all failed; the destruction of the Portuguese empire was reserved for a later generation of Company servants, using as base the strong position their predecessors had built up in the Archipelago.

In the Archipelago itself, besides Solor, the Portuguese had sovereign authority and military power only in the Moluccas. Bantam was an important trade-centre for the whole area. The Portuguese had a factory there, but were subject to the authority of the Sultan, who was eager to grant the Dutch, as rivals of the Portuguese, similar privileges. The Moluccas owed their great importance to the spices, which they alone produced and which were in extraordinary demand on the European market. Cloves grew especially on Amboina and on the neighbouring peninsula of Ceram, Hoamoal; nutmeg and mace constituted the wealth of the small Banda group to the south. The Portuguese had forts on Tidore, whence they could keep an eye on Ternate, seat of the strongest native sovereign, and on Amboina, which commanded the southern and western approaches, that is to say from Java, to the whole of the Molucca Sea. The inhabitants of the island-realm of Ternate were torn by party strife, Mohammedan against Christian, and this helped Steven van der Haghen to make himself master of the Portuguese castle on Amboina. He had the support of the weaker party, the Mohammedans, although the arbitrary and licentious rule of the Portuguese had made them hated even by the people whom their own Jesuits had converted and among whom even their language had made progress. Van der Haghen paints us the first picture of the Dutchman no longer as a mere trader but as a responsible wielder of power over Indonesian peoples. The capture of the castle of Amboina brought with it, in his words, 'the greatest burden and difficulty' so far, namely, the task of establishing order and settling internecine feuds.

> In the cabin the Amboinese, ten, twenty, yea thirty at a time, reported their affairs, in great confusion and with little resolution. . . . For a full month the Admiral (*that is, himself*) has been engrossed with such head-puzzlings, with great patience hearing now the one and then the other party, and in unbearably great heat, continually wiping off the sweat, has sought in all friendship to reconcile them.

Tidore, too, was conquered from the Portuguese in 1605, but the following year brought an unexpected reverse. This time it was not the Portuguese but the Spaniards who, suddenly pushing South from their old-established settlements in the Philippines, drove the Hollanders from Tidore and put the Company to a much harder struggle to retain its hold on the Moluccas, a struggle which largely occupied the attention of the first Governors-General.

Yet no one ever thought of establishing in the Moluccas those headquarters which were so sorely needed. For that purpose these islands lay much too far to the east, while yet they could not exist without contact with the rest of the Indian world: their inhabitants had devoted themselves so exclusively to the cultivation of their staple export, spices, that they were dependent on imports for food and dress: rice from Java, clothing from India. The Portuguese used their strong town of Malacca as an *entrepôt* for that barter, which after the loss of Amboina they still tried to carry on with the help of such native intermediaries as Surabaya and Macassar. For the Hollanders Bantam was obviously indicated. Bantam was a staple-town for the pepper trade especially; ships from home touched there first, and trade could be despatched thence on its way to India and China. But the Dutchmen's position at Bantam was highly unsatisfactory.

From the Portuguese they had nothing to fear. There were Portuguese merchants at Bantam, but they lay low; under such men as Van Warwijck, Matelieff and Van der Haghen the Company's naval power had grown so formidable that the Portuguese could not assert themselves far beyond their strong places. But commerce was exposed to continual extortion from the Bantamese authorities themselves. Civil war, too, often made the town so unsafe that the foreigners had to maintain their 'lodges' in a state of defence. In 1610 there came to power, on the occasion of a royal minority, a 'State-Governor'—by this title the Dutch generally referred to him—who systematically plagued the foreigners. So bad did the situation become that the Company soon established a factory at Jacatra,[1] a town fifty miles east of Bantam, whose prince (*pangerang*) was a vassal of the King of Bantam and was on bad terms with the latter's State-Governor. The Hollanders thus secured a means of putting pressure on Bantam. Their ships proceeded to use Jacatra more than Bantam and the lodge there became a 'strong good house'. At the same time the *pangerang* of Jacatra felt himself threatened from the other side also, from the East, in particular by the *panembahan* of Mataram ('the Mataram', as he was called by the Dutch), King of Middle Java, who was bent on extending his authority in both directions, towards Surabaya in the East and Jacatra in the West.

Such were the complicated circumstances in which the Hollanders felt it necessary to undertake the forcible establishment of the *rendezvous* at Jacatra, and thus to sow the seed out of which would grow their dominion over Java and the Archipelago. The impulse to action came from their hostility with the English, and that flared up over the question of the Moluccas.

As early as 1610 the Directors at home, the Lords Seventeen as they were called, representing the several 'chambers'

---

[1] This is the form always used in the Dutch documents. When the name was revived by the Indonesian Republic, it was spelt (more correctly no doubt) Jacarta.

of the United Company (united in 1602), had charged Pieter
Both

> to take all possible care that the trade of the Moluccas, Amboina and Banda
> therein included, should ever remain and be assured to the Company, so that
> no part of it should fall into the hands of any other nation in the world save
> to ourselves or to such as we should find good.

The Amboinese had quickly repented of their joy at the
advent of the Hollanders. The new masters did not long remain
neutral, even in the matter of religion. They banished Mohammedan priests as systematically as they did Roman priests; they
destroyed mosques and crucifixes. At first they had no ministers
at hand to assume spiritual charge of the superficially Christianised population, but in time the flocks collected by the Jesuits
were Protestantised, just as well or as badly as it could be done
in halting Malay. At the same time the Hollanders were not to
be trifled with in the matter of trade. The Company officials
clothed their forced monopoly in legal forms; they always
found means of persuading the numerous authorities on the
islands into contracts giving the Company the exclusive right
to trade. Violation of these agreements was called smuggling
and was put down by force. The Bandanese also were made to
feel the mailed fist, Pulo Wai being occupied. But to shut this
extensive and multiform island region off from all traffic with
the outer world was an impossible task. On every side the native
junks slipped through the meshes of the net, carrying spices
to neighbouring harbours, where Chinamen, Indians and
Portuguese came to pick them up.

The English meanwhile, whose Company had been founded
shortly after the first Dutch expeditions to the East, were not
content to be shut out of the Moluccas in this fashion, but
English ships which ventured there were shadowed by Dutch
vessels and thwarted in their commerce with the natives. The
Company, however, did not yet dare employ armed force against
the nation with which the States-General were on friendly
terms in Europe. As late as November 1614 the Directors,
doubtless in conformity with admonitions from the States-
General, gave their East Indian servants express orders (which
did not arrive there until nearly a year later) to prevent the
English from trading with the Moluccas, but without taking
any high-handed action against them. The line of conduct which

they laid down was an impossible one, and they certainly wished their instructions to be exceeded. The Director-General of Trade, Jan Pieterszoon Coen, who resided at Bantam, did not shrink from that course, but the Governor-General, Reael, wanted to wait for positive orders. When Reael sent in an only half-serious request to be relieved, the Directors straightway replaced him by the man who was bold enough to forge ahead. Coen's appointment reached him in June 1618.

The East Indian adventure had already developed out of Dutch stock a throng of sharply defined personalities. Here birth counted for little. Reynst and Reael, it is true, belonged to the class from which the Directors themselves were drawn. But there was never any system—as there was in Spanish and Portuguese colonisation—of keeping the higher posts for the nobility or the ruling class. Character or ability could raise simple middle-class youngsters as seamen, traders or administrators to the highest ranks. In narratives of voyages, in reports and official correspondence, written in a direct and lively style, these men have left a lasting record of their experiences in this strange world, and unconsciously of their own personalities.

Among these remarkable figures, Coen, while not one of the most attractive, was certainly one of the most striking. In 1618 he was still only thirty years of age. Coming to the East Indies as a young clerk, he had distinguished himself by his business acumen and austere way of life. As Director-General at Bantam he kept up direct correspondence with the Directors at home ('the Lords Seventeen'), and one cannot read his letters without feeling that they are the product of an outstanding personality, a man devoted to the cause of the Company, which he identified with the cause of his country, a man with views of his own on the great problems of administration, a man who knew what he wanted.

If some daring thieves should night and day break into Your Lordships' houses (*he had written to the Directors late in 1615, on receipt of their orders not to use force against the English*), what measures would Your Lordships take to meet such fellows and defend your property, if not by using force against them? This is what the English do commit against Your Lordships' estate in the Moluccas, Amboina and Banda. Wherefore we are surprised that it is ordered not to use force against them. If the English have this privilege above nature and all creation, then is it right good to be an Englishman, and true indeed the slander and the calumny which they spread among all princes against the Dutch.

It was not only on the subject of the English that Coen dared to heap reproaches on his principals. No letter did he send home which did not point out how greatly they themselves were jeopardising the future of the Company by sending out 'unserviceable persons' and by continuing to pay them a handsome salary even when they had rightly been discharged for incompetence or malpractices, while faithful servants were stinted.

We request Your Lordships to send no more of these and suchlike persons (*he once wrote, and bitingly added:*) but you may let them join the English.

There was no letter in which he did not censure the economy that withheld necessary capital from the Eastern trade. It is to the credit of the Directors that in this young official who rapped them so sharply over the knuckles they recognised the strong man whom the situation demanded. In 1618 that situation had become critical indeed.

The Hollanders had concentrated their activities more and more at Jacatra in place of Bantam, and the *pangerang* eyed their growing power with suspicion. Ignoring his protests, Coen, who knew that if he were not to lose everything he must push on still further, began to fortify the little island of Onrust (Unrest) lying off Jacatra, and in October 1618 resolved in council to erect 'a proper fort' at that town. It could be foreseen that before this fort was completed it would have to withstand an assault from the united forces of Bantam and Jacatra, and the English now prepared to profit by the difficulties ahead of their rivals. The English Company had put forth a great effort. In December 1618 no less than fifteen English ships, under Sir Thomas Dale, lay before Bantam, empowered not only to take forcible measures in self-defence, but to exact reparation for past injuries. The Bantamese supported him in the hope of coming out on top. After the English had taken a Dutch ship, Coen attacked the English lodge at Jacatra. But when the English fleet thereupon set sail for Jacatra, a critical situation developed, for the Netherlanders' main force lay in the Moluccas and he had only seven ships at hand. Rather than expose this squadron to almost certain destruction and thus 'to hazard the whole state of the Company' for the sake of the new fort at Jacatra, he determined to proceed with the whole squadron to the Moluccas and to return as soon as possible with reinforcements. The fort would meanwhile have to look after itself.

That it managed to hold out was due more to divisions among the enemy than to the garrison's powers of resistance. Following a dispute with his allies Sir Thomas Dale withdrew in dudgeon to his ships, and the Bantamese, who had already treacherously captured the Dutch commander, Pieter van den Broecke, an Antwerper, were determined, even in spite of the Jacatran *pangerang*, to conquer the Dutch fort themselves. Yet so feeble was the attack of their numerous horde that the Dutch flag still flew over the fort when at last in May 1619 Coen reappeared with a fleet of sixteen sail. The English had not waited for him. The Bantamese could not hold their own against Coen's landing-force. Not only was the fort relieved, but Jacatra itself conquered. The palace of the *pangerang*, who had already been driven out of it by the Bantamese, was destroyed.

Despair not, fear not your enemies, there is nothing in the world can hinder or cast us down, for God is with us. And hold the former defeats in no consequence, for there are great things to be wrought in the Indies and every year there can be despatched rich returns.

Thus Coen had written to the Lords Seventeen some eight months before, when the dark clouds were massing. Now he was jubilant:

In this wise have we driven those of Bantam out of Jacatra and become lords of the land of Java. It is certain that this victory and the flight of the proud English will spread great terror throughout all the Indies. Hereby will the honour and repute of the Dutch nation be much increased. . . . The foundation of the long-wished-for *rendezvous* is now laid.

At the desire of the Directors the town and castle of Jacatra were henceforward known as Batavia, a name intended to honour the new North Netherland nation as a whole. It was a condition of Batavia's efficiency as the centre of Dutch power in the East that Bantam, which Dale had used as a base for his attempt to close the Strait of Sunda and which still had an English lodge, should be rendered harmless. Coen straightway took the fleet thither, effected Van den Broecke's delivery and next established a permanent blockade of Bantam harbour. The English could not even attempt to prevent all this. Their fleet was scattered, and seven of their vessels fell into the hands of the Dutch. To put forth a second effort, after the first had failed so disastrously, was beyond the power of the English Company. The foundations had been laid, not only, as Coen had written, for the *rendezvous*, but for the strategic and economic mastery of the Malay Archipelago.

But there was a shock in store for Coen. On 27 March 1620 an English ship brought him tidings of a treaty between the two Companies, concluded in July 1619 in ignorance of what had then already befallen in the East Indies. From 1611 onwards, throughout the years of rivalry and strife in the East, negotiations had been carried on in Europe. Grotius, the champion of the freedom of the seas, had been sent to England to unfold the reasons why the Dutch might close the Moluccan sea to others. The principal argument was that, although they had originally come to the Indies as peaceful traders, the Dutch had been compelled to expend blood and treasure in disputing the Portuguese claim to exclude all other nations, that they still had to maintain warships and castles there, and could not now allow third parties to profit freely from the situation which their sole efforts had brought into being. King James's dissatisfaction was not appeased by these explanations, and so, at the very moment when the victory had been won in the Indies, the States-General let themselves be pressed into a union of the rival Companies. The leading provisions of the treaty were: co-operation in defence, equal shares in the Java pepper trade, and for the English a third part of the spice trade in the Moluccas, but without the right to erect fortifications there. It was enough to arouse Coen's fierce indignation.

If the English laugh for gratitude (*he wrote to the Directors*) your labour has not been in vain. Their great thanks are due to Your Lordships, for they had properly let themselves be thrown out of the Indies, and Your Lordships have set them back in the midst thereof. . . . Wherefore the English have been granted a third of the cloves, nutmeg and mace, we cannot well understand. They had no claim to a single grain of sand on the coast of the Moluccas, Amboyna or Banda.

The weakness displayed by the Dutch in the renewed negotiations of 1618–19 is to be explained by the situation at home. The East India Company was intimately connected with the Holland regent class which was overthrown in 1618. Maurice and the Contra-Remonstrants built on the friendship of England, and the treaty of July 1619 was the price they paid for it.

But the arrangement projected by the treaty accorded too little with the realities of the position in the Indies for a man like Coen to let it tie his hands for long. Outwardly the enemies of yesterday now co-operated as allies. A joint Anglo-Dutch Council of Defence planned expeditions against Manila and Goa. But at Batavia the English found themselves on soil where the Dutch were masters, and Coen made them feel his power. They lagged far behind their new friends in capital resources and naval power, and as early as 1621 they proved unable to co-operate in an expedition undertaken by Coen to subject the Banda Islands. Yet the occasion involved their last chance of keeping some foothold in the Moluccas. They possessed a factory on the most westerly island of the group, Pulu Run, and the Bandanese had clung to them in a forlorn hope of escaping the grip of the Dutch monopoly. The inhabitants of Lontor had even proclaimed the King of England their sovereign.

But now Coen appeared fully determined to put an end once and for all to these shows of opposition to the Company's monopoly. Just now I spoke of 'subjecting'. But subjection was not enough. To force the people to surrender was easy, but it was feared that they 'would quickly rebel again, so soon as the fleet had departed', and it was therefore decided to tranship them 'willingly or unwillingly' to Batavia. Seven hundred and eighty-nine were got on board; thousands sought refuge in the mountains. Of these, a few hundred managed to escape to other islands in their junks. The rest were blockaded, all victuals as far as possible being destroyed, until an assault could be launched, when most of them were found starved to death. Of those who still lived, some threw themselves from the cliffs, but 'a good party of women and children' were taken alive.

About 2,500 are dead either of hunger and misery or by the sword. So far we have not heard of more than 300 Bandanese who have escaped from the whole of Banda. It appears that the obstinacy of these people was so great that they had rather die all together in misery than give themselves up to our men.

Thus Coen, who had left with the main force without being able to see the end of 'the game'. At Batavia forty-five headmen (*orangkais*), who had been brought there, were executed for alleged treason. Coen was scandalised at the unruliness of the 789, already considerably reduced by disease. Before a year had passed they were found guilty of conspiracy, and several put to death.

All the other male persons, to wit 210, have been thrown into chains here (*Batavia*), and the women and children, namely 307 souls, we have sent to Banda to be shared and sold among our people there.

For the depopulated Banda Islands, 'altogether as fair an orchard as may be seen in the world' (as Coen himself testified), had to be peopled afresh, if the Company were to obtain from the trees the nutmeg and mace for the sake of which the original inhabitants had been brought to ruin. Coen's dream was to make it a Dutch settlement.

Meanwhile, at every stage of the long-drawn-out agony of the Bandanese, Coen had gloated over the ill-concealed chagrin of the English at the fate of their protégés. He had always suspected secret understanding between the malicious Bandanese and the deceitful English. It was now the turn of these last.

The gentlemen at home might recommend good relations with the English, Coen roundly declared that he did not believe them possible. The English sought nothing but quarrels.

Pride, presumption, falsity, and, in short, all vices are too great in them.... If Your Lordships desire something great and notable to be done for the honour of God and the welfare of the country, then deliver us from the English.

There was really little further cause for uneasiness. The impotence of the English became more and more apparent until, just before Coen's departure for home early in 1623, they came to inform him that they could no longer keep up their factories in the Moluccas and were even compelled to ask for Dutch ships to bring away their officials and property. Yet after this, in Coen's absence, but still under the influence of his fell spirit, matters ended in a terrible drama. The governor of Amboina, Van Speult, received evidence of a conspiracy against Dutch rule planned by the English lodge there, with the aid of its Japanese soldiers. Confessions were obtained, most, but not all, by torture. Ten English merchants and ten Japanese were put to death. The affair made a violent sensation in England and the 'massacre of Amboina' long hampered relations between the two countries in Europe. In the Indies it helped to make the position of the English Company at Batavia untenable. Efforts to establish elsewhere in the neighbourhood of Sunda

Strait a base capable of maintaining itself against Batavia, met with grievous failure. In the long run the English had to make shift with Bantam, but there they were by no means out of the reach of Dutch power. Very soon the English Company had to recognise that it had no future in the Archipelago.

The significance of Coen's first Governor-Generalship is that the Dutch had laid hold on the Archipelago. True, their position there was very different from what it would later become. Only in the Moluccas and at Batavia did they exercise sovereign authority. Coen himself, during his second Governor-Generalship (1627-29), had again to defend his creation of Batavia in heavy conflict, this time against the Mataram, who, having come thus far in his conquests, attempted to drive the Hollanders out of Java. Coen died during the siege, at the age of forty-two.

Coen—the well-known sentence has been quoted above—felt that *something great was to be wrought in the Indies*. Was he thinking solely of trade? Most certainly not. For him 'the welfare of the country', 'the honour and repute of the Dutch nation', even 'the honour of God', were bound up with the success of the Company. The 'rich returns' were assuredly not to be forgotten, especially when one was writing to the Directors. But Coen felt himself to be, and was, the architect of much more than a flourishing business concern.

History, however, has decided, as it so often does with human creators, that his work should result in something wholly different from what he had imagined. Coen's most cherished hopes centred around those Dutch settlements which were to arise in the Moluccas and at Batavia. So soon as he had secured 'by God's grace', peaceful possession of Banda, he asked repeatedly and insistently for 'honourable men' to be sent out to Banda, Amboina and Batavia 'to plant colonies'. Instead of turning water into land at great expense to provide room for the growing population—an allusion to the draining of the lakes in North Holland, Coen's own district, and to the reclamations in Zealand—people should be sent to the Indies to found a State there which would be able to resist all enemies and in which the Seven Provinces would have an invaluable ally. The Company's servants in the Indies were useless to him for this purpose; they were for the most part 'a godless crowd'.

Let the soldiers and seamen be used against the enemy, to which task they were created of God; few or none can be expected to make good citizens.

Yet in default of better he had to transform much of that unsound material into 'free men, for the sake of keeping people in the country'. Living with slave-girls, since the Company did not send out enough respectable women, these men by their wild conduct too often brought the good name of the Dutch into disrepute and moved Coen to bitter complaints. Nothing grieved him so much in the Directors as their failure to super-intend the quality of the women who were sometimes sent out.

If the Indies, if we and other Your Lordships' servants, are worthy of no better women than the scum of the Netherlands, then do not count upon keeping good people in the Indies or founding a prosperous State there.

It was as a sacrifice to this ideal that he had Sara Specx, daughter of a future Governor-General and a member of his household, publicly whipped for pre-marital intercourse, an act of barbarism which set up an unattainable standard for the Netherland community of his dreams. He was assiduous on behalf of this vision during his sojourn at home. He knew that if it were to be realised, exemptions from the Company's monopoly system would have to be allowed in the interest of the free citizens, and it was in the sphere of the intercolonial trade that he wanted this latitude. Not without difficulty he managed to get a regulation in this sense drawn up by the Directors. But many shareholders, in spite of Coen's argument that prosperous settlements might be taxed to keep up garrisons, protested so strongly against this infraction of the monopoly that the regulation was revoked before ever being put into force. It ran counter, indeed, to the whole spirit of the Company's administration.

Apart from this, a community such as Coen envisaged could not exist in the densely-populated Indies, where trade had to conform to a deep-rooted economic system, unless the treatment of Banda were to be carried out everywhere. And that cruel episode had been fiercely criticised. In passing judgment on Coen's conduct in it, we should indeed do him less than justice if we forgot that such methods were a commonplace in the Indian world at the time, that even in seventeenth-century Europe Cromwell inflicted no less bloody penalties on the Irish, and Catinat on the Waldenses, with equal complacency. But

it must not be thought that all Dutchmen shared Coen's hard-
ness of heart. There were among the humble executants of his
orders some who 'took no pleasure in such transactions'. The
Directors themselves were alarmed and wrote that it must be
'once and enough'. The inhuman policy which Coen prosecuted with so much vehemence, the policy of mastering the
entire intercolonial trade by forcible suppression of native
navigation, was a corner-stone of his great scheme: it was clear
that the Company would never throw open the trade with the
mother-country, and the colonists would therefore have to
subsist on the intercolonial trade. But a critic in Holland—it
may have been Reael—argued with acuteness that it was
precisely this system itself which, by rudely overthrowing the
economic life of the East, blocked the way to the realisation of
Coen's ideal.

What honourable men will break up their homes here (*so ran this remarkable
memorandum*) to take employment as executioners and gaolers of a herd of
slaves, and to range themselves amongst those free men who by their maltreatment and massacre of the Indians have made the Dutch notorious
throughout the Indies as the cruellest nation of the whole world? The freemen (*meaning the settlers*) may well use force against the Indians, but cannot
clear them off the seas by reasonable means, for the Indians equip themselves
at much less cost than our people.

As a matter of fact, the utter ruthlessness displayed by Coen
towards the opponents of the Dutch monopoly not only
constitutes a blemish on his character, it reveals a shortcoming
in him as a statesman. Once, as Director-General, he had
written that a sovereign Dutch rendezvous would draw people
from every side because 'the merciful free manner of our
nation' was in such contrast with the 'tyranny' of these
Eastern kings who 'held all their dominions solely by force'. In
Coen's policy as it developed later neither mercy nor freedom
was apparent; the Indian peoples had no place in it at all. Yet
there they were, and a great task awaited the Dutch with regard
to them. Nor was this a view which could only develop in a later
age. Steven van der Haghen had already been dimly aware of
it in the Moluccas. We have seen him restoring peace between
the Amboinese parties. Banda, he thought, should also be
conquered:

These lands of Banda with those of Amboina would also suit well together
under a single lord, for the Bandanese often wage war with one another, and

so lay waste their own lands, hewing down the nutmeg trees, and each side doing as much hurt as possible to the other; so that if they stood under one lord, therewith would all that evil cease.

Here was presented a political programme not less noble than that of Coen's Dutch settlements, one, moreover, which time was to prove practicable. In more than one way Coen offended unpardonably against this tenet that Dutch power in the East Indies 'should make all that evil cease'. Yet his conquests laid the foundations on which not his, but that other dream, was later to be realised.

ii. Van Diemen: the Moluccas, Malacca and Ceylon

To the mighty efforts under Coen there succeeded a period in which the Directors' fear of any expenditure not immediately productive set the pace. No extension of territorial rule, that was the permanent lesson they drew from the cost of military enterprises and of maintaining castles and garrisons. But out there even less forceful authorities felt that Coen's work could only be preserved by being carried further, until in 1636 a strong man became Governor-General and, either disregarding or contriving to overcome opposition from his principals, set on foot a new forward movement. This was Antonie van Diemen, son of a burgomaster of the little town of Culemborg, who had come to the Indies a bankrupt, but had rehabilitated himself under Coen.

First ranked the task, which was still to exact great efforts even after the ten years of Van Diemen's governorship, of consolidating Company rule in the Moluccas, or, to use Company terminology, consolidating the spice-monopoly.

Amboina is not Banda; it will not be settled there in a matter of ten or twelve months.

So a Company servant once wrote in despair at the stubborn resistance of an island which, while several times larger than the Banda group, does not equal the area of a single Dutch province, even if the small Uliassers and the peninsula of Ceram, Hoamoal, be included. The Amboinese were not left wholly to themselves in their frequent revolts to shake off the grip of the Dutch monopolists. On one side they were supported by the Sultan of

Ternate, their nominal sovereign, on the other by the ruler of Macassar in South-West Celebes, centre of the independent trade in the Eastern archipelago, and a refuge for English and Portuguese. In 1638 Van Diemen himself came eastwards with a fleet and induced the Sultan of Ternate to conclude a treaty giving the Company a free hand in the Amboina group. This was quickly followed by a war of subjection, which Antonie Caen, after first destroying a fleet from Macassar, brought provisionally to an end in 1643. The savage punishment of the rebel *orangkais* was carried out in the name of their overlord in Ternate.

The Company's supremacy meant that it was able not only to exclude foreigners from all trade in the valuable produce of these islands, but also to restrict production to the demands of the European market, which might easily be glutted. Outside Amboina, the Uliassers and the Banda Islands, all clove and nutmeg trees were destroyed, either by amicable arrangement with the natives or by force. This was often judged necessary even in the producing islands, and it is easy to see that the white settlement of the depopulated Banda group could not flourish under a system by which a surplus was much more to be feared than a shortage. At the same time, the high-spirited native life of the entire Eastern archipelago was rudely disturbed.

A gruesome story. But in the profits of the spice-monopoly the Company saw the only source from which to make good the heavy charges involved in the system of territorial rule. The Company's position in the East was based on forts and garrisons, and above all, warships. That was inevitable owing to the circumstances of its rise in open hostility to the monopolistic Hispano-Portuguese empire. In any case, it meant that in the Company's books a liability occurred with which the English, Danish and French companies, now everywhere limiting themselves to peaceful penetration, did not have to reckon. Hence the grim, the fell conviction that

we must work heart and soul to remain masters of the profit-yielding Molucca spices of nutmeg, cloves and mace, to the exclusion of all other nations.

The conquest of Amboina did not mean the end of the tragedy. It was still to be feared that Ternate, reconciled perchance with Tidore and with the Spaniards pressing forward from the Philippines, would awake from its lethargy and attempt a restoration of its position in the South. Macassar still stood there, the hope of all independent traders. But these were problems which a subsequent generation of Company servants was to be called upon to solve. Meanwhile, in a wholly different direction as well, Van Diemen had given a powerful stimulus to the development of the Dutch empire in Asia.

In 1642, under his leadership, the Spaniards were driven out of the Northern corner of the island of Formosa. The Dutch, who in Coen's time had made fruitless efforts to bend the immense Chinese empire to their will by raiding expeditions along the coast, had already set foot in South Formosa to establish a base for their China trade. Now they succeeded in conquering the whole island. But even before that Van Diemen had made a start with the forcible demolition of the Portuguese Empire, which his predecessors, following the failures of the early years, had done little more than undermine. The superiority of the Netherlanders over their enemies and rivals was especially marked at sea. To strike at the Portuguese strong-holds, therefore, the weapon of blockade lay to hand. Thus first Malacca, commanding the passage from the Indian to the Chinese Ocean, and the fixed central point of what still remained to the Portuguese of their trade and influence in the Western Malay Archipelago, and afterwards also Goa, their capital itself, were regularly blockaded by the Dutch at the season when they were due to receive fleets from the mother country. Then, in 1638, the policy of conquest was launched with an attack on Ceylon.

Ceylon was more than a nerve-centre of the whole Portuguese system; it was also desirable in itself as affording the prospect of capturing yet another valuable monopoly, namely, that of cinnamon. The cinnamon region is situated in the south-west of the island; there the power of Portugal was concentrated, and there lay the principal towns, Colombo, residence of the Portuguese governor, Negombo and Punto de Gale. The mountainous interior was still under the rule of the Prince of Kandy, Rajah Singha, who had not indeed abandoned his claim to the cinnamon region. To shut him off from the outer world, and in particular from the Hollanders, the Portuguese had only recently completed their chain round the island. Rajah Singha

had contrived all the same to establish contact with the Dutch
factories on the Coromandel coast, and it was at his invitation to
liberate him from the Portuguese usurper that the Company's
ships and troops came to the attack in 1638. They straightway
obtained a firm footing on the island, though not in the cinnamon
districts; a Portuguese fleet was destroyed, and the 'High
Government' at Batavia saw possibilities of success far beyond
Ceylon.

> The time is come to throw the Portuguese out of India. . . . The oppor-
> tunity presents and offers to Your Excellencies the mastery of the Orient.

Thus wrote Van Diemen to the Lords Seventeen at home.
Ceylon, Malacca, the Malabar pepper-coast, all seemed to await
their grasp. But it proved to be less easy than that. The Directors
did their utmost to furnish the extra ships and troops which the
Governor-General asked for; to expel the Portuguese and to take
their place in Asia became the Company's policy in the Council
Chamber of the Seventeen as well as at the castle of Batavia.
But however rotten the foundations of Portuguese dominion,
however incapable of withstanding the Netherlanders' fleets, in
open conflict on land it still showed stubborn powers of resistance. The Portuguese were fighting not merely for a Company,
not even for the abstract idea of their national greatness; they
were fighting for their very existence. Van Diemen himself
wrote of them:

> The greater number regard India as their fatherland, thinking no longer
> of Portugal; they trade thither little or not at all, living and enriching them-
> selves out of the treasures of India, as though they were natives and knew no
> other fatherland.

No other Europeans have ever been so deeply involved in the
social and cultural life of the Asiatic races as the Portuguese at
Malacca, in Ceylon, at Negapatam, Cochin, Goa and elsewhere.
We have seen what progress Catholicism had made in the
Moluccas under their rule. Everywhere, even in the rest of the
Malay Archipelago, where they had never been more than
traders, their language had already before the arrival of the
Hollanders penetrated so deep that the new rulers themselves—
to the displeasure of their leaders—used it all too often in their
transactions with native princes and merchants. The Company's
language of trade and administration abounded with Portuguese

terms. Even at Batavia, with its inhabitants and slaves drawn
from all quarters, Portuguese long disputed with Dutch the
place of language of intercourse; ministers even used it in the
pulpit. A generaticn of hard fighting was needed to destroy
the Portuguese position in Asia.

Only in 1640 did the Hollanders succeed in their designs
against the cinnamon ports and capture Negombo and Gale.
But they now straightway fell out with Rajah Singha, their
erstwhile protégé, who vainly demanded of them the return of
those towns. Their leader, Coster, was murdered on an expedition into the interior, and the Portuguese recaptured Negombo.
Simultaneously, the Company had to sustain a mighty effort to
conquer Malacca. Long hampered in its trade, deserted by the
two powerful princes of the neighbouring country, the Sultans
of Atjeh and Johore, deprived of all prospect of relief from Goa
or the mother-country, the town was in a hopeless position, yet
the siege lasted throughout the second half of 1640 and 'cost
much human flesh'. The capitulation made a great stir throughout the Archipelago and beyond.

Meanwhile, events were taking place in Europe which, to
Van Diemen's undisguised chagrin, threatened to put an end to
his whole policy of conquest. In November 1640 the Duke of
Braganza was called to the throne of Portugal, and the union
with Spain, which had exposed the country's colonial possessions to the assaults of Spain's Dutch rebels, was, after sixty
years, dissolved. In April 1641 peace negotiations were begun
at The Hague between the Republic and the new kingdom, now
enemy of the Republic's enemy. The importance of co-operation
in Europe was too obvious for the Company's ambitions to
be suffered to prolong the state of war. But those ambitions were
not overlooked, and one of the provisions of the ten years' truce
which was concluded declared that it should only come into
force in Asia one year after the exchange of ratifications (which
took place in November 1641).

Van Diemen thus obtained a period of grace, during which,
however, the conquest of Ceylon made no progress. The Dutch
were masters only of Gale, and sat there as though locked up,
without access to the coveted cinnamon country. But Europe
was far away, and to acquiesce in a position of inferiority
because a treaty had been concluded there accorded as little

with Van Diemen's character as with Coen's. The Viceroy of
Goa was in an over-confident frame of mind as a result of the
successful defence of Ceylon, and so it was not difficult to find
a pretext for continuing the war. Goa was again blockaded, and
late in 1643 the Netherlanders succeeded in taking Negombo
for the second time. Van Diemen had great plans still in store.
But the Directors, taken to task by the States-General, made
clear to their over-zealous servant that it would not do to ignore
the official armistice so completely. Joan Maetsuycker, the
commander of the blockading fleet which had reappeared before
Goa in the autumn of 1644, now negotiated an arrangement with
the Viceroy, by which Gale and Negombo should remain to the
Company, with access to the cinnamon country.

So peace came in 1644 with Van Diemen in possession of
Malacca and two of the cinnamon ports in Ceylon. But the
Portuguese had not been 'thrown out of India'. They were still
in Ceylon, where the cinnamon trade had to be shared with
them; they still had strong places on the southern end of the
Coromandel coast, where the textiles were made; they continued
to hold the Malabar coast, whence, as from Sumatra, pepper
was exported; they were still known to be hanging on here and
there, in China, on Timor. It would clearly be impossible to
procure an equilibrium between the rising and declining
empires in the Indies. As we shall see, the struggle in another
part of the world for Brazil between Dutch and Portuguese was
soon renewed, despite the armistice, and thereby relations
strained still more. But even so the Company's servants in Asia
were hankering after the moment when they should be free to
revive those schemes of conquest interrupted from European
motives on the restoration of Portuguese independence.

The Dutch East India Company was, in the Indian world, the
power of the sword. The Directors might sometimes shrink
from the terrific cost of a policy of force, but they had chosen a
road whence there was no turning back. Armed forces, warships
and soldiers, these distinguished the Company from all other
groups or rulers in the East. With these it consolidated all its
monopolies, which in their turn defrayed the cost of those
armaments. And although for the masters at home it was a
question of monopolies only, what was coming into existence
in the process was a colonial empire of the first rank. Yet how

perfectly natural seems the reluctance with which the Directors sometimes resolved upon new conquests, when it is noticed that the peaceful trading-posts under the authority of this or that powerful native prince, such as those at Surat under the Great Mogul, on the Hooghly under the Nabob of Bengal, on the island of Desima under the Emperor of Japan, or in Persia, almost always figured on their books with larger profits than the places over which they had themselves assumed sovereignty and which they had therefore to administer and defend.

There would be no point in blaming the Directors, who were bound to think first of the solvency of the Company, but it is obvious that under such direction opportunities for the Dutch nation were lost. There were, for instance, the explorations of Abel Tasman. His despatch to explore "the Southlands" is a striking testimony to the breadth of Van Diemen's vision. But the Company was not looking for empty lands; when Australia did not appear to contain either the thickly-populated regions with which trade might be carried on, or the rich mines with their treasures ready for the finding, no more attention was paid to what lay south of the Archipelago.

c. THE WEST INDIA COMPANY

i. *The Conquest of North Brazil*[1]

USSELINX'S conception of settlements to plant Dutch civilisation overseas and to create a market for home industry[2] had equally little to do with the establishment of the West India Company, which was taken in hand immediately after the expiry of the Truce. This Company was, it is true, heir to the New Netherland Company, which during the Truce had made a modest beginning with the fur trade on the Hudson River in North America. The Wild Coast, as Guiana was called, also lay in the new Company's territory, and repeated attempts had already been made, and were again made under its auspices, to colonise there, now on one now on another of the great rivers which

---

[1] See map at end.
[2] See *The Revolt of the Netherlands*, pp. 253/4.

traversed the tropical jungle, but for the most part these were short-lived enterprises. As we shall see, the conquest of Brazil was soon to engage a large share of the Company's energies; that, however, was forced upon her by circumstances. Even trade was not the primary object.

The Company's foremost task was to carry on hostilities against Spain, with the aim of striking the enemy at the source of his wealth. In its inception, then, it differed wholly from the East India Company. Trading operations such as those in North America for fur, and navigation to Guinea and South America, in which the Zealanders were especially interested, were certainly not unimportant; besides the forts on the Wild Coast already mentioned, there were also several factories for gold and ivory in West Africa. In the main, however, the Company was not, as the East India Company had been, an amalgamation of flourishing concerns, but a new creation and one which was only with great trouble got under way. The organisation of predatory raids in Spanish America demanded great outlay, while profits were uncertain. The States-General had themselves to contribute money and warships, besides compelling the East India Company to contribute, and they had to extend the scope of the monopoly, before the capital was fully subscribed. They could therefore also claim more immediate control over the directorate than they possessed over that of the East India Company.

The Company that came into being in this way was certainly an impressive affair, the pride of the Contra-Remonstrant war-party. Of its capital of about seven millions, Their High Mightinesses held 500,000 guilders; Amsterdam subscribed nearly half the remainder and Zealand a considerable share (1,380,000 guilders), while—as was not the case with the East India Company—a 'Chamber' was also established in Groningen and Friesland. The Company certainly did not answer badly to its immediate purpose. Joannes de Laet, of Leiden (originally from Antwerp), a Director, begins his historical account in 1644 on a note of triumph:

With scant power and at small burden to the community, by means of the contributions of a small number of the inhabitants of this State, the operations of the Company have been carried out so successfully that the pride of Spain has not been able to withstand them, and it has plainly appeared

therefrom in what wise this mighty sovereign may be damaged through his
own resources, and the American treasures with which he has these many
years plagued and kept in lasting unrest the whole of Christendom, be
snatched from him or rendered useless.

And he supports this view with a survey of the Spanish ships
taken or destroyed each year by the Company, amounting by
1636, large and small, to 547. Piet Hein's capture of the Plate
Fleet in 1628 was naturally a significant item in this tale: the
booty was estimated at 15 millions and the Company paid out
50 per cent. in one dividend to its fortunate shareholders. But
what came off once never occurred again, and as time went on
the struggle for Brazil in particular swallowed up more money
than the Directors had at their disposal.

It was with the backing of the millions brought in by Piet
Hein—which, as we have seen, had already contributed to the
siege of 's Hertogenbosch—that the Brazilian adventure was
embarked upon. After a short-lived occupation of Bahia, the
capital itself, an attack was launched early in 1630 on Olinda,
the capital of the province of Pernambuco. The fact that here in
America, too, it was a Portuguese possession that had to bear
the brunt of the attack was due to the strategic advantages
offered by Brazil's position on the jutting-out north-east corner
of South America, as well as to the attraction of the country's
sugar and mahogany supplies. The fleet under Hendrik Lonck
numbered no less than 35 large and 30 small vessels with 3,780
sailors and 3,500 soldiers on board, a much more numerous
force than Van Diemen had disposed of for his expeditions
against Ceylon or Malacca.

The Dutch succeeded in taking Olinda, but the position into
which they wedged themselves there remained for years
dangerous to a degree. The Portuguese population of Olinda,
estimated at two to three thousand, fled inland. The governor
(who bore the famous name of Albuquerque) maintained himself
in a fortified camp a little way off. The conquerors could do
nothing with the town and destroyed it, confining themselves to
the barren spit of land, the Recife, which had served the town
for harbour. Soon, with the aid of the fleet, which had first been
called upon to defend the approach to the scene of operations
in a great naval battle, they undertook successive expeditions,
now towards the North, now towards the South, and so got a

footing at other points on the coast. But it was a long time before they could make their power felt in the interior, that is to say, before they got any grip on the production of sugar and mahogany. Not until 1635 did they manage to capture the fortified camp behind the Recife. Shortly before this, when the port of Parahyba had fallen into their hands, they had issued a proclamation promising civil equality and freedom of religious observance to Portuguese who would submit to the Company's authority. This was not without result. From Porto Calvo in the South to, ultimately, beyond the corner of Cape St. Roque, the Company got effective possession of a slice of that vast country —a slice nearly twice as big as the whole Dutch linguistic area at home—and it was now at length possible, after six years of unproductive struggle, to make the new colony pay. It was high time. The Company was already millions in debt.

To inaugurate this new period the Directors ('the Lords Nineteen') once more felt in their pockets and in 1636 sent out as governor a man of high rank, no less a person than a nephew of the Stadholder, Count John Maurice of Nassau, then thirty-two years of age. It is a striking fact that the West India Company was much less fortunate than the East India Company in the quality of its higher personnel on the spot. No man had risen in the government of New Holland (as Company's Brazil was now called) who appeared equal to the situation, no Coen or Van Diemen. In New Netherland, as we shall see presently, the case was no better. The explanation must, in my view, be sought in the different system pursued by the West India Company. While in the East Indies great responsibility was laid on individual servants, in whom functions of trade, government and war were intermingled, the government of the territory conquered in Brazil had been entrusted to a Political Council sent out fresh from Holland, for which the officers—who were nothing, nor could ever be anything, but that—were never inclined to feel much respect. The chief among these officers were foreigners, the Pole Artichofsky and the German von Schkoppe. The Council itself, in which no member rose above the others, was suspicious of the military commanders, and, following a home custom which did not work so badly there, often sent deputies along with them into the field. One attempt had already been made to resolve this confusion and disharmony

by means of an extraordinary mission of two Directors, Van
Ceulen and Gysselingh, under whom the authority of the
Council did indeed increase. These two gentlemen, with a
third, now accompanied John Maurice on his journey.

For nearly eight years the Count directed the government of
New Holland and he undoubtedly showed great ability. But he
was also very fortunate indeed in the moment of his arrival, just
when the work of construction could begin. Not that there was
no further fighting to be done. The first task before John
Maurice was the suppression of the hideous ravages with which
bands of Portuguese and Indians visited the plantations of
Portuguese who had submitted to Dutch rule; and with that in
view the southern frontier especially needed strengthening.
The Directors had hoped that the evil could be attacked at the
root by the destruction of Portuguese power throughout Brazil,
but an expedition which the Count led against Bahia in 1638
resulted in a reverse, although it is true that he brought further
wide areas under the Company's authority, particularly along
the north coast. Moreover, in order to meet the demand for
negro labour in the plantations, St. George d'Elmina, centre of
the Portuguese slave trade on the Gold Coast opposite, was
captured by an expedition from the Recife, and later, after the
conclusion of the armistice with newly independent Portugal,
but before its taking effect abroad, St. Paul de Loanda was
added with the same object in view.

What were now the possibilities for construction in this
New Holland? The Portuguese plantation-colony—Portuguese
owners, working with Indians and negro labourers—was not
swept away; on the contrary, the conquerors did what they
could to restore it. The zealous priesthood had already partly
Christianised the Indian population, at the same time causing
it to adopt the Portuguese language. Was there room for a
veritable Dutch community in addition?

There were indeed some Dutchmen, mostly come to the
colony as officials, who applied themselves to sugar cultivation,
but they found the Portuguese owners of sugar-mills in possession. If only these had been exterminated at the conquest! sighs
an eye-witness, at the same time considering that this would
have been unchristian. If, at least, their right over the surrounding country had been taken away, or if the free men had been

helped to acquire land or slaves! The best chance for Dutch settlement outside the coast towns lay in the Northern provinces, where Reformed missionaries were already beginning to convert the Indian tribes hostile to the Portuguese. But of any regular emigration of Dutchmen to Brazil there was no question.

Later historians have too frequently allowed their attention to be monopolised by the capital, as it was developing under John Maurice. The narrow Recife itself was no longer sufficient. On the island behind it arose Mauritsstad (Mauricia). Here was crowded together a preponderantly Dutch world of officials, soldiers, sailors, and merchants; here, too, came artisans and small business men from the mother-country to seek their fortunes. The Company always hoped that soldiers whose service had expired would settle in the country. But the soldiers died like flies in the hot climate and the bad living conditions; the continual despatch of fresh troops augmented the Company's expenses; and those who survived were eager to go back to Europe. Thus the Portuguese element maintained itself even in the town, especially in business, and the Portuguese Jews who flocked there, attracted by Dutch toleration, also played an important rôle. There was little chance that this Portuguese society would condescend to learn the newcomers' language for official or legal matters. The reverse was the case. Dutch life and language still lacked a firm foothold in Brazil; the basis of it all was the mother country's naval power.

John Maurice realised quite well that the goodwill of the submissive Portuguese was indispensable. When in 1638 he urged the liberation of private trade—a concession to which, after heated discussions both in the privacy of the committees and in public, the Company agreed, although for a long time not unconditionally—it was partly with a view to encouraging immigration, but not less in order to remove one of the grievances of the Portuguese population. One great obstacle to good relations with the former inhabitants was religion. The Reformed ministers at Mauricia and at Parahyba were not content with ordering the lives of their fellow-countrymen and with keeping their national sentiment up to the mark—a sufficiently difficult task in that cosmopolitan and heterogeneous society! They declaimed, just as at home, against the popish wickedness of the original population. The current policy of toleration towards

Catholics and Jews was a thorn in their flesh. The West India Company was the creation of Contra-Remonstrantism. It was indeed an ironical dispensation that this organisation in its principal possession should have to bear with popery; and it did not always do so with a good grace. Strong measures were sometimes taken against monks suspected of intrigue with Bahia. Apart from that, there is no evidence that the Political Council was any more disposed to allow the ministers to lay down the law than were the regents in the mother country, but the constant urgings of the consistory naturally did not sweeten the relations between Dutch and Portuguese. For example, in the benches of magistrates, established on the Dutch model, the two nations met, but co-operation left much to wish for in cordiality. All things considered, it remains a question whether the Company's occupation could ever have led to anything other than the situation which actually came into being: the domination of a Catholic and Portuguese population by foreign Protestant newcomers.

The administration of Count John Maurice gained lustre from his princely establishment. He brought intellectuals and artists with him from Holland. His Court physician Willem Piso of Leiden and the German astronomer Marcgraf studied tropical diseases and vegetation; De Laet, whom I mentioned above, later published their work in a celebrated book *Historia Naturalis Brasiliae*. Frans Post painted the Brazilian landscape for the Count, and Pieter Post (who was later to build for him the Mauritshuis at The Hague, where a few of Frans' pictures are still to be seen) built his palace of Vrijburg, whose gardens were as much admired as the house itself.

But behind all this splendour the settlers never felt certain of the future from one day to another. The peace with Portugal in 1642 was no more welcome to the West than to the East India Company. But now at least the Nineteen hoped to be able to economise on the garrisons. The men on the spot, however, knew only too well that strong garrisons were more necessary than ever to hold down the Portuguese subjects, animated as they were by the recovery of their mother country's independence. The wealth of the sugar-plantations, the trade in dye-wood, all this had not freed the Company from its burden of debt. This financial stress, which compelled the Directors to cut down all expenses of their officials, unsettled the already precarious situation. Much as they appreciated his success, the Directors found John Maurice expensive. In 1644 he was honourably recalled, and the government again put into commission.

If John Maurice had been fortunate in the moment of his arrival, he was even more so in the moment of his departure. In 1645 there broke out a revolt against the heretical usurpers, secretly supported by the Viceroy at Bahia and led by a mulatto, Vieira, who is still to Brazilians a great patriotic figure, the hero of a war of liberation. The whole interior once more lapsed into indescribable confusion. When the Dutch army, after fierce and courageously renewed assaults, had to retreat from the rebel headquarters, even Mauricia lay in such imminent danger that the government evacuated this new seat, demolished Vrijburg and its beautiful gardens, and withdrew with everything on to the Recife. The fleet under Lichthart was still able, as ever, to repulse any attack by sea from the now overtly hostile Portuguese of Bahia. Communication with the mother country remained open, and there the States-General came to the assistance of the bankrupt Company to save a possession in which national prestige was so closely involved. A relieving fleet was sent out; it found the besieged (for that was the position) half-starved on the Recife. A Director and member of the States-General for Groningen, Walter van Schoonenborch, had sailed with it and now took charge of affairs in their desperate state (June 1646). It appeared impossible to do more than hold what remained. The Portuguese now penetrated even into the Northern provinces, where the Indians had hitherto been on the Dutch side, and a second relief fleet, sent out in December 1647 under Witte de With, found the Recife still more closely besieged and as hungry as before.

The costs of this second expedition were to a large extent met from a contribution that the East India Company was obliged to make on the occasion of the second renewal of its charter. The more fortunate Company might congratulate itself on having got out of the business for a million and a half. A warm pen-and-ink war had been waged, in which old Usselinx as well as John Maurice had argued, though in entirely different ways, that Brazil could only be retained, or rather recovered, by a

fusion of the two Companies. Bitter attacks were launched—
especially in the famous pamphlet *The Brazilian Money-Bag*—
against the short-sightedness and covetousness of the Directors,
to which the disasters of the West India Company were
attributed. Others in reply attempted to rally support for the
hard-pressed Company by recalling that its load of debt had
been accumulated in the struggle against the national enemy.
It would have been an unfortunate decision for the future
development of Dutch potentialities if the live and healthy
body of the selfish but successful East India Company had been
shackled to the rotting corpse of Dutch dominion in Brazil.

At a superficial glance one would say that the situation in
Brazil was a return to that of 1630, and why should not the West
India Company succeed in the reconquest of what it had
previously conquered in that and the following years? But
the peace of Münster, which put an end to privateering at
the expense of Spain, robbed the Company of all hope of
permanently reviving its finances. Moreover, adversity had
produced wrangling not only in Holland, but on the Recife
itself. Some of the citizens

railed, as folk without brains, against the High Councils with all filthiness,
intolerable reproaches, slanderous contempt and a deal of collected false-
hoods.

In contrast to this, the rising which now had to be faced in
Brazil was permeated by a national passion and a hatred of the
Dutchman such as had been unthinkable before Portugal's
separation from Spain. The next period, which would see the
East India Company dealing still further destruction to
Portuguese power in the East Indies, was also to witness the
final collapse of the Dutch position in Brazil.

ii. Colonisation in New Netherland[1]

'NEGLECTED BRAZIL!' wrote Onno Zwier van Haren more than
a century later, with melancholy reflections on what might have
been. These possibilities were, it seems to me, altogether
chimerical. But look at New Netherland—what was neglected
there does rightly call for melancholy.

[1] See map at end.

In 1609 Henry Hudson, an Englishman, but sent out by the Amsterdam Chamber of the East India Company to search for a North-West passage to India, discovered the river which has since borne his name. His first belief was that its broad mouth was the entrance to a sea-passage that would speedily bring him into the Pacific; no one suspected how wide the American continent really was. When the through-route failed to materialise, the East India Company lost all interest, but a number of Amsterdam merchants, attracted by the reports of the journey, began to voyage there for furs. A New Netherland Company was founded. From 1613 there appeared blockhouses under the Dutch flag, one on the island of Manhattan, at the mouth of the Hudson, and another, Oranje, higher up where now stands Albany. When everything was transferred to the West India Company (its Amsterdam Chamber assuming particular responsibility for the acquisition), the settlement consisted only of trading-company officials, whose business was to buy from the Indian tribes furs, especially beaver and otter pelts, and collect them for transhipment. The thing now was to attempt real colonisation.

For the English were already only too active on the East coast of North America. In 1606 King James had chartered the whole territory between the French settlements in Canada and the Spanish in Florida (to quote the charter: between the 24th and the 45th parallels and from ocean to ocean—from Atlantic to Pacific!) to two English companies, the London and the Plymouth. We have seen how the Dutch owed their success in the Indian world to force of arms, imposed upon them by their war with Spain. England on the other hand, being at peace with Spain, was free to give more undivided attention to the colonisation of this hitherto unclaimed and therefore eminently attractive coast, and colonisation, not trade or piracy, was the object for which the two English companies were established amid lively public interest. There followed settlements in Virginia on Chesapeake Bay and in what was soon to be called New England, much further north. In 1622 the population of the first was estimated at four thousand. In New England, where the first attempt had come to nothing, there landed in 1620, in the bay behind Cape Cod, a hundred or so English Puritans, who had previously settled at Leiden to escape episcopal persecution. From 1629 onwards there came over directly from England whole fleets of like-minded groups intent on living according to their beliefs in this new world. This stream flowed rapidly southwards and westwards in America, impinging upon the Dutch sphere of influence which began at the Fresh River (the Connecticut).

The English government had repeatedly protested against the incursion of Dutchmen into what it considered its territory. But the reply from the Dutch side had been—and the argument was one that Queen Elizabeth had been wont to use against the Spaniards—that a proclamation of sovereignty is void unless followed by actual possession. The English had never established control over the stretch of country between the settlement in Virginia and that in New England: the discovery of 1609 on behalf of the East India Company and that Company's entry into possession of New Netherland in the name of the States thus gave the Dutch an unimpeachable title. Under James I and Charles I the English government was, as we have seen, less inclined to take vigorous action than to make lofty pretensions; but although it did not follow up its protests by deeds, it was careful both then and later to avoid recognising the legitimacy of the Dutch position on the East coast of North America. For this reason, prudence dictated an influx of settlers as rapidly as possible to consolidate that position. And here the West India Company fell grievously short of the mark. When every year counted in the race with Virginia and especially with New England, we see the colonisation of New Netherland conducted with exasperating supineness and incompetence, and even if it now and again received a helpful stimulus, promptly exposed again to wanton reverses.

Not that the Company—or rather the Amsterdam Chamber —did not go beyond the irregular settlement of fur-hunters; it soon did try to create a real colony, capable of providing for its own needs by means of agriculture. The first small group of families (Walloon emigrants) was taken out in 1623; a second followed in 1625, accompanied this time by "the engineer and surveyor" Crijn Fredericxsz, who was instructed to build a large fort, Amsterdam, on Manhattan, and to fence off the estates on which certain colonists were established as tenants of the Company. Everything was arranged beforehand down to the smallest detail, the distribution of the land and the cattle taken out from Holland, the judicial system, the powers and composition of the Council. This Council, purely official, under a Director—Willem Verhulst was the first Director, soon succeeded by Pierre Minuit—was tied down by a peremptory set of instructions. The Chamber intended to remain master of its colony.

Soon the Chamber attempted colonisation on a larger scale, but along lines demanding as little activity on its own part as possible. In this it was following the example of the Zealand Chamber, which in 1627 had come to an agreement with one of its Directors, the Flushing merchant Van Pere, by which he was to send sixty men to the Wild Coast (Guiana) to establish a settlement. That was the origin of a colony, named Berbice (after the river on which it lay, while some distance inland was established Fort Nassau), which, unlike so many others before and since in that region, did not afterwards go under. The Wild Coast had always stirred Usselinx's imagination more than North America, but he had never realised that the tropical climate would make slave-labour indispensable. The stringent limitation of the colonists' freedom of trade, both here and in New Netherland, also conflicted with his views; only the emphasis laid on the national and Reformed character of the settlement accorded with his ideas. Van Pere became 'patron' of Berbice, which he financed from Flushing. The development of this colony really begins only later and we shall not pursue it here.

In 1629, then, the Amsterdam Chamber made a general offer of as much land as they could cultivate to settlers who went out at their own expense, but held out especially attractive conditions to any shareholders of the Company who were willing as patrons' to send each fifty souls to New Netherland. The Company reserved the island of Manhattan for its own tenants, but beyond that gave a choice of extensive territories along the rivers or on the coast, where patrons while owing allegiance to the Company should govern their own farmers. Nothing is more curious than this introduction of feudal relationships and even forms amid the virgin forests of America, and that from a country where feudalism had long since disappeared. The offer of 1629 did not remain wholly without result. A number of independent colonists came out and some enterprising share-holders, among whom were several Directors, took land on 'perpetual lease' as patrons. It was not so easy, however, to find colonists for these 'patronages'. The position was not very attractive, especially as little attention was paid to the regulation giving tenants a right of appeal to the Company against their patrons. Relations between patrons and Company, too, soon became strained. Patrons and free colonists alike set their face against the many restrictions to which they were subject: the prohibition of trade in furs and the obligation to despatch all wares through the Company's staple at Manhattan and to use the Company's ships for all export and import. The upshot was that the big men had engrossed the best land without seriously clearing it, and would-be settlers at home were scared off by rumours of dissension and jobbery.

Such was the situation under Wouter van Twiller, whom the Company had sent out from its Amsterdam office in 1632 as Director-General in succession to Pierre Minuit, who had fallen into disgrace. For five or six years the new man set his subordinates an example of corruption, mainly at the expense of his masters, on whose fur-trade monopoly he and the colonists made large inroads. Since at the same time agriculture languished, and colonists who had taken up land from the Company began to return home, the Lords Nineteen came more and more to look upon that very monopoly as the sole source of profit. When the Fiscal of the colony, Lubbert van Dinclagen, an honourable man, was manoeuvred out by Van Twiller and came home to expose the Director's practices, a certain Willem Kieft —as much a newcomer to the colony as Van Twiller had been on his appointment—was sent out as Director-General to put affairs in order.

To the Directors that meant above all else the strict enforcement of their fur-trade monopoly. But Van Dinclagen's reports had drawn the States-General's attention to the broader aspects of the mismanagement of New Netherland, to the tardiness of emigration and to the danger threatening from the much more rapid growth of the adjacent English colonies, and so the recalcitrant Directors were now compelled by the country's sovereign assembly to embark upon a new colonial policy. The change involved nothing less than the sacrifice of the monopoly system; it had, indeed, come to a choice between that and utter ruin. In 1638, therefore, the Company issued a declaration offering much better terms, designed especially to attract independent emigrants. The patronage system was not abolished; on the contrary, it was now possible for non-shareholders to take up patronages, but the exorbitant powers which patrons had been able to exercise under the regulations of 1629 were cut down for the future.

There was only one man who had made a success of patronage under those regulations: Kiliaen van Rensselaer, a merchant of Amsterdam, who had become patron of a stretch of land—one and three-quarter million acres in extent!—higher up on the Hudson, near Fort Oranje. Van Twiller was a nephew of his and looked after his uncle's interests. From Amsterdam (for he died in 1646 without having set foot in America) Van Rensselaer administered his vast estate, Rensselaerswijk, in masterly fashion. Not only did he fight for its interests on the stormy battlefield of the Amsterdam Chamber; not only did he bestow the greatest care on the selection of men and material for its exploitation; in spite of the scant and uncertain communications he controlled the administration of that little community, which, lost in the wilderness, formed a colony within the colony— controlled it down to the minutest details (lay-out of farms, clearing of land, purchase of cattle). Van Rensselaer had experience of land clearance in the Gooi and the Veluwe, whence came many of the colonists he kept sending out year after year. He made his bailiff wear a plumed hat and a silver sword. He had a fort, Rensselaerstein, built on an island in the Hudson, and exacted a salute for it from passing vessels. That Van Rensselaer was earnest in his devotion to the ideal of colonial settlement is certain. In 1635 he wrote to Van Twiller:

> We seek to populate the country and at the same time to propagate the doctrine of Holy Writ by settling a multitude of people there; they (*the Directors*), on the contrary, want with but few people only to gorge themselves with the profits of the pelts.

But the excellent patron Van Rensselaer was could see good only in the patronage system and seems to have regarded the free colonists with such mistrust that in 1638, in his capacity of Director, he advised against the granting of free privileges to all and sundry. Nevertheless, this came to pass, and now for the first time the population of New Netherland, hitherto made up of Company officials and patrons' agents, together with the essentially servile multitude of patrons' and Company's tenants, began to include a considerable number of substantial and enterprising immigrants. Besides farmers, there came traders, who found in New Amsterdam, as the growing town by Fort Amsterdam on Manhattan was called, a port excellently located for coastal trade to Virginia and New England as well as for navigation to the Company's other possessions, Brazil and Curaçao (captured in 1633).

The drawback was that it was left to the reluctant Company to carry out the policy imposed upon it. There was little likelihood that the Nineteen, or the Chamber of Amsterdam, would put themselves to real trouble to find potential settlers.

The Dutch colonisation could therefore offer no barrier to the flood-tide of the English. It remained confined almost exclusively to the banks of the Hudson. In the early days of his Director-Generalship Van Twiller had established a small fort, called the Goede Hoop, on the Versche Rivier (the Connecticut). Soon English settlements had come into existence there and it was now coming to be surrounded by a completely English region, where nobody dreamt of recognising the West India Company's claims. Along the coast of Long Island Sound the English were pushing their townships even further westward; they were even settling on the island itself. Towards these intrusions the representatives of the impecunious Company, which had its hands full with the war in Brazil, were compelled to adopt a cautious and patient attitude. Van Twiller was bold enough to pounce on a party of Englishmen who had nestled on the other side of New Amsterdam, at the mouth of the South River (Delaware); his successor Kieft had to look on passively when the same spot was occupied by Swedes under the leadership of Minuit, the former Director-General of New Netherland, and with the secret support of a Director at Amsterdam, Samuel Blommaert! Kieft himself forced the settlement of Greenwich, which had brought the English from New England to within thirty miles of New Amsterdam, to acknowledge the Company's authority. Incidentally, this was far from being the only English settlement by which the Dutch composition of the population owing allegiance to the Company was diluted:

Englishmen were continually coming to live on the free Hudson, especially such as had been exiled on religious grounds from the far from tolerant New England settlements. For the most part the Dutch officials let it go at remonstrances and warnings. What a contrast with Coen's conduct in the East Indies! David Pietersz. de Vries, son of a burgomaster of Hoorn, shipper and contractor, who at one time and another in his chequered life was through patronages deeply involved in New Netherland affairs, observed it with vexation:

> I told him (*i.e. Van Twiller; thus De Vries in his "Short History"*) that if the English did us some outrage in the East Indies, a counter-blow would soon follow; that otherwise you cannot preserve anything from that people, for so haughty are they by nature that they think everything is theirs by right.

The real Coen spirit! But after all things were different in America. It is no use blaming Van Twiller and Kieft for their timidity towards the English. They yielded nothing to each other in unfitness for their task. Where the first was an easy-going toper, the second was a martinet and at the same time a rabid little despot. Loose living, corruption, narrow-minded greed of power were, indeed, far from unknown among the officials of the East India Company: the conditions were themselves a temptation to these failings. But they seldom penetrated to the higher ranks, let alone to Batavia; only men with real ability to wield authority were likely to rise to the top. How different in "the West"!

> I told the secretary (*writes De Vries*) that I was surprised the West India Company sent such fools to the country, who knew nothing but how to drink themselves drunk. In the East Indies they would not be allowed to serve even as Assistants. (I said) that such doings would bring the Company to ruin. For in the East Indies they appoint no one Commander unless he has done long subordinate service, so that they can see that he is capable, first from Assistant to Under-Trader, then Trader, and afterwards Chief Trader, and they promote them further according to merit. But the West India Company sends out straight to posts of great authority over people men who have seen no command in their lives. And therefore it will end in ruin.

It will be recollected with what profound conviction Coen, in a country alas! unsuited to the carrying out of his ideas, used to urge on his principals the cause of the free citizens. Kieft systematically treated his colonists with the most offensive hauteur. A right to some say in the administration was conceded with a sour face, afterwards to be whittled down again. In a

province such as New Netherland was now on the way to
becoming, this could not fail to develop into a burning question.
Usselinx had always maintained that 'free Netherlanders'
would have to be granted self-government. The example of the
English colonies, where, in Virginia as well as in New England,
representative assemblies assisted the governors, made doubly
impossible the maintenance of the absolutist Company regime.
In the proclamation of 1638, as one more means of attracting
colonists, the Directors themselves had promised that as soon
as villages and townships arose, they should be given their own
government, to be nominated by the Director. On Kieft's
assuming power, however, the position was still that the
Director in Council—and Kieft put on his Council one official,
with one vote, while he himself had two!—was supreme.

There now arose a question of vital importance to the colony,
which compelled Kieft to consult the independent colonists:
this was the question of relations with the Indian tribes. So far
these had in the main been friendly. But now that the white
intruders were devoting themselves more and more to agriculture, occasions for collision became much more frequent.
Kieft wanted punitive expeditions. Before undertaking any, he
called together the heads of families, who elected a Committee
of Twelve to assist him with advice. De Vries, whom we have
already met, was one of them; he was now a joint patron with
others on Staten Island and higher up, where he had named the
country Vriesendael. But it was contrary to the express and
urgent advice not only of the citizens but of his fellow-councillor
that Kieft in 1643 had his troops attack and massacre the wholly
unsuspecting Algonquins, who had sought refuge with the
Hollanders from their hereditary enemies the Mohawks. This
barbarity, which De Vries and others relate with deep-felt
indignation, led to fearful vengeance. An Indian war began, in
which the Director was so little capable of protecting the citizens
and their estates, that in their despair they thought of calling
on the neighbouring English colonies for help. In 1645, following an Indian defeat, the pipe of peace could be smoked, but the
development of the colony had suffered a bad check. Vriesendael, like many highly promising estates, was reduced to ashes;
De Vries returned home, an embittered and dispirited man.
The number of colonists was said to have fallen from 3,000 to

1,000. There was universal anger against Kieft, who had wantonly provoked the disaster, and who now arbitrarily, and without heeding the protests of the citizens' representatives (now a Committee of Eight), introduced taxation to cover the costs, especially of the English troops who had been taken into service.

This is what we have, in the sorrow of our hearts, to complain of (*thus wrote the Committee of Eight to the Amsterdam Chamber, 28 October 1644*); that one man, who has been sent out, sworn and instructed by his lords and masters to whom he is responsible, should dispose here of our lives and properties at his will and pleasure, in a manner so arbitrary that a king would not dare to do the like. . . . It will be impossible ever to settle this country until a different system be introduced here, and a new Governor sent out with more people, who will settle in suitable places, one near the other, in the form of villages or hamlets, and elect from among themselves a Bailiff or Schout (*Sheriff*) and Schepens (*Aldermen*), who will be empowered to send their deputies and give their votes on public affairs with the Director and Council; so that the entire country may not again hereafter, at the whim of one man, be reduced to similar danger.

To retain Kieft had become impossible. His successor was appointed as early as 1645, but such was the slowness of communications between mother country and colony that he did not land on Manhattan until 1647. Kieft had employed the interval in violent disputes—especially with the minister, Bogardus—and it is not to be wondered at that his successor's arrival evoked demonstrations of riotous joy.

Pieter Stuyvesant was a retired soldier, who had served the Company as governor of Curaçao and had lost a leg there in battle against the Spaniards. He was an active and honest man, but the citizens who hoped to see him introduce new principles of popular participation in the government were making a grievous mistake. True, Stuyvesant brought with him his own solution of the constitutional problem, but it was an extremely conservative one. Out of a 'double number' of eighteen men, for once nominated by the citizens, he appointed nine. These 'Nine Men' became a permanent body; each year six had to retire, at the same time proposing a 'double number' of twelve to the Director and his Council, from whom these would appoint their six successors. The Nine Men, thus elected with a minimum of popular participation, were to assist the Director with their advice—when he asked them for it. But what was even worse, Stuyvesant had seized the very first opportunity to demonstrate in what spirit he proposed to uphold the Directoral authority. The complaints brought against his predecessor by the Committee of Eight he took to heart as if they had been directed against himself, and he fell upon them, and in particular upon their leaders Cornelis Melyn, a native of Antwerp, who was a patron on Staten Island, and Jochem Kuyter, a German, with unexpected severity. The words 'high government', 'subjects', 'high treason', and the like, were constantly on his lips. The two burghers were brought to trial, and for writing the letter of 28 October 1644 ('a false and libellous letter') as well as for uttering menaces against Kieft,

at the time when he was lawful governor and leader—all matters of dangerous consequence, tending to rebellion, defamation of justice and high authority,

in short, for *lèse-majesté*, the Council sentenced them to fine and exile. The ship which bore Kieft home (with his ill-gotten fortune, so his enemies said) had Melyn and Kuyter also on board. It was wrecked on the coast of England and Kieft was drowned, but his accusers were saved, and soon they were laying their complaints and charges, not before the Company, but before the States-General. There they found ready hearing, and in 1649 Melyn reappeared at New Amsterdam bearing not only a safe-conduct from Their High Mightinesses, but a summons to the Director to repair to The Hague to answer for himself. Melyn came just in time to support the Nine Men in the struggle which they were already waging against the fire-eater of Fort Amsterdam. But that struggle, as it was finally to be fought out in The Hague and Amsterdam, really belongs to the succeeding period.

The doom of New Netherland was not so much an accomplished fact at the time of the Peace of Münster as was that of Brazilian New Holland, but we have seen enough to understand how perilous was the position into which the Company's neglect of emigration had brought the colony. It cannot be pleaded in extenuation that no one in Holland realised the importance of emigration. I need only mention Coen and Usselinx. A man like Van Rensselaer was certainly a disciple of the latter. And the States themselves, though in drawing up the conditions for the Company they neglected Usselinx's advice, were far from intending to hinder the colonisation of New Netherland. On the contrary, we have seen how more than once they intervened to coerce the Directors into measures to promote it. But although the West India Company was less favourably placed than the East India Company to ignore hints from the country's high assembly, yet it retained the initiative, and the misfortune was that the States entrusted the execution of that great undertaking, the settlement in America, to a body which was wholly engrossed, and soon ruined, by the struggle with Spain, first by privateering, later by the futile establishment in Brazil; a body, moreover, whose directors could not but regard all problems primarily from the standpoint of profit, and immediate profit, for the shareholders.

The fact of the matter is that the States themselves were equally engrossed by that struggle and, even apart from that, that their constitution rendered them exceedingly unsuited to direct and finance overseas enterprise themselves. All things considered, the monopoly system with which they made two such formidable fighting-machines of the two great Companies was by no means an unhappy find. De Laet was not wide of the mark when he asserted that the State, using its own weapons, would not have found it easy to inflict as much damage on the Spaniard. Damage to the Spaniard—that was the justification for the monopoly, and only we who know the future are able to estimate how weighty an interest was sacrificed when the development of New Netherland was allowed to suffer under the immediate pressure of circumstances.

IV

Cultural Life

LONG-CONTINUED political disruption had brought into existence in the Dutch linguistic area two foci whence radiated the impulses of intellectual life, even though the rays still crossed one another. In the South, dominated by Church and monarchy, deprived of all outlet for political self-expression, and held in the tenacious grip of economic stagnation, there reigned the great international culture of Counter-Reformation and Baroque; older Netherland traditions were assimilated into this, but caused no more than ripples on the broad main stream. In the North also this potent influence was at work, but there it had to compete with the infinitely varied manifestations of more indigenous processes of thought and expression.

A. RELIGION AND SCIENCE

THIS essential characteristic of the North's culture resulted from the break-up of medieval Catholic unity. To put the fact in this negative way is what the realities of the case require. How often do we not see the civilisation of what is called in the North the 'golden century' represented as a Calvinist civilisation in contrast with the Catholic civilisation of the South! Flemings in particular are prone to do this, and yet how far removed from the actual facts is this interpretation. A culture so abundant, so free, so receptive as that which was vouchsafed to Holland at this time could not have found in Calvinism either its sole inspiration or even its standard of values.

Calvinism undoubtedly ranked among the principal cultural forces in the North. With its conception of a 'chosen people', of the Netherlands as a second Israel, whose history embodied the profoundest sense of the grace of God, it gave style to a larger body of opinion than that of its professed adherents. In literature this conception, together with other features of

Calvinism which touched the individual more deeply, was an inspiring factor. Yet the positive significance of Calvinism belonged primarily to the political and social spheres. In the realms of science and art the exclusiveness of its system, the singleness of its aim, could easily have a stifling effect. But in fact these branches of intellectual life—and this is what characterises the situation in the North—were far less completely dominated by the Reformed Church than they were in the South by restored Catholicism.

Even within the Reformed Church herself the Synod of Dort fell far short of establishing at one blow the desired orthodoxy. A doctrinal oath might now be demanded of ministers, professors, schoolmasters, but that did not put an end to the matter. Some subscribed to the oath under the reserve of an individual interpretation; others even declined to take it. An unceasing struggle went on, with synods and 'classes' needing to be constantly on their guard. For generations that irrepressible community kept bursting through the barriers designed to keep it in order. And the secular authorities usually protected the unruly; at Utrecht even a Remonstrant was admitted as professor in 1649, with the proviso that his appointment was not to prejudice the principle of excluding Remonstrants!

Barely half the population of the province of Holland belonged to the Church which at Dort had purged herself so very incompletely. Outside her ranks there stood a considerable body of Catholics and heterodox Protestants, Baptists or Remonstrants. Strikingly enough, each of these three religious attitudes found a spiritual leader to give it poetic realisation. If the passionate Revius, minister at Deventer and afterwards regent of the States Seminary at Leiden University, is the poet of militant Calvinism, the two other tendencies are represented no less purely by the gentle and peace-loving Camphuysen, ejected from his living in 1619 as a Remonstrant, but who in course of time found even Remonstrantism too narrow and wished to bear no other name than that of Christian; and by the tender, melodious Stalpert van der Wiele, who tranquilly laboured his life long at Delft as a Catholic priest.

It must not be thought, however, that the contribution of the Catholics to North Netherland civilisation was proportionate to their numbers. We have seen that these were still very considerable,[1] and that the Papal organisation under Sasbout Vosmeer and later under Rovenius had succeeded in arresting further decline. In some towns (Rotterdam, for example) the number of communicants even multiplied during the first half of the seventeenth century. This certainly does not mean that many of those who had already taken their place in the Reformed Church were reclaimed, but that out of the multitude which had remained without firm attachment to any creed since the collapse of the established organisation a generation before, many now streamed back. Yet the Catholics, while enjoying considerable freedom in comparison with other minority groups in Europe, were never allowed to forget that they existed only on sufferance. They were compelled to purchase their opportunity for religious worship in degrading negotiations with sheriffs and bailiffs. They were more and more rigorously excluded from municipal and national government. With some stifling of conscientious scruples they could study, they could practise as advocates, but neither the professor's chair nor the judge's seat was for them attainable. If Catholic thought shone with brilliant lustre, so that Protestants were often painfully conscious of their own disunity and were never able to drop their defensive attitude, that was the work of the great South European civilisation, in which North Netherland Catholics took little active part. In the realm of art we shall see how deeply what was an essentially Catholic style would impress even the North Netherland Protestants, but they admired it principally in Flemish and Brabant exponents. The North Netherland Catholics came to be a community of the quiet and obscure.

This in spite of Vondel, who went over to Catholicism in 1641 (when he was 54) and whose voice certainly did not decline in power in this new service; in spite also of the fact that Tesselschade and Anna Roemers went over practically at the same time, and that Grotius came so near doing so that it is a matter of dispute whether or no he had taken the final step before his death in 1645. These conversions of highly developed minds were purely personal. We may see in them proof of the power of attraction which reborn Catholicism could exercise over seekers after unity and authority, admirers of style and tradition. But these converts introduced no new tendency into

[1] See above, p. 63 ff.

North Netherland civilisation. They continued to be esteemed, though not without some friction, for what they had already achieved and for what, despite their straying, they still were. They laid no foundation for a Catholic poetry or a Catholic philosophy; on the contrary, as the generations succeeded each other, everything became more and more Protestant.

Catholic unity as against Protestant disunion—that was a contrast which the dispute between Remonstrants and Contra-Remonstrants illustrated painfully indeed. And yet all was not peace and concord in the Catholic camp. Jealousy was rife and found vent in interminable quarrels over competence between the secular priests and the regulars, notably the Jesuits. In the South the principal battle-ground was education, and in particular the Jesuits' efforts to gain control of Louvain was bitterly resented; in the less ordered conditions of the North, where bishops were no more and the Vicar Apostolic had to administer a large area from abroad or from a hiding-place, these differences had worse consequences.

Yet it was in the South that the situation was prepared in which the struggle over organisation was to become a struggle of principle, of dogma. The theological issue which had recently split the North Netherland Reformed Church was nothing new; the Catholic Church knew it of old and was wont to bear it. The Jesuits laid stress on freedom of will. Their emphasis on morals was bound up with it, even when that found expression in a mystic form, as in Father Hugo's fine book *Pia Desideria*, which appeared at Antwerp in 1624 and speedily acquired great influence, and not only in the Netherlands. Largely under Jesuit auspices, an extensive devotional literature sprang into existence. But more dogmatic natures, or those more intent on individual earnestness, often complained of the Jesuits' flexibility, their readiness to bear with human weakness and to win advantage for the Church by worldly concessions. It was opposition to their attitude which caused the Louvain professor Jansenius, at the close of his life Bishop of Ypres, to build up systematically with the aid of St. Augustine the doctrine of predestination. Jansenius—we met him before, polemising across the newly established frontier[1]—was a native of Leerdam in Holland and had been to school at Utrecht, but

[1] See above, pp. 94, 115.

before his appointment to the chair at Louvain he had passed some years in France and formed a close friendship with a French theologian. It was through Arnaud that his book, published after his death, became such a potent influence in French religious life; but it also made a deep impression at Louvain, whence Jansenism radiated over the Southern as well as over the Northern Netherlands. To Rovenius, as to Vosmeer before him, Louvain was a spiritual home; he was a friend of Jansenius and was imbued with his spirit. The Jesuits, too, with whom he had to wage what was sometimes a bitter struggle, relied on superiors in the South or themselves originated from there. In many respects, and especially with regard to the broader aspects of cultural history, North Netherland Catholicism seems like an appendage of the Catholicism of Flanders and Brabant.

The quarrel over Jansenism belongs to the ensuing period. In the years under review it was the Reformed Church which had to contend with the more vital break in the uniformity which was *their* ideal as well. The Protestant dissenters constituted a standing problem. The Baptists, by reason of a certain other-worldliness, and in particular because of their ideas on the duty of non-resistance, were indifferent to political life, and yet as the pioneers of the Reformation in the Netherlands they bore themselves a little more confidently towards the authorities than did the Catholics. The Remonstrants belonged, even after their overthrow, to the leading circles, where they formed an active oppositional element. Between these two groups there existed close relations, and both helped to nourish the peculiar dissenting movement of Collegiantism, which advocated free 'prophesying' and individual Bible exposition, and which produced, especially in the next generation, a number of remarkable personalities, remarkable chiefly for the adventurousness and unconcern with which they broke through all dogmatism.

The orthodox ministers, who regarded themselves as the watchmen on the turrets of Zion, might sound the alarm as zealously as ever against all such errancy and presumption; yet the regents, as we have seen, usually lent only half an ear and on occasion even cast down the prophets of the new Israel no less resolutely than did of old the monarchs who walked not in the paths of righteousness. The independence of the Holland regents with regard to the ministers was the greatest obstacle which the gradual Calvinisation of social and intellectual life had to overcome. Their opposition did not always proceed from deep-felt religious or philosophic conviction. It was before all else the instinctive reaction of secular rulers, thinking of their own authority, of the interests of commerce, of the privileges of their town. One result of the decentralisation of authority was that anyone threatened with persecution was likely to find shelter in one body or another, be it town, committee, or corporation. There was, indeed, much that was attractive in this state of affairs, for it was far removed from the arbitrariness of pure anarchy. Every resistance was founded upon a right. When Hooft is insulted by a nobleman, he reminds him

> that we live here in a free country, and that of justice.

The famous Netherlandish liberty was inseparable from the conception of law. In this respect (as I have already pointed out[1]) North and South remained one. Even Descartes, the Frenchman, who, devout Catholic but revolutionary philosopher, passed the best part of his life in Holland, praised next after the liberty, which men enjoyed more in that country than elsewhere, the order and security reigning there.

If one bears in mind this characteristic feature of Netherland society, does not the work which, of all those that flowed from Netherland pens during this period, obtained the greatest hold on world thought—Grotius' *De jure belli ac pacis*, written in exile (1625)—appear a typical product of the Netherland spirit? It is an attempt by a theologically and classically educated jurist to base upon law order and security in the community of states as well as in the national society in which he had grown up. In the rather naive rationalism, the belief in reason as the lord of life, is revealed the spiritual son of Erasmus. How, then, came this typical Dutchman to be so permanently at variance with his country? In another respect he was the reverse of typical, namely, in his desire to construct closed systems that had made him exalt the authority of the States of Holland against religious dogmatism carried to extremes. It was this that brought him into conflict with the particularism and individualism as they had developed in the North, and we have

---

[1] See above, p. 20.

already seen that it carried him, once abroad, further and further away from the attitude which prevailed in Holland, even to the threshold of Catholicism.

Descartes, who prized Netherland liberty, was himself, in the fortunes that attended his ideas, to experience that limitation of it at which I have just hinted, and which may be called its empirical character.

The great activity in the sphere of the natural sciences which was to be observed at the end of the sixteenth century[1] had not slackened—quite the reverse—but it was on the eve of discoveries which shook the very foundations of philosophic and religious thought and forth at reason was meeting with resistance. Protestantism had rooted itself as firmly as Catholicism in positive dogma, and both regarded the Aristotelian philosophy, blended into one with the scholastic system, as part of the eternal verities. Everything which could not be comprehended within its customary formulas and modes of argument was rejected. That system ruled at the Reformed universities in the Republic as much as at Louvain.

Not all scientific progress was restricted by it. Philology at least for the time being succeeded in reconciling itself very well with the reigning system. Philology was an indispensable auxiliary to theology, and the theological preoccupation of the universities, regarded as they were by their founders, the various provincial States, first and foremost as props to support the Reformation, explains the extraordinary vogue which the study of ancient languages continued to enjoy. The names of Daniel Heinsius and Salmasius, of Gerard Vossius and Caspar Barlaeus, were renowned throughout Europe. It is true that the two last, especially Barlaeus, were numbered amongst the Remonstrants and, finding their careers at Leiden cut off or hindered, were to add lustre to the Amsterdam 'Illustrious School'[2]; but these private opinions of theirs had little to do with their humanistic work. Vossius' international reputation as an authority on antiquity, and as an exponent of its literary laws, was unconnected with his ideas on predestination. Nor did Dutch scholarship confine itself to Latin and Greek. The Dutch universities were the nurseries *par excellence* in Western

[1] See *The Revolt of the Netherlands*, pp. 236–7, 268, 288.
[2] As mentioned already: see above, p. 76.

Europe of the study of Oriental languages, of Hebrew and Arabic. At Franeker there taught successively Drusius, Amama, who died young, and Cocceius. At Leiden there were Erpinius, also cut off in youth, and Jacobus Golius, whose brother Petrus, won over to Catholicism at Antwerp by their uncle Hemelarius and admitted a Carmelite, was also a great Arabic scholar and eventually obtained a chair at Rome. The new translation of the Bible finally resolved upon, as we have seen, by the Synod of Dort, could draw upon abundant skill and preparation. It is true, here too, that Drusius, who had long urged the great undertaking, fell, like Amama, under ministerial suspicion, and later it was to be seen even more clearly in the case of Cocceius that philology was fraught with theological dangers.

But it was the natural sciences that were driven into a conflict of principle with Aristotelian orthodoxy. In 1633 Galileo was compelled by the Inquisition at Rome to renounce his theory that the sun did not revolve about the earth, but the earth on its axis; and at the new university of Utrecht, Voetius, its principal professor of theology, rejected that theory no less decisively as contrary to the Scriptures and to reason. Harvey's discovery of the circulation of the blood, incompatible as it was with the ideas of Galen, the Aristotelian physician of antiquity, was refused admittance.

During his long career at Utrecht (he did not die until 1678, at the age of eight-seven), Voetius personified the ambition of Reformed theology to span the whole compass of life, spiritual, moral, social. A man of intense conviction and unshakable fixity of principle, of iron will and inexhaustible combativeness, he won a personal authority in the Reformed Church such as no man has exercised before or since. Under his influence the Puritan strain in Dutch Calvinism became stronger. In this connection the English example was important. Amesius, a professor at Franeker, was himself an Englishman. The Middelburg minister Willem Teellinck, whom I quoted before[1] and whose preaching and numerous writings wielded great influence, had been in England and was married to an English-woman; after his death in 1629 his work was carried on by his sons, one of whom was later to be a minister at Utrecht. Teellinck adopted the Contra-Remonstrant position uncondi-

[1] See p. 18.

tionally; yet in a certain sense he went right against the essential implication of the electionist doctrine.

He knew (*so wrote a follower afterwards*) that not only belief but also conduct must distinguish Christian from pagan.

At the same time, and although he believed that minute precepts of conduct were necessary to keep the world at a distance, there was a mystical strain in Teellinck; his pietism was akin to the Jesuitical mysticism of Father Hugo. In Voetius, undaunted scholastic that he was, insistence on the law came uppermost. Not that he was lacking in fire. Listen to him inveighing against those who were

weak-kneed and half-hearted, below water and above water, half this and half that, left and right, half fish half flesh, neither too loose nor too stiff, not too godless nor yet too godly, not too holy and not too profane, something for the flesh and something for the spirit, something for heaven and something for the earth, betwixt and between, half Christian half the world; a monstrous compound.

At Utrecht he lectured at great length on Sunday observance, on the unlawfulness of dancing, card-playing and gaming, of extravagant fashions in clothes and coiffure—all illustrated with a wealth of Biblical texts and quotations from the Fathers. But we have already seen him engaged in more important questions: the suppression of Catholic worship at 's Hertogenbosch and the dispute over the Fraternity in that town.[1] He also argued with the Utrecht magistracy on the lawfulness of banking (here he was defending the old Catholic thesis against usury); he attacked the use of the organ even to accompany psalm-singing by the congregation, and thus drew forth from his tent Huygens, a zealous Churchman but also a keen music-lover.

Such was the scene upon which in 1636 Descartes descended with his *Discours de la méthode* (that it was written, not in Latin, but in French, may be called an event in itself), in which he sought to liberate thought from all preconceived axioms and cramping terminologies. Among the Dutch intellectuals several were eager to accept and apply the new philosophy. But it did not pass without a struggle. There had already been one or two who had joined issue with traditional conceptions, even without the assistance of so developed a theory; in particular, Jan Baptist van Helmont (1579-1644), of Brussels, whose work was

[1] See above, pp. 92, 172.

to be of prime importance for the foundation of modern chemistry. He was a physician, and it was his medical theories especially which, on account of their deviation from the Galenian and Aristotelian system, caused him to get into trouble with the archiepiscopal law court of Mechlin. Van Helmont also understood the importance of writing in the vernacular, but the original version of his chief work only appeared long after his death, and in the North.

The situation there was certainly more propitious for the progress of scientific thought. But we must not imagine that the tyranny of tradition was essentially different there, nor that it surrendered without a struggle.

For example, Regius, professor of medicine at Utrecht, had been made to promise on his appointment that he would keep within the current theories in his lectures. It was only when lectures in natural science were also entrusted to him that he felt at liberty to broach the theory of the circulation of the blood, and even then he first consulted with Voetius on the possibility of harmonising that theory with theology. Such incidents show how difficult it must have been to develop science at the universities, and one is no longer surprised that none of the pioneer investigators to whom seventeenth-century science and philosophy owe their great progress is to be found there. But in the North Netherland universities authority at least lacked the hold necessary to stifle discussion, although that was the solution to which it inclined most naturally. At Utrecht the impetuous Regius became a storm-centre. At the public defending of theses, then still usual, wild scenes sometimes occurred.

Yes, what you cannot defend with arguments (*thus a pamphleteer later addressed the Cartesians*), you do with stamping, hurling of beans, blowing of trumpets, if not with fists and sticks.

In 1642 the Senate of the university, under the chairmanship of Voetius, then Rector, and with the approval of the town magistracy, adopted a resolution rejecting the new philosophy:

first, because it is contrary to the ancient philosophy, which the universities of the whole world have thus far taught with wise deliberation; . . . finally, because several false and preposterous notions, which conflict with the other sciences and faculties, and above all with orthodox theology, either proceed directly therefrom or may be deduced from it by inexperienced youth.

Regius was silenced for the moment, but Voetius was still not satisfied. He persuaded his ex-pupil Schoockius, professor at Groningen, to write a sharp attack on Descartes himself. Descartes now went straight for Voetius. The Utrecht magistracy summoned him before them, with ringing of bells, to prove his allegations against their professor. The Frenchman was at first terrified, but he quickly realised that being in Holland he had nothing to fear from the fulminations of Utrecht, and he soon got sufficient grasp of the strategy of the country to strike at Voetius in the person of Schoockius at Groningen, where some were well-disposed to the new ideas. Meanwhile Regius had finished a work on the principles of science, which he was bold enough to publish, having first used the intercession of Huygens, whose intellectual curiosity had led to a friendship with Descartes, to obtain permission to dedicate it to Huygens' master, Frederick Henry. The new spirit was now stirring at Leiden also. The sub-regent of the States Seminary and professor of philosophy, Heereboord, avowed himself a Cartesian in an oration with the unequivocal title *De Libertate philosophandi*. Whereupon great discussion arose, in which the Regent, Revius, was his colleague's most violent antagonist; then followed intervention by the curators, a ban on uttering the name Descartes, and instructions to Heereboord:

that in future he shall please to confine himself within the limits of the Aristotelian philosophy subscribed to in this Academy.

But in 1648 the curators themselves hauled in the Trojan horse (although it is much to be doubted whether they had ever intended their own prohibition very seriously) by appointing to the chair of theology Abraham Heidanus, who was to be the great Cartesian of the following period.

The picture which takes shape out of all this is certainly not that of an ideal State imbued with the spirit of liberty; nor, seen by the side of the exiled Grotius and the foreigner Descartes, are these native theologians and professors figures of the first magnitude, save perhaps Voetius through the force of his personality. But of life and strife there was no lack, and it was in this atmosphere that art and literature flourished—and *they* certainly did not lack real greatness.

B. ART

RUBENS died in 1640. His marvellous creative powers remained undiminished right up to his death, and he maintained a sovereign rule over artistic life in the loyal provinces. His delight in handling mass-motion, his feeling for full, luxurious form, contended victoriously against the fatigue of his sixties. In the whole history of art there has rarely been anything so impressive as the appearance made by Rubens, by reason both of the amazing, almost superhuman, fecundity of his genius and of the admiration and appreciation which he enjoyed from fellow-countrymen and foreigners alike. He worked in France for a short time to paint the series of triumphal pieces of the Queen Mother; he sojourned in Spain; from Italy, from England, commissions poured in.

And Rubens did not stand alone. In the first place there was his pupil of genius, Van Dyck, precocious (before the expiry of the Truce he had already painted a host of works which were long attributed to Rubens himself), of a natural distinction both in form and spirit, his master's superior in portraiture, but without his master's glowing and inexhaustibly self-renewing vitality. Van Dyck worked for several years in Italy, and later as Court painter in England, where the quality of his work, which he left largely to assistants, markedly declined, although it shows to fine effect again in the lovely portrait of young William II and his little Stuart bride. On Rubens' death Van Dyck returned to his native land, dying quite soon after (1641). Then—to dismiss lesser lights such as De Vos, Van Thulden, Gonzales Coques, with no more than a mention—there was Jordaens, equally hard at work on the altar-pieces and festal secular subjects in the fashion that the great leader had made supreme, and at the same time exhibiting a very real and natural feeling for the monumental, and a vigour and a clarity full of character, which render him a wholly distinct personality. A significant figure, too, was Frans Snyders, who painted large decorative still-lifes and hunting scenes; a feature of his paintings, as of those of his much younger pupil Jan Fyt, is the way in which the traditional Netherland feeling for detail is assimilated to a monumental concept of style. His work, too, fits into the aristocratic and showy life of the Antwerp Baroque.

Trade might be suffering a decline, but the Gild of St. Luke and the closely-connected 'Gillyflower' Chamber of Rhetoric enjoyed a period of splendour; nor did architecture and sculpture lag behind. Frankaert and Father Huyssens continued to build fine churches, at Brussels, at Mechlin, at Ghent, at Bruges (mainly for the Jesuits), while wood-carvers and sculptors were everywhere active. Two of the very best, it is true, the brothers Du Quesnoy, passed the greater part of their lives in Italy. At Rome there was a large Netherland group of painters, Hollanders and Flemings together. Some of their doings are described by a poet from Dort, Van der Merwe. Artus Quellin was yet only at the beginning of his career. But the important point is, that while in the North, as we have seen illustrated in the case of De Keyser,[1] conditions no longer encouraged religious sculpture, in the South there was being formed, under the influence not only of Italy but also of all that was characteristic in Rubens, a rich tradition of decoration and of the sculptor's art.

Now, is the whole of this artistic movement permeated by the spirit of the Baroque? A certain luxuriance tending towards external appearance and a stylistic ideal is certainly predominant. Yet there were undercurrents in which we can see the persistence of the older Netherland traditions of loving attention to immediate surroundings and of spiritual introspection. Rubens' delightful landscapes followed a native tradition in the true Baroque manner, but in the work of Jordaens the man's own personality occasionally breaks through the eternal flourish of the style's rhythm, in the realistic rendering of an apostle's head, or in such a portrait as that of Van Surpele, whose bourgeois gravity is but superficially accommodated to the demands of the aristocratic convention. There is, too, the rendering of the Snoeck family by Cornelis de Vos: its transposition into the legend of St. Norbert and its devotional postures accentuate the difference between the attitudes in Flanders and in Holland society since the separation, but how closely akin has remained in both regions the lucid feeling for personality! Side by side with Snyders and Fyt, moreover, there still were

---

[1] See above, p. 35.

numerous painters who handled still-life after a less monumental, more bourgeois manner, and in so doing proceeded to develop, in traditional Netherland fashion, a vision wholly different from that of the Baroque. Indeed, one of the great Holland masters of this art, De Heem, worked for a time at Antwerp and had great influence there. Pictures of lower-class life were even more difficult to treat in the Baroque style, and that subject, once exalted to such a height by Pieter Bruegel, was still held in honour. David Teniers became Court painter on the strength of it and enjoyed an amazing popularity; it was as if a comic interlude were needed as repose from the high-flown drama of the Baroque. Greater still (and rightly so!) with art-lovers, was the reputation of Brouwer,

who was mean of spirit, but in art most rich,

as De Bie, the notary of Lierre, rhymed a generation later in his *Golden Cabinet of the noble free Art of Painting*. Brouwer's wild habits, his mockery of all established order and dignity, attracted nearly as much attention during his brief life—in North as well as South, for he worked for a time at Haarlem and there belonged, as he afterwards did at Antwerp, to a Chamber of Rhetoric—as did the villains, soldiers and poets he painted, so unmistakably alive and so crudely dissolute. What a dissonance in the majestic harmony of Contra-Reformationist art! And what a testimony to Rubens' breadth and openness of mind that Brouwer excited such lively admiration from him!

Yet the vast, dramatic, courtly style expressed in historical and altar paintings, a style primarily for church and palace, remains the chief thing; and even in the eyes of the Northerners, whose own middle-class and Protestant society found such a style hard to keep up, it was this achievement that gave the Antwerp school its dazzling radiance.

The traditional Netherland love for art was by no means weakened in Holland and Utrecht. The spirit of Calvinism might lend it no inspiration, might even be hostile to it, but that is only one more proof that the cultural life of the North derived from many other sources besides Calvinism, for never in any country has the painter's art been more truly popular. Nearly every town had its painters, members of a St. Luke's Gild and often of a Chamber of Rhetoric, as their brethren were in the

South, while Delft, Leiden, Haarlem, Amsterdam and Utrecht were important centres. The loss of ecclesiastical patronage was made up for by the eagerness of townsfolk and farmers to adorn their houses with pictures. At inns the rooms were hung with paintings. There were picture-stalls at the fairs. Moreover, here, as at Antwerp, there was plenty of work to be done for export.

And these conditions called forth an amazing artistic florescence, essentially indigenous in character, in which both the older Netherland—not exclusively Northern—traditions were carried on and entirely new ground was broken. In the general history of seventeenth-century art this was a truly remarkable phenomenon, just as the entire Republic, politically and socially, was a remarkable phenomenon. In a Europe where the monarchical idea was in the ascendant and States were everywhere conforming to a centralised and rationally designed pattern, where everything was beginning to be reduced to an order that tolerated no more than the trappings of nobility and ceremony, where even spiritual life was seeking after all-embracing systems and identifying civilisation with heavy formalism—in such a Europe as this the bustling and loose-knit middle-class society of Holland was something quite apart; and in the same way a feeling for directness, for individuality, for unstyled life made the art of Holland into something unique in the period. It approached man for his own sake, with shrewd observation, but also with a profound sympathy: for to talk of mere realism is to ignore the intimate relationship into which the observer entered with landscapes and material objects, and to be blind to the imagination that inspired some of the finest of these painters.

This contrast which I have sketched here between the Baroque art which we admire in seventeenth-century Flanders, and the national Dutch art which enchants us in seventeenth-century Holland—how often has it been broadened by native writers and foreign into a contrast between the Flemish and the Dutch native temperaments! Yet it is obvious that the style of Rubens, so far removed from the style of former generations of Flemings, was the product, not of the Flemish native temperament, but of the Counter-Reformation in Flanders, imposed there, as we have seen, by victorious Spanish arms; just as the style of Hals (who was born at Mechlin!) or of Van Goyen was the outcome of the destruction of Hispano-Catholic civilisation in Holland, a process to which, as we have also seen, both assistance from abroad and the purely material factor of the country's geographical configuration had so largely contributed. The contrast was there, but, like the political and religious cleavage, it was brought into being by the vicissitudes to which the nation had been subject, and not as the inevitable consequence of a supposed dualism in its nature. It was a historical phenomenon, bound up with time and circumstances. Moreover, granted the contrast was there, let us for once consider the qualifications which have to be made as much on the one side as on the other. We have already seen that not everything in the South was Baroque. But still less was everything in the North what might be called 'national Dutch' in style.

Least of all in architecture. In a period of such rapidly increasing prosperity, much building was done in the North. In contrast to the picturesque, playful style, which, originating with Vredeman de Vries, had found its most brilliant exponent in Lieven de Key, Hendrik de Keyser already represented a more academic tendency,[1] while Jacob van Campen, whose assistant, Pieter Post himself, also designed many buildings in his master's style, went a long way further in the same direction. While here and there, especially in the smaller towns, town-halls, weigh-houses and gates in the lively traditional manner were still going up, to the intelligentsia Van Campen was already the outstanding man.

Who vanquished flowing Gothic folly with Roman stateliness
And drove old heresy forth before an older truth.

So wrote Huygens, for whom Van Campen had built a house on the Voorhout, and who did his best to get the architect commissions from the Prince of Orange. Van Campen built the palace in the Noordeinde and the House in the Wood, and also designed the Mauritshuis for John Maurice of Nassau, although in this case Post carried out the work. And when the municipality of Amsterdam wanted a town-hall in keeping with the power of the city they selected Van Campen's strictly classical design; the work of construction was begun in 1648 amidst the respectful admiration of the intellectuals.

[1] See *The Revolt of the Netherlands*, pp. 278–9.

We shall now better understand how it was that those painters who broke away from the Italian manner, and whom today we most admire, did not enjoy the greatest prestige among their contemporaries in Holland. The reputation which Flemish artists enjoyed in Holland shows that people there were impressed by what they themselves lacked. Indeed, the higher the Hollander's individual position in society, and the more charged with humanistic elements his culture, the more he demanded style; and style now meant convention, florid ornament, classical scholarliness, Italianism, the Baroque. Nor should it be thought that there was no work done in the North itself in response to this demand; in fact, the painters who engaged in it were regarded as the leading men and made the highest prices.

As the centre of this style Haarlem, where Corneliszoon continued a somewhat antiquated classicism, was surpassed by Utrecht. Here were the studios of Moreelse, Bloemaert, Honthorst, Both, Poelenburgh—a whole crowd of talented artists, who had all spent years in Italy and had adopted the Italian manner. They painted Biblical and mythological subjects, landscapes adorned with shepherds and shepherdesses, nymphs and satyrs—a panorama wholly alien to the picture that one usually forms of the Dutch art of the time. These painters cut quite a figure in the world. Poelenburgh for a time painted at the Court of Charles I. Honthorst, who had become famous in Italy for his lighting effects under the name of 'Gherardo delle Notti', did more work for the Prince of Orange than any other painter, being entrusted, for instance, with the decoration of the palace of Honselaarsdyk. His work, too, was in vogue in England, and the princes of Bohemia took lessons in his studio. When in 1627 Rubens made a tour of the North—one is continually reminded that in those days war offered much less hindrance to intercourse than now—he went to Utrecht on purpose to visit the artists there in their studios, and but for an illness Honthorst would have accompanied him on his further tour. The Italian-Baroque movement was by no means lacking at Amsterdam. Its most esteemed exponent was Pieter Lastman, to whose studio the young Rembrandt came to learn the art of painting.

Against this background of aristocratic, academic and

'European' art there now begins to emerge a separate Holland school—if, indeed, 'school' may be called what had so little intrinsic unity. For what characterises these de-Italianised and non-Baroque painters is their individualism: they dared to be themselves and for that very reason they are all different. It was not, of course, impossible to express a vivid and personal feeling of life and character through the medium of the Italian-Baroque style. Among the Utrecht painters there was one whom I have not yet mentioned but whom on account of his very strength and truth in observation and sentiment I can regard with a warmer appreciation than any of the others, namely, Verbrugghen. Yet, speaking generally, when one wants those qualities one has to go to the new Hollanders.

There is, first, Frans Hals, of Mechlin—and it is indeed remarkable that one of the first typical artists of the Holland school was by origin a Brabanter. Hals developed his art in a centre of Italian classicism, Haarlem. To be sure, there were undercurrents and counter-tendencies. The more realistic style of painting naturally held its own best in portraiture, and especially in that typically Dutch product, the group portrait. Another noteworthy figure of these times was Willem Buytewech, who was working at Haarlem while Hals, in his slow development, was presumably still following in the footsteps of Goltzius and Corneliszoon. Buytewech's speciality was the 'merry company', which he painted with masterly spirit and wholly without pose. From about 1620 Hals becomes clearly visible as an interpreter of the life around him. He presents types from the lower classes with as complete a lack of moralising ulterior motive as did Brouwer, but without that painter's vehemence, sparkling with life but light-hearted; then portraits, and among them the famous civic guard festivals. The Baroque subordinates mankind to a larger unity, to a style, one would sometimes say to show and spectacle. In that Holland, however, where a stormy public life, together with an economic expansion of revolutionary consequences, had sharply accentuated individual personality, man was himself the portrait-painter's primary concern. Hals was not unsympathetic to the Baroque: his feeling for effect and for contrast belongs to it. But what a love for personality as such! He has bequeathed to us a matchless portrait-gallery in which that society itself lives on, with all

its self-confidence, its positiveness, its zest for life, its unconscious swagger.

And just as the Holland personality now spreads itself in the
painter's art, so the Holland landscape also came into its own.
A great figure in the history of landscape painting is Hercules
Seghers, whose tragic career has left behind it a very few
visionary pictures of unusual beauty. But although some of his
etchings are founded directly on the Netherland scene, the real
pioneers of the Holland landscape school were Salomon van
Ruysdael and Jan van Goyen. (In passing, I may mention the
first of the great architectural painters, Saenredam, who
perceived the beauty of the dismantled and whitewashed
interiors of the Reformed churches.) Seghers dreamed for
himself a landscape according to his mood—just as did Rubens,
though his was a very different mood; Ruysdael and Goyen
accepted the landscape they saw around them and found it full
of mood. Landscape painting, although its beginnings reached
far back into the Middle Ages, had only recently dared to make
an appearance without some apology in the shape of figures;
and as I have pointed out before,[1] it was a Flemish rather than
a Holland conquest for art. If it now flourished in Holland, on
the root of Flemish traditions which the Baroque encouraged
but little in Flanders itself, this was, like the corporation piece,
an expression of the self-confidence which inspired this rejuvenated society. But how tranquil, how unforced is that
expression! The painters do not expressly set out to glorify
their own town or region, but how they did love those pale, soft
shades, those sweeping lines!

And what of Rembrandt? Rembrandt is not to be comprehended in either the one or the other movement, the Baroque
or the national Dutch. It is part of his greatness that he fought
out and ultimately resolved within himself the contrast that
dominated his age—a struggle and a triumph both so personal
in character that often, especially in his later period, contemporaries looked upon it with incomprehension.

Rembrandt began in the Baroque. It responded to his lofty
conception of art. But from the first there is an unrest noticeable
in him. He was no Rubens. Because he was of lowly origin, while
the other was of good birth and upbringing? Not at all. It was

[1] See *The Revolt of the Netherlands*, p. 279.

because from his very nature Rembrandt stood on difficult terms
with life. Even in the animation of his youth, when fortune
smiled on him and he bade fair to become the fashionable
Amsterdam portraitist, this lack of adaptability sometimes
proved to belong to the very root of his being. He sought his
art where people were not likely to follow him; as he himself
proudly put it, he yearned for freedom, not for honour. The
'Night Watch' was what people mockingly dubbed the great
corporation piece in which he had played with dramatic
composition, with light and shade, until most of those portrayed
could not find themselves in it. This was the Baroque with a
vengeance! Yet at the same time this breath-taking seeker after
effects was more interested than anyone in human personality,
and there are no more penetrating, more devoted portraits than
his. A life-long student of the Italian masters, he also revelled
in sketching directly from nature. Following Seghers, he
painted purely imaginative landscapes as expressions of his
inner life, but in his etchings and drawings he rendered the
surroundings of Amsterdam with tender fidelity. The pomp
and mystery of Old Testament temples, the simplicity of a
multitude of the faithful assembled to hear the word of
Christ; whatever was romantic, whatever profoundly human,
Rembrandt pursued it. In 1648 he was forty-two years of age.
Saskia was dead, but the great social disasters of his life as well
as the great triumphs of his art were yet to come.

c. LITERATURE

In Dutch literature of the seventeenth century, especially
between about 1610 and 1660, there is to be found—in the
North, that is to say, for here the South offers but a pale
reflection—everything that goes to make a veritable golden age;
not only are there works of imperishable beauty, in poetry,
prose and the drama, but also a vigorous intellectual intercourse,
with centres of its own (the Amsterdam theatre, the Muiden
circle), and above all personalities of perennial interest, whose
attitude to the problems of their time belongs to history.

I shall first treat of these personalities. Everyone of them has
been mentioned in a more general context in the preceding

chapters. They are four in number: Cats, Huygens, Hooft and Vondel. I shall not return to Breero, who was dead before the expiry of the Truce, and shall also leave aside the figures of more limited interest, even though their poetic appeal may be even purer (as is the case with Revius, Camphuysen or Stalpert van der Wiele) or the witness they bear of that society may be profoundly interesting (as with Heemskerck or de Brune). Dozens of others I shall simply have to pass by altogether.

Yet before coming to the four outstanding personalities mentioned it will be necessary to indicate, however briefly, the background against which they are set. There was a great deal of writing done, and much, of which the history of literature does not as a rule take notice, possessed style. The pamphlets are for the most part clumsily written, they are often coarse and even vile. Nevertheless in a good many the language is handled with striking precision and vividness. The same is true for the accounts of sea voyages, although the writers, here, too, were generally men little used to the pen. The chronicles, the large works devoted to the great church quarrel, the political disquisitions and memoranda, generally seem hopelessly dry and long-winded to the modern reader, yet the historian's eye will despite all discern behind them interesting personalities realising themselves by their style. Indeed, letters like those of Coen are very far from dry, and how excellently written! The official language was interlarded with latinisms which are apt to offend the modern reader because they were not permanently absorbed into the Dutch language (as happened in the case of English). The literary writers never admitted these bastard words and in the latter half of the eighteenth century they were largely driven out even for official use. Once one can accept this peculiarity, however—to contemporaries, of course, it did not seem peculiar—the style of the seventeenth century clerks and politicians often charms by its forcefulness and aptness. Reading, for instance, Grotius' speech in the Amsterdam town council or his Justification,[1] one cannot help admiring the supple vigour of the language, nor is this exclusively due to the writer's uncommon personality. The same qualities can be observed in the writings of obscure personages: I remind the reader of the letters of Hondius[2]; I would cite the memorial in which a simple

[1] See above, pp. 53, 73.   [2] See above, p. 111.

Contra-Remonstrant minister[1] gives a spirited account of the treatment that had been meted out to him by the magistracy of the town; and I should like to quote a dozen more instances. In all these writings can be observed the reflections of a time full of life and character, spontaneous, direct.

Jacob Cats, a Zealander of the regent class, began his career as a lawyer. Won over to the pietism of Teellinck through the influence of his wife, he became obsessed with a single problem: how to safeguard the soul against the dangers of the senses. His poetry he intended to help his fellow-men in this task. A moral arbiter as unswervingly devoted to his ideal as Maerlant had been three and a half centuries before him, Cats was a much less noble personality and professed a much more limited outlook on life. In his view the major part of education consisted in cautioning; moreover, for him the dangers were concentrated in the relation between the sexes. This is the subject treated in his greatest didactic poems. *Marriage* (1625) and the *Wedding Ring* (1637)—twenty and twenty-five thousand lines long respectively —and he continued to busy himself with it in all his other works down to his *Thoughts of An Eighty-Year-Old* and *Eighty-two Years' Life*. Cats filled the office of Grand Pensionary for a number of years, but if one searches these reminiscences, or indeed the whole of his work, for sidelights on the politics or the political thought of his period, one is bound to be disappointed. His work bespeaks infinite attention to the details of domestic life, wide knowledge, experience and insight into the human mind. But everything is always on the same low plane. Never does the poet rise.

For this reason Cats is at his best in the brief and usually short-lined pieces of his *Mirror of the Old and New Time*, 1632, a collection of 'Emblems', aphorisms subjoined to pictures with explanatory inscriptions, a form long held in affection, which he made into something quite original with his inexhaustible gusto and juicy humour. In the long didactic poems the perpetual drone of a mediocre spirit through interminable alexandrines is apt to become unbearable. Cats loves to hand out precepts reminiscent of cookery-books or manuals for newly-weds. But

---

[1] "Verweerschrift van Willem Crijnsze", in *Bijdr. en Meded.*, H. G. Utrecht, XVII (1896).

whether he is dealing with table manners or with the duty of parents towards their children, his tone never varies. All his opinions and moralisings—and this is the keynote of his personality—are inspired by distrust of human nature. His good-life philosophy (for this was what he developed in his writings) set a standard before the crude and thoughtless; it demanded constant deliberation and self-control. But it did so in virtue of a principle which rejected 'love and desire' together as 'a poisonous weed':

> Loving is a strange pursuit
> It bringeth folk into dispute.

How little of the grandeur of Augustine or of Calvin is revealed in this Calvinist's contempt for the human passions! He is continually pointing to the consequences, practical as well as spiritual. His philosophy of life is one of fearfulness, with greed too often squinting round the corner. According to the doctrine of Teellinck 'the renunciation of the world' was necessary to perfect the 'union betwixt the soul and Jesus'. Cats would rather have come to terms with the world. In the midst of a passage wherein considerations on the danger of exorbitant wealth are pressed into service as a consolation for an unlucky venture in land reclamation, a sigh escapes him:

> It is a work of skill and worthy to be praised.
> To be allowed to be godly and at the same time rich.

His was a philosophy, too, of the mean—his own beloved word: how little of the true spirit of Voetius is seen in him!

> Neither too sweet, nor yet too sour,
> Neither too soft, nor yet too dour
> (*and so on, for thirty-four lines, and then:*)
> The happy mean is what I look for in a wife,
> Neither of high nor yet of low estate in life,
> (*etc., etc.*).

Cats exercised great influence over the tone of North Netherland civilisation. As late as the nineteenth century all respectable Protestant households possessed, alongside the Bible, a copy of his *Collected Works*. He had the qualities proper to a popular poet. His prolixity and flatness repel impatient intellectuals, but even they have to admire, however unwillingly, the mastery of language, the force of metaphor and the gift of narrative which were his. His influence has none the less on the whole been unfortunate. He peremptorily assigned to woman a position of inferiority to man; Anna Roemers Visscher (a friend of his), and Anna Maria Schuermans, the Utrecht 'bluestocking', he dismissed with a joke:

> Although a clever maiden may perchance be found,
> One swallow, as we say, does not a summer make.

In marriage his advice to the wife was:

> Let not thine own brain rule, but turn thy feelings round
> And to thy husband a good sunflower be.

He had grave suspicions of that free intercourse between the sexes for which Dutch society was known; and in general his petty-bourgeois circumspection, his tamely cerebral worldly wisdom and his fear of passion and spontaneity acted as a damper on all that was fresh and spirited.

Constantijn Huygens, son of a Brussels father (Secretary of the Council of State in the days of Maurice), and an Antwerp mother, was from 1625 secretary to the Prince of Orange. As firm a Protestant as Cats, nearly twenty years his senior, he, too, came under the influence of English and Zealand pietism and gave great attention to the conduct of his personal life, which he attempted to control with the intellect. (Perhaps his thinking here was in closer touch with Stoicism, which exercised as powerful a sway over that generation of intellectuals as it had over their predecessors.) He, too, wanted to keep women in subordination, and liked to manifest an unromantic view of love. The similarity is sufficient to suggest that Cats's view of life was no purely individual matter, and to explain how it was that Huygens and other enlightened contemporaries so greatly admired him. But in Huygens there grew out of this common ground a spirit and a personality which contrasted all the more strikingly with that of Cats.

Its first characteristic was crisp forcefulness. Huygens' matter-of-factness often turns to harshness; his sensuousness is never sneaking but often gross; at times coarse, it is always manly and forthright; and when Huygens pours out his soul in all simplicity—his zeal for Fatherland and Church, his grief at the loss of his wife, his longing (if it should please God) for rest—a deep note of sincerity strikes the ear. And besides all

this, he displays a broad and lively interest in the higher
intellectual life as well as in the political occurrences of his time.
We have already met him as the friend of Descartes, as the
admirer and patron of Van Campen, as a lover of music.
Descartes wrote of him after their first meeting:

Despite what I had heard of him, I could not believe that a single mind could
occupy so many things and acquit itself so well in them all.

The talmudic and scholastic trend of Voetianism was alien to
Huygens. His Calvinism was a fighting creed. He was quick to
pour scorn on popish superstition, and it was his heartfelt
conviction that the honour of God was bound up with the war
and with the well-being of the fatherland.

> Close not thy clouds, who above thy clouds there
> Sittest guarding the people,
> O God, and judging
> Those who among us are withstanding thy honour.

Huygens' poetry is in the highest degree personal. Whether
his poems are didactic, satirical, or descriptive, in reality what he
gives us is nearly always the meditations, the sallies, the ideas of
Constantijn Huygens, expressed after his very peculiar fashion
in a terse style which pressed words into unwonted service and
whose unexpected metaphors and allusions only half reveal the
thought beneath. Even his contemporaries found Huygens'
poetry difficult, nor would he have wished it otherwise; but to
the modern reader, in addition, that entire sphere of thought,
wherein religious and moral arguments bulk so large, is far from
easy of comprehension, while the hair-splittings and witticisms
of which the age was enamoured strike us all too often as feeble.
Nevertheless, in Huygens' work there stands written the story
of a mind that reflects a rich humanity in relation to the movements of a great age.

Through his post at the Court (which as long as Frederick
Henry lived meant every summer a post in the army camp),
Huygens belonged to a very different world in addition to that
of Dutch society. His poems were written as a recreation amidst
his multifarious activities. But what is more remarkable is to
observe him being a courtier among courtiers. We have seen
how French in tone was Frederick Henry's Court. From youth
up Huygens spoke and wrote French—French poems, a French

diary—and he employed Latin with equal fluency. He corresponded on the one hand about their problems with the greatest French writers of his age, Corneille and Guez de Balzac, on the other with the humanists, Barlaeus and Salmasius. No Dutchman commanded a more European culture; no Dutchman was more thoroughly Dutch.

The Dutch literary movement exhibits the same two currents as did Dutch art, namely, that of the Renaissance tending towards the Baroque, and that of the inspiration sprung from the native soil, individualist and realist in character. In literature the two are mingled even more inextricably; in every individual case their influence makes itself felt in different proportions. We have seen something of this already in Breero and the youthful Hooft, of whom the one could be himself only when emancipated from alien leadership, while the other achieved a harmonious fusion between foreign ideals and his own genius. Cats and Huygens exemplify the effects of this confluence each in a fresh fashion again.

Cats was no less immersed in French and Latin culture than were Huygens and Hooft; what the intelligentsia admired in him was his 'learning', manifested in the infinite variety of reference or quotation with which he supports or illustrates his moral precepts. But he addresses himself so directly, so ingenuously and in so homely a fashion to his middle-class public, his pen extracts such wealth from the living vernacular, that both as poet and moralist, alexandrines and all, he constitutes an altogether original phenomenon. As for Huygens, no desire to be understood by a wide public restrained him from artifice; on the contrary, in his search for contrast, his striving after wit and point, he lapses into it only too often. Not content with the regular verse-structure which had by now found general acceptance and thus no longer set a poet apart, he even experimented with hexameters and pentameters. But while in architecture Huygens might admire the 'stately' restraint of Van Campen, and in painting the flourish of the Antwerpers, he was in reality too much interested in the particular, in the life of the individual, in the workings of his own mind and spirit, to follow their example in his poetry. He was too matter-of-fact ever to be a true Renaissance poet, too individualistic to be a poet of the Baroque. Theory and practice were not too well harmonised in his work, yet the result was eminently personal and sincere.

More than either Cats or Huygens, Hooft and Vondel were primarily poets, that is to say, intent on the creation of beauty, and in them the current of the Southern style ran much more deeply. Hooft's career as a poet was nearly at an end with the expiry of the Truce. Of his plays there is only one that has stood the test of time. I mean *Warenar*, but the collection of lyric poems he wrote in his youth rank with the finest produced in the Dutch language; the best among them are perfect in form and structure, in rhythm and music. And how different the world into which Hooft leads us from that of Cats and Huygens! When 'Dutchifying according to this country's occasion' the *Aulularia* of Plautus into *Warenar*, then indeed he appears completely at home in bustling, populous Amsterdam, but his lyrics move with a lightness and grace, and throb with a purity of passion, over which neither human triteness nor the moral code of pietism hold sway. No feeling of sin obtrudes, sensuousness is good, and in Hooft we meet neither the sneaking hypocrisies of Cats nor the coarseness of Huygens. Love is not the only theme of his poems; in them, and especially in the sonnets, we find his whole philosophy of life, stoical, resigned.

In the historical work to which Hooft devoted his middle and later years he carried the culture of his time to a high pinnacle. Based on a wide knowledge of the literature on both the rebel and the Spanish side, and on family papers and traditions, it excels in subtle observation and clear exposition. History proper had not yet been written in Dutch, but in Hooft's *History* the chronicle-form, as practised by Bor or Van Meteren, is completely left behind. The power of description is maintained on a rare level; no matter where one opens the book, it lives. And the whole panorama of a complicated story is envisaged through a well-thought-out philosophy. It is the Revolt seen by a libertinist, by an aristocrat who believes in the mission of his class to defend liberty not only against the foreign despot, but against the stupidity of the mob and the unscrupulousness of the fanatic. A passage such as the following (comment on the Gelderland Calvinists' campaign under John of Nassau against

the Pacification of Ghent) is characteristic of the son of Burgomaster Hooft and of the admirer of Montaigne:

> In truth a husky time to govern. Neither divine nor human law, nor yet
> the need for unity, permitted the breach of plighted troth; yet whoever was
> disposed to gainsay or prevent it was denounced as a papist, or a friend of
> papists, yea in the end as a turncoat and traitor. That man who owned the
> most insolent mouth for abuse, was held the most loyal upholder of his
> country's freedom and the true faith.

The book would be an even more valuable possession to the
Dutch people, it would have played a greater rôle in their
cultural history had it not been written in so difficult a style.
Hooft, who appreciated so clearly the national significance of
his work, who so zealously proscribed bastard words and, what
is more important, dared to pick up the plastic, the colourful
word, the idiomatic phrase, even out of the gutter,[1] borrowed
his structural principles from the most difficult of the Latin
historians, Tacitus, whose work he translated by way of preparation. For a long time now in Europe the modern languages
had been evolving a new prose style after the Latin model, but
a reaction against the excess of artificial Latinity constituted the
most recent phase of that process—in England linked with the
work of Hooker, who died in 1600, in France with that of Guez
de Balzac, Hooft's contemporary. That Hooft could so err in
this respect (a real set-back for Dutch culture) is perhaps
a reflection of his typically Dutch individualism. I am more
inclined to explain it by the social weakness of the Dutch
language, which had to do without the support of Court and
aristocracy, and was too much at the mercy of intellectuals,
artists and preachers.

Nevertheless, in his own circle Hooft had helped to fashion
Dutch into a light tool for exquisitely courteous intercourse.
His merits as letter-writer and host, already touched upon,
deserve to be mentioned, next to those of the poet and historian.
In his letters, animated and witty, exceptionally beautifully
written and much less mannered than his historical prose, we
see him exercising his office as representative of justice in the
Gooi, or, full of intelligent interest in the events of the outer

---

[1] 'To pick up outcast words off the streets and make them do such service
as they are fit for, even though it were among the nobility, is a thing one can
take credit for.' Hooft to Huygens (1630) *Brieven van Hooft*, II, 1.

world, waiting for the news-reports at his quiet castle of
Muiden,[1] or again, collecting material for his History; but above
all we watch him in friendly intercourse with Huygens, Tesselschade (Roemer Visscher's daughter), Barlaeus (Van Baerle),
Vondel and a number of others, as the active centre of what is
known as the Muiden circle. The blend of literary interest and
sociability recalls the tradition of the Chamber of Rhetoric,
but the circle was as far removed as possible from the lower
middle-class plane to which those institutions had now sunk.
Tesselschade's voice and that of her friend, the Portuguese
singer from Antwerp, Francisca Duarte, ring across the years;
we know of the grief, so variously borne, that overcame all
through the death of their loved ones, of the reactions set up by
the conversion of Tesselschade and of Vondel to Catholicism.

Their profound differences notwithstanding, the ·personali-
ties of Cats, Hooft and Huygens were linked by fundamental
similarities; all three were intellectual natures, all three were
absorbed in the workings of their own hearts and captivated by
the human spectacle around them. Vondel stood alone as the
man of feeling and imagination, the man who found the stuff
of his poetry, not in nature, not in his own surroundings or in
his fellow-men, nor even in his own inner life, but in the idea,
in the ideal, through which to him all these were illuminated.
The truth and the beauty which Vondel served flowed from
one source alone, from God—he was a believer with all his
being. Born in a Baptist circle he threw himself passionately
into the dispute over predestination, denouncing the orthodox
doctrine as an insult against God, and struck right and left at
whatever seemed to him a violation of justice or an outrage on
truth.

> Truth—that's an old story—can nowhere find shelter.
> Therefore is he to be praised as a wise man who keeps his mouth shut.
> Would I too were expert in that art. But whatever lies in my heart
> Rises up to my throat. I am pressed too hard.
> It goes like young wine which bursts the stop.

He was about forty years old when he wrote like this at the
height of the crisis of 1618. Would he not be lost in political

---

[1] The Gooi district was at that time under the jurisdiction of Amsterdam.
The castle, on the Zuiderzee, was the sheriff's official residence. Cf. above,
p. 68.

wrangling? No; amidst the turmoil he steadily kept in sight the great ideal. And after a while it beckoned him irresistibly to other service than that of denouncing its calumniators. Reverence, respect for authority and unity, that was the real soul hunger which drove him onwards. Glorification of his town and its lawful governors, the lords burgomasters, due submission to all established authority, in the secular as well as in the spiritual sphere, in these things Vondel sought harmony. Similarly in his literary work he humbly, or rather eagerly, accepted the highest conventions known to his time. As a child of the lower middle class he had learned French, but not, as had the regents' sons Cats, Hooft and Huygens, the classical tongues. In later life, with unwearying labour, he learned Latin, writing dramas after the model of Seneca and satires after Horace. He also mastered Greek and learned to regard Sophocles as the master rather than the bombastic Roman dramatist. In this he was helped by young Vossius, whose father's literary precepts were law to the docile poet. Vondel's intellectual interest ranged over the whole world and all its history. The Emperor Constantine was to become the hero of his epic; among living men Grotius won his greatest admiration. He did not on that account become any less enthusiastic an Amsterdammer and Dutchman, but only in the widest European thought, in classicism and the Baroque, could he find intellectual contentment, and only in Catholicism peace of mind.

All this does not explain why Vondel was so great a poet, by far the greatest of his time. On the contrary, it leads one to expect powerful obstacles, and it is the greatness of Vondel that he was able to raise up his poetry against their obstruction, that he managed to carry with grace his heavy burden of classical learning and Renaissance ornament, the whole paraphernalia of Jupiter and the Muses, and that the tremendous gestures which he undertook did not falter in their sweep. The inward power and the singleness of aim which fitted him for these feats were his personal possession.

Poems of praise, of exultation, of mourning streamed forth from Vondel in flowing rhythm with the effortlessness of breathing. He accompanied every public occurrence of his great period in the manner of a master of ceremonies—a master of ceremonies upheld by a profound conviction. After his conversion to Catholicism he wrote a number of long poems in honour of his new faith; the first, *Altar Secrets*, he dedicated in 1645 to the Archbishop of Mechlin. His greatness comes out best in the few arrestingly personal poems which great sorrow wrung from him, in the polemical poems to which indignation moved him, and in the imaginative evocations of the long series of dramas which opened with *Gijsbrecht van Amstel* (written when he was already fifty years of age). It is obvious that a poet such as the Vondel I have sketched could not create any real tragedies, could not, that is to say, depict clashes of personalities or clashes within a single personality. Vondel's most typical dramas live by virtue of his imagination, they are poems flowing rhythmically through five acts and designed to set forth an everlasting truth. The finest of them were still to be written in 1648, when he had passed his sixtieth year.

In 1653 (if we may glance for a moment beyond the limit of this volume), Vondel was crowned as chief of Dutch poets by painters and writers assembled at a St. Luke's Gild festival. In 1647 a high-flown funeral oration (a pity that young Brandt had copied it largely from a French model) had been pronounced on the Amsterdam stage in honour of Hooft. We see here that Vondel, despite his idealism and Catholicism, and Hooft, despite his aristocratic refinement, were recognised as masters by their contemporaries. But Cats was the poet who was read, and it is difficult to avoid the impression that the others, however conscious they may have been of their call to leadership and however great the admiration which they evoked, roamed too far and too high in the exotic realms of the Renaissance and of Classicism for literary life to keep pace with them.

That comes out most clearly in the theatre. During the Truce the Amsterdam stage had been fulfilling a function in intellectual life. But although in 1637, following the struggle between the Old Chamber of Rhetoric and the Academy,[1] a permanent theatre under the patronage of the burgomasters was inaugurated with Vondel's *Gijsbrecht* (the profits were to be devoted to charity, in order to appease Puritan opposition), it would be a mistake to think that therefore he and the intellectuals dominated the theatre during this period. The tremendous hit

[1] See above, p. 69.

made by the bloody melodrama of *Aran and Titus*, the work of an illiterate glazier, Jan Vos, was in any case an ominous portent for the future. It is a striking fact that no one was more enthusiastic about this monstrosity than was the famous humanist Barlaeus. In the following period Vos, who became director of the theatre, flattered the taste for elaborate spectacle and ingenious stage machinery.

So now the eye as well as the ear will have its share in what is being played,

so an admirer testified.

There were thus certainly weaknesses in the North's cultural florescence, yet if we turn from it to the South the contrast that we observed already during the Truce appears in still more glaring colours. To enable its middle-class society to bring forth such vigorous, enterprising and varied personalities as in the North, the South lacked the indispensable condition of liberty. Religious uniformity, guarded by the censorship, was not all; worse was the foreign domination under which it continued to live. Men from the governing class like Hooft and Huygens, who, using the vernacular, built up literary personalities full of style, could hardly exist in a country where there were no world-famous achievements, no sovereign independence to create in that same class national pride or belief in themselves as Netherlanders; where on the contrary it experienced its happiest moments in feeling at one with the entire Counter-Reformationist world and focussed its pride on the Spanish masters' championship of Catholicism. I am far from suggesting that the Antwerp patricians were for that reason devoid of culture. A circle such as Anna Visscher[1] encountered at Antwerp —the pensionary Edelheer, the secretary Gevaerts, the old canon Hemelarius (who was perhaps instrumental in converting her), the merchant De Romer, Plantin's son-in-law Balthazar Moretus, and Duarte, the father of Francisca—possessed highly cultivated minds, but their constant intercourse with priests and Spanish officials gave them a wholly different orientation from their counterparts in Holland. There were certainly a few among them who wrote poems in Dutch—Richard Versteghen, who led in that respect, had died just before Anna Visscher's

[1] A convert to Catholicism, see above, p. 211; *cf.* also below, p. 259.

first visit; his poetic merit was somewhat slight, but his was an interesting personality and I shall come back to him. There existed no conscious prejudice against the literary use of the popular language. The Dutch poetess, who knew no French, was a great success.

Yet the intellectual aristocracy of Antwerp had virtually ceased to regard Dutch as a language of culture. Intellectual life as a whole was at an ebb. Side by side with the decline of the great Antwerp printing-house of Plantin-Moretus, the rise in Holland of presses of international repute, of Blaeu at Amsterdam, and of the Elseviers (who hailed from Louvain) at Leiden and later at Amsterdam, almost seem to have a symbolic significance. Blaeu's splendid atlases and town-books travelled the world over, the Elsevier classics no less, and foreigners increasingly had their works published in the free Republic. Whereas the Moretuses, although they still steadily made money through their monopoly of liturgical books, were prevented by the censorship from exploring any fresh realms of culture. So depressed was the position of book-publishing in the South that the priest Sanderus had to go to an Amsterdam publisher with his great illustrated work on his own province of Flanders, to one moreover who made no secret of his bitter anti-popish feelings.[1]

Sanderus wrote his book in Latin. And indeed, to set against the historical works produced in the vernacular by the North, including not only so powerful a work of art as Hooft's, but also

[1] Hondius, whom we have already heard speaking so strikingly about letting 'those who speak Dutch join and unite with us who speak Dutch' (p. 112), permitted himself the most cutting remarks because the 'little priest' (Sanderus) introduced too many descriptions of 'relics, images and suchlike trivialities, as even the Catholics here poke fun at, for the world is now become too knowing and suspicious to believe in such childish things'. Moreover, he made haste to lay the drawings and plans, so soon as he received them from Flanders, before the Northern commander 'to the promotion of the good cause', to 'rid the fatherland from the black swine' (the Spaniards) and 'to teach' the Flemings 'to speak good Hollandish' (by which he certainly meant: to cure them of their Catholicism); the drawings and plans for which the Flemish towns and the Spanish authorities themselves were subsidising Sanderus! No more striking proof of the helplessness of the South than the story of how the famous *Flandria Illustrata* came into being! This story has yet to be told in full. It is characteristic of the attitude of historians in North and South in present conditions that the Flemish biographer of Sanderus in the Belgian *Dictionnaire de Biographie Nationale* does not know the correspondence published in *Oud-Holland*, nor the Dutch biographer of Hondius in the *Nieuw Nederl. Biog. Woordenboek* that in the publications of the *Société d'Emulation de Bruges*.

Utenbogaert's and Trigland's folios on the religious quarrels, Baudartius' continuation of Van Meteren, Velius' *Chronicle of Hoorn* (which is only the first of a splendid series of town histories), De Laet's *Year by Year History* of the West India Company, and the reports and descriptions of travels which were collected during this period under the title of *Rise and Progress of the East India Company*;—to set against all this wealth of culture one can find on the other side little more than Adriaan van Meerbeck's bald, insipid and uncritical *Chronicle of the Whole World, and especially of the Seventeen Netherlands* (1620). This brings home what the contrast in political fortunes signified in the intellectual life of the sundered provinces.

Versteghen, whom I mentioned a moment ago, made use of the Dutch language to discuss the great problems of the day. Curiously enough he had spent the first thirty years of his life in England, and then eight more in Paris and Rome. He was at home in the circle of English refugees who in agreement with, and often in the pay of, the Spanish Government, were trying to bring about an overthrow of the existing state of affairs in their country. Gradually, nevertheless, Versteghen became a true Antwerper. In that town, where he had settled in 1588, and where at first he still published in English, he began, in 1611, when he was past sixty, a whole series of half literary, half political-polemical works in Dutch. It is significant that the Brussels town secretary Numan, in the laudatory poem with which he honoured Versteghen's *Dutch Epigrams*, of 1617, felt obliged to praise the Dutch language, rated below 'the foreign languages' by so many, for its antiquity, abundance and force.

> But lack of writers causes it to lag behind.

Versteghen did what he could. His bitter taunts at the North-Netherlands Calvinists are often amusing. Compared to Costerus,[1] to whom the honour of God and his Church came first, he is the earthly fighter, taken up with the quarrel of the moment. He also wrote for Verhoeven's *Antwerp Tidings*. It is again significant that the three issues per week of this paper had from 1629 on to be cut down to one. Versteghen, in his old age (he did not die until 1640), did succeed in stirring up the

---

[1] See above, p. 28.

intellectual life of the Southern Netherlands a little, but he could not avert the decline.

Nor, to turn to the field of pure literature, was the somewhat timid dawn represented by De Harduyn and his friends[1] followed by any bright day. The work which appeared during the last period of the war either did not rise above the rhetoricians' level or else was limited to purely devotional literature. Infinitely numerous as were the dramas and farces, written on every hand for the Brabant Chambers of Rhetoric, one man alone has remained a name in Dutch literature with work of that kind, the Antwerper Ogier, who in his youth wrote some comedies on the deadly sins. Ogier had studied Breero, but is not fit to hold a candle to him. Even his sometimes intolerably squalid stuff had to be presented with a moralising purpose, and for the rest devotional literature is the order of the day.

De Harduyn himself did nothing further than translate Hugo's *Pia Desideria*, although he appears to have lived until 1641. The Renaissance style at which he had aimed, first in love poems, then in religious verse, and which one might imagine would have formed so natural a counterpart in Flanders to the pictorial and sculptural production of like inspiration, faded away before it had well and truly blossomed, and this at a time when it was achieving triumphs with Hooft and Vondel in the de-Romanised North. Clearly, it was robbed of all vitality by the low esteem in which the educated held the vernacular. Besides Hugo, the Society of Jesus produced several other religious writers of some importance, who expressed themselves in Latin: the most celebrated of them was Sidonius Hosschius (De Hossche, of Merxem), whose *Elegiae* were collected and published under papal direction after his death in 1653. It goes without saying that devotional reading matter for the people also had to be produced, but this was long confined to translations of works often projected in Latin by Dutch-speaking authors and to collections of religious songs which contained scarcely anything new.

The two writers who eventually did once more create something original in the vernacular did not employ the loftier style which De Harduyn had attempted and which in Holland was within the reach of Protestants and Catholics alike, but wrote

[1] See above, p. 30.

as simply and directly as possible. I am thinking of Boëtius à Bolswert and of Father Poirters, and I am far from wanting to belittle the literary talent of either. But after having observed that the whole domain of culture was in the South brought under the dominion of the Counter-Reformation, it is no less necessary to emphasise that the share of the vernacular was being confined to mere popularisation, to what could actually reach the multitude.

No doubt in that way the two writers mentioned best realised their literary gift. Boete of Bolsward (in Friesland) was an engraver who worked at Antwerp, by no means the only one whose Catholicism had driven him into exile from the North. *Dovekin's and Willykin's pilgrimage to their loved ones in Jerusalem*, which appeared in 1627 with illustrations by the author, proceeds from a long medieval tradition and at the same time owes a debt to Jesuit mysticism. The descriptions of the wanderings of the worldly Willykin are charmingly written, and the book was widely read even in the North.

Father Poirters was himself a Jesuit, and his output was much more extensive than that of Boëtius and, always within strict limits, more varied. Born at Oisterwyk in the territory of 's Hertogenbosch, his studies and labours had taken him to live in every corner of the Spanish Netherlands, Mechlin, Louvain, Maastricht, Roermond, Dunkirk, Bruges, before he and his superiors became conscious of his gift as a popular writer. He had collaborated in the translation of the great work in which the achievements of his order were celebrated on the occasion of its centenary (1640). In 1644 appeared the first version of the popular book which he was finally to entitle *The World's Mask Withdrawn* and whose importance was realised in his own lifetime. In its first form it was no more than a version of one of the many devotional books of emblems which had been produced in Latin under the auspices of the Jesuits; Otto Vaenius (Van Veen), the painter, had written one at the instigation of Isabella herself. By means of the inclusion of examples from everyday life, sketches and stories, and using the colourful language of common speech, Poirters made something very striking of the humdrum *genre*. It is true he had had a precursor, none other than Cats, in whose *Mirror of the Old and New Time* moralising emblems had been so attractively popularised. Cats was as highly prized in the South as in the North. His Protestantism was not of the dogmatic variety; his pietism with its moralising tendency and aversion to the world did not accord ill with the Jesuits' view of life. Poirters could thus without apprehension learn much from Cats, but he is not really a second Cats. The Jesuit allows his own personality to come into the foreground much less than did the Zealand regent, and for that reason does not so often strike an unpleasant note; he is much more purely, and also much more fervently, teacher and preacher, but at the same time, despite his popular wit and vivid style, by which in his prose he surpasses Cats, a much less significant literary personality.

V

Social Conditions

LET US glance back for a moment at the society, in both North and South, which gave birth to all this. Political occurrences, economic expansion or regression, cultural life—here and there in our account of these various activities and processes we have been able to observe social conditions from varying points of view. It remains to make one or two more direct remarks.

In this respect, too, if we take in the whole of the Netherlands at a glance, there was still a great deal that all the provinces had in common. We have seen how deeply society, in both North and South, was permeated by a conception of law in the form of respect for particular rights, and how everywhere there existed a broad middle class, which strove to defend itself by gild regulations against the inroads of capitalism, and to share in literary and intellectual life through the medium of Chambers of Rhetoric (though in the North-Eastern provinces these were but weakly represented). Above this middle class there rose everywhere an aristocracy, a regent class, differently composed and with a constitutional basis varying from province to province. Disregarding for the moment the difference in political weight which the separation brought about between this class in the North and its counterpart in the South, the sharpest contrast was between Holland and Zealand on the one hand, and the landward provinces of the Republic on the other, while the position in Flanders and Brabant offers similarities to both these extremes.

Throughout the Republic the nobility formed an absolutely closed caste, but it wielded great political power only in the landward provinces. In these, save in the towns of Utrecht and Groningen, town magistrates commanded but slight prestige. The towns were relatively small and, compared with the great towns of Holland, Zealand, Flanders and Brabant, economically backward; the trade boom passed them by. Moreover, most of their magistrates were still more or less dependent on their citizens (through "commoners' committees" and the like), and this was also to a certain extent true of Flanders and Brabant, and even of Zealand. Burgomasters of Arnhem or Zwolle or Leeuwarden certainly appeared in the States-General as members of their provincial deputations, but among the representatives of these provinces only the nobles cut any figure at The Hague and in the general political life of the Republic. In Holland and Zealand, on the other hand, it was the middle-class town regents who had the real power in their hands and played the leading rôle on the national stage. The Holland nobility, numerically weak as it was, allied itself as little with the great burgher families as did that of the more agrarian and feudal provinces of the East.

Now in the South there were at once a numerous nobility, as in Gelderland or Utrecht, and important towns with wealthy oligarchical families, as in Holland; but the two classes did not remain apart, they blended with one another and with the monarch's ennobled bureaucrats. To obtain an idea of the difference, one should picture to oneself the country houses and their occupiers in the various provinces. In Flanders and Brabant, no less than in Utrecht and the North-East, the castles of medieval origin and lordly air are to be counted by the dozen; the Flemish ones are depicted in *Flandria Illustrata*, some more modernised than others, but all moated, with drawbridges and towers. The castles in Gelderland or Overysel were inhabited by the old families intimately attached to the region, many of them still enjoying exorbitant feudal privileges. But where Flanders is concerned, if one looks beyond the names of these ancient dwellings for the names of their owners one lights upon a motley collection; some go back to the earliest age of the province's history, but in other cases the titles conceal town magistrates or officials arrived at greatness, these last not seldom foreigners. In Holland there stood here and there among the medieval ruins some castles with their moats and battlements intact; they were sometimes occupied—like the 'high castle' of Muiden—by the representatives of towns which ruled neighbouring rural districts, and in a few cases by surviving members of the ancient nobility. But the gentry of the Holland countryside were for the most part municipal patricians lately waxed rich, who sometimes also derived fine-sounding titles from a manor they had purchased and along with them acquired certain extremely limited privileges (perhaps the most substantial of them being the appointment of ministers and teachers). On the whole, however, the town remained these men's real abode, and their country houses or farms were no more than places of relaxation lacking even the outward appearance of ancient noble origin.

All things considered, this Holland regent class is not only the most important political factor, but also the most notable social phenomenon in the Netherlands throughout the seventeenth century and beyond; and certainly the most peculiar. Probably for this reason historical tradition has shown this class little favour. This intermixing of commerce and government, this concentration of political power in middle-class hands, often roused the antagonism of foreign visitors, as indeed did the whole of the sudden outburst of commercial capitalism in the Northern Netherlands. The Catholic Church had never succeeded in properly fitting into her system this mercantile class, which on its first appearance she had detested, indeed treating as suspect the whole institution of money-capital increasing itself through interest. To the aristocratic conception of society as much as to the petty bourgeois gild-ideal, to all such feelings and views associated with the more stable conditions of the past, the changes which took place in rebellious, Protestant, republican Holland represented a reckless overthrow of all restraints. I do not mean that the condemnation, even when made by Italian or French observers, usually proceeded from a positive Catholic view. It is a fact, nevertheless, that numerous witnesses hailing from the Catholic countries of Europe were shocked to find that greed of gain seemed the prime motive power, not only of the leading class, but of the entire community.

In this great town (*writes Descartes from Amsterdam*), where apart from myself there dwells no one who is not engaged in trade, everyone is so much out for his own advantage that I should be able to live my whole life here without ever meeting a mortal being.

And this was the Amsterdam where dwelt Vondel and Rembrandt, P. C. Hooft, Barlaeus and Vossius!—but is any proof needed to show that this is a ludicrous verdict? All that it proves is that the visitor had remained an outsider. And the little esteem with which foreigners spoke of the regents (we have heard[1] what Charles I said of them) belongs to the same category of prejudice. Sprung from the brewers, the tanners and the soap-boilers of a few generations back, who at that time still ranked equally with the merchants and shipowners, the burgo-master families of Amsterdam, the cream of the whole class, had risen by the middle of the seventeenth century to cut the figure of merchant princes and capitalists—in their own sur-roundings a *great* figure, with their fine houses on the Singel or the Heerengracht and their country-seats in the reclaimed Beemster or on the river Vecht. Many of the leading Amsterdam regents remained business-men, managing great concerns, or at least directly interested in them, but public office occupied an ever more important place in their lives, and often they trained themselves for it from youth up. Nevertheless, in the eyes of foreign observers they remained tradesmen, and it was a commonplace to suspect them of knowing no other rule of statecraft than covetousness.

This commonplace is by no means current among foreigners only. I have had occasion to show that at times the regents did subordinate the problems of the country to those of their own particular town or of trade. But one must bear in mind that once the opposition between States supporters and Orangists had come to dominate political life, there was always an eager audience for the most hateful interpretations of the other side's actions. Of the two party views, the Orangist one was in the nineteenth century (for both survived the Republic of the Seven Provinces) by far the most popular, and modern historical scholarship has not always been sufficiently on its guard against the legend's distorting effects. The regents' shortcomings were sometimes serious, but they should in fairness be viewed in relation to the whole. Just as the trade itself which raised the Republic to a high level among the nations without assuring it a solid basis for the future was the result of forces beyond human volition or control, so the Holland regent-class with its peculiar outlook was a natural phenomenon, an expression of the nation's history. If one begins by recognising that the policy of an organism such as Amsterdam *must* attach immense

[1] See above, p. 137.

importance to trade, then there remains much in the life and work of its oligarchic exponents that, in the conditions such as they were settled for good or ill by the separation, has possessed great positive value for Dutch life.

The drawbacks of the oligarchic regime in government were to make themselves only too apparent in the history of the Republic. This makes no difference to the fact that it began by creating generations of real rulers, and at the same time a theory of the State in which their relation towards the ruled could find long-standing stability. The commonalty was required to submit to its lawful rulers; government in town and country was the exclusive privilege of municipal councils and States assemblies, constituted according to ancient usage, that is to say, without any direct intervention on the part of the commonalty. At the same time no one was supposed to be excluded on grounds of birth, and there was a well-established doctrine that the deputies 'represented' everybody and must keep faithful watch over the interests of all. It goes without saying that this ideal arrangement was never fully translated into practice; sometimes the reality fell very far short of it. We have seen to what a severe test it was put by the religious disputes, when the Reformed citizens and their guardians were here and there fiercely opposed to one another. Moreover, many regents early misused the irresponsible power entrusted to them. Burgomaster Hooft was much exercised over the 'self-seeking' of some of his colleagues. Vondel depicts in his *Curry-comb* the degeneration of the paternal authority into unfeeling oppression, when he makes the regents declare to the 'public ass';

> Our office is to drive, the pack is thine to bear.
> And be content that thou hast fought thee free,
> If not perchance in body, yet so in the spirit.

But in 1626 (the probable date of the poem) Vondel was still feeling bitterly hostile towards his Counter-Remonstrant regents. As soon as he again saw in the Calvinist clergy, whom he hated so intensely, the rivals and enemies of his town authorities, his tone altered noticeably. In these later utterances of the poet, in his glorification of the burgomasters and impassioned expressions of loyalty and devotion to the powers ordained of God, the element of partisanship cannot therefore be ignored; moreover, as he grew older, Vondel came to be dominated by an inward craving for authority. But all this notwithstanding, his attitude may well be called typical of the feelings that inspired large sections of the public in all the Holland towns, and especially at Amsterdam.

And, indeed, neither nepotism nor corruption assumed their worst forms in Holland during this period. In monarchical countries such as England or France the standard of political morals was certainly lower, and in the Republic itself these evils flourished worst in Zealand, and, above all, in Friesland, where the very word *kuipen* (intrigue) took its origin. The venality of a man like the Greffier Musch, and of many of the deputies of the nobility from the landward provinces, was an attendant phenomenon, not of the rule of the Holland oligarchy, but of the growing monarchism against which that oligarchy set its face. It was otherwise with the scandalous speculations at the country's expense of which the members of the Rotterdam Admiralty were proved guilty in 1626. But these provoked a very effective outburst of public opinion and after a strict investigation by the States-General were visited with severe punishments. The oligarchy was not yet so based upon itself but that public censure could affect it and cause it to react.

The disintegrating influence of the rising capitalism that preached the doctrine of every man for himself and lifted one group high above the rest by providing fortunes of a magnitude hitherto unknown, had not yet badly shaken the feeling of solidarity which used to envelop the whole of a town. Be the leading regents never such fine gentry, the rise of their families from humbler circumstances usually remained fresh in the public memory. Not all regents, indeed, were as wealthy and important as some. Between the town council taken as a whole and the well-to-do citizen class there existed numerous ties of friendship and kindred. The merchant class, though it grumbled from time to time that the regents had sunk too much money in land to be still intimately concerned in trade, knew its interests were in safe hands and indeed found a ready ear for its desires and opinions; and with such amazing prosperity in every branch of life, no section of the community felt the urge to dispute the direction of affairs with 'the gentlemen'. There was to be no question of a democratic movement for a long time yet. Meanwhile, all found common ground in civic pride. How strong the old community feeling still was may be seen in the many benefactions and foundations on behalf of the poor established in every Holland town. Who does not know them, the almshouses, the orphanages, the old men's and old women's institutions, which arose in the seventeenth century? This was naturally no peculiar merit of the oligarchy, it testifies to a spirit active through a much wider circle, but one which the regents shared to the full. In municipal administration the spirit manifested itself at Amsterdam in the boldly designed and vigorously executed plan of extensions, which gave the town that splendid series of concentric semi-circular canals abutting on the river Y; and again, in the building of the town hall on the Dam, furnished with a splendour in which the pride and the artistic feeling of the time were both reflected, a real citizens' palace, which to be sure afforded the burgomasters an inaccessible sanctum in their council chamber, but whose public hall and galleries were open to the entire population.

P. C. Hooft, the Amsterdam burgomaster's son, is in himself sufficient proof that this class yielded fruitful soil for the growth of a refined and fundamentally Dutch culture. So fine a mind could not spring from the broader middle-class ranks, so purely Dutch a figure was not possible among the aristocracy. And in the political sphere, too, the Amsterdam regent class produced some really great figures during this period, men who from their council chairs helped to shape the policy of the Republic; such men as Reiner Pauw and Andries Bicker. Pauw, who filled the leading position at Amsterdam (which was called 'the magnificat') during the last years of the Truce, was a large shipowner and one of the original directors of the East India Company. Bicker controlled the municipal government from about 1627 in alliance with his brothers and with his relatives the De Graeff family, all of them wealthy merchants and shippers. In spite of the wide difference in outlook between the fierce Counter-Remonstrant and the imperious Libertinist, one is struck in both cases by the strong, passionate personalities, characterised by conviction and assurance of power. These traits correspond to the proud upsurge of the town, but they must also be partly ascribed to the peculiar election customs of Amsterdam, which tended to concentrate power in one leading man's hands. In any case, when faced with these sharply marked figures of true statesmen risen from the broad regent class, it is to misjudge both national character and historic truth to keep harping on petty-minded commercialism or greed of gain.

VI

Epilogue

THE SENTIMENT OF UNITY AND
ITS LIMITATIONS

IN THE foregoing chapters, whether dealing with cultural, social or political matters, we have watched the progressive effects following upon the violent disruption of a natural entity described in the previous volume *The Revolt of the Netherlands*. Yet even now Flanders, Brabant and Upper Gelderland still had much more in common with the Northern provinces than their language; the community of social and cultural traditions still showed dogged powers of resistance.

In the first place, the new (and still so uncertain) frontier was bridged by numerous personal connections. The exiles from Flanders and Brabant and their descendants played an important rôle in the North and they often kept in touch with relatives remaining in the South. I recall a few names already mentioned in various connections: Usselinx, De Laet, Pieter van den Broecke, Melyn, the Elseviers, Gomarus, Daniel Heinsius, Vondel, Huygens, Hals; Cats's wife and Hooft's second wife were both from Antwerp. On the other side, too, there were many men whose origins were in the North as for instance: Boëtius à Bolswert, Jansenius, Otto Vaenius; Vaenius' brother, who returned to the North and became secretary of The Hague, reflected in his family the spiritual disruption of the nation.

Nowhere does the basic unity come out more clearly than in the art of the painter. Since it has become usual to ignore the Utrecht school and all Italian influence in the Holland school, and at the same time simply to equate the Flemish school with Rubens, it has been found possible to postulate a plain North-South contrast. We have seen how little this accords with reality. Just as during the Middle Ages, so now the bent towards painting was a trait in which the cultural unity of Holland, Utrecht, Brabant and Flanders expressed itself, and the persistence of the traditions and the constant interchange of influences and personalities had been scarcely diminished even by the war. Art-lovers in the North had a thorough knowledge of the work of the Antwerpers and set the highest store by it: Vondel and Huygens loved to praise not only Rubens, but Snyders, Jordaens, Van Dyck, and even the less important floral painter Daniel Seghers, a Jesuit; all were patronised by the Stadholder. No one thought of speaking of two schools of painting, a Dutch and a Flemish, or a North- and a South-Netherland school. When about 1630 Huygens enumerates the 'history painters', he includes those of Amsterdam, of Utrecht. of The Hague, of Antwerp, in a word, of the Netherlands ('Belgium' in his Latin[1]):

and the chief and Apelles of them all is P. P. Rubens, whom I rank as one of the wonders of the world. . . . He has not escaped the envy of the Italians, nor, save the mark, of the English, who imagine that their buying up of foreign pictures fits them to pass judgment on Rubens! But how often has he not dispersed these mists with the splendour of his sun! For myself I have always cherished the conviction that there is no one, nor that there shall easily rise up anyone from outside the Netherlands, who in wealth of invention, in daring beauty of form, or in perfect variety of all kinds of painting, shall rival him.

One sees here Huygens, when on the defensive against Italians and Englishmen, drawing national pride from the greatness of Rubens. Even when at a later period the history of painting as told by Van Mander was continued, the authors always keep to Van Mander's plan,[2] the Southerner De Bie no less than the Northerner Houbraken, treating Hollanders and Flemings indiscriminately as Netherland painters.

The idea of unity was no less strong in literature, notwithstanding that conditions were so different here. For while in painting the Flemings enjoyed the greatest repute, in the literary sphere the Northerners no longer paid much attention to what was doing in the South—and is it to be wondered at? Huygens and Anna Visscher, who corresponded with Southerners, inevitably came into contact with circles whose cultural language was Latin. The same is true of Vondel. On *their* cultural plane Dutch was hardly used any longer in Flanders and Brabant. Nevertheless, those who did use it felt strengthened

[1] See note on p. 260 ff.
[2] See *The Revolt of the Netherlands*, p. 281.

by the example of the celebrated Hollanders. What an unheard-of situation in relations between North and South, that the North should have set the literary tone—but indeed, so it was now! In 1622 Willem van der Elst, a parish priest at Bouchoute, wrote in the preface to a collection of his *Religious Poems*:

> Who seeks the rightful law of poetry to learn,
> To Heinsius and Cats with profit he may turn.
> These two, now faméd long by men who understand,
> Give splendid proof thereof throughout all Netherland.

That clerics did not shun the lessons of Cats we have already seen in the case of Poirters. But over and above that, when a few years later a Bruges literary man, De Wree, wanted to celebrate the exploits of the Duke of Bucquoy, he made bold to do so in Dutch solely because 'that language-master Heins' had done so before him: true, he calls him 'the Ghent nightingale' and says that he had published verses 'in Flemish', but it is irony enough that he should cite the example of a professor at the heretical university of Leiden for his paean in praise of a commander in the service of the Habsburgs. Meanwhile the coyness of his 'Flemish Muse' is characteristic. Generally speaking, polemical and political poetry, in which the best minds in the North at times produced work of undying beauty, in the South remained in the hands of rhetoricians and popularisers. Men of that stamp it was who occasionally carried on controversies across the frontier in connection with the happenings of the war. The great North-Netherland poets did not find their match in the South for this purpose; even Father Costerus and Versteghen they could hardly accept as such. When figures of national stature engaged in mutual vituperation, like Voetius and Jansenius after the capitulation of 's Hertogenbosch, then the Southern theologian's broadsides were in Latin.

I have already observed in passing that the development of a universal civilised language in the North was still a long way from having gone as far as it might. Ministers of religion, politicians and writers, the three groups to which it owed most, each wrote their own variety of Dutch, while owing to the gallicising influence radiating from the Orange Court, to which the aristocracy were exposed, the unifying factor was lacking. The North-Netherland nobility was, indeed, more deeply gallicised during this period than it had been under the pressure of the Burgundian influence, which had been somewhat less potent in Holland than in Brabant and Flanders, and in the North-Eastern provinces much less potent than in Holland itself. Yet on the whole, there was progress in this sphere in the North, while in the South we observe a retrogression.

Side by side with the writers, I mentioned ministers and politicians. The Reformed Church exerted an immense influence on the spread of a standard Dutch, not only through the translation of the Bible, but also by way of the pulpit; and the States assemblies not less so, however studded with bastard words their 'town-hall speech' might be. The influence of the Catholic Church in the South certainly worked in the same direction; it is no accident that the two best-known writers of Dutch poetry of this period, De Harduyn and Poirters, were clerics. But that influence was not so far-reaching, because in the higher ranks of the Church there was the obstacle of Latin. A writer like Costerus, who, excellent as he was, had no other ambition than to reach the people, was really more typical than were the poets who tried to fly higher. And while it is true enough that the States of Brabant and those of Flanders and Upper Gelderland, as well as the provincial law-courts there, continued to use a Dutch very little different from the 'town-hall speech' of the North, how insignificant, indeed, was their rôle compared with that of the corresponding organs in the Republic! Above all, there was in the South no central focal point such as the North had in its States-General; and when once again for a short time there was such a body, as in 1632–33, then the presence of Walloon deputies necessitated the use of French. Meanwhile, the whole of the permanent administration at the centre was conducted in French; not only were officials and jurists obliged to use that language continually in their correspondence with Brussels, but it was becoming the everyday language of all who rose to the top. To this situation the Republic offers a sharp contrast. From top to bottom Dutch was the language of politics, of administration, of law. The Orange Court was a centre of gallicisation, but that must be understood in a social sense; in his Stadholderly functions and transactions with organs of State, no Prince of Orange could ever use any language but Dutch.

So there began, between North and South, that divergence

in the matter of the language of polite intercourse which in the fullness of time, in the nineteenth century, would come to appear an unbridgeable gulf.[1] Dutch as spoken in Holland, backed by the superior power of this leading province, conquered the entire Northern Union. Supported by the same political and religious factors, it even crossed the Eastern frontier: through the medium of the garrisons, through dependence on The Hague, but above all through the influence of the Reformed ministers, Holland-Dutch secured a strong position in East Friesland and in Cleves. The process whereby the Holland dialect was becoming the basis of the new civilised language did not of itself present any danger to relations between North and South. For this dialect was much more akin to the Flemish-Brabant language than to the Saxon of the Eastern Provinces, not to mention Frisian. Moreover, no breach was attempted with the tradition of literary language hitherto built up in the South, and in this work of construction, too, Flemish and Brabant exiles played a leading part. The real difference is, that whereas in the North the accepted cultural language was continuing to develop and at the same time extending its sway, in the South it was decaying and loosening its hold over the dialects. The South, too, had its East. Remember the jargon that the Upper Gelderland noble Van den Bergh (a subject of the Archdukes) wrote to his North Gelderland relative Culemborch[2], the same dialect that Culemborch's grandfather had spoken[3]; but the Culemborch of the day (a product of generations of Northern independence) replied in standard Dutch.

One must not imagine, however, that these linguistic developments were already making for estrangement between North and South. The time was still far distant when gentlemen of Flanders and Brabant would not dare to use their own language in intercourse with their Northern equals, while in the matter of dialectic differences, the civilised language of the North had certainly not yet penetrated so deep that Hollanders were not

---

[1] I must add, however, that the decisive factor, by which the slow undermining process suddenly made way for a relentless and purposeful policy of gallicisation, was the twenty years' annexation of Belgium to France following upon the conquest by the armies of the Revolution in 1792–94.

[2] See above, p. 98.

[3] See *The Revolt of the Netherlands*, p. 168.

sometimes treated in the States-General, by Groningers and Overyselers, to accents much stranger than, for instance, the Archbishop of Mechlin's speech of 1632 can have sounded to them.

In the literary sphere the Southerners clung to the traditional unity. We have already seen something of this in the extent to which they permitted themselves to imitate Heins, Cats and Vondel. It is also curiously illustrated in the indignation with which an Antwerper, in the course of a political paper-war over one of Frederick Henry's campaigns, repulsed the derision of the Deventer poet Jan van der Veen, who had thought to caricature him and his fellow-countrymen by writing verses brimful of the most outrageous bastard-words:

> Why dost reproach us with these foreign-court effects?
> Know'st not, O stupid mule, that everyone was wont
> Such speech to use, who e'er was trained in rhetoricians' school,
> In Holland just as much as under Brabant's rule?

Notwithstanding the ready amusement with which the North received Breero's caricature of the Spanish Brabanter, there can be no doubt that the feeling engendered by community of language gave substance to the idea of Netherland unity, albeit this generally found expression in the phrase 'the seventeen provinces'. The idea of unity was still current. Maps and descriptions of the country were still constructed on its basis; even in legal documents the seventeen provinces remained a recognised entity, and in the names 'Netherlands' and 'Netherlander' (*Belgium, Belga*) North and South were still comprised. But it hardly needs to be repeated that the political significance of this idea of unity was restricted. The men of the seventeenth century had great respect for the existing State; in any case they deduced its rights from wholly other considerations than those of cultural cohesion. We have already seen that between this and the possibility or desirability of a reunion of the Netherlands some connection was at times made; but it was at best a passing thought. Anna Roemers Visscher was oppressed by the monstrous fact of the state of war which had now existed for so long between North and South. After one of her visits to the South she described in a famous letter to Pieter Roose, president of the Secret Council at Brussels, how a distinguished company gathered at the house of Grand-Pensionary Cats had toasted his health.

> In the midst of this jovial banquet my heart was heavy and distressed within me at the misery of the beautiful Netherlands, ravaged and oppressed by this devilish fury, the accursed war.

Yet in the same letter she made a distinction between her 'fatherland', the North, and her 'friends' land', the South. And when in 1648 Vondel, he too a Catholic, celebrated the peace of Münster with his play *The Liondalers*, he accepted the political dualism without hesitation.

> Land's Crown (Spain) recognised the North part of Liondale as a LIBERTY on its own. From both sides people welcomed and embraced each other, whereupon the wedding-feast began. . . .
>
> The cows yield milk and cream.
> It is butter from ceiling to beam.
> And all is Peace and Joy.

That the peace of Münster not only left the Spanish Netherlands crippled and exhausted in face of the menace from France, but perpetuated a situation in which the Dutch civilisation of the South was bound to wither—was there anyone who appreciated that momentous fact?

NOTE ON THE WORD 'BELGIUM'

THE word *Belgium* in sixteenth and seventeenth century Latin has caused a good deal of misunderstanding among later generations. The editor and translator of Huygens' autobiography, in which the passages quoted on p. 255 occur, Worp (*Oud-Holland*, 1891), translates *Belgium* by *the Netherlands* and *Belga* by *Netherlander* whenever the context unmistakably requires this translation; and yet when Huygens writes: 'Delphi, Batavi (? Batavia), Belgium, Europa' (p. 121), he translates: 'Delft, Netherlands, Belgium, Europe', while what Huygens intended was a climax: 'Delft, Holland, Netherlands, Europe'. The Fleming Dr. Sabbe makes the same mistake in *De Moretussen en hun kring*, 1928, p. 13, where he makes B. Moretus pray for peace 'for the Belgians': Moretus (this was still only in

1589!) was naturally thinking of the whole of the Netherlands. Similarly on p. 119, in rendering remarks by Grotius, Gevartius and Schottus, Dr. Sabbe falls into this error. Even in the quotation from Grotius' letter, where the context clearly demands the translation 'Netherlands', Sabbe writes 'Belgium': 'This was one of the chief reasons why I wish to visit the part of Belgium where you live: the war has for a long time prevented this, and after the armistice the fear that it would be taken in ill part restrained me.' Why should the war have made one part of the loyal provinces more difficult for Grotius to visit than another?

But indeed, the use of *Belgium* or *Belgica* for the Netherlands is well established, quite apart from the context in a particular passage. Even where 'the Netherlands' already means in fact the Northern Netherlands, it was usually rendered by *Belgium* or *Belgica*. This was even official usage. In diplomatic documents the Northern States-General styled themselves *Ordines Generales Foederati Belgii*; the Dutch East India Company was called *Belgica Societas Indiae Orientalis*; an example in Anglo-Dutch diplomatic exchanges is to be found in Aitzema, VIII, p. 1537. In the later part of his *Annales et Historiae de Rebus Belgicis* (which naturally cannot be translated otherwise than by 'Netherland affairs'), Grotius uses the word *Batavus* to render North-Netherlandish (in the official privilege, however, prefixed in the Blaeu edition of 1658, the Northern States-General are called *Ordines Foederatae Belgicae*). But *Belgica* always means the Netherlands, *e.g. Ordines totius Belgicae* (p. 62); and at the end, too: *validum esse, se cohaereat, Belgicae corpus* ('that the whole of the Netherlands, if they remain united, are strong'; p. 781: 1608). I would point also to the title page of Bor's *Nederlantsche Oorlogen*, 1626 (reproduced on p. 282 of Vol. I of my *Geschiedenis van de Nederlandse Stam*, second edition): *Belgica*, who is there shown mourning the corpse of William the Silent, naturally does not represent 'Belgium'; to the *Nimpha Belgica* of the allegory mentioned on p. 223 of *The Revolt of the Netherlands*, who wishes to reconcile the two groups of the then (1594) warring provinces; and to the map of the W. I. Company settlement in North America (also reproduced on p. 51 of Vol. II of *Geschiedenis van de Nederlandse Stam*, second edition) with the legend *Nova Belgica sive Nieuw Nederlandt* (1656).

Finally, I will mention the title of a translation of Guicciardini's description of the seventeen provinces published at Amsterdam in 1648: '*Belgium, that is; the Netherlands* . . .', and of a work which appeared at Amsterdam in 1715: *Antiquitates Belgicae, or Netherlands antiquities. Being the first origin of Holland, Zealand, the Bishopric of Utrecht, Overijsel, Friesland, Brabant, Flanders, etc.* . . .

These are examples chosen at random, which could be multiplied indefinitely. Had our contemporaries not smuggled in the word *Belgium* so eagerly where the context did not clearly rule it out (or even where it did!) none of this would need to be said. As it is, I would once again expressly warn my readers that in a multitude of cases satisfactory evidence of the persistence of the idea of Netherlands unity has been effaced by this mistranslation.

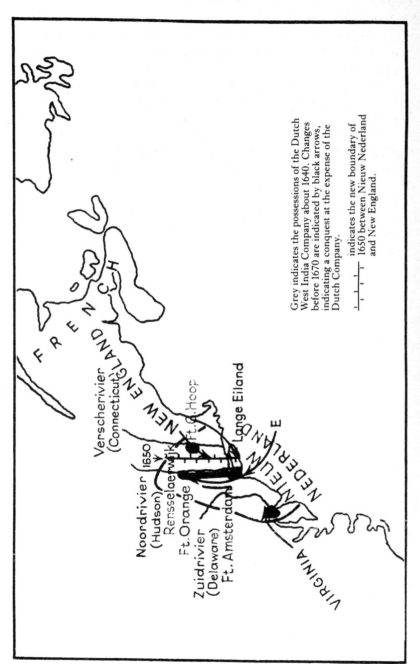

Grey indicates the possessions of the Dutch West India Company about 1640. Changes before 1670 are indicated by black arrows, indicating a conquest at the expense of the Dutch Company.

–––––––– indicates the new boundary of 1650 between Nieuw Nederland and New England.

THE COLONISATION IN NEW NETHERLAND

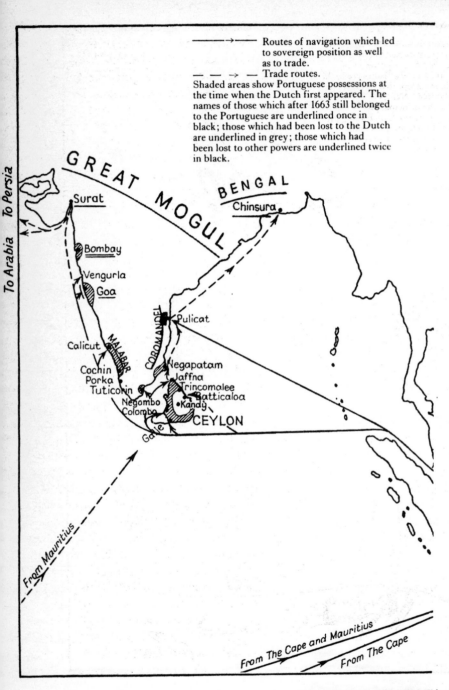

Routes of navigation which led
to sovereign position as well
as to trade.
— — → — Trade routes.
Shaded areas show Portuguese possessions at
the time when the Dutch first appeared. The
names of those which after 1663 still belonged
to the Portuguese are underlined once in
black; those which had been lost to the Dutch
are underlined in grey; those which had
been lost to other powers are underlined twice
in black.

To Persia   To Arabia

GREAT MOGUL

BENGAL

Surat

Chinsura

Bombay

Vengurla

Goa

Calicut

Cochin
Porka
Tuticorin

MALABAR

COROMANDEL

Pulicat

Negapatam
Jaffna
Trincomalee
Batticaloa

Negombo
Colombo   Kandy

Galle   CEYLON

From Mauritius

From The Cape and Mauritius

From The Cape

THE DUTCH EAST

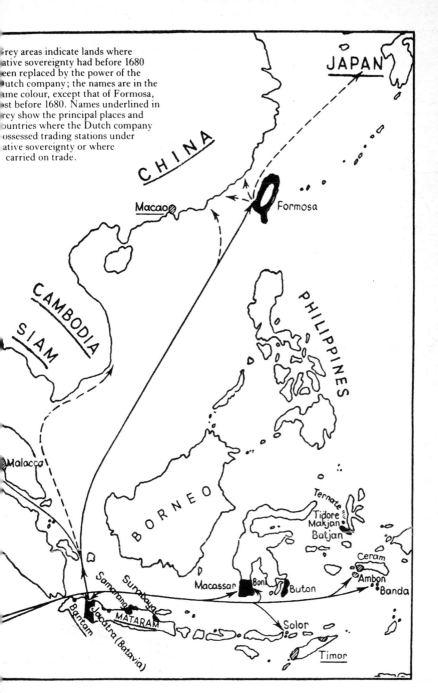

Grey areas indicate lands where native sovereignty had before 1680 been replaced by the power of the Dutch company; the names are in the same colour, except that of Formosa, lost before 1680. Names underlined in grey show the principal places and countries where the Dutch company possessed trading stations under native sovereignty or where carried on trade.

JAPAN

CHINA

Macao

Formosa

CAMBODIA

SIAM

PHILIPPINES

Malacca

BORNEO

Ternate
Tidore
Makjan
Batjan

Ceram
Ambon
Banda

Macassar
Boni
Buton

Solor

Samarang
Surabaya
Bantam
Jacatra (Batavia)
MATARAM

Timor

NDIA COMPANY

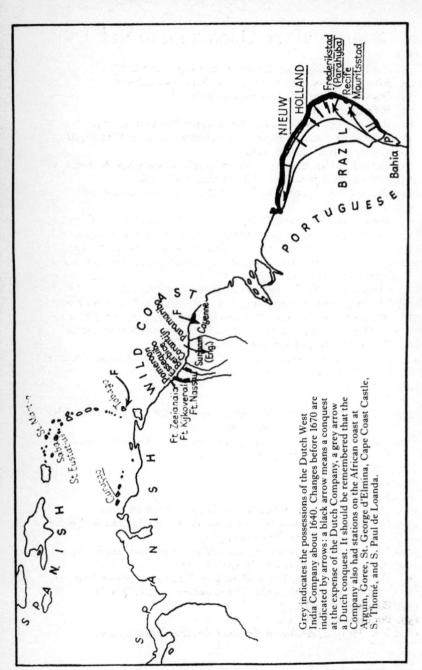

Grey indicates the possessions of the Dutch West
India Company about 1640. Changes before 1670 are
indicated by arrows: a black arrow means a conquest
at the expense of the Dutch Company, a grey arrow
a Dutch conquest. It should be remembered that the
Company also had stations on the African coast at
Arguin, Goree, St. George d'Elmina, Cape Coast Castle,
S. Thomé, and S. Paul de Loanda.

THE CONQUEST OF NORTH BRAZIL

Sources of the Quotations to Vol. I

PAGE

38. See Henne, *Règne de Charles V aux Pays-Bas*, VIII.
44. After p. 154 of the contemporary French translation.
54. Quoted in Roersch, *L'humanisme belge*.
57. *Refereinen*, 154.
60. Burgon, *Life and Times of Sir Thomas Gresham*, I, 175.
78. Quoted by Fruin, *Verspreide Geschriften*, I, from *Vita Viglii*.
80. Lasco, *Opera*, II, 349, note 2.
81. Quoted in Van Schelven, *Nederduitsche Vluchtelingenkerken*, 112.
83. *Bibliotheca Reformatoria Neerlandica*, VIII, 374.
84. *Kroniek van G. van Haecht*, edited by Van Roosbroeck, 66.
91. *O.c.*, 72.
93. Marcus van Vaernewijk, *Van die beroerlijcke tijden van Ghent*.
94. Quoted by Knappert, *Opkomst van het Protestantisme*, 241.
99. The latest edition of collected Beggar Songs is by E. Kuyper.
102–3. Quoted after Fruin, *Verspreide Geschriften*, II, 89, and Rachfahl, *Wilhelm von Oranien*, III, 142.
113. Quoted after Fruin, *Verspreide Geschriften*, II, 172.
115. Conyers Read, *Walsingham*, I, 154 (Walsingham to Leicester).
118. *Archives de la Maison d'Orange-Nassau*, III, 512, and IV, 4.
119–20. *O.c.*, IV, 29; letter from Count Neuenahr (Nieuwenaer).
122. Pieter Bor, *Nederlandtsche Oorloghen*, I, 269.
123. J. van Vloten, *Nederland's Volksopstand tegen Spanje*, volume on 1572–1573, p. xliv.
127. Bor, I, 275.
128. Bor, I, 266 ff.
130A. Kluit, *Hollandsche Staatsregering*, I, 378; letter from the Prince to the town of Gouda.
130B. Bakhuizen van den Brink, *Cartons tot de geschiedenis van den Nederlandschen vrijheidsoorlog*, II, 202.
130C. *O.c.*, 205.
132. Bor, I, 302 ff.
134A & B. Bor, I, 327.
137. *Oude verhalen van het beleg van Leiden*, edited by Fruin.
147. *Resolutiën der Staten-Generaal*, edited by N. Japikse in "Rijks Geschiedkundige Publicatiën," I, 8.
152A & B. Bondam, *Verzameling van onuitgegeevene stukken*, I, 283.
152C. De Jonge, *De Unie van Brussel*, II, 17.
153. Quoted after Blok, *Geschiedenis van het Nederlandsche Volk*, II, 131; the original in the *Correspondance de Philippe II*.
155. Bondam, *o.c.*, III, 55.
159. Bondam, *o.c.*, IV, 282.
162A & B. Hessels, *Archivum Ecclesiae Londino-Batavae*, 626.

PAGE

165. De Schrevel, *Troubles religieux en Flandre* (edited for the Société d'Emulation de Bruges), II, p. xviii.

167. Van de Spieghel, *Bundel van onuitgegeevene stukken (voornaamelijk Unie van Utrecht)*, I, 34.

168A & B. Account of the Diet held at Arnhem, published in *Bijdragen voor Vaderlandsche Geschiedenis*, I, 126.

169. *O.c.*, 328.

171. Bor, II, 164.

172A. In a poem entitled "Nieuwjaar, 1678."

172B. Report of Van Leyden, burgomaster of Utrecht, published by Blok in the *Bijdragen en Mededeelingen van het Historisch Genootschap te Utrecht*, 1919.

178. In a pamphlet entitled *Bedencke van der Nederlanden noodt ende hulpe.*

182. *Politieke Balladen*, edited for the "Vlaanische Bibliophielen," II, VII, 293.

185. Q. Janssen, *Kerkhervorming in Vlaanderen*, II, 209.

188A & B. Everhart van Reyd, *Voornaemste Geschiedenissen in de Nederlanden*, 39, 41.

190A. P. Verheyden, *Antwerpsch Letterkundig Leven*, 13.

190B. Janssen, *o.c.*, II, 275.

193. *Archives de la Maison d'O.-N.*, VIII, 133.

195. Printed in Bor, III, 28 sqq.

199. *Calendar of Foreign State Papers*, 1584–1585, 622; Le Sieur to Walsingham.

205. Thus Vrancken in the discourse mentioned above, p. 198 (Bor III, 33).

209. Joris de Bye, in a memorandum printed *Bijdragen en Mededeelingen van het Historisch Genootschap*, 1888, p. 424.

212A & B. *Calendar of Foreign State Papers*, 1586, 63.

213. After the Dutch translation given by Bor.

220. Published by Haak, in *Bijdragen voor Vaderlandsche Geschiedenis*, 1920, 23.

223. Van Meteren, *Belgische ofte Nederl. Historie van onsen tijden.*

229. Ypey en Dermout, *Geschiedenis der Nederlandsch Hervormde Kerk*, II, 108.

230A, B, C, D, & E. The report was published in the *Bijdragen en Mededeelingen van het Historisch Genootschap*, 1884.

233. *Memoriën en Adviezen van C. P. Hooft*, edited for the Historisch Genootschap, 1871.

234. Elias, *Schetsen van het Nederlandsche Zeewezen*, I, 71.

239. Van Meteren, *o.c.*

241. Gachard, *Etats-Généraux de 1600*, p. cxlii.

243. *O.c.*, 764.

PAGE
244. Van der Kemp, *Leven van Maurits*, II, 460.
245A & B. *Gachard, o.c.*, 780.
246. Van Meteren, *o.c.*
247. Extracts from his correspondence were published in the *Codex Diplomaticus* of the Historisch Genootschap.
252A. Published in Bor.
252B. Van Meterren, *o.c.*

Sources of the Quotations to Vol. II

306. Quoted in Engelberts, *Willem Teellinck*, 84.
308. (a) Eryci Puteani, *Des oorlogs ende vredes waegschale*, translated from the Latin by C. D. Muliers, The Hague, 1633. Knuttel, W. P. C., *Catalogus van de Pamfletten-verzameling . . . in de Koninklijke Bibliotheek* (Den Haag), 4304.
(b) *Antwoordt op 't Munsters Praetie*, 1646. Knuttel, *op. cit.*, 5296.
309. *Opere storiche del Cardinal Bentivoglio* (ed. 1806), I, 161.
310. Dated 31 March 1619. Lonchay and Cuvelier, *Correspondance de la Cour d'Espagne sur les affaires des Pays-Bas au XVIIe siècle*, I, 527.
316. See R. Hardeman V.J., *Franciscus Costerus, en Vlaamsche aportel en volksredenaar*, 1933.
319. The phrases quoted descriptive of Harduyn and his circle are from O. Dambre, *De dichter Justus de Harduyn* (1926), 141.
321. Ch. Ruelens and Max Rooses, *Correspondance de P. P. Rubens*, V, 14.
331. (a) J. Trigland, *Kerckelycke Geschiedenissen . . . ende aenmerckingen op de Kerckelycke Historie van Joh. Utenbogaert* (1650), 428.
(b) Quoted in Maronier, *Jacobus Arminius*, 142.
332. (a) Thus Utenbogaert in 1611. Quoted in Rogge, *J. Utenbogaert en zijn tijd*, II, 86.
(b) Thus Robbert Robbertsz. in 1610. Quoted in Meinsma, *Spinoza en zijn kring*, 21.
(c) *Verhooren van Oldenbarnevelt*, in *Kronijk van het Hist. Gen. te Utrecht* (Utrecht Historical Society), 6de jaarg. (1850), 40.
334. Dated 3 October 1611. Motley, *Life and Death of John of Barneveld*, I, 307.
335. Quoted in L. H. Wagenaar, *Van Strijd en overwinning; de groote Synode . . .* (1919), 118.
336. From the Preface of Utenbogaert's *Treatise* mentioned in the text.

PAGE

337. (*a, b* and *c*) The resolution of 1614 in pamphlet-form: Knuttel, *op. cit.*, 2503.

(*d*) Trigland, *op. cit.*, 678.

338. To Caron, 21 January 1612. Motley, *op. cit.*, I, 312.

339. Quoted in Wagenaar, *op. cit.*, 196.

342. *Verhooren van H. de Groot*, in *Werken van het Hist. Gen. te Utrecht*, N.R. XIV, 12.

348. (*a* and *b*) Quoted in Wagenaar, *op. cit.*, 229.

380. G. Brandt, *Historie van de rechtspleging . . . omtrent de drie gevangene heeren . . .* (ed. 1723), 199.

351. (*a*) *Ibid.*, 210; (*b*) *ibid.*, 212.

353. Vondel, *Het Lof der Zeevaert* (1623).

355. From the Preface to Breero's *Geestigh Liedtboeck*.

356. S. Coster, *Spel van Tüsken van der Schilden* (1613), vs. 1116.

357. (*a*) S. Coster, *Duytsche Academi* (1619), vs. 42 ff.

357. (*b*) *Iphigenia, Treurspel* (1617), vs. 570 ff.

359. Trigland, *op. cit.*, 1137; Rogge; *Utenbogaert*, 512; Wagenaar, *op. cit.*, 357.

364. 1 August 1629. Quoted in Gallée, *Academie en kerkeraad*, 38.

365. *Verantwoordringh van de Wettelücke Regieringh van Hollandt ende West-Vrieslant . . . geschreven by M. Hugo de Groot*, second impression, 1623, p. 11.

373. The phases used by Peckius are quoted from M. G. de Boer, 'De hervatting der vijandelijkheden na het Twaalfjarig Bestand', in *Tijdschrift voor Geschiedenis*, 35ste jaarg. (1920), 41.

377. To Baeck, 31 July 1630. *Brieven*, II, 42.

379. Coloma to Villela, 20 September 1629. Lonchay and Cuvelier, *op. cit.*, II, 478.

380. Duker, *Gijsbert Voetius*, I, bijlage CXII.

383. Quoted in *Annales de l'Académie royale d'archéologie de Belgique*, LV (1903), 267.

385. L. van Aitzema, *Saecken van Staet en Oorlogh* (1657–68), III, 12th book, 4 (quarto edition).

386. (*a*) Quoted in M. G. de Boer, *Die Friedensunderhandlungen zwischen Spanien und den Niederlanden 1632–33*, 24.

386. (*b*) Gerbier to Coke, Secretary of State, Brussels, 10 July 1632. Public Record Office, S.P. For. Flanders/22. Cf. Geyl, 'Een verzuimde kans; Noord en Zuid in 1632', in *Leiding*, 1931.

388. (*a*) Gerbier to Coke. Hardwicke, *Miscellaneous State Papers*, II, 75.

388. (*b*) J. Heinsius, 20 January 1633. In *Kronijk van het Hist. Gen. te Utrecht*, 1867, 309.

389. The references to Aitzema are to *Saecken van Staet . . .*, III, 12th book, 55.

PAGE

390. (a) J. Heinsius, as above under 100 (b).

390. (b) Carleton and Boswell to Coke, 14 October 1632. Public Record Office, S. P. For. Holland/145.

391. Gachard, *Actes des Etats-Generaux de 1632*, I, 369.

392. (a and b) Aitzema, *op. cit*, III, 13th book, 39, 43.

393. *Ibid.*, 43.

398. Quoted in Waddington, *La République des Provinces Unies*, I, 432.

400. (a) Knuttel, *op. cit.*, 4268.

400. (b) Hondius to d'Hondt, 23 August 1640. In *Annales de la Société d'Emulation de Bruges*, XXIII, 239.

401. *Ibid.*

402. Quoted in M. Sabbe in *Verslagen en Mededeelingen van de Koninklijke Vlaamsche Academie*, January 1928; and in the same author's *Brabant in 't verweer*.

404. (a) Quoted in Dambre, *op. cit.*, 283.

404. (b) Quoted by M. Sabbe, as above under 116, July–August 1928.

405. As above under 112 (a).

409. Quoted in M. Sabbe, *Brabant in 't verweer*, 114.

413. Wagenaar, *Geschiedenis van Amsterdam*, I, 537.

419. The passage relating to the Orange family's noble connections is from P. J. Blok, *Frederik Hendrik*.

425. (a) The words quoted relating to the Stuart marriage are from a letter of Nicolaes van Reigersberch to Grotius, 9 November 1643, in *Brieven van N. van Reigersberch aan H. de Groot*, in *Werken van het Hist. Gen. te Utrecht*, 3de serie, XV, 740.

425. (b) *Mardachai ofte Christelijken Patriot*, Middelburg, 1632.

425. (c) The words attributed to Charles I are quoted by Arend, *Alg. Gesch. des Vaderlands*, III, v. 261.

426. (a) Letter of Charles de la Fin from The Hague, 20 March 1641, in *Somers Tracts*, IV, 152. The episode of the Orange-Stuart marriage and its effect on party feeling in the Dutch Republic as well as on its foreign policy will be found treated more fully in the author's "Frederick Henry of Orange and King Charles I", *Eng. Hist. Review*, 1923, and "William II of Orange and the Stuarts", *Scottish Hist. Review*, 1923, reprinted together under the title "Orange and Stuart" in his *Encounters in History*, 1961.

426. (b) The word 'insensiblement' occurs in a letter from Goffe to Jermyn, 8 June 1645, published in *The Lord George Digby's Cabinet*, 1646.

427. Aitzema, *op. cit.*, V, 555. Observations on the wrecking of the Secret Committee by means of this new instruction are to be found in Van der Capellen's *Gedenkschriften*, II, 173;

Waddington, *La République des Provinces-Unies*, II, 35 (d'Estrades) to Masarin); and in a French memorandum of 1647 published in *Bijdragen en Mededelingen*, Hist. Gen., XV, 124. — The instruction: Aitrzema, V, 552 ff.

428. (*a*) *Ibid.*, VI, 3.

428. (*b*) Van der Capellen, *Gedenkschriften*, II, 98.

430. (*a*) Quoted in W. P. C. Knuttel, *Toestand der Katholieken onder de Republiek*, I, 136.

430. (*b*) Voetius to Lemannus, quoted in Duker, *op. cit.*, II, 102.

431. Aitzema, *op. cit.*, V, 676.

433. (*a*) Van der Capellen, *op. cit.*, II, 8.

433. (*b*) The phrase relating to the South Netherland subscription in aid of the war is quoted in H. van Houtte, *Les occupations étrangères en Belgique sous l'ancien régime*, I, 278.

433. (*c*) Aitzema, *op. cit.*, V, 784.

434. J. Focanus, *Adoni-Beseck . . . Straffe Godts over de Tyrranen* (1632; reprinted 1643), 140.

437. *Grafschrift op een Musch.* Vondel's authorship of this is questioned by his most recent editors: *De Werken van Vondel*, Wereldbibliotheek, V, 946.

442. The Treaty of Münster in Dumont, *Corps Universel Diplomatique*, VI, i, 429–35.

448. 'Advies van Amsterdamsche kooplieden tegen het plan van oprichting eener Compagnie van Assurantie, 1629', published by P. J. Blok in *Bijdragen en Mededeelingen vanhet Hist. Gen. te Utrecht*, XXI (1900), 47.

450. Huygens, *Stedestemmen* (1624).

459. P. A. Tiele, 'Documenten voor de geschiedenis der Nederlanders in het Oosten', in *Bijdragen en Mededeelingen van het Hist. Gen. te Utrecht*, VI (1883), 272, 282.

461. J. C. de Jonge, *De opkomst van het Nederlandsch gezag in Indië*, III, 131 (paraphrase).

462. H. T. Colenbrander, *J. P. Coen, bescheiden omtrent zijn bedrijf in Indië*, I, 158.

463. *Ibid.*, 168.

464. (*a*) *Ibid.*, 399; (*b*) *ibid.*, 472.

465. *Ibid.*, 544.

466. (*a*) *Ibid.*, 630; (*b*) *ibid.*, 643.

467. (*a*) *Ibid.*, 705; (*b*) *ibid.*, 662, 735.

469. (*a* and *b*) *Ibid.*, 644.

470. (*a*) The phrases relating to the treatment of Banda are quoted in Colenbrander, *Koloniale Geschiedenis*, II, 117.

470. (*b*) *Ibid.*, 122.

470. (*c*) Coen's remarks are from Colenbrander, *J. P. Coen*, etc., I, 215.

PAGE
470. (d) Tiele, *loc. cit.*, 352.
471. J. E. Heeres, *Bouwstoffen voor de geschiedenis der Nerderlanders in den Maleischen Archipel*, III, 16.
472. The Seventeen Directors to Governor-General and Council, 23 September 1649. *Ibid.*, xxxiv.
474. (a) Extracts from two letters from Van Diemen to the Seventeen Directors, of 22 December 1638 (quoted in Colenbrander, *Koloniale Gesch.*, II, 145), and November 1640 (Heeres, op. cit., III, 11).
474. (b) Heeres, *op. cit.*, III, 48.
478-9. J. de Laet, *Jaerlyck verhael van de verrichtingen der Geoctroyeerde West-Indische Compagnie* (Werken uitg. door de Linschoten-Vereeniging, XXXIV, 1931), I, 1-2.
485. J. Nieuhof, *Gedenkwaerdige Zee en Land-reize door de voornaemste landschappen van Oost- en West-Indiën* (1682), 228.
490. Quoted by N. de Roever, 'Kiliaen van Rensselaer en zijne kolonie Rensselaerswijck', in *Oud-Holland*, 8ste jaarg. (1890), 243.
492. (a) D. P. de Vries, *Korte Historiael ende journaels aenteyckeninge van verscheyden voyagiens . . .* (Werken uitg. door de Linschoten-Vereeniging, III, 1911), 175.
492. (b) *Ibid.*, 178.
494. J. R. Brodhead, *Documents relative to the Colonial History of the State of New York*, I, 213.
495. *Ibid.*, 213-14 (paraphrase).
502. Hooft, *Brieven*, I, 80.
505. (a) Fr. Ridderus in the dedication of his *De Mensche Godts*, 1653. Quoted in Engelberts, *op. cit.*, 37.
505. (b) Quoted in Duker, *op. cit.*, II, 230.
506. (a) Quoted in De Vrijer, *Regius*, 33 *note*.
506. (b) Duker, *op. cit.*, bijlage LVI.
507. P. C. Molhuysen, *Bronnen tot de geschiedenis van de Leidsche Universiteit* (Rijks Geschiedkundige Publicatiën, XXXVIII, 1918), III, 5.
510. De Bie, *Gulden Cabinet der edel vrij Schilderconst* (1662), 90.
512. Huygens, *Dichtwerken*, ed. Worp, VI, 247.
519. (a) Cats, *Tachtighjarige Bedenckingen*.
519. (b) Cats, *Twee-en-tachtighjarigh Leven*.
519. (c) Cats, *Houwelick*.
520. (a and b) *Ibidem*.
521. (a) Quoted in G. Cohen, *Ecrivains français en Hollande*, 493.
521. (b) Huygens, *Biddagsbede* (October 1624). In *Dichtwerken*, II, 77.
524. Hooft, *Historiën*, fol. 588.
525. Vondel, *Roskam* (? 1626).

PAGE
528. Quoted in G. Kalff, *Literatuur en Tooneel te Amsterdam*, 177.
529. 1. The quotations from Hondius are from the correspondence
     published in *Annales de la Société d'Emulation de Bruges*,
     XXIII, as above under 113 (*b*), and in *Oud-Holland*, 9de
     jaarg. (1891), 190–3.
530. See Edward Rombaut's *Richard Verstegen, een polemist der
     Contra-Reformatie*, Kon. VE. Ac. var Taal en Lett., 1933.
536. Quoted in G. Cohen, *op. cit.*, 464.
538. Vondel, *Roskam*.
543. J. A. Worp, 'Constantyn Huygens over de schilders van zijn
     tijd', in *Oud-Holland*, 9de jaarg. (1891), 118–19.
544. Quoted in Dambre, *op. cit.*, 140.
547. Published in M. Sabbe in *Verslagen en Mededeelingen van de
     Koninklijke Vlaamsche Academie*, 1927, 1033.
548. (*a*) Quoted in Sabbe, *De Moretussen en hun kring*, 77.
548. (*b*) Vondel, *De Leeuwendalers*.

Notes on Sources and Secondary Works to Vol. I

The mass of published material available for the study of the Netherlands revolt is enormous. Dutch and Belgian historians have filled a library with their volumes and series containing the correspondence of Philip II, Margaret of Parma, Granvelle, William the Silent, Leicester, and Oldenbarnevelt, or illustrating the activities of the States-General (both of that of 1576,which was continued in the North, and of the loyal assembly called together in the South in 1600), the formation of the Union of Utrecht, the beginnings of the Reformation in the whole of the Netherlands, the religious troubles in Flanders, the relations of the insurgents with Anjou and with England. In addition there are numberless *mémoires*, especially on the royalist side and for the first years of the rebellion, and the invaluable Dutch chronicles have their counterpart in excellent Spanish descriptions of the war.

In the preceding list of references for the quotations in the text the titles of several of the most important of these collections of sources as well as of some secondary works will be found, but that list was not intended to give a complete or well-balanced survey of either category. To append a fuller bibliography would be beyond the scope of this work. The studious reader may be referred to the *Bibliographie de l'histoire de Belgique*, by H. Pirenne, third edition, 1931, which covers the whole of the Netherlands down to 1598, and which is especially useful for the sources. The reader in search of a guide to the modern literature on the subject would be well advised to begin with the chapter bibliographies in Gosse's and Japikse's *Handboek tot de Staatkundige Geschiedenis van Nederland*, second edition, 1927.

The lack of modern contributions in English has been noticed in the Preface. Much excellent work was done by Dutch nineteenth-century historians, like Bakhuizen van den Brink, Fruin (especially Fruin[1]), Van Vloten, P. L. Muller, Bussemaker. All these writers, it is true, viewed the events from a strictly Protestant and North Netherlandish standpoint. Unconsciously they projected the "Belgium" which seemed so alien to them in their own day back into the sixteenth century, when it was, in fact, still far to seek. The mental attitude of Belgian historians was the complement to that of their Northern neighbours. M. Pirenne gives in the third and fourth volumes of his *Histoire de Belgique* a striking and brilliant version of the story,

---

[1] A minor work of Fruin, which is a good specimen of his method, is now available in a translation by Elizabeth Trevelyan: *The Siege and Relief of Leyden in 1574.*

but he ignores practically the work of his Dutch predecessors while proceeding, like them, on the tacit assumption that the severance of Flanders and Brabant from the rest of the Dutch-speaking area was a perfectly natural consummation. The period still repays original research, and the years since the war have witnessed the appearance of a number of interesting monographs both in Holland and Belgium; Flemish historians are more and more frequently using Dutch for their publications.

Notes on Sources and Secondary Works to Vol. II

FOR THE chapter dealing with the religious disputes in the North I have, as in the case of *The Revolt of the Netherlands*, trod ground which was traversed in an earlier generation by the famous American historian Motley. His *Life and Death of John of Barneveld* (1873) is a much less known book in the English-speaking countries than his *Rise of the Dutch Republic* (1858), but for the working historian it is far more useful, as in preparing it Motley delved deeply into unpublished material. As for the value of its presentation of the facts, this is marred by the same essentially unhistorical attitude of mind which characterises the earlier work, the same violent partisanship and incapacity to appreciate the other side's point of view. To Motley, Oldenbarnevelt was the champion of republican liberty, Maurice the ambitious and unscrupulous soldier, and there was an end of it.

Apart from Motley's last work, there is not a great deal of literature in English on the period of Netherlands history treated in the present volume, and certainly no comprehensive account that is more than superficial and conventional. Of monographs I mention G. Edmundson, *Anglo-Dutch Rivalry during the first half of the Seventeenth Century* (1911); A. W. Harrison, *The Beginnings of Arminianism* (1926); W. S. M. Knight, *Life of Grotius* (1925); Baroness van Zuylen van Nyevelt, *Court Life in the Dutch Republic* (1906); E. Cammaerts, *Rubens, Painter and Diplomat* (1932).

It is, of course, quite impossible to enumerate even the more important monographs by native historians. The student may be referred to Pirenne's *Bibliographie de l'histoire de Belgique* (third edition, 1932) and to the chapter bibliographies in Gosses-Japikse, *Handboek tot de Staatkundige Geschiedenis van Nederland* (second edition, 1927).[1] It will be realised that my attempt to deal with the whole of the Dutch-speaking provinces in one connected account is unusual, and that as a rule historians confine their attention either to the Republic or to the Spanish Netherlands, 'Holland' or 'Belgium'; for while the present political frontier is allowed to play its dividing part already in the presentation of the past, the permanent linguistic division is ignored and the Flemish and Walloon provinces now composing Belgium are treated as a whole. This difference of method accounts for certain differences of opinion. In Pirenne's famous and masterly *Histoire de Belgique* there is the deliberate intention, as stated in the

---

[1] It will now be wise to consult also the *Algemene Geschiedenis der Nederlanden* (i.e. Holland and Belgium), 12 volumes, (1949–58).

avant-propos to the first volume (1900) with respect to the Middle Ages, 'to bring out before all the character of unity of Belgian history'. I believe that as a result of my plan of work the artificiality of that unity becomes at times unmistakably clear, while on the other hand one is forced to see that the dividing line drawn across the Dutch linguistic area and separating Flanders and Brabant from Holland and the rest of the Northern provinces did violence to a living organic unity.

In the references to sources of quotations will be found many of the more important works containing first-hand, contemporary information. I will here remark only that in the North there was a rich crop of political literature, pamphlets, and other controversial matter, as well as chronicles not of course unbiassed, but still primarily intended to be informative. The best index to the pamphlet literature is Knuttel's Catalogue of the pamphlets in the Royal Library at The Hague. Among chronicles, Aitzema's large work, which was continued into the 'sixties of the century, stands out. In the South there is much less of this kind of literature. Dr. Sabbe, of the Plantin Museum, Antwerp, has recently been unearthing the Dutch political verse in which, during this and the succeeding periods, the Flemings and Brabanters commented on great events, a real contribution to our knowledge of public opinion in the South, of which grateful use has been made in this work.

Among other records of the period there is a certain scarcity even in the North of intimate political correspondence. The *Archives de la Maison d'Orange-Nassau* are disappointing in what they contain from both Maurice and Frederick Henry. Other private correspondence of a political nature is mostly to be found in the publications of the Utrecht Historical Society and of the State Historical Publications (R.G.P. Series). However much one may wish that there were more, what has been preserved is wealth compared with what the South has to offer. Here the scholar is confronted first of all by the Spanish official correspondence which has quite recently been published (or rather calendared) for the Commission d'Histoire of the Belgian Academy. Important also is Gachard's publication of the records of the States-General of 1632.

The material for the history of religion and civilisation is to a certain extent mentioned in the text and in the sources of the quotations; it is impossible to give anything like a comprehensive survey within the limits of this Note. On art and literature, as well as on ecclesiastical or religious history, a vast modern literature is in existence.

One word may be said on colonial history. Dutch historians have been very industrious in this field, but not unnaturally their attention has been largely directed to the regions which are still under the Dutch flag. For the Dutch in what is now British India I refer to the bibliography appended to my chapter in the *Cambridge History of*

India, vol. V. For the general history of the Dutch East India Company, De Jonge's large work, with its continuations, is still of prime importance. Coen's correspondence has lately been published much more fully by Colenbrander. For the history of the West India Company the historian finds himself less well documented. Works like Netscher's *Les hollandais au Brésil* and Wätjen's *Das holländische Kolonialreich in Brasil* are based on unpublished material, but the independent investigator would like to possess far larger extracts *in natura*.[1] For the history of New Amsterdam and New Netherland, the necessary work has been done by New York historians; unfortunately (from the Dutch point of view) they published their large collection of extracts from the archives at The Hague in English translation.

[1] We have now, of course, the excellent work of C. R. Boxer, *The Dutch in Brazil, 1624-1654* (1957).

INDEX

Bogerman, Johannes, the younger
(1576–1637), of Uplewert in East
Friesland, Reformed minister,
theological writer, president of the
Synod of Dort, 355, 358–9
Bohemia, King and Queen of, see
Elizabeth; Frederick V
Boisot, Charles de (d. 1575), of
Brussels, employed in the
negotiations of Breda (1575), killed
before Zierikzee, 141, 142
Boisot, Louis de (d. 1576), of Brussels,
Admiral of Zealand (1573), of
Holland (1574), killed before
Zierikzee, 124, 135, 137, 141, 142
Bombergen, Antoine van, of Antwerp,
97
Boonen, Jacob (1573–1655), of
Antwerp, Archbishop of Mechlin
(1621–55), 368, 387, 395, 403; and
negotiations of 1632, 389, 399, 403,
547; Vondel and, 527
Bor, Pieter (1559–1635), of Utrecht,
notary public and historian, 282
Borchgrave, Daniel de (1550–90), of
Ghent, uncle of Daniel Heinsius,
secretary of Leicester's Council of
State, 210, 215
Borluut, Joost (d. 1597), of a famous
Ghent family, pensionary of Ghent
(1567), 103
Bossu or Boussu, Count of, see Hennin,
Maximilien de
Boswell, Sir William (d. 1650), English
diplomatist, 390
Both, Jan (?1618–58), of Utrecht,
painter, 513
Both, Pieter (d. 1615), of Amersfoort,
Governor-General of Dutch East
Indies (1609–14), 458, 461
Bouillon, Duke of, see Tour
d'Auvergne, Henri de la
Bourbon, Louis de (1621–86), duc
d'Enghien, afterwards Prince de
Condé, French military commander,
victor of Rocroy (1643), 416; and
Lens (1648), 444
Bournonville, Oudart de (1533–85),
Baron of Capres, commander of
Walloon troops, 107
Brakel, Heer van, Utrecht nobleman

involved in the revolt of 1610, 327
Brandenburg, Elector of, see John
Sigismund
Brandt, Geeraert, the younger
(1626–85), of Amsterdam, historian
and poet, 527
Brant, Isabella, daughter of Jan Brant,
first wife of Rubens, 325
Brant, Jan (1559–1639), author and
municipal secretary of Antwerp, 321,
325
Bray or Brès, Guy de, of Tournai,
Reformed minister, 82, 93, 98, 138
Brederode, Hendrik, Count of
(1531–68), Holland nobleman, 85–9,
91, 92, 96–100, 104
Brederode, Johan Wolfert, Count van,
Governor of Den Bosch, 430
Breero, Gerbrand Adriaenszoon
(1585–1619), of Amsterdam, poet
and playwright, 286, 353, 355–6,
517, 522; his Spanish Brabanter, 355,
357, 547; studied by Ogier of
Antwerp, 531
Breughel, Jan, the elder (known as
'Velvet') (1568–1625), painter, 321
Breughel, Pieter, the elder (1525–69),
Brabander, painter, 49, 50, 64, 263,
510
Brimeu, Charles de (d. 1572), Count of
Meghen, Knight of the Fleece and
Councillor of State (1555),
Stadtholder of Gelderland (1559), of
Friesland, Groningen and Overysel
(1568), 76, 77, 79, 87, 91, 98, 101,
154
Brizuela, Fray Inigo de, Dominican
father-confessor to Archduke Albert,
309
Broecke, Pieter van den (1585–1640), of
Antwerp, in East India Company
service, 464, 542
Broek (Paludanus), Van den, brothers,
Crispin (1524–1601) and Hendrik
(1522–1600), of Mechlin, architects
and sculptors, 323
Bronkhorst, Dirk van (d. 1574),
governor of Leyden for Orange, died
during the siege, 137
Brouwer, Adriaan (1608–40), of
Oudenaarde, painter, 510, 514